The Oriental Question

The Oriental Question

Consolidating
a White Man's Province,
1914-41

Patricia E. Roy

UBCPress · Vancouver · Toronto

09 08 07 06 05 04 03   5 4 3 2 1

Printed in Canada on acid-free paper

National Library of Canada Cataloguing in Publication

Roy, Patricia, 1939-
    Consolidating a white man's province : British Columbians and the Oriental question, 1914-41 / Patricia E. Roy.

    Includes bibliographical references and index.
    ISBN 0-7748-1010-6 (bound); ISBN 0-7748-1011-4 (pbk.)

    1. Chinese – British Columbia – History. 2. Japanese – British Columbia – History. 3. British Columbia – Race relations. 4. British Columbia – Politics and government. 5. British Columbia – Emigration and immigration – History. 6. British Columbia – Emigration and immigration – Economic aspects. 7. Immigrants – British Columbia – History. I. Title.

FC3850.C5R687 2003   971.1'004951   C2003-911110-5

Canadä

UBC Press gratefully acknowledges the financial support for our publishing program of the Government of Canada through the Book Publishing Industry Development Program (BPIDP), and of the Canada Council for the Arts, and the British Columbia Arts Council.

This book has been published with the help of a grant from the Canadian Federation for the Humanities and Social Sciences, through the Aid to Scholarly Publications Programme, using funds provided by the Social Sciences and Humanities Research Council of Canada.

A reasonable attempt has been made to secure permission to reproduce all material used. If there are errors or omissions they are wholly unintentional and the publisher would be grateful to learn of them.

Printed and bound in Canada by Friesens
Set in Minion by Artegraphica Design Co. Ltd.
Copy editor: Robert Lewis
Proofreader: Deborah Kerr

UBC Press
The University of British Columbia
2029 West Mall
Vancouver, BC V6T 1Z2
604-822-5959 / Fax: 604-822-6083
E-mail: info@ubcpress.ca
www.ubcpress.ca

Contents

Acknowledgments

Like every historian, I am indebted to many archivists and librarians who have collected and preserved documents, organized them, and cheerfully retrieved them. Since this research has taken place in so many archives and libraries and over so many years, it would be impossible to list all of them by name. Nevertheless, my thanks are sincere.

I also thank students who have patiently endured my enthusiasm for the subject and my colleagues, who have not read this manuscript, for making kindly inquiries about its progress and for providing an environment in which research is appreciated. In addition, my thanks are due to the anonymous readers of the manuscript who gave me many good ideas for improvement, and, of course, to my good friends at UBC Press, especially Jean Wilson, who gently encouraged me to finish the volume; to Holly Keller-Brohman and Ann Macklem, who coordinated the editorial process; and to Robert Lewis, whose careful and astute copy-editing saved me from some errors and smoothed out my prose.

Finally, I wish to thank the Social Sciences and Humanities Research Council for providing a leave fellowship many years ago that enabled me to begin this research and the Aid to Scholarly Publications Programme for the funds that assisted in the publication of this volume.

The Oriental Question

Introduction

One of the joys of teaching is that students remind one to ask basic questions. Some years ago I was explaining the federal powers of reservation and disallowance to an introductory Canadian history class. To give the subject some relevance to a British Columbia audience, I used as examples the various acts that the legislature passed in the first decade of the twentieth century as it attempted to halt Asian immigration. After explaining that provincial legislators eventually realized the limits of their powers over immigration, I mentioned that in 1923 Parliament had passed a Chinese exclusionary law. An alert student asked the obvious question: Why, after having rejected British Columbia's efforts to stop Chinese immigration, had Ottawa capitulated? I suggested a few generalities by way of explanation and the student seemed satisfied. I, however, was not and so revisited the handful of secondary sources for a fuller answer. They added nothing to my knowledge but did pique my interest. Shortly thereafter, Susan Mann invited me to present a paper on some aspect of the 1920s to the Western Canadian Studies Conference that she was organizing at the University of Calgary. As a young and naive historian, I was sure that a little work in the National Archives and some digging into the Mackenzie King papers would provide me with the answer and a paper. The paper, "The 'Oriental Menace' to British Columbia,"[1] was well received but I was not convinced that I had the whole story and so the research continued.

Since then, I have published one volume of this study, *A White Man's Province*,[2] a number of articles, and a preliminary overview, "British Columbia's Fear of Asians." In that essay, which dealt with the first half of the twentieth century, I argued that the hostility of white British Columbians toward Asians "was rooted in fear of Asian superiority," concern about a province in its formative years being "swamped" by an influx of Asians, and the fact that "Asians provided sufficient, effective competition in the fishing grounds, in the fields, in the market place, in the classroom, and on the battlefield to warrant deep fears about the ability of white British Columbians to maintain their dominant position in the province."[3]

That is the origin of this, the second volume of a trilogy on the response of white British Columbians, especially their politicians, to the immigration of the Chinese and the Japanese. The first volume covered the story from the arrival of the first Chinese settlers in 1858 to the eve of the First World War. The third will cover the years from the outbreak of the Pacific war on 7 December 1941 to the 1960s when Canada ended racial discrimination as a principal feature of its immigration laws.

By then, British Columbia had repealed its discriminatory laws and Asians could become full Canadian citizens.

Now that the research is complete – or as complete as historical research can ever be – it is time to modify some earlier observations with particular reference to the years between 1914 and 1941. The overall arguments hold, but it is clearer that concerns about Asians "swamping" British Columbia declined without disappearing, that agitation was episodic and was largely confined to a limited number of economic interests, that anti-Asian agitation shifted from a focus on both the Chinese and the Japanese to one that was almost exclusively anti-Japanese, and that the issue evolved from being almost exclusively a British Columbia matter to one of national concern.

This volume starts with the outbreak of one war and ends with the beginning of another. During the intervening twenty-seven years British Columbia grew and consolidated itself as a settled white society. Yet, its white residents continued to use "the other" as part of their self-definitions. In 1911, the province had just under 400,000 residents, of whom almost 8 percent were of Asian origin. By 1941, the total population had doubled to slightly over 800,000 and the Asian portion had fallen to about 5 percent. Throughout the period, the percentage of British ancestry hovered around the 70 percent mark but the number of home-made British Columbians increased. In 1911, only 17 percent of the non-Aboriginal population was provincially born; by 1941, that figure had more than doubled to 37 percent.[4] Among the leading anti-Asian agitators were a few native British Columbians, some migrants from elsewhere in Canada, mainly Ontario, and several of Scottish[5] or English birth. Like Asians, the Aboriginals lacked the franchise but when they came into contact with Asians, mainly Japanese fishermen, their views were similar to those of their white counterparts.

British Columbians also consolidated their "white man's province" through the virtual end of Asian immigration. Thus, there was less reason for them to fear being "swamped" by Asian immigrants but old fears reappeared at times of large real or perceived immigration. The end of the First World War and the resumption of normal trans-Pacific travel saw an influx of Chinese and Japanese. It seemed even larger as many Chinese, having "registered-out" under provisions of the Chinese Immigration Act, returned after going home during the war or the prewar depression. Unfortunately, their arrival coincided with the winding down of war-related industries, serious economic dislocation, the return of war veterans, and anticipation of the 1921 federal election. In response to a well-organized national campaign, discussed in Chapter 3, the federal government passed an exclusionary Chinese Immigration Act in 1923. With that, anti-Chinese agitation sharply declined. Renegotiations of the gentlemen's agreement by which Japan restricted emigration to Canada reduced Japanese immigration to a trickle but Japanophobes extrapolated from their high birth rate a fear that Japanese might still swamp white

British Columbia. That fear was reinforced by rumours of extensive illegal Japanese immigration in the late 1930s.

Many other basic arguments against Asians remained but less was heard of "cheap labour." By 1914, through custom and legislation or "institutional racism,"[6] white British Columbians had largely circumscribed Asian economic activities as they consolidated their "white man's province." That development, and organized labour's own internal divisions, contributed to its relative lack of interest in the Asian question. Politicians, however, continued their efforts to curtail Asian competition in lumbering, the fisheries, agriculture, and small business, with mixed results. Post-war efforts to enforce a 1902 law denying employment to Asians on certain timber lands led to complicated court cases but did little to reduce the number of Asians in the industry. The 1926 Male Minimum Wage Act made up for this. Earlier, after intense lobbying by British Columbia MPs, especially by A.W. Neill (Independent, Comox-Alberni), the federal government had introduced a licensing policy designed to eliminate the Japanese from the fisheries. Until the affected Japanese won a legal battle in 1929, the policy went far toward accomplishing its goal. As the Japanese left the fishery, they increasingly moved into other industries, chiefly agriculture and small business, which required relatively little capital and where there were few constitutional ways of limiting them. Chinese, of course, already had a foothold in agriculture and small business. This trend added to complaints of Asians merely being pushed from one industry to another. Some farmers lobbied for legislation similar to the alien land laws of some American states but such laws would be unconstitutional in Canada. Organized white retail merchants successfully lobbied for exclusionary Chinese immigration legislation, but attempts to regulate the retail trade and to prevent the employment of white women by Asian restaurateurs had limited effects. Appeals to patronize white merchants were not very effective since Asian grocers, restaurateurs, cleaners, and launderers often offered better service and prices than did their white competitors.

The attitudes of white British Columbians toward Asians did not fall along neat lines of economic interest. The major industrialists A.D. McRae and H.R. MacMillan were as hostile to Asians as were some of their white employees. Fish canners were of several minds about the Japanese. They relied on them as efficient fishermen but, worried about their dominating the industry, accepted Ottawa's decision to reduce the number of Japanese fishermen in 1923 provided that it was done gradually. Union leaders did not agree on the place of Asians in the workplace or in the union movement. Although Japanese and white fishermen occasionally co-operated in seeking better deals from the canners, Alicja Muszynski, a sociologist, observes that racism divided "groups of workers against one another, thus retarding the formation of class consciousness that would unify labourers in their relations with employers."[7] Discussions of efforts to restrict Asian competition appear in several chapters but principally in Chapter 4 of this volume.

By 1914, less was being heard about Asian threats to public health because the Japanese never had a reputation for uncleanliness and the Chinese had tidied up Chinatowns. Allegations of Asians corrupting white morality reappeared during the campaign for a new narcotic drug act in 1923, when municipal politicians tried to score points by halting Chinese gamblers, and when they and provincial legislators sought to "protect" white women from Asian employers. Although concerns about morality were only episodic, the notion of inassimilability survived, for example, in the concern of Attorney General A.M. Manson about "ethnological differences" and the fears of racial intermixing expressed by C.F. Davie, MLA (Conservative, Cowichan-Newcastle). This notion is examined in Chapter 2 and appears in almost every other chapter as it reinforced arguments for a variety of restrictions on Asians.

In the first volume, I argued that "the Asian question was always political."[8] It remained a politicians' issue but was seldom partisan. Federally and provincially, the two major parties, the Liberals and the Conservatives, agreed on the need to halt Asian immigration and to limit Asian activities. Their only disagreement was over which party had done the most (or the least) while in office to restrict Asians and which was more likely to adopt stronger anti-Asian measures. In Ottawa, British Columbia's MPs set aside party differences to campaign for anti-Asian measures, particularly immigration restrictions and a stiffer Opium and Narcotic Drug Act and some, notably Neill and Thomas Reid (Liberal, New Westminster), paid special attention to the fisheries, a matter of particular interest to their constituents.

Alicja Muszynski found British Columbia's racist legacy especially instructive given the state's role "in perpetuating a racist consciousness."[9] Because only they could legislate, politicians retained a major role in the story, but whether they merely reacted to public opinion or led it depended on circumstances. In the 1921 federal election, politicians responded to popular concerns about unemployment and apparently high immigration. In 1935, when the upstart Co-operative Commonwealth Federation (CCF) party challenged Liberals and Conservatives, the traditional parties led the agitation in appealing to old prejudices by claiming that the CCF would enfranchise Asians. Similarly, in 1937-38, as explained in Chapter 7, very few British Columbians paid much attention to eastern Canadian rumours of Japanese espionage on the west coast until MacGregor Macintosh, MLA (Conservative, the Islands) exploited rumours of illegal Japanese immigration and espionage to launch a campaign to remove all Japanese. In Vancouver, Alderman Halford Wilson used the situation to strengthen his campaign against Asian competition in small business. Because almost every legislator, provincial or federal, favoured checking Asian immigration and economic competition, the anti-Asian organizations that appeared from time to time had brief lifespans because they were redundant.

As in the past, the intensity of anti-Asian agitation fluctuated over time. Journalist Bruce Hutchison wrote in 1938 that "when you look back over the history of the Oriental here you see that public interest in it rises and falls in waves. For a while British Columbia will be acutely aware of its Orientals. There will be viewing with alarm in the Legislature, resolutions from public bodies, impassioned speeches. Then British Columbia seems to walk away and forget about the whole thing."[10] Hutchison's observations are easily illustrated. During the First World War, as described in Chapter 1, and especially in the early 1930s, as outlined in Chapter 5, anti-Asian agitation virtually disappeared. In the first case, Premier Richard McBride deliberately ended it. During the remainder of the war and again in the early years of the Depression of the 1930s, British Columbians were preoccupied with other problems. In contrast, agitation peaked at certain times as in 1921 and again between 1937 and 1941 as Japan followed an aggressive course in Asia. So vigorous was the latter agitation, especially in Vancouver, that even the federal censor could not completely silence Alderman Wilson and his allies.

Given the nature of the province, regional variations also developed. Antipathy to Asians was widespread but particular regions focused on matters of local concern such as agriculture in the Okanagan and Fraser Valleys; fishing, especially on the west coast of Vancouver Island; and the retail trade in Vancouver and Victoria. The reasons for opposing Asians were variations on the realistic worry of economic competition as well as a constructed concern: the challenge that Asians posed to the white race. Municipal politicians in Vancouver, Victoria, and some smaller centres, for example, linked the alleged corruption of Chinatowns to calls for the reform of police departments. Where there were few Asians, as in the northern interior and in the Kootenays (vigorous opposition in the heyday of the mining industry had discouraged their presence), little was said about Asians, but Kootenay residents reacted very much like other British Columbians when they heard rumours that Asians might move into their region. Only occasionally, as at Prince Rupert where the Japanese were prominent in the fishing industry or in parts of the Fraser Valley where Japanese and white berry growers co-operated, did Asians and whites work out a modus vivendi.

Though few British Columbians could instantly distinguish visually between the Chinese and the Japanese, long before 1914 they had noted some differences and that trend continued. The Chinese population of British Columbia was overwhelmingly male. This imbalance in the distribution of the sexes created images of immorality among the Chinese and concerns about the protection of white women, the illegal drug traffic, and gambling.[11] The passage of laws in the early 1920s that were designed to halt the illegal use of narcotic drugs and to protect women and girls against working in compromising situations defused much agitation over these alleged corrupting influences. The fading of interest in the "drug evil" after the passage of the Chinese Immigration Act suggests that Sinophobes exploited interest in illegal drugs to secure support for an exclusionary immigration law. The passage of that immigration act also shows that China had little diplomatic clout. Although the consul interceded, he failed to halt the passage of the immigration law and had only limited success in solving the segregated school dispute in Victoria.

In contrast, the Japanese were backed by a powerful nation. The Anglo-Japanese Alliance expired in 1921 but Japan's roles at the 1919 Paris Peace Conference and as a permanent member of the Council of the League of Nations showed that it was a major power. Even as the British Empire became the British Commonwealth, Canada and its courts remained conscious of international considerations in dealing with Japan. Thus, Canada restricted Japanese immigration by negotiation, not statute, and even in the late 1930s and early 1940s, as shown in Chapter 6, it moved cautiously in imposing export embargoes. Increasingly, British Columbians perceived the Japanese to be the greatest challenge to "a white man's province." John Nelson, a Vancouver journalist, captured this when he wrote that the Japanese were "not disposed to accept a secondary position to the whites, either socially or commercially, and they press with much vigor for political recognition."[12] In addition, many Japanese immigrants were women in their childbearing years. Thus, the population of Canadian-born Japanese, the Nisei, grew rapidly. In the early 1930s a number of British Columbians recognized that these young people, as Canadians by birth and education, deserved certain privileges of citizenship. That talk of toleration is examined in Chapter 5. Alas, before the Nisei got any concessions, as explained in Chapter 6, Japan's expansionist policies in Asia stimulated rumours of extensive illegal immigration and raised fears of Japan's military ambitions. This led to suspicions of the loyalties of all Japanese residents of Canada as described in Chapter 7 and ended the nascent sympathy for the Nisei who had been seeking the franchise. The Sino-Japanese war did engender some sympathy for China and the Chinese but the citizenship concerns of the small Canadian-born Chinese population got lost in the shuffle.

Even though about 95 percent of the Japanese in Canada resided in British Columbia and mainly on the coast, as the province's share of Canada's Chinese population fell from 70.5 percent in 1911 to 53.8 percent in 1941,[13] complaints about Asians increasingly resonated nationally. As historian James Walker points out, "ideology of race" infected views on both sides of the Rockies.[14] Indeed, if other Canadians had not agreed, it is unlikely that the federal government would have ended Chinese immigration or reduced the number of fishing licences issued to Japanese residents. Because their views were so widely shared, British Columbians found that their demand for a "white man's province" became a less useful "common rallying cry"[15] by which they could distinguish themselves from other Canadians or by which their politicians could "fight Ottawa." Moreover, its premiers had learned the constitutional limits of provincial powers.

In exhibiting antipathies to Asians, Canadians were not unique in the Western world. In the nineteenth century, British Columbia drew on the Australian colonies for ideas to check Asian immigration but by 1901 Australia had built its "great white wall" and so ceased to provide new examples. The United States, however, provided plenty of ammunition. References to the "Negro problem" appeared occasionally but more relevant were claims that British Columbia could be "overrun" by the Japanese as had supposedly happened in California and Hawaii. Many farmers and some urban businessmen wanted legislation similar to the alien laws of several western states, which denied immigrants the right to buy land. British Columbians followed the controversy over Japanese exclusionary legislation in the United States in 1924 but heeded warnings that a law that seriously offended Japan might lead to a worse fate than the entry of a few hundred Japanese under the revised gentlemen's agreement. From time to time editors cautioned that discriminatory treatment of the Chinese or Japanese could impede trade prospects but such importunings had little effect on those who wanted a "white man's province."

In the first volume, I argued that the Asian question evolved from being primarily an economic one with racial overtones to one that was mainly racial with economic underpinnings. This trend away to an emphasis on race continued after 1914 in large part because so many Asian economic activities had been checked. But, as H.L. Keenleyside shrewdly observed in his 1938 report on alleged illegal immigration, "a prejudice may be just as important as an economic fact but it is much more difficult to evaluate."[16] Indeed, it is often impossible to disentangle motives within the rhetoric around the issue. For example, it is evident that retail merchants were primarily concerned about direct economic competition from Asians but their largely successful campaign for Asian exclusion appealed to racial prejudice because they knew that their campaign would not get very far if they focused only on their own needs. Racial prejudice or "racism" was often rampant in British Columbia and echoed throughout Canada. Seldom, if ever, did it have a single biological, social, or economic cause; rather it was based on combinations of these factors, whose relative weight varied according both to the individual or group affected and to the time in which the antipathy was expressed.

What is "racism"? First, a comment on "race" is necessary. As demonstrated by the quotation marks, a library of books and articles, and a variety of definitions, "race," like its cognates "racism" and "racialization," is a problematic term. My argument in the first volume, that "race" was more than just skin colour, still has merit.[17] To bring the analysis up to date, it is helpful to look at some recent literature, especially since internationally the understanding of the idea of "race" in the interwar years was "in a state of flux"[18] as it moved from a biological interpretation to one of social construction. It is also useful to try to comprehend how British Columbians at the time might have viewed the concepts, if they thought about them in the abstract at all.

British Columbians would have had little trouble with the observation of one of the foremost students of race and racism, the British sociologist Robert Miles, that the "biological conception of 'race'" was "an important presence in 'common sense'"[19] and would have readily understood the modern description of Asians as a "visible minority." Miles's statement, that the "biological conception of 'race'" has been "discredited scientifically," however, would have been "news" to them as it would be to most people in the Western world before the Second World War. Some British Columbians were aware of recent thinking that "race" was socially constructed but their most likely source of "scientific" information was Lothrop Stoddard's *The Rising Tide of Color against White World Supremacy* (1920). Stoddard warned that the "yellow" and "brown" races could easily overwhelm the superior white race. People influenced by this notion spoke of "ethnological differences." To white British Columbians it was "common sense" that there were different races, though they were not confident that whites could retain their hegemony. With the benefit of hindsight, it is evident that white British Columbians entertained "socially constructed" ideas of race. Among the best illustrations of the mutability of their ideas about "race" are the gradual move from discussions of the "Oriental" or "Asiatic" question to specific references to the Chinese and the Japanese and the emergence of divergent attitudes toward them.

Definitions of "racism" vary but modern scholars agree it is socially constructed. In a British Columbia context, Muszynski defines it as "a social construction rooted in complex and specific sets of social, cultural, economic, and political relations and patriarchal consciousness" and adds that it "also informs the ideology that categorizes groups of people by the colour of their skin."[20] The American social theorist David Theo Goldberg calls it "the irrational (or prejudicial) belief in or practice of differentiating population groups on the basis of their typical phenomenal characteristics, and the hierarchical ordering of the racial groups so distinguished as superior or inferior."[21] Following either definition, it is easy to accuse British Columbians of the time of being "racist." They would not have appreciated the suggestion that their beliefs were irrational. In the first place, they considered that their concerns about Asians were very real; in the second, in their rankings, Asians sometimes came out on top! They feared Asians as potential superiors who might gain a numerical advantage through immigration, or in the case of the Japanese, through a high birth rate and a militarily ambitious ancestral land. Moreover, in daily encounters, they saw the Japanese as very effective economic and academic competitors. As some rhetoric surrounding Chinese gambling, drug use, and the employment of white women suggests, white British Columbians were also unsure of young whites' ability to withstand challenges to their morality. In this last sense, the claim of Michel Foucault that racism is part of a "state's 'indispensable' defense of society against itself" has some resonance.[22] In sum, to white British Columbians, Asians were different and unless their immigration and activities were checked, they were also a danger to the idea of "a white man's province."

British Columbians were, of course, unaware of the term "racialization," which only came into common use after 1977 when the British scholar Michael Banton used it to refer to the "social process" by which people developed "a mode of categorization" to organize their "perceptions of the population of the world."[23] In the British Columbia context, Audrey Kobayashi and Peter Jackson, though noting that racialization is a "complex and contradictory process," use the concept to argue persuasively that in the sawmill industry "the process of racialization had produced a remarkably entrenched division of labour" that depressed the wages of all. They contend that in *A White Man's Province*, I fail to take account of "*how economic competition came to be structured along 'racial' lines*."[24] It is a "chicken or egg" question. Did white workers object to Asian competition because Asians were "cheap labour," or were Asians "cheap labour" because they were racialized Asians? Kobayashi and Jackson stop their study just short of the introduction of the Male Minimum Wage Act, a "racialized" action that eliminated the "cheap labour" claim in the sawmills. The act did not completely remove Asians from that work but it may have contributed to a brief waning of hostility toward the Japanese.

Although racialization "does not denote a precise action,"[25] as other scholars have argued, many of its attributes were also in the imprecise notion that British Columbians called "inassimilability"[26] – a notion that they used as the basis of their arguments for restrictions on Asian immigration and activities. In its simplest form, "inassimilability" meant that the "races" could not and should not mix. British Columbia racists, like their counterparts elsewhere,[27] often used such claims to justify proposed restrictions on Asians, such as segregated classrooms and denying them access to the land. Mention of "inassimilability" faded somewhat in the early 1930s but later reappeared. Whether the apparent toleration for Asians described in Chapter 5 was a cause or an effect of the declining concern about "inassimilability" is unclear. Paradoxically, Nisei efforts to assimilate by seeking the franchise revived old agitation. The Native Sons of British Columbia claimed that giving voting rights to the Nisei would lead to the enfranchisement of all Asians in the province and that, in turn, the Orientals, "once our servants" and "now our competitors in industrial occupations and commercial and economic spheres," would become "our masters."[28]

In the 1980s, British Columbia scholars joined the debate about whether "race" or "class" is more important in shaping a society. Internationally, Benedict Anderson, for example, argued that racism derives from class whereas Michel Foucault saw the reverse.[29] Drawing on research that dealt mainly with "race," Peter Ward readily concluded that "the major cleavages" in British Columbia's society had "been those of race."[30] Ward's critics, however, argued that "class" was a fundamental factor in explaining the province's history.[31]

Later scholars questioned the race/class debate itself. One American noted that it pivots "on an axis bounded by two unhelpfully formalistic, artificially separated poles";[32] another described deciding "whether class or race factors were more powerful" as a "silly and unproductive exercise" since "racial ideology constituted only one element of the whole ideology of each class."[33] David Roediger, an American labour historian, also warned that the "privileging of class over race is not always productive or meaningful."[34]

A basic problem in the debate is that of defining terms. As explained above, "race" is a problematic word. So too is "class." Although E.P. Thompson said simply that "class is defined by men as they live their own history, and, in the end, this is the only definition,"[35] his disciples have read far more into the notion of class and have engaged in lively debates on its complexities and nuances. Indeed, a good part of the discussion in British Columbia over "race" and "class" revolved around definitions of "class." Nevertheless, the debate stimulated some scholarship. For example, in examining Asians in the labour market, sociologist Gillian Creese found that "the racist content of Euro-Canadian labour organizations, with its exclusionary policies and anti-Asian demands, cannot be interpreted simply as racism overshadowing class-consciousness."[36]

In British Columbia, both "class" and "race" were factors in shaping society but they were often intertwined and their relative importance varied according to time, place, and the individual or group concerned. It is difficult to ascertain the motives even of individuals. For example, did "race" or "class" interests motivate the workingman's wife as she chose to patronize a white or a Chinese grocer or did she simply consider service, price, and quality of the produce?

Since a simple dichotomy between "race" and "class" has not satisfactorily explained the complexities of British Columbia society, scholars have turned to other concepts. Robert A.J. McDonald argues that at least in the case of Vancouver before 1914, both class and race were factors. He suggests that "status," or "respectability," is a better analytical tool. According to his definition, "to be 'respectable' was to be of good character: pious, sober, honest, industrious and self-sufficient," and "respectability" was associated with rootedness or stability, families, and British culture.[37] Although Asians could be of good character, and the evidence suggests most were – paradoxically their industriousness was a major complaint against them – the perception was that they were not respectable. Moreover, their travels across the Pacific, the lack of families among the Chinese, and language limitations among immigrants automatically excluded Asians from this definition of respectability. In concluding that the segregation of Asians "ultimately rested on the hardpan of racial prejudice," McDonald is close to the mark.[38] However, he deals only with the period before 1914 and his definition of "respectability" becomes less relevant for Asians as a generation of Canadian-born Asians, particularly Japanese Canadians, grew up and showed every intention of remaining rooted in the province, raised families, and tried hard to adopt what, by the 1930s, was more of a Canadian than a British culture. In the larger coastal cities, Asians remained very definitely the "other," or outsiders, until after the Second World War. Limited anecdotal evidence, however, suggests that this may have been less so in smaller centres where Asians' respectability could be judged on an individual basis.[39] In Prince

Rupert, for example, the social columns of the local newspaper listed both Occidental and Japanese guests at a bridal shower, and both Chinese and Japanese residents donated to the construction of a new civic centre.[40]

By 1914, British Columbia was no longer a traditional colonial society either constitutionally or in practice, for an elected government represented the overwhelming majority of the adult male population.[41] Nonetheless, the observation of Ann Laura Stoler that in colonial societies "what sustained racial membership was a middle-class morality, nationalist sentiments, bourgeois sensibilities, normalized sexuality, and a carefully circumscribed 'milieu' in home and school" has some applicability in British Columbia.[42] Whether British Columbia was still intellectually a colonial society or whether the phenomenon described by Stoler was not necessarily confined to colonies merits further investigation.

This is a study in "racial relations,"[43] but it is not a complete story. As Timothy J. Stanley rightly observes, understanding the effects of racism "requires engagement with the meanings of the excluded."[44] A comprehensive examination awaits more research on the internal dynamics of the Chinese and Japanese communities in British Columbia and their responses to the situations in which they found themselves. Asian communities were not monolithic. Conflicts between merchants and labourers[45] and between political factions[46] divided Chinatowns; merchants and members of the Japanese Labour Union vied for control of the Japanese Association that claimed to speak for all of them. The union itself had splits between owner-operators of small businesses such as laundries and those who were employees.[47] How such divisions and conflicts between the Chinese and Japanese communities may have affected responses to discriminatory measures deserves a study of its own. Fortunately, the relevant literature is growing. The older but still valuable historical studies such as those by Adachi, Takata, Li, Con et al., Chan, Lai, and Yee[48] are now complemented by memoirs and historical analyses.[49] Particularly as the Canadian-born grew up, more Asians in British Columbia became articulate in English. Thus, it has been possible to include some "Asian voices" here.

As a study of how white British Columbians acted toward Asians and why they acted as they did, this work fits into the growing literature by "outsiders," including myself. James Walker and Constance Backhouse have examined the legal manifestations of Canadian racial laws. The geographer Kay Anderson has used theoretical constructs of race to examine Vancouver's Chinatown and to analyze race relations in that city. And Peter Ward, in a book now in its third edition, has explored policies and attitudes against a background of stereotypes.[50] Their approaches are useful but underplay the complex origins of the opposition to Asians in British Columbia. As will become evident, I rely more on empirical evidence than on theories to make my arguments.

A few words on terminology are necessary. In his collection of essays, *The Resettlement of British Columbia,* the historical geographer Cole Harris boldly asserts that "whiteness became the first and most essential marker of social respectability."[51] Although Harris focuses mainly on the nineteenth century – during which, until the 1880s, another non-white group, Native Indians, formed the largest portion of the total population – the idea still has some relevance to the twentieth century. The fit, however, is not perfect. As recent American critics of "Whiteness" studies have observed, "white" is a moving target; people can "become" white depending on how they are perceived.[52] That is a problem in British Columbia too where Doukhobors were often not considered "white" despite their skin colour and European origins and where, according to folklore, French Canadians were told to "speak white." I define "whites" simply as those people who were defined by themselves and others as "white" – that is, who were not Asian, Aboriginal, or African and who had European ancestors.

The term "Oriental" was always at least slightly derisive and is now considered offensive. Thus, I have substituted "Asian" except in quotations or close paraphrases where substituting "Asian" for "Oriental" would shift the tone of the statement. Curiously, the pejoratives "Chink" and "Jap" long survived in British Columbia speech.[53] The word "Chink," however, rarely appeared in print. Headline writers, however, seldom resisted the abbreviation, "Jap." The terms "Oriental" and "Asiatic" frequently appeared and were always at least a slight term of derision and are now considered offensive.[54]

The word "man" also requires explanation. At the time, it was a collective noun that included both women and men. Thus, for example, women's institutes passed resolutions to keep this "a white man's country."[55] There were no discernible gender differences in attitudes toward Asian immigrants. Women's organizations and individual women could be just as hostile to Asians as could men. There was little to distinguish for example, between the views of most women's institutes and those of the Great War Veterans' Association (GVWA) or between the propaganda work of J.S. Cowper and that of Hilda Glynn-Ward. On the other side, individual women such as Nellie McClung were as scarce as such men as Professor Henry F. Angus who publicly expressed sympathy for enfranchising Canadian-born Asians. Although the evidence is scattered and only anecdotal, one variable among whites in their attitudes to Asians appears to have been age; at play or in school, but not in their homes, children seem to have ignored "racial" differences.

As the notes reveal, this book relies mainly on the papers of politicians, the records of relevant government departments, and the newspapers of the time. The newspapers do have a problem with bias; most had a clear political slant. But the existence of competing dailies even in smaller centres such as Prince Rupert, however, helps to compensate for that. Whether newspapers make or reflect public opinion or whether they can create an "imagined community" is, of course, open to debate.[56] Had they followed lines of argument incompatible with the majority opinion of their readers and advertisers, they were unlikely to survive.[57] And almost all of the newspapers operating in 1914 were still in business in 1941. The only significant exceptions were the *Vancouver World* and its successor, the *Vancouver Star,* that went out of business in 1924 and 1932 respectively. That the *World* was perhaps the most virulent anti-Asian journal in the province was probably not the cause of its demise; its anti-Asian sensationalism may have been a bid to win readers. Certainly, the *Vancouver Sun,* which did survive, advertised its anti-Japanese campaign in the late 1930s as it sought new readers. Yet the *Sun* did not always oppose Asians. At times, for example, it warned that anti-Asian agitation could impair trans-Pacific trade. Such inconsistency was not uncommon among the province's newspapers whose opinions shifted with the times. After the outbreak of the European war in 1939 the press was censored. Editors generally co-operated with the censor and, as tension with Japan mounted, many counselled readers to distinguish between Japan and the Japanese in Canada. In the short run, that may have had a calming effect but it did not long survive Pearl Harbor.

Although I have not read every page of every newspaper published in the province between 1914 and 1941, I have read the major dailies for Vancouver, Victoria, New Westminster, Nanaimo, and Prince Rupert and most of the weeklies for Kamloops, the Okanagan and Fraser Valleys, and Vancouver Island. For other communities, mainly in the Kootenays, I looked at the local press in times of province-wide controversy, or when other evidence suggested that there might be a local issue.

The organization of this volume follows the mixture of thematic and chronological chapters used in *A White Man's Province.* Thus, a recurrent issue, notably fears of Japan's military ambitions, is in a chapter covering the entire time frame. Chapter 2, on "inassimilability," focuses on the 1920s, when that notion was most frequently expressed. The other chapters fall into more or less chronological units as they explain the fears and prejudices that developed as the Far Eastern conflict evolved into the Pacific war. This volume, as a prelude to the events following Pearl Harbor that led to the removal of all Japanese from the coast in 1942, shows how politicians, by exploiting the complex fears of an "Oriental Menace," kept racial prejudices alive even after they had seemingly consolidated the whiteness of their province.

1

"The Least Said, the Better": The War Years, 1914-18

On the first day of the First World War, Premier Richard McBride advised Prime Minister Robert L. Borden that "owing to the war situation, the least said [about the Asian question] the better." Other politicians apparently agreed.[1] In 1916 federal officials saw neither evidence "of improved feeling" nor hostility toward Japanese residents. Asians were scarcely mentioned in the 1916 provincial election and were noted in the 1917 federal election only when anticonscriptionist Liberals on Vancouver Island suggested that conscription would allow Asians to take conscripts' jobs.[2] Politicians had turned down the heat, but the Asian question bubbled up when Asians competed for jobs or when particular economic interests sought to import them to cope with labour shortages.

After becoming premier in 1903, McBride vigorously campaigned to halt Asian immigration, but *Sir* Richard McBride, conscious of possible imperial repercussions, denied being hostile to Asians. Nevertheless, on the eve of the war, as the Sikh passengers on the *Komagata Maru* challenged the "continuous voyage" clause of Canada's Immigration Act, he repeated the widely held belief that the "Oriental civilizations are so different that there never could be an amalgamation of the two, nor could the Asiatics conform to our ways and ideals." He wanted "to conserve the province of B.C. for the white man and the Dominion of Canada for our own race." To avoid offending other nations he emphasized "economic and social conditions," namely lower standards of living and "unfair" competition, rather than "racial reasons" for restrictions on Chinese and Japanese residents. He warmly received two visiting Japanese naval training vessels in the spring of 1914 to demonstrate "that our attitude ... to [the] Japanese ... is not based on any national dislike, but ... [is] purely and simply the outcome of economic and social conditions."[3]

Several editors observed that Japan was a "valuable" ally and encouraged readers to reflect on what might happen if its friendship were lost. Though critics of federal naval policy found it humiliating, under the Anglo-Japanese Alliance, Japan's navy protected British Columbia's weakly defended coast from the German fleet that was rumoured to be in the North Pacific. Commander Kabayama of the Imperial Japanese Consulate in Ottawa gave the Department of Naval Services useful advice. In Esquimalt he and his successor, Lieutenant Miyata, developed cordial relations with Canadian naval officials. Even after the German danger passed,

British Columbians were grateful for the "fortunate stroke of diplomacy from Downing Street" that had made Japan "our ally." J.D. Taylor, MP (Conservative, New Westminster), told Parliament in 1917 that he welcomed "the presence of the Japanese fleet on the Pacific." A year later the *Penticton Herald* reminded those who wished to prevent Asians from acquiring land of British Columbia's debt to Japan for protecting its coast. When Consul S. Ukita hosted a banquet in honour of Emperor Yoshihito's birthday in 1920, several guests, including the mayor of Victoria, praised the Japanese navy's assistance during the early years of the war.[4]

Yet there were stories of British Columbia being "practically a school for Japanese seamen," of Japanese spying inland, and of Japan's military ambitions. The *B.C. Federationist*, the voice of the BC Federation of Labour, claimed that Japan was "rapidly building up a naval and military fighting machine ... to make the world sit up and take notice of them and their aspirations." McBride also feared Japan's ambitions. When Prime Minister Borden argued that the strength of the British and Japanese fleets made the danger of a significant attack "exceedingly remote," a resigned McBride replied: "I trust with all sincerity that your hopes are well founded." McBride feared that if Britain lost the war, Japan might co-operate with Germany. He cited potential danger from Japan when he sought American assistance to build a railway through northern British Columbia en route to Alaska.[5]

Nevertheless, at the legislature's first wartime meeting in January 1915, McBride thanked Japan for its "immense service" in defending the coast. He reiterated that Asian immigration policies were made for economic reasons and that they did not reflect "against the Japanese people." When he could grant concessions or courtesies, he did. He responded to a request from the Canadian Japanese Association and the Japanese consul to use the wartime importance of the Anglo-Japanese Alliance, possible timber markets in Japan, and the absence "of ill feeling against [the] Japanese" to stop enforcing the 1902 ban on employing Asians on certain timber lands. When the Cabinet rejected this as a permanent policy, McBride warned the consul that maintaining "friendly relations" required "not emphasizing" any past disputes. In the fall of 1915, visiting Japanese naval officers sought permission to hunt. The Game Act required that hunters be licensed but made it illegal to sell licences to Japanese applicants; McBride had the game warden issue the licences free of charge. To improve relations with Japan, he privately informed the consul that the attorney general was considering omitting a clause in the Companies Act prohibiting the registration of Japanese-owned companies. And, when Parker Williams, a Socialist MLA, proposed adding a "no Mongolian" clause to an act licensing kelp reduction works, McBride told the legislature that British statesmen had advised him that it was "most inopportune" to take any action that might be an affront to Japan's "dignity." Yet his government refused poolroom licences to nonvoters, a measure particularly discriminatory to the Japanese.[6]

Despite discrimination, the Japanese in British Columbia enthusiastically demonstrated their loyalty to the British Empire. Within days of the outbreak of war, the Steveston Fishermen's Benevolent Association contributed $1,000 to the Canadian Patriotic Fund; a smaller group in Cowichan donated $73.50. After Rev. Fumio Matsunaga and others spoke of loyalty to Britain and Canada at the Japanese Methodist Church, several hundred Japanese residents applied for naturalization "to show their sympathy for the British flag and British institutions." Japanese British Columbians offered to fight for Britain or to serve Canada at home or abroad; one said that only army height requirements deterred more from enlisting. Although members of the Canadian Japanese Association recognized the irony of being allowed "to fight for their adopted country" while being denied its franchise and entry to British Columbia regiments, they drilled on their own and offered themselves as a battalion on "no conditions except to be treated as citizens."[7]

While some white British Columbians questioned their motives, many praised the "spirit" of the Japanese. The Daughters of the Empire and individual women donated socks to a Japanese women's campaign in order to provide comforts for the unit. The *Vancouver World* favoured accepting the "kindly generous offer" of these effective fighters "to leave the workshop and the store and take the field on behalf of the land in which we live and in which they live and labor"; it also noted that enlistment would remove competition in the workplace. Observing that Japan had proven to be an "honorable nation," the *Vancouver Sun* warned against refusing "recognition of their faithfulness and bravery" because of suspicions that the Japanese contributed to the war effort only to gain "definite recognition as the equals of the European races." The Canadian Japanese did cite their contributions when, in 1916, they petitioned the provincial government to remove such disabilities as disfranchisement and employment restrictions.[8]

Although the British Foreign Office favoured enlisting Japanese residents, Canadian military authorities believed that the proposed battalion was probably "nothing more than a weak company of 200 men" and so declined the offer with thanks. This refusal did not surprise the would-be soldiers, who had, in anticipation, also offered their services to the commanding officer of Military District No. 13 in Calgary. Several Alberta regiments were delighted to have them. Indeed, they were such impressive soldiers that the officer commanding Military District No. 11 in British Columbia later asked permission to recruit 200 of them after the fishing season and "to handle them entirely in this district." In the meantime the federal government awarded the Canadian Japanese Association $4,000 for training expenses. At least 166 Japanese men served in the Canadian Expeditionary Force, with 4 winning the Military Medal and 2 earning the Russian Cross of St. George. When Vancouver's Japanese community erected a monument in Stanley Park to honour their fallen countrymen, the *Vancouver Province* described the unveiling ceremony as "creditable to the generosity and good taste, as well as the patriotism and valor of the Japanese members of this community, and it is only British fair play to say so."[9]

British Columbia's Chinese residents did not display quite the same patriotic fervour. With the encouragement of the local consul, many bought Canadian war bonds, but few, if any, heeded the *Victoria Colonist*'s suggestion in 1917 that they sacrifice high wartime wages to raise one or two labour battalions for service with the Canadian army and thereby demonstrate their "willingness to share in the country's dangers" and their appreciation of "the blessing" of living in Canada. Unlike many of the Japanese residents who had become naturalized British subjects, if only to secure fishing licences, few Chinese residents were naturalized. Moreover, the weak Chinese Empire had few ties with the British Empire and little diplomatic clout, especially since it was preoccupied with Japanese ambitions to acquire part of its territory.[10]

In the first two years of the war, the Chinese in British Columbia endured severe unemployment and suffered as scapegoats for white unemployment. Early in 1915 a Presbyterian missionary estimated that over 70 percent of the Chinese in Vancouver were out of work. The consul warned the Board of License Commissioners that if it ordered the dismissal of Chinese hotel employees, "a situation now strained to the breaking point will be aggravated a thousand fold." Nevertheless, the Chinese sought neither city relief nor help from outside charities. They looked after their own by such ingenious means as having naturalized Chinese residents obtain crab fishing licences in order to supply food to poverty-stricken compatriots. To encourage people to return to China, the consul urged federal authorities to refund the head taxes of recent arrivals and to permit Chinese immigrants to stay out of Canada without penalty for more than the year provided by the Chinese Immigration Act. The government was unlikely to refund head taxes, but the minister of immigration liked the idea of letting them stay out of Canada for a longer period. The Vancouver Trades and Labour Council endorsed any move to relieve the plight of the Chinese since "any move to help them helps whites," but in a prescient observation Premier McBride opposed extending the "registration-out" period lest returning Chinese residents "seriously compete in the labor market" when "our own people" would be re-establishing themselves. Nevertheless, because of shipping problems, Ottawa relaxed the time limit.[11]

In the interim, the Chinese continued to lose jobs. China was neutral before joining the Allies in 1917, but xenophobic British Columbians associated the Chinese with enemy aliens. A Victoria laundry advertised that it employed "not a single German, Austrian or Asiatic." The Victoria Trades and Labour Council accused employers of Orientals of being "decidedly unpatriotic," while its Vancouver counterpart asked members not to patronize bars, restaurants, or hotels employing Asians and urged that such businesses be denied liquor licences. Women's organizations complained that the Chinese competed for jobs with white women. Despite warnings from the Chinese Benevolent Association that dismissing "dutiful" Chinese residents would be unjust, Helena Gutteridge, secretary treasurer of the Trades and Labour Council, on behalf of the Women's Employment League, asked the Board of License Commissioners to create work for women by means of a "white labour only" clause in hotel licences. They rejected her plea. A few white restaurateurs replaced their Chinese employees with whites, but hotelkeepers claimed that some hotel work was unsuitable for women. Mayor L.D. Taylor objected to singling out particular kinds of business.[12]

A year later, amidst popular feelings of duty to "our own people" who spent their money at home and to white men fighting overseas, the Vancouver Trades and Labour Council demanded that rooming houses employ "white labour only." Aware of rising opposition to Asians, the licence commissioners decided not to renew the licence of any hotel employing Asians after 31 December 1916. Only about forty Japanese residents worked in hotels, but their consul warned that the Anglo-Japanese Treaty made it necessary to substitute another word for "Asiatic." The *Vancouver World* agreed that "for the sake of such a small number the giving of offence to an ally would seem gratuitous." It was less generous to the Chinese, who tended "to lower the standard of living for other races." The debate was academic. Finding that they had no legal power over Asian employment, the licence commissioners dropped the matter.[13]

Moral suasion seemed the way to preserve jobs for whites. "If you believe in the superiority of the white race," admonished the *Prince George Herald*, "do your duty" by not patronizing Asian businesses. After seven white laundries in Vancouver closed for lack of business, the *Vancouver World* repeated an old allegation that Chinese businesses did not build up the country since the Chinese sent most of their earnings "home to the Flowery Kingdom to await the exigencies of a pleasant old age." Throughout the province, white laundries exploited images of Chinatown with "secret doors and tortuous passages ... filthy and slimy walls with an entire lack of ventilation." Saying that they had reduced prices to provide work for white men and women, white laundry owners appealed to racial loyalty. One advertisement portrayed the scales of justice: on one side were happy, neatly clad white washerwomen; on the other, dishevelled opium-smoking Chinese employees in dingy quarters. Under the sketch was a question: "To Which Are You Lending Your Support?" Other businesses did the same. A Kamloops restaurant asked: "Do you realize what it means to you to eat in a Restaurant which employs ALL WHITE HELP, where the kitchen is sanitary, airy, large and where the help does not sleep on the premises?"[14]

Agitation against Asians and unemployment continued to go hand in hand. In 1915, when unemployment was at its worst, many complained of Chinese labourers in the lumber industry. Shingle workers in New Westminster and workers at the Genoa Bay mill near Duncan protested that the low-paid Chinese worked while white men were unemployed. Fraser Valley merchants and settlers claimed that the presence of large numbers of Asians in the mills and in the woods retarded the local economy. In Victoria the mayor heeded a request of the Central Employment Bureau (Municipal Free Labour Bureau) and called a meeting of the Board of

Trade, the Trades and Labour Council, friendly societies, and others to urge inclusion of a "white labour only" clause in government lumber contracts. Labour representatives charged that the mills were chiefly interested in profits. Saying that American competitors did not use Asian labour, they demanded that British Columbia be a white province. Operators argued that replacing reliable and experienced Chinese labourers would greatly reduce productivity. The Board of Trade questioned the timeliness of such a move with the mills expecting new export orders. City council tabled the matter.[15]

In the Vancouver Island coal fields, bitter memories of Asian strikebreakers during the strike of 1912-14 complicated the question. Then, responding to anti-enemy alien sentiment, the Cumberland mine began replacing Austrians with Chinese workers. District 28 (Nanaimo) of the United Mine Workers of America and a committee of Comox Valley miners protested the use of Chinese and Japanese miners when white men were unemployed and their families destitute. Canadian Collieries Ltd. (Dunsmuir) said that white miners had not objected to the Chinese and Japanese working underground at times of full employment. It noted that unlike white miners, Asians remained in slack times and were available when required. Nevertheless, anticipating a crackdown on non-English speaking miners, the *Vancouver Chinese Times* urged Chinese miners "to study English hard." Early in 1916 the *B.C. Federationist* warned that a "gradual increase of Asiatic labor in the coal mines of Vancouver Island" would doom Caucasian miners "to be supplanted by the Asiatic workman."[16]

The provincial Conservative government, though sympathetic to white miners and aware of a pending election, could do little because the Asians were properly certified and the province knew the limits of its jurisdiction over the employment of Asians in coal mines. When Liberals, who stood "for a white British Columbia," attacked the government for not acting, A.E. Planta, the Conservative candidate in Nanaimo, promised to do all that he could "to have the Orientals kicked out neck and crop, from all industries in the province." More telling was the attempt of Premier William J. Bowser (McBride retired in December 1915) to evade the issue by referring to his government's lack of jurisdiction. He claimed that a Royal Commission was investigating the genuineness of certificates held by some Asian miners – a comment that William Sloan, the successful Liberal candidate in Nanaimo, correctly described as a "vote-catching job." Sloan proposed a minimum wage law as "the only true and feasible solution of the Oriental question."[17]

Using a minimum wage law to discourage the employment of Asians was attractive. In 1916, when Sloan became minister of mines in Harlan C. Brewster's new Liberal government, the BC Federation of Labour expected a sympathetic hearing and, acting on a request from the United Mine Workers, asked the government to enforce a minimum wage of $3.50 per day for all adults working underground. If this minimum were not paid, the federation proposed a fine of $25 for any miner failing to report it and of $100 for the guilty mine manager and company. The new government, however, had so many problems with finances, railways, and prohibition that it did nothing about a male minimum wage. In 1918 J.H. Hawthornthwaite, the Socialist member for the nearby mining constituency of Newcastle, revived an old idea under a new name. His Employment in Dangerous Industries Bill would have required workers in coal and metal mines, sawmills, shingle mills, and other "dangerous" industries to have a reading knowledge of a European language. He frankly admitted that the bill's object was "to get rid of Oriental labor" since "in the struggle for existence" every race had to protect itself. In office Sloan realized the ramifications of anti-Asian legislation. In opposing Hawthornthwaite's bill, he recalled that Japan's navy protected British Columbia's coast, that earlier laws requiring language tests had been disallowed, and that barring Asian labour might "open wide the gate to a motley crew of alien labor of questionable origin." Moreover, he argued, the bill was contrary to British policies. Reflecting their different international standings, the Chinese consul exhorted his countrymen to learn English and fight for their rights whereas the Japanese consul persuaded the legislature to kill the bill.[18]

Reduced agitation against the Japanese in industry eased the consul's task. When the Pacific Mills Company of Ocean Falls on the northern coast opened a paper mill, there was no protest about Japanese workers, who formed about a third of the labour force, being paid eight cents an hour less than their white co-workers. By 1917-18 the demands of the armed forces and the munitions and shipbuilding industries had caused a labour shortage. Citing this development and a high demand for timber, the consul revived requests that the Japanese be permitted to work through the issuing of special timber licences and that the 1908 Land Act be amended to expand opportunities for Japanese hand loggers. Given the generally unsettled labour conditions, the nervous Brewster government referred the problem to Ottawa lest removing such disabilities should cause a "complete tie-up of all Provincial industries." Nothing happened. Similarly, when a contractor for the Imperial Munitions Board arranged for "a large number of Japanese" labourers to cut airplane spruce on Crown timber limits in the north, a worried Brewster urged the federal government to use soldiers as loggers. Ottawa evaded the matter, as timber licences were a provincial matter. Brewster's fears were unnecessary; there was no public reaction to the employment of Japanese workers in isolated areas. The consul continued discussions but received only an admission from John Oliver, who became premier after Brewster's death in March 1918, that the 1902 resolution was contrary to the Anglo-Japanese Treaty.[19]

The employment of Japanese loggers in the northern forest industry attracted little public attention, but concerns about overfishing, the failure of past licensing policies to encourage white settlement on the north coast, and a wartime decline

in the number of white fishermen did. In reporting that Japanese labourers represented over half the fishermen on the Fraser River, the *Vancouver Sun* complained
that "the Japanese are a people who possess many admirable qualities but they are
an alien race." Among the fleeting references to the Asian question in the 1916
provincial election were allegations by New Westminster Liberals that the Conservative government was responsible for the Asian "peril to white fishermen" and
Conservative accusations that Brewster employed many Chinese workers in his
cannery. Fisheries, however, were largely a federal matter. In 1917 the federal government established a special commission to investigate and recommend changes
in cannery and fishing licences. Some witnesses appreciated Japan as a wartime
ally, but there was little sympathy for Japanese workers in the industry. Orlando
H. Nelson, a member of the federal Fisheries' Pacific Coast Advisory Board, explained that as allies the Japanese were "fighting our battles" but that he would
"wipe out the Jap" because "he does not go to the building up of the country as we
would like to have it." Native Indian and white fishermen complained that the
Japanese were driving them from the industry.[20]

Debates on the place of Japanese labourers in the fisheries often seemed as much
a consequence of class conflict as of racial rivalries. Most canners claimed that the
Japanese were law-abiding, reliable, efficient, undemanding, and hard-working;
fishermen blamed canners for Japanese successes. Members of the Fishermen's
Protective Association, a union, accused the Pacific Coast Advisory Board of acting solely for canners and of replacing whites with Asians. In the 1917 federal election campaign, J.H. McVety, the Socialist candidate in Vancouver South, and the
B.C. Federationist claimed that the minister of militia had refused to recruit a Japanese battalion because cannery and mill operators feared losing cheap labour. The
suggestion was not entirely off the mark. When conscription came into effect in
the fall of 1917, rumours circulated that many naturalized Japanese residents were
returning to Japan to avoid serving in the Canadian army. The Canners Association expected to use its influence to get them exempted from military service, but
this tactic was never tested. Given the refusal of British Columbia regiments to
admit them, it was unlikely the Japanese would be conscripted. The exodus was
part of a traditional seasonal pattern, and high wartime wages enabled more Japanese residents than usual to take holidays in their homeland. In the spring, as
expected, they returned.[21]

Discussions about employing the Japanese in the fisheries, in the mines, and on
timber lands were isolated echoes of old grievances about Asian economic competition; debates on the place of Asians in agriculture were relatively new. Before the
war, there was scattered talk of importing Asian agricultural labour and of adopt-
ing something akin to California's Alien Land Law of 1913, which denied Asian immigrants the right to own land. Wartime conditions brought these questions to the
fore. Suggestions of importing Asians to relieve a chronic shortage of agricultural
labour aroused emotional passions about control of the land. Many British

Columbians agreed with J.C. McIntosh, MP (Unionist, Nanaimo), "that the man who tills the land will eventually own the land, and the man who owns the land will ultimately govern the state." The argument that British Columbia must be preserved for the white race was compelling. With 9.5 percent of the white population having enlisted, there seemed truth in the claim of one labour leader that the proportion of Oriental to white males had dropped from one in seven to one in four.[22]

For some years before the war, Japanese and Chinese farmers had been buying or leasing agricultural land in the Fraser Valley, in the northern part of the Okanagan Valley, and in some valleys on Vancouver Island. The war and the prewar collapse of the real estate boom accelerated the process by making land available cheaply. Efficient and hard workers, Asians became effective competitors; as proprietors they ceased to be cheap labour for white farmers. The magazine *The Week* warned that the practice of white farmers leasing dairy, stock, and vegetable farms to Chinese farmers would make it impossible to attract white settlers and force the province to choose between being either "a white man's country or the exploited paradise of a Helot race." A Mission district resident told the attorney general that "when a white transfers his right & title to any oriental, it breaks up the chain of tradition, citizenship, civic improvement and all things we all have interest in." The advisory board of the farmers' institutes sought legislation to "debar Orientals from acquiring title to agricultural lands." Since the province had no means to "prevent a Chinaman from renting and tilling land," farmers used other methods to keep Asians off the land. The Vernon Farmers' Institute urged members to do all they could "to keep our land, our production and the business interests of this valley in the hands of the white race." Chilliwack farmers pledged not to transfer cleared land to Asians for five years. The 1917 and 1918 conventions of the British Columbia Fruit Growers' Association (BCFGA), the United Farmers of British Columbia (UFBC), and women's institutes also discussed the land question.[23]

Nevertheless, white farmers who were overseas – one Okanagan resident claimed that a third of the male population of Kelowna was "with the colors" (i.e., serving in the military) – or who had difficulty securing hired hands, sold or leased land to Asians. Asians had the significant advantage of adequate help. The Japanese used family members on their berry farms; Chinese vegetable growers hired countrymen allegedly for as little as seven cents a day. Chinese farming techniques were also suspect. The provincial inspector of fruit pests said that "Mongolian parasites" could ruin the industry by "planting diseased seed and selling diseased potatoes, in competition with careful white planters." With their own organizations and with door-to-door delivery, the Chinese were effective marketers. To meet the competition, some whites suggested boycotting Chinese produce, pressed white farmers to organize their own marketing, and called for laws either to prohibit the Chinese from selling their produce except in Oriental stores or at least to halt peddlers from working on market days. Others demanded stronger action. H.H. Stevens, MP (Conservative, Vancouver City), told the BC Consumers' League that

Chinese truck gardeners used such an "invidious" "system of slavery" that "demoralized labor conditions" might have to "be proclaimed in large notices addressed to Canadian and British workmen and inscribed over the entrance gates to British Columbia: All Hope abandon ye, who enters here."[24]

Not all white farmers opposed the presence of Asians; some wanted to import Chinese workers. In the fall of 1916, a joint meeting of Fraser Valley fruit growers and the Mission Board of Trade considered asking the federal government to suspend the Chinese head tax until the labour situation improved. Like an earlier proposal from the Cowichan Valley, the idea received little support. The local newspaper called it a mistake to admit Asians; David Whiteside, MLA (Liberal, New Westminster), condemned it as "very short-sighted"; the New Westminster Trades and Labour Council protested. Nor were Japanese growers satisfied; they suggested relaxing the gentlemen's agreement to allow for the entry of more Japanese nationals! Vancouver women made the only practical suggestion. Mrs. Kemp, president of the BC Consumers' League, accused Asian fruit and vegetable growers and vendors of "usurping the rights and privileges and doing the duty of white men and getting control of the food supply of the province." The league, which claimed 10,000 members, organized the YWCA, the Local Council of Women, and other groups to recruit 3,000 women and girls as berry pickers. Most growers were satisfied with these helpers, but some complained that the women could not do heavy work. Fearing that they could not pay sufficient wages to secure enough women for the 1918 season, growers asked the government to allow them to use interned enemy aliens or to import "coolies."[25]

Fruit growers also expected a labour shortage but, like other farmers, had conflicting interests. At both the BCFGA and UFBC conventions, delegates observed that Asians were gaining control of agriculture as white men were forced to abandon farms. "Every cent paid to an Oriental," said one delegate at the founding convention of the UFBC, "went to China or to buy a mortgage on a white man's farm." The farmers' institutes wanted laws to prohibit the sale or lease of land to Chinese residents and to guarantee that the "coolies" would neither stay nor encroach further on the land. After heated discussions, both farm groups reluctantly called for the temporary admission of Chinese labourers free of the head tax. After telling the Vernon Farmers' Institute that the Chinese sent most of their earnings to China and exhausted the soil, a speaker concluded nonetheless that at present it was "useless to talk of getting rid of the Chinaman, we need him in our businesses and require his labour on our ranches and to develop our country." Several Okanagan Valley boards of trade and newspapers opposed the idea. "It would be better to allow acreage to remain untilled rather than use Chinese labor," said the *Kamloops Standard-Sentinel*. A Victoria area farmer said that "the proportion of Orientals to whites in B.C. is too great but only [because] ... they are in business for themselves and are not, as they should be, working for white men." His was a common view.[26]

"A 'White' British Columbia," *B.C. Federationist,* 31 August 1917.
The caption reads, "JOHNNY CANUCK (home from the trenches):
'So this is the BRITISH Columbia I have been fighting for! Well, it will have
to be a bit more British when all the boys get back, I guess.'"

With the exception of some socialists, such as E.E. Winch, who denied that Asians lowered the standard of living of white workers, most labour leaders opposed Asian competition and framed the debate as a class war. The Vancouver Trades and Labour Council called the Chinese "unfair competition" and attacked the hypocrisy of farm organizations that sought coolie labour but wanted to deny Asians the right to acquire land. After outlining the extent of Asian activity in provincial industries, the *B.C. Federationist* asked, "what has become of that white Canada slogan? Those who stay at home during the Great War owe it to the brave lads to fight against the Oriental invasion while they are fighting the attempted Prussian invasion." The BCFGA executive tried to explain its position, but the BC Federation of Labour claimed that the fruit growers only wanted "cheap labor."[27]

The Canadian Pacific and Grand Trunk Pacific railways also wanted cheap labour, but no one wanted indentured labour, which was considered "only a classy name for slavery and wherever slavery is introduced there is trouble." There was concern to protect "our own labour" and defend it against a "scheme to Orientalize" the province. R.F. Green, MP (Unionist, Kootenay West), asked Parliament: "How can you possibly expect to build up an industry with a class of labour that you cannot assimilate and do not want to assimilate?" Categorizing Orientals as a class of slave labour who worked under contract for substandard wages, he concluded that "the only way to build up Canada is to ... build it up with our own people, white people ... who will grow up and become part of us." Noting an "already alarmingly large" number of Asians, others warned of increased immigration menacing the province's future "as a white man's country."[28]

Few Asians arrived during the war. The number of Japanese immigrants fluctuated around an annual average of slightly more than 600 and in 1915-16 only 20 Chinese arrivals paid the head tax.[29] Until the last year of the war, low immigration levels, the importance of Japan as an ally, preoccupation with the European war, and divided opinions on the need for Asian labour helped politicians generally to adhere to the principle of "the least said, the better." But their constituents had not ignored the Asian question, which had simmered throughout the war; increased immigration and a new consideration, racial equality, put the question on the boil soon after the war ended.

"We Could Never Be Welded Together":
The Inassimilability Question, 1914-30

We must have a white man's country and now is the time to start making it so.
The Asiatics, no matter how good they are, cannot assimilate with us.
Our mode of living, temperament and ideals are all different
and we could never be welded together.

– Vancouver *Critic*, 3 May 1919

White Canadians generally believed that Asians were inassimilable. Like most anti-Asian arguments, the catch-all term "inassimilability" was, as a contemporary noted, often an "irrational and blindly jingoistic" expression of racial prejudice. It had several intertwined manifestations and was neither consistently nor clearly defined nor free of paradox. It was an abstract concept but usually appeared in concrete situations. It did not imply inferiority but rather differences in habits, morals, customs, and standards of living. In such instances it was socially constructed, but some people thought that it was biological, as they objected to miscegenation, a prospect that was thought to have unfortunate results for both Asians and whites. Even Prime Minister Mackenzie King believed that cultural intermingling, the exchange of things of the mind and soul, was good for both Asians and Occidentals, but "we cannot intermingle physically on any wholesale or unlimited scale without mutual misfortune."[1]

Because it transcended particular economic interests, the concept of inassimilability frequently appeared in arguments for restrictions on Asian immigration and economic competition. Yet it also had a life of its own. It appeared in allegations about the corrupting environment of Chinatowns and sometimes became caught up in moral crusades to "clean up" cities. It was conspicuous in situations of interracial contact – real or potential – in such largely white institutions as schools. And, while the notion is irrational for those who now recognize that race is socially constructed, British Columbians then were undoubtedly sincere in their beliefs, misguided as they were. Because inassimilability was so widely mentioned in the 1920s, this chapter focuses on the notion in general and on situations where it was the principal anti-Asian complaint. Later chapters will show how it was used to justify other objections; the antipathy of white British Columbians to Asians seldom had a single cause.

The notion of inassimilability persisted partly because Asians and whites had limited contact outside economically competitive situations. A visiting Chinese labour leader, who was a Cambridge graduate, correctly told the Vancouver Board of Trade that the average Canadian largely gathered his conceptions of the Chinese "from the laundryman and cook." Some theatres denied Asians admission or "herded" them into special seats; Vancouver's Crystal Pool permitted "coloured races" to swim only at specified times. Asians and whites met in integrated athletic leagues, but baseball teams such as the Asahi of Vancouver (who also had a basketball team), the Taiyos of Victoria, the Royston Japanese, and Vancouver's Chinese Students soccer team, formed along racial lines. Interracial, postgame social gatherings were rare. Asians participated in music festivals, Alfred Quan Lee sang at concerts, Japanese residents entertained at an Empress Hotel tea dance, and the "great horned dragons" of the Chinese Free Masons Lions Brigade and a Chinese Benevolent Association float were part of Victoria Day parades in Victoria and Cumberland respectively. "On stage," these Asians were separated from their white audiences.[2]

White hosts rarely had Asian guests or invited them to participate in their activities, a Nisei who grew up in Vancouver's Kitsilano neighbourhood recalled having "white friends or even buddies. But there was a cut-off point ... I was never in their homes. And essentially, neither were they in mine." Muriel Kitagawa (née Fujiwara) "lived in the orbit of the small Japanese community" in New Westminster and knew no other after school life since fellow students "took it for granted that parties were not for one of my colour ... not with them anyway." A wise young Nisei later wrote that "white children never coming into contact with the Japanese grow up with an inherited prejudice against the Japanese firmly implanted in their minds." Similarly, the guest lists of teas, parties, and family celebrations of the Chinese and Japanese rarely had non-Asian names. Through kindergartens run by some Christian churches, however, Japanese mothers did invite white parents to social events in an attempt to establish contact with other parent-teacher associations.[3]

Though one complaint about Asians was their propensity to live in enclaves such as Chinatowns or "Little Tokyo," when they sought to raise their living standards by moving into white neighbourhoods, Asians encountered hostility. K. Iwashita of Kelowna explained that "we are segregated because white people have publicly protested that they do not like my people living in their neighborhood." Except for restrictive covenants applied to a few luxury subdivisions, to the University Endowment Lands on the edge of Vancouver, and to the Uplands near Victoria, barriers to Asian settlement were social rather than legal. Vancouver aldermen sympathized when taxpayers sought reduced assessments because Asians had moved into their neighbourhoods, but the matter was outside the jurisdiction of the Court of Revision. Kelowna City Council persuaded Japanese Methodists to build their church in Chinatown in order to avoid scattering Orientals or letting them "invade" residential areas. Members of Victoria's Chamber of Commerce objected when they learned that a Chinese resident was building a large home on fashionable Rockland Avenue.[4]

Businessmen sometimes met on formal occasions. For example, in 1919 General J.A. Clark gave a dinner marking a successful Victory Loan drive among Chinese residents in Victoria, but only prominent merchants attended. More often the Chinese or Japanese issued the invitations. In Cranbrook, Chinese Masons invited some white men to a ceremonial. When Japanese businessmen invited about twenty of their white counterparts in Vancouver to discuss promoting trade with Japan, one white businessman observed a desire to suppress the "anti-Oriental feeling ... among the more ignorant of the population" and to establish friendships. Given that, apart from businessmen, few first generation immigrants could easily communicate in English, the latter objective was mainly wishful thinking.[5]

Christian churches sponsored missionary work in Asia and among the Chinese and Japanese in British Columbia but seldom provided meeting places. They might have shared the same faith, but whites and Asians seldom shared the same pews. Whites attended their own churches, and the Chinese and Japanese, their own missions. When the popular Pentecostal evangelist Rev. G.S. Price visited Victoria and Vancouver in 1923, hundreds of Chinese residents heard his words through translators at a separate meeting.[6] Language was not the only problem; not all members of white congregations wanted to mix with Asians. The supervisor of Presbyterian missions said that his biggest fight was "not against the Chinese non-believers but against the narrow, racial, colour prejudice of our own kind," which was aggravated by unemployment. Another Presbyterian minister noted that some parishioners had such blatant prejudice and disrespect for the Chinese that they did not attend services when the Chinese were the announced sermon topic. At a Kamloops presbytery meeting, economic and religious problems caused "an animated debate" over mission work among Asians. In Victoria, the Society of Friends rejected the idea of discussing matters of common interest with representative Asians "in view of the several prevalent conditions and circumstances connected with this problem locally." At its 1915 general synod, the Anglican diocese of New Westminster encouraged ministrations to the Japanese but not "in ordinary parish churches, which were occidental preserves." In 1920 the Oriental mission reported that the laity's attitude toward "the yellow man ... seriously hampered" its work. In reply the synod pledged to try to give practical demonstrations of Christian fellowship to Asians. Nevertheless, before the motion passed, J.H. MacGill, a lay delegate, strongly opposed "the sentimental view that white people were remiss in their Christianity if they did not mingle with the Orientals in social and political life." Great embarrassment resulted when Wesley Church in Vancouver arranged to have Chinese and Japanese participants from its missions and members of the Asiatic Exclusion League set up booths at the same bazaar. Tolerance won out, and the league had to withdraw.[7]

Conflict between clergy who preached tolerance and the laity who acted like other white British Columbians continued in the new United Church of Canada. At the church's First British Columbia Conference in 1925, a storm of protest followed the call of Rev. Dr. S.S. Osterhout, former superintendent of Oriental work for the Methodist Church, for equality for Asians and other aliens. Two years later the conference appointed a commission to study the "Oriental question" in co-operation with other Christian denominations. Yet, despite their belief in fair treatment for the Chinese and Japanese in Canada – a point reaffirmed at subsequent conferences – some committee members realized that United Churchmen who were "shopkeepers, produce growers, industrialists ... labor union men, Fraser Valley farmers, Vancouver merchants of the third rank, and others" would approve only further study. The Committee on Christianity and Race Relations agreed. Under the chairmanship of Rev. Hugh Dobson, it limited itself to conducting further study, to distributing study guides, and to giving lectures to lay groups, both religious and secular, about the need to overcome "the roots of fear" that caused racial and other prejudices and to discourage "candidates for public office who fan racial or other prejudices." Some Anglican clergy also sought to educate the public. Rev. F.W. Cassillis-Kennedy, who worked among the Japanese, so actively opposed racial discrimination that critics accused him of being in the pay of the Japanese government. Suggesting that apparent inassimilability might not be the fault of Asians, he advised letting "our attitude be one of sympathy, of welcome, of invitation to assimilation and it will yield a result diametrically different from that of coolness or persecution or ostracism."[8]

Some church leaders, however, believed in the "Yellow Peril" and advocated stricter limits on Asian immigration. For example, Rev. John Mackay, a Presbyterian, told the Vancouver Kiwanis Club in 1919 that admitting large numbers of Orientals meant "either that they will overrun the country or [that] there will be war between this country and the one from which they came." At the Smithers Union Church, Rev. James Evans warned that "unless the Western races take steps to guard their own interests, Japan with her fifty millions of people allied with China with her 400 millions, will, within the next 50 years dominate the world." He recommended a rigid exclusion policy. During the war Bishop Doull of Kootenay told a Toronto gathering that because white men were overseas, the "Yellow Peril" had increased ten-fold, as the Chinese and Japanese were taking over agriculture and industry. "If British Columbia is to be Oriental," he admonished, "let us take care that it is Christian." Another Anglican, Bishop A.U. de Pencier, stood for an immigration policy that would make the province white, British, and Christian. He referred to the high Japanese birth rate, the Asian takeover of certain branches of agriculture, and a "particularly reprehensible" situation of a wealthy Chinese hotel owner in Ashcroft employing a white veteran and his wife to do his work. De Pencier, however, was anxious to convert Asians in Asia to Christianity. When he ordained George Lam Yuen, who had done "excellent work" among his country-men in British Columbia, he urged his flock to exercise great energy and zeal in efforts to "Christianize those who are strangers within our gates, and who, return-ing as they do to their own land, will carry the Gospel message to their fellow countrymen."[9]

Many religious leaders, however, called for the toleration of Asians already present. As a Presbyterian missionary noted, "it is impossible to jostle a Chinaman six days a week and expect him to listen to your message on Sunday." Rev. N.L. Ward, a former missionary and superintendent of Anglican missions to the Chi-nese in British Columbia, expressed sympathy for the Asiatic Exclusion League's objective of forbidding the entry of more Chinese and Japanese nationals but chas-tised those who would persecute Asians already in Canada. Rev. Dr. S.S. Osterhout was pleased that the number of Orientals had declined during the war and thought that Canada should admit no more Asians than it "could hope to assimilate and Canadianize." But he opposed the Chinese head tax and the virtual ban on female Chinese immigration, arguing that since Canada had admitted the Chinese, they were "entitled to the privileges of our country."[10]

Assimilation and Canadianization were limited to membership in Christian churches, to the acquisition of citizenship rights, and to the adoption of Canadian standards of living and morality. Church leaders hoped, of course, that the adop-tion of Canadian standards of living would eliminate "unfair" Chinese economic competition and that the acceptance of Canadian morals would justify admitting Chinese wives to Canada. The major denominations expected that their missions would prepare the Chinese and Japanese for limited assimilation through reli-gious services, social welfare work, and English language lessons. As a Presbyte-rian cleric in Prince George wrote, "Left to themselves, the Chinese ... become the prey of the basest influences at work in every city, and ... a menace to the city's or country's life." He suggested that if they knew English and realized that "the best influences are making an effort to help them," they could become "a real asset to civic and national life."[11]

Missions also sought to counteract the potentially overwhelming influence of Buddhism, Confucianism, and other Asian religions on Christianity. Some cleri-cal rhetoric may be explained by the need to secure moral and financial support for missions, but it also reflected insecurity. "Unless the Christian churches of British Columbia rise up in earnest to convert these Oriental peoples in their midst," warned Rev. N.L. Ward, "the history of the North African church will be repeated and Christianity will be wiped out by an Oriental wave of theosophic Buddhist thought ... The day may come when there will be Buddhist and Shinto temples on Shaughnessy Heights and Rockland Avenue, and a temple erected to Confucius where now stands the cathedral of the Holy Rosary!" Reverend Ward expressed his ideas more vividly than most, but his sentiments were not unique. Even the moderate Rev. Dr. S.S. Osterhout thought that Christianity did "not seem virile enough ... to impress very seriously the heart of the Oriental."[12]

More common was a belief that Asians were very different from Caucasians and would remain so. For example, after a Presbyterian cleric called for extending brotherhood to the Chinese in British Columbia, the *Kamloops Standard-Sentinel* remarked that the Oriental "belongs to another hemisphere and temperamentally is far apart from the white race. So divorced in sentiment is he from us that his very bones must not lie in the country of his temporary adoption."[13] This view, of course, ignored Asians who had been born in British Columbia and reflected an old grievance over sojourners.

In the case of the Chinese, there was some justification for the perception that they were only temporarily in Canada for economic gain for themselves and their families in China. Most Chinese residents in Canada were immigrants. Whether the sojourning mentality arose from "racist rejection" or was part of an immigrant's cultural baggage is a moot point. No one knows how many Chinese nationals achieved the sojourner's ambition of making a fortune and returning to China to live in comfort. Nevertheless, the Chinese practice (under the provisions of the Chinese Immigration Act) of "registering-out" at British Columbia ports and returning after familial visits to China, of sending money to China, and of following China's politics was clear evidence that many Chinese residents retained close ties with their homeland. Given the demography of the Chinese in British Columbia, the sojourning mentality was largely a male phenomenon but Denise Chong's grandmother also "saw China as home and Canada as but a temporary exile."[14]

Complaints about sojourning were less valid when directed at the Japanese. Although some came as *dekasegi*, intending to return to their home villages, and sometimes returned to Japan with Canadian-born children, many Japanese nationals established families in British Columbia. In a pamphlet prepared in 1940 to counter anti-Japanese sentiment, the Canadian Japanese Association asserted that early immigrants had hoped to make money and return to Japan but had "learned that this attitude towards the life in the new land" created a situation detrimental to their welfare and decided to remain permanently in Canada. Moreover, the Japanese desired to assimilate. A fisherman described assimilation

as living in unison with people, different in racial origin, but of common ideals, honoring the common flag and cherishing the common institutions ... When the meaning of assimilation is interpreted in this way, the question of biological assimilation in our opinion is only a question of time ... The Japanese born in this country are losing some of their racial characteristics. Their pitch black hair is becoming dark brown. The color of their skin is becoming fairer and the average height is taller than the average height of children of the same age in Japan. These tendencies seem to indicate that the Japanese people after all like all other races are endowed with an inherent adaptability to new environments.

Another fisherman thought that biological assimilation through intermarriage was already underway. This possibility was an exaggeration, but as the consul pointed out, his countrymen were "doing everything they can to become assimilated into the country. But you will not let them. We are doing our best but we cannot change our color in a day."[15]

White British Columbians often associated inassimilability with the supposed evil of miscegenation, a theory that had attracted new attention through the efforts of two Americans, Madison Grant and his disciple, Lothrop Stoddard, who refined and popularized the nineteenth-century racist ideas of such Europeans as J.A. Gobineau and H.S. Chamberlain. In *The Passing of the Great Race* (1916), Grant argued that when "two distinct species are located side by side," either one race drives the other out of the way or they amalgamate to "form a population of race bastards in which the lower type ultimately preponderate." In Stoddard's hierarchy, the Nordic was "far and away the most valuable" race, but "white men cannot, under peril of their very race existence, allow wholesale Asiatic immigration into white race areas." In the United States so popular were their works that scholars have linked them with the restrictive immigration laws of the early 1920s.[16] The British Columbia press gave no special attention to Grant but widely noted Stoddard's *The Rising Tide of Color* (1920), which the United Church recommended to its study groups on race relations.[17]

The ideas expressed by Grant and Stoddard – which in other places were linked with the notion of "race degeneration" – had appeared in British Columbia school geography texts and at Royal Commissions on Asian immigration in 1885 and 1902. Journalists and politicians had long classed Asians as undesirable immigrants and those of "Teutonic stock" as acceptable since the latter were "more or less allied to our own race by common descent and by characteristics similar to our own." After August 1914, references to the "Anglo-Saxon" or "British" races, or simply to "Canadians," replaced references to the "Teutonic" race.[18] Otherwise, the concept of inassimilability changed little in the postwar decades. In 1921 H.H. Stevens, MP (Conservative, Vancouver City), whose copy of Grant's book is carefully annotated, claimed that "the offspring of an intermarriage between an Oriental and a white invariably results in a lower and inferior type than either of the present race." A decade later Thomas Reid, MP (Liberal, New Westminster), said that "intermarriage between whites and Asiatics is usually repugnant to both races." In the legislature, Minister of Lands T.D. Pattullo suggested that there were "biological reasons" why Asians "should not come to our province. We do not believe that the white and yellow races will properly mix." In 1927 Attorney General A.M. Manson asserted that "ethnological differences" between Asians and Europeans were great. After telling an interprovincial conference that the result of interracial marriages "would seriously affect the social structure of the province," he asked, "are you prepared to see your daughter married to an Oriental boy?"[19]

Such biological notions were not limited to politicians. Judge David Grant of the County Court in Vancouver, who wanted to save British Columbia "for the Anglo-Saxon race and the Empire," contended that the Japanese believed that they were a superior race "because their king is the son of heaven." Thus, he concluded, "intermarriage becomes impossible, because a Japanese would be marrying into an inferior race and so would lose caste." Judge Grant's arguments were not wholly biological. In court he drew on California examples to argue that the Japanese were "determined to retain their national traits and customs in a foreign land" by educating their children in Japan and by preventing women from "becoming imbued with Occidental ideas." He refused a naturalization application after asking whether the candidate could "divorce himself from his citizenship in Japan."[20]

Some Christian churchmen also thought that intermarriage was impossible. Rev. N.L. Ward argued that Asians were "human beings, not animals," and that they had souls "just as precious in the sight of God as our own," but he called the marriage of Asians and whites a "repugnant" idea. For him the "acid test" was "Would you like your sister to marry a Chinaman or a Japanese? ... Surely, God does not expect that we should call anybody and everybody a brother-in-law!" Anglican Bishop A.U. de Pencier of New Westminster said that except in rare instances "the Occidental and the Oriental cannot successfully intermarry." Some observers warned that miscegenation could lead to something like the "negro problem" in the United States.[21] Intermarriage was rare but legal.[22]

Journalists also opposed miscegenation. In his series "The Rising Tide of Asiatics," J.S. Cowper wrote of the "instinctive repugnance" of marriages between the Chinese and whites and of "hybrids" with the vices of both parents being produced by marriages between the Japanese and whites. The *Vancouver Sun* argued that Europeans and Asians should not marry for the "purely biological" reason that "with few exceptions the 'half-caste' had the bad qualities of both races." However, the newspaper was not consistent. In the fall of 1923, its series "Canadians All" favourably described the background of a ten-year-old local girl whose father was a native of China and whose maternal grandparents were Irish and German. Two months later, in some horror, it reported how parents, the police, and a clergyman had failed to stop a thirty-two-year-old Nelson woman from following her lover, a twenty-five-year-old Chinese man, to Vancouver![23]

Biological claims were part of the argument for racially segregated schools. Hilda Glynn-Ward's anti-Asian novel, *The Writing on the Wall,* tells of the scandalous misfortune befalling a young white girl who marries her former classmate, a Chinese boy. Members of the Women's Conservative Association applauded when former premier William J. Bowser spoke of the "great social menace" of Chinese and Japanese children "commingling" with white children, which "might lead to destruction in the future." Harry Langley, secretary of Victoria's Oriental Exclusion Association, relocated his family because he did not want his children growing up with Orientals and would have prefered "to *murder* them than see them fall prey to Orientals for husbands." In *Maclean's* magazine C.E. Hope of the White Canada Association admitted that Oriental pupils were generally "exemplary pupils" who learned quickly and mixed well and who were clean, tidy, and well behaved, but he asserted that "the school question is the most serious phase of the whole problem" and predicted that interracial marriages would produce inferior half-castes who would increase the Asian population but be despised by both whites and the Japanese.[24] Similarly Captain C.F. Macaulay of the Asiatic Exclusion League urged the Vancouver School Board to establish a separate Asian school since familiarity with Asians was "sure to tend" toward lower national standards. In 1924 the school board's Major M.J. Crehan, who had made school segregation an electoral promise, told the Putman-Weir Commission, then investigating education in the province, that "most of our dope trouble starts in the Chinese section of the city and as a father I object to my little girl sitting next to a Chinese boy in school on general principle." A member of the Great War Veterans' Association warned the New Westminster School Board that "white children, through the environment, would learn the ways of the Jap or Chinese." Some mothers at Vancouver's Henry Hudson School feared corruption from an eighteen-year-old Japanese boy – presumably a recent immigrant – in classes with white children aged twelve and under. Its PTA had considered educating Japanese parents by inviting them to its meetings until one member threatened to leave if Japanese parents attended. The Asiatic Exclusion League, the Native Sons of British Columbia, and the British Progressive League, a Vancouver women's group, wanted segregation in order to protect the white race, to spare "the sensibilities of parents who do not wish their children to mingle with Asiatics," and to enable the schools to "frame a curriculum adapted to the peculiar needs of the Asiatic children."[25]

As Canadian-born Japanese children reached school age, their numbers affected school accommodation. In 1920 the Vancouver School Board scattered new students throughout several schools to avoid overcrowding. For financial reasons and due to the lack of evidence of Asian children as "a serious disturbing influence," the board rejected the request of some white parents for segregation. The principal of Strathcona School, which served Chinatown and "Little Tokyo," said that Asian children were "above reproach" in cleanliness and deportment and were intelligent, polite, generous, refined, dignified, and scholastically inclined. Both Chinese and Japanese community leaders urged parents to ensure that their children were clean and well behaved in order to "try to make good impressions on the whites." To allay complaints of language problems, many Japanese communities, sometimes in co-operation with Christian churches, established kindergartens where Asian children could learn English before going to public school.[26]

Until they went to school, many Chinese children did not venture outside Chinatown. Sometimes this was a problem of geography, as in Cumberland, where Chinatown was distant from the main community; sometimes it was the result of parents telling children that "the white people were devils." Some Chinese residents recall being called "yellow bellies" or "cowards" by "white kids" and disobeying their parents by fighting taunters; when anti-Asian agitation was high in 1921 and 1922, white children showed some prejudice. Usually, however, children had few problems integrating. As an example, the principal of Strathcona School cited a snowball fight in which Canadian-born Asians sided with white children against newcomers from China who had not seen snow before.[27]

Asian children generally found classrooms to be welcoming places. Almost every published reminiscence by Asians who grew up in the province in the 1920s and 1930s comments on the encouragement and respect given them by white teachers.[28] Educators favoured exposing Asian children to a Canadian way of life. When some white parents in Haney complained that high school students had elected a Nisei as a maid of honour for the May Day celebration, teachers defended the students' choice, and Miss Fujishiga carried out her royal duties. At the 24th of May celebration in Mission, white and Japanese girls performed a Highland fling. Such private groups as Boy Scouts and Brownies, however, segregated children by race.[29]

Pedagogically there was little reason for segregated schools. Even the few principals who preferred the segregated classes, which Vancouver had for children who did not know English, agreed that Asian children did not impede class progress. Despite anecdotal evidence suggesting weak language skills, Japanese children were "very proficient in arithmetic and other subjects," and Chinese children, in penmanship and drawing. Overall, there was evidence that Asians were superior students. In a survey of the intelligence of British Columbia school children, Dr. Peter Sandiford of the University of Toronto found that Japanese children scored higher marks on intelligence tests than did Chinese children and that both were "greatly superior to the average white population." Vancouver School Board officials correctly noted flaws in Sandiford's methods and said that Asian children succeeded through better application rather than through mental superiority; the *Vancouver Sun* suggested that "the Oriental is bright and energetic in Canada because he HAS to be."[30] Many Asian students and their parents shared that feeling. Although some parents needed to have children contribute to the family economy or believed that education was a poor investment since Asians could not obtain good jobs, others told their sons and daughters to learn to "be as self-sufficient as possible" because no white person was going to hire them. One Chinese woman recalled that young Chinese women did not even seek jobs in white-owned businesses, for "they wouldn't even look at you."[31]

High school entrance and matriculation examination results confirmed the superior achievements of Asian scholars. In 1924 Shuichi Enomoto of New Westminster won the gold medal for the highest marks in the high school entrance
examinations in his district; in Victoria a Chinese student came second. "We hold
no brief for Chinese children, nor to the mixture of the Orient and the Occident
in the school," said the *Victoria Colonist*, but if they "arouse our own to a keener
appreciation of their ability, and a necessity for spurring themselves to greater
intellectual activity, instead of being a menace, this competition ... may prove a
blessing in disguise." Then, in 1925, Nobuichi Yamaoka, who had known no English when he came to Canada three years earlier, led the province in the high school
entrance examinations. To many whites this was a frightening event. "The 'yellow
peril' is not yellow battleships nor yellow settlers but yellow intelligence," warned
the *Vancouver Sun*. The *Prince Rupert Daily News* demanded "personal efforts as
well as government measures" to overcome the situation, and so too did the *Vancouver Star*, which suggested that Yamaoka's secret was available to all, hard work.
In an essay that the *Vancouver Province* had commissioned from medal winners,
Yamaoka wrote "that as a Japanese Canadian I would endeavor to accomplish a
Canadian's duty." He explained that "a country must have her own loyal people. It does not matter to what race they belong and what kind of work they do,
so long as their purpose is to prosper their country and to expand their natural
pride."[32]

This was also the view of the Japanese consul, who hosted a banquet for Vancouver school trustees and principals to discuss preparing Japanese children to be
good Canadian citizens. Some Canadian groups assisted with the work. A service
club, the Canadian Daughters' League, sought to encourage Asian children "to
study our customs," learn "to love Canada," and become "good Canadian citizens."
The idea that Asians educated in Canadian ways were better than those who were
uneducated also explains why school boards with heavy Asian enrolments did not
pursue complaints about educating children whose parents paid little or nothing
in school taxes. Burnaby, for example, withdrew a proposal to relieve school boards
of the duty of educating Asians after some trustees argued that since Asians paid
taxes, "it would be better to educate them."[33]

Despite abandoning its segregated school in 1916 because so few Chinese children attended it, Victoria maintained a primary class for older children – almost
exclusively male – with limited knowledge of English. By 1921 the number of Chinese students in Victoria was increasing, as fathers took advantage of student ex-
emptions under the Chinese Immigration Act to bring in their sons. Much to the
chagrin of Vancouver's Asiatic Exclusion League, which complained that an "Oriental, while being given an education, must be under the guidance and supervision of one whose whole heart is centred in the British Empire," the Victoria School
Board appointed a young Chinese woman, a Nanaimo native and graduate of the
Provincial Normal School, to teach the Chinese class. Nevertheless, apparently

because she could not establish discipline in a class where it was already a problem, the experiment failed.[34]

In the meantime a Victoria Chamber of Commerce committee on "Oriental Aggression" recommended establishing schools exclusively for Asians. Prominent mill operator and committee member J.O. Cameron complained that "white children sitting side by side with Orientals tended to develop the idea of social equality" whereas he believed that the white race should be able to look upon itself "as a little better than the uneducated colored stock." Recognizing that the pending Arms Limitation Conference made discussion of the subject inopportune, the full chamber tabled the report.[35]

Nevertheless, Municipal Inspector G.H. Deane described the presence of approximately 200 Chinese students as a "growing menace" to the health of white children. He saw danger in Chinese boys "coming from their unsanitary living conditions downtown and mixing with other children." He claimed that their lack of English impeded the progress of others, a suggestion that the *Victoria Times* endorsed. In announcing its plan, the school board said that the arrangement, including a special curriculum emphasizing English, was "in the interests of efficiency" and would promote the progress of students. Despite Deane's complaints, the board specifically denied health or social concerns. When some members of the Local Council of Women noted that Chinese children were conscientious and well behaved, Mrs. Spofford of the school board agreed but said that white parents complained that children who did not know English retarded the progress of their children. Some parents were simply prejudiced.[36]

At the beginning of the 1922 school year, the Victoria School Board opened a special school for all Chinese children below the level of Grade 8.[37] White neighbours complained that the school would reduce property values and expose their children to Chinese residents; the Chinese community strongly objected to the "humiliation" and discrimination that would slow their children's progress in learning English and keep them "permanently ignorant, so that they must remain laborers to be exploited." The Chinese were, in the words of historian Timothy J. Stanley, simply demanding "access to the cultural capital of the dominant group." Moreover, approximately 85 percent of the children affected were Canadian-born, and at least one child was a third-generation Canadian. Victoria's Chinese residents raised funds for a legal campaign and enlisted the aid of the Chinese consul. Their most effective protest, however, was refusing to send children to the segregated school. The Chinese "students' strike" found some support among whites. The *Victoria Colonist*, noting that municipalities were obliged to educate children, questioned the policy of singling out specific nationals. Since there was no discrimination in tax collections, it argued that proficiency should be the only test for school promotion. It called narrow-minded discrimination "the sure precursor of racial animosities." Other allies of the Chinese had their own causes for concern. The Victoria Ministerial Association believed that the board, "sadly misguided" by the municipal inspector, had blundered; it feared for its missionary work. And the *Vancouver Sun* worried about the effect on trade with China.[38]

In such an atmosphere, the board permitted all the children, except twenty-one beginners, for whom it said that space was not available, to attend regular schools. Chinese parents replied that the precedent of admitting their children to public schools only "when there is room, implies that the schools are no longer 'public schools,' but only schools for non-Chinese students." The board denied this claim, but the Chinese boycotted the schools until the following September, when seventeen children, who were very deficient in English, attended a segregated class but were promised admission to regular classes once they had mastered the language. In his annual report to the provincial Department of Education, Deane said that the matter had been "adjusted satisfactorily."[39]

Despite Victoria's limited success in segregating Chinese students, other communities considered it. Nanaimo had a de facto segregated school, known to its Chinese pupils as the "Indian School" because, as one student recalled, "that's where the Indians and non-whites went." In 1926, Cumberland, which had both Chinese and Japanese residents, proposed segregating children in the primary grades because of alleged language problems. Ironically the same page of the *Cumberland Islander* reported that a local Japanese student had graduated from the University of British Columbia. When Chemainus proposed putting an overflow class in the Japanese Community Hall, white parents protested against the inadequacy of the facilities and the "environment in the Japanese quarter" while Japanese parents opposed an all-Japanese class. After the superintendent of education told the board that it could not segregate children by race, it found other space.[40]

The school question did not go away. A "startling" 74 percent increase in the population of Japanese children in provincial schools between 1922-23 and 1925-26 led C.F. Davie, MLA (Conservative, Cowichan-Newcastle), to propose forbidding the education of those of "Asiatic Mongolian origin or race" and white children in the same classroom. He warned that educated Asians would later compete with whites and wondered why white children should "be compelled to sit beside children of the yellow race" who had different traditions, conduct, and manners and "whose presence we would not for a moment tolerate as playmates for our children when at home." He persuaded the sympathetic Duncan Women's Conservative Association to approach other women's organizations. The *Victoria Times* suggested that Victoria had tried segregation to overcome a language problem and accused the Duncan women of being inspired by "racial reasons." The *Vancouver Sun* called the bill unjust and unreasonable, arguing that segregating Chinese school children would be "the most stupid course British Columbia could possibly take" because the only Chinese now coming to British Columbia were students who would return to China as "trade missionaries." In any case, few legislators supported Davie since the proposal, which referred to "Asiatics" generally, was *ultra vires* the Anglo-Japanese Treaty and would give Chinese traders an unfavourable impression of Canada. Moreover, the number of Chinese children was not increasing although the number of boys, including recent immigrants, was disproportionately large.[41]

Advocates of school segregation rarely referred to Japanese children. The treaty with Japan was a factor, but many Japanese residents were Canadian-born and could speak English before going to school, and the number of boys and girls was approximately equal. Nevertheless, a report that the Japanese community was importing four teachers for Japanese language schools aroused interest in the Canadianization of Japanese children. Y. Sato of the Japanese Consulate explained that such schools were necessary to facilitate communication between children and their parents, who spoke little English. He noted that when one of his secretaries had greeted a fourteen-year-old Japanese girl in Japanese, the girl had replied, "I do not understand Japanese." Critics of language schools rarely mentioned the Chinese language schools in Vancouver and Victoria, possibly because they expected that the Chinese would remain in their own communities whereas many Japanese residents wanted to participate in mainstream society.[42]

Though some white British Columbians welcomed language schools as a way of segregating Asian children, others feared that they would retard Canadianization. The Vancouver Ministerial Association complained that the schools kept "the rising generation in their ancestral faith, namely Confucianism and Buddhism." The Canadian Daughters' League protested the "thin edge of the wedge of bi-lingualism ... and Oriental bi-lingualism at that." When the Richmond School Board hired a Japanese woman to teach English to the children of Japanese fishing families in Steveston, some ratepayers protested that even though Hideko Hyodo was Canadian-born and a graduate of the Vancouver Normal School, she could not instill "the true principles of Canadian citizenship" in her charges. The *Vancouver Star* replied that denying her employment would be a form of "helotry" inimical to the "true principles" of Canadian citizenship and that a Japanese girl, born and educated in Canada, was unlikely to teach anti-Canadianism.[43]

The *Vancouver Star*'s observations were true, but Miss Hyodo, a leader in the Nisei community, and her fellow Nisei did not enjoy the full principles of Canadian citizenship. The Japanese and Chinese, even those who were Canadian-born, could not vote in the province. They were, as one newspaper put it, "in the same position as the Uitlanders in the old Boer republics." Exclusion from the voters' list also meant that they could not vote in federal elections, run for public office, serve as jurors, or practise the professions of law and pharmacy.[44] Few white British Columbians questioned that discrimination.

During the First World War, the Canadian Japanese Association asked the legislature to enfranchise naturalized Canadian citizens, who were effectively people without a country. If they went to the Japanese consul with a problem, they were "outside of his jurisdiction, being no longer citizens of Japan, but citizens of British Columbia." The association explained that "we go to our authorities here, and if we get no redress, we have no other source of appeal, being debarred from the vote." Premier Harlan C. Brewster was sympathetic but deferred action, citing likely postwar "important readjustments" in racial and international relationships. As the European war ended, the *Vancouver Sun* suggested that since there was "no longer a danger of the Pacific coast becoming anything but a white man's country," excluding a class of citizens from the franchise served no useful purpose, but the matter drew scant attention.[45]

Theoretically the By-Election Act of 1919 gave the federal franchise to all Asians who were otherwise qualified. When Ottawa realized this "oversight," a few Liberals, such as Rodolphe Lemieux, MP (Gaspé and Maisonneuve), referred to racial equality and suggested that Asians, especially the "highly intelligent" Japanese, should be able to vote. Provincial Conservatives opposed their enfranchisement, and the Union government amended the act to disqualify those who lacked the provincial franchise unless they were veterans of the Canadian Armed Forces. Before politicians plugged the loophole, 515 of Victoria's Chinese residents, all of whom were naturalized or native-born British subjects, objected to "our rights being thus unjustly taken away." Noting their status as taxpayers, they reminded the prime minister of the Uitlanders and asked that their naturalization papers not be made "scraps of paper." The question would have been academic, but a by-election was in progress following the appointment of Simon Fraser Tolmie as minister of agriculture. When the Federated Labour Party (FLP) found that thirty "wealthy" Chinese residents were on the voters' list, it sought to register several thousand Chinese workingmen at a rate limited "only by the speed of Judge Lampman to swear them in [and] ... the capacity of their motor cars to bring them to the courthouse." Nevertheless, its candidate, T.A. Barnard, believed that Asians belonged in Asia. Some recently enfranchised women said that they would not vote if they had to go to the polls with Chinese residents. Returned soldiers argued that the Chinese should not vote since they had been exempt from military service. Tolmie denied that his workers had put any "wealthy" Chinese residents on the list. When he promised that no Chinese would vote, the Chinese lost interest in registering to vote. In 1920, Parliament amended the Franchise Act. Despite the protestations of China's consul general that laws in British Columbia and Saskatchewan denying British subjects of Chinese race the right to vote injured "the respectability of China and the Chinese" and was contrary to "British fair play," Parliament enfranchised only Asians and Native Indians who had served with Canadian forces. As the *Victoria Times* noted, "anybody who was ready to lay down his life on the battlefield for the protection of our institutions – which includes our institution of Government and the right to vote – ought to be permitted to participate in the maintenance of those institutions at home."[46]

Asian veterans still lacked the provincial franchise. Several branches of the GWVA, including the large Vancouver branch headed by Ian Mackenzie, a future Liberal MLA and MP, and the branch in Mission, where a number of Japanese had settled, favoured showing gratitude to the veterans. The Japanese consul endorsed the idea, and the Canadian Japanese Association joined Mackenzie in seeking the enfranchisement of 142 British subjects who had served Canada overseas. Conscious of the "wedge" argument, they denied wanting to enfranchise all naturalized Japanese residents. When critics suggested that they had enlisted only to receive the vote, the Japanese veterans replied in a newspaper advertisement that "our Canadian comrades will not believe that we offered our lives, and endured suffering, and so large a proportion of our number met death on the fields of France and Flanders, for selfish reasons, or for any cause less than that of patriotism."[47]

The Native Sons of British Columbia, the Vancouver and New Westminster trades and labour councils, several Victoria women's groups, and, significantly, some branches of the GWVA opposed enfranchising this "thin edge of the wedge." William J. Bowser, leader of the opposition, wondering what the Japanese "knew of our institutions," suggested that few could read or write English and that they had really fought for the mikado. Warning that Asians might be bloc voters, Bowser painted a verbal picture of M.A. MacDonald, who had resigned as attorney general over an election-day scandal, marching "a battalion of brown men" to the polls. Bowser thought that having to mix with "Japs" at the polls would insult women. Several of Victoria's women's organizations, self-proclaimed guardians of "the race's chastity," agreed that it would affect "the very woof and fabric of our Anglo-Saxon civilization." Premier John Oliver said he had an "open mind," but reminded the legislature that "these Japanese gave their bodies as bulwarks against Britain's enemies." However, when soldier MLAs and opposition from some branches forced the GWVA to withdraw support, he abandoned any idea of enfranchising Japanese veterans.[48]

In a pamphlet published as part of its campaign for enfranchisement, the Canadian Japanese Association argued against taxation without representation and declared that the Japanese were more easily assimilated "to British and Canadian ideals, customs and institutions" than were many Europeans. The pamphlet backfired. The *Vancouver Sun*, which had once supported the association's cause, described it as "dangerous propaganda" and argued that biologically the Japanese could not be assimilated; the *Vancouver Province* implied that the Japanese should not complain since they had known the conditions under which they would live when they had come to Canada.[49] For the Japanese, the prospect of the franchise was dim.

Meanwhile, the legislature received a petition, originating in Kamloops and signed by about 200 people from all parts of the province, asking that Chinese residents born to naturalized British subjects and educated in British Columbia be enfranchised. Among those lending their signature were several clergymen and some prominent businessmen, including W.C. Woodward, a Vancouver department store owner, and George Straith, whose family had a fashionable clothing store in Victoria. After hearing Mrs. E.B. Shaw declare that women of the British Empire should stand for "the purity of the white race, the standards of Anglo-Saxon civilization and the ethics of Christianity," the Kumtucks Club, a Victoria businesswomen's group, circulated a resolution against Chinese enfranchisement. Groups as diverse as the Victoria Trades and Labour Council and the Vancouver Women's Conservative Association endorsed it. Nothing happened.[50]

The franchise issue, however, was not quite dead. During the 1921 federal election, local Conservatives quoted eastern Liberals who, in debating the By-Election Act, had argued the "sound Liberal principle" that anyone fit to pay taxes "should have the right to vote." The Liberal leader, Mackenzie King, accepted the "sound Liberal doctrine" that the franchise was a provincial matter. As a federal candidate, former attorney general MacDonald called the enfranchisement of Japanese veterans "the thin edge of the wedge." Just before the election, *Danger: The Anti-Asiatic Weekly* published a cartoon. In it, a Japanese workman, wielding a mallet, is drawing a wedge into a log labelled "Canadian solidity." The thin edge of the wedge is labelled "1921, 150 soldiers"; the next segment, "1925, 10,000 Japanese votes"; the third, "Japanese candidates"; and the final one, "1933, Jap majority at Ottawa." A.W. Neill, an Independent candidate in Comox-Alberni, epitomized the argument by accusing Prime Minister Arthur Meighen's administration of "deliberately" arranging for "some hundreds of Japs to VOTE AT THIS ELECTION." At the next election, he warned, "there may not be two hundred but two thousand Oriental votes, and good-bye to our hopes of a white B.C."[51]

Although King had said that the franchise was a provincial matter, the legislature feared that as prime minister he might change his mind. Thus it unanimously opposed, "on economic and social grounds," letting any Asian vote in provincial or Dominion elections. With such unanimity, the Asian franchise all but ceased to be a political issue except among some Labour Party and Socialist Party members. When the Canadian Labour Party (CLP) sought the endorsement of the Vancouver and New Westminster District Trades and Labour Council in 1928, a heated debate ensued over its support of Asian enfranchisement, which some called a Communist idea. To the assertion that Asians who were "good enough" to participate in the council were good enough to vote, others replied: "That does not say we are prepared to give them an equal voice in the government of the country." Some delegates thought that this stance would "kill" any chance of Labour electing anyone. In the end, the council did not support the CLP, which retained its enfranchisement plank and elected three members in the 1928 provincial election, but the franchise was not a major issue.[52]

Federally, however, just before the dissolution of Parliament in 1925, A.W. Neill introduced a resolution to disfranchise Asian veterans in British Columbia. Despite his claim that defeating the bill would mean "friction and riot, and possibly bloodshed," Parliament rejected it. A month later when a wire service erroneously reported that the prime minister had told the Imperial Labour Conference that Canada would enfranchise Asians, the conservative *New Westminster British Columbian* asked whether King's "Oriental policy" commended his government to British Columbia electors. Asians, however, were barely mentioned in the 1925 election, and the franchise received no mention at all.[53]

One argument against enfranchising Asians was the need to protect white women at polling places. Yet only after Ontario, Saskatchewan, and Manitoba tried to protect women and girls from immorality by forbidding their employment by Asians, did British Columbia amend its Municipal Act to forbid Chinese residents to employ white women or girls in any capacity.[54] The idea occurred in Vancouver in 1915 when the Social Service Council asserted that three-quarters of the "lost womanhood" of the city was "manufactured" in Oriental restaurants. As in Saskatchewan, the motives were both economic and moral. The BC Federation of Labour sought such legislation in 1917, but little happened until 1919 when the legislature cheered as George Bell, MLA (Liberal, Victoria), introduced the necessary amendment to the Municipal Act. An officer of the Vancouver Juvenile Detention Home underscored its desirability by reporting the recent need to remove a white girl "in a delicate condition" from a Chinese restaurant. Chinese diplomats argued that the law was *ultra vires,* disgraced the Chinese nationality, discriminated against subjects of a friendly nation, and affected only a handful of Canadian girls. Premier Oliver, saying that the courts must decide on its validity, saw no reason to repeal it. It did not apply to Vancouver, which had its own charter, but was occasionally enforced elsewhere until its replacement by the Women and Girls Protection Act of 1923, which applied throughout the province.[55]

As introduced by Mary Ellen Smith, MLA (Liberal, Vancouver), the Women and Girls Protection Act would have made it a criminal offence for Chinese establishments to employ white or Indian women. Mrs. Smith admitted an economic consideration, the availability of "enough white people to run our restaurants," but the bill appeared to confront a moral issue. Thus such groups as the Ministerial Association of Victoria endorsed it. In the wake of Chinese charges that the bill was "an unwarranted reflection" on all of them, the consul's observation that yellow and black women were also entitled to protection against the "black sheep ... found in every flock," and the argument of a lawyer hired by the Chinese Consolidated Benevolent Association that the bill was unconstitutional, the legislature amended it to forbid any person to employ or lodge a white or Indian woman or girl if local police officials deemed it inadvisable "in the interests of the morals of such women and girls." In sum, the bill protected women "from whatever characters, of whatever nationality."[56]

This amendment removed a blatant racial sting but did not satisfy Mrs. Smith, especially after the sensational murder of Janet K. Smith (no relation), a Scottish nursemaid employed in the home of a wealthy Vancouver family. Because the prime suspect was a Chinese servant, the Amalgamated Scottish Societies, other patriotic groups, and some labour organizations demanded that the Women and Girls Protection Act be amended to ban the employment of any white female in a household where a male Chinese or Japanese servant was employed. "If there is any discrimination to be shown," Mrs. Smith argued, "it should be in favor of our own British race." "It is not morally in the eternal fitness of things that a white girl or woman should be placed in a position where she is constantly coming into daily personal touch with a Chinamen under the same roof," said the *Vancouver Star*, "it is simply a question of racial and economic incompatibility." Not all agreed. The Vancouver Trades and Labour Council, a Victoria businesswomen's club, and some MLAs feared that employers would dismiss white "girls" in favour of the generally more "valuable" Chinese servants. Others agreed with China's consul that the law would impair employment rights and be "an unwarranted reflection on the morals of the whole nation of a friendly country." The *Vancouver Province* noted that convicting all Orientals without any evidence was contrary to "British justice." Attorney General Manson thought that white girls should not be employed in close proximity to Orientals, who might give them narcotic habits, but admitted that despite increased crimes against women, no Asians had been prosecuted for such offences. Because it was a private member's bill, the Oliver government let it die, readily acceding to federal hints that the bill, with its references to the Japanese, would cause diplomatic embarrassment.[57] The 1923 statute, with its limited restrictions on employment, remained on the books.[58]

The notion of contagious Oriental immorality – immorality by white standards – underlay arguments in favour of the cessation of Asian immigration, segregated schools, and restricted contact with white women, arguments against enfranchisement, and arguments generally intended to reinforce antipathy to Asians. It had a long pedigree, but its only "factual" basis was the popular image of Chinatowns. Over the previous half-century or so, British Columbians had, with some reason, created a vision of Chinatowns as exotic places that were centres of crime, intrigue, and disease – a vision that made them, in the words of geographer Kay Anderson, "a collection of essences that seemed to set the Chinese fundamentally apart."[59] Whites knew little of the real inner workings of these communities apart from occasional reports of "tong wars" – or, more accurately, factional strife – in Vancouver, Victoria, and smaller centres such as Prince George and Lytton. Newspapers pictured Chinatowns as dens of iniquity inhabited by gamblers and opium smokers living in filthy and cramped quarters marked by ingenious arrangements

Men were crouched over
tables tossing money,
here and there where
fancy prompted.

"Chinese Here Gamble Secretly," *Vancouver Sun,* 3 May 1924

of doors, partitions, corridors, and warning signals that enabled inmates to escape
police raids. A *Victoria Colonist* reporter who followed a census taker through
Chinatown in 1921 noted that many men were proud that they could speak English and that many were Christians, but his story featured dark alleys and stair-
cases and living quarters "found in unexpected places." The *Vancouver Province,* in
describing a visit to Vancouver's Chinatown, noted shops that sold "dried bats and
snails and birds, curious, knobby, shapeless things that might be animal or vegetable, ... strange, twisted shrunken things that make you shiver." Stories of gambling
and drug raids added to the image of intrigue.[60]

In one respect, the image of Chinatowns did improve. Concerns about their
danger to public health declined. Residents usually responded, at least temporarily, to pressure to improve sanitary conditions. In May 1915, for example, Vancouver aldermen and officials found "filthy and slimy walls with an entire lack of
ventilation" in Chinatown. When they returned in September, conditions were as
sanitary as could be desired. In 1918, however, the mayor decided that it was time

to "clean out the disease breeding dens which had existed in the Oriental quarters in defiance of city bylaws and health regulations." A year later the city's chief sanitary inspector reported that the clean-up had been temporary and that the prevalence of tuberculosis threatened "the health of the entire city." He ordered a major crusade against unsanitary and overcrowded conditions. Concern for the spread of tuberculosis continued, but the director of the Rotary tuberculosis clinic suggested that Asians increased Vancouver's death rate from tuberculosis "on paper and not in reality" and that "propinquity" was a minor factor in spreading the disease. A Chinese resident, he argued, might contract the disease and die of it "without endangering the life of one single white citizen." Similarly the *Vancouver Province* observed that despite outward appearances there was "personal cleanliness in Chinatown" and "no crime to speak of." Public health officials quietly enforced health bylaws and educated Chinatown residents about them. Victoria's medical health officer said that sanitary conditions in Chinatown were "far from good" but did not endanger public health and that there had been no "serious infectious disease" for years. He explained a relatively high death rate as resulting from the habit of tubercular Chinese patients from other parts of the province going to Victoria's Chinese Free Hospital. New Westminster's building inspector described Chinatown as a menace, an eyesore, and a fire hazard and called for its removal. However, despite the city's desire to expand its retail district and later attributions of disease to Chinatown, its condemned buildings remained a "bone of contention." In the mid-1920s several Saanich residents complained that Chinese greenhouse growers had no "sense of cleanliness" and that they lowered the value of nearby property, but the municipality does not appear to have responded.[61]

Outside the larger cities, the provincial government was responsible for public health. In July 1918 the minister of education, J.D. MacLean, himself a medical doctor, told Victoria's Civic Improvement League that the foreign sections of the cities were "great breeding-grounds for disease." He suggested that living conditions might be "all right for Orientals" but noted that they came "in contact with citizens of every class every day, and we cannot afford to shelve the responsibility." Occasionally women's institutes and farmers' institutes asked for strict enforcement of health regulations among "Orientals," but there is no evidence of any follow-up. In the legislature, G.S. Pearson, MLA (Liberal, Nanaimo), complained that Nanaimo's Chinese residents were "housed under conditions which would not be tolerated by respectable Anglo-Saxon laboring men." He suggested that forcing them to live under better conditions would lessen "the pressure of their competition." Again, there is no evidence of a follow-up.[62]

What continued to attract the attention of the press and politicians and to stimulate "clean-up" calls were moral issues: gambling and the use of illegal drugs. The evidence about Asian criminality was contradictory. Statistics on jail inmates in 1921 suggested that Chinese residents, with only 5 percent of the total population, formed 16 percent of the province's prison population and that they were the "worst citizens from a law-abiding point of view." That year there were but nineteen Chinese and three Japanese nationals in federal penitentiaries. A decade later, probably reflecting stricter drug laws, there were seventy-six Chinese inmates but only one Japanese convict.[63]

Of course, Asian gambling and drugs could compromise the morals of whites. Ironically, controversies over enforcing gambling laws suggest that immorality was as great among whites as it was among the Chinese! Nevertheless, suppositions that unscrupulous Chinese residents drew unsuspecting and vulnerable young white people into their dens added to the image of "no race [being] more adept than the Chinese in the exploitation of all the varied forms of vice." "Individually we like and admire them," said the *Nanaimo Free Press* in 1915, "but those foreign characteristics we find interesting and amusing in casual acquaintance, lead to a veritable Chinese puzzle when these people are placed in the same social conditions as ourselves ... by reason of their divergent standards of living and conduct." "Since these people are with us, apparently to stay," the *Western Methodist Recorder* suggested, "the least we can do is to inculcate into their minds a wholesome respect for Canadian laws, ideals and institutions, remembering that if we fail to Canadianise the Oriental, he will not fail to Orientalise us."[64]

Enforcing the law was always a problem. A New Westminster police officer suggested that "you can't stop the Chinese absolutely from gambling unless you cut their hands off." During the war, the police had other priorities and largely ignored Chinatowns. By 1918 the situation in Vancouver was such that the Chinese Benevolent Association circulated a petition in city churches. Asserting that over forty gambling dens employed 700 to 800 men full time and that over 3,000 Chinese gamblers were often led into idleness, opium-smoking, licentiousness, theft, and even suicide, the petition asked civic and provincial authorities to enforce the law and provide "wholesome means of recreation for the Chinese." The press saw the petition as an indictment of both the Chinese and law enforcement officials. The police claimed to have driven white men from Chinatown gambling establishments and used the Idlers' Act to clean up the clubs. The Shingle Agency of British Columbia, however, reported a "severe" labour shortage, noting that many Chinese employees quit their jobs when their luck was good, because, if their luck turned bad, they could easily find other work. Criticism of the police continued. Rev. Dr. S.S. Osterhout told the Vancouver Police Commission that a wealthy Chinese syndicate paid fifteen dollars per month in protection money per table to operate without interference. Denying this claim, Chief W. McRae said that over 1,000 Chinese residents had been arrested for gambling in 1918 but admitted that there was "always a certain amount of gambling in the Oriental section." With the attorney general's co-operation, he promised greater efforts to suppress gambling, including a new undercover squad.[65]

The Chinese consul was aware of the bad image of Chinatowns. After two Chinese residents were arrested for smoking opium and gambling in a room with a decomposed corpse, he admonished that law breaking gave "people occasion to despise us" and advised that such criminals should be "publicly punished or deported." Since few gamblers or opium smokers read English language newspapers, in which the consul's advertisement appeared, the message was clearly designed to assuage white readers. Despite more Chinese requests for stricter enforcement of the law and support from the Vancouver Ministerial Association for recreational centres, police raids on gambling dens became routine.[66]

Vancouver politicians often discussed Chinese gambling in terms of police efficiency. In October 1924, after the murder of David C. Lew, allegedly because of a "tong war" over gaming houses, Mayor W. Owen ordered the police to clean up Chinatown and stamp out lotteries. Several raids followed, but the *Vancouver Sun* cynically noted that "every time anybody hollers about vice in the city all the [police] department has to do is go down and knock over a game of dominoes ... It is a good, easy way of keeping the city 'clean.' It has a nice, fattening effect on police statistics. And above all, it enriches the city's coffers." In the 1924 election Owen sought votes from those who rejected "Chinatown's hopes for a wide open town," but voters chose L.D. Taylor, who accused many complainants against Chinese gamblers of ulterior motives. Arguing that Chinatown was not the city's "worst place," he opposed using the police against Chinese gamblers to "the neglect of other parts."[67]

Nevertheless, from time to time, the police raided Chinatown. During an inquiry into the police in 1928, several witnesses alleged that proprietors of gambling dens paid protection. A city detective said that he had wanted "to go out with an axe" to wreck new gambling "joints" but that superior officers had advised him that the mayor would not allow it. A private detective claimed to have seen Shue Moy, the reputed "king of gamblers," visit Taylor's home "arm in arm" with the mayor. Shue admitted going there but denied discussing gambling. Taylor had no objection to gambling in Chinatown if it were confined to Orientals. In the election later that year, W.H. Malkin declared that "he would rather go down to defeat with the women and churches of Vancouver than with the election of supporters of Joe Celona, the alleged king pin of non-Chinese crime, and Shue Moy." That complemented his successful promise to confine Chinese merchants to Chinatown and to clean up the city morally. Police Chief W.J. Bingham, however, believed that gambling, a "natural instinct" of the Chinese and one of their few recreations, could not be suppressed.[68]

During the war, Victoria largely abandoned raids on Chinese gambling quarters since raids and maintaining prisoners cost more than the revenue in fines. In 1919 the suppression of gambling in Vancouver increased it in Victoria. Some Chinese residents obtained licences to operate retail stores, put in a small stock, but only sold lottery tickets. When Chen Yuen San complained of extensive gambling by his countrymen and white men, Victoria City Council condemned the inability of the police to deal with the problem. The police staged a raid and arrested sixty-two

Chinese residents. Raids continued. Magistrate George Jay told white gamblers to spend their money on their families "instead of throwing it away on a Chinese game at which you cannot win." Joseph North argued that he did not want to "build an imaginary Chinese wall around the district," that a total prohibition of gambling was almost impossible, and that Chinatown must be "for the Chinese." Mayor R.J. Porter ordered a "clean-up" and claimed that the police had halted gambling. After easily winning a seat on the Police Commission, North toured Chinatown but found "only Chinamen." Nevertheless, the commission proposed to clean it up and to demolish barricades and partitions. Despite advice that health conditions were good, that partitions were fireguards, and that interfering with private dwellings challenged British liberty, city council sought to regulate Chinatown buildings.[69]

North was not done. Together with Police Commissioner Dr. Ernest Hall, he allegedly prepared a grand scheme in co-operation with Charlie Bo, a Chinese tailor and purported agent for the gambling dens, which resulted in Bo being charged with attempting to bribe Police Chief John Fry. The plan was to permit twenty-eight Chinese gambling "resorts" to open with the commissioners' "supposed compliance" and then, after a day or two, to have the police make a "grand concerted raid" and round up inmates and keepers. Fry rejected the idea because the police had already closed all establishments that could be legally closed. After a case that "was more than a nine days' wonder," the grand jury found "no bill" against Bo. The courts had earlier acquitted Fry on a charge of failing "to prevent crime by allowing the Chinese lotteries and gambling houses to remain open" and had dismissed charges against Hall and North for procuring the chief to neglect his duties because of a lack of evidence. The *Victoria Colonist* correctly blamed the Police Commission for infusing "a feeling of utter disorganization throughout the Police Force" and for dragging it into municipal politics. Gambling and occasional raids continued, including an adventure in which Fry disguised himself as an Indian "squaw" to raid a gambling den. In 1928, after a factional feud in Chinatown and a request from Chinese merchants and citizens, the commission ordered the closure of all gaming houses; as usual, this was a temporary phenomenon.[70]

One of the most scandalous cases of police corruption occurred in Kelowna. A provincial police constable accused city police chief R.W. Thomas of laxness in enforcing gambling and drug laws in Chinatown. Thomas, who had served eleven years with the Shanghai Police, had been chief since 1914. He claimed that he strictly enforced laws on prostitution and narcotics but thought gambling a "trivial matter" that gave the Chinese "some amusement." A provincial inquiry determined that Thomas had permitted "virtually unrestricted" gambling to take place in Chinatown because "public opinion favored Orientals being allowed the same latitude in this respect as whites." Several Chinese witnesses, however, said that they had paid Thomas in order to avoid prosecution for opium possession or prostitution.[71]

The police in many communities continued to raid gambling dens, but attitudes to gambling were changing. Victoria's police commissioner, Andrew McGavin, questioned the wisdom of breaking the doors of Chinese buildings and tearing down partitions "to secure a few poker chips and a few nickels and dimes and occasionally, but very rarely, an opium pipe." He persuaded the commission to license some Chinese gambling clubs in the same manner as white clubs where poker and bridge were played. Similarly the *Courtenay Free Press* wondered why so much was heard of raids on Chinese gambling houses and so little about white men's gambling. Tongue in cheek, the *Vancouver Sun* suggested that mah-jong parties were so cutting into housewives' time that husbands were thinking of forming a Husbands' Protective League.[72]

Far more serious was the drug traffic. In 1920 Chief McRae of the Vancouver Police reported that 80 percent of those arrested under the Drug Act were Chinese. "If the only way to save our children is to abolish Chinatown," said the *Vancouver Sun*, "Chinatown must and will go and will go quickly." The president of the Chinese Benevolent Association admitted that the Chinese had engaged in the trade, but a police commissioner reported that "persons other than [the] Chinese" controlled it. Undeterred, the *Sun* published related stories, including an interview with a "hophead" who said that "they'll never stop the 'dope' by throwing 'hypos' in the can. They want to go after the Chinks that sell it and give us guys a chance to beat the 'dope' out." When the Chinese consul warned Vancouver City Council that the *Sun*'s attacks might cause "great loss and damage" to innocent people, the acting mayor reminded him that people believed that the Chinese, more than any others, were "connected with the trade." The *Vancouver Province*, while critical of the drug traffic, did not blame the Chinese. Similarly, in calling for more drastic laws on the sale of opiates and heavier penalties for abusers, Chief McRae did not mention Asians and said that Vancouver was no worse than some other Canadian cities. The *Province* called the federal Opium and Narcotic Drug Act of 1920 "the beginning of a vigorous campaign in Canada against illicit trade in opium and its derivatives" but argued that the act did not solve a national problem. Under the penname "Janey Canuck," Emily Murphy, a Juvenile Court judge in Edmonton, published articles critical of the drug trade in *Maclean's* magazine and a book, *The Black Candle*, in which she argued that "the illicit [drug] traffic in our Dominion has grown to menacing proportions."[73]

British Columbians continued to agitate against the illegal drug trade. While conceding that it was not confined to Asians, the *Vancouver Sun* described Chinatown as "a cancer corroding the vitals of this community" and referred to the ruinous "habit-forming traffic" that brought "hundreds of white girl addicts into moral slavery." It published sensational "confessions" by Dora M., "a young girl who, after many months' struggle," had escaped from its "clutches." The Chinese formed the Anti-Drug Association; the Returned Soldiers' Council, in association with the Ministerial Association, called a mass meeting to protest the "appalling proportion" of the drug trade and to seek more severe penalties for offenders. A short-lived White Cross Society publicized the evil, calling for stiffer laws and enforcement and for the rehabilitation of traffickers. Speakers at such meetings usually referred to Chinese drug dealers, but others noted that China had rid itself of opium and that the local Chinese were "most likely only pawns in the game."[74]

Drugs were a key part of the plot of Hilda Glynn-Ward's novel, *The Writing on the Wall*. A main character, a white lawyer, collaborates with Chinese agents to smuggle opium into the country. "Once the most brilliant barrister in British Columbia," he becomes an addict and last appears "writhing on the floor like a worm dropped from a spade." *Danger: The Anti-Asiatic Weekly* suggested that Chinese and Japanese drug peddlers might have been the first great effects of "an insidious Oriental campaign to take away the health and strength of our coming generations." Exploiting such notions, white taxi-cab owners advertised that their drivers were "free from the dope evil" and would "protect the younger generation" and "white women."[75]

Although two mayoral candidates who called for stiffer penalties for drug traffickers were defeated in Vancouver's 1922 civic elections, the *Vancouver World* agitated against "the corruption of the little tawdry girls who are taken around in curtained taxis to the Chinese labor camps and lodging houses – so that they might earn the money to purchase more of the foul stuff." It promised "tales of the traffic in illicit drugs that would make red-blooded men feel like taking a gun and ridding a number of places from Chinatown to Shaughnessy Heights, of some of its citizens." Subsequent articles described the drug peddler as "a worse menace than a mad dog," declared that the drug trade knew "no color line," and urged a cleanup of Chinatown slums and the "absolute banishment by deportation of every Oriental who lends himself to the drug ring." Such articles stimulated public interest. Public service organizations and the Ministerial Association asked Vancouver City Council to correct the perceived evils in the Asian quarter – drugs, gambling, white slavery, and plural marriages – and to enforce laws in order to give Asians a "wholesome respect" for Canadian law. After hearing "particularly distressing details ... of the ravages of the drug habit among a large number of girls," the Rotary Club took up the cause. With other service clubs, it sponsored a mass meeting chaired by department store owner Chris Spencer. One speaker claimed that "drug fiends" had committed 98 percent of the crime in the city. Another, the recently elected Conservative MP Leon J. Ladner (Vancouver South) promised to seek measures ensuring that Chinese deportees did not return. Practically every women's organization was represented at a meeting called by an organization of women reformers, the New Era League, that advocated taking "up arms against the alleged illicit traffic in drugs being carried on here by Orientals." Mary Ellen Smith suspected that "the wily Oriental with his trickery and chicanery and oily methods" was "using this drug traffic as a means of overcoming the white race." Another featured speaker, Mrs. James O'Brien, suggested that drugs made boys steal and drove girls "to lives of shame." She later intimated that certain white men had opposed her campaign. Church groups, women's organizations, patriotic societies, lodges, and the Board of Trade called for stiffer penalties for traffickers. The proposed punishments – the deportation of aliens and the cancellation of the naturalization certificates of those convicted of drug offences – would have been particularly effective against the Chinese.[76]

The antidrug campaign spread to the hinterland. The *Cumberland Islander* said that Cumberland did not suffer from the "dope traffic" but endorsed the campaign. The *Nanaimo Daily Herald* complained that the *Vancouver World* had libelled coal mining communities by saying that the companies aided the drug traffic in order to keep Asian labourers at work. A few days later, the Nanaimo police, "acting on information, presumably obtained from several girls of the city who have become addicts," raided Chinatown and discovered cocaine, opium, and ammunition. Nanaimo residents listened with interest to visiting Vancouver speakers. Mrs. O'Brien attacked the lax administration of the law and the ability of Asian traffickers to hire clever lawyers and avoid conviction while addicts, "our own Canadian boys and girls, and sometimes men and women," went to jail. Captain C.F. Macaulay said that Chinese drug peddlers were tools of Japan's imperialist plan to undermine the physical and mental culture of Canada. His observations, like those of Mrs. Glynn-Ward, anticipated an increasing sense of the Japanese being a greater threat to a white society than the Chinese.[77]

Yet the image of a contagious drug-related immorality in Chinatown persisted; interior centres feared that "drug rings" driven from larger cities would re-form in their communities. An ecumenical group of clergymen and members of Vernon City Council organized a public meeting to consider the threat of drug traffickers bringing "their nefarious trade" to the Okanagan. When Rev. Hugh Dobson of the Board of Evangelism and Social Service came to Vernon, local Methodists cancelled a Valentine's Day social to hear him speak on the drug evil. Before a small audience in Penticton, Rev. Nelson A. Harkness, secretary of the Social Service Council of British Columbia, tried to launch "The New Crusade: A Fight Against the Disease of Society." Primarily concerned about boys and young women who fell under the influence of drugs, he alleged that most Chinese dope peddlers were agents of a larger ring that included many Anglo-Saxons. Six months later several women's institutes in the Kootenays called for "drastic action on the Oriental question in connection with the illicit traffic in drugs" but did not answer the attorney general's request for more information. The police in the Okanagan enforced drug laws, but a raid on Armstrong's Chinatown resulted in only two residents being arrested for liquor offences and only one for having opium.[78]

In Ottawa, under the leadership of H.H. Stevens, MP, and using evidence assembled by Ladner, "a solid delegation" of British Columbia members lobbied for increased penalties for traffickers. They secured an amendment to the Opium and

Narcotic Drug Act in 1922 making the lash a possible penalty for peddlers. That did not fully satisfy the *Vancouver Sun,* which warned that "the children of Vancouver parents, promising sons and daughters, will never be safe from the ravages of this evil until these drugs are banned entirely from the country." The *Vancouver World* was more optimistic; it hoped that once they realized that narcotics offences could lead to deportation, residents of Chinatown "would get religion." Members of Parliament used the drug traffic, a matter of national interest, to gain support for an exclusionary immigration law. In defending this idea, W.G. McQuarrie (Conservative, New Westminster) cited the responsibility "to a certain extent" of the Orientals for the drug traffic. Developing this theme, Ladner described "snow parties" at which wealthy Chinese residents introduced white girls to narcotics and quoted Captain Macaulay's claim that doing away with the Asiatic would save "the souls and bodies of thousands of young men and women who are yearly being sent to a living hell and to the grave."[79]

Mrs. O'Brien continued to talk about Chinese drug peddlers debauching white boys and girls, but an Anti-Narcotics League formed in Victoria by church leaders and service clubs scarcely mentioned the Chinese. Once Chinese immigration ended, interest in the drug traffic waned. The *Vancouver World* and its successor, the *Vancouver Star,* occasionally referred to the "drug dragon" or the "drug octopus" but did not pursue it. Evidence given to a Royal Commission investigating methods of the RCMP narcotics squad in 1923 sometimes read "like a dime novel," but neither this evidence nor well-publicized police raids on Vancouver's Chinatown revived the crusade. The police and health officials said that the problem was declining. Even Attorney General Manson admitted that the Oriental was not the only offender and that "many conspicuous members of our own Anglo-Saxon race" engaged in the "nefarious trade." A candidate for Victoria's Police Commission who referred to a Chinese drug ring came a distant fourth. The victor, a former member of the Anti-Narcotics League, said that there were few addicts in the city. The police enforced the law, and the courts sent white and Chinese residents to jail for selling drugs illegally, but the end of Chinese immigration removed much of the antidrug crusade's raison d'être.[80]

In responding to anti-Asian rhetoric that often referred to them collectively as Orientals or Asiatics, the Chinese and the Japanese took pains to point out that they were different. In 1918, for example, a Chinese resident of Victoria complained that the government never dared to "apply strict regulations on the Japanese, nor ... hurt their feelings, as their nation is far more superior than other powers. You treat us as though we were not God's children." In fact, despite their rhetoric, white British Columbians did perceive differences between the Chinese and the Japanese. For example, J.S. Cowper suggested that "the Chinaman remains a Chinaman always relying on his ability to undercut the white man in his market; the Japanese aspires to become a white man in all but pride of race and loyalty to the nation he makes his home with. And he succeeds; that is the bite of the Japanese problem."[81] This distinction continued but inassimilability was applied to both peoples. It was unlikely that white men would "become yellow," but few white British Columbians were willing to allow Asians to be anything but "Oriental."[82] By transcending specific economic complaints, appealing to racial prejudices, and resonating nationally, inassimilability was useful ammunition for those who sought to halt Asian immigration, check the competition of those Asians already present, and consolidate British Columbia as a white man's province.

3

"Putting the Pacific Ocean between Them": Halting Immigration, 1919-29

If the good Lord had intended orientals and white people to live in the same country, he would not have put the Pacific Ocean between them.

– T.G. McBride, House of Commons, *Debates*, 30 April 1923

The end of the European war and "a striking advance in British Columbia's Oriental population" in 1919 intensified anti-Asian agitation.[1] Returning soldiers swelled the labour market, the closing of war industries reduced employment, and the restoration of regular trans-Pacific shipping enabled Chinese labourers, who had gone home to visit or escape economic depression, to return. Moreover, during the war, Asians had entered new fields of endeavour. The Japanese took advantage of distress sales of land to expand their agricultural holdings in the Fraser and Okanagan Valleys; Chinese and Japanese merchants opened shops in white neighbourhoods. Farmers and retail merchants became zealous advocates of Asian exclusion and adapted the arguments of labour and fishermen about inassimilability to buttress campaigns for more restrictions on Asian immigration and activities. British Columbia's politicians exploited these feelings. In the 1920s they largely succeeded, as Parliament passed an exclusionary Chinese immigration law and diplomats renegotiated the gentlemen's agreement with Japan.

Many British Columbians erroneously thought that other Canadians shared their fear that Asians could quickly "swamp the white settler ... and throw our entire social and economic life into confusion." Of British Columbia's half-million residents in 1921, slightly less than half had been born in Canada; only 27 percent were natives of the province. In this "formative period of our national life," explained the *Prince Rupert Daily News*, "we cannot afford to take any chances in regard to the building up of a nation with ideas and standards of living different from our own." To keep their province "British" or "Anglo-Saxon," white British Columbians called for encouraging immigrants of the "right kind." Attorney General A.M. Manson urged "our white people to beget children, in other words, to buck up the birth rate."[2]

Despite the gentlemen's agreement, the Japanese population rose from 6,526 to 15,006 between 1911 and 1921. In 1927 the registrar of vital statistics reported that

The Lonely White

A REAL Problem for the Birth Control Enthusiasts.

"The Lonely White," *Danger: The Anti-Asiatic Weekly*, 1 December 1921.
The caption reads, "A REAL Problem for the Birth Control Enthusiasts."

the natural increase of the Chinese was at a virtual standstill. If there were no new immigration, the number of Chinese residents would decline as its largely male population returned to China or died. The birth rate of the Japanese, however, was 40 per 1,000. Overall, excluding Native Indians, the province's birth rate was 18 per 1,000. The high Japanese birth rate partly resulted from a disproportionate number of women of childbearing age among immigrants. Calling the "ever increasing flood" of Japanese births a Sword of Damocles, propagandists such as J.S. Cowper, a former Liberal MLA, claimed that Japanese girls were taught that it was their patriotic duty to have as many children as possible. He predicted that the yellow races could outnumber whites in five years! H.H. Stevens, MP (Conservative, Vancouver Centre), claimed that one Japanese woman had recently borne her twenty-third child in twenty-five years. Premier John Oliver admonished Prime Minister King that it was Ottawa's duty to grapple with the situation since even a complete halt to immigration would still leave "our present large Oriental population and their prolific birth rate." He recommended eliminating "this menace to the well-being of the white population of this Province" by deporting Orientals or by some other "legitimate means."[3]

While the "prolific" birth rate posed future problems, in 1919 the immediate worry was an apparent dramatic increase in immigration. After falling to a low of 88 new Chinese immigrants in 1915-16, the number rose rapidly. In the first nine months of 1918, there were 2,670 Chinese arrivals. Federal regulations still prohibited the landing of labourers and artisans, but over 5,000 Chinese residents, who had "registered-out" under the Chinese Immigration Act, were eligible to return. In late January 1919 the *Monteagle* arrived with 866 Chinese passengers, mostly students and returnees. Four days later, the *Asia* brought 1,100 BC soldiers home from Europe. By 31 March 1919, 4,333 Chinese individuals had entered Canada, as had 1,178 Japanese people, the largest number since 1907-8. There was also concern that Chinese nationals who had served in labour battalions in France might escape en route home. Finally, loopholes in the Chinese Immigration Act admitted "students" and "farmers" without defining their qualifications. China's consul freely admitted that many of the 2,000 recently arrived "students" were really labourers. This conjunction of events aroused fears that "a rush of Orientals" would take jobs needed for veterans.[4]

At the same time, xenophobia was sweeping North America. Labour organizations, the BC branch of the Canadian Manufacturers' Association, branches of the Great War Veterans' Association, local councils of women, and others called for the dismissal of aliens in order to create jobs for returning soldiers. China had been an ally during the war, but many British Columbians regarded the Chinese as enemies in all but a diplomatic sense. In what the *Vancouver Province* correctly described as "a first determined step against the Asiatic influx," a divided Vancouver City Council asked Ottawa "to entirely prohibit" foreign immigration until returned soldiers had been satisfactorily settled. A few weeks later it demanded an end to Chinese and East Indian immigration and strict enforcement of the gentlemen's agreement with Japan. It pointed to the veterans' difficulty in securing employment, the presence of "too many Chinese" residents, the undesirability of their assimilating "with our citizens on account of racial prejudice," and problems created by competition from Chinese farmers and storekeepers. Similarly, the Great War Veterans' Association wanted to ban Asian immigration for at least twenty years because their working and living conditions were "a detriment to Canada." To solve the "Returned Soldier Problem," New Westminster City Council demanded the end of all Asian immigration and the deportation of Chinese residents who had entered under false pretences, Asiatics who had not "attained a reasonable standard of citizenship" after five years, and aliens "who rendered no service to the State."[5]

Given the prevailing "spirit of unrest," the Chinese consul admitted the wisdom of halting immigration until a new arrangement such as a gentlemen's agreement or literacy test could be devised. Many voices of influence – including immigration officials, Simon Fraser Tolmie, who was federal minister of agriculture and British Columbia's cabinet member, and the Labour Industrial Reconstruction

Committee of Victoria – agreed that riots could ensue unless Asian immigration was halted until every veteran had "permanent and profitable employment." Heeding advice from its officials and British Columbia MPs, the Department of Immigration had already instructed trans-Pacific shipping companies to sell transportation only to Chinese passengers who had "registered-out" or who were bona fide merchants. It also refused head tax payments except from students under the age of sixteen and refunded the tax to approximately 1,200 Chinese individuals en route to Canada and to any Chinese resident who would return to China. By stiffening regulations and their enforcement, the government relieved a potentially explosive situation. By the end of 1920, however, the rules were being evaded in "a wholesale way," as labourers and small merchants secured identity certificates that styled them as merchants and thus exempted them from the head tax.[6]

In the first six months of 1921, 1,068 Chinese and 285 Japanese immigrants entered the country. Stevens feared that political opponents would "precipitate a crisis." Suspecting a conspiracy to evade the law, he persuaded the Department of Immigration to pay careful attention, but many "students" still arrived. The number of merchants rose from 3 or 4 per year to over 1,000. "If Premier Meighen wants to do this Province a service," said the *Vancouver World*, "he must improve the facilities for checking this influx." To stop abuses, in May 1921 Parliament required merchants and students to satisfy the controller of Chinese immigration of their honest intentions. Mackenzie King, leader of the Liberal opposition, agreed that Chinese immigration must be restricted and fraud prevented, but he urged that Chinese people be treated with courtesy.[7]

This did not happen. Victoria's Chinese Benevolent Association complained of the "difficulties and harsh treatment" facing would-be immigrants. It wanted the head tax replaced with an arrangement similar to the gentlemen's agreement. Koliang Yih, the Chinese consul in Vancouver, told a Retail Merchants Association (RMA) luncheon that "the unreasonable and unmerciful hand of your money making Chinese Immigration Act has been very hard on my people." He quoted Canadian statistics to demonstrate that more Chinese nationals had left Canada than had entered between 1911 and 1921. Citing a low birth rate and a high death rate, he predicted that "the next census will show a greater reduction in the number of my people in this country." Finally, he warned that "any attempt on the part of demagogues and good-for-nothing politicians to breed national prejudice and petty strife would be exaggerated ten-fold on the other side of the Pacific, and would retard trade relations."[8]

At the same time, Japan took "the greatest care" in granting certificates to labourers desiring to go to Canada. Canadian immigration authorities admitted that the secret gentlemen's agreement applied only to "coolies" and that Japan was honouring it. Though Japanese immigration was on an upward trend after a modest wartime flow, only 879 Japanese individuals entered Canada in the first nine months of 1918, and most were returnees. Yet the journalist John Nelson claimed that the high Japanese birth rate, their "independence and initiative in industrial development," and their "insistence upon racial equality and demand for political rights" had "done more in one decade to render the Oriental question acute than half a century of economic pressure from the bland and passive Chinese."[9]

British Columbians were alert to anything that might relax controls on Japanese immigration. In 1919, as the Paris Peace Conference discussed Japan's request for a racial equality clause in the League of Nations Covenant, the legislature asked Prime Minister Borden to ensure that Canada could prohibit the immigration of "races which will not readily assimilate with the Caucasian race." Many editors agreed. The *Nanaimo Free Press* feared "mixing unassimilable races," arguing that immigration was "an economic question" and that each country must settle on its own standards. The *Vancouver Province* insisted that the resolution did not impute "race inferiority" but rather recognized "race difference." But there were dissenters. The *Vancouver Sun* asked how Canadians would feel if a world body intimated that they were to be regarded as an inferior people.[10]

British Columbians did not have to pursue the issue. In defending "White Australia," William Hughes, premier of Australia, scuttled the racial equality clause.[11] British Columbians, however, did not favour Hughes's desire to renew the Anglo-Japanese Alliance in 1921 as "White Australia's insurance policy." They appreciated Japan's wartime assistance and wanted friendly relations, but some believed that the alliance had outlived its usefulness and might prevent a check on "an influx of Orientals." They feared that "given a strong foothold" the Japanese would soon take control of every branch of industry. Shortly before the Imperial Conference opened, F.C. Wade, British Columbia's agent general in London, wrote a long letter to the *Times* (London) warning of danger if Canada did "not retain the right to protect herself against the Asiatics, who now threaten to swarm the shores and crowd the valleys of British Columbia." Former attorney general M.A. MacDonald said that Canadians must "preserve our own heritage for our own people." He respected Japan and the Japanese in Canada and denied any "arrogant superiority to race or culture" but noted "economic and race prejudice" against them, their impossible economic standards, and their fecundity. Drawing on California examples, he called for "even more restrictive legislation in line with the undoubted right of all countries – which Japan freely admits – to control our own immigration."[12]

MacDonald's views reflected popular and long-standing sentiment. The provincial government, city and municipal councils, and special interests such as the Native Sons of British Columbia and the Retail Merchants Association of Canada (RMA) urged Prime Minister Arthur Meighen to ensure that any renewed Japanese treaty preserve Canada's right "to restrict Japanese immigration in the interests of a white British Columbia." Oliver, whose critics accused him of trying to embarrass the Meighen government, sought a guarantee that the treaty would not interfere with provincial restrictions on the employment of the Japanese or with control of provincial lands. Meighen's reply was simple: The Anglo-Japanese Alliance had nothing to do with immigration, and the 1911 Treaty of Commerce and Navigation, which did, was not due for renegotiation. This position allowed the local press to reiterate its respect for Japan, its gratitude for wartime help, its desire for peace, and its insistence that Canada control immigration. Debate continued. The legislature, whose main concern was Asian economic activities, unanimously asked Ottawa to take steps to terminate the Anglo-Japanese Treaty and to amend the Immigration Act "to restrict totally as far as possible Asiatic immigration" so that British Columbia could "be reserved for people of the European race."[13]

Race certainly influenced ideas about the Chinese and Japanese. Yet direct economic competition inspired such groups as retail merchants and some unions affiliated with the Vancouver Trades and Labour Council to agitate for the cessation of Asian immigration – that is, for Asiatic exclusion. Several small-town newspapers suggested that Asians were "flooding" the province and prospering, that few were unemployed, and that some were acquiring expensive automobiles, a hallmark of wealth. Realizing the limits of local efforts to halt competition, the British Columbia branch of the RMA initiated a national campaign "to make this a white man's country."[14] At the national convention in 1920, a Vancouver delegate referred to Chinese competition in Vancouver and Victoria; others warned that "the presence of so many Orientals had a bad effect on the moral and social status of western communities." Nova Scotia and New Brunswick delegates reported Chinese competition in laundries. The convention asked the government to prohibit Oriental immigration. The next year, George S. Hougham, secretary of the British Columbia branch, urged the "complete exclusion of Orientals as the only means of combatting the Japanese and Chinese menace on the western Coast and in other parts of Canada." He persuaded the RMA to ask the federal government "for drastic action" on Chinese immigration.[15]

Minister of Agriculture Simon Fraser Tolmie was sympathetic, having recently said that Asians in British Columbia were rapidly gaining supremacy in certain industries and were undesirable citizens, as they sent all of their profits to Asia. Referring to a less satisfactory answer from Meighen, Hougham told the provincial convention that "a tremendous force of public opinion" was necessary before any government would consider exclusion. Reminding retailers that the public patronized Chinese grocers, he warned them of "severe criticism" if they attacked the question only from their own viewpoint. Thus the local RMA magazine said that it was more than a matter of labour or competitive merchandising but "purely and simply an economic and racial question" on whose solution depended "the future of Western civilization." California examples also inspired retail merchants. After Paul Findlay of the California Fruit Growers Exchange told them that Oriental exclusion was "a matter of life and death for our civilization," the grocers' sections of the Vancouver and Victoria RMAs protested continued Asian immigration as "the most serious social measure facing the citizens of B.C."[16]

While pressing for national action, coastal retailers lobbied their interior counterparts. In the Okanagan they emphasized that unless white merchants united to "combat the growing evil they will find themselves crowded out by Orientals." The RMA also co-operated with farm organizations and in Vancouver had F.W. Welsh, president of the Trades and Labour Council, participate in a series of talks on the "Oriental question." Welsh prophesied a menace within twenty years if immigration laws were not made more rigid but, reflecting labour's ambivalence, told retailers that businessmen, rather than a labour organization, must solve it. Three months later, however, Welsh used similar words and a reference to cheap Asian labour to convince the Trades and Labour Congress of Canada to pass resolutions for Oriental exclusion and against renewal of the Anglo-Japanese Alliance. An editorial in the *B.C. Labour News* argued that a "vast number of unemployed" made it necessary to take immediate "drastic action" to stop Asian immigration. The GWVA called for the total exclusion of Asians and for their dismissal from employment in order to make room for white men. Anticipating co-operation with the Trades and Labour Council, the Soldiers' Council of all lower mainland veterans' groups prepared statistics to demonstrate the need for action to maintain Canada as a white man's country.[17]

In 1921 unemployment was widespread. The economy had improved slightly after the initial postwar maladjustment, but unemployment rose sharply in 1921; the net value of production in the primary and secondary industries fell by about 13 percent. J.W. de B. Farris, the provincial minister of labour, estimated in July that there were 5,600 unemployed in Vancouver, 3,500 in Victoria, and 2,000 to 3,000 elsewhere. He anticipated 20,000 unemployed by the fall because of inactivity in lumbering and mining (except in the coal industry), declines in the pulp and paper industry, and the end of shipbuilding. The *Vancouver Sun* warned in November that several thousand unemployed men in Vancouver could create a difficult situation. The decision of many Canadian and imperial veterans to settle in British Columbia added to the problem. Asians, none of whom applied for relief, were convenient scapegoats.[18]

In July the Vancouver Trades and Labour Council organized a meeting to discuss the Oriental "penetration of industries" and to form an "Oriental Exclusion League." In attendance were representatives of the RMA, veterans' groups, unions of carpenters, iron moulders, teamsters, machinists, hotel and restaurant employees, observers from the Rotary Club, and, "in a watching capacity," two members of the Board of Trade. The meeting unanimously called for exclusionary legislation. After the Board of Trade's own special committee reported that "national racial prejudice has resulted in a general cry being raised to exclude the Oriental," the board said that "absolute exclusion" was "the only ultimate solution." Although the board, which had Chinese and Japanese members, stopped short of endorsing what was now called the Asiatic Exclusion League, A.D. McRae, a prominent businessman, accepted the league's honorary presidency and contributed to its finances. McRae, who had political ambitions, later boasted of this link to counteract criticisms of the employment of Asians by his firms the Canadian Western Lumber Company and Wallace Fisheries Ltd.[19] At the official founding meeting of the Asiatic Exclusion League in Vancouver in mid-August 1921, delegates from the Rotary Club and the Board of Trade did not attend, but representatives of the tailors, the bakery salesmen, and the Imperial Order of the Daughters of the Empire did. Although the RMA offered moral and financial help, it wanted more information on the league's "constructive policy." Organized labour was also ambivalent, but some of its leaders were prominent in the league. Five hundred people, including Japanese and Chinese residents, attended a meeting on Asian exclusion organized by the Federated Labour Party under Angus MacInnis. Saying that their only enemy was "the capitalist class of all countries," they opposed any measure that would "tend to exclude any workers from Canada."[20]

British Columbia's Asiatic Exclusion League had three main aims: "to educate the white population to the terrible menace of the Oriental immigration; to pledge every federal candidate to state his policy on Oriental exclusion; and to press for the immediate registration of all Orientals in British Columbia." In an interview with the Japanese Workers' Union, which feared that the league wanted its members repatriated, Captain C.F. Macaulay stressed that its primary object was ending the Asiatic influx in order to "provide more work for white men." Unlike its namesake, which gained notoriety when its parade and rally turned into a riot in 1907, the new league did not organize mass rallies but did have Alderman Philip Tindall of Seattle speak to it on the situation in the United States. The league also sought clarification of any imperial authority over Canadian immigration policy and informed Britain's prime minister, David Lloyd George, of its concern that "the Yellow Race will outnumber the white" and of "unbearable" economic competition such that businesses and trades, particularly the fishery, "the training ground for Canada's future sailors," were falling to Oriental control.[21]

The league hired V.H. Johnston to run its membership campaign and to crystallize "public opinion in order to put up a strong front to both Federal and Provincial governments." He hired fifty canvassers to sell 40,000 memberships at twenty-five cents each. Union business agents also sold memberships. By 7 September the league had claimed over 2,000 members; by 12 September, 4,000; by 23 September, 15,000; by 28 September, 18,000; and by early October, 23,000. In Vancouver, canvassers reported enthusiastic welcomes, except in fashionable Shaughnessy Heights, where Asian servants often answered doors. Macaulay spoke to such diverse groups as the Federated Association of Musicians and the Grandview Chamber of Commerce. The league sent organizers to Powell River, Port Alberni, and Milner. In Courtenay it signed up members after Macaulay and J.S. Cowper spoke to a "fair audience." Cowper addressed the annual meeting of the Lower Mainland Women's Institutes. Since July he had been writing articles for the *Vancouver World*[22] under the title "The Rising Tide of Asiatics: An Investigation of the Oriental Peril." Sometimes in sensational fashion, he described Chinese and Japanese domination of aspects of agriculture and retailing, the presence of the Japanese in logging, their high birth rate, and their continued ties with Japan. After Hilda Glynn-Ward addressed a joint meeting of the Duncan Board of Trade and the RMA, several individuals joined, and the Board of Trade endorsed its aims. In Prince Rupert the Trades and Labour Council and the GWVA planned to invite an organizer to help establish a branch. Despite such activity, membership levelled off well short of the league's objective of 100,000 members.[23]

Hilda Glynn-Ward's novel, *The Writing on the Wall*, was published by the *Vancouver Sun*, which advertised it as a story "so startling and lurid that it surely cannot fail to awaken those unbelievers in Eastern Canada who still wonder why the West is crying out on its knees for new immigration regulations." The book has scant literary or other merit, but the contemporary press reviewed it favourably. The *Vancouver World* noted that it "vividly" portrayed the impact of Asians on the province; the *Victoria Colonist* suggested that it would "disturb the complacency of those who regard the Oriental problem as a 'local issue'" and later described it as "a story with a moral"; and the *British Columbia United Farmer* said that it would "bring home to its readers in a striking manner the real dangers of the situation." The *B.C. Federationist*, however, called its attack on the "Asiatic invasion" a "failure" while a *Vancouver Sun* review, although claiming that "patriotism, not sensationalism" had inspired it, editorially counselled tolerance and warned of the danger of offending "450,000,000 people only eight days away" and of confounding efforts to establish "perpetual peace on the Pacific."[24]

Another exercise in anti-Asian propaganda was *Danger: The Anti-Asiatic Weekly*, which was published in Vancouver beginning in October 1921. This magazine was "devoted to an expose [sic] of the perils of the Oriental menace, and to an effort to keep Canada, and especially British Columbia, a white country, for white men." Despite sharing the objectives of the Asiatic Exclusion League and carrying a free advertisement for it, *Danger* criticized the league's employment of canvassers whose commissions represented 60 percent of the membership fees. In response, the league advertised its "thousands" of members and denied having "been associated in any way with the publication called 'DANGER.' Nor do we endorse its policy." *Danger* replied that the league executive, dominated by the Trades and Labour Council and returned soldiers' organizations, did not represent the population and lacked a business-like approach in lobbying governments and soliciting memberships.

Danger had some advertisements, especially from candidates in the 1921 federal election, but its pre-election issue appears to have been its last whereas the league survived the election.[25]

The "Oriental question" had largely ceased to be a provincial issue since the province had reached the limits of its ability to restrict immigration. During the 1920 provincial election, the question was mentioned in only a few constituencies although Liberal Premier John Oliver's stock speeches mentioned "a White B.C."[26] The 1921 federal election, however, stimulated the question. In this election British Columbians were as much interested in tariff, trade, and railway policies as were other Canadians, but no candidate opposed a "White Canada" – not even F.B. Stacey (Liberal-Unionist, Fraser Valley), who was concerned about international relations. There was so little difference in the candidates' policies that the *Nanaimo Herald* cynically observed that "they will be just as unanimous when the next election comes round, and the Orientals will be just as numerous as ever." The candidates of all three major parties spoke of impressing eastern Canada with the need to resolve British Columbia's problem although the intensity of the debate varied by region. Their arguments anticipated subsequent parliamentary action, and most politicians used the generic terms "Asiatic" or "Oriental," which in many contexts were a code word for "Japanese."[27]

Exclusion was mentioned even in areas with few Asians. In Cariboo, which covered most of the northern two-thirds of the province, T.G. McBride, the successful Progressive, was as much concerned with a government abattoir in Kamloops as he was with Asians, but he alleged that the Japanese obtained money to buy land through their consul (an accusation that the consul had already denied). In Prince George his Conservative opponent advocated exclusion to avoid "competition with the Japanese in all industrial pursuits." In East and West Kootenay, each of which had fewer Asians than any of the other constituencies,[28] the Asian question was of little local interest, but in the latter the successful Farmer-Labour candidate, L.W. Humphrey, listed "Exclusion of all Asiatics" in his platform and attacked his Liberal opponent for employing Asians. When two Liberals from Vancouver, Victor W. Odlum and M.A. MacDonald, asserted that "for the sake of our children, British Columbia must be kept white," a large audience in Cranbrook was unresponsive. Nevertheless, a few weeks later in Cranbrook, H.H. Stevens said that Laurier had disallowed British Columbia's exclusion laws but that Meighen was working to abrogate the Anglo-Japanese Treaty, a point echoed by Conservative incumbent Dr. Saul Bonnell. Captain C. Carmichael of Vancouver toured West Kootenay for the Conservatives, saying that "if you want the Japanese, vote Liberal."[29]

In Skeena, outsiders also initiated anti-Asian discussions, although its 2,403 Japanese and 1,041 Chinese residents formed one of the heaviest concentrations of

Asians in the province. In opening the Conservative campaign in Prince Rupert, the main population centre, Tolmie said that if their immigration were not halted, Asiatics would soon "own this country"; at a Liberal meeting, MacDonald warned that without exclusion British Columbia would become like Hawaii, where Orientals represented 10 percent of the voters. The Liberal candidate and ultimate victor, A.W. Stork, "absolutely and unalterably opposed" the entry of even one more Asian. The liberal *Prince Rupert Daily News* added that Conservative inaction had left the "Oriental question" in "exactly the same state" as when the Liberals had left office in 1911.[30]

In Yale, which included the Okanagan Valley, the incumbent and victorious Conservative, J.A. MacKelvie, boasted of his record in upholding Canada "as a white man's country"; his Liberal and Farmer opponents also favoured Asian exclusion. However, despite the presence of 1,080 Chinese and 490 Japanese residents, as well as concern about Asian land ownership, the issue received only passing mention. The other main agricultural constituency, the Fraser Valley, had 1,600 Chinese and 1,142 Japanese residents, prompting the National Liberal Conservative (Unionist) nominating convention to call on the federal government to investigate and to legislate a halt to Asian immigration and land holding. Stacey, the incumbent Unionist, advertised his past advocacy of greater restriction of Oriental immigration and his belief that it could be accomplished without international complications; nevertheless, the Liberal, E.A. Munro, won the seat. Much of the adjacent riding of New Westminster was agricultural, but sawmilling and fishing were also important. Because of fishing, New Westminster had more Japanese residents, 3,189, than any other constituency. It also had 1,935 Chinese residents. The Federated Labour Party candidate so equivocated on the "perennial Oriental question" that C.E. Hope, speaking for W.G. McQuarrie, the Conservative, wondered whether "Oriental money" was helping him. McQuarrie, who was re-elected, asserted that "if you want to keep this a white man's country, you will make no mistake to vote for Meighen." His Liberal opponent also supported "exclusion of Orientals and all other immigrants not easily assimilated."[31]

Although Vancouver had three separate constituencies – Burrard, Vancouver Centre, and Vancouver South – for purposes of mass meetings and newspaper advertisements, Conservatives and Liberals treated it as one. Thus, although Burrard and Vancouver South had relatively small Asian populations, the popular image was that of Vancouver Centre, whose 5,994 Chinese and 3,017 Japanese residents represented 14.8 percent of its total population. There was little to differentiate between the main parties. M.A. MacDonald, the Liberal in Burrard, predicted that if unchecked the "Oriental menace" would dominate the province. Leon J. Ladner, the Conservative in Vancouver South, said that the "Oriental question" struck "at the root of our social and economic well-being and happiness." Victor W. Odlum, the Liberal in Vancouver South, did "not think the white and yellow can mix" and called for a "scientific" immigration policy, but he suggested that subnormal

European immigrants were more dangerous because they were more likely to be added "to our own families." Stevens declared that "the Oriental was unfit socially, mentally, morally and industrially, to take any part in the building up of a national type." When R.H. Gale, the Liberal in Vancouver Centre, said that easterners did not understand the problem, Ladner agreed.[32]

Where the parties differed was on tactics. Ladner criticized Liberals for raising the matter during the Washington Conference on naval armaments and Far Eastern matters; MacDonald contended that "total exclusion" could be accomplished without "offending" nations with "great and promising" markets. When Ladner blamed Liberals for the number of Asians in Canada, Odlum replied that both parties "should stand shoulder to shoulder" to face eastern Canada on the matter. Stevens praised Meighen for standing "fearlessly" for abrogating the "unfair" Anglo-Japanese Treaty, which the Laurier government had accepted, and noted that the Oriental population of British Columbia was no longer increasing greatly. Ladner claimed that local Liberals had instructed Odlum "to say nothing about the Oriental question"; Odlum contended that "business interests," who wanted Asian immigrants, supported Ladner. Mackenzie King, who had told an Ontario audience that it was a "bad time" to discuss Asian exclusion, sent a telegram to Gale endorsing "more effective restriction" of Oriental immigration to maintain Canadian labour standards and avoid international complications. Stevens noted that Liberals promised only "effective restrictions" on Chinese immigration, had not mentioned the Japanese or Hindus, and advocated Asian enfranchisement. The Liberals ran a large newspaper advertisement under the slogan "Liberal Candidates Are Pledged to a White British Columbia" and a cartoon of an arch that straddles a map of the province and bears the inscription "Meighen Welcomes You." Beneath the arch, Meighen welcomes an endless stream of immigrants. The text cites statistics of Asian penetration in industry to suggest that Stevens had done nothing to halt Asian immigration. The same day a smaller Conservative advertisement listed in parallel columns Liberal and Conservative policies under the heading "Who is Responsible for the Asiatic?" The Conservatives won all three Vancouver seats.[33]

In Victoria, where the Japanese population was small and the Chinese population stable, the Liberal candidate favoured "total exclusion of Oriental labor" but was not reported as speaking on it. Several supporters, however, including Major Richard J. Burde, MLA (Independent, Comox-Alberni), and J.S. Cowper, referred to Japanese encroachments in fishing and agriculture. Tolmie called for "wise immigration" and recalled watching "the Oriental spread throughout the whole of Canada," but his full-page newspaper advertisement did not list the "Oriental question" as a reason for voting for him. He was re-elected.[34]

Victoria's suburbs, Oak Bay, Esquimalt, and Saanich, were part of the Nanaimo constituency, in which Asians were widely discussed even though they represented only 5.5 percent of the population. The Liberal candidate, T.B. Booth, referred to "the Oriental menace in all lines of industry," which endangered "the very existence of white people"; the Conservative candidate, C.H. Dickie, decried the unemployment of white men while Asians held jobs. Booth supported any move to expel all Orientals from Canada; Dickie would not "drive the Orientals out of the province" but would do all in his power "to replace the Orientals with whites." Booth complained of federal indifference; spokesmen for Dickie blamed Laurier's government for the influx of Asian immigrants. Booth referred to Japan's "secret aspirations ... for world domination"; Dickie, the successful candidate, conceded that Japan had helped in the war but hoped that Meighen's work at the Washington Conference would allow Canada to deal with the problem.[35]

In Comox-Alberni the incumbent Conservative, H.S. Clements, insisted that the tariff was the main issue. Veterans' organizations and fishermen supported his chief opponent, the Independent candidate A.W. Neill, whose slogans were "Self-preservation and Self-representation" and "A White B.C. and a home-made MP." Neill declared that "little brown men" were swamping the west coast; the presence of 1,795 Japanese and 2,295 Chinese residents, who together formed 12.8 percent of the constituency's population, gave some credibility to his claim. He called for bringing a "complete stop" to Oriental immigration and attacked the Meighen government for issuing large numbers of fishing licences to Orientals and accused it of arranging for the Japanese to vote. Neill called for aid to settlers to "help build up a permanent White fishing population ... instead of having every strategic point on our Pacific Seaboard in possession of Orientals." Clements rightly replied that the Asian "menace ... always sprang up just before an election." Nevertheless, he averred that he had always opposed Asian immigration and blamed Burde for letting Japanese come to the west coast. While endorsing the enfranchisement of Japanese veterans, he boasted of instructing returning officers not to put any Asiatic names on the voters' lists.[36] Only in Comox-Alberni was the Asian question decisive, but British Columbia MPs considered it an important issue.

In Ottawa, irrespective of their party ties, the British Columbia members formed a "solid thirteen" on Asian immigration. W.G. McQuarrie entered a resolution on the order paper stating that since "the immigration of oriental aliens and their rapid multiplication is becoming a serious menace to living conditions, particularly on the Pacific coast, and the future of the country in general, ... the Government should take immediate action with a view to securing the exclusion of future immigration of this type." Then, on 31 March 1922, the British Columbia MPs interviewed Charles Stewart, minister of the interior, who was responsible for immigration. Ladner, who claimed credit for bringing them together, recorded that "each person spoke a little, having prepared a particular aspect of the case. It is undoubtedly a difficult question on account of the apathy here in the East and the idea that it is unChristian-like to keep out these people. It shows what fool ideas people are capable of. Some of these people professing such ultra Christian ideas should have a Jap family living on one side of them, a Chinese family on the other with a Hindu child sitting on each side of their only girl in the public school." When Stewart did not satisfy them, the MPs orchestrated arguments for the debate on McQuarrie's resolution. In inviting members to attend, McQuarrie stressed that the "Oriental menace is rapidly spreading over the whole Dominion" and warned that without immediate "drastic action" "to stop the influx of these unassimilable people" an "alarming situation," as in California and Hawaii, could occur in Canada.[37]

Anticipating the debate of 8 May 1922, Prime Minister King discussed the matter in Cabinet. He was sympathetic to excluding the Chinese and claimed partial credit for putting "more effective restriction of Chinese immigration" in the 1919 Liberal platform. He determined from the consul, Dr. Chilien Tsur, that China would accept restrictions on the admission of labourers if Canada admitted bona fide students and merchants, as well as the wives and children of men already in the country, and abolished the head tax. Department of Immigration officials did not think that the head tax harmed trade but complained of labourers evading the tax by claiming to be students or merchants' wives. A.L. Jolliffe, controller of Chinese immigration, favoured exclusion. In the meantime, an Order in Council required Chinese emigrants to have their passports checked before leaving China. Through administrative regulations, such as requiring Asians, other than the Japanese, to possess at least $250 before they could land, lowering the maximum age for students joining their parents, and requiring merchants to have at least a $2,500 investment, the Department of Immigration reduced immigration from China to only twelve emigrants in August 1922. King also had discussions with the Japanese consul, but Japan's international stature and the gentlemen's agreement limited options in dealing with that nation.[38]

When McQuarrie introduced his resolution, the galleries were "packed with delegations from all parts of Ontario, where Oriental penetration was increasing." The RMA had done its homework. In Ottawa E.M. Trowern, its national secretary, met McQuarrie and Stevens daily. Outside Parliament it so effectively co-ordinated lobbying that McQuarrie attributed much of his success in getting the resolution through Parliament to its educational work across the country. From Alberta to Nova Scotia, RMA branches, chambers of commerce, farmers' organizations, and patriotic groups sent resolutions to the minister of immigration and their own members of Parliament supporting exclusion. In its annual presentation to the Cabinet, the Trades and Labour Congress of Canada pressed for "partial or total exclusion of Asiatics." Several national railway unions called for "further restriction of Asiatic immigration." In British Columbia many organizations reaffirmed their opposition to Asian immigration. A new Provincial Farmers Progressive Party included "a strict policy of Oriental exclusion" in its platform.[39]

In explaining his resolution, McQuarrie sketched the history of immigration arrangements with China and Japan, noted the "alarming" Japanese birth rate, recent advances of Asians into industries, and their invasion of Alberta and other eastern provinces. He cited as evidence of national support, the RMA, the GWVA, the Trades and Labour Congress of Canada, and articles in the *Winnipeg Free Press,* the *Toronto Telegram,* and *Maclean's* magazine. He referred to a serious race problem in the United States arising from the presence of negroes and the Japanese and concluded with eight reasons for exclusion that focused on inassimilability and the expectation that "peaceful penetration" would "lead to racial conflict and international unpleasantness." He admitted that the government would have to work out the details but unequivocally demanded Chinese exclusion and cancellation of both the gentlemen's agreement and the Anglo-Japanese Treaty.[40]

To demonstrate that it was more than a British Columbia issue, the seconder, W.T. Lucas (Progressive, Victoria, Alberta) argued that the question "vitally affects the Dominion as a whole." George Black (Conservative, Yukon) echoed this sentiment and warned eastern Canadians that they would soon "be battling with these people for an existence." The British Columbia members dominated the debate, which carried on until 1:45 a.m. Speakers stressed particular aspects: the history of Asian immigration, the Anglo-Japanese Alliance, the particular circumstances of their constituencies, the illegal drug traffic, Oriental occupation of land, the need to give the problem national attention, California's experiences with the Japanese, the potentially huge number of Asian immigrants, and the imperial government's admission of Canada's right to determine its own immigration policy. Common threads were: the desire to retain Canada for the white race, the impossibility of economic competition with Asians in light of their low living standards, and less concern about the Chinese than about the Japanese, whose industry was admired and economic aggression feared. Prime Minister King and other Liberals agreed with the need to protect white labour and "the desirability of a country having a homogeneous people" but, for diplomatic reasons relating to Japan, rejected "exclusion." The British Columbia members opposed a government amendment to replace "exclusion" with "effective restriction." As Stevens said, "we want immigration from the Orient stopped." Of the BC members, only Dr. J.H. King, minister of public works, voted with the government. The *Vancouver Province* agreed with Stevens that "effective restriction" would probably not solve the problem, but other journals, including, after reflection, the *British Columbia Retailer,* were prepared to try it. They were satisfied that the BC members had drawn eastern attention to the problem, a point reinforced by a *Toronto Globe* editorial asserting that "it is manifest that restriction of immigration and restriction of land holding are alike necessary if British Columbia is to remain a white man's country."[41]

Meanwhile, the provincial RMA continued its campaign. With the assistance of Attorney General Manson, it persuaded Charles Stewart to visit the province in order to see the "Oriental question" first-hand, and it convinced its national body to renew its support. Stewart did not seem very sympathetic, but other federal cabinet ministers who visited that summer were. Minister of Agriculture W.R. Motherwell told a Victoria audience that the question "seemed to be overwhelming here." Minister of Labour James Murdock said that observing Chinese and Japanese competition in industry had made him realize that "some action was needed to prevent a situation developing that might become a real danger." Solicitor General D.D. Mackenzie told 15,000 people at a Vancouver Liberal picnic that the prime minister had promised to "exercise every constitutional power that we have to see that you are not imposed upon by people that you do not want" even if it were necessary to amend the constitution.[42]

Despite such promises, British Columbia's exclusionists continued their national campaign. At the annual national conventions of the Army and Navy Veterans Association, the Grand Army of United Veterans, and the Imperial Order of the Daughters of the Empire, British Columbia delegates secured resolutions favouring Oriental exclusion. The Trades and Labour Congress of Canada noted that the "yellow menace exists in an ever increasing degree throughout the entire Dominion" despite the head tax. After unanimously endorsing the "total exclusion of Oriental immigration," it asked for the repeal of the clause in the Anglo-Japanese Treaty relating to the Japanese in Canada. Elsewhere individuals spread the exclusionist message by means of "startling statistics" of "the menace of yellow race penetration." For example, Charlotte Whitton, convenor of immigration for the National Council of Women, advised the council to study Oriental immigration.[43]

In British Columbia the RMA took the lead in reorganizing the Asiatic Exclusion League, which had been relatively quiet since the election. It designed membership buttons with the white letters "B.C." on a blue background to show their support for a white British Columbia, wrote letters to politicians, and sponsored a mass meeting in Vancouver on 1 October 1922, at which Stevens, McQuarrie, Cowper, and Mrs. James O'Brien, a specialist on the drug evil, repeated old arguments. In Nanaimo sixteen organizations, including city council, the GWVA, farmers' institutes, the Board of Trade, women's groups, and labour organizations attended a mass meeting chaired by the mayor. Among the speakers were Captain Macaulay of the league and R.T. Crowder of the RMA. Macaulay raised the spectre of Japanese nationals being brought in secretly through the Queen Charlotte Islands, of doing military drills, and of promoting the dope traffic as part of an imperialistic policy to undermine Canada's physical and mental culture. Crowder drew on California material to show that Japan planned to colonize North America. The meeting formed a branch of the Asiatic Exclusion League. The Victoria RMA pledged support for the league, but the Kamloops branch offered only donations from individual members. In New Westminster the RMA did not work with the league but did join the GWVA in sponsoring a public meeting to endorse McQuarrie's resolution. After hearing Cowper and others, attendees unanimously endorsed a resolution asking the federal government to prohibit Asian immigration; they pointed to unemployment, the impossibility of economic competition with Orientals, and their inassimability as justification. The Nanaimo and Prince George branches of the RMA also subscribed to the "Oriental fund," but other branches were indifferent.[44]

In rural areas, women's institutes heard papers on the growth of the Asian population and its increasing penetration of the economy. Their district conferences urged members to do what they could "to make this a white man's country" and encouraged them to write to Ottawa. Many followed this advice, and their individual letters often expressed vivid opinions. The secretary of the Pitt Meadows Women's Institute, for example, wrote that "'a White Man's Country' is the cry heard on every side. B.C. is today overrun with members of the yellow race whose mode of living is so far below our standard that they can afford to work for a much smaller wage than a white man. In these years of struggle, 'the Aftermath' of the Great War, who has a greater right to employment than our own race?" At the 1923 national convention of the women's institutes in Fredericton, Mrs. McLachlan of Victoria urged members "to use their influence in keeping British Columbia a white man's country." Similarly the forty-three delegates at the January 1923 annual convention of the United Farmers of British Columbia (UFBC) agreed with guest speaker J.A. MacKelvie, MP (Conservative, Yale), that Oriental immigration was a "deadly menace" and agreed to continue "the fight for the exclusion of Orientals." One of the thirteen campaign planks of the new Provincial Party, organized after the UFBC convention, was "the gradual replacement of Oriental labor by white labor, coupled with all possible measures towards the exclusion of Orientals."[45]

Both mainstream provincial parties repeated their opposition to Asian immigration at their 1922 conventions. Premier Oliver believed that there was no doubt of the "overwhelming feeling amongst British Columbia electors that nothing short of total exclusion will meet the situation." Manipulating "the race idea," however, was not a major source of his "political legitimacy";[46] transportation policies, for example, were much more important. Nevertheless, William Sloan, MLA (Liberal, Nanaimo), who had long fought against Asian competition in coal mines, took "the winds out of the sails of the opposition" on the first day of the fall 1922 session by giving notice of an exclusion motion. Citing the threat to Canada's "industrial and economic life" by competitors "with a lower standard of living [than that] necessary for the well-being of Anglo-Saxon civilization," he called for a complete prohibition on Asian immigration. Denying any "racial or national superiority," he said that "a single State" could not "long continue to contain two conflicting and distinct civilizations." He asserted that everyone in the province was affected, "with the possible exception of doctors of divinity, of medicine, and of law, and a few other callings with which the Oriental does not compete." The legislature "loudly applauded."[47]

In seconding the motion, Attorney General Manson made an "almost fervid appeal" for the white race "to stand together to oust the Oriental." Manson agreed that it was mainly a federal matter but noted that Ottawa did not appreciate "the acuteness of the situation." If Asians were not stopped at the coast, he warned, "the mountains will prove no barrier to the swelling tide," and the prairies would soon have the problem. Expressing begrudging admiration for "the little Jap," for "his steadiness, his thrift, and his hard working qualities," but "perhaps not [having] that same admiration for the class of Chinamen that come to British Columbia," he described the "progressive menace" as Asians entered new industries. When two Federated Labour Party MLAs, Thomas Uphill (Fernie) and Sam Guthrie (Newcastle), gleefully noted that business and professional men were making the same complaints as labour, Manson agreed that "it is wonderful how a man begins to think when his pocket is touched." His "real *objection* to the Oriental," however, was "permanent and incurable, the ethnological differences as between the white and Oriental races." Several MLAs deplored the issue being a political football, a point underscored by Conservative leader Willian J. Bowser's attempt to embarrass federal Liberals by demanding a provincial veto over any treaty that did not allow the province to prohibit the employment of Asians in industries. No one spoke against Sloan's motion in principle or voted against it. Moreover, outside the legislature, several agricultural organizations, the New Westminster Board of Trade, Saanich Central Ratepayers, and the Victoria branch of the Canadian Legion commended its intent.[48]

Even in Ottawa the resolution spoke to the converted. Prime Minister King favoured restricting "Oriental immigration to the point where it will vanish completely" but would not use the phrase "exclusion" lest it raise serious diplomatic complications within the British Empire. Nevertheless, he was preparing to regulate Chinese immigration. He advised Consul Tsur of interest in a treaty to replace the head tax with some means of "effective restriction." Tsur replied that China's new government would limit the number of labourers emigrating rather than endure the "humiliating" head tax or an "open expression of exclusion of Chinese labour." While an arrangement along the lines of the gentlemen's agreement was diplomatically attractive, Percy Reid, controller of Chinese immigration, said that removing the head tax would "open Canada's doors" to Chinese immigrants from places other than China. He argued that the lack of stable central government or authority in China would make any arrangement "of little value" and that to avoid fraud Canada would have to station a Department of Immigration official in China. Reid proposed a more draconian measure: that of subjecting even Canadian-born Chinese residents to an immigration law. After consulting the Department of External Affairs, however, the Department of Immigration modified the proposal in order to remove references to the Canadian-born and to suggest that China permit only bona fide merchants, clergymen, and students to emigrate. College and university students were a special case. Department of Immigration officials thought that it would be difficult to single them out for special exemption, but some British Columbians favoured admitting such students to benefit trade.[49]

In the meantime, because of continuing unemployment, an Order in Council forbade the entry of all Asians, other than Japanese nationals, except for farmers, farm labourers, female domestics, and wives and children under eighteen of those Asians legally resident in Canada and capable of caring for them. Department of Immigration officials offered advice about timing the announcement lest the Chinese try to bring in family members before the new limits became law. When Tsur arrived in Vancouver in late January 1923 after a visit to China, he was unaware of the policy changes. He told reporters that through a reciprocal treaty Canada would remove the head tax and that China would not let labourers come to Canada. Rumours circulated in Ottawa of legislation based on negotiations with China to settle "the troublesome question of Oriental immigration."[50] In fact, negotiations were over; the government was planning legislation.

During the 1923 parliamentary session, the British Columbia members again called for restrictions on Chinese and Japanese immigration. Neill proposed a New Zealand model in order to restrict immigrants from entering Canada until they had secured permission from the minister of immigration. In support McQuarrie said that the name of the policy did not matter as long as Asians were "kept out of the country," noting that British Columbians wanted "absolute exclusion" rather than "effective restriction." As evidence he cited resolutions by the legislature, women's institutes, a statement by Anglican bishop A.U. de Pencier, and letters from "prominent" but unnamed citizens indicating that without "effective measures" to keep Asians out, people would "take matters into their own hands." He recalled the 1907 riots. Ladner, concerned about stemming the increasing Asian control of retail and wholesale business, argued that "the question is purely an economic one." MacKelvie reported that the UFBC and others were "absolutely determined" to continue the fight for "absolute and complete restriction of oriental immigration." Stevens was even more dramatic. Quoting statistics on Japanese birth rates and rebutting government arguments that harsh immigration regulations could impede trade, he warned that without effective measures "it will not be a question of considering the effect on trade; it will be a question of whether British Columbia is going to be merely a colony of the Orient or a province of the Dominion."[51]

On 2 March 1923 Acting Minister of Immigration Charles Stewart introduced the expected Chinese immigration legislation. It limited the entry of Chinese nationals to diplomats, children born in Canada who were returning after having been educated in China, merchants, and students. He believed that admitting only students seeking university degrees would end the student problem but saw difficulties in defining merchants. The RMA too was naturally concerned about the definition of merchants. "I have no quarrel with the elimination of the head tax, it is an insult anyway on any man," Crowder told the Victoria branch, but "what is to prevent them all from coming as merchants? What is to prevent them, once in, from farming potatoes at Ashcroft or apples at Okanagan?" The Vancouver branch took up the matter with Stevens, who found other loopholes. In Ottawa RMA representatives interviewed government members about the looseness of the definition. Their magazine conceded that the legitimate Chinese merchant was "an honorable, keen and efficient businessman" and suggested that the bill insulted all retailers by making it legal for Chinese "coolies" to enter as merchants. Several British Columbia branches suggested substituting "trade representative" for "merchant." Nevertheless, the RMA's provincial secretary believed that the new act was "one of the greatest steps forward that has been made on this vexed question in the history of the Association."[52]

While waiting for the debate, several British Columbia Conservatives pressed for changes that would make "effective restriction" tantamount "ultimately, to exclusion." Stevens criticized so many details of the bill in a speech to the Vancouver RMA that a Department of Immigration official could not "grasp the reason" for Stevens's doing so unless "anti-Asiatic sentiment in British Columbia is evidently not strong enough to survive the realization" that the bill was an exclusion act. Tolmie feared that the bill would "leave wide open the entry of merchants." The *Vancouver Province* explained that since "almost all the Chinese farmers and gardeners are also traders ... Unless there is some restrictive definition of the term, any Chinese resident may bring all his relatives and friends to this country disguised as merchants or students."[53]

Early in an anticlimactic debate during second reading, Prime Minister King urged the house to consider Canadian economic conditions and the need to avoid offending "an entire nation." He could not see how a "self-respecting" Canada "could impose a poll tax on working people coming from another country, and at the same time have its population subscribe to funds for missionary purposes to teach the heathen the most elementary principles of Christianity." Yet he boasted that the new law was really "an exclusion law" directed at Chinese labour because it did not list them among the permissible classes. Only a few British Columbia members – none of them Liberals – spoke in the debate. They welcomed the bill's principle but anticipated Chinese evasions. Other than T.G. McBride, who wondered why British Columbia "should educate the people of the Orient," they agreed that to promote trade, university students should be admitted if there were safeguards to ensure their departure after they had completed their studies. Merchants were another matter. The BC members quoted telegrams from RMA branches suggesting that they already had too many Chinese competitors and that the bill did not ensure that a "merchant" remained a merchant. While most arguments were economic, some MPs cited inassimilability and forecast that continued immigration and the natural increase of the province's existing Asian population would soon mean "there will be very few white people in British Columbia." They warned that eastern Canada was already facing Asian competition, an argument echoed by

Senator R.F. Green, who admonished that "if you want these people in eastern Canada, bring them here; we do not want them in British Columbia, and we will not have them there."[54]

Not everyone favoured the law. In letters and by lobbying senators, Protestant missionaries and their friends complained of injustice, the hardship of retroactive legislation on those Chinese residents in Canada who could not bring in wives or children, the limitations on students and religious workers, and the indignity of requiring the Chinese to carry certificates and be fingerprinted. Some asked why such legislation was imposed on the Chinese when there seemed to be "far more apprehension about the Japanese." In contrast Dr. S.S. Osterhout, N.L. Ward, and David A. Smith, three clergymen prominent in Oriental work in British Columbia for the Methodist, Anglican, and Presbyterian churches respectively, thanked the prime minister for abolishing the head tax and for admitting bona fide students but, warning of abuses in the "merchant" class, recommended admitting only as many Chinese as we "could hope to assimilate and Canadianize."[55]

The people most affected, the Chinese in Canada, protested restrictions and regulations that were more humiliating than the head tax. Many Chinese organizations in Vancouver united to fight the measure before it became law. Student clubs and theatre groups helped raise funds. The Victoria Chinese Consolidated Benevolent Association sent Dr. Joseph Hope to Toronto for a mass meeting sponsored by the newly formed Chinese Association of Canada to discuss the "Forty-Three Harsh Regulations on Chinese Immigration." The association did not object to "effective restriction" but complained that the law curtailed the Canadian citizenship of the naturalized, did not guarantee the retention of rights granted on entry or the ability of present or future merchants to bring in their wives and minor children, and made no assurance that students could enter. They warned of "a danger of international misunderstanding" resulting from the harsh conditions, especially from retroactive measures that "might result in deportation of many now in this country." To reinforce their arguments, representative Chinese residents waged "a quiet propaganda" campaign in Ottawa to kill the bill. For several days they gathered in the Senate gallery and distributed an eighteen-page brief "so voluminous that the majority of the recipients discarded it without perusal." They had organized late and, except for a few missionaries who were concerned about the admission of church workers and families, had few friends with political influence.[56]

Through diplomatic channels, the Chinese government responded to the proposed law. When the appeals of Sun Yat Sen, president of the Kuomintang (the Nationalist Party in China), to delay passage in the interest of commercial cooperation failed, Peking recalled Consul Tsur. As he passed through Vancouver, Tsur warned that the new law would create a "revulsion of feeling in China towards Canada" and hinted that China might boycott Canadian goods. In warning that the policy could harm trade, the *Vancouver Sun* was a lonely voice. Other commentators had no sympathy for China. The *Victoria Times,* for example, contended that "threats of severing relations and boycotting Canadian goods, teachers and missionaries, will not bring about the relaxation of a solitary condition of the law." Nevertheless, China continued to protest "the most drastic" act.[57]

So too did the Chinese in Canada. On 1 July 1924, the day that the law took effect, they held a "Humiliation Day" throughout Canada to protest the act and to mourn such indignities as the registration of even those Chinese residents who were Canadians by birth or naturalization. In Vancouver, despite several meetings, the closure of Chinese businesses, and the absence of Dominion Day flags in Chinatown, white reporters saw no signs of "a day of mourning." That was not so in Victoria, where 700 Chinese residents met at the Chinese Theatre with banners bearing such mottoes as "We are compelled to go through a criminal process, registration"; "Chinese women and children are barred from joining their husbands and homes in Canada"; and "The crux of the problem is not immigration, but the question of the treatment of Chinese already admitted." For three hours the audience heard speeches with messages to the effect that the act was "merely a political move to gather votes at the expense of the Chinese." After the meeting, several automobiles paraded the city, and every Chinese resident in attendance wore a lapel pin "exhorting him" to remember the humiliation. The Victoria daily newspaper *Chinese Times* used the occasion to reiterate its anti-Christian argument that "Canadians were not really Christian, and [that] they did not practice the teachings of Jesus, although they called themselves Christian. They discriminated against our countrymen, and issued various laws excluding our people from Canada." For several years Chinese shopkeepers in Victoria closed their stores on 1 July, not for a Canadian holiday but because it was "Humiliation Day."[58]

The Chinese in Canada, their missionary friends, and China's government repeatedly reminded Canada of the injustice of the act, especially of the ban on wives or children. In 1927 Chinese businessmen contributed advertisements to a "Chinese Unity and Goodwill Section" in the *Vancouver Star*. One asked whether it was right for a law to separate a man from his wife and family. It noted that if their families were with them, they would spend money in Canada and not send it to China. Editorially, the *Star* was unsympathetic. It conceded that the Chinese were hard-working and law-abiding and admitted that the problem of second generation Chinese residents required study but claimed that it was "better for Canadians to stay in Canada and for the Chinese to stay in China." The comment was not surprising. Although three years earlier, during the first "Humiliation Day," the *Star* had seen some "right" in the protest since children of naturalized Chinese residents "should not be required to register under the Immigration Act," the newspaper had concluded that "if they intend to become really truly British subjects and Canadian citizens they would overlook a discrimination which, under existing circumstances, is unavoidable."[59]

Generally, the few comments made by white British Columbians about the passage of the Chinese Immigration Act were favourable. The *Vancouver World* welcomed it as being "not anti-Chinese" but "protective of Canadians." M.A. MacDonald, president of the provincial Liberal Association, described it as "the greatest advance for many years in dealing with the Oriental problem so far as [the] Chinese are concerned;" Crowder told the New Westminster Kiwanis Club that although he was a Liberal, he thought that businessmen owed a vote of thanks to McQuarrie for his work on Oriental immigration. And R.J. Cromie of the *Vancouver Sun* personally congratulated Prime Minister King for his "immigration policy." Nevertheless, *Sun* editorials attacked the government for the "stupidity" that might allow the "prejudice of a few Canadians against Orientals" to "result in a serious breach of friendship between Canada and China" and impair trade. After the legislation had been in effect for over a year, Neill told Parliament that feelings between the Chinese and the whites had improved now that the Chinese knew exactly what their limitations were and now that the white man, satisfied that there would be little new Chinese immigration, left them alone.[60]

One reason for the lack of white excitement over the exclusionary law was the decline in Chinese immigration. Although 2,435 Chinese immigrants entered in the fiscal year ending 31 March 1921, that number dropped to 1,746 in 1921-22 and to only 711 in 1922-23. A second reason was the belief that there were still too many Chinese in Canada. The *Victoria Colonist* repeated an earlier suggestion to refund the $500 head tax to Chinese residents who would "return from whence they came." The idea of repatriating the Chinese did not disappear. In 1927 the Army and Navy Veterans Provincial Command suggested confiscating all the personal property of the Chinese in Canada and deporting them. Premier Oliver immediately replied that such a measure was beyond the scope of provincial jurisdiction. Two years later when the Nanking government announced that it would denounce extra-territoriality clauses in treaties with foreign powers, the *Colonist* saw an opportunity to bring about "a final solution of the Chinese problem in our midst" by bargaining to repatriate the Chinese in British Columbia and elsewhere in the British Empire.[61]

Nature and the Chinese Immigration Act were reducing the Chinese population. Although the census revealed that there were 3,606 more Chinese residents in British Columbia in 1931 than in 1921, this increase was largely the result of immigration early in the decade. A provincial government survey based on 1925 statistics found that the natural increase of the Chinese had been practically at "a standstill" since 1921, with an "an aggregate surplus of 62 births in three years being offset by an aggregate surplus of 41 deaths in the other two years." As aging men returned to China or died, the Chinese population fell sharply. By 1941 the province had only 18,619 Chinese residents.[62] This decline in the Chinese population, concerns about trade, and sympathy engendered for China by the Sino-Japanese war led to a brief reconsideration of immigration regulations in the late 1930s.

The Chinese Immigration Act, of course, did nothing to check Japanese immigration. In noting that only six Chinese nationals, comprising five students and a consul's servant, had entered Canada in the first four months that the act was in effect, the *Port Alberni News* asserted that "this looks like genuine Chinese exclusion. The only matter for regret is that the word 'Oriental' was not used in the place of 'Chinese' so as to include the Japanese." Though the Japanese were less numerous than the Chinese, many British Columbians regarded them as a more serious menace. As John Nelson explained, they were "not disposed to accept a secondary position to the whites, either socially or commercially, and they press with much vigor for political recognition." When Prime Minister King told Parliament in 1923 that with one exception fewer than 400 Japanese labourers had entered each year, McQuarrie concurred that Japan might have honoured the agreement but, citing recent ship jumpers, insisted that its people had not. The Department of Immigration proposed tightening identification procedures and making departing Japanese residents register, but Japan protested this measure as discrimination and an unwarranted inconvenience. It argued that more Japanese nationals returned to Japan than left for Canada and that population growth reflected natural increase. Nevertheless, it agreed to co-operate in examining passports, and Canada dropped the registration idea.[63]

The prime minister's immediate concern was Neill's bill to amend the Immigration Act in order to make it a Japanese exclusion act. To maintain goodwill and trade with Japan, King repeatedly adjourned a second reading. He asked Japan to help avoid an embarrassing debate by voluntarily restricting the emigration of labourers. In the interest of "international good will," Japan offered to negotiate arrangements "consistent with a sense of justice and a regard for fair human rights" but reminded King that it also had to consider public opinion. Thus, when Meighen, the leader of the opposition, asked about Japanese immigration, King revealed Japan's offer to put greater restrictions on labourers. He hoped that Parliament would not have to legislate in a way that would embarrass Japan but said that if the contemplated restrictions did not meet the situation, legislation might be necessary. Japan subsequently proposed reducing the annual number of domestic servants and agricultural labourers to 150 from the 400 authorized in the 1907 gentlemen's agreement.[64]

The promise of these restrictions elicited little comment in British Columbia, but Neill did not forget the Japanese issue. Several times in the 1924 session, he praised the Chinese Immigration Act, which, coupled with a low Chinese birth rate, meant that "we may look to their gradual elimination and the final solution of the Chinese question in Canada," but he continued to complain of a more acute "nigger in the woodpile," the Japanese. Unless Japanese immigration were halted, he predicted, "the dominance of the white races over the brown, black and yellow races of the world will be lost." He claimed that the gentlemen's agreement was so loosely worded and applied that in a recent year 1,178 Japanese nationals had entered Canada. "We want the exclusion of all but Japanese diplomats, Canadian born Japanese and merchants and students," he asserted, but his immediate concern was an apparent lack of a limit on wives, a matter that the prime minister said was under negotiation. Neill urged cancelling the agreement to regain control of immigration and to create a "wholly" white and Canadian citizenship. Like other anti-Asian agitators, he feared that American exclusionary and alien land laws would cause more Japanese immigration to Canada and create a California-like "crisis" in British Columbia. Rhetoric and information crossed the border. For example, V.S. McClatchey, the leader of California's Japanese Exclusion League, sent information to Premier Oliver and to the Department of Immigration in Ottawa; Oliver sent McClatchey a copy of a provincial survey on Oriental land ownership.[65]

Many comments on American exclusionary measures criticized the lack of diplomacy by both the United States and Japan. The *Vancouver Province* called the Japanese ambassador's protest to the United States "masterly in its tactlessness" but made no direct link with local problems. The *Vancouver Sun,* whose international coverage consisted of brief wire service stories, merely carried a Victoria report that provincial officials expected the lumber industry to benefit from any Japanese boycott of American goods. Later, in commenting on Ottawa's plans to restrict Japanese immigration, the *Sun* indicated that it hoped the Canadian government would have "the good sense to impose these restrictions in a plain, frank manner and without the emotional nonsense that made the United States exclusion measure so distasteful to the Japanese." Both Victoria papers, the *Times* and the *Colonist,* suggested that statesmanship could have avoided conflict while permitting exclusion. The conservative *Colonist* praised Mackenzie King's "correct attitude" in trying to limit immigration through diplomacy. Even a Canadian academic flaunted Canada's superior approach. In November 1925 historian Walter N. Sage told the Pacific Coast branch of the American Historical Association that Canada was "trying to solve the Asiatic problem without injury to the feelings of the Asiatics."[66]

Japanese diplomats agreed that Canada "had treated Japan with perfect courtesy" and was wise not to admit a large number of foreigners until those already there were "well assimilated." The British ambassador in Tokyo, however, warned that if Japanese newspaper reports that Canada was considering a ban on Japanese immigrants were true, "nothing could be more fatal" to the "Anglo-Japanese friendship." Fortunately for King, Neill agreed with a diplomatic approach, but privately he said that the time was opportune to press Japan to accept exclusion. If the government halted Japanese immigration and imposed registration, Neill predicted that King "would sweep British Columbia" in the next federal election.[67]

The popularity of Japanese exclusion was evident. Although only the upstart Provincial Party referred to Oriental immigration in its 1924 provincial election platform, during the campaign William Sloan attacked federal Conservative MPs for not doing enough to exclude Orientals. When the provincial legislature met that fall, he introduced "the most drastic" immigration resolution ever to come before the legislative assembly. It called for a complete prohibition on Asian immigration and the denunciation of any treaties denying Canada the power to control it. He wanted "to dam completely the stream of Orientals." The real danger, he said, was not economic competition but the inassimilability "of the white and yellow types." In the brief debate, the only criticism came from three Labour MLAs who suggested that the solution was "to improve the Orientals' standard of civilization." The legislature unanimously passed the resolution, which members hoped would "have a stronger effect on imperial policy than any previous anti-Asian action."[68]

Public interest, however, had waned. By 1924 the Asiatic Exclusion League was almost moribund. The British Columbia Fruit Growers' Association and the UFBC still passed resolutions for exclusion, but few others did. Then, in Vancouver and Victoria, the Native Sons of Canada invited a number of "white" organizations to form an Oriental Exclusion Association. At its first meeting in Vancouver in January 1925, eighty-four delegates from thirty-nine groups, mostly labour and veterans' organizations and fraternal orders, began planning "a united drive for the exclusion of Orientals." The new association incorporated the Asiatic Exclusion League. At subsequent meetings, which for a time occurred weekly, members heard "startling allegations of schemes to outwit Canadian immigration policy," such as a story of 300 Japanese women admitted to pick herbs who were in fact "picture brides" and another of "students" whose only purpose was to found families. Guest speakers such as McQuarrie observed that "excellent progress had been made in spite of lack of interest in the East." He exhorted the association to "get together and demand exclusion. Do not let public opinion die down – keep it alive." But the association could not meet this demand; the RMA apparently remained aloof, no prominent names appeared in the list of twenty-seven founding members, and a request to individual politicians for financial assistance yielded only two donations and a promise of five dollars from Leon J. Ladner. The association issued a few press releases and sent a resolution to Ottawa demanding the prohibition of "further immigration of Orientals to Canada" but soon disappeared.[69]

The Victoria branch survived a little longer, possibly because one of its founders and first president, Rev. Clem Davies, the controversial but popular pastor of the Victoria City Temple, had a high profile.[70] Late in 1924 Davies gave a sermon on "British or Oriental Columbia – which?" Two thousand people, including many MLAs, attended while others heard him over the radio warn that the Ku Klux Klan was growing in the province and would "take the law into its own hands unless legislators realized the gravity of the economic and oriental problems." He recited notions about the unknown size of the province's Oriental population, the high Japanese birth rate, the inroads of low-paid Orientals "into every department of trade and commerce," and the immorality that resulted from young whites being "thrown into intimate association" with young Chinese men. The congregation unanimously called for a reduction in the number of Oriental workers, an inquiry into enforcement of the Opium and Narcotic Drug Act, and "active steps ... to bring about the ultimate elimination of Orientals from British Columbia." Davies's popularity helped attract 181 delegates from 80 groups to a preliminary meeting; a follow-up meeting attracted delegates from 60 groups, and representatives from 100 groups attended the June meeting that formally organized the Oriental Exclusion League. According to Davies the goal was not to expel Asians but to ensure that no more be admitted. The league called for the total exclusion of "Orientals, both Chinese and Japs," the refunding of the head tax to Chinese under the age of forty who volunteered to leave, and a Royal Commission "to inquire into all phases of the Oriental problem as it affects British Columbia."[71]

The time for such lobbying was opportune. The Department of Immigration had advised the prime minister of plans to tighten procedures concerning Japanese immigration because of evasion of existing regulations, the large percentage of female immigrants, and demands from British Columbia MPs. King did not

UNDER THE COAT OF THE JAPANESE QUOTA

"Under the Coat of the Japanese Quota," *Vancouver Province*, 3 April 1925 respond until British Columbia's Liberal MPs reminded him that one of their strongest electoral arguments in 1921 had been the failure of the previous government to deal with the "Oriental question." They warned that the Chinese exclusion act, a cut in the number of fishing licences issued to the Japanese, and reductions in numbers under the gentlemen's agreement did not fully meet the problem since women and children seemed to be arriving "in practically unlimited numbers." "What the people" wanted, they declared, was "total exclusion of Orientals, or the equivalent of 'effective restriction,'" as in the Chinese Immigration Act. As evidence they claimed to have telegrams and letters from British Columbia calling for "definite action" at the present session. In conclusion, they reiterated that without "definite action," they would "be badly handicapped" in the pending election.[72]

How many such letters and telegrams they had or from whom they did not say. The lack of press comment or news of anti-Asian resolutions suggests that they exaggerated the number. Dr. G.L. Milne, one-time controller of Chinese immigration in Victoria, did "not agree with the alarmists" since the only Chinese entering were genuine merchants and the number of Japanese immigrants had declined. The *Vancouver Sun* said that before further restricting Japanese immigration, the government should demonstrate that such immigration menaced "the well-being of Canadian workers" and "the economic life of Canada." Anxious to promote Pacific trade, it argued that "goodwill between Japan and Canada is just as important to the prosperity of this country as the jobs of a few white fishermen." In congratulating the *Sun,* a Vancouver businessman claimed that many people shared its views but were wary of speaking "their minds for fear of being howled at by the small mob of hysterical fanatics who ascribe all their own failures to the competition of the Oriental or because they are afraid of being dubbed pro-Oriental."[73]

Nevertheless, the electoral concerns of British Columbia Liberal MPs, as well as Conservative plans to ask embarrassing questions in Parliament, led to action. The press reported that Ottawa would curtail the Japanese influx, check for illegal immigrants, and negotiate with Japan. Neill agreed that negotiations were preferable to any "hasty action that might offend the Japanese people," as the United States had done. In relaying concerns about the increased number of female and teenaged immigrants, King warned Japan's consul that it might become an election issue. He suggested that Japan issue no new passports while negotiating limits on the entry of women and children. Fearing "political disturbance" of its own, Japan refused to include wives and children in a quota of 150 emigrants. Disappointed, King repeated that the problem was economic rather than racial and threatened that, given the "strong feeling, irrespective of party," in western Canada, Japan must reduce the number of immigrants or face legislative action. The British government, which acted as a go-between since Canada did not yet have diplomatic representation in Tokyo, did not want trouble with Japan at a time of high "anti-foreign and nationalistic feeling" in China and urged Canada to avoid cause for friction.[74]

King had no desire to embarrass Britain but feared that he could not avoid public discussion and, given the legislature's unanimous demand for total exclusion, avoid criticism for failing to act. Since a federal election was pending, King stalled. As the parliamentary session ended, he told Neill, and possibly some other British Columbia MPs, that delaying a statement for a few weeks would facilitate negotiations. He also warned the consul that during the parliamentary recess, Canada could deal with the question by an Order in Council. This threat had some effect. Although Japan rejected Canada's proposal to deny males who had emigrated after 1925 the right to bring in wives and children as discriminatory and "repugnant to the natural laws of social justice and humanity," it did offer to exclude picture brides, to define children as those under the age of eighteen, and to limit emigrants to a maximum of 300, but without restriction on their distribution. King accepted most points but worried that public opinion would interpret "unrestricted distribution" as leading to a large proportion of females. He proposed a compromise: unrestricted distribution, including families of immigrants already in Canada, within a maximum of 150 emigrants. Japan rejected this idea, and Canada presented counter proposals, but the 1925 election delayed negotiations.[75]

News of the negotiations that leaked to the press and knowledge of the tension created by the American exclusionary law inspired several comments. The tone varied, but all noted the need for diplomacy. In a striking departure from its usual policy, the *Vancouver Sun* repeated traditional shibboleths about the Asian economic menace, their low standards of living, and the biological impossibility of mixing their blood with that of whites, suggesting that exclusion would be mutually beneficial. It subsequently emphasized using diplomatic methods to keep North America white. The *Vancouver Star* agreed that Japan was a good neighbour and customer and that her people were virtuous, but the Japanese were unwelcome immigrants "due to their estimable qualities of loyalty to the fatherland, and their inability to undergo assimilation by the white race." It wanted "firm but kindly" restrictions. The *Victoria Colonist* quoted the *Montreal Star*'s warning that in imposing new immigration barriers, North Americans must remember Japan's sensitivities. Nevertheless, news "of an entirely friendly exchange of the white and yellow viewpoint" at the unofficial Institute of Pacific Relations conference was promising although a later report indicated that the debate had become "rather sharply joined."[76]

That debate was reflected in Ottawa, where, because King was electioneering, O.D. Skelton, the undersecretary of state for external affairs, continued intermittent negotiations with Japan's consul. The main conflict concerned numbers, particularly of women and children; a lesser conflict focused on the treatment of merchants. Delays in communicating with Japan meant that no agreement was likely before the election and particularly before the prime minister had campaigned in British Columbia. Neill, an Independent but a Liberal in all but formal affiliation, told constituents that he hoped for a revision of the gentlemen's agreement.

Because of the minority government, Neill, known as the House of Commons's "chief anti-Asiatic campaigner," had more influence than most backbenchers. And, given the number of Japanese fishermen and lumber workers in his constituency, fighting for exclusion was a popular stand. As the campaign began, Neill pressed for an announcement because anti-Oriental feeling in BC was "growing greater." His platform had a simple statement: "Immigration. Absolute exclusion of Asiatics." But he generally honoured the prime minister's request not to introduce the issue into the campaign. He explained to electors that the Japanese immigration question "was not quite so satisfactory, owing to diplomatic relations." Nevertheless, he told Skelton, who kept him informed of the negotiations with Japan, that Ladner was canvassing Comox-Alberni while attacking "the slavish support [Neill] was supposed to have rendered the premier" and accusing him "of supporting a Government which substituted 'effective restriction' for 'exclusion'" in McQuarrie's resolution. Neill suggested that only "complete exclusion" would "completely satisfy B.C." but thought that he could defend alternatives, such as admitting 150 Japanese immigrants per year, of whom no more than 50 would be wives and children, or legislation similar to the Chinese Immigration Act.[77]

Elsewhere, trade, the tariff, and freight rates were more important. Early in the campaign, Dr. J.H. King, the province's leading federal Liberal, urged the prime minister's office to continue seeking the "greatest limitation possible" although the question was "not prominent" at present. That lack of interest continued. In Victoria, Tolmie occasionally mentioned the work of the British Columbia members on McQuarrie's 1922 resolution, but only in Nanaimo and New Westminster did the "Oriental question" receive more than passing mention. McQuarrie made much of his work in educating the east and in uniting the province's MPs to work on the problem, attacked Elgin Munro, MP (Liberal, Fraser Valley), for being absent at the time of the vote, and boasted of how Mackenzie King had complimented his handling of the resolution even though King had voted against it and thereby gained "the thanks of the people of Japan." The Liberal challenger, A. Wells Gray, stood "for the total exclusion of Orientals." In Nanaimo the debate was reminiscent of that of 1921. The Liberal candidate, T.B. Booth, repeatedly boasted of the practical end to Chinese immigration, called for total Oriental exclusion, and attacked the Conservative incumbent, C.H. Dickie, for not supporting the complete elimination of the Japanese from the fisheries. Dickie claimed that he had been overruled in his desire to cut the number of Japanese fishermen in half and that he favoured "a white Canada as much as any man in B.C."[78]

During the campaign, negotiations between Canada and Japan petered out. But officials prepared to resume them once the election was over, especially after H.J. Barber, the newly elected Conservative in Fraser Valley, gave notice of a motion for an exclusion law. King also faced diplomatic pressure. The Tokyo press had complained of the British Columbia Legislature wanting to denounce immigration treaties. The British ambassador warned of possible trouble although Japan was not anxious to see people emigrate since some returned from the United States and Hawaii with ideas that were "not to the taste of the present regime." Provided that legislation did not imply that the Japanese belonged "to an inferior race," the ambassador thought that Japan's demands would be quite moderate. This led to negotiations that, at Japan's request, were conducted in Ottawa.[79]

In the meantime British Columbia's MPs precipitated action. Sensing that it would not be discussed, Barber withdrew his exclusion bill, but Neill and Alfred Stork (Liberal, Skeena), noting that McQuarrie had mentioned the "Oriental question," warned that if an exclusion motion were "sprung" on the House of Commons, they would have to vote for it unless negotiations with Japan were concluded satisfactorily. On Skelton's advice, news of the likelihood of a minority Parliament passing the measure was relayed to Japan with a request for early action. Japan promptly agreed to a maximum of 250 entrants to be divided equally between wives and children in one category and between domestics and agricultural labourers in the other. It apparently accepted a time limit on the admission of families, but negotiations stalled over merchants and clerks. Canada was willing to admit merchant investors engaged in international trade and, once they were established, their wives and children, but not ordinary clerks as Japan wanted. Negotiations also bogged down over the right of individuals born in Canada or who had emigrated as children to bring wives from Japan. Skelton denied Japanese claims of a "disregard of humanity" by observing that since "presumably as many girls as boys are born in Japanese families in Canada, or are brought by their parents to Canada," young men should have no hardship finding wives in Canada. By the time diplomats sorted out the details, chaos caused by the defeat of the King administration in Parliament, by Meighen's failure to secure Parliament's confidence, and by the subsequent 1926 general election had ended negotiations. The "Oriental question" was not an election issue, but the idea of limiting Japanese immigration persisted. When the press reported that Japan would colonize Hokkaido, Formosa, and other possessions rather than have emigrants go where their presence caused "much trouble and ill-feeling," the *Vancouver Province* welcomed the move. The *Vancouver Sun*, having little patience with anti-Asian agitators, suggested that the report would reassure "some of those hysterical jingoes who have set up a yellow bogey." The report was based on a misunderstanding; Japan had not changed its emigration policy. Since Japanese immigration had not been an election issue, it was not a priority for King's government.[80]

In the spring of 1927 the provincial government, especially Attorney General Manson, urged Ottawa to halt Oriental immigration and, through "deportation or other legitimate means, seek to bring about the reduction and final elimination of this menace to the well-being of the white population of this Province." Manson specifically suggested that the federal government provide funds to buy the holdings of Orientals, who would then be transported out of the country. The main reason for such measures, Manson argued, was ethnological, the problem being that "the blood of the two races" could not be mixed, but the legislators were now more interested in restricting Asians already in the province than in exclusion. Nevertheless, the Native Sons of British Columbia and the *Vancouver Star* heartily agreed, as did the Ku Klux Klan, which was trying to organize itself in the province. The *New Westminster British Columbian* favoured Oriental exclusion but accused Manson of simple vote seeking. Federally, Stevens publicly admitted that the immigration situation, while not wholly satisfactory, gave no cause for alarm, but at that fall's Conservative convention, he fought hard for a resolution favouring Oriental exclusion. Senior party members, notably Sir George Foster, argued that it was neither wise nor courteous to suggest that contrary to the spirit of the League of Nations, the Conservative Party wanted to bar certain peoples from Canada. Conservatives, however, saw more votes in British Columbia than in Geneva and passed the resolution.[81]

British Columbia politicians continued to seek publicity. Premier J.D. MacLean, who became premier after Oliver's death in August 1927, told the Ottawa Rotary Club that British Columbia had "no complaint against the individual Oriental, who was, as a rule, honest, industrious and thrifty, but it was a question of preserving the British white race." MacLean's formal letter to the prime minister on the "more important" questions of the Dominion-Provincial Conference in November 1927 did not mention Asians, but at the conference, in a "forcible" speech, Manson referred to their "fecundity" and to the danger of interracial marriages in arguing for Oriental exclusion. In reply Prime Minister King spoke of "the grave danger of arousing the Orient against this continent"; privately he envisioned helping "save another war on this issue." A censored conference communiqué merely said that "Mr. Manson dealt briefly with the Oriental problem from the standpoint of his province and the Dominion. He advised consideration of this by the Federal Government." Grant Dexter reported that Manson had received "the unqualified support" of most provinces and that action would probably be taken at the next parliamentary session. Dr. J.H. King advised Premier MacLean that the prime minister had "done a great deal" toward solving the problem, that he favoured a white British Columbia and a white Canada, and that negotiations could accomplish more than could offensive actions against friendly nations.[82]

Nevertheless, Manson continued to agitate. He told the legislature that he had not pressed "the economical argument" but rather had underscored his case by "picturing all the Cabinet Ministers' daughters married to Orientals." He claimed to have "astonished" other premiers by warning that British Columbia would soon be "nothing more than a British-Oriental community" and that "the yellow races" would "invade the provinces in the East as they have done on the Coast." He urged the legislature to solve the problem. A few days earlier Prime Minister King had scolded Conservatives for endorsing Oriental "exclusion" since it offended Japan but had declared his own desire for "a white Canada and a white British Columbia," agreeing that there were "too many Japanese of the labouring classes in" the province. Perhaps, as the *Vancouver Province* suggested, when Manson spoke he had been unaware of King's admonishments about referring to "exclusion." The newspaper agreed with King that the problem had to be viewed in an international context. The liberal *Vancouver Star* supported exclusion but noted that Asian immigration had "been reduced to comparatively small proportions" and that "hasty action" might "militate" against Japan making a real effort to solve the immigration problem. The Japanese consul in Vancouver had already warned that anti-Japanese motions could harm the timber trade. Thus a month later, in a "carefully worded speech," Manson changed his tune, quoted King's statements in support of a white Canada, and urged the legislature not to embarrass the Canadian and British governments by passing Conservative motions for abrogation of the Anglo-Japanese Treaty and the total exclusion of Asians. He suggested that the province send details of the growth of the Oriental population and its effects on British Columbia to every member of Parliament, and he invited all MLAs to meet informally to draft the document.[83]

The result was a motion introduced by Dougal McPherson (Liberal, Grand Forks-Greenwood) and C.F. Davie (Conservative, Cowichan-Newcastle). It was designed "in a compelling way" to call Canadian attention to British Columbia's problem while avoiding resentment from China and Japan by referring to diplomatic negotiations. Although some Conservatives wanted an outright exclusionary resolution, the legislature unanimously urged Ottawa to initiate negotiations with China and Japan to bring about exclusion and repatriation until "the proportion of Orientals in Canada to the Canadian population shall not exceed the proportion of Canadians in China and Japan respectively to the population of China and Japan." Referring to the legislature's inability to restrict many economic activities of the Japanese, the motion called for replacing the Anglo-Japanese Treaty of 1911 in order to empower British Columbia to legislate with reference to property and civil rights.[84]

The daily press reported the debates with little comment. The *Prince Rupert Daily News* considered deporting Orientals "a fantastic" idea but not "feasible." It speculated that unanimous passage of the resolution would put "the Oriental question out of provincial politics." More cynically the *Vancouver Province* predicted that the resolution would be more effective in the pending provincial election than in Ottawa. There was, in fact, little pressure for a resolution on immigration. Only six groups expressed any interest. Three were small groups on southern Vancouver Island, where there were few Japanese residents and a declining Chinese population; the sixth, the "A B.C." group, was an informal association of Vancouver merchants organized by T.R.E. (Tom) MacInnes, a professional lobbyist. The resolutions were more atavistic responses than reflections on realities.[85]

In Ottawa a few British Columbia MPs still mentioned their desire to halt Asian immigration but did not press the issue – although McQuarrie did cite the provincial legislature's debate in arguing that "the situation in British Columbia has become most acute inasmuch as the orientals are getting into all lines of industry." Meanwhile, the Department of External Affairs conducted desultory negotiations with Japan. When disagreements over the total number of new immigrants (Japan wanted 200; Canada, 150) and the admission of wives and children of future immigrants hampered negotiations, Skelton cited the legislature's resolution in order to suggest that public opinion would likely require a stiffer proposal than one that might have been acceptable in 1925. Perhaps this warning had some effect. Japan agreed to the 150 limit and promised not to "considerably exceed" an average maximum of 75 females per year. In informing Parliament of the successful negotiations, Prime Minister King remarked that Canada had "made clear the difficulties created in western Canada by the economic competition of Japanese immigrants." He stressed that the total would not exceed 150 new emigrants per year and that "picture brides" would no longer be admitted. As in other countries, Canadian officials would pre-investigate prospective immigrants and issue visas.[86]

In British Columbia a provincial election overshadowed the news. The *Victoria Times* reported that the provincial government saw the new agreement as the "most important step in recent times to halt Oriental penetration into British Columbia" and credited Attorney General Manson, Dr. J.H. King, and Neill for the agreement's negotiation. The *Times* praised Prime Minister King for adjusting "the matter without disturbing the friendly relations" with Japan. Otherwise, the press gave the news no prominence. In the campaign, some Liberals noted the new 150 maximum and asked why Tolmie, the Conservative leader, had done nothing when he was in the federal Cabinet. Although the Conservatives' promise to continue "efforts for a white British Columbia and persevere in its policy of Oriental Exclusion" ranked twenty-third in a twenty-four-point platform, a pamphlet said that they stood "as always four square for a white British Columbia for white British Columbians – diminution and extinction of non-assimilable Asian elements in the population by all constitutional methods and at every opportunity." In Dewdney, which included Mission and Maple Ridge, the Conservative candidate, N.S. Lougheed, emphasized the serious problem of Oriental competition in horticulture. On a northern tour Tolmie said that Conservatives had always favoured Oriental exclusion. Nevertheless, Japan's consul in Ottawa complained that with "ill information or some selfish natures," Tolmie was "making a big noise" on Oriental exclusion that would not go unnoticed in Japan. The matter may have been news overseas, but in British Columbia the "Oriental question" was no longer a significant provincial political issue. Discontent with Liberal policy on the Pacific Great Eastern Railway largely explains why British Columbians elected Tolmie's Conservatives. In a by-election to replace Tolmie as Victoria's member of Parliament, Dr. J.D. MacLean mentioned that the federal Liberals had stopped Chinese immigration completely and had sharply reduced immigration from Japan. Nevertheless, the seat remained Conservative.[87]

Asian immigration was no longer an issue, but some federal and provincial politicians continued to act as though it were. Until spy stories and allegations of illegal Japanese immigration appeared as part of prewar jitters in the late 1930s, constituents seemed satisfied with the end of Chinese immigration and with the sharp reduction in Japanese immigration that followed revisions to the gentlemen's agreement. The virtual cessation of immigration, however, did not end demands for controls on Asian economic activity within the province.

4

"Shoving the Oriental Around": Checking Economic Competition, 1919-30

*This business of shoving the Oriental around out of one industry into another
is not solving the problem. Humanity is selfish. When the Oriental invaded the
labour world, with his lower standard of living and his willingness to accept a
lower wage, the labour man was very energetic in decrying his invasion.
The businessman and the farmer were not interested. When he began to invade
the farm the farmer protested and now that he has established himself on
Granville Street and Government Street the businessman is valiantly and
patriotically shouting for relief, but, in the meantime, the Oriental, particularly
the Jap, has raised his standard of living, he has joined the union and the
white labourer is not half so much interested as he used to be.*
– A.M. MANSON TO V.W. ODLUM, 28 SEPTEMBER 1927

Attorney General A.M. Manson, who wrote those words in 1927, was a frustrated
racist.[1] Despite his efforts and those of his federal counterparts, Asians were almost as much a factor in the economy at the end of the decade as at the beginning.
What disheartened Manson and like-minded individuals was the lack of sustained
public interest. Whites patronized Chinese stores, laundries, and restaurants. Agricultural groups condemned Asian occupation of the land, but some farmers sold
or leased land to Asians and co-operated with them in marketing schemes. In the
more prosperous fishing and lumbering industries, where labour organizations
were weak, the Asian question was a source of division. Nevertheless, federal and
provincial politicians legislated to push Asians out of fishing and lumbering respectively. They were among the few British Columbians with a persistent interest
in checking Asian economic competition and preserving the province for the white
race.

Severe unemployment marred the immediate postwar years. Union leaders and
veterans accused Asians of taking their jobs. The Vancouver Repatriation and Community Service League threatened mill managers with "trouble varying all the way
from a veterans' boycott to something more drastic" unless they replaced Asians
with returned soldiers. At an August 1921 labour conference, the provincial minister of labour, J.W. de B. Farris, predicted that another 8,000 to 9,000 would soon

join the 11,000 to 12,000 already unemployed. A representative of the Army and Navy Veterans warned of permanent unemployment unless the Asian question were solved. Although an estimated 3,500 Chinese residents were unemployed, with the provincial Department of Labour reporting that the "foreign races were not gaining ground at the expense of our own flesh and blood," the image persisted that few Asians were ever out of work. So bitter were anti-Asian feelings that Japanese residents of Vancouver feared that their 4 August 1919 lantern procession celebrating the peace might lead "very anti-Japanese" workingmen to attack them. Census takers in 1921 attributed Chinese aversion to the census to strong anti-Oriental feelings among returned soldiers and the unemployed.[2]

Ideological splits within organized labour influenced its views. Some members of the executive of the Vancouver Trades and Labour Council were prominent in the Asiatic Exclusion League. Trades and Labour Congress of Canada conventions regularly called for Asiatic exclusion and, in 1929, for repatriation. We want a "clean sweep" of all the Chinese, a sawmill worker told the 1919 Royal Commission on Industrial Relations because the Chinese deferred to their "bosses," accepted whatever pay was offered, and rejected white men's unions. Socialists, however, saw capitalists as the enemies. A contributor to the *B.C. Federationist* wrote that "all of us are exploited by a master-class who cares not what nationality we are so long as we remain willing slaves." Since the Chinese had been admitted to the country, he argued, it was "right" and "essential" to give them "full rights of citizenship" and raise their standards to ours. Otherwise, he warned, "we are bound to go down."[3] Some labour advocates, such as J.S. Woodsworth, wanted to prevent "scabbing" by getting Asians into unions. The ill-fated Lumber Workers Industrial Union, an affiliate of the One Big Union (OBU), did so. In 1919 even the Trades and Labour Congress of Canada agreed to "co-operate as far as possible" with unions that were "trying to organize Asiatics." When Japanese drivers applied for membership in the Teamsters Union, the president of the Vancouver Trades and Labour Council said that they had "a perfect right to do so," but delegates laughed at a suggestion that the Teamsters might regard a Japanese driver as their "best delegate." In 1927 the Vancouver and New Westminster District Trades and Labour Council admitted the 700 Japanese members of the Mill and Camp Workers Union as affiliates, a decision that caused conflict within both the labour movement and the Japanese community.[4]

Workers who saw Asians as a threat to their livelihoods did not have to agitate; others did it for them. The *Vancouver World* and its successor, the *Vancouver Star*, frequently urged that industry be preserved for white men. The *Star* believed that a shortage of unskilled work in 1924 had resulted from "the fallacy of so-called cheap Asiatic labor" and "the insidious ousting effect of Orientalization with its baneful degradation of standards of living and the handing over of a province in which Anglo-Saxon civilization should prevail to the dominant influences of coolie

Asiatics." Attorney General Manson favoured "attrition" as a means of wearing down Asians "already in the country." He admired their industry, thrift, and thoroughness but called them unfair competitors because of their low living standards.[5]

Many employers wanted Asian labour because whites would not take "heavy, dirty work"; moreover, cheap labour was necessary to compete in export markets. Shingle manufacturers could not train sufficient returned soldiers as sawyers and packers to replace the 1,100 Chinese workers in New Westminster and elsewhere who struck in 1919 rather than accept a pay cut. In 1920 Okanagan fruit packers offered free classes to "WHITE Fruit Packers" but, despite unemployment, could not find sufficient white help. After 500 people attended a meeting in Kelowna chaired by J.W. Jones to protest "the Chinese peril within our gates," an investigation found that the Chinese were essential workers in the packinghouses. By then anti-Asian sentiment was at a flash point. In Keremeos, where poor conditions and the low wages offered by the cannery attracted only "yellow" labour, a Chinese resident's house was burned.[6]

Employers said that they wanted to abolish Asian labour, especially since it was not always docile, but to do so gradually. Despite a reputation as strikebreakers, Asians joined strikes and occasionally led them. In greater Vancouver they had a prominent role in thirty-nine disputes between 1914 and 1939, and some Chinese labourers belonged to the radical One Big Union during its heyday, 1919-21. At Fraser Mills, when Chinese workers struck for higher pay in 1920, white workers affiliated with the OBU organized a sympathy strike. The next year, when seventy-five Japanese lumber workers in Vancouver struck to protest a pay cut from thirty to twenty-five cents per hour, the OBU picketed, but the mill reopened with a white crew paid thirty-six to forty cents per hour. An official of the Soldiers Civil Re-Establishment Commission said that lumber operators paid veterans more because they did "so much more work." Some farmers, however, preferred Chinese labourers for such chores as land clearing since they were more willing and energetic workers. Several editors suggested making country life more attractive to white labour, but once the immediate postwar unemployment crisis had passed, the Chinese were tolerated as cheap and efficient farm labour.[7]

The proportion of Chinese and Japanese residents employed in lumbering, the province's largest resource-based industry, declined steadily from 40.7 percent in 1919 to 20.46 percent in 1925. Yet the editor of the *Port Alberni News* and Independent MLA for Comox-Alberni, Major Richard J. Burde, lamented that industries over which the government should have the greatest control employed the highest percentage of Asians. In the summer of 1924, when the lumber industry suffered a temporary depression resulting ironically from the end of a boom caused by the rebuilding of Tokyo and Yokohama after the 1923 earthquake,[8] the *Vancouver Star*

told of white men losing jobs to Asians. It cited old statistics and pointed to the shingle industry, where Asians did dominate, to buttress its claim that "the Oriental battalions have advanced all along the line."[9]

The provincial government was anxious to eliminate Asians from all aspects of the lumber industry – logging, shingle bolt cutting, sawmills and shingle mills, and pulp and paper. Not everyone agreed. In 1921 entrepreneurs asked Prince Rupert City Council for concessions relating to a water supply for a proposed pulp mill. After council narrowly rejected a clause forbidding the company to employ Asians, members of the Trades and Labour Council, the Great War Veterans' Association (GWVA), the Sons of England, and the Loyal Orange Lodge urged residents to reject the necessary bylaw in order to "protect Prince Rupert, our home town, against yellow labor." Prince Rupert's *Evening Empire* urged readers to "Vote only for a White Man's Town" while the liberal *Daily News* agreed that the "Oriental question" was acute but maintained that solving it was beyond the city's jurisdiction. Voters, preferring a new industry to an anti-Asian clause, passed the bylaw.[10]

The province, however, continued its efforts to restrict Asian employment on Crown lands. Since 1902, provincial timber leases had included a clause against their employment. The regulation was not enforced during the war, but in 1919, when a Japanese syndicate obtained an option on a million dollars worth of timber on the Queen Charlotte Islands, the government refused to allow the transfer. Forestry officials subsequently found Asians working as loggers and shingle bolt cutters and blamed inexperienced Asians for the "butchery of good timber and deplorable waste." Standing "at all costs for a white country," the chief forester believed that provincial regulations had kept the Japanese out of logging except on privately owned land, but he feared that lowering the barriers would enable them to monopolize the industry. During the war they had moved rapidly into logging, and since then sawmills and pulp mills had started training Japanese and Chinese labourers to replace whites.[11]

In the spring of 1920, district foresters warned holders of timber licences that they could lose them if they employed Asians. The Japanese consul protested a violation of the Anglo-Japanese Treaty of Commerce and Navigation and explained that Premier Richard McBride had admitted that the 1902 Order in Council was not legally binding and had instructed the chief forester not to enforce it. Neither Premier John Oliver nor Minister of Lands T.D. Pattullo was aware of this. When the federal minister of justice advised that the order seemed to violate the Anglo-Japanese Treaty, J.W. de B. Farris, now attorney general, contended that the province should control its own property and had the right to make contracts. The province referred the matter to the Court of Appeal but in the meantime enforced the regulation, which angered employers. The Shingle Agency of British Columbia claimed that the order was *ultra vires* the province, an opinion confirmed by the provincial Supreme Court's ruling in November 1920 that the policy conflicted with federal powers over naturalization and aliens and was repugnant to the Japanese

Treaty Act. Contrary to the attorney general's advice, Pattullo had cancelled licences and, shortly before the 1920 provincial election, promised to pursue the
matter to the Privy Council if necessary. In court Farris argued that excluding
Asians from government contracts or lands did not affect treaty rights and that
the Japanese could seek no more than the "freedom to contract with those who are
willing to contract with them." In April 1921 the province passed retroactive legislation to validate the 1902 Orders in Council.[12]

A few months later Pattullo advised Brooks-Bidlake & Whittall, a manufacturer
of red cedar shingles, that by employing Japanese workers it was breaching the
terms of its licence. Mill owners were unhappy. A trade journal, though concerned
about the number of Asians in the industry, predicted that legislation would "make
a bigger mess of the business." The Japanese were even more upset. Vancouver
lawyer and one-time federal Conservative cabinet minister Charles Hibbert Tupper
advised his client, the Canadian Japanese Association, that "the authorities are
truckling to the extreme views of the voters in this Province" and "for political
reasons" are inviting Ottawa to find the Japanese Treaty Act void. Japan asked
Ottawa to disallow the act validating the 1902 Orders in Council as *ultra vires* and
contrary to the Treaty of Commerce and Navigation. The *Vancouver World* called
this argument "crowning evidence of the aggressive quality" of Japan and accused
Ottawa of "tampering with the foundations of British national life in this province." The Meighen government, perhaps realizing that the Liberals might exploit
disallowance, honoured the province's request for a further appeal. Farris arranged
a test case in co-operation with Brooks-Bidlake & Whittall by not cancelling its
licence pending an appeal to the Supreme Court of Canada.[13]

The matter was technically *sub judice* but remained in the political arena. Using
an outline history provided by the attorney general as electoral ammunition, M.A.
MacDonald, a Liberal candidate in the 1921 federal election, repeatedly attacked
the Conservatives for ratifying the Anglo-Japanese Treaty in 1913. George S. Hanes,
MLA (Independent, North Vancouver), demanded that Pattullo resign as minister
of lands for not enforcing the regulations. In reply Pattullo cited his letter of 1 May
1920 urging Oliver to hold "to the last ditch" against employing Japanese workers
on timber land and reiterated that the government would not allow timber leaseholders to employ Japanese residents or "allow Japs to get possession" of any provincial natural resources. He conceded their industry but said that the "yellow race"
"could not be assimilated." Referring to the court case, Pattullo declared that the
government "was anxious to preserve the rights of the Anglo-Saxon."[14]

The Supreme Court of Canada considered the Brooks-Bidlake case partly in
light of the Treaty of Commerce and Navigation. Lawyers for Brooks-Bidlake had
earlier told the Court of Appeal that the Oriental Orders in Council Validation Act
was "insufficient in law" to validate the "no Chinese or Japanese" clause in their
special timber licences and that interference with the employment of Asians was
beyond the powers of the provincial legislature. Acting for the province, Attorney

General Farris argued that, like a private owner, the province had a right to insert stipulations in contracts for the use of its land without contravening the Anglo-Japanese Treaty. Early in 1922 the Supreme Court ruled that the province had this right and upheld its cancellation of the Brooks-Bidlake licence.[15]

Simultaneous with the Brooks-Bidlake case, the Supreme Court heard arguments relating to the request of the federal minister of justice that it consider the constitutionality of the Validation Act. This was the minister's response to the Japanese consul's request that he disallow the Validation Act and possibly his attempt to avoid dealing with the matter during a federal election campaign. The arguments for both sides were similar to those presented during the Brooks-Bidlake proceedings. The provincial government maintained that it had power over its public lands and resources, that it only wanted to regulate its own property, and that because the Validation Act merely confirmed existing provincial laws concerning the "management of Crown property," there was no conflict with the Anglo-Japanese Treaty. On the other side the attorney general of Canada submitted that the law was *ultra vires* because it interfered with federal powers over naturalization and aliens and had been "devised to deprive [the] Chinese and Japanese, whether naturalized or not, of the ordinary rights of the inhabitants of British Columbia, and in effect to prohibit their continued residence in that province, since it prohibits their earning their living there." He noted, moreover, that it violated the Anglo-Japanese Treaty, a point also argued by Charles Hibbert Tupper on behalf of the Canadian Japanese Association and by Charles Wilson, acting for the British Columbia Shingle Manufacturers' Association. Although they announced their decision in this constitutional reference only six weeks after the Brooks-Bidlake decision, the Supreme Court ruled that the Validation Act was *ultra vires* since it infringed on a provision in the Anglo-Japanese Treaty giving Japanese citizens the same rights in respect to industries and occupations as those guaranteed to subjects of the most favoured nation. Even Mr. Justice Lyman Duff, a British Columbian who had "no revulsion" against anti-Asian legislation[16] and who thought that the province should be able to encourage the settlement of people of its choice, concluded that the Validation Act was repugnant to the Anglo-Japanese Treaty and, since it viewed the Japanese and Chinese as "a single group ... must be treated as inoperative *in toto*." The judges gave different reasons for their conclusions, which provided grounds for an appeal to the Judicial Committee of the Privy Council.[17]

In the meantime the new federal Liberal government disallowed the Validation Act as *ultra vires*. Then in 1923 the Privy Council decided that the federal government could not regulate the management of provincial public lands. Although it did not express a judgment on the effects of the Anglo-Japanese Treaty, it appeared to uphold the provincial policy at least insofar as it related to the Chinese.[18] Attorney General Manson welcomed the news as helping to "strengthen the hand of the government in dealing with the Oriental menace." N.R. Whittall, the disappointed plaintiff, warned that the decision would "cause serious injury" to the lumber industry. The Privy Council's decision was only "the first round" in the controversy. Because the treaty rights of the Japanese were still an open question, the province made a second appeal to the Privy Council, which decided that the Validation Act was invalid since it violated the 1913 treaty but hinted that the act could be redrafted to exclude Japanese nationals from its provisions.[19]

The province, however, had other ways to restrict Asian employment. While waiting for the courts' decisions, Manson, who had succeeded Farris as attorney general, appealed to industrial leaders "to do their duty as Canadians" and replace Asian workers. He urged railways, shingle mills, pulp and paper mills, and logging companies to co-operate in creating "a white British Columbia" and to develop its "natural assets," which "belong to our Anglo-Saxon people." He asked whether it was "not right that white labor should be employed throughout your industry even if it does absorb a portion of your margin of profit?" The railways eventually replaced over 2,000 Asians. Manson later boasted that the Powell River pulp and paper plant had replaced all Asians and that Ocean Falls was gradually reducing its number. The Shingle Manufacturers' Association, while sympathetic to white labour, reported that sawyers performed highly skilled work to which the Chinese had "become particularly adapted," that higher wages did not attract sufficient white sawyers, and that white men would not cut shingle bolts at a reasonable price. Mill owners received some sympathy. When the Esquimalt Board of Trade called for laws to compel lumber manufacturers to curtail the use of Chinese labour, other members of the Associated Boards of Trade of Vancouver Island agreed that British Columbia should be "a white man's country" but noted that mill owners could not always obtain white men and that "the Chinaman was a faithful and law-abiding worker." When the new legislature met in 1924, only the three Labour MLAs opposed Manson's resolution that all employers "should employ members of the white race exclusively." As for unemployed Asians, Manson said that they could go back to Asia.[20]

Meanwhile, Burde sought to reduce the Asian presence in lumbering by replacing the average fifty-five-hour work week with a maximum eight-hour day in sawmills and shingle mills. When he first introduced the idea in 1920, he received support from the Vancouver Trades and Labour Council and from at least one branch of the Army and Navy Veterans. Although the government did not oppose the principle of a shorter day, it responded to protests from the Lumber and Shingle Manufacturers, the British Columbia Loggers' Association, the Canadian Manufacturers' Association, and the Salmon Canners' Association. Burde's private member's bill got the six months' hoist, but he persisted. He introduced another bill in 1922. Averring that because Orientals formed half of the workforce in lumber mills, workers in this "slave driving industry" had been unable to organize, he proposed that taking "two hours a day from the Orientals" and giving them to the white workers would do "more to relieve the Oriental menace than all your Oriental exclusion resolutions." Again the legislature rejected his bill. When Burde raised the matter again in 1923, the Timber Industries Council told the government that its members wanted "to eliminate the Oriental from the lumber business" but noted that its 3,496 Asian[21] employees were an "inconsiderable number" in the total labour force. Moreover, the council noted, contrary to common belief approximately 6,000 Orientals worked in the industry in Washington State and Oregon; thus the eight-hour law would put them at a disadvantage in foreign markets. J.G. Robson, owner of a large sawmill near New Westminster, warned that it would encourage operators to employ more Asians "in preference to the higher wages necessary to be paid to white labour." He threatened to resign as president of the New Westminster Liberal Association. The government ignored the timbermen and at the 1923 session brought in eight-hour legislation.[22]

Referring to the eight-hour work day as "the white man's day," the *Vancouver World* declared that it would strike a blow "at the very foundation of the Asiatic menace." Indeed, the legislation did not have the dire effects that mill owners had predicted. Rather, a trend away from the employment of Asians, especially of Hindus and the Japanese, was established, and the provincial Department of Labour attributed the increase in Chinese workers to a reserve labour force that was being drawn on in busy times. By 1923 the Rat Portage Mill in Vancouver had replaced its 90 percent Asian workforce with one that was 90 percent non-Asian. In the province as a whole, the number of Asians in sawmills fell from 40 percent in 1922 to 34 percent in 1924 although the number in shingle mills rose from 54 percent to 56 percent. Mill managers reported that "we can get better service out of the white workmen" but that retaining them was difficult whereas Asian labourers were generally faithful and steady. Yet, because it was "a white man's country," one manager preferred "to give the white workmen the first chance."[23]

Burde was not satisfied. Complaining that thousands of young British Columbians had gone to Washington State and California, where they did not have "to work in close contact and competition with the Orientals," he said that mill owners must recognize "the long despised rights of the white man in what is supposed to be a white man's country." If the lumber industry could not operate without half of its workforce being Asian, he told the legislature, it was "not a white man's industry, and ... this is not a white man's country." He revived the idea of a minimum wage law to make Asian labour less attractive to employers. In 1919 a delegate at the New Westminster Trades and Labour Council, who had "nothing against the Oriental ... except that his place is in Asia not here," had proposed such a law to make Asians less profitable employees. Similarly Helena Gutteridge, a tailor and active craft unionist, told the National Industrial Conference in September 1919 of unfair competition and argued that we "should pay to the Chinaman or to any other man employed, a wage which should be a living wage." Several veterans' organizations favoured a minimum wage law, as did F.R. Carlow of Victoria's Oriental Exclusion League. Carlow said that sawmills paid Orientals $2.25 per day and whites $3.25. He ascribed "the spread" to "the greater ability of white workers" but claimed that white men could not demand better pay lest Orientals be given their jobs. The differential, though possibly caused by racialized ideas about Asians, engendered much of the hostility toward them as "cheap labour."[24]

In introducing a male minimum wage bill in December 1925, Burde attacked the lumber industry for using cheap Asian labour and not paying white workers a decent wage. Mill owners protested against "class legislation of the worst kind." In a classic statement of the needs of free enterprise, J.G. Robson complained of "hampering legislation" that made it difficult to compete in world markets. Oliver may have sympathized but voted for the Minimum Wage Law, as did most members. One MLA forecast that it would "accomplish more to solve the Asiatic question in British Columbia than all the resolutions on the subject the Legislature had ever sent to Ottawa."[25]

Although the Male Minimum Wage Act was described as "an extraordinary experiment" in North America, it was an anti-Asian measure rather than a sweeping social reform. It could be applied to all workers except in domestic service and in such seasonal industries as fruit canning. The Board of Adjustment (also known as the Minimum Wage Board), which administered the act, first applied it to lumbering. With approximately 40,000 employees, lumbering was the province's largest industry, and over 20 percent of its workforce was Asian. White workers complained of low wages but earned about 25 percent more than Asians. The board observed that a few large firms near the larger population centres relied more on Asian labour than did the industry as a whole and that some of them were the loudest objectors to the minimum wage. Weighing conflicting claims of employers and employees, the board set forty cents per hour as the minimum wage. A mass meeting of the Canadian Lumber Workers' Association applauded J.D. McNiven, chairman of the Minimum Wage Board, when he told them that the minimum wage would be set on a white man's scale to drive out Orientals. The left wing *Canadian Labour Advocate*, however, claimed that employers wanted "to purchase Occidental efficiency for the Oriental wage scale."[26]

The only concession to employers was almost a year's delay in implementation to give them time to adjust. Describing the act as "a crude specimen of vote catching law-making passed in a disgracefully crowded session by a House either afraid or unable through lack of time to tear it to pieces," employers complained that they could not find steady, unskilled white labour and that raising wages would draw Asians into the industry. They proposed a voluntary gradual reduction in the Asian workforce and suspension of the law until a commission could investigate. Knowing that the legislature would not agree, Premier Oliver advised them to lobby individual members. Liberal MLAs, such as Ian Mackenzie (Vancouver), described the law as "the only way to grapple with the Oriental labor question"; the press called it "the most vigorous blow ever delivered by Canada against Oriental penetration."[27]

Not everyone was convinced. The rabid anti-Asian C.F. Davie, MLA (Conservative, Cowichan-Newcastle), regarded the Minimum Wage Act as "a joke" that would not free the industry "from Oriental domination," but the act did go some way toward this goal. A year before it came into effect, 55.2 percent of the employees in thirty-one principal coastal sawmills were white; a year after the act was in force, the percentage of whites had risen to 65.7 percent; and a year later, to 68.86 percent. These figures, concluded the Department of Labour, relieved "any apprehension that the chief result of the order would be to benefit Oriental workers." Liberals included data on the increased number of white lumber workers in their speakers' handbook for the 1928 election, and Manson noted the increase at a campaign speech in Prince Rupert.[28] Asians, however, were a minor issue in a campaign dominated by the Pacific Great Eastern Railway.

In the meantime mill owners, in co-operation with the government, went to court to test the constitutionality of the Minimum Wage Act. Ultimately the Supreme Court ruled that the Minimum Wage Act was *ultra vires*. In asking the new Conservative government of Simon Fraser Tolmie to refrain from amending the act to make it constitutionally acceptable, the timber companies again focused on foreign competition, discouragement to new industry, and hardship. The British Columbia Lumber Manufacturers' Association, whose members produced over 85 percent of the lumber on the coast, said that the act had resulted from political expediency rather than from "public demand or necessity." They claimed that its chief beneficiaries were Asians, whose number in the industry had declined by less than 2 percent and who had received 74 percent of the increased wages.[29] The new government was no more sympathetic than its predecessor. The legislature amended the act to validate the board's rulings on minimum wages. Industrialists could not budge the government on a law that the politicians wanted.

During the First World War a major cause of agitation against Asian labour was their employment in Vancouver Island's coal mines. The provincial government still wanted to keep them out. Between 1916 and 1921 it issued only ten coal miners' certificates to Asians and in 1919 amended the Coal Mines Regulation Act to set a minimum wage for coal miners "working at the face" in certain districts, specifically Cumberland. There is no evidence of enforcement. Minister of Mines William Sloan delayed the act's implementation for a year lest Ottawa disallow it. The company, Canadian Collieries (Dunsmuir) Limited, claimed that all employees on contract work were paid the same wages, but a member of the Employees' Grievance

Committee said that Asians were paid less than white men for day work.[30] In the 1920s the number of Asians in the industry declined absolutely and relatively without the intervention of the weak United Mine Workers or specific new legal discrimination. In 1919, 1,164 Chinese and Japanese miners represented 15.62 percent of the total number of miners employed. By 1923 there were only 582, or 9.5 percent of the total; Canadian Collieries (Dunsmuir) Limited in Cumberland employed the largest single group of Asians, 317, and the limited agitation against Asian miners was directed at them.[31]

The federal government was also concerned. When several veterans' organizations complained that the Canadian Government Merchant Marine used coal mined by Asians in Cumberland, Prime Minister King asked Sir Henry Thornton, its president, to discuss the matter with federal and provincial politicians no matter their party. It may only be coincidence, but the number of Asian miners dropped noticeably between 1922 and 1923. An equally plausible explanation was an explosion on 8 February 1923 that killed fourteen white and nineteen Chinese miners. A few days later a miners' grievance committee demanded the expulsion of Asians, a detriment "to life and limb," from the mines. Management agreed not to hire Asians on new work and to remove them from the mines as soon as possible. An overwhelming majority of white miners accepted this measure as the "only concrete proposal" in thirty years for removing Asians. Slightly over two hundred Asian miners were dismissed within the year. Yet the coroner's conclusion that a Chinese miner who had illegally lit a cigarette had caused the explosion led to criticisms of the government for not enforcing regulations about smoking materials. Minister of Mines Sloan increased penalties for violations of such regulations, but politicians were generally more interested in the presence of Asians than they were in safety. Sloan used the Asian question to good advantage in the 1924 provincial election. In his Nanaimo constituency his boasts of having reduced the number of Orientals working underground from 407 in 1916 to 263 in 1924 drew loud applause. He promised to continue the work. When Conservatives suggested that he should remove all of them, he accused them of having allowed Asians into the mines in the first place. Sloan readily dismissed his strongest rival, the Socialist candidate, William Pritchard, for favouring Asian enfranchisement.[32]

Early in 1925 Paul Phillips Harrison, MLA (Independent-Liberal, Comox), warned the provincial government of a "very tense" situation because Canadian Collieries had dismissed or put on short time 200 white employees while retaining Asians. Then the Western Fuel Corporation in Nanaimo called in Chinese workers to break a strike. The effects of these events spilled over into the 1925 federal election, when Socialists and Conservatives attacked the Liberals for letting the Chinese work underground; the Conservatives retained the Nanaimo seat. At their 1926 convention, provincial Conservatives demanded the removal of Asians from underground work even though Senator A.E. Planta of Nanaimo said that it was impossible to legislate the Chinese out of mines. Nevertheless, a few months later, in a throwback to turn of the century legislation, C.F. Davie, claiming that it was "now or never ... to stop this invidious invasion," proposed excluding from "dangerous occupations ... any person, whether naturalized or not, who belongs to the Asiatic Mongolian race" who could not prove his competence in reading, writing, and speaking English. As examples of "dangerous occupations," he cited coal mining, sawmilling, and logging, in which machinery or signals were used. The Chinese consul complained that the bill was discriminatory, contrary to Anglo-Chinese treaties, and *ultra vires.* Moreover, he noted that "in the present delicate diplomatic situation between Great Britain and China," it "might embitter diplomatic commercial relations." No MLA objected to its purpose, but the bill had little political advantage. Only a few hundred Asians were still employed in the mines, and only atavistic Conservative politicians complained about them. Given the bill's doubtful legality and, as the Japanese consul pointed out to Premier Oliver, its inconsistency with the Anglo-Japanese Treaty, the provincial government had it killed in committee.[33]

Whereas their numbers in coal mines declined, the Chinese remained prominent in laundries and restaurants. As an oblique method of limiting Chinese laundries, in 1919 the legislature amended the Factories Act to prevent laundries from operating between 7 p.m. and 7 a.m. When white laundry owners complained of poor enforcement and of Chinese launderers defying the act by working on statutory holidays, the provincial government replaced token fines with penalties that rose to $200 for second violations and included jail sentences for those who did not pay. To appeal to white patrons of Chinese laundries, some white laundry operators advertised employing "All White Help" and associated Chinese laundries with disease, but public health officials denied any danger. Nevertheless, in the 1924 provincial election, Liberals boasted of checking "the unfair competition of Oriental with white laundries."[34]

Restaurants, another traditional Chinese business, also depended on white customers. In reporting plans for a "first class white restaurant," the *Penticton Herald* suggested that eliminating "the Chink will take the form of a crowding out process." Whereas white laundry owners took the lead in fighting Asian competition, white workers led the campaign against Chinese restaurants. In 1919 the Cooks and Waiters Union in Vancouver complained that union men ate in such places. Chinese restaurateurs often disguised their proprietorship by giving their businesses "white" names, such as the Maple Leaf Café, and hiring white waitresses. Many hotels and restaurants not owned by the Chinese hired Chinese help, who worked longer hours and at lower wages than did whites. In 1921 the Vancouver Trades and Labour Council estimated that over half of the city's hotel and restaurant employees were Asian. Stimulated by the Hotel and Restaurant Employees

Union, the council tried to exclude Asians from restaurant kitchens and suggested prohibiting the Chinese from working alongside white women; in fact, a law forbidding the Chinese to employ white women was already on the books.[35] At its 1922 convention, however, the Union of British Columbia Municipalities (UBCM) rejected a Nanaimo proposal to amend the Municipal Act in order to forbid white men to employ Chinese help in restaurants and laundries because it was an "international" question. The Trades and Labour Council urged members to patronize union employers and businesses that did not hire Asians. In 1926 the council discussed organizing Oriental restaurant workers in order to raise their wages and make them less competitive but did not hire a Chinese organizer until 1938.[36]

Cooks and waiters complained that it was almost impossible for white men to secure jobs in hotel and restaurant kitchens or to learn the trade because Chinese chefs demanded that only their countrymen be employed. In 1927 the province invited employees and employers to present their cases for applying the Minimum Wage Act to catering. An official of the Vancouver Waiters and Caterers Union hoped that the Minimum Wage Law would give work to white women and encourage white men to stay. Like mill owners, white restaurateurs did not like the minimum wage. They complained that they could not attract or retain reliable white help for menial jobs such as dishwashing, that white women could not work as well as the Chinese, and that using Chinese labour enabled them to compete with Chinese restaurants and to provide cheap meals, which was good for the tourist industry. Because entering the business required little capital, white restaurateurs feared that those Chinese workers dismissed from white restaurants would open their own establishments. Nevertheless, the Minimum Wage Board extended the act to catering effective 1 April 1928. Deputy Minister of Labour J.D. McNiven admitted that the act did "not discriminate against any race or color" but noted that calling it "a veiled attack on the Oriental" was not far off the mark. Saying that white men could not compete with the Orientals' wages, he suggested that "we shall put them on the same wage basis and see who survives."[37]

Asians had limited access to other occupations. The provincial civil service would not hire them, and the Ministry of Finance warned government agents who employed Asian janitors that it would not honour vouchers to pay them. When R.W. Bruhn, MLA (Conservative, Salmon Arm), claimed that Asian university graduates were displacing whites, Dr. Edward Banno, a dentist and leader in the Japanese Canadian community, called this fear "ridiculous" since Asian professionals had to go elsewhere to find jobs. In the case of medicine and dentistry, this claim was not quite true; both professions admitted qualified Asians, presumably to practise among their own people.[38]

Nurses were another matter. Most hospitals had training schools and used students as cheap labour. In the fall of 1920 several members of the medical staff of the Vancouver General Hospital favoured admitting Japanese and Chinese students. One doctor noted that a graduate Japanese nurse was "well liked." Two aldermen on the Hospital Board, however, argued that "plenty of girls of our own race ... are ready and willing to do the work." Graduate nurses at Vancouver General agreed, and Asian students were not admitted.[39]

A few aspiring Asian nurses went to other hospitals, but other would-be professionals had no such opportunities. In 1918, when Gordon Won Cumyow, a native of British Columbia, applied for admission as an articled student and at least one other Chinese and one Japanese resident were interested in enrolling, the Vancouver Law Students' Society sought an amendment to the Legal Professions Act in order to exclude Asians. The benchers achieved this objective by denying enrolment to anyone who, if twenty-one years of age or over, would not be entitled to be placed on the provincial voters' list. Since Asians lacked the franchise, they were excluded from the legal profession in British Columbia. Pharmacists adopted a similar regulation.[40]

The lumber and service industries were largely within provincial jurisdiction; fisheries were mainly a federal responsibility. The annual reports of the Department of Marine and Fisheries and a Royal Commission on British Columbia fisheries echoed the desirability of a white-dominated fishery. Canners protested that they needed Japanese fishermen and that not all white fishermen were hostile to the Japanese. Nevertheless, until the courts ruled otherwise, the federal government responded to the demands of British Columbia MPs by dramatically reducing the number of Japanese labourers in the industry. As for those Chinese residents who worked seasonally in the canneries, usually under the direction of a Chinese "boss" or contractor, no one paid them much attention, probably because few whites wanted such miserable work.[41]

The key to controlling the fisheries was the licence. Different licences were issued for various species of fish, fishing methods, and geographic areas, but only British subjects could secure them. It was widely alleged – and with some reason – that the Japanese illegally traded licences and naturalization papers, "that when a Japanese fisherman is about to give up the ghost there is standing beside him on the boat, ready to take over the tiller, another Japanese who stands in his place and takes possession of his naturalization papers." Canners denied Major Burde's claim that they kept naturalization papers on hand, but F.H. Cunningham, director of the western division of the Fisheries branch of the Department of Marine and Fisheries, warned that if veterans, who had preference in getting licences, could not raise the capital necessary to enter the industry, they might sell their licences to Japanese fishermen.[42]

During the war, the scarcity of white labour and the demand for food created new openings for the Japanese. By 1919 they held 3,267 licences, or about half of the total issued; new, expensive equipment testified to their prosperity. Amidst postwar xenophobia, old complaints reappeared. Economic issues did not disappear, but racist arguments became more evident. Declaring that good white fishermen could not compete with the cheap-living Japanese, W.G. McQuarrie, MP (Conservative, New Westminster), claimed that the Japanese now monopolized the industry. "I remember the time when a good run of fish meant prosperity of that district," he said, "but now the money received by the fishermen goes ... to build up a foreign country." Other critics were harsher. "The fact that more than half the fishermen of the Canadian west coast are Japanese and only 15 percent British is one more proof of a dangerous social disease in this province," declared the *Nanaimo Free Press;* the *Port Alberni News* feared that the fisheries would soon "pass entirely into the hands of the brown men from the Orient." Several members of the Associated Boards of Trade of Vancouver Island predicted violence between white and Japanese fishermen. At Smith's Inlet, white gill-netters destroyed about $3,000 worth of seine nets and boats and promised "even more drastic action" if Japanese seiners resumed fishing. Premier Oliver warned the Department of Marine and Fisheries of a "grave risk of bloodshed." Others accused the Japanese of plundering "resources which belong to Canadians" but admitted that they were not alone in using seines and traps. A spokesman for the Native Indians of Barclay Sound accused the Japanese of "taking everything out of the country."[43]

Despite concern about the extent of the salmon stock, early in 1920 the Department of Marine and Fisheries adopted an "open door" policy in the salmon fishery. To satisfy canners and increase the proportion of white men, the department granted unlimited licences to white British subjects and Native Indians. For the Japanese, euphemistically listed as "others," the number of gill-net licences was frozen at the 1919 level. This was less harsh than an earlier proposal by the Department of Marine and Fisheries to carry out annual cuts and issue salmon cannery licences only to British subjects "of the white race." "Jubilant" Fraser River fishermen, their position relatively secure, organized a British Columbia Fishermen's Protective Association and invited representatives of the Steveston Fishermen's Benevolent Society, a Japanese organization, to attend their meeting. Because as British subjects they had "lost all their rights in Japan," E.S. Yoshida explained that it was in "their interest to work in harmony and good fellowship with their white fellow-citizens." His group did not expect to amalgamate with the new organization but, wanting "to co-operate wherever the interests of all the fishermen of B.C. are concerned," donated $100 to assist the association. The two organizations launched a joint fight against an embargo on the export of raw fish, called for the use of motorboats in all districts, co-operated in negotiating fish prices, and tried to "arrange for mutual protection in connection with the fishing industry from the fisherman's standpoint." Veterans' organizations did not approve. The association's acceptance of a donation from the Japanese upset the Army and Navy Veterans, whose Vancouver branch opposed the new regulations and called for more gill-net licences for returned men and white British subjects and for freezing the number of licences issued to Asians. The GWVA would let Japanese veterans obtain gill-net licences but otherwise wanted fishing to be "purely a white man's industry." Its national convention called for gradually reducing purse-seine licences until the Japanese comprised no more than a tenth of the industry.[44]

Hostility toward Japanese fishermen was stronger on the west coast of Vancouver Island. A travelling Presbyterian missionary warned that the industry was in "immediate danger of passing absolutely into the control of the Japanese." The *Port Alberni News* claimed that Japanese fishermen were so numerous that "the place now scarcely shows any signs of being a white man's country" and "so arrogant" that many white settlers were losing their tolerance. Moreover, the Japanese were going into commerce and taking trade from white storekeepers. When the *Victoria Colonist* retorted that the Japanese operated within the law and should not be singled out among aliens, the *Port Alberni News* stiffly replied that their competition was "of a kind and extent, that the white British subject should not be put up against in his own country inasmuch as successful competition would mean moral degeneration." Burde speculated that in a Pacific war, British Columbia would be fortunate if Japanese fishermen merely refused to supply food. The sympathetic minister of marine and fisheries had already decided not to increase the number of herring licences issued to Asians.[45]

The question slowly simmered until the 1921 federal election. Like Conservatives elsewhere, H.S. Clements, the incumbent in Comox-Alberni, tried to focus on the tariff but took credit for breaking a ring of cannery men who employed Japanese workers and for opening the fisheries to white men. He believed that only those of British birth should have fishing licences. His opponent, the Independent candidate A.W. Neill, complained that Ottawa was letting the Japanese swamp the fisheries. Neill, who would have a political career of twenty-four years opposing the Japanese, won. On the northern mainland in Skeena, Colonel C.W. Peck, the Unionist incumbent, spoke of "our national life," took credit for the gradual replacement of Japanese with white fishermen, and recalled the role of the fisheries in training seamen. His Liberal opponent, and the victor, A.W. Stork, opposed Asian immigration but did not specifically mention the fisheries.[46]

Under the new Liberal government, the Department of Marine and Fisheries continued to limit the number of licences issued to Asians. To encourage whites and Native Indians to enter the industry, in 1922 it issued one-third fewer salmon trolling licences to the Japanese. After allegations that some Japanese residents on the west coast of Vancouver Island made "deals" with white licence holders and that unlicensed Japanese fishermen plied their trade outside the three-mile limit, the department confiscated sixteen vessels for operating without licences. Fifteen operators were found guilty. After redeeming his boat and paying a $1,000 fine, one Japanese fisherman, exploiting Canadian suspicions of Japan's military ambitions, warned officials in a menacing manner that "by and by, when Japanese soldiers come, they [would] fix 'em." Then, he and the other Japanese fishermen left port without their lights on and "in a reckless manner."[47]

In the meantime, after pressure from the British Columbia MPs and evidence presented to the Fisheries Committee of the House of Commons, the government set up a commission on the British Columbia fisheries. Its main focus was the depletion of the Fraser River salmon fishery, but it had a broad scope. Inevitably Asians were an issue. The commission's composition (two MPs from Nova Scotia, including William Duff, who had said that he did "not believe in oriental fishermen," and four MPs from British Columbia) ensured that it would not be sympathetic to the Japanese.[48]

In late summer 1922 the commission visited fishing communities before hearings in Vancouver and Victoria. Canners denied any partiality for the Japanese. Several suggested that the Japanese should never have been admitted but should be justly treated and that any reduction in their number should be gradual. In the north, canners said that it was impossible to find sufficient, reliable white or Native Indian fishermen. Moreover, the Japanese produced "the most fish," and their work was "indispensable to the successful operation of the canneries." Native Indian witnesses alleged that the canners gave better equipment to the Japanese, who landed more fish by breaking regulations, using long nets, and fishing twenty-four hours a day. "We object to their fishing," said Charlie Barton of Kincolith, "because it reduces our supply."[49] White fishermen agreed that "the Japanese is too good a fisherman. He doesn't want to let that net out of the water." They accused them of "juggling" licences and naturalization papers, using illegal nets, avoiding the strenuous halibut fishery, practically exterminating cod, sole, and herring in enclosed waters off southern Vancouver Island, and being "under the thumb" of the canners. Some white fishermen objected that Japanese buyers, some from Seattle, would buy only from Japanese fishermen. By listening to such people as Burde and Hugh Thornley, president of the Disabled Veterans' Association in Vancouver, the commissioners heard what they wanted to hear about the Japanese. Burde accused Japanese fishermen of bribing government officials to obtain licences and naturalization papers. When asked for evidence to justify his demand that "Orientals should be excluded from all our industries," he answered that "we want a white man's country here." He claimed that "the Japs ... have very covetous desires on the Commonwealth and the Dominion." In questioning Japanese witnesses, the commissioners scarcely mentioned the fisheries but asked about intermarriage and living standards. An eighteen-year-old Nisei, Yoshio Oda, replied that "marriage is not the only way to assimilate. If they can get into the country and get around well and be good, that is assimilation ... They keep the laws and pay their taxes regularly." He alleged that white men "loaf in town" until the fishing season started but that Japanese fishermen arrived early to secure the best gear, study tides, and be where the fish were.[50]

The commission's interim report recommended a 40 percent reduction in licences for all methods of fishing issued to "other than white fishermen and Indians" for the 1923 season. A delighted British Columbia Fishermen's Protective Association said reducing licences would "let more fish go up the river" and help restore the Fraser River fishery. Few others were pleased. A lawyer for Japanese herring packers remarked, "such phraseology deceives no one" because the Japanese were the only ones affected. One Japanese fishermen's association reminded the government that they were "fellow citizens" who were guaranteed rights on becoming citizens. Reducing licences, Japanese fishermen asserted, would mean "absolute ruin" for them and their families. They urged that those who evaded regulations should be treated "purely as violators of the law." The 40 percent reduction was "somewhat greater" than the department had contemplated; it was so drastic that some white fishermen feared it might discourage fish buyers from going to Vancouver Island's west coast! Canners, who regarded Japanese as their best fishermen, called the proposal "far too drastic" and "entirely unfair" to Japanese who would then go "into some other industry, thereby causing ill feeling and change of policy again." Concerned about getting competent white and Native Indian fishermen, they argued for a more gradual reduction.[51]

Given such protests, the minister of fisheries waited for the final report before making any reductions. Officials initially suggested that the commission's plan was feasible but realized that a 40 percent reduction might force some firms on the Skeena into liquidation. The commissioners were not impressed; some wanted an immediate 100 percent cut. In their final report released on 7 March 1923, the commissioners suggested solving the urgent problem of "the squeezing of white men out of the fishing industry" by immediately reducing the number of licences issued to the Japanese by 40 percent and making further reductions as soon as possible "without disrupting the industry." The only concession to the Japanese was preference to those who had served overseas or had lived and fished in the area for a long time. Henceforth, in applying for certain licences, fishermen had to declare that "the operations as conducted by me under such license are neither directly or indirectly, wholly or partially on behalf of other than white British subjects, Canadian Indians or a company or firm authorized by the Provincial Government to do business in the province of British Columbia." In announcing that more than 800 Japanese licence holders had been barred from fishing, Chief Fisheries Inspector Major J.A. Motherwell said that "our aim is to induce the white man to take care of the fishing more than before" and to avoid closed seasons for certain fisheries.[52]

The canners' protest produced a strange sight in the House of Commons. Two Vancouver Conservatives, General J.A. Clark and Leon J. Ladner, who had opposed Asian immigration, complained that canners would suffer serious losses since they had not expected the 40 percent reduction for the 1923 season. Ernest Lapointe, minister of marine and fisheries, taunted "members who want to exclude the orientals, except those whom they employ themselves, or who are employed by their friends." An embarrassed Ladner accused Lapointe of "a political twist" and reiterated his belief in preserving British Columbia's natural resources and industries "for the white people of Canada." When Lapointe visited the coast in the fall of 1923, canners told him that white fishermen did not work as hard as the Japanese, but he decided that the policy was working well. A year later Motherwell reported an overall 40 percent decline in the number of Asians holding salmon gill-net licences. In the province as a whole, 9.5 percent more whites and 7.4 percent more Native Indians took up such licences, but the total number of fishermen fell by 534, or 11.9 percent. In later annual reports, Motherwell noted that the policy of "eliminating the Oriental from the fisheries ... with a view to placing the entire industry in the hands of white British subjects and Canadian Indians appears to be working out well."[53]

Canners said that difficulties in finding white fishermen meant a choice of "the Jap or the trap," a reference to a fishing method long outlawed as a conservation measure. Although fisheries officials denied any protests over a policy that was "reclaiming the great Pacific fishing industry for Canadian citizens," Henry Bell-Irving of Anglo-British Columbia Packers, one of the larger firms, correctly noted that those Japanese labourers forced from fishing were moving into agriculture and trade. The Berry Growers Co-operative Union complained that many fishermen were growing fruit in the Fraser Valley. In Alberni some fishermen found work in the lumber mills. Nevertheless, the government briefly sped up the removal of Japanese fishermen from the herring industry and ordered that, except for two executives, all employees of dry salteries must be whites or Native Indians. This did not satisfy Neill, who persuaded the Marine and Fisheries Committee to recommend removal of Asians from the salmon and cod fisheries by 1937. In the 1925 and 1926 federal elections, he promised that the gradual elimination of the Japanese would continue. In Nanaimo, Sloan attacked incumbent Conservative C.H. Dickie for a minority report to the Royal Commission asking for a 15 percent rather than a 40 percent reduction, but Dickie was re-elected. In Vancouver North, when a heckler accused the King government of not enforcing the law to curtail Japanese fishermen, Liberal G.G. McGeer accused A.D. McRae, the Conservative candidate, of employing Orientals in his canneries, but McRae said that he had replaced Japanese fishermen with whites. In Nanaimo and Vancouver, however, the fishery was a minor issue.[54]

Protests by the Japanese against their removal from the industry had little effect. By 1928, of the 14,493 licences issued for all branches of the fishery in British Columbia, they held only 2,261, or about 16 percent. Then the Amalgamated Association of Japanese Fishermen orchestrated the launch of a court challenge by having twenty-two Canadian-born Japanese residents apply for salmon gill-net licences. Their lawyers contended that some regulations in the Fisheries Act were invalid and that the Department of Marine and Fisheries was "interfering with civil rights" in a way not justified by the British North America (BNA) Act. Provincial officials feared that the case was "freighted with grave possibilities" and, if successful, "would give Asiatics virtual domination of fishing on this coast." In the words of the *Vancouver Province,* the existing regulations were Canada's "most successful attempt ... to stem the tide of Oriental penetration."[55]

At about the same time, the Supreme Court of British Columbia in the separate Sommerville Canneries case ruled that the federal government lacked the power to license salmon canneries. This ruling also threw into question the discretionary powers of the minister of marine and fisheries to grant or refuse fishing licences, so he asked the Supreme Court of Canada to determine whether he in fact had this power and, if not, whether Parliament could give it to him. In the meantime Asians "flocked back" to fish reduction and packing plants on the west coast of Vancouver Island, displacing a "considerable" number of white workers. William Sloan, the provincial minister responsible for fisheries, warned that if federal control of canneries were not restored, the province would take over. After Neill accused herring packers of "not playing the game," they began replacing Asian labour with whites. Meanwhile, Japanese fishermen, with the financial help of the Japanese government, hired a lawyer to represent them before the Supreme Court since the minister's discretionary powers had resulted in the reduction of the number of licences issued to them. The lawyer referred to Mr. Justice Lyman Duff's comment in the Brooks-Bidlake case that under the Anglo-Japanese Treaty, "with respect to the right to dispose of their labour, the Japanese are to be in the same position before the law as the subjects of the most favoured nation." In May 1928 in a split decision, with Mr. Justice Duff in the minority, the Supreme Court ruled that the minister could not discriminate among British subjects. The latter decision, observed the *Vancouver Province,* upset the policy of "gradually weeding out the Japanese." Neill warned the prime minister that "every naturalized Jap" would immediately apply for a fishing licence, leading to "a tremendous upheaval." By an Order in Council, the government authorized the minister of marine and fisheries to control licences pending an appeal to the Privy Council. The uncertainty of the situation was demonstrated when a Japanese fisherman in Prince Rupert accepted his licence under protest because it carried the usual stamp on Japanese licences "that in the operations conducted thereunder a motor boat will not be used." When he later fished from a motorboat, a white fisherman charged him with contravening his licence, but the Department of Justice said that nothing could be done pending the Judicial Committee's decision. Its ruling in October 1929 that the government could not withhold licences from naturalized citizens ended the licence reduction policy, and in January 1930 the Department of Marine and Fisheries announced that in the forthcoming season the number of licences issued to "others" than whites or Native Indians would not be reduced.[56]

Neill was wrong; there was no "upheaval." White and Japanese fishermen on the Fraser River jointly struck for higher fish prices. When fishermen and canners met federal and provincial officials late in 1929 to discuss new regulations, only Neill complained about Asians. Indeed, 250 fishermen at a mass meeting of the British Columbia Fishermen's Protective Association agreed to co-operate with the Japanese Fishermen's Association in seeking relief from a new provincial licensing system that permitted the Japanese to fish only "for a specified cannery." By 1930 the number of Japanese fishermen had been much reduced, but such co-operation among fishermen suggests that politicians such as Neill were responsible for much of the conflict. The solicitor for the Berry Growers Co-operative Union had rightly noted that the policy of eliminating the Japanese from the fishery had a "purely political genesis."[57]

Despite new land acquisitions during the war years, Asians controlled less than 5 percent of the total acreage of improved land in British Columbia in the 1920s. They were concentrated in a few areas: Japanese berry growers mainly in the Maple Ridge-Mission district of the Fraser Valley; Chinese market gardeners in greater Vancouver, greater Victoria, North Okanagan, and the Kamloops-Ashcroft area; and Chinese and Japanese farmers in the mixed farms of the Comox Valley, where the only Asian dairy farms were located. The intensity of opposition to Asians varied over time, space, and particular aspects of agriculture. Nor did opposition apply equally to the Chinese and the Japanese. The Chinese tended to lease land whereas the Japanese preferred to own it. Moreover, as farmers experimented with marketing schemes, they distinguished between the Chinese, who tended to flout marketing laws, and the Japanese, who often participated in co-operative marketing.

Throughout the 1920s, farmers' organizations, the British Columbia Fruit Growers' Association (BCFGA), farmers' institutes, and the United Farmers of British Columbia (UFBC) used old arguments in repeated demands for a law to deny Asians the right to own or lease land. They accused Asian farmers of sending most of their earnings out of the country, of low living standards, of working longer hours and more efficiently than white men, of depressing property values so they could spread their "colonies," and, in the case of the Chinese, of "cutthroat" pricing. Propaganda from the intense campaign preceding California's decision in 1920 to stiffen the Alien Land Act and stories of how "brown-skinned sons of Nippon" controlled California's land informed British Columbia opinion.[58]

Farmers who had once sought cheap Chinese labour now feared competition from "the industrious and thrifty Oriental," who was "in many respects ... a better man." The *Kamloops Standard-Sentinel*, in dismissing lamentations on the "yellow menace" that "savor too greatly of party politics," observed that honest, hardworking Chinese farmers could "vastly improve lands and make hopeless-looking places fit for good returns." The ambitious Japanese farmer, however, was a worry, for "he aims to be a landowner and an aggressive force in the community." The

Kamloops Telegram attributed an increased Asian presence in the Okanagan Valley to the fact that "white men will not work, learn, save and invest, and the Japanese will." Whether inspired by Arcadian, agrarian, or country life ideals, British Columbians commonly endowed the land with a special mystique. The *Comox Argus* suggested that "a house can be burnt down and a business destroyed but the land passes on from generation to generation." "For biological reasons," the *Vancouver Sun* declared, the "Japanese must not be allowed to settle on Canadian farms."[59] City dwellers found the idea of protecting "our own people" appealing and sought laws to deny Asians the right to own land, protested the use of Asian labour, and expressed fears of Asian takeovers of certain districts. Sometimes they were more concerned than the residents of the affected areas.

Maligned communities protested insults to local pride. When J.S. Cowper referred to Chinese farmers on leased lands in Enderby, the *Enderby Commoner* replied that the lands were "entirely in the vicinity of Armstrong, the nearest to Enderby being seven miles away." The *Ashcroft Journal* accused Chinese potato growers of being detrimental to land and crops, but when the *Vancouver Province* called Ashcroft "to all intents and purposes a Chinese community," the resentful *Journal* listed the town's white-owned businesses and noted that only seven of eighty students in the school were Chinese. When A.U. de Pencier, Anglican bishop of New Westminster, cited Chinese domination of Ashcroft to suggest that Asians were taking over the province, the *Journal* answered that no more than 10 percent of Ashcroft's population was Chinese. The Board of Trade condemned those who called Ashcroft "the place where the Chinese come from." Yet the image persisted. When the provincial minister of agriculture in 1928 said that Chinese farmers owned 90 percent of the land in the area and exploited serf labour, the *Journal* responded that all but one Chinese farmer merely leased land, that all operated according to strict business principles, and that many shared profits with their workers.[60]

Ashcroft's difficulty in convincing others that it was not a Chinese community demonstrates how imagination could inspire an "oriental menace." Rumours of Japanese interest in Comox Valley farm land led the Courtenay-Comox Board of Trade and the Comox Farmers' Institute to demand laws preventing Asians from acquiring or leasing land. A Kelowna Board of Trade member admitted that "fear" was a major reason for opposing Asian land ownership. The *Penticton Herald*, observing Penticton's "good fortune" in being "practically free from their ownership," wondered when Asians would arrive "insidiously and slowly at first, but gradually gaining in strength and numbers until we find ourselves in the same unenviable situation as Armstrong or points in the Fraser Valley?" The Vanderhoof District Farmers' Institute, while not yet directly affected, took a stand "for the sake of those to whom the question is a vital one." There were no Asian dairy farmers in the Fraser Valley, but producers blamed a milk surplus on Asian vegetable growers who drove white vegetable growers into dairy farming. J.W. Berry, MLA (Conservative, Delta), said that the Japanese provided 40 percent of Seattle's milk and warned that if British Columbians did not take "heed, they would find themselves collectively with 'Oriental backbone' in place of the sturdy backbone stock of pioneer agriculturalists."[61]

In a few cases, there appeared to be reason for fearing Asian domination. In Maple Ridge, Japanese land holdings increased four-fold from 272 acres in 1914 to 1,120 acres in 1918. Local residents pressed the government to prevent further land acquisition by the Japanese, who, they claimed, borrowed money at 3 percent from their consul in Vancouver and brought in countrymen as cheap labour. The opposition's objections had a distinctly racial basis. One resident complained that "a whole host of desperate looking savages bought 30 acres within a stone's throw of my place here, thereby in one quick strike cutting my years of work & expense in two." A local clergyman warned that "in a few years the Canadians will be driven out of these municipalities, or we will have tragedies here in such conflict between the two people." Would-be soldier settlers warned that the Japanese could "turn our fair Province into a colony of the Mikado's."[62]

Asians comprised less than 5 percent of the population of the Yale census district, but its most populous area, the Okanagan Valley, strongly opposed them. The southern part of the valley had few, if any, Asians, and its inhabitants wanted it to stay that way. Late in 1919 two Chinese residents bought a lot on Main Street in Penticton. The Board of Trade was indignant; the *Penticton Herald,* claiming "an Oriental invasion" had virtually ruined the Armstrong district, threatened that "even if we have to take the law into our own hands, in a manner of speaking, these gentry should get it plainly and strongly that we do not want them on Main or Front streets as land owners." Under the heading "Keep Penticton White," the GWVA sponsored a public meeting to consider how to make "our town unattractive for the yellow man." Participants emphasized Chinese inassimilability and the need to preserve Canada for "those of Anglo-Saxon birth." One suggested expropriating Asian land and shipping its owners "back from whence they came." All three candidates for reeve promised to keep Penticton white. The editor of the *Summerland Review* was more concerned about the Japanese. He admitted that many were "fine, clean young men," but alleged that because of the "wide difference between the two races," continuing sales to Orientals would narrow social life by reducing the white population and "making others more inclined to sell out and move elsewhere."[63]

In North Okanagan, where the Chinese had owned market gardens for many years, the idea of prohibiting Asian land ownership had been popular before the war. Early in 1919 white farmers in Rutland, just east of Kelowna, complained that the Japanese, who already owned 125 acres and leased another 394, had almost bought three more properties. No one else seemed anxious to check the Japanese. Without enthusiasm the Kelowna Board of Trade responded by asking the government to prevent Asians from purchasing land in the area until all returned soldiers were settled; the GWVA merely discussed the subject; and, after a vigorous discussion, a

BCFGA committee collected data on Asian land ownership. Then the *Toronto Globe* reported that English capitalists had sold the 13,000-acre Coldstream Ranch near Vernon to a Japanese syndicate. Since its British owners were trying to sell the financially troubled ranch, the rumour had a ring of reality. Hitherto there had been no Japanese landowners near Vernon though Chinese truck gardeners leased 1,142 acres. Local residents reacted quickly. Pointing to Japanese control of parts of California, the *Vernon News* feared that they would soon control much of the valley. Delegates to a meeting arranged by the Board of Trade described this prospect as "the worst thing that could happen to the Okanagan Valley." They asserted that British Columbia, "by possession and settlement a white man's country," must be preserved as such and that assimilation was neither likely nor desirable because of the very different "standards and habits of living" of "the white and yellow races." The Associated Boards of Trade of the valley told the provincial Board of Trade that, if unchecked, Asians would drive out the whites. Asserting that no Japanese resident in British Columbia could afford to buy the Coldstream Ranch and that "Japanese capitalists would keep away" until public feeling changed, the Japanese consul denied the *Globe* report. Calling his intervention impertinent, the provincial Board of Trade asked the federal government "to make it impossible for Orientals and undesirable aliens to own, lease or otherwise control land in Canada."[64]

Meanwhile, Martin Burrell, MP for Yale and secretary of state, told the owners' agent that thousands of returned soldiers lived in the area and warned of violence if the property passed into Japanese hands. In London F.C. Wade, the provincial agent general, advised the British owners that "a greater blow could not be struck against British Columbia" than the sale of the ranch to Japanese interests. Premier Oliver expected that the matter might "become acute at any moment." Advice from the Okanagan seemed to confirm this fear. The secretary of the BCFGA warned of "serious trouble" if the government did not quickly "debar Orientals from owning land." At the BCFGA convention in January 1920, "no resolution would have been too drastic." Members proposed sending a "strong delegation" to urge the federal government to give "careful and immediate consideration" to the matter in view of the forthcoming expiry of the Anglo-Japanese Treaty. The *Vernon News* heartily agreed that "grave" international questions were involved but insisted that "self-protection ... is the first law of nature." The UFBC heard claims of Orientals "blocking the whole future of white agriculturalists in this Province" by reducing prices for produce and thus lowering land values.[65]

Okanagan businessmen easily received province-wide support. At the provincial Boards of Trade convention, James Vallance of Vernon predicted that without legislation "to rid ourselves of this canker, which is fastened to the backbone of the Okanagan, we are done." A long discussion revealed similar concerns elsewhere. The provincial board asked Ottawa to appoint a commission to find a means "to make it impossible for Orientals and undesirable aliens to own, lease or otherwise control land in Canada." At the Western Boards of Trade convention in Calgary,

British Columbia delegates "put up a stiff fight" for a similar resolution, but prairie delegates warned that denying citizenship rights to the Japanese and Chinese might force Canada "to build up an army and navy to protect the principle." They would support investigation only. H.B. Morley of Penticton complained that prairie delegates had little knowledge of the situation and that "Ottawa is too far away to see what is going on in the West." J.A. MacKelvie, a Conservative and editor of the *Vernon News,* warned Burrell that the Union government was already unpopular in the province and that "if no determined effort is made to keep our lands from passing into Oriental ownership, it will certainly be the 'last straw' as far as B.C. is concerned." Apparent eastern indifference frustrated British Columbians.[66]

Local MLAs exploited the land question. Dr. K.C. Macdonald (Liberal, North Okanagan) and J.W. Jones (Conservative, South Okanagan) joined the protest. Jones spoke to over 300 people at a Kelowna meeting sponsored by the GWVA. He mentioned the Coldstream rumour, the extent of Japanese land ownership in California and Washington State, the declining British proportion of the population, and the province's unique problems with Doukhobors and Asians. He concluded that "the passage of the ownership of the soil, on which our whole civil foundation rested" could not be tolerated. Even though K. Iwashita, a prominent Japanese resident, argued that the proposal would deny British justice, the meeting referred to Asian inassimilability and unanimously protested Asian land ownership. Jones also spoke in Peachland, where the GWVA complained that competition from Asians and unnaturalized aliens depreciated land values and reduced returns for British settlers. "Industries made profitable by the British settler ought to be available to such citizens only," the GWVA declared, and warned that the legislature's apathy was making British settlers "seriously consider the necessity of direct action." The GWVA's national convention endorsed the resolution against Asian land ownership.[67]

Stating that one-ninth of the population was Oriental, Jones told the legislature that British Columbia should be preserved "for the white race" and complained of Japanese competition in fishing and agriculture. Referring to "determined" and "alarming" efforts by the Japanese to acquire "the very best lands" in the province, he said that Canada should "profit" from the lesson of the United States. There, he claimed, the Japanese had "swarmed in their thousands" and now controlled "the great industries," the legislature and municipal offices of Hawaii, and the small-fruit industry of California and had extensive land holdings in Oregon and Washington State. He proposed laws against land passing into "undesirable" hands and urged Ottawa to admit only immigrants who could be assimilated and "imbued with the principles of liberty and constitutional government so characteristic of the Anglo-Saxon." Premier Oliver sympathized but wondered about the Anglo-Japanese Treaty. Although Ottawa had ignored his requests for clarification, he explained that since the treaty gave Japanese residents the same liberty to acquire and possess property as citizens of any other foreign country, the province could not legislate against Asian land ownership. A general law against alien land owner-ship would antagonize Americans while a law applying only to Asians would prob-ably violate the Anglo-Japanese Treaty of 1911. Aware of this diplomatic problem and of "pretty strong feeling" against Asian land ownership, Martin Burrell gave similar advice to his constituents who demanded an alien land law but also urged the Japanese consul to discourage Japanese residents from trying to acquire land "where so much feeling exists."[68]

Meanwhile, at its 1920 session the legislature merely received a report from its Select Standing Committee on Agriculture, which drew attention to "the rapidly increasing menace to white agricultural settlers" from the purchase and lease of land by Orientals and called for more information. The BCFGA, farmers' insti-tutes, the UFBC, the British Columbia Stockbreeders, and others continued to protest the rapidly increasing number of Chinese and Japanese residents on the land and the inability of white farmers to compete. Some MLAs described "acute" situations in their districts; witnesses had told the committee that Asians were "getting control of the land in the best agricultural districts." At its 1921 session the legislature endorsed the committee's recommendation that someone with a "thor-ough understanding" of the problem should attend the forthcoming Imperial Conference. It also heeded requests from the farmers' institutes and the UFBC to gather information "on the extent of Oriental land holding" in order to make other Canadians "aware of the seriousness of the menace" and to provide evidence in order to argue for treaty revisions at the Imperial Conference. Forty typed pages of statistics, collected in response to earlier requests, were published in June 1921 and sent to Prime Minister Meighen and Simon Fraser Tolmie, federal minister of agriculture, to use at the Imperial Conference. The statistics revealed that 1,080 Chinese and Japanese residents owned or leased a total of 26,918 acres. The Chi-nese tended to lease land, and the Japanese to own it; most Chinese landowners engaged in truck farming while the Japanese mainly grew small fruit – that is, berries. Many newspapers published the press release without comment, letting the figures speak for themselves.[69]

Citing the data, Premier Oliver asked Prime Minister Meighen to ensure that any new treaty preserve British Columbia's "right to deal with its own resources." Oliver had the support both of farmers, especially in the Fraser Valley, and of municipalities and organizations in the form of resolutions asking that a renewed treaty not affect provincial efforts to forbid the employment of the Japanese on public works contracts and on Crown lands. H.H. Stevens suggested that refusing to renew the Japanese treaty without protection for Canada's right to legislate on land holding and to control immigration would be a "knock-out" blow to the Liberal opposition. Confusion, however, reigned. The treaty being considered was the Anglo-Japanese Treaty of Alliance – a defensive pact – rather than the Treaty of Commerce and Navigation, which affected the rights granted to nationals of the contracting parties. In any case, Prime Minister Meighen said that the treaty did not restrict Canada's right to legislate on matters relating to land, a provincial concern; however, during the 1921 election campaign, his Department of Justice advised him that the overriding Naturalization Act allowed aliens to hold real and personal property in the same way as it did native-born British subjects.[70]

Undaunted, provincial politicians sought a constitutional change. In what one newspaper called "the most drastic resolution" ever passed by a provincial political convention, the Liberals urged negotiations with Ottawa for legislation to debar "Asiatic aliens" from owning land and other natural resources. Ian Mackenzie said that "economically we cannot compete with them; racially we cannot assimilate them; hence we must exclude them from our midst and prohibit them from owning land," which instead must "be peopled by those descended from the white stock." Favouring "peaceful means" to halt "peaceful penetration," he wanted to amend the BNA Act in order to allow the province to prohibit Asians from acquiring any proprietary interest or employment in agricultural, timber, and mineral lands or in fishing and other industries. He asked Ottawa to reject any treaty or "binding international obligation" limiting the legislature's power in such matters. Minister of Agriculture E.D. Barrow agreed that the measure was necessary since it was "practically impossible to buy any produce not grown by Orientals," who raised 90 percent of the local produce consumed in Vancouver and 55 percent of the potatoes grown in the province. William J. Bowser, leader of the opposition, noted difficulties in amending the BNA Act and implications for imperial relations; Federated Labour Party members Sam Guthrie (Newcastle) and R.H. Neelands (South Vancouver) accused Liberals and Conservatives of using the issue for political purposes. Nevertheless, the legislature unanimously endorsed Mackenzie's resolution as "the only logical way" to "prevent the peaceful penetration of the Asiatic into British Columbia." The idea was popular. The BCFGA and boards of trade in New Westminster and Vancouver passed similar resolutions. The Vancouver board told Prime Minister King that "intensive cultivation" by the Japanese, "the greatest menace to the future development of our Province," had practically ousted white settlers in parts of British Columbia. Given the "natural repugnance inherent in the souls of our own people to fraternize with the Oriental," the board explained, they get "control of the surrounding land" and, as its owners, will "eventually control" the nation's destiny.[71]

To no one's surprise, the federal minister of justice reminded the province that since the BNA Act gave powers relating to aliens and treaty obligations to the Dominion government, granting British Columbia's request "would be incompatible with the compact of union." Attorney General Manson agreed, and the provincial Liberals did not fight their federal counterparts. Their 1924 provincial campaign book included a memo from the deputy attorney general stating that the province lacked power to limit the rights of Orientals to hold or acquire lands or personal property. Nonetheless, the new legislative assembly asked Ottawa not to adhere to any treaty that would limit its power to regulate the "social and industrial activities" of Asians.[72]

This request did not satisfy British Columbia's agricultural organizations, which still wanted to prohibit "the owning or leasing of land in Canada by Orientals," particularly after Asians bought an additional two farms near Kelowna and rumours circulated that the Canadian National Railway (CNR) would permit Asians to buy 120 acres of celery land along its right of way. R.C. Neish, the secretary of the United Farmers of British Columbia, complained of land around Kelowna being "honeycombed by oriental owners, who even if they are able to grow a few more onions to the acre, weaken through their unassimilability the social structure of the rural population." After discussions with the legislature's Select Standing Committee on Agriculture, the advisory board of the farmers' institutes and the BCFGA sent the board's secretary, C.E. Whitney-Griffiths, to Ottawa to interview O.D. Skelton, under secretary of state for external affairs, and to present the case to Dr. J.H. King, the only British Columbian in the Cabinet. Apart from sympathy from Progressives in Parliament, Whitney-Griffiths received only promises that the matter would be considered.[73]

In the meantime the Vernon Board of Trade sent a brief to sympathetic Conservative MPs. It did not quite agree with agricultural groups. Believing that Oriental farmers stimulated trade, it accepted temporary leases but opposed "the cancerous conditions engendered by the actual sale of land to these people," fearing that such ownership might create "orientalized districts" that, "owing to racial peculiarities," would always be "out of sympathy with the white population" and, in a time of conflict, a possible "source of great danger to the nation." In a follow-up letter, Grote Stirling, MP (Conservative, Yale), suggested that since Japan did not allow foreigners to own agricultural land, Canada could enact similar legislation. The prime minister replied that a new Japanese land law permitted foreigners to own land "on condition of reciprocity" and that under the 1911 treaty Canada had given reciprocal property rights to the Japanese. Amid the political and constitutional crisis and federal election campaign that summer, his promise of a policy became lost. British Columbians, however, did not forget. Although Attorney General Manson and Premier Oliver recognized that a proposal to prevent disenfranchised individuals, other than Native Indians, from acquiring land by purchase or lease was *ultra vires* and "inconsistent" with the Japanese treaty, Provincial Secretary William Sloan introduced a motion asking Ottawa not to adhere to any international obligations limiting provincial powers over "the regulation of social and industrial activities within the province" and to take steps to denounce existing treaties affecting immigration. Sloan's resolution did not come to a vote, but observers interpreted it as the government's official view. Privately Manson told the BCFGA that the problem was eastern Canada's inability "to appreciate the extent of the Oriental menace." He urged "a campaign of education ... throughout

Canada." In the meantime, he observed, if British Columbians refused "to have anything to do with the Oriental," he would be compelled to make other provinces realize "the seriousness of the Oriental question." A year later, as part of a sweeping anti-Asian resolution, the legislature unanimously asked Ottawa for power to control the ownership of land by Orientals.[74]

Although the provincial government changed from Liberal to Conservative after the 1928 election, the Agricultural Committee continued to consider ways to prevent Asians from owning land. A major witness, C.E. Hope, a Fraser Valley farmer, said that Asian competition made it difficult to keep white boys on the farm. Noting California and Washington State laws against alien land ownership, he suggested disobeying Ottawa's rulings unless the federal government conceded to "the just demands of the Province." Committee members agreed that there was a problem but were not inclined to fight Ottawa; they suggested that white farmers not hire Asians or rent land to them. Farmers' institutes in the Fraser and Okanagan Valleys still called for restrictions on Asian land ownership and worked with Hope's White Canada Association. Although it denied wanting to upset international relations, in 1930 the association, in concert with with the advisory board of the farmers' institutes and the Native Sons of British Columbia, made a presentation to the Agricultural Committee. Some delegates feared becoming "Chinese Columbia"; others complained that whites could not compete with the Japanese. The association wanted the removal of all Asians from the country, expropriation of their property, and a $5,000 grant for its campaign to revise all laws restricting action against Orientals. One of the few press comments called expropriation talk "foolish." The Conservative government found, as had the Liberals earlier, that the province had no jurisdiction; there is no record of a reply to the request for funds, but given the Depression a grant was unlikely. In Ottawa, McQuarrie proposed a reference to the Supreme Court to determine what powers, if any, the Dominion and the provinces had in respect to Orientals owning and leasing land, but the minister of justice said that the Supreme Court was unlikely to answer such an academic question. Before the members could pursue the matter, Parliament was dissolved.[75]

Given doubts about the constitutionality of land laws, British Columbians had already considered other ways to keep Orientals off the land. A decade earlier Stevens had urged Vancouver residents to buy Fraser Valley land, clear it, and plant crops. Since white men had not rushed to take up farming, Minister of Agriculture Barrow urged farmers to copy his Chilliwack neighbours by making a gentlemen's agreement not to sell or lease land to Asians. Similarly, former attorney general M.A. MacDonald chastised farmers who "would sell land to a Japanese one day and join in a clamor against it the next." The provincial secretary advised women's institutes to send resolutions against Asian land ownership to those who leased land to Orientals. The government rejected applications from Asians who wanted to buy rich agricultural land reclaimed from Sumas Lake, but its legal counsel indicated that any clause denying Japanese residents the right to buy irrigated lands in Oliver would be in "absolute conflict" with the Anglo-Japanese Treaty. He noted, however, that it might be possible to discriminate against the Chinese. Some municipalities refused to sell land to Asians.[76]

From time to time, farmers' groups recommended the same idea. The president of the UFBC urged farmers not to sell or lease land to Asians, but only farmers in Delta, where the Chinese dominated potato growing, pledged not to lease land to Orientals for five years. By 1927 white farmers concerned about an Oriental "stranglehold on the potato business," which had lead many farmers to give up in despair, had organized the Delta Co-operative Owners Association. Members signed a "binding agreement" stating that for five years they would not sell, rent, or lease land to Orientals. The Union of British Columbia Municipalities (UBCM), "numerous" boards of trade, Chilliwack potato growers, and the farmers' institutes of several districts endorsed it, but enthusiasm was not matched by action. Even Delta farmers "gradually broke away." The BCFGA refused to bind members to a similar scheme proposed by a Vernon member. Indeed, the Department of Agriculture found that some of those who petitioned against Asian land holding leased land to Asians. Refusing to sell or lease land to Asians was too great a personal sacrifice for some landowners.[77]

In the Cowichan Valley, where white farmers had long wanted to restrict Asian land ownership, the Duncan Municipal Council, anxious to maintain "a white man's country," called for legislation to require municipal approval for "all transactions bearing upon the conveyance of title to lands and leasing of lands." Municipal councils in Vancouver, Nanaimo, Prince George, Chilliwack, Abbotsford, Penticton, Spallumcheen, Cumberland, Saanich, Surrey, Richmond, and elsewhere supported such legislation. Others had reservations or rejected the resolution, as did some boards of trade and the GWVA provincial executive. Port Coquitlam thought that approving every land transaction would be tedious; Victoria feared that Asians driven from the land would undercut white wages; Prince Rupert considered Asians a federal responsibility; and Revelstoke considered the issue a matter for the UBCM. Given these reservations, nothing came of the idea, but it did not go away.[78]

Those who wanted to impose restrictions on Asians in agriculture needed firm evidence to convince Ottawa and other British Columbians of "the danger" of Orientals. The Cabinet was reluctant to spend money to find well-known facts, but in 1925 the legislature accepted a recommendation of its Agricultural Committee to learn "just how far the Orientals had penetrated into the farming industry of B.C." The resulting survey, the Legislative Assembly's *Report on Oriental Activities*, issued early in 1927, revealed that between 1921 and 1925 Orientals had purchased an additional 5,000 acres and leased a further 1,500, had greatly increased their number of greenhouses, and had come to control 30 percent of the acreage in small fruit and to dominate the sale of fresh vegetables and produce by peddlers and in stores.

The findings so impressed farmers' institutes and the Agricultural Committee that they asked that the survey continue as part of a campaign "to halt Oriental encroachment." After studying the survey, the Brotherhood of Locomotive Engineers, whose members were unlikely to encounter direct Asian competition, endorsed any action the government might take to eliminate or restrict oriental activities. So too did the Associated Boards of Trade of Vancouver Island.[79]

The few editors who commented on the survey saw, in the words of the *Revelstoke Review,* no great "cause for alarm." The *Vancouver Star* noted a "startling and perplexing" increase in the Asian population but thought it impossible to get general consent to "proposals to drive the Orientals out of the country, or to starve them out, or to make their lot so intolerable that they will go out voluntarily." In any case, it admitted, those Chinese and Japanese residents born in Canada "have rights which cannot be disregarded" even if they did not enjoy all the privileges of citizenship. *Farm and Home* magazine suggested that no survey would remove Asians who, although an economic problem, were not a menace to well-established farmers. The *Vancouver Sun* was even less alarmed. While insisting that Canada "must remain white," it believed that as long as Asians were required to "conform to our standards," they would not be "a serious menace." Some editors rightly recalled the survey's major purpose of providing information for people on the "other side of the Rockies." Oliver sent a copy to Prime Minister King as a means "to indicate why British Columbia is alarmed about the increase of its Oriental population."[80]

Within the province various laws were proposed to limit Asian competition. Among them were special taxes on their produce, a ban on their Sunday work, a requirement for an occupational licence that would have obliged applicants to take an examination devised so that Asians could not pass, and changes in the traffic law that would have required drivers to show that they could "read and understand the Motor Vehicle Act and city traffic by-laws." No one, apart from their proponents, seriously considered these ideas, but the Trade Licenses Board Act of 1928, designed to restrict competition in retailing, also empowered the board to control the leasing of land by Asians. However, no board was set up. The Retail Merchants Association (RMA) tried to organize white growers and to educate consumers to buy white-grown produce; the BCFGA and the UFBC proposed labelling produce from Asian farms. Okanagan fruit shippers asked prairie wholesalers not to handle Asian produce if white products were available, but Asians sold tomatoes there at less than half the price demanded by white growers. Some observers suggested that white growers compete by raising top quality products, such as certified potatoes.[81]

Many white growers decided that salvation lay in co-operation with Asians rather than in competition. As the *Okanagan Commoner* noted in 1921, "if, instead of condemning the Oriental, we could get together and organize and work with the same spirit of community betterment as the Orientals show in the handling of themselves, the 'problem' would disappear as the morning dew." Others had doubts.

One white berry grower said that his associates could not decide about admitting Orientals to their co-operative because it might encourage more to enter the industry whereas leaving them out would make it harder for them to market their produce and hence discourage Oriental production.[82]

White vegetable growers realized the importance of co-operating with Asians. Some were already co-operating by way of crop share agreements. Onion and other vegetable growers in Kelowna talked about forming an organization "to control the marketing of crops grown on a half-share agreement with Orientals," which made them "practically partners" in raising and marketing produce. Under such agreements white owners of a tomato field, for example, did the "horse work" of ploughing, levelling, and disking the land and in some cases of manuring it. "Then, the Japanese, who goes in with him in this enterprise, does all the rest, including planting, cultivating, pruning and irrigating. The bargain between the two varies, but generally on a 50-50 basis." In the Okanagan, white growers admitted a leading Asian grower, K. Iwashita, to their marketing organization but did not want ordinary Asian growers. Without full co-operation, prices fell. Thus, when Aaron Sapiro brought his ideas for co-operative marketing to western Canada early in 1923, 100 percent of Kelowna area tomato growers – white, Japanese, and Chinese – signed up. Iwashita was elected to represent tomato growers on the Kelowna Growers' Exchange. In justifying his election, R.C. Neish of the UFBC told the *Kelowna Courier* that Iwashita was the best man for the job because he was experienced and, as a Japanese person, could represent nearly half the tomato growers. Nevertheless, Neish continued, "we are trying to make the best of a very bad job," as he asked rhetorically whether "racial matters" could drift until Asians completely occupied the province's richest lands and there were "permanent social cleavages." In calling for the prohibition of the sale or lease of land to Asians, the UFBC damned their refusal to join co-operative marketing organizations but specifically excluded "the majority of the Japanese, who are good co-operators."[83]

In Maple Ridge most Japanese berry growers belonged to one or more of a succession of Japanese co-operative marketing organizations.[84] By 1923 white men were ploughing under berry patches because of a lack of markets. Others were selling out to the Japanese – many of whom were former fishermen – who made "their wives and children work all day and night in the fields," allegedly living happily despite a standard of living that was 50 percent lower than that expected by white men, and whose "non-assimilability makes them undesirable neighbours and more undesirable competitors." The Japanese quickly became major players. By 1925, 192 Japanese growers owned 2,378 acres of land worth $330,487 in Maple Ridge. Despite their ascendancy, or perhaps because of it, Japanese growers, who were adopting Canadian ways, worked with whites in such ventures as establishing a precooling plant in Haney. When the Berry Growers Co-operative Union was formed in 1923, white organizers called Japanese participation simply "plain justice" and boasted that increasing the "existing friendliness" between both groups of growers did much to "make impossible the repetition of the unhappy racial discord of California" and to prevent "unfair competition." The latter promise was not initially fulfilled; white growers alleged that the Japanese sold berries independently in Vancouver and Calgary. When the Co-operative Union failed in 1927, hard-hit Japanese growers replaced it with the Maple Ridge Co-operative Scheme. The British Columbia markets commissioner in Calgary reported that few Japanese growers undercut prices; with the help of the Canadian Japanese Association, he organized them for the 1927 strawberry season and received good prices. That year the province passed the Natural Products Marketing Act, which allowed growers of particular crops in a given area to accept market control under a committee of direction. In what officials in Victoria called "one of the most significant developments in the history of the Oriental problem in Canada," Japanese berry growers accepted market control, joined the BCFGA, brought in others, and, with white growers, criticized Chinese wholesalers in Vancouver who collected "bootleg" berries and bypassed the marketing scheme.[85]

In greater Vancouver, where the Chinese controlled 25 percent of the greenhouse business, growers decided to stay out of marketing control until they had seen how it worked elsewhere. White hothouse tomato and cucumber growers in greater Victoria wanted a committee of direction, especially since the Chinese, by pooling capital and labour through loose family relationships, had rapidly expanded their activities to gain control of two-thirds of the greenhouse production.[86] "Unless we avail ourselves of the Marketing Act," said a spokesman, "it will be a short time before our industry will go the way of the potato industry." Chinese growers were opposed, and the Capital City Co-operative Hothouse Tomato Growers' Association rejected market control.[87]

Whereas Japanese and white growers recognized advantages in co-operation, there was no co-operation between the Chinese and whites in the potato fields. When the idea of a potato marketing organization was discussed in the early 1920s, Minister of Agriculture Barrow, himself a potato grower, urged lower mainland and Vancouver Island growers to include Asians, who produced 55 percent of the crop. He claimed that a goal of the Natural Products Marketing Act was "to restore the industry to white men." R.G.L. Clarke, chief Dominion fruit inspector, told potato growers that "it was better to admit the Chinaman as a man whose active co-operation they could secure rather than have an enemy outside." George Challenger, manager of the Mainland Potato Committee of Direction, admitted that the committee could "not discriminate against Orientals" but suggested reading between the lines of the Marketing Act. "The Oriental in our midst," he declared, "must live and work among us by our own British standards."[88]

The potato industry gave the act its severest test. Interior potato growers were the first to form a committee of direction to overcome problems of "over-production and Oriental competition." Participation was mandatory. Despite publication of explanations of the law in Chinese and the advice of the consul to obey it, Chinese growers shipped potatoes and other vegetables to Vancouver and Calgary at low prices. F.M. Black, chairman of the Committee of Direction for the interior, called them a major problem since the Marketing Act did not differentiate "between the honest white growers and the Oriental, who has his cousins and connections in Vancouver making it impossible for the Committee of Direction to trace shipments and prices." At a meeting called by Black, Vancouver produce dealers observed that "the Oriental" had quickly become "practically the master of the situation" and without control might eliminate white men from the industry. Chinese growers knew of the committee's activities; certified copies of its confidential correspondence on potato prices were found in the office of the Chinese consul. When the *Vancouver Star* tried to make this an issue, the *Ashcroft Journal* objected to an "unwarranted" attack, implying "that the B.C. Dry Belt was behind the Chinaman as a grower of potatoes, which is no disgrace under present conditions in the dry belt."[89]

Chinese growers, who dominated the interior industry, were partly pawns in a conflict between white growers who favoured marketing control and white landowners who leased land to the Chinese. Barrow claimed that Chinese "serf labor" produced 90 percent of the potatoes grown in the Ashcroft and Kamloops districts on leased land. Shortly after the Marketing Act came into effect, the Committee of Direction charged Mah Chong of Kamloops with shipping several carloads of potatoes without a licence and selling them at less than the committee's price. His lawyers argued that the Marketing Act was *ultra vires,* but the magistrate fined him $50. At a meeting of white growers, the Chinese question, though seldom mentioned, "lurked in the background as everyone knew." The Chinese, added the *Kamloops Sentinel,* "are proverbially non-co-operative and there were men at the meeting who made money out of Chinese growers." The real problem was a surplus of potatoes caused by good crops in the United States and on the Prairies.[90]

Fraser Valley potato growers put themselves under marketing control for the 1928 season. During that summer's provincial election campaign, Alex Paterson, the Liberal incumbent in Delta, alleged that "Oriental wholesalers" were raising funds to challenge the Produce Marketing Act. Attorney General Manson added that "all the energy of the government" was behind the act. During the campaign, the government charged Chung Chuck and eight other Chinese growers with "unlawfully marketing potatoes without written permission of the Mainland Potato Committee of Direction." In this instance, the first of Chung's many trips to court on charges of "potato bootlegging," the magistrate let him and the others off lightly because theirs were the first cases under the act, but he warned that the Marketing Act would be "rigidly enforced." Chung and the others refused to pay their fines and were sent to jail. The situation caused confusion until the Appeal Court confirmed Chung's conviction and reversed the lower court's decision in the case of Wong Kit, who had shipped two carloads of potatoes to Calgary. In short, the Appeal Court said that the Natural Produce Marketing Act was valid. Chinese potato growers on the lower mainland said that they would submit to the control of the Committee of Direction; their problem was with its administration rather than with the act itself.[91]

White growers claimed to be "facing serious financial loss" because the act was not working well. They cited problems with white landowners who stayed outside the scheme and secured "enhanced prices in selling or leasing their lands to the Chinese growers." They conceded that white growers would remain subservient until they produced a better potato at a lower cost but appealed to local prejudices. In describing "the tentacles" of Oriental competition, which "was a menace to the business, social and political life of the community," George Challenger rhetorically asked a New Westminster service club: "Do we want the Fraser Valley populated with prosperous white farmers and producers, or do we desire Orientals with dirty, ill-kept shacks lining the highways?" He accused the Chinese of "ravaging" the land by draining "the soil of its richness" through "intensive farming."[92]

The marketing legislation was the real problem. Both Chinese growers and wholesalers, as well as some whites, had little difficulty breaking with marketing controls because of inadequate enforcement of the legislation and uncertainties about its validity. White wholesalers in Vancouver, feeling the "menace" of Chinese jobbers, joined growers and retailers in urging the Cabinet to force Chinese growers to obey the law, pay taxes, and keep account books in English. Attorney General R.H. Pooley privately advised the judiciary that the government did not want to assist an "organized attempt among the Orientals to defeat the intention of the Act" by delays in hearing cases. He was particularly concerned about a case in which the Mainland Potato Committee had sued Tom Yee, a Chinese wholesaler, for money he had collected for the committee from Chinese growers. When the court questioned the committee's legal existence, some white growers in the Fraser Valley, with the assistance of the minister of agriculture, asked the interior Committee of Direction, which had known some success in co-operating with Chinese growers in Kamloops, to take control. It could not repeat its earlier success. When told that Orientals were raising money to fight control, Premier Tolmie replied that "no Chinaman can run the province. If they have $100,000, we have a million." Pooley promised that the government would "stand behind the Committee and pay all reasonable costs of prosecution." Determined to enforce the law, he personally chose a magistrate to deal with the cases and suggested that the highest possible fines be imposed in order to end the controversy quickly. In February 1931, however, the Supreme Court of British Columbia ruled the Natural Produce Marketing Act *ultra vires*. In the words of a *Vancouver Province* reporter, "credit for launching the fight against the Act goes chiefly to Chinese growers who objected to being branded criminals because they sold sacks of potatoes for the best price obtainable in the local market."[93]

The marketing question had not been solved, and the Depression made it worse. The campaign to keep Asians off the land had shallow roots on farms and in orchards.

By the mid-1920s, anti-Asian resolutions were a less regular feature of the annual submissions of agricultural organizations to the legislature, but politicians and urban businessmen with their own reasons for opposing Asian competition exploited anti-Asian sentiment and the complex marketing question for their own ends.

When the Dominion secretary of the RMA visited British Columbia in 1913, he found that most merchants looked favourably on the Chinese and Japanese as industrious, law-abiding citizens who bought quality goods and paid bills promptly. Most Asian merchants catered to their own communities or sold Asian imports, such as curios and silk. Apart from scattered references to Chinese fruit and vegetable merchants violating Sunday closing laws or profiteering, few whites noticed the first Asian stores in previously all-white districts in Victoria and Vancouver and to some extent in smaller cities such as Kamloops. By the time the armistice of 1918 was signed, the change had become apparent. A tragic anecdote illustrated the process. It told of "a little woman [who] eked out a living on an Oak Bay Ave. store during the war; her son was killed overseas; a Chinese grocer moved into a store across the street. She 'carried on.' 'It's all I have,' she said, 'and the Chinaman over there is cutting prices, but if I can only keep going till the war is over I know the "boys" will see that I have fair play.' By war's end, her shop too was run by an Oriental." White grocers complained that the Chinese cut "the heart out of prices," camouflaged their stores with the "the names of Allies," worked with fellow Chinese employed in white homes, and ignored or evaded early closing bylaws. Most of Victoria's Asian merchants were Chinese whereas in Vancouver, except in green groceries, which were almost a Chinese monopoly, the Japanese were prominent.[94]

Early in 1919 merchants in the middle-class Vancouver districts of Grandview and Fairview organized to drive Oriental stores from their areas and asked real estate agents and owners to evict Asian tenants in order to create "a clean, white Grandview." Much to the chagrin of the Chinese consul, a neighbourhood newspaper asked, "do you want the yellow race to control the business on the Drive?" Merchants on three major downtown shopping streets objected to an influx of Chinese retailers and asked city council to segregate the Chinese in one section of the city. "Each store," explained Alderman Joseph Hoskins, eventually becomes "a Chinese rendezvous, which generally spreads in the neighborhood." The consul reminded council that the law "fully protected" the Chinese and that discrimination would have effects in China. Moreover, the city solicitor advised that council had no power to confine Asiatic retail stores to a specific area. Thus, a few years later, when the RMA complained of "an influx of Chinese shopkeepers in residential districts, and districts heretofore exclusively served by white storekeepers," Mayor C.E. Tisdall immediately replied that the city could not refuse licences on the basis of nationality.[95]

In Victoria, too, Chinese retailers were "scattering their stores in the outlying residential districts." Some forty to fifty Chinese stores, displaying mainly fruit and confectionery, but selling almost every line of groceries and at all hours, operated outside Chinatown in 1919. Alderman Albion Johns claimed that by living in their stores the Chinese had few expenses whereas a white shopkeeper had to maintain a home and family and pay high wages for help. He proposed forcing fruit stores to keep the same hours as grocery stores, but white fruit sellers, who claimed that only the large stores had inspired the agitation, objected. Johns subsequently reported that "the wily" Chinese partitioned their stores to sell fruit legally and groceries illegally after hours. This finding spurred members of the retail section of the Board of Trade to become "vigilantes" in order to enforce the early closing bylaw. Some Chinese merchants were fined, but the number of their stores increased. Late in 1921 the Chamber of Commerce's special committee "on Oriental Aggression" called for the strict enforcement of shop closing bylaws and an end to partitions within stores. City council, however, merely filed a proposal from the local RMA branch suggesting that it and the Chamber of Commerce vet applications for business licences from Orientals because of the "deteriorating effect on surrounding property and business."[96]

When a Chinese resident applied to the Vancouver suburb of Burnaby for a licence to open a grocery, municipal council refused to issue any more retail licences to Asians; the attorney general's office quickly advised that refusing a licence on grounds of race or nationality would be "absolutely illegal." Burnaby went ahead with measures intended at least to cause "considerable trouble" to Orientals who sought business licences. The British Columbia board of the RMA, which supported Burnaby's original plan, revived the idea of legislating to restrict Orientals to particular parts of a municipality. Attorney General Manson was sympathetic but ascertained that any amendment to the Municipal Act intended to give municipalities discretion in issuing licences would fail legally if their decision were based on "nationality or race." Manson referred them to the federal government; W.G. McQuarrie, MP (Conservative, New Westminster), told them that it was a provincial matter. Vancouver's solicitor believed that such legislation was beyond municipal powers and that legislation affecting the Japanese would be repugnant to the Anglo-Japanese Treaty. In short, no one could restrict Asians to a particular part of a city.[97]

Meanwhile, the RMA worked on changing laws in order to regulate the operation of stores but could not get Vancouver's early closing bylaw changed because 57 of its 290 retail grocers were Orientals or foreigners. There was also conflict between small and large grocers. In 1925 the Small Storekeepers Association submitted a petition signed by white and Asian grocers asking that corner stores and delicatessens be allowed to stay open indefinitely in the evening. Despite opposition from larger groceries, the city relaxed its early closing bylaw.[98]

The number of Asian merchants in Victoria and Vancouver increased significantly in the early 1920s. By 1925, of the 2,235 business licences issued in Victoria, 331 were held by Asians: ninety were peddlers, sixty-five owned confectioneries or fruit stores, and forty-five were licensed as butchers or grocers. In 1926 Vancouver's Chinese merchants held 74 of 85 green grocers' licences; of 348 licences for candy stores, the Chinese held 22 and the Japanese 62; and of 493 licences for general groceries, the Chinese held 67 and the Japanese 68. Moreover, Asians were venturing into dry goods and jewellery and into such services as barbering and cleaning-dyeing.[99]

Asian merchants succeeded in large measure because of convenient service and lower operating costs that allowed them to offer lower prices. One Victoria alderman accepted Chinese peddlers as a "great convenience" to working-class families and as competitors for downtown grocers. Mayor R.J. Porter of Victoria admitted that "the mushroom growth" of Chinese stores "was a real and serious menace" to white proprietors but explained that they operated "attractive stores" in neighbourhoods where whites ran "tawdry establishments" and that they did not circumvent early closing bylaws. Merchants knew this. In a speech on "What a Grocer Should Know About the Grocery Business," the provincial president of the RMA told its annual convention that "attacking" the matter "solely from the retail grocers' point of view" would lay its members "open to serious criticism."[100]

In appealing to racial pride, white merchants aroused some class conflict. The Victoria Board of Trade invited civic organizations to join it and the RMA in their effort to "popularize exclusive trading with white merchants." The Local Council of Women was interested; the Trades and Labour Council was merely amused. Board of Trade members wondered whether white labourers "deliberately" bought from Chinamen in order to convince retailers to take "steps to remove the Chinaman from the labor market" or because of lower prices. Patronizing Oriental stores, said the board's retail group, was "a blot on the racial conscience" of Victorians. White merchants urged Grandview residents to "trade with white merchants, employ only white men and we will soon have a WHITE CANADA." Although no appeal seemed "potent enough to keep white women shoppers from patronizing the Chinese grocery and vegetable stores," the idea of boycotts became part of anti-Asian rhetoric. The *Vancouver World* admonished that "the man who saves 60 cents a week on his grocery bill by buying from a Chinese grocer is a loser thereby, for he is helping to undermine his own job." The *Prince Rupert Daily News* thought it "vain for white people to bemoan the penetration of the Oriental" yet patronize his stores because of slightly lower prices. The women's institutes of the lower mainland proposed boycotting Oriental products, a move also favoured by Mary Ellen Smith, MLA (Liberal, Vancouver). Sid Leary, MLA (Liberal, Kaslo-Slocan), said that "blue-blooded Canadians" should stop doing "business with [the] Chinese in this province in any way." Yet white people did patronize them. A Saanich councillor thought it useless "to ask white people not to" do so.[101]

Municipal politicians occasionally tried to exploit the matter for electoral purposes, but in the 1920s it was not a defining issue. In 1922 Vancouver alderman P.C. Gibbens was re-elected with a call to "strengthen his hand in the fight to drive the Chinaman out of the retail districts of Vancouver," but mayoral candidate L.D. Taylor, who called for "full supervision and revision of [trades] licences given to Orientals," was defeated. Four years later mayoral candidate G.H. Worthington complained that permitting Oriental merchants to operate "day and night without interference" was an injustice to "ourselves"; Taylor noted that anyone could sell fruit and vegetables at night and, on this occasion, won easily. In 1928 he told electors that his opponent W.H. Malkin, a wholesale grocer, was directly bribing small-volume storekeepers by calling for "the curtailment of Oriental competition in retail and residential districts." Malkin said that his plank would be costly since Chinese merchants would no longer buy from his firm but that concentrating the Oriental shops in one locality was more important than personal gain. In a newspaper advertisement, a group calling itself the White Food Merchants of Greater Vancouver endorsed him. Voters, probably more impressed by promises to improve public works and reorganize the police force than by his Oriental policy, elected him. When RMA members complained to New Westminster City Council that Chinese merchants had opened stores in some of the best locations on Columbia Street, the main shopping thoroughfare, the mayor, a grocer, said that there was no legal way to prevent it. Chinese and Japanese competition in retailing was largely a south coast phenomenon, but other communities expected that it might spread. After visiting the coast, the editor of the *Vernon News* warned interior fruit growers that "the advance made by these people in the sale of fruit to the ultimate consumer will necessitate vigilance lest the Orientals become so firmly entrenched that they will control this particular trade."[102]

The Chinese also peddled fruit and vegetables door to door. Vancouver and Victoria tried to limit their competition by raising hawkers' licence fees. Vancouver raised the fee to a prohibitive $100 per year (the average profit was only $500 per year) whereas it charged shopkeepers only $10. The consul interceded, and city council reduced the fee to $50. Peddlers raised prices to cover the fee, but the RMA claimed that white retailers could still not compete because of heavy taxes. In 1924 council raised the fee to $75 to help them. Victoria doubled the licence fee from $20 to $40 per year in 1919, but this increase did not put peddlers off the streets. Some white entrepreneurs tried to beat Chinese peddlers at their own game. In Vancouver the White Service Co. Ltd. set up two fruit and vegetable stores and a fleet of trucks to deliver produce grown by white farmers door to door, but the business failed. In 1925 the Oriental Exclusion League in Victoria organized a "white service" of thirty-two men with sixteen trucks. City council, however, would not exempt them from the licence fee, and the Chamber of Commerce refused to help with an advertising campaign, noting that competition should have "no distinctions as to race." White Service disappeared. Women's institutes and farmers' institutes complained of the sale of Chinese goods in Victoria's public market. Surrey farmers proposed setting up a stand in the New Westminster city market featuring garden produce grown by Women's Institute members but withdrew when they learned that the Chinese, who dominated the market's vegetable sales, could not be excluded.[103]

The continuing advance of Asians in British Columbia provided sometime-journalist, sometime-lawyer T.R.E. (Tom) MacInnes with material for a series of articles in the *Vancouver Province*. Attorney General Manson asked MacInnes to suggest remedies since pushing "the Oriental from one occupation to another will not solve our problem." MacInnes drafted a bill empowering municipal councils to control retailers, wholesalers, service businesses, and tenant farmers by appointing Trade Licenses Boards that could "refuse to issue, continue, transfer or renew a license to any person whose name does not appear on the Provincial Voters' List" or who was not qualified to be on the list. Since Asians were the only large group so affected, the bill's intent was clear. Vancouver merchants liked the idea, and 143 of them, including representatives of the three major department stores and of some smaller stores, petitioned for such legislation in lieu of "more radical measures to curtail and eliminate unfair competition" in agricultural, industrial, and mercantile activities. Reportedly the Liberal caucus saw it as an alternative to Conservative demands for the total exclusion of Asians and the abrogation of treaties with Japan. On the second last day of the session, Victor W. Odlum (Liberal, Vancouver) introduced the "MacInnes Bill," which no longer referred to the voters' list. Despite claims that it would infringe on municipal authority and Manson's complaint that he had not had time to review it, the legislature passed the bill. Premier J.D. MacLean was not very enthusiastic. In the subsequent election campaign, he mentioned the "peaceful penetration" of Oriental stores and businesses on Vancouver streets, but his platform did not refer to the "Oriental question." He had little time for MacInnes, who admitted that "the further away I am from home the more I am listened to." Thus MacLean rejected Ian Mackenzie's suggestion that he hire MacInnes, "if only until the Election is over," in order to exploit the support of his "influential" "A B.C." group and that he distribute copies of MacInnes's book in order to identify the government "with the movement to abate the evil of overmuch Oriental competition."[104]

Spurned by the Liberals, MacInnes offered to secure "strong support" for the Conservatives "from practically all retail grocers ... who are being crowded to the wall because of the intrusion on our best streets of Chinese and Japanese shops." There is no evidence of a reply from the Conservative leader, Simon Fraser Tolmie. With the Trade Licenses Board on the statute books, Vancouver merchants lobbied the new Tolmie government for action on the "Oriental question." They suggested segregating the Chinese within cities and sought both strict enforcement of laws related to taxes and closing hours and the cancellation of the business licences of any Asians who broke such laws. They also approached city council. The city license commissioner, whose statistics showed an increased number of Asian businesses in the previous half dozen years, claimed that the Trade Licenses Board would not check competition. Council was sympathetic to having a board, but the city solicitor questioned its constitutionality. Vancouver also considered a Saskatoon bylaw that allowed that city to refuse a trade licence to anyone without stating the reason. However, both the *Vancouver Province* and *Vancouver Sun* agreed that any civic measure would "embarrass the federal government" and might impair immigration and trade negotiations. The *Province* considered it "highly probable that the economic consequences of the Oriental's presence in British Columbia has been absurdly overrated." It contended that maintaining "friendly relations with the Orient" would ultimately bring in thousands of times more money than was lost through Oriental competition.[105]

By 1929 British Columbia's political leaders had done much to curtail Asian competition. The impetus came largely from their own ranks and was increasingly inspired by racial prejudice. Economic arguments against Asians and their cheap labour so prominent before the First World War did not disappear, but minimum wage laws and fishing regulations provided new ways of checking Asian competition. Nevertheless, there was concern about Asians being driven from one industry to another. Employers often had the ear of the politicians, but, as was evident in lumbering and to a lesser extent in mining and fishing, government did not pander to the owners and managers of industry. Its only concessions were delays in implementing policies. Organized labour, which had once led the movement against Asians, was weak, and its socialist elements believed that they could gain more by working with Asians than against them. Such too was the case in agriculture, as many farmers realized that working with Asians, particularly the Japanese, was more profitable than fighting them. Conflicts with Chinese potato growers were as much a commentary on marketing legislation as on race. Politicians were sometimes frustrated. Manson, one of the most racist provincial politicians, complained that he had no "crystallized and stabilized public opinion" on which to rely in dealing with the problem. Indeed, most British Columbians had accepted a modus vivendi with their Asian neighbours and, to the chagrin of farmers and retailers, continued to patronize them.[106]

5

"A Problem of Our Own Peoples":
An Interlude of Apparent Toleration, 1930-38

It is becoming increasingly a problem of our own peoples, of Chinese and Japanese
born in Canada, educated in Canadian public and high schools,
and in everything but descent more Canadian than Oriental ...
What are we going to do about them?

– VANCOUVER PROVINCE, 14 MARCH 1930

The virtual end of Asian immigration in the 1920s, the maturing of the first generation of Canadian-born Japanese, the Nisei, and the emergence of Canadian-born leaders in the Chinese community gave a new perspective to the Asian problem in the 1930s. Three basic attitudes emerged. A small, vocal group, repeating atavistic arguments, continued to agitate against Asians. Though seldom challenged, they received little support. Similarly white potato growers found little sympathy for their campaign against Chinese producers who defied marketing regulations. A second group, including many newspaper editors, in some cases inspired by humanitarian and civil libertarian motives, urged greater toleration for Asians already in the province. And some white fruit and vegetable growers joined Japanese growers in co-operative marketing arrangements. Most British Columbians, however, no longer perceived Asians as an immediate "menace" and were more concerned about the Depression. Given this atmosphere, it seemed possible to consider relaxing immigration restrictions in order to encourage trade and to extend the franchise to Canadian-born Asians. In retrospect what appeared to be toleration was apathy.

The individual most concerned about apathy was C.E. Hope. Trained as an architect in his native England, he came to British Columbia in 1888 and worked variously as a land surveyor, realtor, Fraser Valley farmer, and writer of national magazine articles describing the "Oriental threat" to British Columbia. A sincere believer in the notion of "an unassimilable and unabsorbably alien race ... peacefully conquering" British Columbia, he founded the White Canada Association in November 1929 with the assistance of Alderman E.H. Bridgman of North Vancouver and the Union of British Columbia Municipalities (UBCM). Delegates at a recent UBCM convention had complained of a Chinese foothold "in practically every city and town in the Province and in all branches of business" and had suggested requiring Orientals to conform to Canadian standards of living. The convention called on senior governments to assist in solving questions related to immigration, land ownership, and competition. About thirty representatives of municipal councils, boards of trade, farmers' institutes, ratepayers associations, the British Columbia Fishermen's Protective Association, the Retail Merchants Association (RMA), the White Canada League, and the Native Sons of British Columbia attended the founding meeting of the White Canada Association at the Hotel Vancouver. Among those present were William Atkinson, provincial minister of agriculture; J.W. Berry, MLA (Conservative, Delta); W.C. Woodward, a department store magnate, a former Liberal MLA, and president of the Vancouver Board of Trade; Thomas Reid of Surrey Municipal Council; and Alderman F.J. Hume of New Westminster. Having a Japanese resident on its executive put the Vancouver Trades and Labour Council in an "anomalous position," and it declined to "support any movement which would relieve the pressure on one class of the community at the expense of other classes."[1]

According to the invitations, the conference was called because of increased Oriental landowning, "the continuing displacement of white labor in many lines by both [the] Japanese and Chinese," the "serious situation" in many schools, and the desire for legislation to "stop this silent oriental penetration and to gradually reduce the general menace." Hope's main concern was limiting the occupational opportunities of Asians. The conference favoured legislation prohibiting Orientals from acquiring further land by purchase or lease. Seeking support across the country, Hope wrote many letters but aroused little sympathy. Premier Simon Fraser Tolmie refused to accept an honorary position in the White Canada Association or to offer financial assistance lest any official connection embarrass federal and imperial authorities.[2] Unlike the Asiatic Exclusion Leagues of 1907 and 1921, the association remained "a small group which might be called a Research Committee," primarily serving to provide like-minded federal and provincial politicians with speech material. Hope blamed the association's ineffectiveness on the unwillingness of businessmen to be associated with the movement for fear of unspecified Japanese reprisals and on "the feeling of 'what's the use, Ottawa will do nothing.'" In the early 1930s only Hope, a few other self-proclaimed "patriots," such as the Native Sons of Canada, and two members of Parliament, Thomas Reid (Liberal, New Westminster) and A.W. Neill (Independent, Comox-Alberni), agitated against Asian immigration. In the 1930 federal election Liberals listed the Chinese Immigration Act as an accomplishment, but the "Oriental question" was discussed only in New Westminster, Fraser Valley, and Comox-Alberni. When Neill complained that labour could "not understand" why the Japanese still emigrated to Canada whereas European immigration was strictly regulated, only Hope and a "patriotic" group, the Maple Leaf Association of Vancouver, joined his protest. Reid's suggestion that Canada "close the gates" until British Columbians no longer feared "domination by the Asiatic" remained buried in Hansard. Hope and his allies were fighting a non-issue. There was no evidence of Japanese "threats," and Ottawa had reduced the "menace" by passing the Chinese Immigration Act and renegotiating the gentlemen's agreement with Japan.[3]

Japan strictly honoured its 1928 agreement to issue no more than 150 passports per year to emigrants. When the new minister at the Japanese legation in Ottawa, Iyemasa Tokugawa, passed through Vancouver en route to Ottawa, he told British Columbians that trade, not emigration, would solve Japan's problems. Most British Columbians accepted this reassurance. Rumours of illegal immigrants attracted little attention even though Fred Yoshi, the Department of Immigration's interpreter, was found guilty of conspiring to violate immigration laws. An RCMP investigation located only a handful of illegal immigrants.[4]

In the case of the Chinese, trade concerns – which were especially important because of the Depression – led to suggestions that the exclusionary law be relaxed. Canadian diplomats, businessmen, missionaries, the Chinese community in Canada, and the Chinese consul general recommended permitting the entry of wives and children of Canadian nationals and simplifying restrictions on merchants and students to improve Chinese attitudes toward Canada and to encourage trade. So too did delegates returning from the Kyoto Conference of the Institute of Pacific Relations. Businessmen on a Chamber of Commerce tour of the Orient reported frequent references to the insulting exclusion law as an impediment to trade. The Foreign Trade Bureau of the Vancouver Board of Trade wanted Chinese nationals to study in Canadian universities. Major provincial dailies favoured visits by Chinese merchants and students. When N.S. Lougheed, the provincial minister of lands, urged excluding all Asians, the *Victoria Times* warned that "our economic recovery" largely depended on more trade with the Orient. Similarly the *Vancouver Province* noted that trade required paying "some attention to Chinese susceptibilities." Even Hope proposed making it easier for Chinese nationals to visit Canada for trade or educational purposes but wanted to limit their occupations, "the idea being that our White Man Power should not be displaced by unassimilable aliens." Ultimately he favoured a similar treaty with Japan, but China seemed "by far the best bet" for increased trade.[5]

More significantly the idea had political support. Both H.H. Stevens, who had become minister of trade and commerce after the Conservatives won the 1930 federal election, and Ian Mackenzie (Liberal, Vancouver Centre) urged the R.B. Bennett government to relax restrictions for merchants, but the new prime minister feared angering those who were sensitive about Asian immigration. The government's only concession was to advise immigration inspectors to avoid giving "any appearance of different treatment" to Chinese merchants or students entering for legitimate purposes. This policy persisted. Soon after the Liberals returned to power in 1935, H.L. Keenleyside of the Department of External Affairs saw that the situation was still unsatisfactory but thought that relaxing the Chinese Immigration Act was politically impossible since it would revive the Conservative Party in British Columbia.[6]

Nevertheless, the fact that immigration laws could be rationally discussed boded well for a moderation in attitudes toward Asians. So too did the paucity of complaints about Asian labour despite severe unemployment. Three reasons explain this lack of concern. One was the realization that, since the Depression affected most of the world, British Columbians could not blame Asians for their economic problems and might benefit from trade with Asia. Secondly, the notion of an "Oriental menace" had declined as new immigration laws and regulations had taken effect. Even the *New Westminster British Columbian* admitted that "there is not a burning hatred of the Chinese and Japanese as such in the white breast. When these trans-Pacific voyagers are so reduced in number as to form only a small proportion of the population, when their presence does not endanger the white man's chance of earning a livelihood, they will be treated with equanimity." Thirdly, British Columbians realized that Asians driven from one industry entered another. As the *Vancouver Province* explained, "we have hunted the Orientals out of the fishing industry and they have gone to the woods. We have chased them out of the woods and they have gone to the farms. We have made it uncomfortable for them on the farms, and they have gone into business in the cities. We haven't diminished their numbers; we have simply pushed them about." When the provincial government announced that unemployed white miners from Nanaimo had replaced forty-one Chinese miners at Cumberland, the *Vancouver Star* warned that it still had to ensure "that the evicted Chinese do not create a new problem for white men elsewhere." The Duncan Chamber of Commerce suggested making it difficult for Asians to shift employment, but Attorney General Pooley immediately said that such a measure was unconstitutional.[7]

On the few occasions that organized labour discussed Asians, its opinions were divided. In the spring of 1930 a Vancouver Trades and Labour Council delegation asked the visiting Australian minister of trade and customs to deny preference to British Columbia lumber since the industry resisted unionization and employed cheap Asian labour. Yet the Trades and Labour Council had as an affiliate the Vancouver Camp and Mill Workers Union, a Japanese body. When the Trades and Labour Congress of Canada met in Vancouver in 1931, delegates from the Camp and Mill Workers asked the congress to remove Asiatic exclusion from its platform. Some delegates called for international brotherhood. Others would concede only "the right to live" to Asians already in the province. Percy Bengough, a founder of the Asiatic Exclusion League in 1921, admitted that the Japanese were good unionists but strongly opposed an "open door" policy. Ultimately the convention accepted a compromise: the "exclusion of all races which cannot properly be assimilated into the national life of Canada." This resolution and others calling for equality in applications for naturalization and the enfranchisement of all native-born Canadians might have assuaged Japanese sensitivities by removing blatant racial prejudice but did not change the congress's policy on immigration.[8]

The affiliation of the Camp and Mill Workers with the Vancouver Trades and Labour Council was not the only example of labour recognizing the advantages of co-operation with Asians. During the bitter Fraser Mills strike in 1931, both Japanese and white workers protested the "chattel slavery" imposed by a Japanese labour contractor. An observer commented that "the Asiatic Exclusion League, dead and presumably buried, must have turned in its grave the other night when an Oriental stood on the same platform with Occidentals and was received with applause as he aligned his compatriots with the Fraser Mills strikers." In 1935 the Shingle Weavers' Union in Vancouver, which had once tried to eliminate Chinese labourers from the mills, increased its membership almost ten-fold by granting an associate charter to Chinese workers, unionizing the Chinese at one mill, and discontinuing the "contract" system, whereby the Chinese worked for substandard wages under the direction of a boss.[9] During the depths of the Depression, some Chinese mill workers and unemployed Chinese residents joined unions affiliated with the Workers' Unity League, a Communist organization. While their gains in wages and improved working conditions were limited, sociologist Gillian Creese suggests that their experience in collective action during the Depression helped the Chinese to "place ethnic equality on the political agenda for the future." In the meantime, minimum wage legislation and the American National Recovery Act, which forced British Columbia mills to maintain American standards in wages and working conditions if they wanted to export goods to the United States, helped to raise Asian wages. The rarity of complaints about "cheap labour" confirmed the claim of the provincial minister of labour that the Minimum Wage Law had ended the "obnoxious practice" of lower wage rates for Asians. As Angus MacInnis explained in 1938, Oriental labour still competed, but the objections came "from small business men, farmers and fishermen who own and operate their own gear."[10]

In the fisheries, the federal government's abortive licence reduction program had reduced the number of Japanese fishermen. In the 1930 election A.W. Neill boasted of this accomplishment. Thomas Reid, who was elected that year, became the self-appointed champion of white Fraser River fishermen. In 1933 he said that issuing fishing licences to the Japanese was "practically" letting them "build up a part of Japan on the Canadian Pacific Coast." He claimed that they were becoming increasingly arrogant and dictating terms to canners and that many were naval officers "spying" on the British Columbia coast. That the only reaction to the latter charge was embarrassment at the Canadian legation in Tokyo indicates a lack of public interest.[11]

Fears of competition continued, but there was some sympathy for Japanese fishermen. In what the *Vancouver Province* called a "decidedly hopeful" state of affairs, in 1930 the British Columbia Fishermen's Protective Association endorsed giving Japanese fishermen additional licences. Fishermen joined canners in persuading federal authorities to allow Japanese fishermen north of Vancouver Island to use powerboats in salmon gill-netting. In Prince Rupert, however, a mass meeting of white fishermen and citizens under the auspices of the Northern British Columbia Salmon Fishermen's Association protested. One speaker claimed that the Japanese had "never stood by or co-operated with the white fishermen" and were but "pawns in the hands of the cannery interests"; another, hinting at the superior fishing skills of the Japanese, said that "a white man had to have a gas boat in order to compete with the Jap in a rowboat or under sail." Once federal authorities had stopped the "virtual slavery" of attaching Japanese fishing licences to particular canneries, Prince Rupert fishermen agreed that the Japanese should "fish on a basis of equality with his competitors, the white man and the native born Indian." They accepted them in the Northern British Columbia Fishermen's Association and supported the Canadian-born in their quest for the franchise. The province's Trollers' Association, however, regarded Japanese enfranchisement as anathema. On northern Vancouver Island an unwritten agreement kept white and Japanese fishermen on their own fishing grounds. Yet at Bull Harbour when sixty trollers manned by white fishermen pushed out a Japanese fish buyer and seven Japanese vessels, Neill reminded white fishermen of the legal rights of the Japanese and persuaded them to withdraw. His words suggested growing tolerance.[12]

Despite a claim by J.E. Armishaw of the almost moribund United Farmers of Canada (B.C. section) that the "government was sacrificing the province's agriculture for Oriental trade and imperial reasons," politicians paid scant attention. C.E. Hope did persuade the legislature's Select Standing Committee on Agriculture to seek inclusion of the "oriental problem" on the agenda of the 1932 Imperial Economic Conference, but Premier Tolmie merely passed the matter to Stevens. In the depths of the Depression, no one pursued it. In 1937, when Cowichan Valley farmers revived the idea of denying Asians the right to own or lease agricultural land, the local newspaper did not support them, noting that the Chinese would drift into other industries. The Vancouver Island Farmers' Institutes and the B.C. Trollers' Association endorsed their petition, but Premier Pattullo would not see their delegation.[13]

Whereas Chinese competition was an old issue in Cowichan, it was a new phenomenon in the Creston Valley. Saying that white men could not compete with Chinese truck gardeners and farmers, the Creston branch of the BCFGA sought legislation to keep them out. In support, the Kootenay Central Farmers' Institutes demanded that the district remain "a white man's country." Vancouver Island and Fraser Valley farmers' institutes and MLAs R.W. Bruhn (now an Independent, Salmon Arm) and G.M. Murray (Liberal, Lillooet) agreed, but neither the legislature nor Parliament acted. H.H. Stevens, who had been the MP for West Kootenay since 1930, was now a member of the opposition. He agreed that the matter was serious but recognized that it was a provincial one. He suggested that farmers refuse to lease land to the Chinese.[14]

To most white farmers, Asians were a problem only in respect to marketing schemes, in which they were often scapegoats. Of more immediate concern were low prices and a 1931 ruling that the Natural Products Marketing Act was unconstitutional. Both white and Asian growers hoped that a federal Natural Products Marketing Act passed in 1934 would improve matters. In the case of the marketing board for hothouse tomatoes and cucumbers, the government specified that it include an Asian member. In parts of North Okanagan, where Asians were relatively numerous, they co-operated in trying to make the Marketing Act work, probably since they had the most to gain. In Vernon, white, Chinese, Japanese, and "even Ukrainian" vegetable growers formed a local board under the new act. So successful was the board in securing good prices that the *Vernon News* described its "Oriental brains" as "the sensation of the marketing season thus far."[15]

As plans to establish a more permanent Interior Vegetable Marketing Board proceeded, Chinese and Japanese growers raised many questions. So vigorous a debater was S.G. Ogasawara, a young interpreter, that T. Wilkinson accused him of being a "mouth-piece" of certain shippers. At the Vernon-Oyama meeting, a British grower asked whether Orientals should vote for the board since "the law in general is made by white men." Wilkinson, the driving force in the movement, replied that "all the growers, regardless of race, want better conditions and the elimination of internal competition." The Chinese and Japanese dominated the meeting, electing Charlie Kwong of the Chinese Vegetable Growers' Association and Ogasawara as their representatives for the Interior Vegetable Marketing Board convention in the spring of 1935. Several other districts also elected Chinese representatives, but co-operation was short-lived. Later that summer the Chinese Growers' Association, which represented all but two or three Chinese growers, advertised that by requiring them to ship through a single agency, the board had forced them to reduce prices. Chinese growers in Kamloops were unhappy about arrangements for tomatoes. Meanwhile, in Ashcroft, the touring journalist Bruce Hutchison suggested that if the "handful of old Chinese" residents working long hours at low wages on their tomato farms "were to die tomorrow, the industry would collapse."[16]

In the Fraser Valley, where the Japanese operated about 63 percent of the berry farms and produced about 85 percent of the crop, co-operation often succeeded because the Japanese were so important. There were conflicts, but, as in other aspects of agriculture, racial issues were red herrings in disagreements over marketing schemes. After the demise of the provincial Natural Products Marketing Act, Japanese and white shippers discussed ways of stabilizing markets, jointly founded the Pacific Co-operative Union in the Mission district in 1932, and joined the British Columbia Coast Growers Co-operative Association, which was formed in 1933 to represent about two thousand fruit and vegetable growers on the lower mainland and to promote better production and marketing. Y. Yamaga of Haney was elected to its executive and other Japanese members served as directors or on committees. At its 1935 annual convention about 65 percent of the 150 or so producers present were Japanese. White and Japanese growers of small fruits and rhubarb agreed "to avoid any racial controversy insofar as possible" and formed a marketing board under the new federal Marketing Act. The board included a Japanese member but, allegedly at the request of the Department of External Affairs, specified that it be "a Canadian national of Japanese origin." One constituent of the Federated Coast Growers at Mission and Hatzic complained that the larger body had accepted a new marketing scheme at a meeting "packed with Japanese growers, brought in by white agents." Two years later, executives of the Federated Coast Growers argued that market control would give control of the industry to Orientals and brokers, "with consequent high prices to the consumer and loss to the grower." Many Japanese growers objected to the new scheme, and, at a meeting attended by many Japanese members, the Federated Coast Growers unanimously opposed including berries and rhubarb in the arrangement. The Coast Growers Co-operative Association elected two Japanese directors. In early 1938, however, when anti-Japanese propaganda was at a peak, many white farmers withdrew or retrenched apparently because of Japanese success and price cutting. The strength of the Japanese was evident; the Pacific Co-operative Union in nearby Mission elected several Japanese directors and a Japanese vice president, T. Nakashima, by acclamation.[17]

The new marketing laws often succeeded because many Japanese growers were keen co-operators, but in the potato industry, in which the Chinese were prominent and overproduction was common, conflict remained. The Marketing Board believed that Chinese growers, who produced less than 20 percent of the crop and only 7 tons to the acre, could not compete under market control with white growers, who produced 8.75 tons to the acre. White growers in the Fraser Valley and on Vancouver Island complained that the Chinese farmer "lives like a rat and works like the devil" and undercut prices. Yet white growers and produce dealers told the legislature's Agricultural Committee that "a lot of darned good Chinamen ... want to live up to the laws of the country." Nevertheless, competition between Chinese and white potato growers led to the courts and to physical confrontations that fortunately were more comic opera than war. The issue had racial overtones but was really an economic dispute going back to the early days of market control. Chung Chuck of Ladner and other Chinese potato growers had first been prosecuted for "bootlegging" potatoes – that is, for bypassing the Marketing Board and shipping directly to Chinese wholesalers in Vancouver – in 1928. Before his long career ended, Chuck boasted of having been in court over eight hundred times and had "a reputation of being wholly in contempt of the very law of the land – and those who made it."[18]

Chung won some court battles because of uncertainties about the validity of marketing laws. Shortly before the new Natural Products Marketing Act came into force, almost all white and Asian growers in the Ladner area agreed to set prices for early potatoes. When a provisional board was set up, white and Japanese growers signed on, but few Chinese growers were interested. The problem began with the early harvest of 1935 when some Chinese growers repeatedly tried to smuggle potatoes into Vancouver. Once, as police seized potatoes, the well-organized Chinese created a disturbance during which a police officer was allegedly bitten on the hand; Chinese truck drivers broke through and "escaped" into Vancouver. The board saw many villains: landowners who rented land to Chinese growers, some lawyers, and a few disgruntled whites who spread propaganda maligning the board's intentions. Its greatest enmity was directed at "Tyee Chinese" wholesalers who led Chinese growers "by the nose" to defy the law and demoralize the market and at growers such as Chung who took "advantage of dark nights and foggy mornings" to smuggle potatoes from Lulu Island to Chinatown in Vancouver, "where they seem to have an underground method of distribution." Some Chinese growers sought an injunction to restrain the Marketing Board from interfering. The courts refused, saying that the Chinese would not "suffer irreparable harm." A few weeks later a mysterious organization calling itself the Federated Vegetable Producers of British Columbia circulated "violently pro-Chinese" pamphlets and dodgers accusing the board of unwarranted attacks on the Chinese and of not letting them serve on the board.[19]

Dr. K.C. Macdonald, the provincial minister of agriculture, fully supported the board and refused to tolerate "a planned attempt by Orientals to override and defy the laws of this country" by running the blockades. At bridges leading into Vancouver, the provincial police stopped "all trucks driven by Chinese ... irrespective of nature of load" and allowed a board inspector to seize bootleg potatoes. Macdonald accused the Chinese of working "the daylights" out of leased land, breaking market prices and, after exhausting the soil, moving to new land to repeat the process. He said that lessees should not be voting members of marketing boards. Like the board, he was highly critical of the few Chinese who controlled the vegetable business. He complained that Ottawa did not comprehend the problem but did not explain how it might be solved.[20]

The federal Liberal government elected in October 1935 was unsympathetic to the federal marketing law and referred its constitutionality to the courts. The Supreme Court ruled it *ultra vires*, a decision confirmed by the Privy Council. Anticipating such an outcome, the province had given its marketing boards the same powers as Dominion boards, but the legal position of the British Columbia Coast Vegetable Marketing Board was unclear, particularly relating to exports. Early in 1937 the Low Chong Company, a produce merchant, challenged the Vegetable Board and announced that it would bring fifteen sacks of potatoes to its Vancouver warehouse. At the Lulu Island bridge, the board seized the sacks because they did not bear its tags.[21]

Certain Chinese growers were determined to ignore the board, which was just as determined to enforce its regulations. Encouraging the white growers was Clive

Planta, MLA (Independent, Peace River). In the *Vancouver Province* he attacked Chinese methods, citing "the serfdom of some Chinese farmers," and protested the "tie-ups" between Chinese farmers, wholesalers, and retailers that allowed the Chinese to dominate the wholesaling and retailing of vegetables. He told the legislature that the Chinese had reduced the courts "to the status of kangaroo courts" and had "made puppets of our judiciary." "If controlled marketing legislation were upheld," he asserted, "the present combine of Chinese family groups would not obtain." D.W. Strachan, MLA (Liberal, Dewdney), who had earlier warned of an "Oriental invasion ... sweeping up the Fraser Valley," said that a "sort of chain gang of grower-distributor-wholesaler Orientals" was gradually ousting white men. Commenting on Strachan's speech, the *Province* complained that "Mr. Chinese Merchant is going a step too far when he insists upon producing by cheap Oriental methods and manpower, and then asserts unlimited rights as a free-born Canadian to control selling in the most profitable city markets." Few legislators were as concerned. By an overwhelming vote of thirty-four to six, they upheld the speaker's decision that Planta's motion for a Royal Commission to inquire into social and economic conditions among the Oriental population was out of order. Planta persisted. Despite an assertion by A.W. Greenwood, president of the grocers' section of the RMA, that Chinese growers often provided white merchants with left-over goods from Chinese peddlers and shops, Planta could not persuade the Select Standing Committee on Agriculture to inquire into Chinese methods of marketing and distribution when it investigated the Coast Vegetable Marketing Board.[22]

Planta was not discouraged. He took his message to the Vancouver Island Farmers' Institutes convention, the Kiwanis Club, and the Local Council of Women in Vancouver. Most importantly, during February and March 1937, vegetable growers in Cloverdale, East Delta, Richmond, Ladner, and Langley held mass meetings often attended by several hundred people "to bring public opinion to bear on the 'open defiance' of the Marketing Act by certain interests." Among the speakers were officials of the Coast Vegetable Marketing Board and other politicians, including Strachan and Barrow, but Planta was the principal speaker. He explained that the "violent opposition" of Chinese wholesalers to orderly marketing was a reaction to the board's interference with the arrangement whereby "the poor Chinese, 'John Chinaman,' is a peon and is bossed by [Chinese] 'headquarters' in Vancouver." The meetings endorsed the idea of a Royal Commission and called for enforcement of the Natural Products Marketing Act.[23]

Without board approval some farmers took matters into their own hands. Violence ensued. On 1 March 1937 white growers, "completely fed up with the overbearing attitude" of the Chinese, gathered at the bridges leading into Vancouver. At the Fraser Street bridge, forty to fifty white growers, armed with sawed-off axe handles and other weapons, stopped Chinese truck drivers, among them Chung Chuck, who claimed that his load was for export and therefore not under the board's jurisdiction. Before Chung managed to escape, his clothes were torn and

The Fraser Avenue Bridge Club

"The bid, gentlemen, is Four Clubs!"

"The Fraser Avenue Bridge Club," *Vancouver Sun*, 2 March 1937

his body cut and bruised, and he had inflicted a minor knife wound on the head of E.A. McKay, a Vegetable Board inspector. Chung charged McKay and six farmers with assault; the police charged Chung with wounding McKay. A wise judge, recognizing "a tempest in a teapot" and believing that Chinese residents were "entitled to British justice," recommended a stay of proceedings.[24]

While the Chinese consul condemned vigilantes for taking the law into their own hands and consumer organizations affiliated with the Co-operative Commonwealth Federation (CCF) Party described the Marketing Board as "a potato family compact," there was sympathy for white growers. The *Vancouver Province* denied that it was "a racial issue" but sympathized with the board's efforts to keep the market for Canadians against an "increasing tide of ruthless Chinese competition." It noted that "big Chinese corporations" owned large well-equipped farms

141

"manned by the cheapest Oriental labor, working from dawn to dusk," and sent produce "to market in trucks owned by Orientals, driven by Oriental chauffeurs, delivered to Oriental warehouses, sold finally through Oriental retail stores – where the salesgirl is very apt to be a brilliant young Chinese graduate of the University of B.C." The *Vancouver Sun*, calling it an "unpleasant little race war," asked whether consumers wanted "low fruit and vegetable prices at the cost of squeezing white growers out of business?"[25]

Minister of Agriculture Macdonald warned white potato growers to accept the board's control or face Oriental domination of agriculture but denied any "desire to discriminate against Orientals." However, he told the Chinese Farmers' Association, which had questioned charges against those who sold or transported potatoes without board tags, that the law would be enforced unless found *ultra vires*. On a province-wide radio broadcast, he alleged that most critics were Chinese growers who had once dominated the profitable domestic market. To the board's regret, Attorney General Gordon Sloan relaxed enforcement of the relevant laws.[26]

By then the courts were deciding the case of the Low Chong Company, for which Chung Chuck was a truck driver. It had sued for the value of ninety sacks of potatoes seized by the board. In passing judgment, Mr. Justice A.M. Manson, who, in 1927 as attorney general had called for the repatriation of all Asians, was able to put justice above his political views. He agreed with Chung that the board was "Just Robbing." He said that the marketing law was *ultra vires* and granted the Low Chong Company an injunction against the board. The "deeply distressed" provincial government feared that no board would be able to enforce its orders. Expecting that the "Manson injunctions" would make it "difficult to get the Oriental educated along the lines of control," the board tried but failed to secure police assistance in enforcing its regulations. An Appeal Court ruling that the marketing legislation was valid and changes in procedures allowed the board to proceed with its work. It continued to fix prices but relaxed other regulations. Chinese wholesalers received fresher produce because they were required only to report transactions and to purchase board tags. A board official claimed that the Chinese were "working 100 percent in harmony with it" and that the inspector's job had become a sinecure. Some white growers, however, were alarmed that the new practices favoured those Chinese wholesalers who were also growers and who could thus easily "shave" prices. The board explained that the Chinese dominated shipments early in the season because they concentrated on early varieties. After several Chinese growers tried to take untagged potatoes into Vancouver and sales declined in October, the board suspected local Chinese growers of bootlegging but found that the cause was an influx of cut-rate potatoes from interior Chinese growers. Of four "die-hard" bootleggers that season, two were white men. The board also cancelled plans to prosecute Tom Yee, a Vancouver wholesaler in whose warehouse its inspectors had found several hundred sacks of untagged potatoes, when it learned that he had received its permission to obtain them.[27]

While white growers on the lower mainland seemed to accept the situation, their counterparts on Vancouver Island did not. Island growers suggested using coloured tags to label potatoes as "white grown" or "oriental grown," but the Marketing Board rejected such a measure as discriminatory. They asked the provincial government to co-operate with Ottawa in order "to find means to combat the menace." Through the Farmers' Institute, they passed a resolution pointing to the "intolerable" and "unfair and unrestricted competition of Orientals" in many branches of agriculture and to widespread "apprehension" of the "alarmingly high proportion" of Orientals in the population. The resolution received no outside support. Premier Pattullo would not grant them an interview but suggested that they might ask an MLA to raise the matter in the legislature. His newspaper mouthpiece, the *Prince Rupert Daily News*, noted that "the men against which complaint is made are citizens of the country and as such have all the rights and privileges of citizens except the right to vote." It added that past legal precedents had shown that the government could enforce laws only "in regard to hours of work, minimum wages, sanitary and housing conditions." In sum, the government recognized that it must tolerate Chinese competition and accept the rule of law. When the Privy Council upheld British Columbia's marketing law, Pattullo expected a more settled period in marketing.[28]

For a time, that seemed to be the case. While white wholesalers still complained of the Chinese ignoring city bylaws and practising unsanitary habits, white farmers took advantage of more stable markets. Instead of renting land to the Chinese, they slowly made "headway" by using better farming methods to get double or triple the crop produced by the Chinese on the same amount of land. Higher yields increased the white growers' share of production and relegated Chinese growers "to an outside position," which meant that many existed "only by bootlegging." The manager of the Coast Vegetable Marketing Board accused some Chinese growers of taking advantage of the war, which had depleted the ranks of white growers, to agitate against controlled marketing. In 1940 Mah Bing Mo, the "Potato Baron," donated 150 tons of surplus potatoes and other vegetables to the armed forces. Instead of praising his patriotism, the board complained of losing the military market.[29]

Minister of Agriculture Macdonald believed that the real solution was to raise the living standards of Asians. He warned that "unless checked by adequate laws, Oriental farmers would flood the produce market with low-price potatoes, bring ruin to the white farmers and create in B.C. a peasantry of which we would not be proud." That fall, as part of a general concern about marketing boards, the government appointed Judge Andrew M. Harper to inquire into the Natural Products Marketing Act. The board denied that a major goal of "orderly marketing" was to reduce Chinese competition, but Chinese growers complained that they had to let surplus potatoes rot, feed them to pigs, or donate them to churches and hospitals. Chung Chuck had been forced to pawn his diamond ring, and, whereas he had owned 100 acres before the board was established, he now had only 11 acres. Harper was not sympathetic. Among his recommendations was to deny voting rights on the board to leaseholders who were not provincial voters in order "to keep control of this industry in Canadian hands and up to Canadian standards." His caution seemed misplaced. The *Vancouver Sun* noted that the Marketing Board had allowed white producers on mixed farms to "get a share of business which some years ago was overwhelmingly in the hands of [the] Chinese."[30]

While the Marketing Board was primarily concerned with large-scale Chinese wholesalers, in the early 1930s about 200 Chinese and Japanese vegetable wholesalers set up shop on sidewalks along Vancouver's Pender and Main Streets, escaped civic control and licence fees, and competed with dealers who rented stalls in the city market or had their own premises. Once the city's market clerk explained the problem, Chinese gardeners co-operated in setting up a new civic market. It was "a cosmopolitan scene" in which Chinese, Japanese, and white growers engaged in friendly rivalry, but the Chinese outnumbered all other nationalities. The friendliness did not last. The market clerk complained that the "un-controlled and disorderly marketing methods" of Chinese wholesalers would lead to their dominating the wholesale produce trade. After the city regulated marketing hours, the Chinese obeyed the law. Then, suddenly in 1938, they began ignoring bylaws.[31] By then the problem had been overshadowed by Alderman Halford Wilson's campaign against Asian competition in the retail trade.

In the early 1930s white merchants complained only sporadically of Asian competition. When some Vancouver grocers discussed general problems with several MLAs and the president of the Local Council of Women, one MLA suggested that they pay attention to Asian competition. The only complaint from a representative of the British Columbia board of the RMA to the Mass Buying Committee of the House of Commons about Asian merchants was their use of cut flowers as loss leaders! Most problems were very local. In Vancouver's Grandview district, white merchants claimed that Asians accounted for 60 of the 177 businesses in their area. They accused Asians, who could sell vegetables until midnight, of selling other groceries after prescribed closing hours. Several aldermen, including H.J. DeGraves, attended a meeting to launch a citywide campaign "to induce citizens to purchase from white merchants." City council was prepared to investigate until it learned that it had no power to discriminate racially in issuing business licences. The consumer education campaign also came to naught; there is no evidence of a proposed mass meeting. Market Commissioner W.J. McGuigan, however, repeatedly noted that the Chinese succeeded because, unlike white dealers, they visited the market early in the morning and were given the first choice of produce "from the farm or orchard." In other provincial centres the issue was limited to an occasional suggestion, as in Victoria and New Westminster, to confine Asian merchants to specific districts. Retail merchants in Smithers proposed prohibiting Asians and Native Indians from starting new businesses on or near Main Street. The provincial board of the RMA persuaded police commissioners and the attorney general to promise better enforcement of the Lord's Day Act, but no action seems to have resulted. In other smaller communities, Chinese merchants were regarded as fellow residents rather than as "unfair competitors." Prince Rupert City Council let Chinese merchants who extended credit to the unemployed receive a share of relief grocery orders; the Kamloops Board of Trade named Peter Wing chairman of its Retail Trade Committee; and in Trail, Harry Pang, a greengrocer, was a member of the Skating Club.[32]

In Vancouver another attempt to arouse public sentiment against Asian merchants occurred early in 1935 when the White B.C. League began publishing a newspaper, the *Weekly Examiner*. The league's promoters, like publishers of earlier journals of this ilk, remained anonymous. Anti-Asian arguments were the sum total of its editorial content. It complained of the Chinese taking jobs as seamen on Canadian ships,[33] the Oriental "peaceful penetration" of Western civilization, the dangers of interracial marriage, and the high Japanese birth rate in British Columbia. The newspaper referred to the danger of disease from groceries or laundries where "any number of people" were housed and of the failure of Orientals to obey closing hour laws. It asserted: "Awake, British Columbians, and give these White Merchants your support before they, along with their white employees, have become forced out of business, as they are eventually sure to be by the cheap labor and subtle subterfuges that only the Oriental mind can conjure." On an accompanying coupon, readers could pledge "to patronize WHITE MERCHANTS" and "those who employ an entire personnel of White Employees." The league solicited advertising from white merchants and publicized its ideas through thrice-daily broadcasts on a Vancouver radio station. Since the only relic of the White B.C. League is a single copy of the *Weekly Examiner*, it is likely that few Vancouver merchants contributed to its cause.[34]

Even concerns about Chinese threats to morality through gambling had faded. "Clean-ups" of Chinatown were almost cause for mirth. Bruce Hutchison suggested that if the Chinese disguised "themselves as prosperous businessmen drinking Scotch whiskey in a well-furnished club, over a poker game, no one would stop their amusement. Or if they would pretend to be society women spending the entire afternoon and a week's wages on their bridge game while they sipped on cocktails, the police would not think of interfering. But these unhappy heathens will insist on playing fantan ... which has the fatal weakness of being a Chinese sport ... but their fatal mistake, of course, is being Chinese themselves." The press occasionally reported alleged violations of the law restricting the employment of white women, but the limited response to the murder of Mary Shaw, allegedly by Dick Lee, a Chinese houseboy who had met her in the Chinatown restaurant where she was a waitress, suggests that the law was largely forgotten. The coroner's jury recommended that the city pass a bylaw prohibiting Orientals from employing white women. Vancouver's police chief told four Chinese café proprietors to discharge their female white employees, but there was no evident follow-up. Like other aspects of the "Oriental question," the issue of employing white women was largely dormant in the early 1930s.[35]

Complaints about Asian competition remained sporadic and isolated. Despite the Depression, Asians were no longer perceived as serious threats to a "white man's province" since Asian immigration had been reduced to a trickle. Secondly, it seemed futile to impose further restrictions on their economic activities. Thirdly, a rising proportion of Asians were Canadian-born and educated. This trend was partly the result of elderly Chinese dying or returning to China but was largely the consequence of a high birth rate among the Japanese who formed families in British Columbia. Past immigration patterns meant that a high proportion of Japanese women were in their childbearing years. In 1933, for example, the Japanese birth rate in British Columbia was 36.4 per thousand in contrast to a rate of 14 per thousand among those of English ancestry.[36]

The public schools provided evidence of the increasing number of Canadian-born Asians. By 1930 the third generation of one Chinese family was attending a Vancouver school. The size of the school-age Chinese population was relatively static, but the number of Japanese students increased from 3,674 to 5,176 between 1929 and 1934. Because Japanese students were concentrated in a few schools, they were conspicuous. In Richmond the Japanese community reduced the resentment of white taxpayers by making cash grants to the school board to compensate for the cost of educating children whose parents paid little in property taxes. In Maple Ridge, when a member of the school board opposed hiring any teacher who was "ineligible for British citizenship," other board members reminded him that the board accepted municipal taxes and high school fees "from such ineligible parents as [the] Japanese." In contrast the Duncan Chamber of Commerce wanted "to relieve the taxpayers of the necessity of educating aliens who never could, under present Provincial voters' regulations, be eligible for registration on Provincial voters' lists." This sentiment was not universal. At a 1934 meeting of Fraser Valley school trustees, several speakers hailed the readiness of the Japanese to adopt Canadian customs and expected that "the native-born would be absorbed into the Canadian race in the second or third generation."[37]

Some educational authorities thought that assimilating Asian children was possible and desirable. J.E. Brown, principal of Strathcona School in Vancouver, where 39 percent of the students were Japanese, observed that the younger generation readily broke away from old customs and predicted that, if given the same treatment as other children, they would soon become Canadian in spirit. In describing Strathcona as a "melting pot," his successor, O.J. Thomas, explained that "we try, first, to make good Canadian citizens of them all, whether Japanese, Russian, Italian or Greek." So successful was the school in obscuring national identities that in a fight among Grade 2 students inspired by the Sino-Japanese war, both "armies" had Chinese, Japanese, white, and black members! Brigadier J. Sutherland Brown, who inspected Strathcona School's cadets, reported that the "Orientals, particularly the Japanese, were much smarter than others of the company, particularly in Physical Training." Members of several Fraser Valley school boards predicted that in a generation or two the Japanese "would be absorbed into the Canadian race." Children did seem to have a facility for working together. In the children's ward of a Victoria hospital, Bruce Hutchison observed white children playing with a Japanese girl "without the least prejudice of race or color" and noted that they "seemed to accept her as the leader of their little group."[38]

Adults became more tolerant. After telling Parliament that "more trouble is caused by the stork than by the immigrant ship," A.W. Neill quickly added that since we have the Japanese "we must put up with them." Similarly, in noting that the Japanese minister to Canada had said that emigration would not solve Japan's problems, the *Vancouver Province* observed that "they are ours and are going to stay with us." When the advisory board of the farmers' institutes called for removing all Asians from the country and expropriating their property, several editors condemned repatriation of the Canadian-born as "impracticable," "foolish," tantamount to exile, and probably illegal.[39] Such comments implied a willingness to see the "Oriental question" as a problem of Canadians.

Nevertheless, old ideas did not disappear. During the Christmas holidays teenaged boys, mainly sponsored by the United Church, annually met in the Legislative Chambers as the Older Boys Parliament. In 1929 predominantly white congregations elected a Nisei from Vancouver and a Chinese youth from Victoria. The presence of Asians in the legislature, even in the Older Boys Parliament, scandalized some. The *Prince Rupert Weekly Empire* said that it should cause everyone in British Columbia to ponder the future. Hilda Glynn-Ward, author of the racist novel *The Writing on the Wall,* declared that "Orientals should not be taught to believe that they will ever be allowed a voice in the government of our country. You can't make a yellow man white by saying so on paper." C.F. Davie, MLA (Conservative, Cowichan-Newcastle), and publisher of a new Vancouver Island weekly newspaper, the *Spokesman,* asked whether the sequel would be "an Oriental premier and cabinet before the century's close maintained by an Oriental majority in the house and country?" Davie argued that members of the Older Boys Parliament should use the chamber only if they were white.[40]

A decade earlier, Davie might have received unanimous approval; now he did not. The *Vancouver Star* warned that unless British Columbians wanted to become like the southern states, that unless Canadian-born Asians were to be denied all but menial employment and "regarded as 'untouchable,' they must be allowed to take part in the communal life as their abilities and education justify." Deprecating Davie's comments, the *Vancouver Province* admonished that "we have put these young people into our melting pot. We have unfitted them for life in the Orient. We have done what we could to make them Canadians. Yet we refuse to accept them as Canadians. What are we going to do about them?" The *Kamloops Sentinel,* which welcomed their competition in the schools, observed that Asian school boys had an edge in manners and urged: "Let us be fair and get rid of our racial prejudices."[41]

In what would become a theme for the Nisei, Minoru Ito, who led the Vancouver polls in the 1929 election of members to the Older Boys Parliament, told the other members that "we have been brought up and educated here along with you as brothers, and we have to live and die in Canada. We are yellow in color but we are Canadians at heart. We were not born in Japan and consequently have no rights as Japanese citizens, but we do not wish to return to Japan. Here we remain, stranded between Canada and Japan, and we aim with our hearts to become true Canadians." In Prince Rupert, Setsuo Kuwahara became secretary of an Interdenominational Young People's Society that had both Japanese and Caucasian members of the United and Anglican churches.[42]

Yet the modest efforts of some Christian churches to promote good relations between their white and Asian communicants through joint services, social hours, and shared fundraising activities could not eliminate prejudice. In 1938, for example, the Anglican synod approved a report urging "fair and just treatment of all Orientals resident in British Columbia." One delegate, however, although agreeing that "Orientals were equal to white people and must be treated in a Christian manner," warned that "definite racial and cultural differences" must be considered. Rev. Hugh Dobson of the United Church told a Student Christian Movement conference, in the presence of Rev. K. Shimizu, that "he would be offended by the entrance of an Oriental into his family."[43]

This was not the only occasion in which the old question of miscegenation arose. Several times, P.A. Boving, a professor of agriculture, cited vegetable experiments to claim that intermarriage would produce inferior human beings. A few years earlier such a statement would have evoked favourable responses, but now the *Vancouver Sun* suggested that Boving's claim meant that there could be no Canadian race, only "a meaningless agglomeration of little colonies." The *Vancouver Star* accused him of generalizing from a few facts. Charles Hill-Tout, an anthropologist, repeatedly advocated interracial marriages to settle race problems and in turn probably produce a superior race, and H.T. Coleman, a former dean of arts at the University of British Columbia, described "the concept of a superior race" as "fallacious" since there was "no such thing as a pure race. We are all mongrels."[44]

Not all British Columbians even wanted Asian neighbours. When a Japanese resident proposed to buy a lot in Duncan, city council persuaded the Union of British Columbia Municipalities to seek action that would make it illegal "for any oriental to acquire title to land in Canada." Delta refused to sell municipal property to the Japanese, but Tofino residents could only complain when a Japanese family bought a house in the middle of the village. The most controversial case arose in Vancouver in 1941 when a young Chinese couple, Tong Louie and his wife, both University of British Columbia graduates, bought a home in an expensive Point Grey subdivision. A delegation, mainly of women and representing eighty-three petitioners, alleged the sale had reduced property values by 20 percent. They asked city council's zoning committee to enact safeguards against such "intrusions" and to lower assessments and taxes. Council could not act retroactively but unanimously proposed to prepare a "Can't reside here" bylaw. This produced a rare instance of Chinese and Japanese co-operation. Consuls and representatives of both communities protested. More significantly, so too did the University Women's Club, the Young People's Union of the United Church, and the Vancouver branch of the Canadian Civil Liberties Union. The *B.C. Federationist* noted, "the Oriental does not become a nuisance and unwanted until he is sufficiently successful in our competitive system to build himself a decent home." In any case, said Alderman George Buscombe, "I don't see that the better class Oriental is any great detriment to any district," and Mayor J.W. Cornett, who earlier favoured segregating Orientals, asserted, "if we cannot live with them here, I don't see how we can expect to get along with them in Heaven." In the end, city council lacked authority to regulate land ownership. The story had a happy ending. The next-door neighbour warmly welcomed the Louies and the protests gradually subsided. Tong Louie, who became a leading industrialist and a widely respected philanthropist, remained in the home until his death in 1998.[45]

A much more common example of discrimination concerned employment. Despite local pride when Asian students did well in examinations, success did not lead to jobs. A Japanese man received a standing ovation at a University of British Columbia convocation for heading the graduating class but said that his opportunities as a physicist in North America were limited. Similarly a Canadian-born Chinese resident, who was a fifth-year mining engineering student, complained that he could not find summer work with the Geological Survey of Canada or with mining companies although more junior students had been hired. He wondered "what is the social or legal discrimination against me and others of my kind?"[46] Some smaller hospitals such as that in Prince Rupert would not accept Japanese student nurses lest patients object. The Vancouver General Hospital and its Alumnae Association, however, despite severe unemployment among graduate nurses, reluctantly agreed that reducing the tuberculosis rate among Asians required the training of Chinese and Japanese nurses "to care for their own race who are ill and in need of attention."[47]

Despite some acceptance of Canadian-born Asians, there was still opposition to admitting Asians to the rights and responsibilities of citizenship. Although a proposed 1931 amendment to the Canadian Nationals Act did not affect the existing law, which stipulated that anyone, regardless of racial origin, who was born in Canada was a British subject and if domiciled in Canada a Canadian national, Thomas Reid argued that Asians could not "assimilate with our Anglo-Saxon stock." He stressed the need "to conserve our heritage for our own people." Some of his words were identical to those used by N.S. Lougheed two months earlier in calling for complete Asian exclusion. Outside Parliament, C.E. Hope, who may have provided the texts for both speeches, was almost alone in opposing "giving citizenship rights to anyone who happens to be born in Canada." A few weeks later the federal government decided that it would naturalize those Japanese residents born outside of Canada only if Japan allowed them to surrender their Japanese nationality. A 1934 Canadian-Japanese agreement made dual citizenship impossible, but few Canadians realized this. In the meantime the government countenanced the refusal of many courts to grant certificates of naturalization to Chinese and Japanese applicants. Thus, despite protests by such groups as the Trades and Labour Congress of Canada, Asian immigrants were denied access to social benefits such as the Old Age Pension.[48]

In the past Asians had rarely sought relief. In 1928 the Chinese Benevolent Association in Vancouver advertised that "no Chinese has had to apply to the city for relief." In fact in 1926 a destitute Chinese widow with seven Canadian-born children applied because her family or clan organization wanted her to return to China with the children. The city relief officer said that the city did not have to help, "as the Chinese were always ready to care for their own people." The committee, sympathetic to the plight of the Canadian children, instructed him not to let them suffer but implied that it would not accept any long-term obligations.[49]

In the early 1930s the Chinese shared a problem with all single unemployed males: they were victims of a relief vacuum between private charity and a disagreement among the three levels of government over responsibility for unemployment relief. They sometimes encountered additional discrimination. In 1931, reports circulated that Asians were automatically being denied civic relief in Vancouver and the opportunity to register at the Dominion Employment Bureau. On 10 August the provincial Cabinet's Committee on Unemployment Relief announced that Asians were "NOT to be registered under the Provincial scheme." The only reaction was hostile. The Vancouver and New Westminster District Trades and Labour Council had already protested when Japanese residents were not allowed to register for city relief. The *Vancouver Star* questioned the justice of denying relief to long-term residents whose people, through taxes, contributed to the cost of relief while "Russians, Finns, Estonians, Hungarians and others, the dust of whose native land has hardly been shaken off their shoes, are to be provided for." It suggested that the government assist the Asian benevolent associations. In response to the protests, the government said that it had only temporarily halted registrations so that officials could process an overwhelming number of applications. Since the benevolent associations cared for them, the government concluded that Asians were the least desperate of the unemployed! This assumption may have been correct, as fewer Asians registered than anticipated, but this statistic was more likely an indication that they did not expect any help. In late 1931 the Chinese Benevolent Association told city council that it had exhausted its funds and that about 260 Chinese nationals were "absolutely destitute." In October 1932, at the nadir of the Depression, more than 250 Asian families were receiving relief, but Vancouver refused to accept responsibility for the sick and indigent lest it set a precedent that would lead to many applications.[50] Similarly, when St. Joseph's Hospital, which cared for Chinese patients under an arrangement with the Vancouver General Hospital, sought financial aid, an alderman told it that "we are afraid to open the gate to any Orientals because Vancouver would then become their happy hunting ground." The city permitted the hospital to have a tag day to raise funds and attacked the Welfare Federation for collecting funds from Chinese residents but not helping them.[51]

Since May 1932 the city had indirectly provided relief to indigent Chinese residents through the Anglican Church Mission, which had accepted the task when unemployed whites had complained that the Chinese received meal tickets and could eat and live where they chose whereas single unemployed white men had to go to relief camps. In return for sixteen cents per day, the mission gave the Chinese two meals per day and medical care. The daily diet included all the rice they wanted plus half a pound each of meat and vegetables. The situation seemed satisfactory. Then in early 1935 the Young Socialist League, the CCF Youth, the Young Communist League, the Provincial Workers Council, and the Chinese Workers' Protective Association alleged that the Anglican Mission's clients received only an ounce of meat daily, two cents' worth of rice, a cent's worth of poor vegetables, and sixty cents per week as a shelter allowance. They accused the mission of "profiteering" and alleged that in the past three years 184 Chinese residents in Vancouver had died of beriberi. The city medical health officer found the food to be of good quality and had no evidence of recent deaths from beriberi.[52]

The Benevolent Association in Victoria also exhausted its funds but, through Premier Tolmie, received a grant under a Dominion-Provincial relief scheme. For a time Victoria's destitute Chinese residents benefited from a soup kitchen organized by the widow of the American consul. The provincial government gave her up to three tons of rice a month; the Chinese provided labour and other food. In 1935, however, when the city refused them aid, "a score" of Chinese indigents appealed directly to the provincial government, claiming that some of them had not eaten in three days. The province said that they were a municipal responsibility. Smaller municipalities often had no fallback positions for destitute Chinese residents. In Mission, for example, when the Chinese Workers' Protective Association alleged that Chinese men had starved, the Village Commissioners replied that the "destitute Chinese" were a joint responsibility of the senior governments. In Cumberland, when local Chinese merchants could no longer give credit to unemployed Chinese residents, the local branch of the Benevolent Association made a "desperate move ... at the cost of losing face" and sought provincial relief to save the destitute from starvation. Cumberland's Chinatown, which had once had over two thousand Asians, by 1940 had only a few hundred residents, mainly unemployed old men who were "largely dependent upon the charity of their countrymen" and "living out their declining years in a foreign land." In unorganized areas the provincial government provided relief but put the Chinese, Japanese, and Doukhobors on a reduced scale because of their allegedly lower standards of living, a practice that Vancouver also followed. By 1935 the province and the city were also paying the fares of indigents who wished to return to China. In 1937 the provincial government boasted of having moved toward solving the "Oriental Problem" by returning over a thousand Asians, mainly Chinese residents, to their homelands.[53]

There were probably fewer Japanese than Chinese residents on relief, but statistics are incomplete and contradictory. In Prince Rupert a number of Japanese fishermen received relief, and two families were on the list for about three years. Provincial officials, who listed 280 Japanese residents on relief, suggested withdrawing the quota of new Japanese immigrants stipulated by the gentlemen's agreement as long as some able-bodied Japanese residents remained unemployed and extending the five-year period during which an immigrant was subject to deportation for those receiving public relief. Norman Rogers, who became federal minister of labour after the Liberals returned to office in 1935, was interested, but the Department of External Affairs warned that Japan would not tolerate any change in the agreement and that humanitarian groups would likely protest extending the deportation period. Two years later, when a Japanese "menace" seemed a reality and unemployment was still a problem, External Affairs officials saw merit in advising Japan that fifty able-bodied male Japanese residents were on relief in Vancouver. Nevertheless, the Japanese continued to receive relief if they were otherwise eligible.[54]

Meanwhile, young Asians retained a fine reputation as law-abiding citizens. When a young Japanese man stole a gold watch and fifty cents from a swimmer near Haney, the newspaper reported that "a Japanese criminal is a rarity in the municipality." Vancouver's police chief attributed the low crime rate among the Japanese to their immediate copying of "the methods of the country in which they reside, whereas the Chinese retain their own habits," such as gambling and using narcotics. Young Chinese residents, however, seldom appeared in juvenile court. In sentencing a sixteen-year-old Chinese boy who had entered a home and stolen $12.60, a Victoria magistrate said that because it had "always been considered safe to leave money around when [the] Chinese were present," his offence "hurt the whole race."

Judge Helen Gregory MacGill of the Vancouver Juvenile Court calculated that between 1928 and 1936 "the white delinquency rate was 15.6 times that of the Oriental." She attributed the good behaviour of Asian youth to "the strong family system
of both China and Japan," which was supplemented "by control of the national
group."[55]

Canadian-born Asians had no more political rights than did their immigrant parents, but as asserted by Thomas Shoyama, one of their leading spokesmen, we "are
expected to assume responsibilities of citizenship" without a voice in government.
S.I. Hayakawa reported the surprise of political canvassers who found that Japanese Canadians could not vote. The Japanese Students' Club at the University of
British Columbia surveyed the status and aspirations of the second generation and
drew attention to the fact that young Japanese residents studied Canadian history,
learned of the injustice of taxation without representation, and were liable for military service but were "not allowed, at least in B.C., compensating rights of voting
citizenship." In a speech to the Vernon Rotary Club on "Commercial Relationships
between Canada and China," David Lim Yuen, "the most distinguished pupil at the
Vernon High School," asked why Chinese Canadians were not "given a say in the
government, so that they may have a chance to learn and know and love their native land, and to work for her prosperity."[56]

The legislature's decision in 1931 to enfranchise Japanese veterans of the Canadian Expeditionary Force gave young Asians some hope and encouraged some white
British Columbians to think of extending them rights. The Canadian Legion had
revived the request of its predecessor, the Great War Veterans' Association, to enfranchise approximately eighty surviving veterans. Premier Tolmie and most of
his Cabinet opposed the request lest it lead to demands for further concessions. A
legislative committee defeated the proposal by one vote; the whole legislature passed
it by one vote. The *Victoria Times* called it "an act of justice" that did "not involve
any fundamental departure from our electoral system"; the *Vancouver Star* saw a
"lesson in citizenship and its responsibilities" when, at the same time, the legislature disfranchised Doukhobors, whose Sons of Freedom sect was notorious for
arson, bombings, and generally flaunting the law.[57] The *Vancouver Province* reminded readers of the need to do something for Canadian-born Asians. It was not
alone. The 1933 Conference of the United Church in British Columbia endorsed
enfranchisement of all Canadian-born citizens.[58] Anglican missionaries told a diocesan synod that the resentment of the Canadian-born over the denial of the
franchise was contributing to "a rising tide of Buddhism and Shintoism." At the
University of British Columbia, where Japanese students formed a Japanese Students' Club to educate British Columbians "to a fair understanding" of the great

problem of the Japanese, an editorial in the student newspaper, the *Ubyssey*, called for equal rights and for encouraging "quality and not quantity in our Oriental citizens." The Canadian Youth Congress and the National Conference of University Students also endorsed enfranchisement. Canadian-born Asians had sympathy in influential places. The Trades and Labour Congress of Canada rejected a resolution to enfranchise "citizens of Japanese parentage" but agreed to ask the provincial government to grant equal franchise rights to all native-born Canadians. In a memorandum prepared for H.H. Stevens, the minister of trade and commerce, O.D. Skelton, undersecretary of state for external affairs, noted the difficulty of defending the disfranchisement of naturalized Asians and particularly of the Canadian-born. If British Columbia would not amend its laws, Skelton suggested that the federal government act on its own. Stevens did not respond; silence implies that he did not object.[59]

The most persistent advocate of enfranchisement was Professor Henry F. Angus. A native of Victoria, Angus had taught economics and political science at the University of British Columbia since 1919 and was active in the Institute of Pacific Relations, an international organization of public-minded individuals on both sides of the Pacific. Among his students were Canadians of Asian ancestry. In a paper presented to the 1930 meeting of the Canadian Political Science Association, Angus argued that removing "racial disabilities of a discriminatory character from men and women of Asiatic race permanently resident in our country" could earn goodwill in the Orient. Initial press reports that he favoured removing immigration barriers drew a hostile reaction, but once it was learned that he had warned of the dangers of unrestricted immigration, the agitation faded. Angus continued his campaign. In his essay "Underprivileged Canadians," published in *Queen's Quarterly*, he argued that Canadian-born Asians must be enfranchised to show them that they need not "look beyond Canada" for the support of a native land and could "rely on time and natural political pressure" to remove economic disabilities. In 1934 he warned *Vancouver Province* readers that large non-voting populations had caused revolutions elsewhere whereas enfranchising Canadian-born Asians would serve justice and lead to cultural assimilation by breaking their solidarity, dispersing them among a variety of occupations, and encouraging them to raise their standard of living and lower their birth rate. He ridiculed three "theoretical alternatives" – wholesale massacre, wholesale sterilization, or wholesale deportation – and challenged the argument that Asians would control the vote in some ridings because it rested "on the assumption that the anti-Oriental group is smaller than the number of Orientals to be enfranchised!" Groups as diverse as the Women's Christian Temperance Union and the Ad and Sales Bureau of the Vancouver Board of Trade endorsed his ideas, but the Native Sons of British Columbia insisted on the inassimilability of Asians. The B.C. Trollers' Association asked the university to dismiss Angus; agitators such as Hope denounced him.[60] Angus persisted. As a member of the Royal Commission on Dominion-Provincial Relations, he had fewer opportunities to speak but a higher profile. In the spring of 1938, at a peak in anti-Japanese agitation, his speech to the Ontario Medical Association attracted attention even though he only repeated old pleas that granting "full nationality rights to the Orientals in Canada" was the best way to solve British Columbia's Oriental problem. Anti-Asian agitators were annoyed. Thomas Reid had already complained of "influential people" such as Angus making his work harder; Neill was so angry that he called for Angus's removal from the commission.[61]

When political opponents of enfranchisement concocted scenarios of its potentially dire consequences, they usually referred to the "Oriental" vote, which included the Chinese even though the number of potential Canadian-born Chinese voters was significantly less than the number of Nisei.[62] On 22 June 1934 J.S. Woodsworth, national leader of the newly formed CCF Party, inadvertently revived old prejudices when he told the House of Commons that "if an oriental in Alberta or Saskatchewan may vote, I think the oriental ought to be able to vote in British Columbia." That November, while visiting Vancouver after a tour of the Orient, he said that there was "no excuse in a civilized country" to deny Canadian-born Asians the franchise. Despite some sympathy with Woodsworth, aghast CCF

"You're Right Mister, But ... " *Vancouver Sun,* 10 November 1934

members deluged the party newspaper with a "small avalanche of letters" and warned that other parties would exploit the issue. As damage control, Angus MacInnis, MP (CCF, Vancouver South), who was also Woodsworth's son-in-law, suggested that "the working class and the small business class can no longer be frightened with the old Asiatic bogey" since "the plight of their respective classes is no better in those provinces in which there is no competition from Orientals." The provincial convention debated publishing a statement "that the CCF did not propose to give votes to Asiatics." MacInnis argued that "as wage slaves we have nothing to lose" and urged the party to oppose racial discrimination. The convention referred the matter to a committee; in the October 1935 federal election, the CCF suppressed internal quarrels to counteract Liberal and Conservative propaganda.[63]

Liberals and Conservatives saw Woodsworth's stand as excellent ammunition against a party that, within a few months of its formal creation, had won 31 percent of the popular vote in the 1933 provincial election and seven seats in the legislature to become the official opposition. In the 1935 legislative session, several MLAs taunted the CCF on the Asian franchise. Clive Planta urged the legislature to affirm its opposition to "any extension of the franchise to British Columbia citizens of Oriental origin." Had CCF leader Harold Winch not successfully challenged the motion on a point of order, CCF members would have been in the awkward position of having to declare themselves on the issue. As unemployment and economic distress continued, federal politicians also feared competition from the new party. In the 1935 election, the franchise was an issue on Vancouver Island, on the lower mainland, in Yale, and in Skeena. These areas had noticeable Asian populations, a tradition of hostility, and often politicians who were experienced anti-Asian agitators. In Comox-Alberni, Neill said that if the CCF gained power the Asian vote in several communities could swing the election and in turn probably bring about relaxed immigration regulations. In Vancouver Centre, Ian Mackenzie said that Woodsworth would "give the franchise to every Oriental in the province."[64]

The CCF was on the defensive. In a radio address MacInnis blamed Liberals and Conservatives for bringing Asians to the country in the first place. He asked whether listeners preferred "an Oriental with a vote who will have to come up to your standard of living or an Oriental without a vote who can be used to break down your income and your working conditions." The idealistic Woodsworth backtracked slightly. Charging that the CCF position had been "entirely misrepresented," he said that Canadian-born British subjects should have the vote but that naturalized Asians would not likely qualify since they lacked an adequate knowledge of English or French and, in the case of the Japanese, could not surrender their original citizenship. He noted CCF opposition to immigration at a time of unemployment and its concern for trade. After the election he mused that "it is better to go down supporting a right principle than to triumph on the strength of injustice." Some CCF candidates, such as Wallis Lefaux in Vancouver Centre, denied that the CCF had pledged to enfranchise Asians. Others stressed that Asians would be enfranchised only after careful investigation of their acceptance of citizenship responsibilities and Canadian standards of living and that few would qualify. Dr. Lyle J. Telford of Vancouver rhetorically asked a Courtenay meeting, "you object to the CCF giving votes to the Orientals. Why not give them the vote? You give them every other damn thing." CCF supporters chastised Liberals and Conservatives for introducing a "yellow herring" to the campaign and, in Quebec, for enfranchising Asians before women received the vote.[65]

The CCF had good reason to attack the old parties. One Liberal advertisement proclaimed in large type: "50,000 Orientals in B.C., C.C.F. Party Stands PLEDGED to Give THEM the Vote. The Liberal Party is OPPOSED to Giving the Orientals the Vote." A subsequent advertisement featured an extract from Hansard quoting Woodsworth in favour of the enfranchisement of Asians. On the radio J. Edward Sears revived old anti-Asian bogeys, such as their high birth rate; their domination of fishing, the grocery trade, and lumbering; their penetration of agriculture; and the unsanitary and immoral habits of the Chinese: "If you men and women want to run the risk of having your children go to bed, figuratively or literally, with Orientals, then cast your vote for a C.C.F. candidate." He asked how much Japanese money was behind the CCF campaign since the "diabolical" promise of a vote encouraged "men of the yellow race to carry on further the undermining of the Anglo-Saxons in the province." Prominent Liberals called for keeping British Columbia "white for white people." A speaker in Victoria asked "how would you like your daughter to apply to a Japanese for a job in the Civil Service? Or to a Chinese for a job in the Public Works Department?" The *Prince Rupert Daily News* predicted that canners would herd droves of fishermen, who knew "nothing about our politics or system of government," to vote as the canners wanted. Yale candidate Charles Oliver suggested that if Asians were enfranchised "in twenty years there might be a Chinese Minister of Education." "The Asiatic simply does not fit in to the white scheme of things," said one Liberal advertisement. Not all Liberals agreed. At one of Mackenzie's rallies, Nellie McClung, who was specially imported from Alberta, dissociated herself from advertisements against enfranchising Canadian-born Asians. That she drew as much favourable audience response as did Mackenzie suggests that there was some goodwill for Canadian-born Asians.[66]

The Liberals were not alone in what Professor Angus described as "stooping to conquer." Six months before the election, Howard C. Green and the Vancouver-Point Grey Conservative Association asked the minister of immigration to survey the Asian situation, especially as it related to the Japanese, and to take steps to "safeguard the interests, the standard of living, and the cultural life of the white population of this Province." Such a move, he explained, "should strengthen our hand considerably in the coming election, as Mr. Woodsworth has stated publicly that he advocates votes for the Canadian-born Japanese." Conservatives in several constituencies used the Asian question. The Nanaimo incumbent, C.H. Dickie, claimed that the Asians would support policies favouring the Orient at Canada's expense and that their unfamiliarity with Canada's problems and history meant that they could not vote intelligently. One of his advertisements told CCF voters that "the clergy and professors at the head of your Party" have committed it to votes for Orientals. The *Prince Rupert Evening Empire* claimed that Woodsworth would invite "teeming millions" who would soon "run our country." A speaker in Victoria asserted that the CCF would give Saanich farms to the Chinese and put "white men to work under them as bosses." In Steveston, Leon J. Ladner described "what might happen in federal, provincial or municipal elections should the Japanese colony in Richmond, estimated to be near the 2000 mark, be given the right to vote." Since the Conservatives shared the Liberals' views on the franchise, they claimed that the Liberals had "dragged in" the "highly-overemphasized" franchise question only "to cloud the more serious questions of the day." The Conservatives related the Asian question to a more familiar fighting ground: the tariff. A Vancouver Island speaker said that "the Liberals want to flood our country with Japanese goods and the C.C.F. want to give the Orientals the vote." Observing the Liberals' rejection of tariff protection, Conservative advertisements proclaimed in large type: "50,000 Orientals in British Columbia to whom neither the Conservative [n]or Liberal Party will give the vote. But, there are 40,000,000 ORIENTALS in JAPAN – who threaten Canada's Workers and Industry." Despite revived anti-Asian rhetoric, Asian policies were a major issue only in Nanaimo, Victoria, Vancouver East, and Vancouver Centre, constituencies where the CCF was a serious contender.[67]

Unfortunately for Asians, the campaign revived old antagonisms. In an attempt to embarrass the other parties, the newly re-elected MacInnis introduced a two-part resolution in Parliament declaring the harm of denying the franchise to certain racial or religious groups and asking the government to "take the necessary measures" to exclude such persons from Canada. The resolution was so phrased that MacInnis claimed that to vote against enfranchisement was to vote for continued Asian immigration. Officials reminded Prime Minister King that pressing the issue might "revive anti-Oriental feeling" and recommended referring the matter to a parliamentary committee examining the Franchise Act. Members overwhelmingly agreed; only seven CCF members and eight Social Crediters supported MacInnis.[68]

The British Columbia press reported the debate with little comment. Some editors recognized MacInnis's political ploy. The *Prince Rupert Daily News,* observing that immigration policies and the Minimum Wage Law meant that "Orientals are no longer a menace," regretted that the CCF had revived the question. The *Vancouver Province* agreed that it was "a bad thing" to have "an undigested and indigestible mass of people" and argued for enfranchising those Asians born, educated, and taxed in Canada. Many, of course, opposed even modest Asian enfranchisement. Reid and Neill found it strange that the CCF had not raised the issue of enfranchisement provincially. In fact, a Conservative MLA, R.H. Pooley (Esquimalt), no doubt seeking "to put the C.C.F. on the spot," proposed a resolution viewing "with alarm any suggestion of extending the franchise to Orientals." The Speaker ruled it out of order on several grounds, including the use of the word "Oriental," which tended to cast "opprobrious reflections upon citizens of other countries with whom we are in friendly relation."[69]

Encouraged by MacInnis and Angus, and by King's promise to refer the matter to a parliamentary committee, members of the Japanese Canadian Citizens League (JCCL)[70] felt confident that "we could present a fair demand on the government," noting that the Nisei were growing up, were "totally different from the original immigrants," and "were ready to share in the responsibilities of our native land." It sent a delegation to Ottawa to present its case. Not everyone in the Japanese Canadian community approved. The Canadian Japanese Association, dominated by the Issei (the first generation Japanese), had close connections with the Japanese consulate and warned that the endeavour would incur the wrath of the white community, but even their intimidation did not discourage the JCCL. In a brief prepared by their lawyer, T.G. Norris, the JCCL argued that denial of the franchise was unconstitutional, contrary to international goodwill, based on misconceptions, and designed for conditions that no longer existed. The brief also suggested that a law applying to only one part of Canada tended to create sectionalism. Its

"Fair-Play?" *New Canadian*, 27 May 1939

key point was that denying Asians the franchise tended to create an economic minority that "will not be assimilated into the life of Canada and [that,] living under a sense of oppression, will eventually become a source of difficulty." Norris drew on a recent survey of Japanese Canadians to demonstrate that, despite legal disabilities, they had adapted to Canadian law and community life. He asked rhetorically, "how can the people of Canada refuse those of them who have become our citizens the franchise merely on the ground of race when illiterate subnormals of the Caucasian race are granted the privilege?"[71]

Appearing before the parliamentary committee were four Nisei: Miss Hideko Hyodo, a teacher; Dr. Edward Banno, a dentist; S.I. Hayakawa, a professor of English at the University of Wisconsin; and Minoru Kobayashi, an insurance agent. They appealed to British fair play, showed that they had been well educated for Canadian citizenship, and argued that while, in the words of Hayakawa, they might be "a little better endowed with the gift of the gab than those whom we represent, we are ... as representative of the Canadian citizens who have sent us, as you of the less articulate Canadian citizens who have sent you to Ottawa." When Kobayashi said that he had been a member of the Older Boys Parliament and hoped one day to be elected to the real Parliament, he was cheered. Even Reid admitted that the Nisei "made a very good impression." The committee decided that this "subject of wide and far-reaching importance" required further study. The delay gave opponents of enfranchisement, notably the Native Sons and Daughters of British Columbia and the Native Sons of Canada, time to protest. The Native Sons of British Columbia claimed that the JCCL was campaigning "for the full rights of citizenship for the whole of the Oriental races, and that means for a dominating place in the control of the country." They explained that "the Orientals," "once our servants," were "now our competitors in industrial occupations and commercial and economic spheres" and would, if they received "full citizenship," become "our masters." In an extensive brief, Reid repeated similar sentiments and the old "thin edge of the wedge" argument. He asked whether Canadians would "allow an unassimilable race of people to control the economic and political life, if not of Canada, then that of British Columbia." Noting Japan's growing militarism, he implied that Japan endorsed the agitation. In any case, said Reid, British Columbia must decide. Neill added that enfranchisement would lead to demands for immigration privileges and fishing licences and make British Columbia "a Japanese state in Canada." Not surprisingly the committee recommended against enfranchising the Canadian-born Japanese before the province enfranchised them. Needless to say, for the Nisei, the "balloon" of optimism had burst in what Muriel Kitagawa later described as "the first of a series of setbacks we were to receive from that time on."[72]

That the province would enfranchise Asians was most unlikely. During the June 1937 provincial election, Gordon Wismer, the Liberal incumbent in Vancouver Centre, told voters not to "forget the growth of the Oriental population and the inroads they are making in business. We don't want Wun Lung Duck for premier in another few years." The *Vancouver Province* properly chastised such "stupid and mischievous nonsense" and the drawing of "a red herring of prejudice across the trail" to obscure the government's poor record. Nevertheless, Wismer persisted, and, in Kamloops and Comox, Senator J.W. de B. Farris declared that the Chinese and Japanese did "not understand democracy as we understand it," predicting that their enfranchisement would lead to "Orientals" in the legislature. In Prince Rupert, the premier's constituency, a Liberal advertisement urged salmon trollers to think carefully before voting for the CCF since the Japanese, if permitted to vote, would soon "dominate trolling as they now do gill-netting." "Are you prepared to give them equal rights with yourselves in your fishing and fraternal organizations? Will you accept them in your boat crews, in your lodges and in your homes?" Pattullo scorned the Conservative plank opposing the franchise for Orientals, arguing that no one intended to extend them the vote, "with the possible exception of the C.C.F."[73]

Opposition to enfranchising Orientals was in the Conservative platform. But neither this stance nor claims that enfranchisement would increase competition for "our" farmers, workmen, and businessmen, thereby giving Asians "a very definite influence in the control of government in this province," helped the party's leader, Frank Patterson, in a 1936 by-election in Vancouver-Burrard.[74] Nevertheless, the Conservatives used the issue of enfranchisement in the 1937 general election. In North Okanagan, Dr. K.C. Macdonald, the Liberal incumbent, held up a copy of the brief that T.G. Norris, the Conservative candidate in South Okanagan, had prepared for the JCCL to present to Parliament. Norris explained that he had written it in the course of his professional work and suggested that Dr. Macdonald, a dentist, had probably pulled a few Japanese teeth. Conservatives also charged the CCF with favouring Oriental enfranchisement. In a province-wide radio address, Herbert Anscomb, the incumbent in Victoria, agreed that Asians might live properly and obey laws but declared that "they do not and cannot live in the same strata of society that we enjoy." He claimed that 36,000 Asians lived in Vancouver and could control the election in one or two constituencies, with the possible result "of having the pleasure of Mr. Hook Long Sing as Speaker of the Legislature." Curiously, in light of his later anti-Asian crusade, Halford Wilson, the Conservative candidate in Vancouver-Burrard, called "the issue of a Chinaman as Premier ... a 'red herring' dragged across the trail to confuse the public on the more important issues of administration."[75]

The CCF was on the defensive. Speakers and advertisements denied that its platform called for Oriental enfranchisement. During a provincial tour, J.S. Woodsworth accused Liberals and Conservatives of trying to distract voters and of having helped the "great corporations" bring in Oriental immigrants. It would have been better if they had never come, he argued, but "for our own sake we must see that the Oriental in Canada is lifted to our status." Angus MacInnis made similar appeals in Prince Rupert, as did several of the CCF candidates on Vancouver

Island. The issue was not decisive. It appeared in only a few constituencies, and, in the popular vote, both the CCF and the Liberals narrowly lost because of a Conservative revival. Nevertheless, as the *B.C. Federationist* put it, the use of "the red herring of the franchise ... to distract attention" from other issues suggested that the toleration of Asians was waning.[76]

What should have been a happy occasion, the visit of Prince and Princess Chichibu to Vancouver en route to the coronation of King George VI, illustrated the difficult position of the Canadian-born Japanese. Two hundred fishing vessels greeted the ship carrying the royal couple as it approached Vancouver, thousands of Japanese residents waited at the pier, school children lined the streets as the royal couple were driven to the Japanese language school, and a crowd saw them off when they left for eastern Canada. As the train made brief stops in the Fraser Valley, more Japanese residents greeted the prince, who spoke briefly to them. Whereas a decade earlier such welcomes had aroused no criticism, now a *Vancouver Sun* reporter remarked how the visit had shown "that in Vancouver there is a Japanese colony, Canadian on the surface, but loyal to the spirit of the old country." For the Canadian Japanese the situation worsened. The *Sun* had greeted the royal couple as "representatives of the great Japanese people, whom Canadians respect and admire and desire to accept as good friends and neighbors" while warning of Canadian suspicions of "Japan's intentions in the Pacific Bowl." In a gesture of goodwill, it published a cartoon showing "Mr. and Mrs. Vancouver" shaking hands with the prince and princess and inviting them to come again. A few days later, the *Sun* printed a letter to the editor purportedly signed by five Canadian-born Japanese residents describing the cartoon as "cheap and disgusting" because it showed the royal couple "in a bowing position." They claimed that by publishing the cartoon and editorially "condemning the peace-loving Imperial Japanese Empire of militarism, while at the same time professing to welcome their Imperial Highnesses," the *Sun* had insulted their Imperial Highnesses and offended the local Japanese.[77]

Nisei who had been campaigning for the franchise immediately informed the *Sun* that the letter was a forgery, that no one knew anyone by the names listed, and that no one resided at the address given. They suspected that a non-Japanese resident had written the letter since "no Canadian-born Japanese would be so asinine as to take it upon himself to speak for the representatives in Canada of the Japanese government." They thought the cartoon inoffensive and expressive of the "natural courtesy of the Japanese people." The Nisei made a strong argument, but the damage to their franchise campaign had been done. The public noted the initial letter, not the rejoinder, and used it to "prove" their unreadiness for the franchise, even citing it after the war to justify continuing restrictions on Japanese Canadians.[78]

"And Come Again," *Vancouver Sun,* 3 April 1937

The Canadian-Japanese community, however, continued to seek goodwill. In Victoria they gave a "generous cheque" toward the celebrations for the Diamond Jubilee of British Columbia's entry into Confederation. In Kelowna they offered a lantern procession and a dancing demonstration to mark festivities in honour of the coronation of King George VI. When the City of Victoria celebrated the seventy-fifth anniversary of its incorporation in the summer of 1937, they contributed to the parade a float with crepe paper cherry blossoms and a showboat featuring folk dancing, a performance by the contralto Aiko Saita, and a march by girls in sailor costumes carrying Japanese and Canadian flags. In Vancouver, in the summer of 1937, the Nisei organized a carnival similar to one that they had held for the city's Golden Jubilee in 1936. They advertised it as "an expression of the loyalty of [the] Canadian-born Japanese to King George VI" and as an appreciation of the city's welcome to Prince and Princess Chichibu. Recognizing the increasing unpopularity of Japan, carnival organizers specifically hoped that this "display of loyalty would not be misunderstood by the public or taken for a demonstration in connection with the present Sino-Japanese friction." In New Westminster hundreds of Japanese Canadians, many of them girls in national costume, made a "picturesque spectacle" when King George VI and Queen Elizabeth visited in 1939. In Victoria and Vancouver, Japanese chrysanthemum fanciers invited the whole community to see their displays; in Victoria they gave the proceeds from a silver collection to the Royal Jubilee Hospital. Despite such efforts, rare indeed were comments such as the *Vancouver Sun*'s that "we have here in Vancouver many Japanese people of charm, intelligence and gentility ... [we] cannot bring ourselves to think that these gracious and cultured folk have been hiding within them a false and treacherous spirit only biding its time to jump at our throats."[79]

In an article commemorating Vancouver's fiftieth birthday, the historian Walter N. Sage wrote that "the Oriental community has, on the whole, ceased to be a very thorny problem, and seems in a fair way to have become a real factor in municipal life." Certainly the place of the Chinese in Vancouver's Golden Jubilee celebrations in 1936 seemed to suggest such a conclusion. A Chinese parade, a festival sponsored by the Chinese Benevolent Association, and a Chinese village featuring a

A NOBLE CONTRIBUTION

— By CALLAN

"A Noble Contribution," *Vancouver Sun*, 16 July 1936

"magnificent spectacle of Oriental art and wonders" were popular attractions. The *Vancouver Sun* praised China's gesture of loaning the treasures in honour of Vancouver and expressed pride in "the energy and initiative and citizenship of our fellow Canadians of Chinese birth or extraction" who had arranged to bring the exhibit to Vancouver.[80]

The Asian community would soon be a factor in municipal life but not in the way Sage had implied. Those who favoured giving the Canadian-born some privileges of citizenship now faced bitter attack. Trade disruptions relating to the Sino-Japanese war discouraged those who urged toleration for trade's sake. And, as farmers and merchants continued to suffer from the Depression, they found that the Chinese were convenient scapegoats. Yet even in 1935 anti-Asian agitation was still somewhat sporadic and tended to be confined to particular issues and areas. Late in 1935 C.E. Hope complained of a lack of leadership in the anti-Asian crusade. He predicted that "it only needs a young man with a little time on his hands, and a little financial backing, energy of the fiery orator type, of which Canada has produced quite a number on different occasions, to take this matter up, and the woods would very soon be blazing." Hope was a greater prophet than he realized. Despite talk of relaxing immigration restrictions, evidence of economic co-operation between Asian and white producers, and sympathetic consideration of the problems of Canadian-born Asians, the toleration of Asians that had appeared early in the decade was not very deep. In 1937 the *Vancouver Province* could recall its 1930 argument that those Asians born and educated in British Columbia were "inoculated" with Western ideas and standards, spoke good English, paid taxes, obeyed laws, owed allegiance only to Canada, and thus deserved a hearing; it suggested, moreover, that the "old problem" of the Oriental immigrant with his low standard of living and cheap labour was gone. But it also listed the fields in which Asians were serious economic competitors. International events were conspiring against Asians in British Columbia, especially against the Japanese.[81]

6

Inflaming the Coast: The "Menace" from Japan, 1919-41

The Sino-Japanese War – with its mass murder of the civilian Chinese population in air raids – has undoubtedly done much to inflame the community on the Coast.

– VANCOUVER NEWS-HERALD, 26 MARCH 1938

In August 1937 Anglican Archdeacon F.G. Scott of Quebec City, a popular Great War padre, told the Ontario Command of the Canadian Legion that in the case of war "the Mother Country might not be able to spare ships in sufficient numbers to guard Victoria and Vancouver, where there are already more than 100,000 Asiatics." That exaggerated story was buried on back pages, as was the claim by an executive of the Navy League of Canada that "secret agents of Japan are working as and with Japanese fishermen making maps and charts of soundings of various parts of the Pacific Coast." Then the *Toronto Star* gave a banner headline to Scott's assertions that "a good authority" had said that there were 40,000 Japanese residents in Vancouver, that Japan knew every inch of the coast, that its naval officers inhabited fishing villages, and that it owned "enormous timber limits." He added that "war in the Orient" and Japan's aggrandizement threatened Canada and the United States. The *Toronto Star* suggested that Minister of Defence Ian Mackenzie would investigate this "latest wave of apprehension." It claimed that "many individuals and various organizations" had made representations; in fact, Mackenzie's office had documented only nine recent references to this "menace" to Canada's safety, including Scott's statement and several letters arising from a recent by-election in Victoria.[1]

"Apprehension" existed mainly in the *Toronto Star*'s imagination. British Columbia newspapers printed Canadian Press reports of the Scott interview but, apart from criticisms of inadequate coastal defences, were more amused than alarmed by reports of spies. The *Prince Rupert Daily News*, for example, could not "see what a spy would learn in this part of the country except that we are undefended, something which everybody knows." The *Vancouver Sun* claimed that "a real spy, with a zest for action, would perish of ennui in Vancouver in less than a week." Mayor G.C. Miller of Vancouver was not alarmed. The police chief said that "the whole statement was not unreasonable as from a military or naval point of view the shipping in question could not be effective" and that the information the fishermen might secure could be readily obtained from naval charts.[2] But the East Asian situation was deteriorating, and Scott's charges fell on fertile ground. British

ARCHDEACON F.G. SCOTT SAYS HE IS "INFORMED ON GOOD AUTHORITY" THAT JAPANESE NAVAL OFFICERS IN DISGUISE ARE LIVING IN SO-CALLED 'FISHING VILLAGES' IN BRITISH COLUMBIA.

"Archdeacon F.G. Scott ... " *Halifax Herald,* 20 November 1937

Columbians, who had heard spy stories before, became concerned about Japanese investments in timber and mines; many joined embargo and boycott campaigns against Japan and, like military and police officials, increasingly worried about inadequate defences against Japan's military ambitions. Suspicions of Japan inevitably affected the Canadian Japanese, reviving agitation for a halt to their immigration and for new restrictions on their economic activities.

Rumours of spies in the Canadian Japanese community had appeared before the First World War but had abated when, through the Anglo-Japanese Alliance, Japan had helped defend the coast against a possible German attack. British Columbians were grateful, but in the postwar civil turmoil military and police officials worried about Bolshevism among the Japanese. They found little evidence, but one officer concluded that since the Japanese considered "it a great honour to report any information of value to their country," they probably spied for Japan. An army major, who had two Japanese speakers investigate the situation in 1919, reported that "the Japs on the Pacific Coast are getting very numerous and very prosperous, and we have noticed that they have a tremendous feeling of hatred for the Americans." The RCMP feared that if Japan goaded the United States into a war and "public opinion were convinced that Canada was harbouring a Japanese spy system," the Americans might demand that Canada allow them to clear out the spies. Civilians noted that many Japanese residents had military experience and had settled on such vantage points as hilltops and in locations near the American border. In 1921 the RCMP investigated reports of Japanese encroachments near a wireless station on the Queen Charlotte Islands but found that the Japanese mine and nearby wireless station had been closed. Army officials concluded that shoals made the coast there of little use as a base for submarines or large war vessels.[3]

The notion that Japan planned to conquer British Columbia had circulated before and during the First World War, providing ammunition for novelists and propagandists. Drawing on a serial story published in 1910 and 1911, the anti-Asian novel *The Writing on the Wall*, published in 1921, wove a fantastic tale that concluded with a final nightmare scene in which Japanese airplanes bombed coastal cities while Japanese residents on the ground cut outside communication links and fired from vantage points on the north side of the Fraser River when the American army attempted to rescue British Columbia. During intense anti-Asian agitation surrounding the 1921 federal election and the campaign for Asiatic exclusion, *Danger: The Anti-Asiatic Weekly* advertised an article with the rhetorical question "Do you know that every move on the part of the Asiatics here in British Columbia is helping in the Japanese Imperialistic Scheme to Dominate the World?" Claiming that Japanese naval officers showed unusual interest in Vancouver Island's coal fields, the *Vancouver World* said that "the menace of having an army of Japanese soldiers, trained in the Japanese army and holding prior allegiance to the Mikado, working our coal fields ... is self-evident." A year earlier a *World* columnist had suggested that in the case of a Pacific war "we would be lucky if the Japanese fishermen would merely quit work and refuse to supply us with this great source of food supply." After denying any hostility to Japan or to the Japanese in Canada and noting that people in Japan did not want war, the *Vancouver Sun* asserted in 1921 that "the class descended from the fighting Samurai ... long for glory, for more land, for the world's recognition as equals ... Where are they to get that land? ... British Columbia, land of fruit, flowers, sunshine, fertility, where the Japanese by self-denial in a different mode of living defeat all native competition THAT is the land for which the Japanese long." Modern Japan, predicted the *Sun*, would come in flying machines. The sensationalist press had no monopoly on such claims. Major Richard J. Burde, MLA (Independent, Alberni), told the legislature that if Japan and the United States went to war "every Jap fisherman" on the west coast of Vancouver Island would immediately "stop work to assist his native country." H.H. Stevens, MP (Conservative, Vancouver Centre), declared that the

Japanese had "every foot of the Pacific coast charted." Rev. N.L. Ward, an Anglican who worked among the Japanese, claimed that fish was only a by-product for the Japanese, who made charts and photographs for Tokyo's benefit.[4]

The conclusion of the Washington Agreement on naval disarmament late in 1921 and Japan's moves toward liberalism and internationalism in the 1920s temporarily called such forebodings into question. The *Sun* admitted that Japan's plan to scrap battleships and reduce its army destroyed many ideas about "that dreaded bogey known as the 'yellow peril'" and was good news for believers in peace. When, during conflict over exclusion in 1924, American newspapers said that Japan was building flying machines to attack the United States, a columnist with the *Victoria Colonist* contended that Japan could not "wage successful warfare against a powerful and wealthy nation like the United States." Even British Columbia's MPs downplayed complaints of inadequate coastal defences although A.W. Neill (Independent, Comox-Alberni), in defending the elimination of the Japanese from the fisheries, saw danger in having "practically the whole coast in the hands of an alien people who might be, at sometime, a potential foe."[5]

The military shared that concern. Intelligence officers in Ottawa instructed their west coast counterparts to follow "very closely" events in connection with Asiatic immigration and to forward information "as occasion may require." In the fall of 1932, given rising tension after the Manchurian crisis, naval headquarters in Ottawa asked the commander in Esquimalt for annual reports on the "general attitude, behaviour, political, economic and trade union aspirations, etc., of the Japanese," especially of those "persons of Japanese nationality who pursue occupations of a seafaring nature." The first, and possibly last, of these annual reports drew extensively from an article in *Maclean's* but included the opinions of senior provincial and RCMP officers that the Japanese in British Columbia, while outwardly observing all laws, were seeking to colonize Canada. In 1934 the provincial police quoted a Japanese informant as saying that many "Jap fishermen belong to the samurai group and are ex-naval men, who know practically every inch of the area in which they fish," had the waters charted in their minds as well as on paper, and regarded the Esquimalt naval base as a "a joke." In Parliament, Thomas Reid (Liberal, New Westminster) said that Japanese fishermen had "better surveys, obtained from their own country, of our Pacific coast than we have in British Columbia." In 1937, while admitting problems in writing a report without being accused of jingoism, the naval staff officer in Esquimalt observed that people with "a thorough knowledge" of the coast feared that Japanese residents might commit sabotage since "it is yet to be proven that a Canadian-born Japanese is other than a Japanese National." He worried about the large number of Japanese fishermen with powerboats and a thorough knowledge of the region; on land the provincial police kept "a wary eye" out for possible Japanese subversives creating "a highly dangerous situation" in an emergency.[6]

Until 1931 the Pacific had seemed as peaceful as its name. Vancouver and Victoria residents warmly greeted a Japanese training squadron in 1925; the press recalled Japan's help in protecting the coast in the Great War; at a formal banquet for officers, Premier John Oliver hailed the late Anglo-Japanese Treaty as "a potent agency in maintaining world peace in past years"; and when hundreds of Japanese from all over the province converged on Vancouver to greet the fleet, no one portrayed them as potential saboteurs.[7]

At the beginning of the Manchurian crisis in 1931, few British Columbians anticipated that the hostilities would affect them directly. In 1932 civic officials attended a ceremony in Vancouver's Stanley Park to plant cherry trees – gifts of the mayors of Kobe and Yokohama – near the Japanese war memorial. Later that year, Herbert Marler, Canada's minister to Japan, told the Japan Society in Vancouver that Canada's good relations with Japan could "be maintained indefinitely, because there is mutual good-will between the two peoples." In 1932 almost no one noticed a locally published pamphlet, *Japan: The Octopus of the East and It's* [sic] *Menace to Canada*. It had sensationalist tales such as that of "Takihashi," a high-ranking Japanese officer who worked as bookkeeper and clerk at a small Vancouver Island hotel before returning to Japan to lecture the Japanese army on the ease of attacking British Columbia. When Neill and Reid told Parliament that there were Japanese spies in the province, the *Vancouver Sun* used the story in its weekly political satire. In this spoof, "Nagasaki," a naval officer disguised as a fishermen, took soundings and positions around the Vancouver harbour while his guide "Tokyo," a local fisherman, assured him that this was unnecessary since the information, including the location of water pipes under Burrard Inlet, was "recorded on a million charts for sale in half a thousand stores." Even while reporting increasing militarism in Japan, the *Sun* suggested the people of Japan were "sane and sound."[8]

This mood changed as Japanese forces moved further into China. When a Japanese training squadron visited Vancouver in 1933, the festivities were modest. The Depression and strained government finances were factors; so too was the world situation. Japan had just withdrawn from the League of Nations. Canadian military officers made courtesy calls on Vice Admiral Hyakutake, but Ottawa relied on the city to supply "the usual hospitality": a banquet for officers and sightseeing for the men. The local Japanese community provided much of the entertainment. When the *Kaiwo Maru*, a naval training ship, visited in 1935, only the Japanese community and the consul offered hospitality.

Coolness toward the Japanese continued with the war in Asia. In the spring of 1937, when Prince and Princess Chichibu passed through Vancouver, the mayor and the attorney general were the only elected officials to greet them although the federal government had an official reception in Ottawa.[9] Japan, however, continued to curry favour by giving Canadian teachers holidays in Japan in exchange for their speaking to service clubs, church groups, and the like on their return. In 1940 the *Japan Times*, in co-operation with the *Vancouver Sun*, organized an essay contest for western Canadian high school and university students on "why Canada and Japan should cultivate friendship." The first two prizes were trips to Japan. What Japan thought of the University of British Columbia winner, who went on to China, where he hoped to have "a front seat at the theatre of war," is unknown.[10]

During the first years of the Far Eastern crisis, most commentators criticized Japan's aggression. Chinese residents raised funds for war relief, circulated pro-China propaganda, and boycotted Japanese goods, but, given the Depression, for most British Columbians possible economic advantages overrode any moral or military issues.[11] Scrap iron, lead, zinc, and copper left British Columbia ports for Japan. Despite concern about competition from Japan for Canadian manufacturers, the federal Liberals argued that Japan had to export processed goods in order to pay for imported raw materials, and attacked Conservative policies that had led to a tariff war and a cessation of lumber orders. During the 1935 federal election, Mackenzie King promised immediate negotiations to restore trade. Without explaining any implications, Ian Mackenzie hinted that if Japan discriminated against Canada in trade, Canada might have to consider that it was "giving a livelihood to 40,000 of her nationals." The Liberals won. Both nations made concessions. The tariff war ended, and ships again loaded logs for Japan. But, as Japan continued its activities in China, concerns began to arise about its intentions for Canada.[12]

Japanese-owned companies had cut some of the logs. For many years they had invested in British Columbia's resource industries, particularly in logging and mining. Prince Rupert welcomed the export of logs; others worried that new investments would parallel Japan's "invasion" of other industries. Military intelligence officers did not deny the possibility of future sabotage but stressed that the Japanese were taking raw materials with "little benefit" to Canada. The provincial police noted that two Japanese residents visiting Queen Charlotte City appeared to be "more the military than the commercial type," were "most reticent" about their business, and showed "unusual interest in the natural features of the coast." They speculated that Japan's government was involved with an iron mine on the Queen Charlotte Islands since "men who were most obviously naval engineers" had taken "extensive soundings" in the inlet. Late in 1936 Commissioner T.W.S. Parsons of the provincial police said that the situation "exactly parallels that of Singapore," where, before defence was an issue, Japanese rubber planters had secured land opposite the new fortifications. A constable reported that the Japanese listened to short wave broadcasts from Japan, that they had an unusual interest in taking motion pictures, and that one fisherman had gone out without bait, possibly to take soundings. In relaying this information, the constable's immediate superior expressed concern about the large number of Japanese workers at the isolated Ocean Falls paper mill, an "ideal position for an emergency naval base," from which they could cut off communications and assist landing parties.[13]

Prince Rupert residents were more concerned about the impact that deep-sea fishermen based in Japan would have on the fishery resource than they were about potential spies. Late in 1936 officials of one of Japan's largest canning companies visited the coast, apparently to establish "elaborate" deep-sea facilities to harvest salmon returning to British Columbia spawning grounds. The Department of External Affairs hoped that there would be no public discussion, but the Prince Rupert Chamber of Commerce asked Ottawa to protect the fisheries. The *Prince Rupert Daily News* admitted that Canada could do little except try to make Japan "see the justice" of Canada's exclusive claim "to the fisheries which we have so assiduously endeavoured to build up and maintain"; the *Vancouver Province* agreed. The B.C. Trollers' Association, whose members were directly affected, voted to retaliate by deporting every Japanese resident in British Columbia if Japan did not withdraw its floating canneries. A.W. Neill warned that Japanese offshore fishermen could wipe out the British Columbia fishery. Premier T.D. Pattullo raised the matter with the prime minister, who advised that Japanese fishermen had not actually "invaded the waters off Canada" but that Canada would co-operate with the United States in the matter. In 1940 the Fishermen's Co-operative Conference urged Ottawa to negotiate an agreement whereby Japan would forbid its nationals to fish within the three-mile limit. This low-key approach to incursions into provincial resources and the lack of response to rumours of Japanese fishing for dogfish and halibut off the Queen Charlotte Islands sharply contrasted with concerns about Japanese investments on shore.[14]

Fears of military incursions increased after the summer of 1937 when Japanese troops began attacking Chinese cities. British Columbia newspapers had almost daily front-page news of the war and its atrocities and frequent interviews with newly arrived travellers and refugees. Service club speeches, sermons, and editorials overwhelmingly sympathized with China and attacked Japan's defiance of international law. A few British Columbians did distinguish between militarists and ordinary Japanese people and between Japan's foreign policy and the views of Japanese Canadians. The *Vancouver Sun,* noting that "we have here in Vancouver many Japanese people of charm, intelligence and gentility," could not believe that Japan's "people are savage barbarians devoting themselves to a remorseless conquest of the world." After visiting Japan, W.T. Straith, MLA (Liberal, Victoria), said that "the domination of a military caste" was obscuring "the true nature of a wonderful nation." The *Vernon News* described Japanese residents as mostly "good citizens, industrious, frugal and often thoughtful. Condemnation of Japan at war with China is one thing. Our attitude to the Japanese in Canada is another."[15]

The expansion of the war coincided with reports of Japanese interests purchasing more than three million dollars worth of timber on Vancouver Island and the

Queen Charlotte Islands and possibly building rayon pulp mills. Japanese interests signed a three-year contract to buy the entire output of 600 miners at the Copper Mountain mine near Princeton; negotiated to buy the entire output of BC Nickel Mines Ltd. in Choate (near Yale); and bought the Iron Duke property at Louise Island in the Queen Charlottes, where they began building a railway with which to reach iron deposits. A Japanese-controlled company reopened an old copper mine on Vancouver Island. Military officials thought that such investments should be a matter "of high Government policy," but the chief of the General Staff determined that the acquisitions did not noticeably "intensify the seriousness" of a problem created by the presence of 24,000 Japanese residents concentrated "in localities of military importance" in British Columbia. He recommended strict regulations about transferring property near points of military importance to foreign nationals.[16]

Although a few British Columbians welcomed new mining operations, most were critical. Members of the Co-operative Commonwealth Federation (CCF) Party contended that the resources helped Japan's war effort, and most civilians did not like becoming, as columnist Bruce Hutchison suggested, "a Japanese colony for the practical purposes of Japan." The *Victoria Times* feared that Japan's acquisition of Vancouver Island timber limits might threaten Canada's leading position in the newsprint industry; the *Langley Advance* was disheartened by seeing Canadians idle while the Japanese got "their feet firmly established in the garden spot of Canada." The provincial Conservative leader called for protection of natural resources against Oriental encroachment; the Fraser Valley Reeves Association suggested creating naval and military reserves in which no Oriental would be permitted to own land. Many objections concerned the export of logs – and thus of jobs. The advisory board of the farmers' institutes asserted that "Canada's raw materials should be reserved for manufacture in the Dominion of Canada"; the Canadian Legion protested "the sale of valuable timberlands to Japanese interests."[17]

The provincial government, which had surrendered control of the land on which the Japanese cut timber, believed that only Ottawa could act because of the Anglo-Japanese Treaty of 1911. When Mackenzie King promised only to consider the complaint, an embarrassed Premier Pattullo told British Columbians that 300,000,000 board feet of timber was not enough to justify erecting a mill in Japan to use it and that the stand was a poor logging show. Nevertheless, Pattullo did not forget. A year later, he warned King of the "increasingly difficult" situation as the Japanese continued "to insinuate themselves into various avenues of endeavour." He asked the prime minister to repeal the 1913 statute by which Canada adhered to the treaty. Advised by H.L. Keenleyside that Pattullo was trying to create prejudice for purposes of the next provincial election, King replied that neither the Canadian nor the British governments thought that international conditions made abrogation of the treaty appropriate. The Department of National Defence advised Ian Mackenzie to make no comment beyond such a generalization as "the map of Canada is no secret."[18]

"But He Leaves the Back Gate Open," *Vancouver Sun,* 4 March 1938

By 1939, as the international situation deteriorated, concern for national security increased. Grant MacNeil, MP (CCF, Vancouver North), continued trying to embarrass the government with reports of Japanese ownership of timber claims and mining properties. Drawing on a report prepared by pulp and paper unions in his constituency, he told Parliament of Japanese interests owning timber and mineral resources on the west coast of Vancouver Island, where they had dredged a harbour to a seventy-foot depth and had constructed tunnels suitable for oil storage. In the summer of 1939 many municipal councils, including some as distant

from the coast as those in Dawson Creek and Nelson, protested "the incorporation of companies dealing in the export of raw materials from Canada, whose
shareholders are nationals of aggressor nations, but whose incorporation papers
indicate that they are purely Canadian." In fact, by 1939 Japan had withdrawn many
of its investments, having gained "little more than a headache" from them. Two
mining properties had been closed, there was no activity on several timber tracts,
and Japan's severe restrictions on capital exports made development unlikely.[19]

To conserve foreign exchange, in the summer of 1939 Japan began importing
only essential raw materials. In British Columbia, lumber sales fell, and almost
four hundred Japanese lumbermen lost their jobs. Japan's "great importance as a
market for British Columbia" declined, but sales of scrap iron, steel, copper, lead,
and zinc increased dramatically. The *Vancouver News-Herald* observed that "how
much of this raw material has been fashioned into bombs and war munitions
which have killed tens of thousands of innocent women and children including a
number of Canadians it is impossible to say, but the figures offer food for thought."[20]

When the idea of an embargo first appeared in 1937, it received more support
elsewhere in Canada than it did in British Columbia. By mid-February 1938 between eight and ten thousand individuals and church, labour, women's, and farmers' organizations throughout the country had sent messages to Ottawa demanding
an embargo on war materials to Japan. The provincial legislature, however, rejected the request of Dorothy Steeves, MLA (CCF, North Vancouver), that it ask
Ottawa to prohibit the export of war materials to aggressor nations. Nevertheless,
her explanation that British Columbia's natural resources "were being fashioned
in Japan into weapons that would be turned eventually against Canada" found
some sympathy. Bruce Hutchison speculated that "the metal in the bombs which
recently damaged British and United States ships may well have come out of the
mines of British Columbia."[21]

In the fall of 1938, the embargo campaign took off in British Columbia. In Victoria the trigger was a speech by Freda Utley on "The Crisis in the Orient" under
the auspices of the Democratic Book Club. Her "sensational book," *Japan's Feet of
Clay,* argued that "the driving force of Japanese Imperialism is primarily loot, and
an attempt to escape from her insoluble domestic problems; and secondarily the
search for raw materials." Three hundred and fifty people attended the meeting,
chaired by Nancy Hodges of the *Victoria Times,* and unanimously accepted Utley's
invitation to demand that Ottawa embargo the shipment of all war materials to
Japan.[22] The idea was contagious. Nanaimo City Council refused a licence to a
Vancouver dealer who wanted to ship scrap metal to Japan, and for more than a
week labour organizations and women picketed "the heap of potential war material." Utley's speeches in Vancouver attracted little attention, but a month later a

mass meeting, sponsored by an unlikely group, the Women's Christian Temperance Union, called for an embargo on scrap iron and metals. A few weeks later two United Church ministers and a Presbyterian clergyman joined CCF MPs and MLAs and about two hundred others in the Vancouver Embargo Council's parade to protest shipments of scrap metal to Japan and other fascist countries. Over the next few months similar embargo councils or clubs appeared in New Westminster, Nelson, and Prince Rupert. Union members, church groups, and Chinese residents were prominent, but such varied groups as the Canadian Daughters' League, parent-teacher associations, the Native Sons of Canada, and the University Women's Club supported the councils. The *Vancouver Sun* and the *Victoria Times* favoured an embargo to help China and protect "ourselves from harm." So too did R.W. Mayhew, Victoria's Liberal MP, who noted that something seemed "out of balance when we could spend so much money on defence ... and at the same time scrap iron and metal is leaving Canada." The cautious prime minister warned caucus that stopping "shipments meant economic sanctions, and economic sanctions meant military sanctions."[23] What was said in caucus affected only Liberals. In Parliament strange bedfellows Grant MacNeil (CCF, Vancouver North) and Howard C. Green (Conservative, Vancouver South) advocated an embargo.

By 1939 few questioned the wisdom of an embargo. People signed petitions, and some municipalities urged Ottawa to stop exports of war materials to aggressor

Thousands of dollars have been spent on guns to protect Vancouver harbor, yet under the very noses of the guns the export of scrap iron and war munitions to Japan continues.

"We Stand on Guard for Thee!" *B.C. Federationist*, 19 January 1939 nations. In Victoria a hundred Chinese picketers stopped trucks carrying scrap iron to city wharves, and six hundred people attended a mass protest sponsored by the Victoria Embargo Council. Though sympathetic the prime minister hesitated to act before learning what the United States would do. In the meantime the Japanese consul thanked him for a decline in criticism of Japan in Parliament and expressed hope that in the forthcoming election he could restrain attacks on Japan and its policies.[24]

Despite the European war and the quiet refusal of licences for the shipment of such commodities as scrap iron and nickel, Ottawa still issued special permits for exports of copper, lead, and zinc. Public concern rose as Japan threatened Hong Kong. The *Vancouver Province* conceded that Japan had been one of Canada's best customers but argued that "there can be no friendship between us and the nation that surreptitiously knifes the cause we have at heart and strikes at our Motherland when the Motherland is in dire extremity." The *Vancouver Sun* agreed, arguing that Canada "does not have to sell Japan the materials of war which are turned against our friends, which ultimately may be turned against us."[25] The announcement of the Rome-Berlin-Tokyo Axis in September 1940 and an American ban on shipments of scrap iron and other war materials to Japan increased support for an embargo. The Vancouver Board of Trade, Canadian Legion branches, the Victoria Assembly of the Native Sons of Canada, and the Vancouver Local Council of Women endorsed it. Longshoremen in Vancouver and New Westminster threatened not to load metals for export to Japan, and the Flying Column, an ex-servicemen's organization with 7,000 members, discussed the loading of copper concentrates onto Japanese ships. Vancouver's mayor, Dr. Lyle J. Telford, asked Minister of Defence J.L. Ralston to "allay public apprehension" over the pact by means of an embargo on scrap metal to Japan or any aggressor nation. In the legislature, the opposition leader, R.L. Maitland, condemned the export of war materials to Japan as "the quickest way to national suicide." While warning of "serious international repercussions" from any violence, the *Vancouver Province* favoured halting the trade, as did the liberal *Prince Rupert Daily News* and *Victoria Times*. Recognizing this strong opinion, the federal Cabinet set aside concerns for the economies of mining communities and halted copper exports except to nations in the British Empire or to the United States for use in Allied munitions contracts. Even if it meant closing "two big copper mines," the *Province* said, British Columbians would not object.[26]

Metals were not the only commodities in question. In the summer of 1940 Canada prohibited the export of Douglas fir sawlogs to non-British countries, a move that British Columbians also welcomed as a conservation measure. By then British Columbia had excellent lumber markets at home and in Britain. Claiming that companies subsidized by the Japanese government were shipping hemlock and balsam logs to Japan for manufacture into cellulose for use in explosives, the Duncan Chamber of Commerce called for a halt to "the traffic in war materials from our own shores which constitutes a serious menace to Canada and the Empire." That plea received wide support. Even the *Prince Rupert Evening Empire*, which had greeted the trade in hemlock logs in 1935, agreed with the Duncan resolution.[27]

When Japan protested the halt on exports, Prime Minister King explained that Canada was trying to avoid riots that might occur in Vancouver if ships left with metal, wheat, or wood for Japan. The Japanese minister in Ottawa did not think that the "risk of local disorders" was great. Ottawa, however, was so concerned about hostile opinion that before permitting the export of pulp logs already on order, King urged British Columbia MPs "to do what they could to discourage anti-Japanese demonstrations."[28] To prevent political capital being made of the situation and "in the interest of international accord," he asked Vancouver's mayor to inform city council and interested officials and organizations to say nothing about a shipment of wheat to Japan. The press censor arranged that editors would not comment; Norman A. Robertson of the Department of External Affairs persuaded Howard C. Green not to raise the issue in Parliament. For a time even Alderman Halford Wilson was silent. When a Saskatchewan Conservative mentioned wheat exports in Parliament, the press admitted that it had been censored. In Prince Rupert the *News* and the *Evening Empire* questioned the wisdom of shipping wheat "to enemies real or potential." As the international situation deteriorated in the summer of 1941, Canada followed British and American precedents, freezing Japanese assets in Canada and notifying Japan of its intention to terminate the Treaty of Commerce and Navigation. Provincial police checked property transfers to see whether any Japanese residents had "cheated" in anticipation of the freeze but did not expect any untoward findings. However, civil servants in Ottawa, meeting as the Special Committee on Measures to Be Taken in the Event of War with Japan, approved a warning to F.J. Hume, chairman of the Standing Committee on Orientals, that "any demonstration against the local Japanese population" in connection with overseas trade "would detract from the moral effect of governmental action." By then there was so little trade with Japan that the effects on the provincial economy were slight.[29]

Paralleling the embargo campaign, calls for boycotts of imports began in earnest late in 1937. Boycotts were an international phenomenon. British stevedores, for example, refused to unload cargo from Japan. As in the case of embargoes, not all British Columbians initially supported boycotts. The conservative *Victoria Colonist* suggested that they would not hasten the end of the conflict but might "strike the fires of lasting racial animosity." Similarly the liberally inclined *Vancouver Sun* warned of engendering hatred that would "work against Canadian goods and Japanese goodwill toward Canada long after the present business in China is past." The *Prince Rupert Daily News*, however, believed that "an effective boycott" would quickly weaken Japan's economy, stop its government's "mad career," and discourage other fascist powers from "similar anarchist terrorism in the hope of saving their racist regimes."[30]

Given that Canada's main imports from Japan were consumer products, individuals, especially women, could initiate boycotts. At first, with "the humanitarian idea" of "teaching Japan a lesson," women asked whether goods were made in Japan and, if so, refused to buy them. Members of such organizations as the South Fraser District Women's Institutes pledged not to buy Japanese goods. Vancouver shopkeepers claimed that the boycott did not seriously affect trade, but Victoria merchants noticed when the Local Council of Women encouraged boycotting stores selling Japanese goods. The *Victoria Times* was pleased that women were helping "to bring the aggressor to his senses." Japan's Chamber of Commerce and Industry asked the Victoria Chamber of Commerce to help stop a boycott "based on false reports and malicious propaganda." The Victoria chamber did nothing, pending investigation. The Canadian Japanese Association of Vancouver said that the boycott harmed members' business and prestige, even though many had never seen Japan, and noted the importance of trade in preserving international goodwill. The association's distribution of a pamphlet explaining the Sino-Japanese conflict from Japan's point of view, however, fuelled suspicions that the Canadian Japanese were loyal to Japan.[31]

Left wing groups such as the League Against War and Fascism, the China Aid Council, and the Vancouver Trades and Labour Council also promoted boycotts. In Vancouver in November 1937 twenty-six young people, thought to be associated with the Canadian League for Peace and Democracy, were imprisoned and fined for demonstrating against the landing of Japanese oranges, a traditional Christmas treat. They did not stop the landing of the fruit but struck a responsive chord. The demand for oranges in 1937 was about 40 percent less than it had been in 1936. The orange boycott waned in 1938 and 1939, but in 1940 local councils of women and women's institutes again urged members not to buy Japanese goods lest they help "an aggressor nation" by providing foreign exchange.[32]

The Vancouver Trades and Labour Council favoured the boycott, but some union members worried about its effects on the local Japanese. K. Iwashita of the Camp and Mill Workers Union failed to persuade the council not to intensify its boycott. Another delegate warned that refusing to deal with Japanese stores would "drive the Japanese out of business and put them on the labor market." Similarly a columnist for the *B.C. Lumber Worker* warned unionists not to allow "local fascist elements" to divert a boycott of "Made in Japan" products into anti-Oriental agitation, a "boycott of small stores owned by Japanese" merchants, and the dismissal of Japanese workers from their jobs. "The Japanese people in B.C., many of whom are Canadian citizens," noted the column, "are not engaged in conquering China." Nonetheless, the Trades and Labour Council supported boycotts of goods from Japan and other fascist countries. Sam Shearer, chairman of its Boycott Committee, spoke to a mass meeting in Vancouver sponsored by the Women's Christian

Temperance Union, which urged a boycott of silk stockings, oranges, toys, and other Japanese goods. Such moves were effective. Shearer reported that trade in Japanese merchandise was down 24 percent during the 1938 Christmas season. As the world situation deteriorated, the council intensified its activities. Early in 1939 it organized the Greater Vancouver Joint Boycott Committee and boycotted German and Italian goods. The new committee included representatives of nine trade unions and such left wing bodies as the Relief Project Workers' Union and The Housewives' League. Only one speaker at the founding meeting, Dr. W.G. Black of the League of Nations Society, reminded boycotters not to discriminate against Japanese residents, who "are our brethren." The boycotts had some effect. By September 1941, when the Canadian government banned imports from Japan except under special permit, trade had been at a "virtual standstill" for months.[33]

Antipathy to Japan often coloured feelings toward the local Japanese whereas sympathy for China brought white British Columbians into friendly contact with the local Chinese, helping them to differentiate between two Asian peoples. British Columbians followed the Sino-Japanese war with interest and generally took the side of China. In locales as separated as Cowichan from Cranbrook and Nanaimo from Kamloops, whites joined the Chinese in boycott and embargo campaigns, attended war films, concerts, and bazaars arranged by the local Chinese to raise money for war relief, contributed to relief funds through tag days and raffles, and listened to visiting Chinese speakers, such as Miss Loh Tsei. Even Vancouver's Alderman Halford Wilson, who was notorious for his anti-Asian campaigns, suggested to his friend Foon Sien that although aldermen were reluctant to authorize more tag days, they might approve a parade, such as one in Victoria during which costumed girls had solicited donations as the parade passed. The provincial censor refused to approve several Chinese propaganda films lest they stir up racial trouble, but white service clubs and other groups invited Chinese visitors, the local consul, and residents such as Dr. Joseph Hope, son of a Victoria businessman and head of the Chinese National Salvation Society, to speak on the war. It was not a one-way street. Chinese residents contributed to funds to relieve British bombing victims, raised money for the Red Cross, and bought war savings certificates and Victory Bonds. Those donations might have been even greater. W.S. Chow, who canvassed the Chinese in the Duncan area for subscriptions to war funds, reported, for example, that many of his countrymen said they would contribute $1,000 for each of their sons that Canada would admit as immigrants.[34] For the Chinese in British Columbia, the glimmers of toleration that had appeared in the early 1930s shone more brightly – but only a little. For Japanese Canadians, however, the Sino-Japanese war snuffed out their faint hopes of acceptance as Canadian citizens. Japan's aggression aroused suspicions that they might be loyal to their ancestral land and assist it in invading British Columbia.

News reports from Asia and the circulation of such books as *Japan Must Fight Britain* stimulated fears of war with Japan. In this volume Tota Ishimaru of the Imperial Japanese Navy argued that England and Japan must collide "because England is trying to hold on to what she has, while Japan must perforce expand." He hinted that even though Canada was "without defence" Japan was unlikely to attack her for fear of bringing in the United States. Nevertheless, notions of the "Yellow Peril" reappeared. In April 1936, articles in the *Vancouver Sun* and the *Vancouver Province* suggested that a "well-trained determined Japan, leading hordes of Chinese able to fight" might cause repercussions "at Vancouver's very doorstep."[35]

As the Sino-Japanese war expanded, so too did concerns about British Columbia's defences. Mayor G.G. McGeer claimed that Vancouver was Canada's "front seat of tomorrow's greatest theatre of conflict." H. Despard Twigg, a Conservative ex-MLA, suggested that British Columbia's coast was extremely vulnerable. The *Sun* reported a warning by Captain H.G. Scott, a one-time British intelligence officer and former Calgary magistrate, that war in Europe might affect the balance of power on the Pacific and on "the coast of North America including British Columbia." Residents of the vulnerable and totally undefended port of Prince Rupert also worried about the lack of defence.[36] In the November 1937 federal by-election in Victoria, defence was an issue. The nearby Esquimalt naval base meant that Victoria was relatively well defended, but the Canadian Legion, the Defence of Canada League, the Vancouver Island Provincial Association, the Native Sons of British Columbia, and the Conservative Association pointed to the presence of Japanese residents at strategic locations. Conservative candidate Bruce A. McKelvie warned that an amphibious bomber based on Japanese timber limits on Lake Cowichan could isolate the coast by bombing railway and highway bridges in the Fraser Canyon. He added that Japanese timber limits near Port McNeill commanded the channel between the island and the mainland, that sites on the Queen Charlotte Islands could dominate the railhead at Prince Rupert, and that large Japanese fishing vessels could cripple coastal freighters. He declared that British Columbia was practically defenceless. The ploy backfired. Liberals spread propaganda "among the women," suggesting that they and their families "would be killed and their property destroyed by shell fire" unless Liberals could continue their "extensive program of protection from land and air." Minister of National Defence Ian Mackenzie urged voters to send a Liberal to Ottawa in order to help him make clear "the necessity for the defensive measures that the government is taking." R.W. Mayhew, the Liberal, won.[37]

While at the League of Nations in 1936, King realized the possibility of war with Japan. Recognizing that the Pacific Coast was unprotected, he persuaded Parliament to increase the defence budget and to focus on the Pacific Coast. To the delight of coastal cities, which hoped to see local investment, the Liberals had already announced studies of specific defence installations. Thus, at the time of Archdeacon F.G. Scott's charges in November 1937, Mackenzie could claim that his department was well informed on all matters affecting the nation's safety. He told the Canadian Military Institute in Toronto of the concentration of defence spending on the Pacific Coast "for strategical reasons which you will appreciate." The King government announced that it would build fortifications on Yorke Island and in Esquimalt, Stanley Park, and Point Grey. After talking to President F.D. Roosevelt, King decided that Japan was "very dangerous" and persuaded Cabinet to place two additional destroyers on the Pacific Coast.[38]

Politically King's actions were timely. By the end of 1937 comments on inadequate defences against a possible Japanese attack were becoming common. "The present expenditures, particularly on the Pacific Coast," said Torchy Anderson in the *Vancouver Province,* "are putting a little flesh – very little – on the skeleton of Canada's defense scheme" as he speculated that enemy bombers could drop "their eggs on the heart of our shipping." Dr. Chang-Lok Chen, the Chinese consul general, told the Victoria Gyro Club that Canadians would "rue the day" they neglected their western defences. The *Toronto Star* claimed that American military officials feared that "an aggressor might use British Columbia coastal territory as a base of attack on the United States." Premier William Aberhart of Alberta cited biblical authority to suggest that "the movement of Japan and the yellow race was not in an easterly direction but in a westerly direction." And Bruce Hutchison, perhaps tongue in cheek, told of a householder seeking "permission to install a machine gun on his front lawn ... to repel the Japanese when they swarm over the Oak Bay golf links."[39]

Others drew on military experience. H.D.B. Ketchen, a retired general, warned of British Columbia becoming a "second Belgium." Colonel H.F. Letson told the Vancouver Board of Trade that a Japanese attack would likely be "hit and run" with long-range bombardment from raiding cruisers, submarines, or seaborne aircraft unless the enemy could establish bases on the coast. He spoke to the New Westminster Board of Trade on "the inadequacy of defence forces in Canada in face of the not remote possibility that Canada will become involved in war." Such stories, a military official in Victoria reported, caused "considerable hysteria among some people." The Victoria Chamber of Commerce, for example, wanted to revitalize the militia for home defence in the case of war between Britain and Japan. In the interior the *Penticton Herald* declared that any Japanese expeditionary force "would probably have to be as far inland as the Rockies before it would be possible to get an adequate vote for national defence through Parliament."[40]

Politicians took up the cry. Premier Pattullo admitted that he would not "be surprised if the Japanese attacked the coast." Howard C. Green told Parliament of Japanese residents in strategic locations and of at least twelve hundred fishing vessels that "might have to be dealt with in the event of hostilities with Japan." Warning that if Japan challenged the Commonwealth the Pacific Coast might "be faced with a raid," he claimed that nothing could prevent Japan "from indirectly acquiring land, timber rights or mineral rights" near fortifications or at strategic

"Contentment 3000 Miles Away," *Vancouver Province,* 28 February 1938

locations. Mackenzie told Vancouver businessmen in April 1938 that if Canada did "not drive off those who seek to use our bays and inlets ... as bases for attacks on another friendly power – somebody else will do it for us." Thus, he asserted, "Canada's defence policy must contemplate 'hit and run' raids by armed merchantmen or submarines each carrying one or more aircraft. Such raids could destroy trade, land parties to destroy important trade and industrial units, create general alarm and despondency." Given such statements, the apprehension of British Columbians was not surprising.[41]

Not all were so pessimistic. Both Victoria dailies thought that Japan would be preoccupied with China for some years. A few British Columbians were amused by Archdeacon Scott's claim that "many villages far inland in British Columbia are entirely Japanese" and by tales of Japanese constructing cement gun emplacements in the Kootenays. Without comment the *Nelson Daily News* reprinted a *Vancouver Sun* editorial suggesting that the Japanese did "some curious and unexplained things" but were "not quite so foolish as to carry out what rumor says they have done." In May 1938 the *Sun* claimed that the crisis in Asia had passed, that Canada was "as safe as any prosperous nation can be considered safe at any time," and that British Columbia should try to profit from Asian reconstruction. Victor W. Odlum, a retired brigadier general, told Vancouver Kinsmen that nature "amply defended" Canada against any military attack by Japan. The Department of National Defence agreed. At the outbreak of the European war, the Chiefs of Staff noted that tension between Britain and Japan was easing. Echoing such confidence, the *Vancouver Province* dismissed the need for blackout tests since "if anything at all is unlikely in this war, it is an enemy air raid over British Columbia."[42]

Nevertheless, Conservatives tried to make local defence an issue in the March 1940 federal election. Retired brigadier general and former MP J.A. Clark said that "against aeroplanes we have no anti-aircraft gun. Against a warship we have no means of seeing its approach from sunset to sunrise." In Victoria a spokesman for the Conservative candidate, Brigadier J. Sutherland Brown, claimed that western Canada, "particularly Victoria and Esquimalt, will be the frontline trenches of Canada if Japan and Russia do start something." The conservative *Prince Rupert Evening Empire* obliquely wondered why Prime Minister King had said that an attack on British Columbia's shores was possible yet had sent British Columbia troops to Ontario for training. Mackenzie and other Liberals, however, convinced voters that military and naval experts thought that British Columbia was among the six best-defended places in the world.[43]

Within weeks the rapidly deteriorating military situation in Europe and Japan's continued Asian adventures had revived defence concerns. Although the *Victoria Times* reported that "thanks to foresight at Ottawa, bank upon bank of heavy guns" were in place to control the entrance from the Pacific and despite the *Vancouver Sun*'s claim that there was no threat since "any war with Japan would be on the western side of the Pacific," these liberal newspapers were exceptions. More representative was the *Vancouver News-Herald*'s warning that if war spread to the Pacific, Canada would have to defend itself without any help from the British fleet. Varying an old theme, columnist Elmore Philpott suggested that "the white man got in [North America] because the red man was not able to keep him out" and concluded that "the so-called yellow man, in his millions, would similarly come if anything ever happened to the white man's navies." In Parliament Thomas Reid declared that British Columbia needed more defences, but his Liberal colleague from Victoria, R.W. Mayhew, told constituents that although he could not give details, "Pacific Coast defences were much better than most people realized."[44]

Increased defence co-operation with the United States following the Ogdensburg Agreement in August 1940 and a visit by the Permanent Joint Board on Defence only briefly reassured British Columbians. While Prince Rupert looked forward to becoming a base for Canadian and American forces, its *Daily News* discussed air-raid precautions and the possible evacuation of women and children. The conclusion of the Rome-Berlin-Tokyo Axis added to the sense of urgency. Fearing "Japanese and anti-Japanese activity" in British Columbia, the Department of National Defence planned to create a Pacific Command and to appoint "a Commanding Officer of reputation and ability" to help "establish local confidence and stability." The commissioner of the provincial police noted that Japanese residents were strategically "well placed from a military point of view" and that "local affiliations and obligations not withstanding, they look to the Japanese Consul for instruction and guidance in all matters pertaining to their welfare and political position." C.V. Stockwell, the officer commanding Military District No. 11 – that is, British Columbia – agreed. The RCMP was less alarmed, for its several Japanese secret agents had found no evidence of subversive activity among the local Japanese. Nevertheless, Assistant Commissioner R.R. Tait recommended discreetly investigating the fishing fleet since most fishermen had received "naval training in their youth in the Japanese Navy."[45]

Meanwhile, civilians fretted. A Toronto magazine publisher told an Association of Canadian Advertisers' convention that Vancouver taxi drivers talked of danger from Japanese residents and possible Japanese air attacks. Mayor Telford urgently asked Minister of Defence Ralston for reassurance about defence precautions and efforts to prevent sabotage. He opposed any unfair or discriminatory action against the Japanese but suggested interning those "suspected of disloyal activities." The fire chief warned of the city's vulnerability "to sabotage by fire from within." Nisei too speculated about the consequences of a war with Japan. Some feared riots against them but expected that the government would stop any such outbreaks.[46]

For the moment, the press was mainly concerned with the external threat. The *Nanaimo Free Press* feared that the linking of the Axis powers might extend the war to the Pacific. The *B.C. Financial News* thought that "Japan might conceivably plan and execute hit-and-run raids on the Pacific coast cities of Canada to cripple the Canadian war effort." Warning that the province was not "immune from attack," the *Victoria Colonist* questioned the lack of anti-aircraft defence, but it also demanded an investigation of Japanese control of certain industries and an increased presence of the RCMP in the province. In addition, complaining that authorities downplayed "potential dangers" in a situation that had "changed for the worse almost overnight," it pressed for a mobile Home Guard "to cope with any dissident element of the population here should Japan precipitate war."[47]

Prime Minister King had long agreed that the external threat existed. On 6 September 1939 he had recorded in his diary: "What may the Japanese not do in the

Orient! ... I have no doubt that we shall have some bombing of our coast and possibly some inland bombing as well." In June 1940 he informed Cabinet that the Tokyo legation recommended serious consideration of Pacific Coast defences. The Department of National Defence did not think that "an overwhelming attack" was probable but admitted that "Canadians cannot ignore the danger." Cabinet agreed to move some troops to British Columbia but, as far as possible, in a manner that would not "alarm the people." Subsequent British dispatches discounting the likelihood of a Japanese land attack because of distance and Japan's reluctance to draw in the United States did not impress King. Nor did the arguments of the Canadian Chiefs of Staff, who believed that Japan's interests were in the South Pacific rather than in Canada. King informed a worried Premier Pattullo that the Department of National Defence thought that in the case of war, British Columbia could expect, at most, "small scale 'hit and run' raids." After listing "precautionary measures" in place in British Columbia, King added a handwritten note: "P.S. Personal. This is an official estimate. Like you, I am far from believing that we can take anything for granted, *vis à vis* the Orient. W.L.M.K." King continued to believe that war with Japan was a real possibility and cited this concern to explain his refusal to attend a proposed Imperial Conference in the summer of 1941. In November 1941 he correctly predicted war with Japan within the month.[48]

The Chiefs of Staff still thought that any attack would comprise only "hit and run" raids, that a serious attack was a "remote" possibility, and that an invasion was "highly improbable." To calm the public, the military gave journalists tours of defence installations. The Chiefs of Staff were not very worried, but their officials in British Columbia were. Intelligence officers in Military District No. 11 concluded that Japan would "strike, without warning, when the time seems right for her to do so" and that the large Japanese population "would be a real threat to industry and commerce." Enthusiasm for promoting civil defence and for recruiting men made local military officials alarmists. Recruiting for his regiment, Major J. Campbell Dow told the Nanaimo Junior Chamber of Commerce that Canada needed to prepare for the Russian and Japanese threats to its Pacific Coast. The officer commanding the Vernon Military Training Centre asserted that Vernon lay in a direct line between the Queen Charlotte Islands and the smelter city of Trail, "the greatest military objective in western Canada." Retired brigadier J. Sutherland Brown told the Saanich Board of Trade of the strong possibility of "Japan striking at Canada ... in fast cruisers striking at Vancouver Island, where defences were not strong enough." Major General R.O. Alexander, the general officer overseeing Pacific Command, claimed that the army was "fully alive to the importance of West Coast defence in the event of Japan entering the war" and commended Attorney General Gordon Wismer for making British Columbians aware of the "danger of invasion on the Pacific seaboard."[49]

Wismer quoted Alexander's letter as he and Commissioner T.W.S. Parsons of the provincial police toured the province promoting "the movement for 'internal

security' to combat any fifth column" and seeking volunteers for the Air Raid Protection force. Wismer referred to between 25,000 and 30,000 Japanese and to thousands of other aliens in the province and repeatedly reminded audiences of "a very
real and grave danger." To generate attention he noted that "he had access to the
documents of the police and the secret service" and stressed local conditions. In
Port Alberni, for example, he said that it and Prince Rupert were likely to be "sub-
jected to enemy raids." Finally, in a province-wide radio broadcast, he warned of a
possible "armed attack" and spoke on "vital civil protection matters" in respect to
the danger from "the current Pacific crisis." Wismer's warnings aroused limited
interest, but the *Nanaimo Free Press* and the *Vancouver Sun* endorsed the need for
Air Raid Protection and a Home Guard. Home defence was a minor issue in the
October 1941 provincial election campaign, but some cabinet ministers listed it
among the government's achievements. In Victoria, Liberal and Conservative candidates referred to the province's vulnerability to Japanese attack; in Vancouver,
Wismer alleged that "Japanese-inspired interests" had financed a pamphlet attacking him on an unrelated matter "to discredit his work as head of the civilian protection branch."[50]

Despite claims that civil defence was in good order, as the crisis between the
United States and Japan deepened in late 1941, civilians became more fearful. After
Germany's invasion of Russia, a Prince Rupert editor referred to the narrowness
of the Bering Strait and warned that the city was "definitely a military objective."
The mayors of Vancouver and Victoria complained of inadequate air-raid precautions; the latter wondered about plans for evacuating the young and the aged. In
arguing for a fireboat, the *Vancouver Sun* quoted Walter N. Sage, a history professor at the University of British Columbia, as saying that Vancouver was "the best
aerial target" he knew of "next to the tinsel and wooden cities of Japan."[51]

By early December 1941, while less fearful of a direct attack, military authorities
had realized that "unless, at the eleventh hour, the saner influences in Japan can
prevail, war in the Pacific seems inevitable." They were preparing the public. Early
in November, Minister of National Defence (Air) C.G. Power referred to the "growing importance of West Coast defences" as he announced that Air Commodore
L.F. Stevenson would return from commanding the Royal Canadian Air Force overseas to take charge of Western Air Command with headquarters in Victoria. Grey
Turgeon, MP (Liberal, Cariboo), announced that two parts of a defence program,
construction of airports and repeater radio stations in the Cariboo, were complete
but that the third part, construction of the Alaska Highway, had been delayed
because Canada and the United States had not decided on its necessity. In praising
the film *War Clouds in the Pacific,* a part of the *Canada Carries On* series, the
Vancouver Sun remarked that "it is encouraging to see scenes of coastal forts, swift
patrol planes, powerful little corvettes. And further afield, the great U.S. naval base
at Pearl Harbor, Hawaii, the strong United States fleet and naval air force in action,
distant defences in the Philippines and at Hong Kong. All are vital links in the

chain that protects our coast – our homes, our existence." While worrying about war with Japan, civilian leaders in Ottawa, particularly Prime Minister King, feared that war might cause anti-Japanese riots in British Columbia coastal cities.[52] This fear was engendered by the revival in anti-Japanese sentiment that had developed in tandem with rumours of a Pacific war.

7

"Poisoned by Politics": The Danger Within, 1935-41

It is no easy problem that faces Canada on the Pacific Coast. On the contrary, the problem is difficult and complicated. It is full of international, racial, economic and social pitfalls. It is wrapped around by old prejudices. It is entangled with personal hurt and thwarted ambitions. It is poisoned by politics.

– VANCOUVER PROVINCE, 9 SEPTEMBER 1940

This comment by the *Vancouver Province* in September 1940 reflected a chronic situation that had recently become acute. In mid-January 1938 Captain MacGregor Macintosh, MLA (Conservative, the Islands),[1] asked a Conservative rally in Vancouver: "Can anyone walk through the environs of Powell Street, ... drive in the vicinity of Steveston or go out towards Mission, or up the coast to the fishing fleets and the herring salteries, and believe that this 'gentlemen's agreement' is being adhered to?" He reported having heard of forty Japanese nationals arriving on the Queen Charlotte Islands from a floating cannery and of new Japanese settlers on Mayne Island. The leading Japanese figure there, he declared, "is reported to be the brother of a Japanese admiral and they openly boast that in a few years they will completely own Mayne Island. There are more Japanese than white children in the Mayne Island school, the young men send to Japan for their wives, and Mayne Island-born Japanese boys are serving their time in the Japanese navy." He demanded a special census to reveal "the actual increase in the number of their nationals in the province." Japanese residents of Mayne Island denied "taking over" the island, proclaimed themselves "more Canadian than Japanese," and chastised Macintosh for not distinguishing between those Japanese residents born in Canada and those born in Japan. In fact, the Japanese, the backbone of the Mayne Island economy, lived in harmony with the island's white settlers. Even a white resident who was concerned about their "peaceful penetration," admitted that they were "very good neighbours."[2]

Macintosh used Mayne Island as an example. Accusing Mackenzie King of sacrificing the province "on the altar of Japanese appeasement," he proposed a survey to "paint the picture as it is – so that Eastern Canada will be forced to take action." In demanding an exclusionary law, Macintosh repeated hoary arguments about inassimilability, but his main concern was "intense" economic competition in fishing, small-fruit farming, and poultry raising and more recently in logging and mining. Macintosh advocated gradually repatriating all of British Columbia's Japanese residents "to Manchukuo or Mexico or elsewhere." He repeated his arguments to

Conservative associations, service clubs, and boards of trade, which often endorsed them and claimed to have "been deluged with letters," many with new information about illegal immigration. The assertions by the Japanese consul that Macintosh's claims were "absurd" and by a visiting Japanese scholar that illegal immigrants would "have to be swimming" did nothing to dispel the image that the Japanese in British Columbia were under Japan's control. What Macintosh's arguments against economic competition and immigration – legal or not – and suggestions of subversion lacked in originality, they made up for in timeliness.[3]

As the brutal Sino-Japanese war continued, reports of new Japanese investment in provincial natural resources, of Japanese aggression in the Far East, and of inadequate coastal defences shifted the "Oriental menace" from an argument against both the Chinese and the Japanese to one that focused almost exclusively on Japanese residents. Even Macintosh admitted that the Chinese problem was less serious. White British Columbians "pulled" for China against Japan, contributed to Chinese war relief funds, and expressed respect for the Chinese. Of course, the Chinese were a declining problem. The quietness of Chinese New Year's celebrations, though attributable to the emergence of the Chinese Republic, the Depression, and the war, and perhaps also to pressure to conform to Canadian customs, was mute testimony to a declining and aging population and to a smaller, younger generation that had "gone western" and paid "no attention to the old traditions." There had been no Chinese immigration for over a decade, and the birth rate was so low that Vancouver's medical health officer predicted that "the Chinese were due for racial extermination."[4]

In contrast, Japan's militarism fed rumours of fifth columnists and illegal immigrants. Whatever goodwill Japanese Canadians had cultivated had long since dissipated. Fearful white British Columbians blurred distinctions between Japanese Canadians and the militarists of Japan, proposed deporting them, and demonstrated such hostility toward the Japanese that federal officials feared violence, especially in Vancouver. Many discussions took place in political settings, but the issue was not a partisan one. While anti-Japanese arguments differed in detail and while some members of the Co-operative Commonwealth Federation (CCF) Party had sympathy for the Nisei, all major parties wanted to halt Japanese immigration. And, contrary to a long-standing belief that the "East" did not understand the "Oriental problem," many easterners shared British Columbians' views.[5]

Bruce Hutchison noted that "the average down-east member thinks of the Orientals here as he would think of the Eskimos – harmless, cheerful fellows that we British Columbians worry about far too much." That was such a common perception that the *New Westminster British Columbian* proposed shipping a thousand illegal Japanese immigrants to King's Saskatchewan constituency so that his government "might take some action to save the best province in the Dominion for white residents."[6] In fact, easterners were interested. British Columbia politicians found an audience in Toronto. Speaking to its Board of Trade, Senator J.W. de B. Farris (Liberal, Vancouver South) claimed that "no man from British Columbia" could "speak to a Canadian audience and gloss over the Oriental Question." A few weeks earlier Conservative MLA R.L. Maitland (Vancouver-Point Grey) had declared that the Japanese had "swamped British Columbia's fishermen and now they are swamping the fruit industry in the Fraser Valley and becoming heavy landowners." He suggested that Japan's recent attitude to the British Empire might "give a wider understanding" of British Columbia's position and strengthen its determination to stop the influx. In fact, since the early 1920s, *Maclean's* and other popular national magazines, including the *Canadian Magazine, Liberty,* and *Colliers,* had run articles on the subject; B.K. Sandwell, editor of *Saturday Night,* occasionally wrote essays sympathetic to Japanese Canadians. The Toronto-based Canadian Institute of International Affairs published C.H. Young and H.R.Y. Reid's *The Japanese Canadians* and C.J. Woodsworth's *Canada and the Orient,* but Japanophobes found little comfort in them. *La Presse* (Montreal) occasionally reported on the "Japanese Invasion" of British Columbia. Toronto papers were very interested – and in British Columbia, Toronto and Ottawa were "the East." In the summer of 1938 the *Toronto Star,* which had publicized Archdeacon F.G. Scott's allegations, sent R.J. Deachman, a Liberal MP and journalist, to the province. After hearing of "thousands of Japanese arriving from mysterious sources," he claimed that British Columbians' feelings were in many cases stimulated by the imagination. This was correct, but ten days earlier the *Toronto Globe and Mail* had said that Japanese residents were fleeing Canada just ahead of an investigation of illegal immigration. In November 1940 the *Winnipeg Free Press* published an article claiming that British Columbians' sentiments had become "unanimously anti-Jap," as Japan's "slimy tentacles ... reached half way round the world." In August 1941 the *Toronto Telegram* noted that British Columbia sensed "peril in case of war with Japan" and that any attack on the province would "be felt through the whole of Canada."[7]

Eastern Canadians increasingly shared British Columbians' antipathy to the Japanese. Howard C. Green, MP (Conservative, Vancouver South), believed that if party whips were withdrawn, MP A.W. Neill's Japanese exclusion bill would carry, "so strong is the feeling in Ottawa, in view of the events of the Sino-Japanese war." Neill (Independent, Comox-Alberni) claimed that the rejection of his proposal had awakened "the Canadian temper" to the realization that Japanese immigration was of interest to all of Canada. He had some evidence. The national conventions of two patriotic organizations, the Imperial Order of the Daughters of the Empire and the Canadian Daughters' League, endorsed ending the gentlemen's agreement with Japan. The Vancouver Junior Board of Trade listed fifteen reasons, most related to "Oriental infiltration" of economic life, for abrogating the agreement, predicting that the "infiltration" would threaten Quebec and Ontario industries, but only persuaded its national convention to urge the government "to restrain the immigration of unassimilable aliens" without specifically referring to the Japanese.[8]

The Conservatives were less tactful. After Herbert Anscomb, MLA (Victoria), warned that if Ottawa did not deal with the serious Japanese economic problem, British Columbians would be forced "to deal with it themselves," the national Conservative convention unanimously approved a resolution demanding "effective measures" to exclude Orientals by strictly enforcing "existing Statutes and Regulations and by taking the necessary steps to secure the rescission of the Lemieux Agreement." Some Conservatives went further. In the summer of 1939 George Drew, the party's Ontario leader, declared that since Japan had said that the British and Americans were "no longer welcome in the Orient," Canada should order the thousands of Japanese residents in British Columbia to leave the country. Not to be outdone, Ontario's Liberal premier, Mitchell Hepburn, recalled that as a member of Parliament he had voted against measures to strengthen defences but said that a visit to British Columbia had since convinced him that once Japan completed her "conquest of China" it would turn to Canada.[9]

While rumours of possible Japanese attacks from outside or potential subversion from within received attention, immigration was still an issue. Complaints about the presence of Asians, especially the Japanese, increased in the fall of 1937. Several British Columbia newspapers described an Ontario professor's suggestion to ease immigration barriers in order to encourage trade with Asia as "drivel" and "gibberish." The Fraser Valley Reeves Association, Thomas Reid, MP (Liberal, New Westminster), and some Conservative constituency associations demanded cancellation of the gentlemen's agreement. Following Scott's allegations, several Fraser Valley Canadian Legion branches called for "drastic steps" to curb Asian immigration and encroachment into the labour market and for the deportation of any Asian who had been "smuggled" in. Alderman Halford Wilson urged Vancouver City Council to ask Ottawa to admit fewer female Japanese immigrants since, he alleged, they came with an unofficial understanding from their government that the "Japanese race is to be propagated in British Columbia." He did not find a seconder, but anti-Japanese agitation was again underway.[10]

Then, early in 1938, Captain MacGregor Macintosh made his charges about illegal immigration. They seemed plausible. Though fewer than 150 Japanese immigrants had entered annually since the 1928 revision of the gentlemen's agreement, the Japanese population seemed larger than indicated both by numbers recorded in the 1931 census and by the natural increase reported by the registrar of vital statistics. Macintosh's arguments gained credibility when Dr. W.A. Carrothers of the Provincial Bureau of Economics and Statistics released "staggering" figures showing that over the previous fifteen years the Japanese population had increased

65 percent and that almost 6 percent of the babies born in the province had Japanese parents. Macintosh predicted that in another fifteen years there would be 70,000 Japanese residents in the province. The Native Sons of British Columbia and junior boards of trade called for investigations, but Macintosh and others, such as the Fraser Valley Farmers' Institutes, subsumed illegal immigration into a broader theme: "Is British Columbia to be a white man's country or not?"[11] In an editorial, published as an advertisement in other papers, the *Vancouver Sun* said that Macintosh was probably "right about Japanese being smuggled in." After observing their high birth rate and economic competition, it declared: "This is a white country ... We have pioneered and developed it and we are not going to permit [the] Japanese to sneak in here and steal the profits." It demanded an immediate census of the Japanese, arguing that illegal entrants could be saboteurs. The *Prince Rupert Evening Empire* favoured a census to check "trade penetration." If Macintosh's allegations were true, Bruce Hutchison wrote, "Japan won't need to invade this country from without. She will have done it quite successfully from within." Anti-Japanese feeling was so high that the *Sun* warned of "a definite possibility ... of violent reprisals" but still had some sympathy for the Nisei and counselled "a tolerant attitude" so that no Japanese child "is humiliated or made to feel sorrow through the sentiment which Canadians have been driven into by economic and social necessity." Similarly the *Vancouver Province* conceded that the Canadian-born were "more Canadian than Japanese."[12]

In the immediate wake of Macintosh's charges, Premier T.D. Pattullo tried to say nothing to "embarrass the national situation, as there may exist a situation of affairs not within my knowledge." Nevertheless, he warned Prime Minister King that British Columbians were "very much exercised" and that the Conservative opposition was "endeavouring to make political capital." Balancing diplomacy and partisan politics, his "carefully worded" press release admitted that Asians had to make a living but also noted that a "mistake" had been made in allowing them "into the country." "To allay public feeling," he asked Ottawa to make "a most careful survey ... to ascertain what number of Japs, if any, are here who should not be here." Apart from announcing that request, he said nothing.[13]

Not all British Columbians appreciated Pattullo's restraint. Reports that Ottawa was watching for alleged "subversive activities" and illegal immigrants and that military intelligence had matters under control did not end agitation. Several Liberal constituency associations, the Fraser Valley Farmers' Institutes, and the Congress of Canadian Organizations demanded banning Oriental immigration, denying citizenship to people of "unabsorbable race," deporting illegal immigrants, and legislating both "to preserve for the white race" jobs essential to national defence and to prevent the occupation of lands that might be "vital in times of national emergency." C.E. Hope warned of possible "serious civil disturbance." Some Vancouver residents formed a British Columbia Guard to combat "Japanese penetration into British Columbia." R.L. Maitland stressed the need to make "the East"

"A Badly Weakened Dyke," *Vancouver Province*, 22 February 1938

understand the province's Oriental problem and to deport any disloyal Japanese residents.[14]

In Ottawa, British Columbia MPs used tales of illegal immigrants and continuing grievances over economic competition to support Neill's Bill 38 to halt Japanese immigration through a language test, a variant on the old Natal Acts. However, Ian Mackenzie pointed to its flaws, including easy circumvention by "intending migrants" learning English or French, and it was easily defeated on a party vote. British Columbia's MPs, however, crossed party lines to endorse Neill's Bill 11, which sought to put Japanese immigration "on exactly the same plane" as Chinese immigration – that is, to achieve "total exclusion." In introducing the latter bill, Neill referred to the "enormous" Japanese birth rate and the impossibility of deporting those already present. He called on Parliament to plug "the loopholes that seem inevitably to be connected with any gentleman's agreement." Eight British Columbia MPs, representing all three parties, spoke in the bill's favour.[15]

Comments on Neill's bills brought out old arguments about the inassimilability of the Japanese. Whatever their merits, argued the *Vancouver Province*, they "are not assimilable. They form a separate and indigestible lump in our body politic, and that lump is already too large"; moreover they directly competed "on terms which are beyond the competition of our own people." The *Port Alberni West Coast Advocate* claimed that the Japanese "are so different it seems hopeless that we should ever amalgamate with them." For the *Vancouver News-Herald*, the only acceptable immigrants were "whites who can be assimilated." The *Trail Daily Times* referred to "problems presented by the penetration of people who cannot be assimilated, who are extremely prolific, whose standards of living are low and who can compete unfairly with local industries." The *Vancouver Sun* wondered, "What must be the feeling of the pioneers who carved our cities, our farms, and our factories and our fine stores out of a wilderness to find these people coming in and multiplying like rabbits to take possession of the fruits of their labors?" MacGregor Macintosh claimed that "in 200 years racial admixtures in the Far East had only produced the vices of both and the virtues of neither." He did not want British Columbia to "be a melting pot or experimental ground for such a theory" since, even if the Japanese became British subjects, they could never be Britons. Senator Farris bluntly said that "intermarriage between the peoples of these two totally different races" was impossible.[16] Even some who were sympathetic to Asians saw a problem. Professor Henry F. Angus of the University of British Columbia, a champion of civil rights for the Canadian-born, argued that intermarriage "would be deplorable at the present time, as our social atmosphere is not yet favorable to it." Interracial marriages were rare; the registrar of vital statistics often reported only one or two per year.[17]

As rumours circulated that the federal government would seek to modify the gentlemen's agreement but not pass an exclusion act out of respect for British interests in Japan, British Columbians let Ottawa know that they disagreed. After Alderman H.L. Corey suggested that "the permeation of [the] Japanese in B.C. might lead to the same situation as occurred when Germany annexed Austria," Vancouver City Council prepared a comprehensive protest to help British Columbia MPs lobby support. Citing inassimilability, low living standards, and unfair competition, and claiming that they were "already here in such numbers that they must be considered from the viewpoint of national defence," city council asked Parliament to legislate or "make such international agreements as will prevent a further influx of these people into our country." Council's request referred to all "Orientals" but was aimed at the Japanese.[18]

As Neill's bill for a Japanese exclusion law went through what he called "nearly four months of stormy passage and many vicissitudes," the provincial press complained that King (who feared diplomatic repercussions) had used parliamentary "tricks" to waylay it. In Parliament, Grey Turgeon, deputy Liberal whip, whose Cariboo constituency had few Japanese residents, explained that the government was investigating Asian immigration but should do nothing to impair the British Empire's relations with Japan.[19] The *Victoria Times* and the *Vancouver News-Herald* agreed that it might be well "to keep cool" at a time of international tension since the eighty Japanese immigrants who arrived annually could not "seriously be regarded as a vital invasion." Other papers chastised King's "super-safe political attitudes," "spineless inertia," and "squeamishness concerning Tokyo's delicate feelings" and accused him of being more concerned with the feelings of Japan than with those of British Columbia.[20]

Contrary to conventional wisdom in the province, Ottawa had listened. In adjourning the initial debate on exclusion, King announced that his government would do everything possible to prevent illegal entries. Officials in the Departments of Immigration and Fisheries and in the RCMP thought that "reports of large surreptitious entries were unfounded," arguing that natural increase explained population growth. Such an increase, O.D. Skelton of the Department of External Affairs wryly explained, "may be a serious factor, but ... cannot very materially be affected by changes in entry regulations." Officials rejected calls for a census or registration of all Asians but recommended creating an interdepartmental committee with general oversight of the matter and a subcommittee or board in Vancouver to investigate violations of the Immigration Act. Without enthusiasm they hoped that a formal inquiry, by demonstrating the absence of extensive illegal immigration, might mollify public opinion. H.L. Keenleyside of the Department of External Affairs cited Neill's comment about anti-Oriental feeling on the coast being more intense than in 1907 to suggest that riotous "incidents" could occur if Ottawa did not "appease local sentiment." Mackenzie also reported that the public was "greatly stirred." Fearing questions during a forthcoming visit to the coast, he sought permission to announce plans to negotiate immigration matters and to "make a thorough investigation of the entire Oriental problem in British Columbia."[21] In Vancouver he announced that a Board of Review, composed of representatives of the Departments of Immigration and External Affairs and the RCMP, would "receive representations from anyone having information about illegal entry." Illegal entrants, he promised, would be immediately deported, but legal residents were "entitled to certain rights." Referring to international conditions, he reminded British Columbians that "our greatest responsibility is to preserve peace in Canada." In welcoming the board, the *Vancouver Sun* predicted that its work would "result in an entirely different attitude in Ottawa." Other papers merely reported its establishment, but Mackenzie thought that the announcement had been made to "good effect."[22]

While Parliament debated Neill's exclusion bill, the Board of Review began investigating illegal immigration. To serve as chairman, the prime minister selected Keenleyside. A former British Columbian who had served in the Tokyo legation, he was familiar with the problem but was not associated with the immigration department, whose work was "in a measure under review." His task was to solicit confidential representations from anyone with information about illegal immigrants and, with the help of an RCMP "flying squad," to evaluate the evidence. Late in March in Vancouver he announced that a "fact-finding body" consisting of himself, Inspector G.W. Fish of the RCMP, and F.W. "Cyclone" Taylor, district superintendent of immigration in Vancouver, would hear evidence but only of specific cases. The board received so much publicity that Keenleyside thought that "few literate persons" did not know of it. MacGregor Macintosh was pleased with the board's attitude and urged anyone with knowledge of illegal immigrants to contact it. "In poker parlance," said the *Nanaimo Free Press*, "Ottawa has called our hand, it is now up to us to play it." Keenleyside was a co-operative dealer; "influencing public opinion in British Columbia" was one of his main purposes, but he insisted on secret hearings to ensure confidentiality and, probably, to avoid giving Japanophobes a platform.[23]

Keenleyside made a point of visiting provincial officials. Pattullo was pleased to have an investigation but expected little; he thought that "the only final solution" was the exclusion and "repatriation" of many Asians. Two weeks earlier he had told the Royal Commission on Dominion-Provincial Relations that "Oriental immigration into Canada should be prohibited upon grounds of ethnological differences of race, and as many Orientals as possible should be returned to the land from which they came." Pattullo almost apologized for introducing a subject that was beyond the commission's scope but explained that people were "very much wrought up; they look upon it as a menace." He presented statistics demonstrating an increase in the Japanese population, especially in the number of females, and a declining Chinese population. Possibly influenced by a pending by-election in Dewdney, a Fraser Valley constituency with a considerable Japanese population, Pattullo continued to speak on the "Oriental question." In a "fireside chat" radio talk, he stressed financial issues but said that "the time is long past for an effective curb on the constant increase of Japanese whose Asiatic standards are disrupting our business and social structure." In a Victoria speech, he explained that the Anglo-Japanese Treaty had once restrained feelings but that Japan's current "aggressive and voracious" interests were alarming. He repeated the familiar refrain that as many Japanese as wished to leave should be repatriated. When the legislature next met, in the fall of 1938, it commended the government for making representations to Ottawa opposing Chinese and Japanese immigration.[24] Neither Pattullo nor Attorney General Gordon Wismer had useful information for Keenleyside, but Wismer was "well supplied with more-or-less lurid stories of the penetration of the Province by [the] Japanese." Senior civil servants disagreed. Dr. H.M. Cassidy, director of social welfare, "denounced as absurd most of the wild stories floating around the Province"; W.A. Carrothers claimed that there were too few illegal entrants "to be significant"; and Colonel J.H. McMullin said that the provincial police had checked many reports of spies but had found no "evidence of improper activities."[25]

The Board of Review also visited constituencies "represented by a strong anti-Oriental member of the House of Commons" and any community where "the Oriental problem is very present to the white inhabitants" in order to "prove the bona fides of the Government's effort to obtain such evidence." Keenleyside found that "hostility towards the Japanese" was "very largely centred in the Lower Fraser Valley, Vancouver and some parts of Vancouver Island." In other parts of the province – including, to his surprise, the north coast – residents were "comparatively uninterested and unexcited." Indeed, C.E. Hope argued that British Columbians outside Vancouver and coastal areas were not "so sure that the present Oriental situation is a real menace" and urged Keenleyside to give more weight to evidence from people in regular contact with the situation. Many British Columbians used the board to draw attention to economic grievances that were often also directed at the Chinese and that had little to do with illegal entries. Kamloops City Council gave information about the size of the city's Asian population, the city's businesses, and its schools; the Kelowna junior and senior boards of trade merely described economic difficulties created by all foreigners. In Vancouver the grocers' division of the Retail Merchants Association (RMA) complained of unfair competition from Asians who violated minimum wage laws and early closing bylaws; Aldermen Wilson and H.J. DeGraves received considerable publicity, as several newspapers printed extensive extracts from their detailed brief on Asian competition.[26]

The board visited more than twenty centres. Its presence temporarily halted "wild assertions" about illegal immigrants and demonstrated Ottawa's desire to solve the problem. Finding little evidence of illegal immigrants, the interim report concluded that most of the "politicians, editorial writers and others who had been most voluble in spreading the impression that Orientals were entering Canada illegally in large numbers" had no "first- or even second-hand knowledge of the facts." It shrewdly observed that "a prejudice may be just as important as an economic fact but it is much more difficult to evaluate." As an additional means of trying to convince British Columbians that there was no problem, Keenleyside recommended that an RCMP "flying squad" and Flight Lieutenant R.M. Wynd, acting as an interpreter,[27] intensively examine certain small and isolated but representative Japanese communities. Although this sampling did not uncover "extensive evidence" of illegal entrants, Keenleyside believed that "the situation so luridly described (without concrete details) by the anti-Oriental elements in the province does not now exist." During the summer, the police quietly made inquiries; Keenleyside revisited the province and invited politicians to submit additional information. The board's interim report indicated that since 1931 the RCMP had found forty-three illegal Japanese immigrants but that the Department of Immigration had allowed them to stay. The department was concerned; it could find only twenty-one such cases, and these, it explained, had not been deported because their Canadian wives and children would have become public charges. The board's final report, completed in October, paid particular attention to the rumour that most illegal entrants came via the Queen Charlotte Islands. It discovered that "the nearer they came to the Islands, local residents put the less credence on a Japanese influx through that channel. Most stories about the Islands emanated from people who live in Vancouver or Victoria and know little about actual conditions in the north." The board concluded that the number of recent immigrants was "very small" and that illegal immigrants numbered "not greatly in excess of 100." Despite "unpleasant connotations," Keenleyside thought that registering all Japanese residents was "the least of the alternative evils." He naively believed that uncovering illegal immigrants would "so appease popular opinion" that British Columbia would begin to "treat its Oriental population in a rational and decent manner." Once the board realized that the government was not seeking a general solution to the Japanese problem, its published report merely recommended continued efforts to apprehend illegal entrants and improved procedures for handling ships at ports of entry. These measures were not implemented, and stories of illegal immigrants persisted.[28]

Most of the scant attention the report received was negative and mainly from Vancouver. The *Vancouver Sun* said that the gentlemen's agreement was "only kept on a gentlemanly basis by erecting what practically amounts to a barbed wire fence to keep hordes of would-be violators out." The *Vancouver Province* attacked the report for not touching the "essential problem": the need for "rigid" Oriental exclusion. Yet, while complaining of the "increasingly irritating intrusion" of an "inherently alien" population that could "not be assimilated," it admitted that the Asian community was "composed of people mainly who are born Canadians" and who "must be accorded the tolerance of our institutions and the protection of our laws."[29]

That a significant portion of Canada's Asian population was Canadian-born was not news to the interdepartmental committee of civil servants drawn from the Departments of Immigration, Justice, National Defence, Labour, Fisheries, External Affairs, and the Dominion Bureau of Statistics, which was studying "various aspects of the presence in Canada of Asiatics." The committee met irregularly but asked the Department of Labour to investigate the success of Asians "in competing economically with white residents." The study was gravely flawed. Because its western representative was busy, the department hired Hugh Thornley to investigate. Given his roles in the Asiatic Exclusion League and the Oriental Exclusion Association and given that one of his major sources was a brief prepared by the White Canada Research Committee, his conclusion was predictable: "The present and prospective infiltration of Oriental labour" was cause for concern. In reporting his findings, the committee cautiously observed that whatever their "justice or accuracy ... they are widely and strongly held throughout British Columbia." In a report designed for internal use, the interdepartmental committee recognized that the "Oriental Problem" was two-fold: (1) an existing population that was "mainly a provincial problem" and (2) future immigration. Because it believed that even slight immigration was "a strong factor in producing the psychological condition that is prevalent in British Columbia," it advised that *"an essential factor in any final solution"* was providing *"for the definite discontinuance of the admission of Orientals to Canada as immigrants."* The committee proposed reciprocal agreements with China and Japan that would forbid Canadians to take up permanent residence there while prohibiting Chinese and Japanese nationals from taking up permanent residence in Canada and that would require the receiving country's approval of those applying for temporary residence for business, professional, educational, or tourism purposes. Such an arrangement, the committee believed, would "save face," deny the Japanese in Canada the right to bring in wives and children, satisfy British Columbia, and "by removing the fear of continued immigration ... allow more time and improve the atmosphere" for solving the problem of those Asians already in Canada.[30]

The idea of a reciprocal arrangement appears to have originated with Keenleyside. While he was at the Tokyo legation in 1933, he drafted a treaty whereby China and Canada would admit to the other's country only individuals who were entering for temporary and specified purposes. In 1935 he revived the plan, suggesting that it could reconcile the political necessities in British Columbia of retaining the ban on permanent immigration and of relieving an irritant to China. The idea might have been acceptable in British Columbia. On several occasions, Hope's White Canada Research Committee suggested a remarkably similar "Treaty of Amity with China (not Trade Treaty) whereby each country acknowledged the complete equality the one with the other, politically, culturally, and in every other way." Under Hope's scheme, Chinese entrants "would be of a decidedly superior class" since the occupations that both they and Canadians might enter, would be specified. Hope said that his committee had once proposed the idea to Sir Herbert Marler, the Canadian minister in Japan. In 1938 Skelton, concerned with the difficulty of defending "more favourable treatment to Japanese than to Chinese immigrants," suggested negotiating "a reciprocal plan" with both China and Japan. Thinking that such agreements "would lead practically to no emigration at all" from China and Japan to Canada and vice versa, the prime minister instructed Skelton to prepare an agreement to exclude certain classes. However, given the situation in Asia, the time was inopportune.[31]

China might have seen such an agreement as a concession; Japan did not. The day before the final vote on Neill's exclusionary bill, King hinted to Baron Tomii, the new Japanese minister in Ottawa, that a reciprocal arrangement might "get rid of agitation on the Pacific Coast." King hoped that the "close vote" of 79 to 42 (including most British Columbia members) against Neill's bill would demonstrate his difficulties to Japan and enable him to reconcile British Columbia opinion without offending Japan with an exclusionary law. King tried to secure British assistance in dealing with Japan, but the Dominions secretary, ironically more conscious of Dominion status than was King, said that Canada could deal with the matter itself; nevertheless, both he and the British ambassador in Tokyo cautioned King against any measure that would whip up nationalists in Japan or lead to retaliation. Cabinet agreed. King also spoke to Neill and to the Conservative leader, Robert J. Manion, about not raising questions that would complicate relations between any part of the British Empire and Japan. Thus, apart from passing comments by Thomas Reid and Howard C. Green, Parliament was silent on Japanese immigration.[32]

British Columbians were also learning diplomatic subtleties. The Associated Boards of Trade of Vancouver Island, the British Columbia Command of the Canadian Legion, and the provincial Liberal convention did not refer specifically to the Japanese but instead used the generic phrase "Oriental exclusion." When Pattullo visited King in late September 1938, he "respectfully but emphatically" urged "the necessity of finding some means of stopping the immigration of Orientals." Everyone knew that "Oriental" meant Japanese. At provincial and national conventions, Conservatives called for the "exclusion of Orientals" while specifically demanding "the rescission of the Lemieux Agreement." In the legislature, Macintosh complained of Ottawa's failure to curb "the continued increase of the Oriental population" and called for abrogation of the gentlemen's agreement. Intimating "that his friend Prime Minister Mackenzie King was doing a great deal about the question, but [that] this was a shush, shush subject, not fit for the ears of the House in view of present international complications," Pattullo forestalled debate, using his majority to uphold the Speaker's ruling that the bill was out of order because the word "Oriental" reflected on Japan, a friendly power. When Macintosh urged further representations, D.W. Strachan, a Liberal, amended the resolution to say that it was "necessary for the social and economic welfare of our people that our population shall be ethnologically homogeneous." Earlier in the session a Liberal backbencher, Captain C.R. Bull (South Okanagan), had decried the harassment of the Japanese and the demands for their exclusion. He explained that the Okanagan's Japanese residents were law-abiding, good co-operators, and the parents of well-dressed, well-mannered children. Recalling that Japan had been an ally in the Great War, he argued that it was "folly to antagonize a nation we could not defend ourselves against without assistance." Only Bull praised the Japanese, but Pattullo pointed out the need to deal "sensibly" with the Japanese who were here and to maintain "amicable relations" with the federal government. The motion to keep the population "ethnologically homogeneous" passed without a recorded vote.[33]

A conciliatory Pattullo accepted King's warning that a demand for "total exclusion" "might embarrass" Anglo-Japanese relations. Mackenzie seems to have taken similar advice but warned that without "very definite" action on Japanese immigration, Liberal candidates in British Columbia would "not even have a fighting chance" in the next federal election. It was already an issue. Green promised that the "first duty" of a Conservative government would be to abrogate the gentlemen's agreement and exclude Japanese immigrants. Although the CCF's position was less blatantly stated and although it proposed to put the Japanese on "the same basis of rights and obligations as people of other nationalities" and to enforce wage and factory laws, it promised much the same as the Conservatives in respect to immigration, opposing all immigration until economic conditions improved.[34]

Fortunately for the Liberals, the European war almost completely overshadowed Japanese matters in the quiet federal election of March 1940. When candidates referred to the Japanese, they did so only in passing. Neill listed among his accomplishments: reducing their number in the fisheries, fighting to end their immigration, and, unlike his CCF opponent, opposing their enfranchisement. The federal Conservative leader, Robert J. Manion, promised to "abrogate the gentlemen's agreement." Green attacked King for not halting immigration and chastised Mackenzie and G.G. McGeer (Liberal, Vancouver-Burrard) for absenting themselves from related votes. In New Westminster, the Conservative candidate, T.R. Selkirk, called for abrogating "the gentlemen's agreement to prevent the penetration of Orientals into Coast industries." He was particularly concerned with the fisheries, but Thomas Reid, the incumbent Liberal, used a strong record on the issue in his successful quest for re-election. G.F. Cameron, the Conservative in Skeena, declared that Manion "was pledged to abrogate the present treaty" in order to keep Orientals out but could not overcome the popularity of the Liberal incumbent, Olof Hanson.[35] British Columbia's parliamentary representation changed little as a result of the election.

As the limited debate in the 1940 election indicated, animosity toward the Japanese often related directly to their place in local economies, but that was not always so. In Prince Rupert the modus vivendi between white and Japanese fishermen generally continued. The Chamber of Commerce had no real complaints about the Japanese who were permanent residents of the district obtaining fishing licences. In the words of the *Prince Rupert Daily News,* "the fish are a northern product and northern people should have a chance to earn a living here." The Northern British Columbia Resident Fishermen's Association, an organization of the resident Japanese, urged members to spend their money in the district in order to create "a better understanding between the Japanese residents in British Columbia and the Canadian people."[36]

On Vancouver Island, however, rumours of war gave ammunition to those wanting to reduce Japanese involvement in the dry-salt fishery. The Japanese had started the industry, dominated its ownership, and sold salmon, a holiday luxury, in Japan and herring in both Japan and China. The Sino-Japanese war hurt markets in both nations. Using this concern as an excuse, the general manager of BC Packers, a major fishing company, said that it was time to develop "a white Canadian fishing population employed by Canadian industries," especially since the herring fishery was in primary defence areas. He argued that the policy would ensure that Canadians retained "an intimate knowledge of the region" and would "lay an essential foundation for naval strength." The province, which had jurisdiction over salteries and canneries, increased the required proportion of white or Native Indian employees from 50 to 60 percent. As the European war began, it ceased granting salmon saltery licences because of uncertain markets and a desire to put all salmon that could be caught "into cans for use by the Empire and its Allies during the present war period."[37]

In the much more important Fraser River salmon fishery, Thomas Reid continued to champion white fishermen. During intense anti-Japanese agitation early in 1938, he proposed reviving the policy of reducing the number of licences issued to Japanese fishermen until the industry was "in the hands of white Canadian fishermen." He noted that in 1927 Japanese residents had held only 1,990 fishing licences but that in 1937 they had held 2,608. What he did not say was that the total number of licences had risen; the proportion held by the Japanese had fallen from 38.9 percent in 1922 to 15.7 percent in 1937 and would fall to 12 percent in 1940. Moreover, only whites and Native Indians were licensed for the important salmon purse-seine fishery. Nevertheless, Reid suggested that Japanese fishermen had exhausted Japan's waters, were present as part of a "studied policy," and were "truly Japanese first." He reiterated old concerns about noncompetitive standards of living, the use of assistants with boat pullers' licences to fish twenty-four hours per day, and the intimidation of white fishermen. Intimidation was a popular cry. The *Nanaimo Free Press* compared the situation "with Capone's gangster reign in Chicago in the beer running days of prohibition." The *Vancouver Sun* concluded that Reid had demonstrated how the fishing industry had "fallen entirely into the hands of shack-dwelling Japanese against whom white men, striving like good citizens to build and maintain decent homes, cannot possibly compete." The British Columbia Fishermen's Protective Association, which took credit for asking Reid to raise the issue, endorsed his motion. Reid did not press it because the federal government agreed to eliminate boat pullers' licences, a class of licence held mainly by Japanese fishermen. This measure affected about only 400 individuals but increased welfare rolls in several municipalities. The Japanese United Church protested the reductions, but the Vancouver presbytery of the United Church, influenced by an argument that the Japanese crowded white men out of fishing grounds, expressed opposition to racial discrimination only if it was directed against Canadian citizens.[38]

The demand for more restrictions on the Japanese continued. Reporters suggested that both Liberal and Conservative MLAs welcomed Reid's ideas, a claim strengthened when Macintosh included fisheries in a catalogue of industries in which the Japanese had made inroads. R.W. Bruhn (Conservative, Salmon Arm) regretted that the federal government had not safeguarded the fishing industry for Canadians. Outside the legislature, George Miller, secretary of the Salmon Purse Seiners' Union, charged that a Japanese fascist organization intimidated local Japanese fishermen, that Japanese capital increasingly penetrated the industry, and that many fishermen were naval spies. Such complaints were not confined to union members; privately, H.R. MacMillan, who had extensive investments in the fisheries, accused the Japanese of using force and economic methods to drive "white fishermen out of certain fishing areas theoretically open to all citizens." A mass meeting in Vancouver sponsored by the Salmon Purse Seiners' Union and the Pacific Coast Fishermen's Union called for a halt to "unfair" Japanese practices, but the immediate concern was the unwillingness of the Japanese to co-operate in raising fish prices and living standards. Some members of the Pacific Coast Fishermen's Union, however, joined the Japanese in refusing to fish until canners paid more for blueback salmon although its president saw little hope of working harmoniously with older Japanese fishermen or with the original Japanese Fishermen's Union under its current leadership. He did advocate working with the Canadian-born Japanese.[39]

Part of the problem with the older Japanese was doubt about their loyalty. For this reason the North Arm local of the Pacific Coast Fishermen's Union endorsed Alderman Wilson's efforts to deny licences to Japanese residents who returned to Japan at the end of each fishing season. Managers of MacMillan's up-coast canneries claimed that three-quarters of their fishermen went home to Japan every year, but the Department of Immigration reported that between October 1939 and March 1940 only 167 adult male British subjects had gone to Japan and that not all of them were fishermen. Wilson later urged the Department of External Affairs to confine Japanese-owned fishing vessels to port pending clarification of the international situation because they had recently been refitted and had many opportunities to do damage. The suggestion was redundant. The Department of National Defence already had plans for the "rapid rounding up" of Japanese-owned vessels in case of hostilities. It advised military personnel to keep vessels "covered by machine guns and small arms until the capture is completed and this situation well in hand" and noted that the anti-Japanese Kyoquot Fishermen's Association had promised "every assistance."[40] Military and economic goals had overlapped.

In the initial debate on Japanese fishing licences, Reid correctly anticipated the old argument that those Japanese residents forced out of fishing would enter other industries. Les Gilmore, chairman of the British Columbia Coast Vegetable Marketing Board, blamed Japanese penetration of farming on the fishing quota. Reid denied this claim but contended that Japan helped its people to acquire land. The Japanese dominated the growing of small fruits, such as strawberries, in the Fraser

Valley. Their use of "mass production methods through labor hired at a scale of living much below that which we desire for our own people," said the *Vancouver Sun*, had given them "virtual control" of the industry. It called for an investigation of the Oriental penetration "in wholesale masses" into industries "that should be reserved for Canadians." The reality was that few Fraser Valley farmers perceived the Japanese as a threat. Even in Maple Ridge, where some white growers complained of unfair competition, Japanese and white growers generally co-operated in marketing schemes.[41]

Similarly, organized labour was not fully convinced of Reid's arguments. When the Vancouver and District Trades and Labour Council met several fishermen's associations, its secretary, Percy Bengough, recounted how as an organizer of the Asiatic Exclusion League in 1921 he had found that "business people and farmers were willing to exclude the Orientals from business competition and land ownership" but not from the labour market. Thus, he explained, trade unions had organized the Japanese and now had two Japanese unions as members. The *B.C. Federationist* suggested that Reid had copied the methods of Hitler and Duplessis in order to gain "personal political capital." Though its president believed that Asians must be accepted "as citizens" and their standards raised, the Trades and Labour Council executive was reluctant to deal with such a controversial matter. After hearing a delegate declare that "racial hysteria only leads to one thing – Fascism" and another assert that the government had allowed "vested interests" to use Orientals, a later meeting almost unanimously reaffirmed its opposition "to the anti-Oriental and racial prejudices being stirred up by the daily press."[42]

Almost all of the prejudice was directed at the Japanese. The Chinese in the province, though declining in number, were increasingly being assimilated into Canadian society. Some were very well-established Canadians. When Mr. and Mrs. Alexander Cumyow of Vancouver celebrated their golden wedding anniversary in 1938, the *Vancouver Province* observed that they were "completely westernized and always have been." Mrs. Cumyow was born in China, but her seventy-nine-year-old husband, a native of British Columbia, had never been there. A journalist noted that the Chinese in Vancouver announced births, deaths, and marriages in the English language daily newspapers and that, whereas the subjects of obituaries had traditional Chinese names, the principles in wedding and birth notices had Western first names.[43]

Nevertheless, old complaints against the Chinese persisted, particularly in Vancouver, where they were linked with political debates over the efficiency of the police department in dealing with alleged corruption and immorality in Chinatown. After being relatively dormant for several years, the issue of the police's apparent

inability to suppress Chinese gambling "within a stone's throw of City Hall" became a political football in the mid-1930s. Alderman Twiss didn't "give a hang
about [the] Chinese gambling among themselves" but complained of their "dealing with white men and getting [the latter's] shekels." Mayor L.D. Taylor thought
that the police should devote their attention to crimes larger than Chinese lotteries; the *Vancouver Sun* criticized city council for "belaboring the police for failing
to stage heroic raids every time a few Chinamen squat around a table on East
Pender Street." In the legislature G.G. McGeer attacked the inadequacies of the
police and charged that Chinese lotteries and bookmaking were "two of the principal rackets, with white men patronizing the former." In December 1934 McGeer
ran successfully for mayor, promising among other things "a crimeless city in three
months." As mayor, he fired the police chief and suspended a number of officers.
Hearings on the suspensions confirmed that Chinese lotteries operated openly.
Shortly before the 1935 municipal election, the Police Commission planned a new
drive against lotteries that permeated "the poorer classes of the community, including whites, Negroes and [the] Chinese." McGeer claimed that he had received
as many commendations from the Chinese for "stamping that evil out" as from
"my own people" and that under a new chief the police had closed all twenty-four
gambling dens and twenty-two lottery houses operated by the Chinese for white
patrons. Even after McGeer retired, the police kept an eye on the gambling houses.
In March 1938 they ordered all Chinatown gambling houses, including one allegedly catering exclusively to female white poker players, to close or face "continuous prosecution." The Chinese community resented that white gambling clubs
operated legally and that they had few other diversions. War in China, poor economic conditions, and the dying off or retirement of "the old Country Chinamen"
helped the police. Canadian-born Chinese residents, the police ascertained, did
not gamble to any extent. Noting that many of the "found-ins" were "aged and
decrepit Chinamen" who did not participate in the games but merely took shelter
on the premises, the police did not charge them.[44]

Gambling was not the only alleged Chinese contribution to white immorality.
Late in 1935 Alderman Wilson told city council that something must be done about
the employment of white girls in Chinatown restaurants, where they committed
such immoral actions as "sitting on Chinamen's knees." Although Vancouver had
396 restaurants, or about twice as many as required, Wilson stressed morality, not
competition. Paradoxically his actions harmed white women more than they did
Chinese restaurateurs. The police, who had discretion under the Protection of
Women and Girls Law, ordered eight Chinese café proprietors to discharge their
white female help, a total of twenty-eight women. The dismissed women protested
that their employers had treated them well and that they had no other jobs. Mayor
G.C. Miller, the police chief, and Wilson devised a compromise that allowed employers to retain white women provided they replaced any who left with Chinese

help. The system broke down; some women gave false names to allow for substitutions, and restaurateurs, who believed the agreement referred to numbers rather than to specific individuals, treated it "as a joke."[45]

Frustrated, W.W. Foster, who had become police chief with a mandate to rid the city of commercialized vice, reported that there was no immorality in the restaurants but that the girls, most of whom were "quite young and without experience," made contact with Chinese customers, became "intimate" with them, and often lived "with individual Chinamen." He cited as a "flagrant" example W. Lee, who met two teenaged girls employed in a Chinese café, persuaded them to live with him, and prostituted them to other Chinese men. Curiously, no one cited a recent divorce case in which a white father gained custody of his three-year-old child whose mother was "Miss Astrid," an eighteen-year-old white waitress. The co-respondent, a "bespectacled and suave" married Chinese man, denied any misconduct but admitted driving the young woman "in his shiny yellow roadster, entertaining her at dinner in Chinese restaurants, and taking her home several times after such entertainment."[46]

Although the employment of white women in Chinatown restaurants caused little excitement generally, in 1937 the city cancelled the licences of three cafés whose operators had not complied with the law. Again the affected women reiterated that their employers treated them well. One girl condemned the "fussy old bridge-playing gossips who are self-appointed directors of morals for the girls in Chinatown." Lum Fun Ting, a businessman, agreed that the problem arose from such meddlers and wondered why the law was applied only in Chinatown while white women could work in uptown Oriental cafés. Nor, for that matter, as the women's lawyer pointed out, was the law applied to Japanese restaurants. As a goodwill gesture, the affected restaurateurs agreed to dismiss white waitresses. Over the protests of Chief Foster, city council did not revoke the licences of two restaurants that had broken the agreement in order to help former employees who lacked jobs and money, but most Chinatown restaurateurs honoured the agreement. When the licence inspector cancelled the licence of the C.K. Chop Suey Parlor in the summer of 1938 because it employed three white girls as waitresses, Foon Sien of the Chinese Benevolent Association complained that the city notified white men of violations before intervening but cancelled Chinese licences without warning. "We should at least be given a Chinaman's chance," he quipped. In fact, about six weeks later, council restored the licence of the C.K. Chop Suey Parlor. The *Vancouver Sun*, however, suggested that the majority of Vancouver citizens did not want Orientals to employ white women and that the Chinese community should "submit to this overwhelming public opinion and conform to the wishes and rulings of the city in which it lives." When, in March 1939, former waitresses had no work and asked city council to reconsider, council accepted Chief Foster's advice to maintain the ban on the grounds that it was "almost impossible" for such employees not to fall "victims to some form of immoral life." As evidence he cited the statement of a former waitress who, after explaining that a Chinese patron of a Chinese restaurant had lured her into prostitution with whiskey and cash, concluded that "had I not gone to work in a Chinatown café I would not be a prostitute now."[47]

By then Alderman Wilson had turned his attention to Asians in business generally. Late in 1936 the chairman of the grocers' section of the RMA had urged members to lobby aldermen and MLAs to require Asians to obey laws applying to all merchants. Wilson was receptive; he had grown up in Vancouver in an anti-Asian tradition, and his father, an Anglican clergyman, had spoken at the infamous Asiatic Exclusion League rally in 1907.[48] Although his first public complaint was against Japanese dry cleaners who cut prices, worked at all hours, and employed children, he soon attacked the competition of all Asian merchants, particularly after widespread concern about both illegal immigration and Japanese military attacks made fighting Asian competition timely.[49]

After gathering information about American measures to control Oriental business activities, Wilson proposed that city council deny new business licences to Asians wanting to set up shops outside the "Oriental areas," or, as the *B.C. Federationist* wryly suggested, that council set up "a sort of Ghetto ... for all the little Japanese shopkeepers." Wilson charged that backed by a "combine," Japanese shopkeepers were "making such serious inroads" into retailing that they "practically" controlled the confectionery business. He wanted "to bring about fair competition" but painted "a picture of Japanese gunboats anchored in English Bay, as Japanese marines landed 'to protect Japan's nationals.'" In seconding the motion Alderman DeGraves declared that "we've got to fight to keep B.C. White before it is too late."[50] After several "bitter discussions," council narrowly accepted Wilson's resolution requiring new applicants for trades licences or transfers to obtain its approval; it continued, nevertheless, to approve most applications. Wilson and DeGraves were so determined to reduce the number of Asian licencees that Mayor Miller complained of their "vaudeville shows of protest against the Oriental penetration" at every meeting. Council knew that the courts would likely reject discriminatory legislation but apparently hoped to quiet Wilson by seeking a charter amendment that would allow it to impose a 5 percent quota on licences issued to Asians.[51]

Wilson documented his claims concerning the striking business success of Asians in a brief that he and Alderman DeGraves submitted to Keenleyside's Board of Review. They provided statistics showing that between 1927 and 1937 the number of business licences issued to Chinese residents in Vancouver had increased by a third; the number issued to Japanese residents had risen by a startling 74 percent, from 459 to 795. Asians dominated certain fields: 91 percent of the licences for green groceries; 89 percent for laundry offices; 64 percent for laundries; 55 percent for hawkers and peddlers; 53 percent for cleaners-dyers; and 53 percent for dressmakers. The Chinese were particularly evident in laundries, green groceries, and hawking and peddling whereas the Japanese dominated dressmaking and dry cleaning and dyeing. Although Wilson often referred to "Orientals," he and his allies saw the Japanese as the main problem. The brief drew attention to the danger, "in the event of hostilities with an Oriental Power" or its allies, arising "from the doubtful loyalty to our country ... of such a large percentage of our population."[52]

Wilson was a prominent Anglican, but neither his church nor other major Protestant denominations wanted such harsh treatment for Asians. Both the Anglican synod of New Westminster (which included Vancouver) and the Vancouver presbytery of the United Church called for "fair and just treatment." Later Rev. Nelson A. Harkness, president of the Convention of Baptist Churches of British Columbia, described the anti-Oriental movement as "unChristian folly" and attacked the movement to refuse trade licences as an example "of one of the greatest problems of the church today, the color question." Churchmen were not the only agitators against discrimination. In the Private Bills Committee two CCF MLAs, Harold Winch (Vancouver East) and Dorothy Steeves (North Vancouver), said that Asians deprived of trade licences would enter other occupations. More telling was the "spontaneous" argument of the committee's chairman, H.G.T. Perry (Liberal, Fort George), that by substituting the word "Jewish" for "Oriental," the legislature would be doing "just what Hitler is doing in Germany." The Private Bills Committee rejected the amendment.[53]

Wilson's accusations of Asians violating early closing laws lost some credibility when, while serving as a witness in a case against a Japanese grocer charged with selling merchandise after 9 p.m., he admitted that he had not checked his watch; further undermining Wilson's testimony was Alderman DeGraves's refusal to turn over the sales slip from the purchase in question. Moreover, the RMA conceded that most Asian stores were small and catered mainly to other Asians. When city council continued to grant trade licences to Asians and refused further requests for a charter amendment, Wilson turned to the Retail Clerks Union, patriotic societies, and other organizations for moral and financial support in his crusade to keep "B.C. British." He also tried to get into the legislature as a Conservative in a May 1939 by-election occasioned by the death of the Liberal MLA in Vancouver Centre. Attacking the Pattullo government for rejecting his attempts to halt the "alarming" Oriental penetration of British Columbia, he argued that to vote for Alderman H.L. Corey, the Liberal, was to approve "the peaceful conquest of the Orientals" and "a standard of living of fish and rice." To vote for Wilson was "to protest against the sweatshops of Tokyo" and to secure "a standard of living of beef and bread." There is no record of Corey referring to Asians, but a supporter of Laura Jamieson, the CCF candidate, suggested that Wilson was planning "a pogrom against the Japanese – as the Nazis have done to the Jews – a pogrom against

Japanese merchants who make a precarious living by selling a few oranges and loaves of bread." In a close race Mrs. Jamieson won; Wilson came third.[54]

Undaunted, Wilson revived his idea of limiting Asian trade licences by citing the medical health officer's report that the Japanese had a birth rate four times greater than that of any other nationality.[55] Asserting that it would be a "splendid thing to ship Orientals out of Canada," he urged council to "hasten the day when they will want to get out ... because they can't do any business." When the European war began, he predicted that returning veterans "would find they had lost to the Japanese or Chinese." Council relented and applied for the charter amendment. The Union of British Columbia Municipalities, encouraged by the City of Victoria, also sought power to permit municipal councils to refuse trade licences, but Vancouver's proposal "ran into a storm of criticism" in the Private Bills Committee. With the help of a new ally on council, Charles Jones, Wilson argued that Asians were "making serious inroads ... upon the commercial life of Vancouver" through their "ability to survive where an occidental will fail in business because they have different standards of living and a tendency to evade or circumvent labor legislation." Despite a complaint from the South Granville District Chamber of Commerce about an Asian influx, council agreed that it was unwise to raise such an un-British measure in wartime, insisting that people could decide whether to patronize Oriental stores.[56] The issue was largely confined to Vancouver, but there were a few complaints about a concentration of Chinese and Japanese merchants on Nanaimo's Commercial Street and of "unfair" competition by Chinese green grocers and confectioners in Victoria.[57]

Wilson then linked his fight against Asian competition in small business with a new interest in alleged Japanese fifth columnists. The RMA supported his bid to have council seek sweeping powers over every business in the city, but the Board of Trade, Real Estate Exchange, and Vancouver Bar Association objected. In the debate preceding the application's rejection by the Private Bills Committee, most observers lost sight of the Japanese. Yet there was sympathy for them. Mayor Telford, who was also a CCF MLA, warned against the "injustice or oppression" of innocent people; the *Vancouver Province* noted that what had been "a problem of alien Orientals has become largely a problem of Canadian Orientals," who, though "not assimilable ... are our people. We must retain them and ... make them good Canadian citizens." In hoping that MLAs would not derive "cheap political capital" from the controversy, the *Vancouver News-Herald* emphasized that the Japanese in the province and Japan's aggression were separate issues and that "any imitation of the Axis psychology and persecution of the local Japanese" would only give Japan an "excuse for further Hitlerism."[58]

Wilson was determined to fight what he called "the peaceful penetration of [the] Japanese into the economic life of the Province," a process achieved, he explained, through "an insidious and destructive method of boring which threatens to establish in the not distant future a standard comparable only to the sweat shops of the

The Patriot?

"The Patriot?" *New Canadian,* 19 January 1941

industrial centres of Japan." It did him no political harm. After "an unusually quiet" election, he headed the 1940 aldermanic poll. Press accounts of the campaign are thin, but his campaign biography called him "a vigorous foe of Oriental penetration." He credited his victory to this reputation and to his support of airport expansion and promised to continue to do anything "to combat most vigorously any tendency which has the effect of reducing standards of living as set by the Canadian people." City council thwarted him. When he tried to delay the issuing of licences to three Japanese dressmakers by having the Health Department investigate claims that they ran unsanitary sweatshops, no one would second his motion. The *Vancouver Province* noted the well-authenticated suspicion "that he is trying by devious means to discriminate, unjustly and unlawfully against Orientals." That summer, when he attacked Japanese confectioneries and dry cleaning shops for violating closing bylaws, Alderman John Bennett accused him of indulging in "political propaganda." Wilson did not persuade city council but was so vigorous an anti-Japanese agitator that federal officials wanted to silence him.[59]

Although Wilson seems to have secured most of his support from small shopkeepers and others who were directly affected by Asian competition, many of his arguments found a receptive audience as British Columbians became increasingly susceptible to tales of Japanese subversion. They had initially laughed at Archdeacon Scott's allegations, but white British Columbians soon drew on their imaginations to report suspicions of the Japanese. In Vancouver the police ascertained that two carloads of Japanese passengers from the *Hikawa Maru* had taken moving pictures in Stanley Park but were "just exercising their privileges as tourists and taking pictures of scenic spots." On Vancouver Island the provincial police traced the story of a secret arsenal of machine guns and large quantities of ammunition to the bar of the Canadian Legion in Cumberland, from whence it had increased in "frightfulness" as it was retold. With difficulty, the police convinced legion members that the rumour was baseless. In the Fraser Valley the police investigated accounts of Japanese residents who were drilling and acquiring arms. One story was traced to a Japanese child who had boasted of his father buying him a cap gun. When the reeve claimed that fencing exercises were military drills, the Japanese in Haney turned to badminton for leisure. The local newspaper remarked that "our local Japanese" were law-abiding and that "the many wild rumors as to war-like preparations on their part have all been shown to be without foundation." If they could not find contemporary examples, people drew on memories. An Okanagan resident said that thirty years ago he had worked on a Canadian Pacific Railway gang with Japanese workers who knew about bridges and tunnels and that, from an aircraft carrier, the Japanese could destroy all railway bridges and the Connaught Tunnel within three hours. Gordon Sloan, a former Liberal MLA, reported having seen two Japanese men with maps and charts in a Vancouver hotel. The RCMP was anxious to dispel the tales lest they cause local conflict; indeed, they found no evidence of espionage. Apart from coastal defence, the authorities' main concern was protecting Vancouver's Japanese population. The *Vancouver Sun* thought it ironic that the first use of Canadian troops in a war with Japan would likely be "to throw an armed cordon around Powell Street to hold back with bayonets a Canadian mob."[60]

Firm evidence was lacking, but some RCMP and military officials doubted the loyalty of all Japanese residents and warned that Japanese people near strategic locations such as harbours, railways, bridges, and power plants were "in a position to cause serious trouble." A naval staff officer in Esquimalt noted that "a very great proportion" of the Japanese were naval or military reserves and that the tidiness of their boats and bunkhouses made them look like barrack rooms. He admitted that the Japanese, including the Canadian-born, seemed to be "very good citizens" but suspected that the "violent rumors" of their having machine guns, arms, and ammunition and of their secretly drilling might be true. If arms were found, he recommended keeping the matter secret, presumably to reduce "scare" sentiments. The Department of National Defence knew Canada's limited defences would not attract espionage but thought that the presence of at least five thousand Japanese residents of military age owing allegiance to Japan made "it expedient to draw up somewhat elaborate plans for the internal security of British Columbia in time of war." Not only was the department unsure of "the peaceful behaviour of even Canadian nationals of Japanese origin at a time when racial feelings will be aroused," but it expected that public sentiment might require it to provide facilities for the detention of over ten thousand individuals.[61]

The latter fear reflected a popular misconception that all Japanese residents, including the Canadian-born, had dual citizenship and were loyal to both Japan and Canada. As H.R. MacMillan explained, "even if born in this country, they support and patronize with national fervour all Japanese institutions here from ships to shops" and treat controversy as "a racial problem" to be settled through the Japanese consul. Noting that many sent their savings to Japan, he described them "as Japanese cells in the Canadian body politic." When Japan's foreign minister, Koki Hirota, suggested that Japanese children born and living in the United States "should be educated as Japanese, think as Japanese and continue to regard themselves as Japanese subjects," British Columbians assumed that he was also referring to Canada. The *Kamloops Sentinel* put it bluntly: Either they "are Canadian – or they are not. If they are not they should return to the land to which they give their fealty." By 1941 the *Prince Rupert Daily News,* in reporting spy stories from the United States, had admitted that the local Japanese were not necessarily foes but warned that they must not be "tempted to play into the hands of our enemy." When Hope hinted that the White Canada Association was considering raiding the Japanese Consulate in Vancouver to ascertain "what nationality or allegiance the Japanese in this province really have," Keenleyside warned him of immediate prosecution and a recommendation for "the heaviest possible penalties."[62]

The outbreak of the European war elicited few comments on the Japanese, partly because the federal government asked the press to say as little as possible that might cause trouble between Britain and Japan and partly because public attention had been diverted. On the eve of the war, a self-proclaimed White Canada Crusade advertised in Vancouver for members by warning that "even if a world war should command our attention we must not forget the Oriental, who will quietly continue to penetrate our economic and social life." The RCMP determined that the crusade had some financial support from businessmen and that it intended to collect information on Japanese economic penetration and to petition Ottawa for a ban on Japanese immigration. The police kept in touch with its organizer, W.R. Page-Wilson, who, by December 1939, reported that because of the war he could not interest people in his movement and promised not to further it.[63]

Japanese Canadians worked to demonstrate their loyalty to Canada. They feared that the Rome-Berlin-Tokyo Axis would mean "concentration camps for themselves." In Vancouver and Prince Rupert they formed units of the Canadian Red Cross. They also contributed funds to the Red Cross, the Dominion war loan, and to aid British air-raid victims. To ensure that their efforts were noticed, they often routed war loan subscriptions through municipal officials and issued press releases. Politicians such as Mayor Telford of Vancouver and Minister of Defence Norman Rogers graciously thanked them. Some newspapers praised their "gratitude and loyalty," but a few considered such generosity the due of those who enjoyed Canadian democracy, noting that the truly sincere would not seek publicity for good works. Doubts about their loyalty grew. The *Prince Rupert Daily News* admitted that many Japanese residents might "well be looked upon as British subjects" but warned that "every Japanese will be more or less under suspicion." The *Vancouver News-Herald* recognized their contributions to the war effort but feared that they "could easily become the 'sudetan Germans' of the Pacific area." The Canadian Japanese Association, which claimed to serve all Japanese residents in Canada and which had close relations with the consulate, discontinued sending parcels to Japan for distribution in hospitals and slums in response to actual complaints. Individuals, too, avowed their loyalty to Canada. Frank Koyama, who had come to Canada forty years earlier as a boy, told the *Nanaimo Free Press* that he regretted Canada's strained relations with Japan but stressed that "I myself will stand by Canada no matter what happens anywhere and I'm pretty sure every one of my Japanese friends will too."[64]

Similarly Tsutae Sato, principal of the Vancouver Japanese Language School and secretary of the provincial Language School Association, vigorously declared that the schools were "NOT Japanese in spirit" and that they sought "to inculcate fine and true Canadian citizenship among our people." As evidence, he proudly showed a *Vancouver Sun* reporter the print of the Union Jack that hung over a stairway with an inscription from Tennyson: "One Life, One Fleet, One Flag, One Throne." Alderman Wilson had attacked the schools as "a menace to Canadian national life" and an indication of unwillingness to assimilate. As the international situation deteriorated, he alleged that they taught a curriculum set by Japan's Department of Education; to make his point to city council, he brandished a textbook supposedly glorifying Japan's military heroes. Wilson was not alone. Arthur Laing, a Richmond school trustee, told the minister of education that the schools taught "Japanese language, literature and a flood of jingoistic nationalism," which he suspected originated in the Japanese Foreign Office. He urged the Department of Education to require all foreign language schools to obtain a permit. Acquiescing, the department implemented the requirement early in 1941 and stipulated that the schools' curriculum not "include guidance in the national aspirations of a foreign power or anything that might be construed as subversive to the interests of Canada." Despite complaints from some school boards, the department issued permits, though some were only temporary, to all applicants.[65]

The Nisei, who had been educated in Canadian schools, proclaimed their loyalty to their native land. Members of the Japanese Canadian Citizens League (JCCL), a Nisei organization, discussed "How Can We Best Serve Canada" and unanimously reaffirmed their loyalty to Canada and Great Britain.[66] They believed that the real test of their loyalty was to volunteer for service in the Canadian military forces. They were among the first to volunteer in September 1939, but recruiting agents usually rebuffed them, as they did the Chinese. Then, in the fall of 1940, Chinese and Japanese residents were called up with men in their age groups for medical examinations prior to training for home defence under the National Resources Mobilization Act. Unfortunately the call went out just when news of the Rome-Berlin-Tokyo Axis had made feelings unusually bitter. Many Nisei and Chinese Canadians welcomed call-ups as acceptance of their status as loyal Canadian citizens. There was support for the idea in the daily press, but the *Vancouver News-Herald* asserted that Canada had "no right to ask them to bear arms when we are not prepared to extend them privileges of citizenship." There was the rub. When the *Tairiku Nippo* (the Vancouver *Continental Daily News*) suggested that the Canadian-born Japanese would welcome call-ups as an opportunity to demonstrate their loyalty, Alderman Wilson sought to ensure that "certain privileges," namely the franchise, would not be granted as a result of military service and that Orientals called up would be dispersed across Canada. Wilson called the bombing of a Canadian passenger ship in Chinese waters a "forewarning" of "Japan's intentions" toward the Pacific Coast and repeated allegations that the local Japanese had not fully co-operated in registering themselves or their firearms. The Finance Committee rejected dispersal as impractical, but council opposed military training altogether unless there was a guarantee that the Japanese would "not receive privileges for their services."[67]

The franchise was still an issue. At its 1938 convention the CCF had narrowly agreed not to enfranchise Asians without a provincial plebiscite but the next year endorsed Asian enfranchisement. Some complaints of Asian expansion in the economy were accompanied by suggestions that such expansion would be even greater if Asians could vote. Yet the president of one fishermen's union believed that it would be possible to develop a good relationship with the Canadian-born Japanese if they had full citizenship rights. Liberals and Conservatives occasionally mentioned their opposition to Asian enfranchisement. Pattullo told the Royal Commission on Dominion-Provincial Relations that people such as Orientals and Doukhobors who did "not share ideas common to Canadians" should not vote.[68]

When it seemed likely that Asians called for military service would demand the franchise, Pattullo informed Prime Minister King that British Columbians could "never tolerate" Asian enfranchisement. Attorney General Wismer warned of "an impossible situation ... as the Oriental vote would be the deciding factor in a great many constituencies." That fall a legislative committee on the Elections Act considered enfranchising Asians in the Canadian forces. E.T. Kenney (Liberal, Skeena) supported the idea, but the committee agreed with R.L. Maitland, the Conservative leader, that Orientals did "not understand Canadian government sufficiently to take part in our legislation." In response, the CCF's leader, Harold Winch, said that "they understand it sufficiently to want to fight for it." If Maitland's comment were correct, suggested the *New Canadian,* the Nisei newspaper, then it was "a sorry reflection" on the province's educational system. There the matter lay. The franchise was no longer a useful election issue. In the October 1941 provincial election, the Liberal candidate in Vancouver East, Winch's constituency, suggested that the CCF had "sold our birthright for a lousy bowl of rice" by recommending the franchise for the Japanese, but Winch was so popular that the Liberal won only 10 percent of the vote. When Professor Henry F. Angus told the Canadian Political Science Association that the political disabilities of Japanese Canadians, which constituted "a *de facto* colour bar," would eventually disappear because British Columbia could not "stand out indefinitely against the force of British tradition and North American practice," only Neill complained.[69]

Meanwhile, as an interim measure to satisfy British Columbia, the Cabinet War Committee did not include the Chinese and Japanese in British Columbia in the first and second calls for military training in the fall of 1940. Believing that the situation was serious, it also set up a special committee composed of representatives from the Departments of National Defence and External Affairs and from the RCMP to report on "the general problem of [the] Japanese and Chinese in British Columbia, from the point of view of internal security, and with particular reference to the question of military training." In confidentially informing Pattullo of the new committee, Prime Minister King urged him to avoid "precipitate action" that might "add to public nervousness and apprehension."[70]

Without publicity Lieutenant Colonel A.W. Sparling of the Department of National Defence and Assistant Commissioner F.J. Mead of the RCMP did most of the work. They drew on existing studies and interviewed the premier; MLAs; municipal councillors in Vancouver, New Westminster, and Maple Ridge; and representatives of military and police forces, the University of British Columbia, businessmen, and the Japanese community. They concluded that the problem resulted from the Japanese being "a rapidly growing and easily identified group" who offered "strong competition in certain economic areas," did not "accept discrimination without protest," and "above all" were seen as representatives of a nation whose ideals were hostile to those of the Allies. They learned that the provincial government wanted all Japanese residents removed from coastal areas. The committee found that prejudice against the Japanese was so strong that whites had exploited and created "an altogether unjustified suspicion and sense of alarm in the public mind"; indeed, they saw no evidence of any "disloyal or subversive activity." They reported that police and military authorities had taken adequate precautions in case of subversive efforts by individuals and "to protect all loyal Japanese [residents] against any attack from misguided members of the white community." With one exception, all their interviewees, including those hostile to the Japanese, agreed that the international crisis meant that anti-Japanese activities and sentiment must be reduced to a minimum. "If this is not done," the committee warned, "there is good reason to fear that riotous outbreaks will occur, with inevitable and possibly dangerous repercussions at home and abroad." They advised the government to reassure the white population and to encourage Japanese residents to follow their suggestions, including watching for signs of disloyal acts. For civil security and to eliminate a cause of complaint, they recommended re-registering the Japanese in British Columbia. They did not think that Canadians of Japanese race should be called for military training. Given the committee's fears of "riotous outbreaks," many recommendations dealt with the white community. They called on the police to provide "for the defence of loyal Japanese" residents, urging that individuals and the press be asked to reduce anti-Japanese propaganda and, if necessary, that the press impose censorship. Finally, the special committee recommended setting up a small standing committee to supervise the implementation of its recommendations and to keep the government informed of the Oriental situation.[71]

Recognizing the underlying issue, the special committee urged that when international circumstances permitted, Canada announce its intention to prohibit Japanese immigration. Because Prime Minister King warned that such a measure would "have a bad effect on our already strained relations with Japan" and "stimulate the anti-oriental groups in British Columbia to demand immediate action," the committee did not publish this recommendation. Heeding a suggestion from C.G. Power, the associate minister of national defence, they also omitted references to the wartime internment of suspicious Japanese residents. While the special committee revised their report for presentation to Parliament, the Cabinet War Committee, subject to Ian Mackenzie's approval, accepted Keenleyside's advice to have Sparling and Mead serve on the standing committee. The other members of this committee were MacGregor Macintosh, a leader of the anti-Oriental movement but "fundamentally a decent and honest man"; Professor Henry F. Angus, "the outstanding advocate of fair treatment for the Orientals in British Columbia"; and Mayor F.J. Hume of New Westminster, a "sensible, level-headed, and highly respected" man. Keenleyside's thumbnail sketches of Macintosh and Angus were fair, but he apparently did not know that Hume's "caustic remarks" on the "Oriental menace" had been the "highlight" of a political banquet in June 1937.[72]

The government did not table the full report of the special committee until mid-February, but on 9 January 1941, after showing it privately to the Japanese minister, the prime minister issued a press release summarizing its recommendations, including the appointment of the standing committee, re-registration of all Japanese residents, and the conclusion "that the most serious danger" arose "from ill-informed attacks against the loyalty and integrity of the Oriental population." The last reference applied chiefly to Wilson. Thomas Reid, thinking that it applied to him, took exception to references to agitators, but the British Columbia MPs indicated that they would set aside their anti-Japanese campaign for the time being.[73]

The news received a mixed reception in British Columbia. Premier Pattullo was pleased that the situation was being watched. The Victoria Assembly of the Native

Sons of Canada disapproved of King's recent sentiments and his unfamiliarity "with the psychology of the Oriental mind, and with the effects of the continued 'peaceful' (?) (but dangerous) penetration of [the] Japanese into our Province." Along similar lines, Arthur Laing told the Vancouver Real Estate Exchange that registration was "only temporizing," that the situation would not be solved until the "Japanese in Canada divorce themselves entirely from Japan." The *Cowichan Leader* agreed that many Japanese residents were loyal to Canada but noted that "Japan is an Axis partner – very unfriendly to Britain – and that blood is thicker than water." Nevertheless, it welcomed re-registration to protect the loyal and check the disloyal. Similarly the *Prince Rupert Daily News* thought that registration would protect the Japanese. The JCCL welcomed appreciations of loyalty but was disappointed that its members were not completely accepted "as full, free and equal citizens of Canada – neither exempt from duties nor excluded from privileges." Nevertheless, the league offered full co-operation and hoped that registration would "allay unnecessary fear and suspicion." Others considered registration wasteful since the National Resources Mobilization Act and the decennial census had recently enumerated the Japanese. Thomas Reid wondered what it was "all about"; Neill thought that since the Japanese looked "all alike," illegal immigrants would borrow registration cards if they needed them.[74]

British Columbia's MPs were interested in broader aspects of the Japanese presence. Angus MacInnis counselled halting discrimination in order to secure Japanese Canadian loyalty, but others rehearsed ancient arguments. Reid still believed that their first allegiance, no matter their birthplace, was to Japan. Howard C. Green claimed that only halting immigration would end "ill feeling" between whites and the Japanese in British Columbia. George Cruickshank offered a solution: "Ship them all to Toronto." Neill blatantly declared that "the white man must be dominant; his word should go. If you adopt an attitude of complaisance or anything which is suggestive of subservience to the brown man, he thinks you are afraid of him." Similarly Vancouver's three English language dailies agreed that the Canadian Japanese should be treated fairly but attacked the government for not confronting the real problem: the gentlemen's agreement and continued immigration. Jack Boothe of the *Vancouver Province* drew a cartoon of a "Local 'Mikado'" in front of an endless stream of "incoming Orientals" disembarking from a gangplank labelled "Gentlemen's Agreement." Not surprisingly Alderman Wilson called it "the height of folly to permit new Japanese [immigrants] to enter the country until we solve the problem of those we already have here." Registration, he averred, would not "eliminate the economic problem." The local press commended Vancouver City Council's tentative approval of his resolution for abrogating the gentlemen's agreement.[75]

In tabling the special committee's report, Mackenzie King told Parliament that Japan would resent a ban on immigration but that he had to consider the claims of men such as Neill that abolishing the gentlemen's agreement "would help quite a

"Local 'Mikado,'" *Vancouver Province*, 10 January 1941

lot to allay the antagonism of the white people in British Columbia." The *Vancouver Province* erroneously interpreted a leak that Ottawa was reconsidering the agreement as news of its cancellation and praised this development as "one good result" of "strained relations in the Pacific." Recalling that most Japanese residents in the province were Canadian-born, it found less reason "to continue to impose difficulties on our Japanese people and greater reason for us to treat them as Canadians." In short, it recognized that Japan, rather than Japanese Canadians, was the problem. Similarly a Vancouver neighbourhood newspaper argued that until proven otherwise Japanese residents must be treated as ordinary, law-abiding human beings. The *Vancouver News-Herald* asked rhetorically whether, "after the manner of the Nazis in their handling of the Jews," it was possible to "make the Japanese scapegoats for our economic ills?"[76]

Registration proceeded smoothly. The RCMP postponed registration of seasonal workers such as berry pickers so as not to interfere with their work. In feeling "out the Japanese on their attitude towards Canada and the British Empire," RCMP interpreters found "no cause for concern" about a Japanese menace to "our internal security" and that those most appreciative of Canada's freedom had recently visited Japan. Registrants were required to carry identification cards, with photographs and thumbprints, indicating their status as Japanese nationals, naturalized Canadians, or Canadian-born citizens. To demonstrate their loyalty, some received permission to stamp the backs of their cards with a notation that they might be Japanese citizens by birth but owed "allegiance to Canada by reason of residence and choice." At first, registration applied only in British Columbia; elsewhere, the prime minister noted, the Japanese were "looked upon more as individuals." When war seemed more likely, the Cabinet War Committee decided to treat the Japanese in the same way as it did Germans and Italians, registering them no matter where they lived in Canada.[77]

Although Prime Minister King briefly believed that anti-Japanese agitation in British Columbia had abated, the situation changed when Canada froze Japanese assets, thus effectively ending trade, and gave notice of its abrogation of the Treaty of Commerce and Navigation of 1911. The special committee still feared that in the case of war "irresponsible elements of the white population" might attack the Japanese community in Vancouver or elsewhere. It had Angus call the standing committee's attention "to the danger of any demonstration against the local Japanese population ... following (or even preceding) any action" concerning economic relations with Japan. A demonstration, Angus warned, "would detract from the moral effect of governmental action." In mid-August 1941 the special and standing committees met in Vancouver to discuss steps "to prevent civil disturbances." Hume thought that the situation was less acute than it had been in the fall of 1940. Sparling reported that Pacific Command had a plan to aid the civil power and mentioned the possible need to remove Japanese residents "from the vicinity of certain areas of military importance," which, Hume remarked, "tied in with the question of civil security." The meeting noted that the province's three Japanese newspapers were generally pro-Canadian but that a newspaper without English translations "would be subject to violent criticism" and possibly to physical action against its staff and premises. Thus, in the case of war, Hume suggested publishing English translations and closing Japanese language schools to reassure British Columbians that the authorities were giving proper attention to the Japanese question. Nevertheless, fear of anti-Japanese outbreaks led military officials to plan the protection of Japanese settlements in Vancouver and Steveston. By November 1941 the military reported that it had adequate strength to deal with any civil disturbance.[78]

There was a real worry. As relations with Japan rapidly deteriorated in early December 1941, the *Vancouver News-Herald* warned that if "Tokyo's aggressive policies" led to war, "British Columbia would be on the 'front line.'" "If we were fighting Japan it would be too much to expect that every Japanese in British Columbia would be on our side." It thought that the authorities were prepared for sabotage or subversion but that "danger would arise from hot-headed minorities, amongst the Japanese and amongst ourselves, whose talk and actions could easily set a match to a dynamite-laden situation." "Those who would stir up racial trouble," it concluded, "would be the real 'fifth columnists.'"[79]

The end of the phoney war in Europe in the spring of 1940 and evidence of fifth columnists helping the Nazis in Norway, France, and other European countries had escalated fears of "fifth column" activities, especially on the coast and in the Okanagan Valley, where the German population was concentrated. Canadian Legion branches, boards of trade, and city councils wanted action. In Kelowna, New Westminster, Victoria, and elsewhere, mass meetings called for interning "enemy nationals and naturalized Canadians of doubtful loyalty, and all other disloyal, treacherous or subversive elements." As one Legion member put it: "We have thousands of enemy aliens and sympathizers in our midst. Today it is the Germans. Tomorrow it may be the Italians. Within a month it may be the Japanese." Many British Columbians shared this fear. Elmore Philpott, in the *Victoria Times,* called for the registration of all residents of alien origin, whether naturalized or not, and suggested that "ex-naval officers, working as secret agents, and disguised in all sorts of occupations" might be working in the province. Mayor Hume of New Westminster and Mayor Telford of Vancouver proposed registering all males, rather than just those who were Japanese, between the ages of sixteen and sixty as possible emergency workers, investigating rumours about alien enemies "to deal with unjustified outbursts on the part of ill-informed, vindictive or emotionally unbalanced persons," and following up on "any disloyal practices ... without permitting unjust or un-British practices against individuals." H.R. MacMillan, "the largest employer of Japanese labour in the province," renewed efforts to have the Vancouver Club replace its Japanese servants with "employees who are by race and birth more suitable to occupy positions which otherwise become posts for potential enemies." Brigadier General J.A. Clark, a former Conservative MP and prominent Vancouver lawyer, told Minister of Defence J.L. Ralston that a well-armed, "large and virile" Japanese population controlled many high-speed boats. Warning that war with Japan was "more than a possibility," he believed it essential to have thoroughly trained troops on the spot.[80]

Residents of a South Vancouver neighbourhood where one ten-acre block was supposedly almost entirely occupied by Germans formed the British Canadian Allied Club to combat Nazism. Alderman Wilson shifted its attention to the city's

"It Can Happen Here," *Vancouver Parashooter,* c. 1940

12,000 Japanese residents. In speaking to the Knights of Pythias on the role of subversive minorities in the fall of Holland and Norway, Wilson stressed the "yellow menace." Anti-Japanese feeling in Vancouver was so strong that the Police Commission asked local MPs to ascertain what was being done to control possible subversion in order to prevent "any undue disturbance" by people who thought that the authorities had not given the Japanese presence "adequate consideration." Japan's consul in Vancouver protested that Wilson's violent propaganda could "only lead to anti-Japanese disturbances and resulting violence." Keenleyside agreed that Wilson's "unscrupulous campaign" might cause riots. Because the police could not "ferret out" all dangerous Japanese residents, as they had done with Germans and Italians, Keenleyside proposed asking Japanese leaders to be responsible for the good behaviour of their community. He wanted police and possibly military resources to protect "loyal and well-behaved" Japanese residents from "hoodlums and super-patriots." He discouraged Mayor Telford from denouncing Wilson lest that give him additional publicity; Telford merely told the consul that he opposed "discrimination against any individual national or group of nationals" and invited him to discuss the matter over lunch with himself and Wilson! To silence Wilson, Keenleyside suggested having Howard C. Green and the federal Conservative leader,

R.B. Hanson, speak to him privately. If this approach did not work, Keenleyside believed that Wilson, a man "of the soft type," would "curl up if given a straight warning by [an RCMP officer] who looks as though he means business."[81]

In the meantime Wilson expanded his campaign. He repeatedly charged Japanese fishermen with an "organized effort" to obstruct seaplanes at the airport. Without distinguishing between the Canadian-born and immigrants, and ignoring Mayor Telford's interjections, he told the Finance Committee that Japanese residents were not loyal to the British Empire but instead "ferociously" worshipped "their government in far-off Japan," menaced "the safety of our people," and had a fleet of fishing boats that "could readily be transformed into torpedo-carrying warcraft." He persuaded the Finance Committee to express "alarm at the presence of large numbers of Japanese scattered along the coast" and to call for the deportation of illegal immigrants, for the removal of Japanese residents' retail trade rights and other privileges "not enjoyed by Canadians in Japan," and for precautions "with persons and property as may be indicated by their military importance." Nisei leaders, who were drawing away from the Issei to fight discrimination, did not take this development silently. Three of them appeared before city council, and one of them, Thomas Shoyama, declared that "if worse comes to worse, we are prepared to defend the shores of B.C. from any invasion of the Japanese Navy." Some Nisei remained fearful of what Wilson might do, but council rephrased the resolution so that it applied to all aliens. The change was cosmetic. The Japanese remained its main target, with the resolution seeming to "crown" Wilson's four-year-long anti-Japanese campaign.[82]

The Nisei replied by showing their support for Canada's war effort. Shoyama, spokesman for the JCCL, vowed that all would "defend the British Columbia coast against the Japanese navy. This is our home to defend." The *New Canadian* denied Wilson's allegations and rightly noted that only the refusal of recruiting officers prevented Nisei from serving in the Canadian Active Service Force. Privately F.J. Mead of the RCMP, relying on assurances from Etsuji Morii, a naturalized Canadian and community leader, believed that most Japanese residents were loyal to Canada. The Nisei found some sympathy, but Wilson's "continued agitations" and "racial persecutions" undermined the morale of the Canadian-born Japanese and threatened to lessen their contributions to the war effort. Mayor Telford tried to ease Japanese sensitivities by speaking to the JCCL on "Citizenship." The *Vancouver Province* warned that treating them "harshly or unjustly" would not solve the problem since most "were born here and belong nowhere else." It called for abrogation of the gentlemen's agreement, as did Angus MacInnis, who admonished readers of the *B.C. Federationist* not to "stoop to the race-baiting tactics of Hitler's Nazis" and reminded them that the Canadian-born Japanese could not be deported. Attorney General Wismer declared that attacks based on racial origin simply bred "animosity and ill-feeling" and were "directed in part at native-born citizens who are loyal to Canada."[83]

Despite this advice and the JCCL's explanation that dual citizenship was only a way to maintain the family tree and that many Nisei had cancelled registration of their births in Japan, the idea that dual nationality compromised their loyalty remained. The *Vancouver News-Herald* noted that "the Canadian-born Japanese have proclaimed their loyalty" but asked rhetorically: "What of the community as a whole? ... To whom does it owe its loyalty? To Japan or to Canada?" The police also had doubts. Provincial Police Commissioner T.W.S. Parsons considered it "not unreasonable to suppose that they have a natural predilection towards the country from which they come." In the case of war with Japan, he expected "a problem of the first magnitude" since, despite local affiliations, the Japanese, including the Canadian-born, looked "to the Japanese Consul for instruction and guidance in all matters pertaining to their welfare and political position."[84]

Examples of the consul's work in promoting goodwill on behalf of Japanese nationals and Canadian citizens abounded. For example, in January 1940 Consul Kenji Nakauchi applauded members of Victoria's "Japanese colony" for assisting Canada's war effort. A few months later he told Prince Rupert Rotarians that their city "was connected with Japan in having a number of his countrymen residing here as peaceful and happy citizens."[85] In answering attacks from the "Japanese baiter," Alderman Wilson, Consul General Tomii asserted that "the Japanese-Canadians and the Japanese residents have proved themselves good citizens and desirable aliens respectively."[86] In a farewell interview with Skelton, Tomii drew attention to the "unfriendly treatment" of the Japanese in British Columbia. In the unlikely event of their causing trouble, Tomii thought that a hundred mounted policemen could control them but warned that public opinion in Japan was not "blind to the indignities" they suffered. Newspapers in Japan reported the anti-Japanese measures proposed by Vancouver City Council following Japan's adherence to the Rome-Berlin Axis.[87]

The Canadian Japanese did not depend entirely on the consul to cultivate goodwill. In Kelowna they contributed to the regatta by bringing in the Vancouver Asahi for a match against a non-Japanese Okanagan all-star baseball team. Vancouver Nisei participated in drama and folk festivals. The Victoria Japanese Chrysanthemum Society invited the public to a show and donated proceeds from a silver collection to the Royal Jubilee Hospital. In Vancouver, in an amazing gesture of goodwill, the Japanese Canadian Chrysanthemum Society had Alderman Charles Jones, president of the Vancouver and District Chrysanthemum Growers' Society, open their show and attend a dinner for Occidental "'mum fanciers."[88]

Such gestures could not overcome fears of war, especially after the formation of the Rome-Berlin-Tokyo Axis. A Vancouver financial newspaper suggested that Canadians "must inevitably consider" the industrious and law-abiding Japanese "as potentially dangerous" if Japan and Britain went to war. City council again asked Ottawa to deport illegal immigrants or law breakers immediately and not to admit any more immigrants. Wilson repeated allegations that the local Japanese

were sympathetic to Japan, did subversive work with wireless sets, and used convenience stores to collect information. The once sympathetic Mayor Telford dismissed any idea of deporting or interning all Japanese residents but argued that
without visiting "hardship on loyal Japanese citizens," military authorities should
investigate and intern any Japanese resident who threatened Canada's war effort
or safety. He encouraged closing "Nipponese schools" for the war's duration but
warned that "we must beware of probing and nipping at the heels of innocent
people who, if pressed too hard, would become formidable opponents." His press
release warned that unless they broke the law or acted contrary to Canada's national interests, the Japanese should "be treated as decent, law-abiding citizens. To
do less is to reflect upon ourselves, our intelligence and our boasted justice." The
Vancouver press agreed. Clearly referring to Wilson, the *Sun* decried the tendency
of some civic leaders to make "inflammatory statements" in the hope of gaining
electoral favour. Similarly the *Province* remarked that even though those Japanese
residents born in Canada were "quite unassimilable," they were "nevertheless, our
people. They are Canadians. We cannot liquidate them. We cannot deport them.
We must keep them." Thus, when F.J. Mead asked them to use their influence to
curb ill-feeling lest violence follow agitation, local editors were amenable. They
agreed that in the case of war, Japanese residents "would become the victims of
mass resentment." Through Maitland, Mead secured an interview with Alderman
Wilson. Wilson seemed to recognize that agitation could lead to violence – he had
received a similar warning from the attorney general – but would only promise to
consult Mead before any organization with which he was associated took "immediate steps." Mead reiterated his concern that violence against the Japanese in Vancouver might "give the Japanese Government the excuse to wreak a terrible
vengeance on all British subjects living in Japanese controlled areas in the Far
East." Wilson insisted that Japanese competition had so destroyed Canadian standards that a vigorous campaign was needed to restrict it.[89]

On 1 October 1940 military and police officials had met at the attorney general's
invitation "to discuss Certain Aspects of Civil Security insofar as they apply to
[the] Japanese in Canada and in British Columbia Particularly." No one could
provide "actual evidence" of possible sabotage, but officials expected that, in the
case of war, "trouble by mobs against Japanese" residents in Vancouver would stretch
local police resources to the limit. To reduce tension, the meeting asked the censor
to have the press refrain from publishing anything "which might inflame the public mind," particularly the anti-Japanese resolutions that were "continually before
the Vancouver City Council." Wilson almost disappeared from newspapers; his
candidacy as an incumbent in the December civic election was scarcely noted.
Keenleyside did not like censorship but believed that "serious action will have to
be taken about that young man if he does not soon show some signs of gaining a
sense of responsibility." He feared that a proposed radio debate between Professor
Henry F. Angus and Wilson would give Wilson publicity and increase "discussion

of a subject which should be allowed to lie dormant." By the time Angus learned of Keenleyside's wishes, cancelling the debate would have given Wilson "a new opportunity to damn the government." Prime Minister King saw censorship as a last resort but agreed that, "if the one or two persons who are chiefly responsible for the virulence and irresponsibility of the present anti-oriental campaign prove impervious to persuasion and blind to the higher interests of their country," censorship might be necessary. Moral suasion by the press censor, and perhaps police interviews and cross-examination by the special committee, kept Wilson largely, but not completely, out of the papers.[90] The sentiments to which he appealed, however, were very much alive.

When the diplomatic situation between Britain and Japan deteriorated in the early summer of 1940, Prime Minister King told the Defence Department to put troops on the Pacific Coast because of the danger of a Japanese attack and "disaffection amongst [the] Japanese population in British Columbia." Lieutenant General H.D.G. Crerar, chief of the General Staff, did not think that Japan was likely to attack Canada's west coast but agreed on the need to have troops in British Columbia "on account of numbers of Japanese there." In a secret "appreciation of the situation in B.C. in the event of war with Japan," the Joint Staff Committee in Victoria said that enemy landing parties might raid Prince Rupert, Esquimalt, and Yorke Island, the latter of which guarded the northern approach to the Johnstone Strait. It considered a raid on Vancouver unlikely but warned that "disaffected enemy aliens" might cause trouble there and in the Fraser Valley, where many of the approximately five thousand Japanese men possessed firearms and were "decidedly anti-British in sentiment," and around the Queen Charlotte Islands and Prince Rupert, where, as in the Fraser Valley, Japanese fishermen owned many small boats that could navigate local waters and carry small parties of men. The Joint Service Committee, Pacific Coast claimed to have "totally inadequate" forces against the sabotage of such military objectives as the Esquimalt and Prince Rupert dockyards; the ammunition magazines in Esquimalt and Kamloops; air bases, especially in Ucluelet and Allieford Bay; and civilian targets, including the Bamfield cable station, the Estevan wireless station, the transcontinental railways and highway through the Fraser Canyon, and harbours in Vancouver, Victoria, and Prince Rupert. As an appendix, they added the report of a special investigation by Flight Lieutenant R.M. Wynd, who was deeply suspicious of the Japanese, their language schools, their close relationship with the consul, their ownership of firearms, and their societies, which were "definitely committed to anti-white activities." He feared that the Canadian-born, who "resent white hostility and are inclined to be sullen and defiant to whites and particularly to investigations carried on respecting them," might indulge in "serious subversive activity."[91]

The European fifth columnists, whose activities in the spring of 1940 inspired many of Wilson's anti-Japanese outbursts, also spurred other civilians to action. Attorney General Wismer harnessed the enthusiasm of military-like groups "who were under no control," such as the Canadian Legion, army and navy veterans associations, and the Flying Column, as a foundation for home defence units. He convinced the representatives of about twenty-seven such groups to co-ordinate their activities and had the provincial police organize an auxiliary service to assist in combatting potential fifth column activity and to guard such utilities as city water systems, power dams, and irrigation ditches. To ensure discipline among the volunteers, Wismer asked Ottawa to put them under military control. In endorsing this request, G.G. McGeer repeated stories of an infiltration of Japanese military officers, admitted that the denial of the franchise gave the Japanese "no reason to feel friendly to the province," argued that "real racial antipathy exists," and concluded that war could put the province "in very grave danger," as "the Japanese, co-operating with our other enemies," could isolate it over night.[92]

The federal government responded by putting Lieutenant Colonel A.W. Sparling in charge of internal security and of liaison between the federal and provincial governments. Ottawa also accepted Wismer's request for more control over firearms. Because the directive making it illegal for aliens to hold guns and explosives was of no use against the Canadian-born Japanese, Wismer announced that after 15 September 1940 all British Columbians would be fined or imprisoned for possessing unregistered firearms. He denied that refusing registration certificates to Chinese and Japanese residents was "intended to cast any reflection on their status" or had any racial bias, insisting that it was "merely a precautionary measure" because China and Japan were at war. The *Vancouver Province* and the *Vancouver Sun* welcomed the news as a way to prevent incidents between Chinese and Japanese residents or between Asians and whites. Vancouver citizens, said the *Sun*, were "not going to kill or shoot any Japanese, but the authorities are justified in making certain that no Japanese shall have the opportunity of using any firearm against any Canadian." Recalling the 1907 riot, the newspaper warned of possible bloodshed. Internal security was also Ottawa's chief concern. Citing the existence of such groups as the Flying Column, the prime minister suggested that the internal danger "was greater than any immediate danger of attack from without." On a visit, C.G. Power, the minister of national defence for air, found that "the danger of anti-Japanese outbreaks was serious" since many British Columbians had a "Japanese complex" and, given their exaggerated ideas of any menace caused by the local Japanese, were talking of "mass internment and deportation of all Japanese."[93]

As early as May 1939, the interdepartmental committee had suggested interning certain Japanese residents in the case of war because of "the strength of public sentiment." Thus the Joint Service Committee, Pacific Coast considered how it might remove the Japanese from dangerous areas. After Wismer urged making arrangements in the case of a "crisis" for the internment "elsewhere" than in British

Columbia of those Japanese residents located at strategic points on the coast, the armed forces consulted the provincial police and the RCMP. The commissioner of internment operations expected to intern no more than fifty Japanese residents whose "attitude or circumstances ... might require their retention for protective custody." By September 1941 the Joint Service Committee had decided that in the case of war it would have to remove Japanese residents from important defence areas and round up their fishing boats and other craft. It believed that some individuals might have to be interned but thought that most Japanese locals "would continue their normal occupations" since they were disinclined to cause any 'serious disorders.'"[94]

"To secure full efficiency," the Joint Service Committee recommended coordinating any action with the United States since inequality of treatment of the Japanese in the two nations could "furnish grounds for grievance by the persons immediately concerned." It noted a major difference: the Nisei in the United States could vote and serve in the armed forces whereas the Nisei in Canada could not. When Colonel B.R. Mullaly of Pacific Command interviewed Etsuji Morii, Thomas Shoyama, and other representatives of the Japanese community about enlistments in the armed forces, they suggested that generous treatment might help to ease tensions with Japan. They agreed that the principal cause of animosity was "economic jealousy tinged with colour prejudice" and that war or an incident involving a Canadian ship or Canadian citizens might raise feelings so high that an anti-Japanese outburst could endanger the community's safety. The RCMP determined that the Japanese expected the internment of certain nationals to benefit their "community as a whole" by reassuring "the Occidental population that the authorities were taking every step to protect the entire community."[95]

Meanwhile, military intelligence officials chased stories of alleged arms caches and secret submarine bases in locations so "secret" that no one knew their exact locations! The RCMP discovered a cache of Japanese army rifles at an unnamed location and found that a naval officer attached to the Vancouver consulate was working at camouflage technique. A detective saw Japanese residents unload heavy packing cases on Galiano Island, and an agent reported that many Japanese fishermen visited the office of the *Continental Daily News,* a Japanese language newspaper, whose editor, described as the "Chief Intelligence Officer in Canada, for the Japanese Government," reported directly to "the Chief of Japanese Intelligence in the Department of Foreign Affairs in Japan." An agent heard a Japanese dry cleaner tell a German that "instead of using mass formations in the event of war, instructions had been issued to organize small groups, who would be told to do certain things." RCMP headquarters saw no "cause for alarm," but Mead, who was "thoroughly acquainted" with Japanese activities in British Columbia, surveyed the situation.[96]

Because they could not be thoroughly disproved, spy stories were easily exploited. As the press reported an Empire-wide roundup of suspected members of a Japanese spy ring, Pattullo told Prime Minister King that British Columbians "were very much concerned" about Pacific Coast defences. The *Vancouver Sun* sensibly reminded readers to keep their heads since "it is easy for the unskilled observer to mistake where the making of a livelihood leaves off and intrigue begins." Rumours did not go away. Even an RCMP officer related a story from New York that Japanese fishermen were picking up packages of money and arms thrown off Canadian Pacific steamers sailing between Victoria and Seattle. His superiors dismissed the story as improbable because of inspections by customs, the navy, and the provincial police. Without citing specific examples, Powell River Liberals asked Pattullo to draw Ottawa's attention "to the grave menace of espionage afforded by the flagrant and extensive operations of Japanese subjects and their second generation descendants residing in this country operating gas and other marine vessels up and down the coast." Japanophobes reported anything suspicious. C.E. Hope was upset because a Japanese nurse at a United Church hospital in Bella Bella frequently visited a nearby Department of National Defence construction project. Neill alerted authorities to the presence of a few Japanese residents near the Ucluelet air base, where they could "keep a watchful eye on everything that goes on" and of a Japanese fisherman getting bait around Seymour Narrows, "a somewhat strategic waterway." An exasperated Keenleyside told Neill that the police had "investigated literally hundreds of charges of espionage, subversive tendencies and related activities, without in any single case finding corroborative evidence." While this did not mean that "no Japanese has been engaged in espionage or has expressed disloyal sentiments," it did show, he suggested, "the quality of charges that have been made, repeated and apparently believed."[97]

Despite censorship, the Japanese question appeared in the October 1941 provincial election campaign. MacGregor Macintosh proposed repatriating all 23,000 Japanese residents to Japan over a period of a decade. Because he was on the standing committee, his proposal embarrassed federal officials; when he lost his seat, members of the Japanese community – having complained that the "antis" were "having a Roman holiday over us" – felt "a certain amount of satisfaction." However, if press coverage is indicative, the Japanese question was a minor campaign issue and only in a few constituencies. In Victoria, Waldo Skillings, a Conservative, declared that "we white people cannot compete against the Japanese because of our standard of living. What will it be like after the war? We cannot deport them, but we can limit their activity by licensing." In Salmon Arm, A.F. Barton, a Liberal, boasted that the provincial Liberal government had cut the number of Orientals in lumbering and that it protected farmers against "under-selling" by "Asiatic competition." In Vancouver East, the Conservative candidate accused the provincial government of making no effort to halt the "Oriental menace." The Liberal replied with such "vicious" and "flagrant and unwarranted charges of disloyalty and treachery" that the JCCL complained to Prime Minister King.[98] No candidate who was reported to have made anti-Asian statements was elected, but this was simply because most provincial politicians realized that the question was a national one. Ironically, voters turned away from Pattullo, largely because he had been one of the three "saboteurs" who had wrecked the Dominion-Provincial Conference, which had been called to readjust the financial relations between Ottawa and the provinces in light of the Royal Commission on Dominion-Provincial Relations.[99] In wartime many British Columbians believed that the national interest was more important than the province's wishes. Prejudice, however, had not gone away. This reality was demonstrated six weeks later when Japan bombed Pearl Harbor. Canada almost immediately declared war on the Japanese Empire, and within weeks British Columbians were clamouring for the removal of all Japanese residents from the province.

Conclusion

When I began this project, I hoped to find a simple answer to the question: "Why did Canada pass a Chinese exclusionary act in 1923?" The answers I soon discovered were not simple and begged a more searching question: "Why were white British Columbians so hostile to Asian immigrants?" Had there been straightforward answers, this book would have been finished much sooner. At times in the research it seemed that some contemporary observers were right in saying that the hostility was irrational. While economic motives inspired many anti-Asian outbursts, the reasons for demanding restrictions on Asians were often couched in racial terms. In short, reasons did reinforce each other.[1] By examining the attitudes and actions of people in a defined area over a relatively short time, it has been possible to study in detail the notions behind British Columbians' desire to consolidate their "white man's province."

Those in responsible positions, such as Premier McBride and Prime Minister King, denied that antipathy to Asians had racial causes, blaming it instead on economic and social conditions. Those were face-saving statements. McBride had earlier said that he wanted to save British Columbia "for the white man" and Canada "for our own race" since there could never be an amalgamation with the "Oriental civilizations," which were so different, but he did not want to insult Japan, a valuable ally during the First World War. Privately King believed that the physical intermingling of Asians and whites would cause misfortune to both races, but he did not want to upset Japan when Britain was concerned about tension in the Far East. In times that were less tense internationally, Attorney General Manson publicly stated that "ethnological differences" between Asians and Europeans were great and that interracial marriages would seriously affect the social structure of the province. He was also anxious to restrict the economic activities of Asians even though "shoving" them out of one field only pushed them into another. Those who sought anti-Asian measures often simultaneously presented racial and economic arguments to increase the chances of gaining popular support. In proposing that the legislature permit the establishment of segregated schools, C.F. Davie feared the "immorality" that would arise from mixing races while warning that educating Asians would improve their competitive position. In the course of lobbying for exclusionary immigration laws, the Retail Merchants Association said that the Asian problem was not merely a matter of competitive merchandising, but "purely and simply an economic and racial question" on whose solution depended "the future of Western civilization." In October 1941 leaders of the Japanese community agreed that the principal cause of widespread animosity and mistrust of the Japanese "was economic jealousy tinged with colour prejudice."[2] They had plenty of recent evidence. Both MacGregor Macintosh and Halford Wilson began their anti-Japanese campaigns with complaints about Japanese economic competition but soon exploited popular concerns about Japan's military ambitions and raised alarms about the loyalty of the Canadian Japanese.

Adding a "racial" twist to the argument could remove the sting of special pleading, especially since economic interest groups did not always agree on the Asian question. When some white farmers proposed solving a wartime labour shortage by importing Chinese workers, the BC Federation of Labour claimed that they merely wanted cheap labour. When the Victoria Board of Trade invited civic organizations to work with it and the Retail Merchants Association in order to promote trade with white merchants, the Trades and Labour Council was amused. Board members questioned the motives of labour men who patronized Chinese businesses. When governments restricted Asian employment, some employers did protest. Lumbermen went to court when the province endeavoured to enforce an old regulation against the employment of Chinese and Japanese labourers on Crown timber licences. When the province checked Asian employment through a minimum wage law, the affected employers were conceded only a delay in its implementation in order to give them time to adjust.

Yet groups espousing anti-Asian ideas do not fit into neat categories. It is simply not possible to construct a grid listing the various economic interest groups (labour, farmers, fishermen, and merchants) on one axis and the attitudes toward Asians on the other axis because there was no consensus among definable economic groups. Organized labour, through the Vancouver Trades and Labour Council, helped to establish both the 1907 and 1921 versions of the Asiatic Exclusion League, but the Federated Labour Party, whose only enemies were capitalists, opposed any measure to exclude any worker. This stand contributed to the relative weakness of organized labour in the 1920s and 1930s. While a "split labour market" was once a factor in British Columbia, by 1914 labour had largely accomplished its goal of limiting Asian competition, and in the 1920s it almost completed its consolidation of a white man's province through federal fish licensing policies and the provincial Male Minimum Wage Act. Employers and employees were sometimes on the same side when it came to anti-Asian ideas. The major industrialists A.D. McRae and H.R. MacMillan employed Asians but could be as hostile to them as could some of their white employees. Fish canners relied on the Japanese as efficient fishermen but, worried about their dominating the industry, accepted Ottawa's decision to reduce the number of Japanese fishermen in 1923, provided it was done gradually. Japanese and white fishermen occasionally co-operated in seeking better deals from the canners, but Alicja Muszynski observes that racism divided fishermen and retarded the development of a class-consciousness that would have unified them in dealing with employers.[3] The Retail Merchants Association had a major role in securing the Chinese exclusionary act, but large- and small-volume retailers did not always agree on such local regulations as closing hours as a means of restricting Asian competition.

Farmers, although a comparatively small group in the province, had a lot to say on the Asian question but often had conflicting views. Some wanted to employ Asians; others sought any other kind of help. Some did not want Asians to acquire any land; others sold or leased it to them. Some white and Asian farmers co-operated in marketing schemes, but conflict between Chinese and white potato growers led to a war resembling a comic opera. By the mid-1920s anti-Asian resolutions were a less regular feature of the annual submissions of agricultural organizations to the legislature, but politicians and urban businessmen with "racist" reasons for opposing Asian competition exploited concerns about Asian possession of the land.

The Vancouver Board of Trade, for example, opposed Japanese land ownership although few, if any, of its members were engaged in agriculture. The board told Prime Minister King that "intensive cultivation" by the Japanese, "the greatest menace to the future development of our Province," had practically ousted white settlers in parts of the province. Given the "natural repugnance inherent in the souls of our own people to fraternize with the Oriental," the board explained, the Japanese gained "control of the surrounding land" and, as its owners, would "eventually control" the nation's destiny.[4] Similarly, because Asian farmers stimulated local trade, the Vernon Board of Trade accepted temporary leases but opposed "the cancerous conditions engendered by the actual sale of land to these people," which could serve to create "orientalized districts" that, "owing to racial peculiarities," would always be "out of sympathy with the white population" and, in a time of conflict, a possible "source of great danger to the nation."[5]

Such racist ideas even infected the Christian clergy. Some clerics called for just treatment of Asians, but others shared the common antipathies. In the Anglican community, for example, Rev. F.W. Cassillis-Kennedy, as noted in Chapter 2, was so defensive of the Japanese that his critics accused him of being in the pay of Japan, but Rev. N.L. Ward was highly suspicious of them. As a member of the United Church Committee on Christianity and Race Relations, Rev. Dr. S.S. Osterhout called for equality for Asians, but the committee, recognizing that laymen who competed with Asians in the workplace would not approve, did little more than study the "Oriental question."

The observations of Edward Said that "European culture gained in strength and identity by setting itself off against the Orient"[6] and of Henry Yu that "thinking about Orientals has always been thinking about what it means to be American"[7] had echoes in the attitudes of British Columbians before 1914. As the province matured, however, the notion of "a white man's province" became a less useful "common rallying cry"[8] by which British Columbians could distinguish themselves from other Canadians, although they did not always realize this. Eastern Canadians, in fact, increasingly showed that they shared many of British Columbians' prejudices and wanted to halt Asian immigration and check Asian activities. Had its members not been sympathetic, the federal government would never have implemented exclusionary measures or attempted to remove the Japanese from the fisheries. Moreover, Saskatchewan, Manitoba, and Ontario preceded British Columbia in legislating to prevent the Chinese from employing white women. In addition, the "Oriental question" became less useful for British Columbia premiers in "fighting Ottawa," especially since they had learned the limits of provincial powers and, in times of international crisis, recognized the need not to upset Japan, an ally in the First World War and a likely enemy in the Second World War.

This book began, in some respects, as a study of the politics of the Asian question, and certainly some of the province's politicians were among the most outspoken critics of the Asian presence. Did the politicians lead or reflect public opinion? There is no simple answer. Clearly they had to listen to the wishes of constituents or respond to what they thought constituents wanted. Their archived papers include many letters from individuals and groups requesting action on the Asian question. Given that immigration, the fisheries, and defence were largely federal responsibilities, British Columbia's members of Parliament, of most political persuasions, kept the "Oriental question" very much alive, particularly since they found sympathy for their ideas elsewhere in Canada. The parliamentary campaign that culminated in the Chinese Immigration Act of 1923 followed popular demand for exclusionary legislation, which had made the "Oriental question" a significant, though not decisive, issue in the 1921 election since every major party had a "No Oriental Immigration" plank in its platform. At other times, politicians led public opinion. In the late 1930s, after anti-Asian agitation had been relatively quiet for about five years, Liberals and Conservatives revived it in the 1935 federal election when J.S. Woodsworth of the CCF endorsed Asian enfranchisement. The fact that some white and Japanese fishermen could co-operate from time to time suggests that politicians such as A.W. Neill and Thomas Reid, MPs for constituencies where fishing was an important industry, may have stimulated agitation against the Japanese rather than simply responded to it.

Because the province had almost reached the limit of its constitutional ability to regulate the activities of Asians, provincial politicians had a much smaller role in the agitation than did their federal counterparts. The legislature, however, passed a resolution endorsing the efforts of the British Columbia members of Parliament to secure exclusionary legislation. On other occasions it urged Ottawa not to adhere to treaties that would affect its ability to limit immigration or Asian land holding. It also asked Ottawa to amend the British North America Act in order to allow it to prevent Asians from owning land. Although usually passed unanimously, these were essentially *pro forma* exercises, and the provincial government accepted Ottawa's advice about constitutional realities. Attorney General Manson, who strongly believed that for "ethnological reasons" the Asian and white races could not mix, recognized the constitutional limits of provincial power and concentrated on "educating the East" about British Columbia's problems.

Individual MLAs, however, did speak out, especially on matters affecting their constituents. Okanagan members were prominent in calling for measures to restrict land ownership, a live issue in their region in the early 1920s. And the most persistent agitators, Richard J. Burde (Alberni) and C.F. Davie (Cowichan-Newcastle), represented constituents with strong views on the Asian question. Burde, whose motives were chiefly economic, persevered in attempts to drive Asians out of the lumber industry and persuaded the legislature to pass the very effective Male Minimum Wage Act. Davie, in contrast, was inspired by racist ideas. He promoted the idea of segregated schools and attacked the presence of Asians in the Older Boys Parliament but received little support. Yet, when circumstances allowed, an MLA could attract a lot of attention. Not until MacGregor Macintosh grabbed hold of the issue of alleged illegal Japanese immigration did this concern become widespread in the late 1930s.

The Asian question spilled over into municipal politics. Questions about morality in Chinatown, particularly gambling, were linked with periodic campaigns in several cities to eliminate vice and to reform police departments. From time to time, municipal councils considered ways to regulate Asian competition in small businesses. Such a concern first set off Vancouver alderman Halford Wilson's anti-Asian campaign, which became so forceful that federal officials censored him to forestall anti-Japanese violence.

By then the international situation was deteriorating. Politicians, both federal and provincial, contributed to apprehension by pointing to the defencelessness of the Pacific Coast. Military officials in Ottawa did not share the anxieties of their officers on the coast about a Japanese attack, but civil servants, particularly in the Department of External Affairs, began setting up committees to study the "Oriental situation in British Columbia" in 1938. Their work represented sensible precautions and well-intended efforts to allay apprehensions but inadvertently gave legitimacy to fears in the province. Their warning of the possibility of "riots" recalled 1907 and occasional past warnings of riots if fishermen were not protected from Japanese competition, if land were sold to the Japanese, if Asians were enfranchised or their immigration continued, or if war materials were shipped to Japan. While most warnings were mere rhetoric, their repetition in the late 1930s and early 1940s threatened to render them self-fulfilling prophecies.

One of the striking changes between 1914 and 1941 was the shift in attention from the Chinese to the Japanese. Because the Western world perceived China as a weak power internationally, the Chinese in Canada could not rely on their home government to protect them against Canadian policies. The Chinese consul, for example, protested Victoria's efforts to segregate school children, but it was the refusal of the Chinese in Victoria to send their children to the segregated school that resolved the matter. The telling example was the inability of the Chinese government to do anything to prevent or reverse the exclusionary act of 1923.

The cessation of immigration, a declining population as elderly Chinese residents died or returned to China, and especially the Sino-Japanese war of the 1930s worked to the advantage of the Chinese in British Columbia. White British Columbians no longer feared being swamped by the Chinese and faced less Chinese competition in the workplace. Moreover, Japan's atrocities in China, which added to British Columbians' distrust of the Japanese, engendered sympathy for China and the Chinese in British Columbia. Chinese and white residents worked together to raise funds for Chinese war relief and to boycott Japanese products. Except in agriculture, where some Chinese farmers flouted marketing regulations while Japanese farmers co-operated in marketing schemes, the acceptability of the Chinese rose as that of the Japanese fell.

In contrast to China Japan was a major power, and its people in British Columbia, unlike the Chinese, who seemed to "know their place," were perceived as being aggressive and ambitious. For example, the *Kamloops Standard-Sentinel,* in dismissing lamentations on the "yellow menace" that "savor too greatly of party politics," observed that honest, hard-working Chinese farmers could "vastly improve lands and make hopeless-looking places fit for good returns" but that the ambitious Japanese farmer was a worry, for "he aims to be a landowner and an aggressive force in the community."[9] Diplomatically, because of various Anglo-Japanese treaties and, until 1921, the Anglo-Japanese Alliance, British Columbians had to treat the Japanese differently than they did the Chinese. In diverse approaches that reflected the two nations' different international standings, when the legislature discussed a bill to limit the employment of Asians in Dangerous Industries such as coal mines, the Chinese consul exhorted his countrymen to learn English and to fight for their rights, whereas the Japanese consul persuaded the legislature to kill the bill. And, when British Columbians forgot about international obligations, as in the fisheries case, the courts did not. Concerns about offending Japan, however, changed in the 1930s as Japan demonstrated its military ambitions. Although the Department of External Affairs and Mackenzie King had feared offending Japan on immigration matters, by 1940 Canada had restricted trade with Japan. Changes in international circumstances inevitably affected the Japanese in British Columbia. Although an increasing number were Canadian-born, most white British Columbians perceived the Nisei as Japanese, rather than as Canadian.

Asians were "hapless" victims of racial prejudice but were not silent.[10] The Chinese Benevolent Association vigorously, though unsuccessfully, protested the Chinese Immigration Act. The Chinese community in Victoria stood fast and forced the school board to end its segregation plans. In the 1930s the Nisei received some sympathy as they campaigned for the franchise but could not overcome the antipathy engendered by their ancestral land. Indeed, a pamphlet published by the Canadian Japanese Association in 1940 observed that while the attitudes and behaviour of both the Nisei and white Canadians were important, the "peace and happiness of the Japanese Canadians depend largely upon international relations between Japan and Canada."[11] Individuals could change their minds. Although Ian Mackenzie, who has been vilified for his behaviour after Pearl Harbor, believed that Asians could not be assimilated, as an MLA he led a campaign to enfranchise Japanese veterans of the Canadian Expeditionary Force.

Not every white British Columbian was hostile to Asians. Attorney General Manson, one of the most racist politicians, complained that he had no "crystallized and stabilized public opinion" on which to rely in dealing with the problem,[12] a view undoubtedly shared by the promoters of anti-Asian organizations, which often disappeared almost as quickly as they had formed. Indeed, many British Columbians had accepted a modus vivendi with their Asian neighbours and, to the chagrin of farmers and retailers, continued to patronize them. Anxious to promote Pacific trade, the *Vancouver Sun* argued, "Good will between Japan and Canada is just as important to the prosperity of this country as the jobs of a few white fishermen." By 1940 British Columbians were also aware of the evils of Nazis; many, not just socialists such as Angus MacInnis, warned against stooping "to the race-baiting tactics of Hitler's Nazis." Attorney General Wismer admonished that attacks based on racial origin simply bred "animosity and ill-feeling."[13]

By then British Columbians had consolidated their "white man's province" by virtually halting immigration and sharply limiting Asian economic activities. With economic issues effectively resolved, they could afford to demonstrate some tolerance. Hints that some British Columbians were questioning racist policies, coupled with the growing acceptance of the Chinese, suggested that, in time, ideas about a "white man's province" could change although no one was prepared to regard Asians as "white." Nevertheless, by differing in their attitudes toward the Chinese and Japanese, British Columbians showed that the theorists are almost right: "race," or more precisely "racist" behaviour, is largely socially constructed. Racism, of course, was often inspired by specific grievances, as would be amply demonstrated after Japan's attack on Pearl Harbor seemed to confirm the tocsins of Japanese treachery. This development is the subject of the next volume.

Since this trilogy is not a mystery story or a serial "thriller," it is appropriate to sketch the subject of the final volume. At the same time that Japan bombed the American naval base at Pearl Harbor, it began attacking Hong Kong, where two thousand Canadian soldiers had recently arrived to reinforce British forces. Within hours, Canada declared war on Japan, civilian defence officials imposed blackouts in coastal British Columbia, the RCMP implemented plans to intern almost forty Japanese nationals whose loyalties to Canada were suspect, and the Royal Canadian Navy began rounding up the Japanese fishing fleet. The police encouraged

Japanese-language newspapers and schools to close; the press advised white British Columbians to be calm and to allow Japanese Canadians to go about their normal activities.[14]

Japanese forces moved quickly in East Asia; Hong Kong fell on Christmas Day. British Columbians became more fearful of the Japanese in their midst, and few distinguished between Japanese nationals and people of Japanese ancestry who were Canadian citizens by birth or naturalization. To panicky British Columbians, all Japanese residents were potential fifth columnists and saboteurs. The government responded in early January by announcing that male Japanese nationals of military age would be moved to useful work inland and that male Japanese Canadian nationals of military age would be encouraged to do so. Making arrangements took time. Meanwhile, Japanese forces moved toward Singapore with frightening speed, capturing the city in mid-February. In Ottawa, British Columbia's MPs demanded the removal of all Japanese residents from the coast; their efforts were reinforced by resolutions from self-appointed "patriotic" groups, municipal councils, service clubs, prominent members of the business community, and others. New anti-Japanese groups appeared and, sometimes in co-operation with the Canadian Legion, planned mass meetings to demand the removal of all Japanese residents from the coast.

Given Mackenzie King's personal recollections of the 1907 riot and repeated references to the possibility of riots if something were not done about one or another aspect of the Asian question, it is not surprising that the federal government worried that planned demonstrations might get out of hand. Thus the federal Cabinet decided to remove all Japanese residents from the coast in order to prevent riots that could lead Japan to exact revenge at the expense of Canadian and other British subjects under its control.

In the spring and summer of 1942, British Columbia's Japanese population was initially dispersed, mainly to the interior of the province but also to sugar beet farms in southern Alberta and Manitoba. The reactions of interior residents varied.[15] Some "ghost towns" such as Kaslo, New Denver, and Greenwood welcomed evacuees as a stimulus to their economies. The Okanagan, which already had some Japanese residents, did not want any more except as agricultural workers under supervision. Kamloops, which had few Japanese residents, wanted newcomers only under military guard. Some communities gradually accepted Japanese residents, but others remained opposed to any permanent settlement for several years after the war. In the spring of 1945 the government told the Japanese that they must choose between moving east of the Rockies or being "repatriated" to Japan. Protests by the Japanese themselves and their white sympathizers, mainly in eastern Canada, eventually halted the repatriation scheme, but not until 1949 were the Japanese allowed to return to the coast except on a temporary basis and with police permission.[16] By then few seemed interested in returning even though British Columbia had dismantled its anti-Asian laws and enfranchised them.

There was little for them to return to. Although arguments for removing the Japanese in 1941-42 were couched in terms of the need for protection against the enemy, few British Columbians failed to see that removing the Japanese would create economic opportunities for white people, especially in the fisheries. Because of the wartime demand for fish, the federal government sold the Japanese fishing fleet to non-Japanese residents, generally at fire sale prices. For most fishermen, boats and gear had been their only capital. The federal government's custodian of enemy property took charge of real property and the personal effects that evacuees could not take as part of their baggage allowance. The custodian was unable to cope with managing either. The storage of personal property was poorly supervised, and vandals frequently stole or damaged it. As for houses, businesses, and farms, the custodian sold them, again usually at fire sale prices and often, in the case of some farms, to the government itself, which planned to make them available to veterans after the war. A few British Columbians protested the confiscation of private property, but most who said anything welcomed the sales as a way to guarantee that the Japanese would be unlikely to return.

The third volume will not ignore the Chinese. China was a gallant ally during the Second World War, and the Chinese in British Columbia benefited from the developing sympathy for their ancestral land. Little by little, governments accepted them as allies and Canadians. The attorney general authorized the return of their firearms, which had been seized in 1940 when federal officials were still thinking of an "Oriental problem"; in 1944 the Department of National Defence called up Chinese men of military age for service. In 1947 Ottawa revised the Chinese Immigration Act so that it was no longer an exclusionary policy. Although only the wives and minor unmarried children of Canadian citizens could enter Canada, the door, which had been slammed shut in 1923, was now slightly ajar. In 1947 both the federal and provincial governments enfranchised the Chinese without any fuss. In the next federal and provincial elections, politicians such as H.H. Stevens, who had once railed against the Chinese, appealed to them as voters. Along the way, the notion of "a white man's province" had disappeared. With enfranchisement, Asians in British Columbia ceased to be political pawns and became full-fledged members of a community that was sufficiently sure of itself to include them in the provincial polity. Nationally, however, both the Chinese and Japanese still endured immigration restrictions. They set aside old antagonisms and, as voters, lobbied the federal government to grant Asians the same standing as Europeans in immigration policy. In 1967, its centennial year, Canada finally changed its immigration regulations and removed the last barrier to "first class citizenship" for Canadians of Chinese and Japanese origin.

Notes

Abbreviations Used in Notes

AGR	Attorneys-General Records, BCA
AMacIP	Angus MacInnis Papers, UBC
AMMC	Angus MacInnis Memorial Collection, UBC
AMP	Arthur Meighen Papers, NAC
BAMP	Bruce A. McKelvie Papers, BCA
BCA	British Columbia Archives
BCLJ	British Columbia, Legislative Assembly, *Journals*
BCSP	British Columbia, *Sessional Papers*
BCV&P	British Columbia, Legislative Assembly, *Votes and Proceedings*
BFM	Board of Foreign Missions, United Church Archives, Toronto
CCLB	Chinese Consul Letter Book, 1914-15, UBC
CHTP	Charles Hibbert Tupper Papers, UBC
CVA	City of Vancouver Archives
CWC	Cabinet War Committee
DAgri	Department of Agriculture, NAC
DCER	Documents on Canadian External Relations
DCIR	Department of Citizenship and Immigration Records, NAC
DEAR	Department of External Affairs Records, NAC
DFish	Department of Fisheries, NAC
DHist	Directorate of History, Department of National Defence
DImm	Department of Immigration, NAC
DJust	Department of Justice, NAC
DLab	Department of Labour Records, NAC
DNDR	Department of National Defence Records, NAC
DSS	Department of the Secretary of State, NAC
ELP	Ernest Lapointe Papers, NAC
FDP	Francis Dickie Papers, BCA
GGMcGP	G.G. McGeer Papers, UBC
GGMcGPA	G.G. McGeer Papers, BCA
GGR	Governor-Generals' Records, NAC
GR441	Premiers' Papers, BCA
GR1222	Premiers' Papers, BCA
GR1668	Provincial Secretary's Records, BCA
HCD	House of Commons, *Debates*
HDP	Hugh Dobson Papers, BCA (microfilm)
HDWP	Halford D. Wilson Papers, BCA
HDWPV	Halford D. Wilson Papers, CVA
HFAP	Henry F. Angus Papers, UBC
HHSPN	H.H. Stevens Papers, NAC
HHSPV	H.H. Stevens Papers, CVA
HRMP	H.R. MacMillan Papers, UBC

IAMP   Ian A. Mackenzie Papers, NAC
JACP   J.A. Clark Papers, BCA
JCCA   Japanese Canadian Citizens Association, NAC
JCCL   Japanese Canadian Citizens League, NAC
JMRC   John Munro Research Collection, UBC
JWdeBFP   J.W. de B. Farris Papers, UBC
JWJP   J.W. Jones Papers, BCA
KD   W.L. Mackenzie King, Diary, available at <www.archives.ca>
KP   W.L. Mackenzie King Papers, NAC
LBP   Lottie Bowron Papers, BCA
LCP   Loring Christie Papers, NAC
LJLP   Leon J. Ladner Papers, CVA
MMP   M. Miyazaki Papers, NAC
NAC   National Archives of Canada
NWFP   N.W. Fujiwara Papers, NAC
PC   Privy Council
PCC   Presbyterian Church in Canada, United Church Archives, Toronto
PCOR   Privy Council Office Records, NAC
POC   Premiers' Official Correspondence, BCA
PTAHHS   PTA, Henry Hudson School, Minute Book, 1919-24, CVA
RBBP   R.B. Bennett Papers, NAC
RBHP   R.B. Hanson Papers, NAC
RCMPR   Royal Canadian Mounted Police Records, NAC
RLBP   R.L. Borden Papers, NAC
SCC   Supreme Court of Canada, NAC
SFTP   Simon Fraser Tolmie Papers, UBC
TDPP   T.D. Pattullo Papers, BCA
TGNP   Thomas G. Norris Papers, UBC
TWSPP   T.W.S. Parsons Papers, BCA
UBC   University of British Columbia, Special Collections
VCCCl   Vancouver City Clerk's Correspondence, CVA
VCCCo   Vancouver City Council Correspondence, CVA
VCCM   Vancouver City Council Minutes, CVA
VMC   Vancouver Mayor's Correspondence, CVA
VWOP   Victor W. Odlum Papers, NAC
WACBP   W.A.C. Bennett Papers, Simon Fraser University

Author note: Since this research was completed, the City of Vancouver Archives has reorganized some official records. When I did most of my research, parts of the Premiers' Official Correspondence (POC) in the British Columbia Archives were in unnumbered boxes. Since then, the files have been organized as GR441. They are now governed by the misnamed Access to Information Law and not all volumes have been "opened."

Introduction
1 Patricia E. Roy, "The Oriental 'Menace' to British Columbia," *The Twenties in Western Canada,* ed. S.M. Trofimenkoff (Ottawa: National Museum of Man, 1972), 243-58, reprinted in *Studies in Canadian Social History,* ed. Michiel Horn and Ronald Sabourin (Toronto: McClelland and Stewart, 1974), 243-55, and in *Historical Essays on British Columbia,* ed. J. Friesen and H.K. Ralston (Toronto: McClelland and Stewart, 1976), 243-55.
2 Patricia E. Roy, *A White Man's Province: British Columbia Politicians and Chinese and Japanese Immigrants, 1858-1914* (Vancouver: UBC Press, 1989).

3 Patricia E. Roy, "British Columbia's Fear of Asians," *Histoire sociale/Social History* 13 (May 1980): 161.
4 Population statistics are from Jean Barman, *The West Beyond the West* (Toronto: University of Toronto Press, 1996), 379, 380, 385.
5 Scottish natives were overrepresented among anti-Asian politicians. A.W. Neill, Thomas Reid, and Ian Mackenzie were all of Scottish birth. This was probably only coincidence but it invites further study.
6 Peter S. Li, *The Chinese in Canada* (Toronto: Oxford University Press, 1988), 33.
7 Alicja Muszynski, *Cheap Wage Labour: Race and Gender in the Fisheries of British Columbia* (Montreal and Kingston: McGill-Queen's University Press, 1996), 243.
8 Roy, *A White Man's Province*, xvii.
9 Muszynski, *Cheap Wage Labour*, 243.
10 *Vancouver Province*, 3 March 1938.
11 The following table shows the population of persons of Chinese and Japanese racial origin in British Columbia by gender, 1921-41 (Canada, *Census*, 1921-41):

	Chinese		Japanese	
Year	Males	Females	Males	Females
1921	21,820	1,713	9,863	5,143
1931	24,900	2,239	12,997	9,170
1941	16,426	2,399	12,426	9,670

12 John Nelson, *The Canadian Provinces: Their Problems and Policies* (Toronto: Musson, 1924), 188.
13 David Chuenyan Lai, *Chinatowns: Towns Within Cities in Canada* (Vancouver: UBC Press, 1988), 61.
14 James W. St. G. Walker, *"Race," Rights and the Law in the Supreme Court of Canada* (Toronto: The Osgoode Society/Waterloo: Wilfrid Laurier University Press, 1997), 119.
15 Roy, *A White Man's Province*, 268.
16 Board of Review (Immigration), Interim Report and Supplement, 14 May 1938, DImm, MfC4752.
17 Roy, *A White Man's Province*, viii-ix.
18 Walker, *"Race," Rights and the Law*, 18. For a detailed analysis see Elazar Barkan, *The Retreat of Scientific Racism: Changing Concepts of Race in Britain and the United States between the World Wars* (Cambridge: Cambridge University Press, 1992). Gordon Allport, in *The Nature of Prejudice* (Reading, MA: Addison-Wesley, 1979, first published 1954), 113, cautions against the danger of confusing "racial" and "ethnic" traits noting that the former "is given by nature" and the latter "acquired by learning." Much of what British Columbians despised in Asians (i.e., their "different" habits) was learned, but to distinguish between "ethnicity" and "race" here would only muddy the waters.
19 Robert Miles, *Racism after "Race Relations"* (London and New York: Routledge, 1993), 47.
20 Muszynski, *Cheap Wage Labour*, 242.
21 David Theo Goldberg, *Racist Culture: Philosophy and the Politics of Meaning* (Oxford: Blackwell, 1993), 93. Goldberg, however, accuses those who "insist that racism is by nature irrational" of repeating a myth.
22 Ann Laura Stoler, *Race and the Education of Desire: Foucault's History of Sexuality and the Colonial Order of Things* (Durham and London: Duke University Press, 1995), 96.
23 Michael Banton, *The Idea of Race* (London: Tavistock, 1977), 18. The *Oxford English Dictionary* cites several earlier uses of the term. Kay Anderson, *Vancouver's Chinatown: Racial Discourse in Canada, 1875-1980* (Montreal and Kingston: McGill-Queen's University Press, 1991),

18, attributes it to Robert Miles, *Racism and Migrant Labour*, but that book was not published until 1982.

24 Audrey Kobayashi and Peter Jackson, "Japanese Canadians and the Racialization of Labour in the British Columbia Sawmill Industry," *BC Studies*, 103 (Fall 1994): 35, 57 (italics in original).

25 Barbara J. Fields, "Whiteness, Racism and Identity," *International Labor and Working-Class History* 60 (Fall 2001): 50.

26 The term does not appear in standard dictionaries although a closely related term, "unassimilable," does.

27 Goldberg, *Racist Culture*, 59.

28 Native Sons of British Columbia, Argument Advanced by Native Sons of British Columbia In Opposition to Granting of Oriental Franchise (New Westminster, n.p., [1937]).

29 Stoler, *Race and the Education of Desire*, 30.

30 W. Peter Ward, "Class and Race in the Social Structure of British Columbia, 1870-1939," *BC Studies*, 45 (Spring 1980): 35.

31 The first critic off the mark was T. Rennie Warburton, "Race and Class in British Columbia: A Comment," *BC Studies*, 49 (Spring 1981): 79-85. Mark Leier, a labour historian, also argues the importance of class in analyzing the province's history. He claims that "class and class struggle are more fundamental than race or gender and other identities" because "class splits racial and gender identities and leads to tensions within these groups that cannot be resolved at the level of theory or practice" ("Response to Professors Palmer, Strong-Boag and McDonald," *BC Studies*, 111 [Autumn 1996]: 95). In that issue, a forum of Bryan Palmer, Veronica Strong-Boag, and Robert A.J. McDonald debated Leier's essay, "W[h]ither Labour History: Regionalism, Class, and the Writing of BC History."

32 Adolph Reed Jr., "Response to Eric Arnesen," *International Labor and Working-Class History* 60 (Fall 2001): 78.

33 Barbara J. Fields, "Ideology and Race in American History," in *Region, Race, and Reconstruction: Essays in Honor of C. Vann Woodward*, ed. J. Morgan Kousser and James M. McPherson (New York and Oxford: Oxford University Press, 1982), 158.

34 David R. Roediger, *The Wages of Whiteness: Race and the Making of the American Working Class* (London and New York: Verso, 1991), 8.

35 E.P. Thompson, *The Making of the English Working Class* (Harmondsworth: Penguin, 1980, first published 1963), 10.

36 Gillian Creese, "Class, Ethnicity and Conflict: The Case of Chinese and Japanese Immigrants, 1880-1923," in *Workers, Capital, and the State in British Columbia: Selected Papers*, ed. Rennie Warburton and David Coburn (Vancouver: UBC Press, 1988), 72.

37 For an overview of some of the relevant historiography see Robert A.J. McDonald, *Making Vancouver, 1863-1913* (Vancouver: UBC Press, 1996), Introduction and 24, 35.

38 Ibid., 104.

39 The evidence is contradictory. One young Nisei said conflict was "especially acute" in some company towns (Fumi Ohori, "B.C. Melting Pot for Second-Generation Japanese," *Vancouver Province*, 3 July 1937).

40 *Prince Rupert Daily News*, 7 January 1939 and 3 November 1941.

41 White women were enfranchised provincially in 1917 and federally in 1919.

42 Stoler, *Race and the Education of Desire*, 105.

43 Robert Miles would insist on the "idea" of racial relations (*Racism after "Race Relations,"* 42).

44 Timothy J. Stanley, "Why I Killed Canadian History: Conditions for an Anti-Racist History in Canada," *Histoire sociale/Social History* 33 (May 2000): 99.

45 Anthony Chan, *Gold Mountain: The Chinese in the New World* (Vancouver: New Star, 1983), 119.

46 Wing Chung Ng, *The Chinese in Vancouver, 1945-80* (Vancouver: UBC Press, 1999), 14-17.

47 Rolf Knight and Maya Koizumi, *A Man for Our Times: The Life-History of a Japanese-Canadian Fisherman* (Vancouver: New Star, 1976), 44-47, 58-59.

48 Ken Adachi, *The Enemy That Never Was* (Toronto: McClelland and Stewart, 1976); Toyo Takata, *Nikkei Legacy: The Story of Japanese Canadians from Settlement to Today* (Toronto: NC Press, 1983); Peter S. Li, *The Chinese in Canada* (Toronto: Oxford University Press, 1988); Harry Con et al., *From China to Canada: A History of the Chinese Communities in Canada,* ed. Edgar Wickberg (Toronto: McClelland and Stewart, 1982); Chan, *Gold Mountain;* Lai, *Chinatowns;* Paul Yee, *Saltwater City: An Illustrated History of the Chinese in Vancouver* (Vancouver: Douglas and McIntyre, 1988).

49 See Patricia E. Roy, "'Active Voices': A Third Generation of Studies of the Chinese and Japanese in British Columbia," *BC Studies,* 117 (Spring 1998): 51-61.

50 Walker, *"Race," Rights and the Law;* Constance Backhouse, *Colour-Coded: A Legal History of Racism in Canada, 1900-1950* (Toronto: University of Toronto Press, 1999); Kay Anderson, *Vancouver's Chinatown: Racial Discourse in Canada, 1875-1980* (Montreal and Kingston: McGill-Queen's University Press, 1991); W. Peter Ward, *White Canada Forever: Popular Attitudes and Public Policy Toward Orientals in British Columbia* (Montreal and Kingston: McGill-Queen's University Press, 1978).

51 Cole Harris, *The Resettlement of British Columbia: Essays on Colonialism and Geographical Change* (Vancouver: UBC Press, 1997), 273.

52 Eric Arnesen, "Whiteness and the Historians' Imagination," *International Labor and Working-Class History* 60 (Fall 2001): 9.

53 Personal recollection. Although the pejorative "coolie" commonly appeared in the nineteenth century, by the twentieth it had largely disappeared from usage in British Columbia.

54 In referring to "Asians," I am referring only to Chinese and Japanese. The *Komagata Maru* affair of 1914 effectively ended immigration from India. Despite a trickle of immigrants, the Indian population declined to under 2,000 by 1941 and little notice was taken of them. On immigrants from the Indian sub-continent see Norman Buchignani and Doreen M. Indra with Ram Srivastava, *Continuous Journey: A Social History of South Asians in Canada* (Toronto: McClelland and Stewart, 1985). The editors of the parliamentary debates used a lower case "o" for "oriental."

55 *Victoria Times,* 3 November 1921; *Victoria Colonist,* 13 November 1921; *Vancouver Province,* 7 October 1922 and 14 June 1922; *Agricultural Journal,* January 1923.

56 Benedict Anderson, *Imagined Communities* (London: Verso, 1991, first published 1983), 62.

57 Although dealing with the last decade or so, Frances Henry and Carol Tator have argued that "readers of a given newspaper usually subscribe to that paper's ideological position, and the relationship between a particular medium and its audience is interactive" (*Discourses of Domination: Racial Bias in the Canadian English-Language Press* [Toronto: University of Toronto Press, 2002], 7).

Chapter 1: "The Least Said, the Better"

1 The idea of setting the debate aside was not confined to British Columbia. In California "responsible leaders ... either exercised restraint or had it thrust upon them" during the war (Roger Daniels, *The Politics of Prejudice: The Anti-Japanese Movement in California and the Struggle for Japanese Exclusion* [Berkeley: University of California Press, 1977, first published 1962], 79).

2 Richard McBride to R.L. Borden, 3 August 1914, GR441, file 600/14; Governor-General to Sir Wm. Conynham Greene, 19 May 1916, DEAR, v. 1187; *Victoria Times,* 29 November 1917; *Nanaimo Free Press,* 3 December 1917.

3 *Victoria Times,* 22 May 1914; *Vancouver Sun,* 27 June 1914; *Kamloops Inland Sentinel,* 30 June 1914. The best account is in Hugh Johnston, *The Voyage of the Komagata Maru: The Sikh*

Challenge to Canada's Colour Bar (Bombay: Oxford University Press, 1979). Mcbride, Speech to Conservative Convention, [c. 22 January 1914], copy in BCA; Miscellaneous Material re McBride, M/M12; R.L. Borden, Diary, 23 March 1914, NAC; *New Westminster British Columbian,* 1 April 1914; McBride to Lieutenant-Governor, 7 May 1914, and McBride to Borden, 26 June 1914, LBP, v. 1; McBride to Yang Shu Wan, 24 February 1915, GR441, v. 65.

4 *Prince Rupert Weekly Empire,* 5 August 1914; *Alberni Advocate,* 21 August 1914; *Victoria Times,* 6 July 1915; *Victoria Colonist,* 28 June 1915; *Vancouver Sun,* 24 August 1914 and 7 October 1915; *Vancouver Province,* 4 November 1914; *The Week,* 23 January 1915; Barry M. Gough, *The Royal Navy and the North West Coast of British Columbia, 1810-1914* (Vancouver: UBC Press, 1971), 238n75; C.J. Desbarats to Under Secretary of State for External Affairs, 11 July 1917, DNDR, MfC5853; *Prince Rupert Evening Empire,* 12 August 1914. Sir Wilfrid Laurier enjoyed the irony of British Columbians damning his Japanese policy but being "grateful to have the Japanese good-will" (King, Diary, 17 November 1914, KD); HCD, 8 June 1917, 2145; *Penticton Herald,* 18 April 1918; *Victoria Times,* 2 November 1920.

5 *Nanaimo Free Press,* 8 October 1915; G.F. Gibson to McBride, 10 August 1914, GR441, v. 59; *B.C. Federationist,* 14 May 1915; *Vancouver World,* 29 June 1916; McBride to J.D. Hazen, 21 December 1914, Borden to McBride, 26 January 1915, and McBride to Borden, 3 February 1915, LBP, v. 1; Borden to W.S. Churchill, 13 August 1914, RLBP, #161134-5; McBride to Franklin K. Lane, 21 December 1914, GR441, v. 397.

In August 1918, the *B.C. Orphan's Friend,* a Roman Catholic magazine published in Victoria, reprinted an editorial from an American journal, the *Pacific Star,* reviving old "Yellow Peril" stories. The *Saturday Sunset* ran a story in which local Japanese co-operated with Germans under Alvo von Alvensleben, whom the kaiser had appointed as military governor (30 January and 6 February 1915). Von Alvensleben, a financial agent and part of Vancouver's prewar social elite, was denied re-entry into Canada when he returned from Europe in the fall of 1914.

6 Kahachi Abe, Memo, 16 November 1914, GR441, v. 62; T.B. Shoebotham to McBride, 15 January 1915, GR441, v. 63; McBride to Abe, 1 February, 21 July, and 2 August 1915, GR441, v. 64; *Victoria Colonist,* 27 January, 2 March, and 3 March 1915; McBride to Rear Admiral Story, 30 September 1915, GR441, v. 399. The *Vancouver Sun* (18 February 1915) and the *Omineca Herald* (26 February 1915) suggested that the poolroom policy was designed to cater to anti-Asian sentiments.

7 *Victoria Colonist,* 19 August 1914; *Cowichan Leader,* 24 September 1914; *Vancouver Province,* 8, 10, and 28 August 1914; S. Kawakami to W.J. Bowser, 9 March 1916, GR441, v. 171; Yashushi Yamazaki to Deputy Minister, Militia, 25 March 1916, DNDR, v. 1246.

8 *Vancouver Sun,* 12 August 1914 and 1 February 1916; *Vancouver World,* 12 August 1914; *Victoria Colonist,* 29 August 1914; *Nanaimo Free Press,* 26 October 1914; Canadian Japanese Association to H.C. Brewster, c. December 1916, POC.

9 W.G. to Christie, 4 April 1916, Bonar Law to Governor-General, 20 April 1916, and Major-General, Chief of General Staff, to Officer Commanding Military District No. 11, 21 April 1916, DNDR, v. 1256. When Rev. Goro Kaburagi, editor of the Vancouver *Canada News,* a rival of Yamazaki's *Tairiku Nippo* (Vancouver), opposed the formation of a battalion, some recruits destroyed his printing plant (S. Fiset to Under Secretary of State for External Affairs, 26 March 1916, RLBP, #16573; *Vancouver Province,* 20 March 1916). See also Roy Ito, *We Also Went to War* (Etobicoke, ON: S-20 and Nisei Veterans Association, 1984), ch. 1.

0 *Vancouver Chinese Times,* 5 December 1917 and 6 November 1919; *Victoria Colonist,* 9 November 1919 and 14 October 1917; F.H. Cunningham, Chief Inspector of Fisheries, New Westminster, to W.A. Found, 31 August 1915, DFish, v. 1812.

1 R. Duncanson to Dr. R.P. Mackay, 16 March 1915, PCC, BFM, v. 3; *Vancouver Chinese Times,* 1 February and 24 June 1915; *B.C. Federationist,* 5 March 1915; Lin Shih Yuan to W.D. Scott, 17

November 1914, and Lih Shih Yuan to Board of License Commissioners, 13 April 1915, CCLB; *Vancouver World,* 23 November 1915; F.H. Cunningham to W.A. Found, 31 August 1915 and 7 April 1916, DFish, v. 1812. Some had lost jobs in the fishing industry because increased use of machinery had enabled canners to replace large Chinese crews with a few skilled white workers (W.H. Barker, President and General Manager, BC Packers, to Royal Commission to Investigate and Report on Salmon Fisheries of British Columbia, Evidence, 12 June 1917, DFish, v. 508). *Vancouver Chinese Times,* 26 August, 8 October, and 27 October 1914; McBride to Yang Shu Wan, 24 February 1915, GR441, v. 65; W.J. Roche to McBride, 15 December 1914, GR441, v. 397; Lih Shih Yuan to W.J. Roche, 31 December 1914, RLBP, v. 183. The consul chastised those who registered to leave and then sold their return cards to new immigrants who sought to evade the head tax.

12   *B.C. Federationist,* 14 August and 9 October 1914; 12 March, 16 April, and 30 July 1915; *Vancouver Chinese Times,* 21 October 1914 and 15 April 1915. The *Vancouver Chinese Times* called on all Chinese residents in Canada to fight attacks on laundries, "the most important and essential business of the overseas Chinese" (12 January 1915).
      Victoria Colonist, 16 May 1915. A riotous mob attacked a beer garden and other German-owned businesses in Victoria after the sinking of the *Lusitania.*
      Her biographer suggests that Gutteridge had friendly feelings toward Asians but "believed they had to take their place in line – behind white workers" (Irene Howard, *The Struggle for Social Justice in British Columbia: Helena Gutteridge, the Unknown Reformer* [Vancouver: UBC Press, 1992], 94). According to Howard, the licensing board later recommended that hotels employ white women, and city council financed renovations to the YWCA to allow for the employment of white women (113).

13   *Vancouver World,* 23 November 1915 and 18 and 28 March and 22, 26, and 28 June 1916; *B.C. Federationist,* 24 March and 14 July 1916. The Licensed Hotelkeepers volunteered to replace Asian labour, but after two hotels hired Chinese workers to replace white cooks, the president of the Vancouver Trades and Labour Council concluded that the hotelmen had merely made a gesture for support in their antiprohibition campaign (*B.C. Federationist,* 5 March 1915); Lih Shih Yuan to Board of License Commissioners, 13 April 1915, CCLB.

14   *Prince George Herald,* 16 October 1915; *Vancouver World,* 6 May 1915; *Vancouver Daily News-Advertiser,* 9 and 18 May 1915; *B.C. Federationist,* 21 May 1915; *Kamloops Inland Sentinel,* 11 November 1914 and 27 March 1916; *Penticton Herald,* 19 November 1914; *Vancouver Sun,* 24 May 1915; *Nanaimo Free Press,* 30 July 1915.

15   *Vancouver Sun,* 18 March 1915; *Cowichan Leader,* 18 March 1915; *Vancouver World,* 2 October 1915. Near Nanaimo, however, the Newcastle Lumber Mill began replacing Chinese labour with white, preferably British, workers (*Nanaimo Free Press,* 9 June 1915; *Victoria Colonist,* 27 May and 8 June 1915). The Cameron Lumber Company, one of the largest firms, claimed that Asians earned about $2,500 of its total $20,000 monthly payroll (*Victoria Colonist,* 5 June 1915).

16   *Nanaimo Free Press,* 2 September 1915; *Vancouver Chinese Times,* 17 May 1915; *B.C. Federationist,* 28 January and 10 March 1916; H.S. Fleming to W.J. Bowser, 3 April 1916, POC. The number of Japanese in the mines declined from approximately 160 in 1914 to about 140 in 1918 (R. Sumida, "The Japanese in British Columbia," University of British Columbia, MA thesis, 1935, 356).

17   Alex Maxwell to McBride, 13 October 1915, and McBride to Maxwell, 27 October 1915, GR441, v. 69; *Platform of the Liberal Policy of B.C.* (Vancouver: Saturday Sunset, 1916); *B.C. Federationist,* 8 February and 8 September 1916; *Vancouver Sun,* 17 January and 10 February 1916; *Nanaimo Free Press,* 30 August and 1 and 9 September 1916; *Vancouver World,* 30 August 1916. During a Vancouver by-election early in 1916, M.A. MacDonald, the successful Liberal candidate, described "the steady increase in the number of Orientals in the province" and

the increase in their employment as "acute" problems. He called the Conservatives' belated interest in a "White B.C." "an election sign" (*Vancouver Sun,* 10 February 1916). On earlier attempts to ban Asians from working underground, see Ross Lambertson and Alan Grove, "Pawns of the Powerful: The Politics of Litigation in the Union Collieries Case," *BC Studies,* 103 (Autumn 1994): 3-31. The idea of a minimum wage was not new. The *Kamloops Inland Sentinel* had mentioned it on 23 June 1914.

18 See Patricia E. Roy, *A White Man's Province: British Columbia Politicians and Chinese and Japanese Immigrants, 1858-1914* (Vancouver: UBC Press, 1989), ch. 6; *Nanaimo Free Press,* 29 and 30 March 1918; *Vancouver Chinese Times,* 8 April 1918; *B.C. Federationist,* 2 February 1917 and 8 March 1918; John Oliver to S. Ukita, 3 April 1918, AGR, 1918-17-2034. The role, if any, of mine operators in leading the government to this decision is unknown. Precedents of disallowance probably convinced the government of the futility of the measure.

19 Consul Ukita, Note Verbale, 5 February 1918, and E.L. Newcombe to Oliver, 22 August 1918, AGR, 2060-17-18; H.C. Brewster to M. Burrell, 6 February 1918, and Brewster to Burrell, 6 February 1918, GR441, v. 189; Sumida, "The Japanese in British Columbia," 340-41; Brewster to N.W. Rowell, 11 February 1918, RLBP, #125938; Joseph Pope to Prime Minister, 18 February 1918, RLBP, #95425-7. Eventually, the matter was referred to the courts.

20 *New Westminster British Columbian,* 11 September 1916; *Nanaimo Free Press,* 1 September 1916; *Vancouver Sun,* 28 June 1916. Report of the Committee of the Privy Council, Approved 21 June 1917, Royal Commission, Evidence, Preliminary Report, and C.C. Ballantyne to G.W. Morrow and O.H. Nelson, 7 January 1918, DFish, v. 508. The commission, after ascertaining that native-born Canadians, other than Indians, held only 102 of 9,126 gill-net licences issued in 1916, recommended encouraging native Canadians to enter the fisheries but ambiguously observed that all immigrants who became citizens should be able to engage "in every kind of honest useful work" on the grounds that this would "bring about real national assimilation." It recommended certifying fishermen and distributing licences among whites, naturalized Japanese residents, and Indians in proportion to their population in the coastal districts.

21 August Forrar, Manager, Wallace Fisheries Ltd., Rivers Inlet, and Robert J. Woods, Superintendent, ABC Packing Company, Skeena River, Royal Commission, Evidence, July 1917, DFish, v. 508; *Nanaimo Free Press,* 1 February 1916; *B.C. Federationist,* 9 November and 7 December 1917; Malcolm Y. Reid to W.D. Scott, 5 November 1917, DSS, v. 799; *Vancouver Sun,* 10 November 1917; A.L. Jolliffe to W.D. Scott, 7 November 1917 and 4 May 1918, DImm, MfC4751.

22 See *A White Man's Province,* 248-50; HCD, 22 April 1918, 1005; C.P. Stacey, *Canada and the Age of Conflict* (Toronto: Macmillan, 1977), I, 235; *Vancouver Province,* 16 February 1917.

23 *The Week,* 27 February 1917; Thomas Cunningham to McBride, 13 and 20 July 1915, GR441, v. 67; McBride to Cunningham, 23 July 1915, GR441, v. 127; *B.C. Fruit and Farm,* March 1917, 1181; *Vancouver World,* 10 January 1918; *Victoria Times,* 15 November 1918; *Chilliwack Progress,* 19 January 1918; *Victoria Colonist,* 27 August 1915; *Armstrong Advertiser,* 23 August 1917. In protesting a 1917 resolution from the Vernon Farmers' Institute seeking to prevent Orientals from acquiring agricultural lands, the Japanese consul reported that only a few Japanese farmers at Vernon were "tilling land on lease or working by wages," that they were satisfied, and that he had heard no objections from Vernon farmers to the Japanese acquiring land (Ukita to Brewster, 14 January 1917, GR441, v. 175).

24 *Victoria Colonist,* 27 August 1915; *Fraser Valley Record,* 28 October 1915 and 18 January 1917; *Agricultural Journal,* April 1916, 14; *Nanaimo Free Press,* 5 June 1915; *Vancouver World,* 16 February 1917.

25 *Cowichan Leader,* 9 November 1916; *Fraser Valley Record,* 30 November and 14 December 1916; *Vancouver World,* 18 December 1916 and 3 January 1918; *B.C. Fruit and Farm,* August 1917, 4.

26 *B.C. Fruit and Farm,* February 1917, 1165, and March 1917, 1181, 1191; *Kamloops Standard-Sentinel,* 12 March 1918.

27 *Vancouver World,* 12 February 1917; *B.C. Federationist,* 16 February and 2 March 1917 and 1 February 1918; *Vancouver Province,* 16 February 1917. Labour organizations in Ontario and Alberta shared these views.

28 The Immigration Department rejected the railways' request to import unskilled Japanese labour but did try to arrange return transportation for 5,000 Chinese who had left because of unemployment (W.D. Scott to Deputy Minister, 20 January 1917, DImm, MfC4750; W.H. Walker to Governor-General's Secretary, 11 September 1917, GGR, MfT1175); *Comox Argus,* 28 February 1918; *Port Alberni News,* 23 January 1918; *B.C. Federationist,* 11 January 1918; Vernon Board of Trade to M. Burrell, 21 January 1918, RLBP, #125184-5; *Vancouver World,* 19 January 1918; HCD, 22 April 1918, 997. In the same debate, Simon Fraser Tolmie (Unionist, Victoria) expressed similar sentiments and noted the propensity of Asians to succeed in business (1002).

29 C.H. Young and H.R.Y. Reid, *The Japanese Canadians* (Toronto: University of Toronto Press, 1938), 203.

Chapter 2: "We Could Never Be Welded Together"

1 T.H. Boggs, "Oriental Immigration," *The Annals of the American Academy of Political and Social Science* 107 (May 1923): 54; E.P. Bell, *Pillars of World Peace: Mackenzie King, Prime Minister of Canada, Discusses the Problem of the Pacific and Gives a Formula for International Good Relations* (Chicago: The Chicago Daily News, 1925), copy in KP, #95042ff.

2 *Nanaimo Free Press,* 31 January 1919 and 27 June 1924; Toyo Takata, *Nikkei Legacy: The Story of Japanese Canadians from Settlement to Today* (Toronto: NC Press, 1983), 45-46; *Victoria Times,* 25 May 1929; *Vancouver Province,* 11 February 1920 and 28 April and 13 June 1930; *Victoria Colonist,* 11 January 1920 and 4 January 1923; Philip C.P. Low, *Memories of Cumberland Chinatown* (Vancouver: P.C.P. Low, 1993), 19-20.

3 Quoted in Barry Broadfoot, *Years of Sorrow, Years of Shame: The Story of the Japanese Canadians in World War II* (Toronto: Doubleday, 1977), 35; Muriel Kitagawa, *This Is My Own: Letters to Wes & Other Writings on Japanese Canadians, 1941-1948,* ed. Roy Miki (Vancouver: Talonbooks, 1985), 21; Fumi Ohori, "B.C. Melting Pot for Second-Generation Japanese," *Vancouver Province,* 3 July 1937; *Vancouver Sun,* 16 September 1921; *Western Woman's Weekly,* 17 March and 1 December 1923.

4 *Vancouver World,* 22 April 1919; "University Hill" (Victoria: Department of Lands, 1925), copy in CVA, RG2A1. Buyers agreed not to sell or lease the lot or any part of it to "any person of Chinese, Japanese, or other Asiatic or Indian race" except Japanese and Chinese consular officials, their families, and their servants. See Kay Anderson, *Vancouver's Chinatown* (Montreal and Kingston: McGill-Queen's University Press, 1991), 127. Burnaby's Ocean View Cemetery would not sell plots to Asians or other "coloured" people. *Vancouver World,* 7 March 1916; *Victoria Colonist,* 29 November 1921; *Kelowna Courier,* 9 February 1922.

5 *Vernon News,* 21 August 1919; *Chilliwack Progress,* 17 May 1917; *Victoria Times,* 15 November 1919; *Cranbrook Herald,* 22 September 1921; *Vancouver Province,* 27 February 1919. Business and professional men organized the Japan Society in 1928 to promote friendly relations between Canada and Japan (By-Laws of the Japan Society of Vancouver, VMC, v. 4). Mitsuo Yesaki and Harold and Kathy Steeves, *Steveston Cannery Row: An Illustrated History* (Richmond: Mitsuo Yesaki and Harold and Kathy Steeves, 1998), 79. In 1921, 32.2 percent of the Chinese and 41.1 percent of the Japanese over the age of ten in Canada could not speak English; in 1931 the corresponding figures were 29.6 percent and 21.5 percent (W.B. Hurd, "Racial Origins and Nativity of the Canadian People," Canada, *Census,* 1931, v. 13, 677).

6 *Victoria Colonist,* 25 April 1923 and 6 December 1924; *Victoria Times,* 25 and 30 April 1923; *Vancouver Province,* 9 May 1923. On Rev. G.S. Price, see Robert K. Burkinshaw, *Pilgrims in*

Lotus Land: Conservative Protestantism in British Columbia, 1917-1981 (Montreal and Kingston: McGill-Queen's University Press, 1995), ch. 5.

7 For example, the *New Westminster British Columbian,* 1 December 1932; *Victoria Colonist,* 29 February 1936; *Fraser Valley Record,* 15 April 1937; *Prince Rupert Daily News,* 16 November 1934 and 30 April 1937. May C. Smith to R.P. Mackay, 12 November 1919, and Smith to Mackay, 21 November 1921, PCC, BFM, b. 4; D.A. Smith to W.H. Noyes, 10 February 1922, and A.A. Gray to Mackay, 11 June 1922, PCC, BFM, b. 5; *Armstrong Advertiser,* 1 March 1923; Religious Society of Friends, Victoria Monthly Meeting, 1 October 1924 and 5 November 1924, BCA, MfA763; *Vancouver World,* 30 January 1920 and 14 November 1922; Timothy P. Nakayama, "Anglican Missions to the Japanese in Canada," *Journal of the Canadian Church Historical Society* 8 (June 1966): 30; *Vancouver Province,* 29 January 1920.

8 *Vancouver Star,* 5 November 1925; Hugh Dobson to W.H. Vance et al., 2 July 1927, and J.K. Unsworth to Dobson, 8 January 1928, HDP; *Western Methodist Recorder,* June 1928, 4; "The Race Problem as it Affects Canada," Address to Vancouver Institute, 7 January 1927, HDP; J.W. Kimura and J.C. Ariga, *The Life of the Rev. F.W. Cassillis-Kennedy: The Father of the Japanese in Canada* (Vancouver: Japanese Anglican Church, 1931), quoted in Timothy M. Nakayama, "Anglican Japanese Missions in Canada: A Historical Survey," Vancouver, Anglican Theological College of BC, essay, 1956, 20; F.W. Cassillis-Kennedy, "Assimilability of Orientals in Canada," *British Columbia Monthly* 26 (November 1926): 3.

9 *Vancouver World,* 25 October 1917 and 17 July 1919; *Victoria Colonist,* 18 July 1919; John Mackay to McBride, 16 September 1914, POC; *Prince Rupert Evening Empire,* 28 September 1921; *Vancouver Province,* 8 February 1923; *Vancouver Sun,* 14 May 1920. See also *Victoria Colonist,* 5 February 1920; *Vancouver World,* 15 September 1922. Doull, a native of Halifax, was bishop of the Kootenays from 1915 to 1923.

10 A.A. Gray to Rev. R.P. Mackay, 11 June 1922, PCC, BFM, b. 5; *Vancouver World,* 26 January 1924; *Vancouver Sun,* 14 May 1920; Rev. N. Lascelles Ward, "The Oriental Problem," supplement to "Further Report on the Oriental Problem, Submitted to the General Ministerial Association, Vancouver, B.C., 9 January 1922," with Rev. B.C. Freeman, to Minister of the Interior, 24 January 1922, DImm, MfC10652. Rev. N. Lascelles Ward's book *Oriental Missions in British Columbia* (Westminster: Society for the Propagation of the Gospel in Foreign Parts, 1925) explained the customs of China in order to help Canadians understand differences in living styles. *Vancouver Province,* 19 December 1925; Osterhout, N. Lascelles Ward, and David A. Smith to W.L.M. King, [c. February 1922], DImm, MfC10661; Osterhout, Report, *Western Methodist Recorder,* January 1919, 4-5. See also W. Peter Ward, "The Oriental Immigrant and Canada's Protestant Clergy, 1868-1925," *BC Studies,* 22 (Summer 1974): 40-55.

11 Rev. Wm. Graham to Mr. Edmison, 3 November 1919, PCC, BFM, b. 4. On the Japanese response to some missionary activities, see Norman Knowles, "Religious Affiliation, Demographic Change and Family Formation among British Columbia's Chinese and Japanese Communities: A Case Study of Church of England Missions, 1861-1942," *Canadian Ethnic Studies* 27, 2 (1995): 59-80.

12 Rev. N. Lascelles Ward, "The Oriental Problem," supplement to "Further Report on the Oriental Problem, Submitted to the General Ministerial Association, Vancouver, B.C., 9 January 1922," with Rev. B.C. Freeman, to Minister of the Interior, 24 January 1922, DImm, MfC10652. *Western Methodist Recorder,* January 1919, 4-5.

13 *Kamloops Standard-Sentinel,* 12 May 1922.

14 Edgar Wickberg, ed., *From China to Canada: A History of the Chinese Communities in Canada* (Toronto: McClelland and Stewart, 1982), 80-81; Denise Chong, *The Concubine's Children: Portrait of a Family Divided* (Toronto: Viking, 1994), 60.

15 *Victoria Times,* 12 July 1920; *Nanaimo Free Press,* 13 July 1920; *Kelowna Courier,* 7 October 1920; *Vancouver World,* 6 February 1920; *The Japanese Contribution to Canada* (Vancouver:

Canadian Japanese Association, 1940), 27; No. 1 District Fishermen's Association, Evidence, [c. January 1923], and Hozumi Yonemura in "Evidence taken in British Columbia," British Columbia Fisheries Commission, 1922, v. 1, and DFish, v. 1233; Daphne Marlatt, *Steveston Recollected* (Victoria: Provincial Archives of British Columbia, 1975), 96.

16 Roger Daniels, *The Politics of Prejudice: The Anti-Japanese Movement in California and the Struggle for Japanese Exclusion* (Berkeley: University of California Press, 1962), 68. John Higham's *Strangers in the Land* (New York: Atheneum, 1967, first published 1953) provides an account of Grant and Stoddard and the background of their ideas.

17 *Western Recorder,* June 1928, 4; Madison Grant, *The Passing of the Great Race* (New York: Scribner, 1916), 69; Lothrop Stoddard, *The Rising Tide of Color against White World Supremacy* (New York: Scribner, 1923, copyright 1920), 162, 231, 420. Stoddard was still cited in 1937 – e.g., P.K. Winch to Editor, *Victoria Colonist,* 11 July 1937. An anonymous writer of a letter to the editor of the *Vancouver Province* recommended Grant's book (13 February 1926); Rev. Hugh Dobson often referred to Grant and Stoddard ("The Race Problem as It Affects Canada," Address to the Vancouver Institute, 7 January 1927, HDP, b. 31). A medical column quoted Stoddard on the "undesirability of crossing races" (*Vancouver Sun,* 4 September 1921). *Maclean's* [1 June 1920], 28, and the *Vancouver Sun,* 30 May 1920, had summaries. A tear-out of Stoddard's October 1920 article on "The Japanese Issue in California" in an unnamed magazine is in the papers of J.W. Jones, MLA (JWJP). In the parliamentary debate on Oriental exclusion, Brigadier General J.A. Clark recommended Stoddard (HCD, 8 May 1922, 1523), and J.S. Woodsworth quoted from its "rather arrogant position" (HCD, 8 May 1922, 1572). A British delegate to the Washington Conference on Arms Limitation told the Victoria Canadian Club that he disagreed with Stoddard's prediction of a racial cleavage between the white and coloured races (*Victoria Colonist,* 26 January 1922). In a full-page advertisement in the *Vancouver Province* (2 November 1922), the *Saturday Evening Post* announced articles on the Near East by Stoddard, "author of The Rising Tide of Color."

18 Timothy J. Stanley, "White Supremacy and the Rhetoric of Educational Indoctrination: A Canadian Case Study," in *Making Imperial Mentalities: Socialisation and British Imperialism,* ed. J.A. Mangan (Manchester: Manchester University Press, 1990), 155-56; R.E. Gosnell, "British Columbia," in *Immigration as Affecting Canada and Her Constituent Provinces* (Victoria: A.C. Flumerfelt, [1909]), 12-14; Patricia E. Roy, *A White Man's Province: British Columbia Politicians and Chinese and Japanese Immigrants, 1858-1914* (Vancouver: UBC Press, 1989), ch. 2. Mariana Valverde, *The Age of Light, Soap, and Water: Moral Reform in English Canada, 1885-1925* (Toronto: McClelland and Stewart, 1991), 108. In colonial British Columbia concerns about miscegenation referred to the mingling of Aboriginal women with European men (see Adele Perry, *On the Edge of Empire: Gender, Race and the Making of British Columbia, 1849-1871* [Toronto: University of Toronto Press, 2001], ch. 2).

19 The copy is located in the JMRC, b. 37. Stevens told the Missionary Society of Mount Pleasant Methodist Church that "assimilation, after all, means inter-marriage." The Asiatic, he said, "may be intelligent, he may be fully educated to Canadian customs and standards, and he may be an asset to Canada in the way of production, but the barrier of race is insurmountable, and he will never be assimilated" (*Vancouver Province,* 2 December 1919); HCD, 26 April 1921, 2591, and 19 March 1931, 143; *Vancouver Province,* 2 November 1921, 25 February and 12 November 1927; *Vancouver Sun,* 25 February 1927.

20 David Grant to King, 24 April 1923, DImm, MfC4751. On another occasion, Grant told a sponsor, "I would rather have a recommendation from a Canadian than from a 'Cockney.' This is our country, and we are better qualified to judge what we want than nine-tenths of the people in the British Isles" (*Vancouver Province,* 3 February 1925). He told a Chinese applicant that his duty required him to reject anyone who would not "make the country better or would keep it as good as it is" (*Vancouver Province,* 5 June 1922). Several

newspapers, including the *Vancouver World* (5 April 1922) and the *Fraser Valley Record* (20 April 1922), praised Grant. So too did the Prince Rupert Trades and Labour Council (*Prince Rupert Evening Telegram*, 15 February 1922) and the Native Sons and Daughters of British Columbia (*Vancouver Sun*, 13 May 1922). When Grant used similar words six years later to reject applications from "sons of Nippon," the press suggested that he was violating the Naturalization Act and expressed concern about trade implications (*Vancouver Star* and *Victoria Times*, 12 June 1928).

Not all judges agreed with Grant, but, citing his instructions, Judge Cayley sent recommendations for or against naturalization to Ottawa (*Vancouver World*, 5 February 1923). In March 1923 the court recommended four Japanese for citizenship. They spoke English, and one, "emphasizing his desire to sever Japanese ties," had adopted the surname London (*Vancouver Province*, 5 March 1923). Attorney General Manson was unclear about federal policy but explained confidentially that the secretary of state had agreed that "they will not naturalize Japs in B.C. No one is rejected except by the local judge or for obvious reasons. Their applications are simply – never dealt with and so stand," but Neill knew that the arrangement could change at any time (Neill to Manson, 15 January 1928, AGR, 1918-17-2060; *Victoria Colonist*, 7 February 1922; N. Matsunaga to King, 19 November 1924, DImm, MfC4951; *Vancouver Province*, 9 July 1924 and 10 January 1928; *Victoria Times*, 30 January 1928; *New Westminster British Columbian*, 11 February and 9 September 1931). British Columbians did not realize, or would not acknowledge, that since 1924 Japan had permitted citizens abroad and their children to relinquish Japanese nationality.

21 Rev. N. Lascelles Ward, "The Oriental Problem," supplement to "Further Report on the Oriental Problem, Submitted to the General Ministerial Association, Vancouver, B.C., 9 January 1922," with Rev. B.C. Freeman, to Minister of the Interior, 24 January 1922, DImm, MfC10652; *Vancouver World*, 15 September 1922; *Penticton Herald*, 8 October 1922; *Victoria Times*, 6 December 1922; *B.C. Veterans Weekly*, 26 November 1921.

22 In 1914 the provincial secretary told registrars under the Marriage Act not to refer applications for marriage licences to the head office in Victoria in cases where one party was Chinese, Japanese, or East Indian and the other "of the white race" (H.E. Young to Registrars, 17 September 1914, BCA, Records of the Government Agent, Grand Forks). The *Vancouver Chinese Times* erroneously reported that because of "numerous marriages between East Asians and Whites," the government had asked judges to withhold, temporarily, licences for such marriages (22 January 1915).

23 *Vancouver World*, 26 September 1921; *Vancouver Sun*, 10 May 1922 and 14 October and 29 and 31 December 1923.

24 C.E. Hope, "British Columbia's Racial Problems," *Maclean's*, 15 February 1930, 45; H. Glynn-Ward, *The Writing on the Wall* (Vancouver: Sun Publishing, 1921); *Vancouver World*, 15 July 1922; Harry Langley to King, 23 March 1925, DEAR, MfT1751 (italics added).

25 *Vancouver World*, 22 November 1921, 25 January, 19 October, and 22 November 1922; *New Westminster British Columbian*, 17 September 1919. New Westminster from time to time had had special classes for Oriental children (*New Westminster British Columbian*, 17 June 1917); *Victoria Colonist*, 11 October 1922; *Vancouver Province*, 9 July 1920 and 10 October 1922; *Vancouver Star*, 6 August 1924; PTAHHS, passim.

26 *Vancouver Province*, 6 February 1920 and 26 March 1923; *Vancouver World*, 21 February 1922; *Vancouver Sun*, 10 June 1923; Victoria Chinese Consolidated Benevolent Association (CCBA), 14 January 1922, quoted in C.P. Sedgwick, "The Context of Economic Change and Continuity in an Urban Overseas Chinese Community," University of Victoria, MA thesis, 1973, 147; Roland M. Kawano, ed., *A History of the Japanese Congregations of the United Church of Canada* (Scarborough, ON: The Japanese Canadian Christian Churches Historical Project, 1998), 17; Yesaki, Steves, and Steves, *Steveston Cannery Row*, 68-69; Jacqueline Gresko, "Catholic

Missions to Japanese Immigrants in British Columbia: The Interwar Years," paper presented to the Canadian Historical Association, 2002. When it heard complaints about unclean Japanese students, the Canadian Japanese Association asked the Simon Fraser PTA for information so that it could deal with the matter (*Vancouver Sun*, 15 September 1921). To counteract propaganda, the association published a pamphlet with extracts from a speech by the principal of Strathcona School, Dr. Peter Sandiford's report on the Intelligence of Chinese and Japanese children, and favourable press comments (*A Few Facts about Japanese School Children in Canada* [Vancouver: Canadian Japanese Association, 1927]). *Vancouver Chinese Times*, 7 September 1920.

27 Low, *Memories of Cumberland Chinatown*, 51; Jean Lumb, quoted in Evelyn Huang, with Lawrence Jeffery, *Chinese Canadians: Voices from a Community* (Vancouver: Douglas and McIntyre, 1992), 32, and in The Women's Book Committee, Chinese Canadian National Council, *Jin Guo: Voices of Chinese Canadian Women* (Toronto: Women's Press, 1992), 51; Sing Lim, *West Coast Chinese Boy* (Montreal: Tundra, 1979), 23; *Vancouver Province*, 18 February 1922; *Vancouver Sun*, 10 June 1923.

28 During the segregated school controversy in Victoria, three Chinese boys drowned while swimming in the Inner Harbour. Their Occidental classmates and teachers attended the funeral and sent wreaths (*Victoria Colonist*, 17 June 1922).

29 Misao Yoneyama, "The Pre-War Haney Community," in *Where the Heart Is*, ed. Randy Enomoto (Vancouver: NRC Publishing, 1993), 17; *New Westminster British Columbian*, 18 May 1923.

30 *Vancouver Province*, 12 January 1930. Between 1920 and 1921 the number of Asian children in Vancouver schools rose by 25 percent whereas the number of white children increased by only 6 percent (*Vancouver World*, 29 December 1921). *Cowichan Leader*, 17 February 1927; *Vancouver Sun*, 27 November and 13 December 1926; British Columbia, Legislative Assembly, *Report on Oriental Activities within the Province* (Victoria: King's Printer, 1927), 21; Peter Sandiford, "The Testing Programme," in *Survey of the School System*, J.H. Putman and G.M. Weir (Victoria: King's Printer, 1925), 508; *Vancouver Province*, 18 October 1925. In lectures to educational groups across Canada, Sandiford repeated his findings (*Victoria Times*, 20 February 1926). For details on flaws in the testing procedure, see Timothy J. Stanley, "Defining the Chinese Other: White Supremacy and Leading Opinion in British Columbia, 1885-1925," paper presented to BC Studies Conference, 1990. In 1919 Vancouver's chief probation officer said that the Oriental races had fewer feeble-minded children than did whites (*Victoria Times*, 31 October 1919).

In March 1942 the provincial Department of Education administered standardized tests in two districts with a high proportion of Japanese students. It concluded that a few of the Japanese were academically gifted but that there was no basis for the "current belief that Japanese children are superior students, outclassing white children." The department did not mention that, at the time of the test, the Japanese community was in turmoil and that that may have affected test scores (British Columbia, *Public Schools Annual Report*, 1941-42, in BCSP, 1944 [Victoria, 1944], B40).

31 The Women's Book Committee, *Jin Guo*, 129, 133; quoted in Tamara Adilman, "A Preliminary Sketch of Chinese Women and Work in British Columbia," in *Not Just Pin Money: Selected Essays on The History of Women's Work in British Columbia*, ed. Barbara K. Latham and Roberta J. Pazdro (Victoria: Camosun College, 1984), 68.

32 British Columbia, *Annual Report of the Public Schools* (Victoria: King's Printer, 1924), T119; *Victoria Colonist*, 8 August 1924; *Vancouver Evening Sun*, 19 February 1927; *Vancouver Star*, 24 July 1925 and 25 February 1926; *Vancouver Sun*, 24 July 1925 and 29 November 1926; *Prince Rupert Daily News*, 24 July 1925.

Almost every public school annual report for the period 1928-41 lists at least one Chinese or Japanese student among prize winners in high school and university entrance examinations. Such successes sometimes generated a feature story in the local newspaper (*Victoria Colonist*, 1 July 1932; *Vancouver Province*, 26 July 1937; *Prince Rupert Daily News*, 6 September 1940).

33 *Vancouver World*, 5 May 1919; Mrs. Matheson, "The Canadian Daughters' League," *Western Woman's Weekly*, 21 July 1923; *Fraser Valley Record*, 3 July 1919; *Penticton Herald*, 11 and 14 October 1922; *Victoria Colonist*, 19 December 1929; *Vancouver Province*, 9 July 1920 and 12 October 1922. In Richmond and Mission, where there were large numbers of Japanese children, the Japanese community offered special financial support to the public schools since their ordinary taxes did not cover the full cost of educating their children (*Fraser Valley Record*, 11 February 1926; *New Westminster British Columbian*, 30 October 1931).

34 In addition to the other sources cited, the following paragraphs draw on: Timothy J. Stanley, "Bringing Anti-Racist Theory into Historical Explanation: The Victoria Chinese Students' Strike of 1922-23 Revisited," *Journal of the Canadian Historical Association* 5, 13 (2002): 141-65, and "White Supremacy, Chinese Schooling, and School Segregation in Victoria: The Case of the Chinese Students' Strike, 1922-1923," *Historical Studies in Education: Revue d'Histoire de l'Education* 2 (Fall 1990): 287-305; David Chuenyan Lai, "The Issue of Discrimination in Education in Victoria, 1901-1923," *Canadian Ethnic Studies* 29, 3 (1987): 54-67; *Victoria Colonist*, 13 October 1921.

35 See Roy, *A White Man's Province*, 24-27. One of the few occasions of actual conflict between Asian and white children occurred in Victoria, where a white boy seriously injured a Chinese student by throwing a stone at him (Lih Shih Yuen to Principal, George Jay School, 24 March 1915, CCLB); *Victoria Times*, 14 September 1916 and 28 November 1921; *Victoria Colonist*, 9 September and 6 December 1921 and 30 August 1922. In a minority report, Christian Sivertz opposed school segregation based on nationality.

36 *Victoria Colonist*, 30 January 1923; *Vancouver Province*, 12 January 1922; *Victoria Times*, 12 January, 10 August, and 12 and 13 September 1922 and 30 January 1923.

37 Admission to high school required passing examinations at the end of Grade 8.

38 *Victoria Colonist*, 3 and 14 October 1922 and 6 April 1923; R.P. Mackay to Rev. D.A. Smith, 23 September 1922, and Smith to Mackay, 16 November 1922, PCC, BFM, b. 5; *Victoria Times*, 11 October 1922 and 5, 6, and 8 January 1923; *Vancouver Sun*, 9, 11, 17, and 18 September 1922 and 1 February 1923; Stanley, "Bringing Anti-Racist Theory into Historical Explanation," 165.

39 *Victoria Colonist*, 8 and 12 April 1923; *Victoria Times*, 12 April 1923; G.H. Deane to S.J. Willis, 1 October 1924; in Public Schools, *Annual Report*, 1924 (Victoria: King's Printer, 1925), T17. The board learned from experience. Early in 1925, when two schools with a large Chinese enrolment were overcrowded, it ascertained the feeling of the Chinese community before transferring some children to a school closer to Chinatown (*Victoria Colonist*, 8 January 1925). There was no controversy over the few Japanese students in Victoria, as most could speak English before going to school (*Victoria Times*, 19 June 1926).

) *Nanaimo Free Press*, 4 November 1921; *Nanaimo Herald*, 9 September 1922; Lumb, quoted in Huang, with Jeffery, *Chinese Canadians*, 32; *Cumberland Islander*, 7 May 1926; *Vancouver World*, 8 January 1923; *Cowichan Leader*, 12 September 1935; *The Hook*, 7 December 1923.

According to Philip C.P. Low, who was born to Chinese parents in Cumberland in 1912, Chinese children did not meet Caucasian children until they went to school because of language difficulties and the concentration of different ethnic groups in physically separated neighbourhoods. After high school in Cumberland, Low graduated from university (Low, *Memories of Cumberland Chinatown*, 50-51). In September 1920 the Chemainus School Board tried to put Japanese students in a separate classroom; a twelve-year-old boy immediately led the Japanese students out of the school. Within the week, the Japanese consul intervened, and the children went back to their regular classes (Catherine Lang, *O-Bon in Chimunesu: A Community Remembered* [Vancouver: Arsenal Pulp, 1996], 219-20).

41 *Cowichan Leader,* 17 June 1926; *Victoria Times,* 19 June 1926; *Vancouver Sun,* 2, 11, and 19 February 1927.

42 *Vancouver Province,* 13 September 1925 and 10 and 14 February 1926; *Victoria Colonist,* 14 February 1926; *Vancouver Star,* 12 February 1926. In fact, only one teacher was admitted to Canada. Japanese parents wanted their children to become proficient in English and Canadian ways but to know Japanese so that discipline could be maintained at home and so that their children would have an opportunity for jobs in the Japanese community and in foreign trade. On Japanese attitudes to education, see C.H. Young and H.R.Y. Reid, *The Japanese Canadians* (Toronto: University of Toronto Press, 1938), 142.

43 *Vancouver Star,* 11 November 1926; *Vancouver Sun,* 11 November 1926; *Nanaimo Free Press,* 10 February and 3 March 1926; Rev. N. Lascelles Ward, "The Oriental Problem," supplement to "Further Report on the Oriental Problem, Submitted to the General Ministerial Association, Vancouver, B.C., 9 January 1922," with Rev. B.C. Freeman, to Minister of the Interior, 24 January 1922, DImm, MfC10652.

44 *Vancouver Star,* 11 and 13 November 1926 (reprinted, *Prince Rupert Daily News,* 18 November 1926); *Cowichan Leader,* 2 December 1926 and 28 July 1927. See Henry F. Angus, "The Legal Status in British Columbia of Residents of Oriental Race and Their Descendants," *Canadian Bar Review* 9 (January 1931): 1-12; Patricia E. Roy, "Citizens Without Votes: East Asians in British Columbia, 1872-1947," in *Ethnicity, Power and Politics in Canada,* ed. Jorgen Dahlie and Tissa Fernando (Toronto: Methuen, 1981), 151-71; Joan Brockman, "Exclusionary Tactics: The History of Women and Visible Minorities in the Legal Profession in British Columbia," in *Essays in the History of Canadian Law: British Columbia and the Yukon,* ed. Hamar Foster and John McLaren (Toronto: Osgoode Society, 1995), 519-25.

45 When, in June 1914, it seemed likely that a new federal Naturalization Act might give naturalized persons the same rights, powers, and privileges as natural born subjects, Premier McBride asked Prime Minister Borden to ensure that the legislation would not affect provincial control of the franchise (McBride to Borden, 5 June 1914, GR441, v. 395; C.H. Tupper and Alfred Bull to H.C. Brewster, 5 December 1916, GR441, v. 175; *Vancouver Province,* 19 March 1917). Early in 1921, when Vancouver City Council sought a charter amendment to ensure that Asian property owners did not vote on money bylaws, the Japanese consul protested to the provincial government on behalf of Japanese ratepayers (S. Ukita to Oliver, 21 February 1921, POC; Brewster to C.H. Tupper, 15 June 1917, GR441, v. 175).

In the debate on the War Time Elections Act, W.A. Buchanan, MP (Liberal, Medicine Hat), suggested that if the government wished to recognize wartime service, it should enfranchise the Chinese and Japanese living in British Columbia. Both Arthur Meighen and R.B. Bennett opposed the idea (HCD, 10 September 1917, 5582-615). British Columbia members did not participate in the debate. Chinese and Japanese residents were not mentioned in the debate on the Military Voters' Act; those Chinese or Japanese serving in the forces could vote in the 1917 federal election.

46 HCD, 26 September 1919, 611-17; Canada, *Statutes,* 16 Geo 5, ch. 2; *Vancouver Province,* 30 September 1919. Lemieux had negotiated the gentlemen's agreement. The Chinese consul complained to the mayor of Vancouver that Chinese residents paid municipal and provincial taxes yet, even if naturalized, could not vote (Koliang Yih to R.H. Gale, 24 January 1919, VCCCl, v. 74); Lee Quong Wai et al. to R.L. Borden, 24 September 1919, DJust, v. 241; *Victoria Times,* 26 September, 9 October, and 10 October 1919; *Victoria Colonist,* 5 October 1919. Someone distributed a crudely prepared circular addressed to women outlining a plot to import a horde of Japanese workers (*Victoria Colonist,* 19 October 1919). The Kelowna

Equal Franchise League urged the provincial government to enfranchise "Hindoos" and naturalized Japanese citizens but did not mention the Chinese (Dora F. Kerr to John Oliver, 12 March 1918, POC). Harry Hastings, a champion of the Chinese, claimed that most registered on their own (*Victoria Colonist*, 16 October 1919; *Vancouver Province*, 30 September 1919; *Victoria Times*, 11 October 1919; *Victoria Colonist*, 15 and 19 October 1919; HCD, 29 April 1920, 1817-22; Yang Shue Men to Acting Premier, 15 March 1920, DJust, v. 249, file 1920-1042. This limited concession probably saved the Liberals some embarrassment, as the caucus was divided (King, Diary, 16 and 23 March 1920, KD); *Victoria Times*, 1 May 1920).

47 *B.C. Veteran's Weekly*, 9 October 1919; *Vancouver World*, 24 February 1920; *Vancouver Province*, 24 March 1920 and 22 May 1919; A.M. Whiteside to John Oliver, 31 January 1920, POC; *Victoria Colonist*, 25 February 1920; Returned Canadian-Japanese Soldiers to Members of the Provincial Legislature and to the Electors of British Columbia, 22 March 1920, published in *Vancouver World*, 25 March 1920; *Victoria Times*, 24 and 29 March 1920; *Vancouver Sun*, 9 March 1920.

48 The letters pro and con are in the POC. *Cowichan Leader*, 18 March 1920; *Victoria Times*, 12, 18, and 20 March and 4 April 1920; *Comox Argus*, 25 March 1920; *Victoria Colonist*, 17 March 1920; *Vancouver Province*, 6 and 18 March and 4 April 1920; *Vancouver World*, 24 February, 10 and 11 March, and 7 and 14 April 1920; Mackenzie to Oliver, 15 March 1920, POC; John Oliver to Victor Odlum, 25 March 1920, VWOP, v. 24. After a "hot" debate, the provincial Great War Veterans' Association convention passed a resolution by a vote of 24 to 11 favouring enfranchising all foreign-born veterans of the Canadian Expeditionary Force (*Vancouver Province*, 7 June 1920). A few opposed the plan because it did not extend to East Indian and Native Indian veterans.

49 *A Short Statement of the Position and Facts Regarding the Japanese in Canada* (Vancouver: Canadian Japanese Association, 1921); *Vancouver World*, 23 June 1921; *Vancouver Sun*, 24 June 1921; *Vancouver Province*, 24 June 1921.

50 *Victoria Colonist*, 5 March and 4 November 1921; *Vancouver World*, 5 March 1921; *Victoria Times*, 14 and 15 March and 3 November 1921; resolutions are in the POC.

51 HCD, 26 September 1919, 614; M.A. MacDonald to King, 1 October 1919, KP, #41176; *Nelson Daily News*, 5 November 1921; *Vancouver Province*, 23 November 1921; *Danger: The Anti-Asiatic Weekly*, 1 December 1921; *Comox Argus*, 17 November 1921. In answering a 1925 Canadian Japanese Association questionnaire, Stevens said that Asians were denied the franchise for "fear that any expression by Japanese or Chinese nationals in British Columbia would be influenced and directed from a racial standpoint rather than from a study of the problem itself." A cynic might accuse Stevens of calling the kettle black, but, he continued, "a solid bloc of Japanese influence would result in a power far beyond the numerical strength of the Japanese population" (*Vancouver Province*, 12 April 1925).

52 Some Conservatives admitted that enfranchisement was a matter of right and necessary for imperial solidarity but warned that it would be politically unwise in British Columbia (Leon J. Ladner to Meighen, 22 October 1922, AMP, #056213-4); BCLJ, 27 November 1923, 106; *Vancouver Province*, 30 October 1923, 17 June 1924, and 3 April, 2 May, and 28 May 1928; *Nanaimo Free Press*, 16 June 1924; *Vancouver Sun*, 28 November 1923 and 4 April and 9 June 1928. After a long debate, the United Sheet Metal Workers rejected enfranchisement by a vote of 25 to 5 (United Sheet Metal Workers International Association, Local 280, Minutes, 12 April 1928, v. 1, CVA). The Canadian Labour Party's MLAs were R.H. Neelands, South Vancouver; Thomas Uphill, Fernie; and F.A. Browne, Burnaby. The dispute contributed to the collapse of the CLP (Martin Robin, *Radical Politics and Canadian Labour* [Kingston: Industrial Relations Centre, Queen's University, 1968], 266; Paul Phillips, *No Power Greater* [Vancouver: B.C. Federation of Labour, 1971], ch. 6).

53 HCD, 25 June 1925, 4905; *New Westminster British Columbian*, 31 July 1925. The editorial was reprinted in the *Chilliwack Progress* (19 August 1925) and also published by Senator J.D. Taylor. The *Prince Rupert Daily News* suggested that if Asians voted, "politicians would fear to say anything against them and they would be pretty well in control of the situation because they could be voted as a bloc. Then they would get everything they ask and a lot more" (20 October 1927).

54 On the Saskatchewan law, see Constance Backhouse, "White Female Help and Chinese-Canadian Employers: Race, Class, Gender and Law in the Case of Yee Clun, 1924," *Canadian Ethnic Studies* 26, 3 (1994): 34-52; Constance Backhouse, *Colour-Coded: A Legal History of Racism in Canada, 1900-1950* (Toronto: University of Toronto Press, 1999), ch. 5; and James W. St. G. Walker, *"Race," Rights and the Law in the Supreme Court of Canada: Historical Case Studies* (Toronto: Osgoode Society/Waterloo: Wilfrid Laurier University Press, 1997), ch. 2. In 1928-29, after the Ontario law, which was never proclaimed, was accidentally included in a revision of the provincial statutes, there was a brief attempt to enforce it in Toronto.

55 Vancouver *News-Advertiser*, 23 July 1915; *Vancouver World*, 12 March 1917 and 28 March 1919; *Vancouver Sun*, 16 April 1919; Consul General to Joseph Pope, 3 April 1919, DEAR, v. 1241; Yang Shu Wen to John Oliver, 4 April 1919, Kichang Sun to City Council, 17 April 1919, and Yang to Mayor, 24 April 1919, VCCCo, v. 74; Koliang Yih to Provincial Secretary, 26 January 1920, DEAR, v. 181; *Victoria Times*, 9 February 1921; Oliver to Lieutenant-Governor, 21 February 1921, POC; *Penticton Herald*, 11 March 1922. Attorney General Manson later said that there had been no prosecutions during the period 1919-23 (*Vancouver Province*, 5 December 1924). Vancouver's lawyers stated that the legislature could not pass such a law until it amended its charter (*Vancouver Province*, 29 April 1919).

56 Ministerial Association of Victoria and District to Oliver, 12 December 1923, Foon Sien, President, Chinese Students Association of Vancouver, to Oliver, 29 November 1923, and Lin Pao Heng to John Oliver, 3 December 1923, POC; *Victoria Times*, 27 November 1923; *Vancouver World*, 6 December 1923; *Vancouver Province*, 20 December 1923; British Columbia, *Revised Statutes*, 1924, c. 275 (Women and Girls Protection Act, 1923). Ontario had enacted a similar measure. The Chinese consul indicated that if the law did not specifically discriminate against people of his race, China would have no complaints (Koliang Yih to Oliver, 14 February 1921, POC; King to Lo Chong, 6 December 1924, KP, #83530-1). On the Chinese Conolidated Benevolent Association hiring a lawyer, see Lin Pao Heng in CCBA records, quoted in Sedgwick, "Context of Economic Change and Continuity," 145.

Chinese fruit and vegetable peddlers remained a common sight in residential neighbourhoods. Children might have taunted them with racist epithets, and some mothers felt uncomfortable about admitting them to their homes. John Norris, who grew up in Nelson in the 1920s, recalls his mother assisting Wo Lee with his business papers but insisting that the children be present as chaperones (John Norris, *Wo Lee Stories* [New Denver, BC: Twa Corbies Publishing House, 1997], 14).

57 *Vancouver Star*, 9 October and 13, 24, 26, and 28 November 1924. Mrs. Smith claimed that J.T. Haig, Manitoba's Conservative leader, had promised to introduce a similar bill in Manitoba (Skelton to King, [c. December 1924], KP, #C61559).

The murder and its investigation (the grand jury found insufficient evidence to try the accused Chinese servant) was a cause célèbre in Vancouver. A detailed account is provided in Edward Starkins, *Who Killed Janet Smith?* (Toronto: Macmillan, 1984). Since few Japanese residents worked in domestic service, the Japanese consul merely noted the bill (Lo Chong to King, 3 December 1924, KP, #83528-9; *Vancouver Province*, 6 and 29 November and 5 December 1924; *Victoria Times*, 21 November, and 2 and 5 December 1924; *Vancouver Star*, 24 and 29 November and 17 December 1924; King to Oliver, 6 December 1924, KP, #90190-1; Oliver to King, 15 December 1924, POC).

58 A police chief placarded a Chinese-owned restaurant as "an undesirable place, from a moral standpoint, for white girls to be employed" because the proprietor paid three women less than the minimum wage and made them work more than forty-eight hours per week (British Columbia, Department of Labour, *Annual Report*, 1929, BCSP, 1931, 156).

59 Anderson, *Vancouver's Chinatown*, 92. See also Roy, *A White Man's Province*, ch. 2. Anderson says that Chinatowns were "in part a European creation" (9). David Chuenyan Lai, *Chinatowns: Towns Within Cities in Canada* (Vancouver: UBC Press, 1988), 34-35, suggests that Chinatowns had complex origins arising from white racism (the refusal of whites to sell or lease property to Chinese), fear of violence and discrimination, cultural barriers (especially language), and economic considerations, including the desire for cheap accommodation and access to a variety of Chinese services. Exploiting the exoticism, a mock-up of Chinatown with wax figures of gamblers, opium smokers, and other "ungraceful" characters toured Canadian fair grounds in 1918 and 1919. In Vancouver the mayor, in a rare expression of sympathy for the local Chinese, pleased them by ordering it closed (*Vancouver Chinese Times*, 22 and 23 August 1918).

60 *Vancouver Sun*, 9 January 1922, 11 February and 20 October 1924, 22 May 1925, and 10, 18, 29, and 30 November 1932; *Nanaimo Free Press*, 24 January 1928; *Victoria Colonist*, 8 November 1932; *Victoria Times*, 7 February 1921, 9 August 1927, 19 January 1928, and 19 November 1932; *Prince George Citizen*, 15 April 1921; *Victoria Colonist*, 5 July 1921; Grace Hope, "Visit to Chinatown of Vancouver City," *Vancouver Province*, 1 April 1928.

61 *Victoria Colonist*, 6 and 20 March 1923; *Vancouver Sun*, 24 May 1915, 17 April 1918, 29 May 1919, 29 January 1920, 12 February 1923, and 28 March 1925; *Vancouver World*, 15 September 1915; *B.C. Municipal News*, April 1929, 7; P.C.B., "Vancouver Chinatown has no mystery – except Chinese," *Vancouver Province*, 12 December 1926; Stewart Murray to Social Service Committee, 16 May 1941, CVA, RG2A1, v. 253; *Victoria Times*, 20 October 1919. In 1921 Dr. J.W. MacLean released statistics showing that the death rates from tuberculosis per thousand were: whites, 0.73; Native Indians, 3.50; Chinese, 3.73; Japanese, 1.20; and East Indians, 4.00. *Victoria Colonist*, 15 December 1921; Timothy Chan, "The Social and Regulatory Relations of Metropolitan Victoria's Commercial Greenhouse Industry: 1900 to 1996," University of Victoria, MA thesis, 1996, 96-97.

62 When Rev. Dr. S.S. Osterhout suggested that the Dominion government provide funds to assist in enforcing laws relating to sanitation, the *New Westminster British Columbian* published a favourable editorial (5 May 1921). The *Nanaimo Free Press* reprinted it (9 May 1921) without acknowledgment. *Victoria Colonist*, 11 July 1918 and 1 March 1929; *Victoria Times*, 21 October 1919 and 17 May 1921.

63 *Victoria Colonist*, 15 July 1921. W.B. Hurd, "Racial Origins," 697. The penitentiary statistics are national.

64 *Kelowna Courier*, 18 August 1921; *Nanaimo Free Press*, 6 February 1915; *Western Methodist Recorder*, February 1921.

65 *New Westminster British Columbian*, 16 February 1915; "Petition to the People of Vancouver, May 5, 1918," [from eighteen Chinese], copy in UBC, Chinese Canadian Project; *Vancouver World*, 7 May 1918; *Vancouver Sun*, 6 and 21 May, 20 July, and 13 and 14 December 1918; *Vancouver Province*, 13 and 17 May, 8 and 14 June, and 4, 13, and 14 December 1918.

66 *Vancouver Province*, 12 December 1926. One raid may have been arranged to entertain a visiting dignitary (*Victoria Times*, 14 May 1920). Several times Rev. Dr. S.S. Osterhout suggested that the churches build a social centre for the Chinese (*Vancouver Province*, 17 April 1920; *Vancouver World*, 20 December 1921).

67 *Victoria Times*, 26 September and 2 October 1924; *Vancouver Star*, 1 October 1924 and 6 February 1925; *Vancouver Sun*, 3 October 1924 and 6 April 1925; *Vancouver Province*, 2 October and 8 December 1924 and 22 January and 2 April 1925. One raid resulted in the surprising arrest of a Chinese woman (*Vancouver Province*, 27 January 1925).

68 *Vancouver Star*, 5, 6, and 8 August 1925 and 20 June and 5 October 1928; *Vancouver Province*, 1, 12, 18, and 19 May and 22 June, 4 July, and 12 October 1928; Greg Marquis, "Vancouver Vice: The Police and the Negotiation of Morality, 1904-1935," in *Essays in the History of Canadian Law*, ed. Foster and McLaren, 248-49.

69 *Victoria Colonist*, 11 and 16 April 1919 and 1 February and 22 April 1921; *Victoria Times*, 8, 15, and 25 April and 18 December 1919, 8 March 1920, and 22 and 23 February, 4 March, 8 and 26 April, and 3 May 1921. A candidate who accused other candidates of picking on the Chinese because "to the average citizen Chinatown is more or less a mystery" came last (*Victoria Colonist*, 25 February 1921).

70 *Victoria Colonist*, 12 June, 26 August, 14 and 23 September, and 20 and 26 October 1921, 26 April 1922, 22 December 1926, and 4, 5, and 10 February 1928; *Victoria Times*, 21 June and 17 and 19 August 1922 and 10 February 1928. A summary of the case against Bo is in the *Victoria Colonist*, 16 October 1921.

71 *Kelowna Courier*, 2 and 16 May, 13 June, and 26 September 1929; *Vancouver Sun*, 21 September 1929.

72 *Victoria Colonist*, 12 September 1922 (re Nanaimo), 8 October 1924, 3 January 1925, 17 January 1930, and 10 December 1931; *Vernon News*, 8 November 1923; *Kelowna Courier*, 25 July 1929 and 21 August 1930; *New Westminster British Columbian*, 23 January, 20 June, and 29 July 1931; *Vancouver Sun*, 11 November 1922 and 4 February 1931; *Courtenay Free Press*, 28 October 1927.
    Public opinion allowed Asians some vices. When it was erroneously reported that the new British Columbia Liquor Control Board would open liquor stores in the Chinatowns of Vancouver and Victoria and carry Chinese liquors and Japanese saké, only the Methodist Conference complained; it opposed making liquor available to anyone! Editorialists suggested that "if a Chinaman wants to buy a bottle of whiskey from a Government store, we know of no reason why he should not get it" (*Victoria Times*, 19 April and 18 May 1921; *Nanaimo Herald*, 20 May 1921; *Victoria Colonist*, 21 May 1921).

73 Between 1 April 1921 and 31 January 1929, Canada deported 677 people, of whom 527 were Chinese, for offences under the Narcotic Drug Act (Statement, Showing Deportations by Nationalities, under the Narcotic Drug Act, DImm, MFC10662); *Vancouver World*, 13 March 1920; *Vancouver Sun*, 18, 22, 24, 27, and 31 March 1920; *Vancouver Province*, 23 March and 17 May 1920; Koliang Yih to Acting Mayor, 25 March 1920, and Acting Mayor to Koliang, 6 April 1920, VMC, v. 2. Emily Murphy, "The Grave Drug Menace," *Maclean's*, 15 February 1920, 11, and *The Black Candle* (Toronto: Thomas Allen, 1922), 26-27.

74 *Vancouver Sun*, 14 and 25 April 1921; H.H. Stevens, HCD, 26 April 1921, 2597; *Saturday Night*, 14 May 1921, referring to an editorial in the *Christian Science Monitor*.

75 Glynn-Ward, *The Writing on the Wall*, 113; *Danger: The Anti-Asiatic Weekly* called for a revival of the White Cross Society (20 October and 13 and 1 December 1921, 6, 25).

76 *Vancouver Sun*, 13 March 1922; *Vancouver World*, 16 and 18 January and 11 February 1922; *Vancouver Province*, 10, 11, 26, and 30 January and 3, 10, 20, and 28 February 1922; Irene Howard, *The Struggle for Social Justice in British Columbia: Helena Gutteridge, the Unknown Reformer* (Vancouver: UBC Press, 1992), 101-3; copies of the petitions are in HHSPV, v. 2; S.S. Osterhout, *Orientals in Canada: The Story of the Work of the United Church of Canada with Asiatics in Canada* (Toronto: United Church of Canada, 1929), 78ff.; *Western Methodist Recorder*, February 1921.

77 *Cumberland Islander*, 4 February 1922; *Victoria Colonist*, 3 February 1922; *Nanaimo Herald*, 26 January 1922; *Nanaimo Free Press*, 29 March and 13 April 1922; *Cowichan Leader*, 27 April 1922; *Vancouver Sun*, 13 March 1922; *Ashcroft Journal*, 3 March 1922. The Chinese consul complained to the Department of External Affairs about a movie, *Dinty*, that allegedly represented the Chinese as "opium smokers, prostitutes, kidnappers, participants in immoral

scenes, and leaders of depraved lives." The department reported that people who viewed it saw no references to opium dens or any attempt to attach a stigma to China or its government. In any case, Sir Joseph Pope explained, censorship was a provincial matter (Pope to Chinese Consul General, 25 April 1921, DEAR, v. 544).

78 *Vernon News*, 9 and 16 February 1922; *Penticton Herald*, 1 April 1922; *Ashcroft Journal*, 3 March 1922; Mrs. M. Matz to Attorney-General, 8 October 1922, AGR, 1918-17-2060; *Armstrong Advertiser*, 23 November 1922.

79 H.H. Stevens to Rev. A.E. Cooke, 31 March 1922, HHSPV, v. 2 (this was a form letter). *Vancouver Province*, 12 and 16 April 1922; *Vancouver Sun*, 16 and 17 June 1922. At an interprovincial conference in 1927, Manson told delegates that "narcoticism has become a serious menace in the Dominion and should be punished by the lash" (Grant Dexter, *Victoria Times*, 10 December 1927); *Vancouver World*, 20 June 1922. See also Shirley J. Cook, "Canadian Narcotics Legislation, 1908-1923: A Conflict Model Interpretation," *Canadian Review of Sociology and Anthropology* 6 (1969): 36-46; HCD, 8 May 1922, 1516-30.

80 *Vancouver Province*, 24 January, 20 October, and 22 November 1923; *Victoria Colonist*, 14 December 1923 and 30 January, 24 February, and 19 November 1924; *Victoria Times*, 6 February and 14 April 1924; *B.C. Monthly*, 23 (October 1924): 14; *Vancouver Sun*, 28 September 1922, 3 February 1923, and 13 May 1924; Cortlandt Starnes to F.A. McGregor, 17 April 1923, KP, #80598ff; *Vancouver World*, 10 July 1923; *Vancouver Star*, 9 October 1924. A resolution in favour of whipping as a penalty for drug traffickers was presented to the legislature but withdrawn (BCV&P, 18 November 1924, 2; *Vancouver Province*, 19 November 1924).

81 W.Y. Way to editor, *Victoria Colonist*, 3 May 1918; *Vancouver World*, 10 September 1921.

82 *Prince Rupert Daily News*, 28 January 1930.

Chapter 3: "Putting the Pacific Ocean between Them"

1 *Victoria Times*, 12 July 1920; *Nanaimo Free Press*, 13 July 1920.

2 *Vancouver Sun*, 25 March 1919; *Prince Rupert Daily News*, 13 July 1921. The provincial government investigated bringing in Hebridean fishermen "to restore to British races the control that has been rapidly passing to the Oriental fishermen" (*Vancouver Province*, 2 May 1923), but neither the government nor the canners provided the financial support required by the Fishery Board of Scotland (Commissioner of Immigration to District Superintendent of Immigration, Vancouver, 18 June 1937, DImm, MfC4760). More significantly, a Department of Fisheries official noted that "no white population can be built up on the salmon fishery that lasts a few months at best" (Notes for File re Final Report, BC Fisheries Commission, Ottawa, 26 April 1923, DFish, v. 1233).

3 *Victoria Times*, 15 September 1923. A member of the Vancouver Island Women's Institutes caused much amusement when she suggested increasing the birth rate (*Victoria Times*, 3 November 1921). *Nanaimo Free Press*, 15 September 1923; C.H. Young and H.R.Y. Reid, *The Japanese Canadians* (Toronto: University of Toronto Press, 1938), 26-33; *Vancouver Province*, 26 March 1923; J.S. Cowper, *Vancouver World*, 14 September 1921; *Vancouver World*, 29 March 1923. Captain Macaulay had made the same argument a year earlier (*Vancouver Sun*, 13 March 1922); *B.C. Federationist*, 21 September 1921; BCV&P, 4 December 1924.

Members of the legislature regularly asked about the number of Chinese and Japanese births. The provincial secretary usually gave figures for several years to reveal trends, but numbers varied. For example, in 1923 the figures for 1922 were 173 Chinese and 553 Japanese births; in 1924 the figures for the same year were 227 and 622; and in 1925, 244 and 700. The discrepancy may be explained by late registrations.

Vancouver Sun, 28 January 1927; *Vancouver Province*, 30 January 1927; Speech to Canadian Credit Mens' Trust Association, 27 June 1927, copy in HHSPN, v. 3; Oliver to King, 21 January 1927, KP, #124777. Oliver's letter is almost a verbatim copy of A.M. Manson to Oliver, 10

December 1926, in AGR, 1918-17-2060. The extreme view was uncharacteristic of Oliver, whose judgment may have been impaired by the cancer that killed him six months later. It did represent the views of Attorney General Manson and ministers such as T.D. Pattullo.

4   W.D. Scott to William McQueen, 18 February 1919, VCCCl, v. 74. Early in 1920 Fred Baker, a Victoria resident, was charged with assisting a member of the Chinese Labour Corps to escape from William Head Prison, near Victoria, where he was awaiting transportation to China. The magistrate decided that coolies en route to China were not immigrants and dismissed the case against Baker for "harboring" the Chinese labourer (*Victoria Times*, 26 January 1920); *Vancouver Sun*, 22 January and 29 March 1919; *Vancouver Province*, 4 and 8 February 1919; *B.C. Federationist*, 28 January 1919. Of the Chinese, 4,066 paid the head tax (Young and Reid, *The Japanese Canadians*, 203). The arrival of the *Monteagle* inspired a doggerel verse, "A White B.C.," in which the "war worn veteran" found that he was unlikely to secure a job because "they're bringing in the yellow men" (Vancouver *Critic*, 25 January 1919). The verse is reprinted in W. Peter Ward, *White Canada Forever: Popular Attitudes and Public Policy toward Orientals in British Columbia* (Montreal and Kingston: McGill-Queen's University Press, 1978), 190.

5   *Kelowna Courier*, 13 February 1919; *Vernon News*, 13 February, 20 March, and 19 June 1919; VCCM, 7 February and 8 March 1919; *Vancouver Province*, 8 February 1919; *Vancouver World*, 14 March 1919; T.J. Thomas to G.D. Robertson, 19 February 1919, DImm, MfC4784. The United Farmers of British Columbia convention unanimously called for restrictions on Japanese immigration (*Kamloops Standard-Sentinel*, 21 February 1919).

6   E. Blake Robertson to W.W. Cory, 5 February 1919, DImm, MfC4784; *Vancouver Province*, 8 February 1919. Responding to protests from the Chinese Benevolent Association and the Chinese Chamber of Commerce about restrictive immigration laws (*Vancouver Chinese Times*, 1 and 4 August 1914) and requests from the Canadian government for a written statement on immigration policy, in 1914-15 the Chinese consul in Ottawa prepared a draft immigration agreement. Under this agreement, Canada would abolish the head tax and give the Chinese in Canada the same rights as citizens of the most favoured nations in return for China agreeing not to permit more than 1,000 labourers per year to emigrate to Canada (Draft Agreement on Admission of Chinese Labourers into Canada, 15 March 1915, copy in RLBP, #100670-2). The *Victoria Colonist* suggested that the "admirable manner in which the agreement with Japan has worked out, whereby British Columbia has been saved from an influx of immigrants, who represent a civilization different from ours and who cannot be assimilated with our population, has shown how the desired end can be accomplished without offending the proper pride of a great people." The paper was optimistic that China would agree "to make Chinese immigration to Canada no longer a menace to white labor" (*Victoria Colonist*, 3 March 1915). When Martin Burrell, British Columbia's representative in the federal Cabinet, wondered if wartime was opportune for such a change, the matter seems to have been dropped (Martin Burrell to George Foster, 28 August 1915, RLBP, #100676-7). Phil R. Smith to Thomas White, 19 March 1919, RLBP, #135328; S.F. Tolmie to White, 21 March 1919, SFTP, b. 29; *Victoria Times*, 21 March 1919; H.H. Stevens to McQueen, 27 March 1919, VCCCl, v. 74; Scott to Yang Shue Wen, 8 March 1919, DImm, MfC4784; W.W. Cory to Blue Funnel line et al., 20 February 1919, J.A. Calder to Cory, 7 April 1919, and Minister of Immigration and Colonization to Governor-General in Council, 22 May 1919, DImm, MfC4794; *Kamloops Standard-Sentinel*, 1 April 1919; *Victoria Colonist*, 23 March and 2 May 1919; *Victoria Times*, 21 and 25 March 1919; *Vancouver Province*, 24 March 1919; Joseph Pope to Governor-General's Secretary, 14 December 1920, GGR, G21 series, no. 332, v. 17a.

7   Blair to J.W. Edwards, 16 November 1921, DImm, MfC10652; Stevens to J.A. Calder, 7 January 1921 and 23 February 1921, JMRC, v. 37; *Victoria Colonist*, 25 January, 29 April, and 26 June 1921; *Vancouver World*, 27 April 1921; HCD, 11 May 1921, 3829, 23 May 1921, 3829, and 25 May 1921, 3830.

8 *Victoria New Republic,* 25 October 1921, translation in DImm, MfC4784; *Vancouver Sun,* 18 and 30 October 1921; *Victoria Colonist,* 27 October 1921.

9 S.J. Crowe to R.H. Gale, 16 March 1919, and Scott to William McQueen, 18 February 1919, VCCCI, v. 74. Some British Columbians agreed (*Victoria Times,* 10 October 1919). Stevens, in HCD, 26 April 1921, 2595. Immigration Department officials later suspected that Japan might not be honouring the agreement but were uncertain because of its secrecy (F.C. Blair to Calder, 10 January 1920, DImm, MfC4751). *Vancouver Province,* 22 May 1919; John Nelson, "Will Canada Go Yellow," *Maclean's,* 15 October 1921, 16. There was considerable support for a 1919 proposal to allow the approximately 500 Hindus in the province to bring in wives and families since the number would be limited (*Vancouver World,* 29 March 1919; *Vancouver Sun,* 29 March 1919; *Kamloops Standard-Sentinel,* 18 April 1919).

10 F.S. Barnard to Secretary of State, 1 April 1919, RLBP, v. 41; BCLJ, 27 March 1919; *Vancouver World,* 28 March 1919; *Nanaimo Free Press,* 21 March 1919; *The Critic,* 3 May 1919; *Vancouver Province,* 19 March and 11 April 1919; *Vancouver Sun,* 15 April 1919.

11 The United States also rejected the racial equality clause, but concerns that membership might affect its ability to restrict Japanese immigration contributed to the Senate's decision not to join the League of Nations (Greg Robinson, *By Order of the President: FDR and the Internment of Japanese Americans* [Cambridge, MA: Harvard University Press, 2001], 29).

12 The *Cowichan Leader,* 27 March 1919, applauded Hughes. Sean Brawley, *The White Peril: Foreign Relations and Asian Immigration to Australasia and North America, 1919-78* (Sydney: UNSW Press, 1995), 73. The premier of Victoria, Australia, noting differences in policy between the Canadian and British Columbia governments concerning the Japanese, asked the prime minister for any published government papers on the subject (Premier of Victoria to Meighen, 14 September 1920, DImm, MfC10652); *Victoria Colonist,* 15 April 1919; e.g., M.A. MacDonald in the *Vancouver Province,* 28 July 1921. Not all editors opposed renewal of the Anglo-Japanese Alliance (e.g., *Victoria Colonist,* 19 August 1920 and 3 and 26 June 1921; *Vancouver Sun,* 24 January 1921; *Vancouver Province,* 22 June and 15 August 1921); *New Westminster British Columbian,* 6 May 1921; *Vernon News,* 13 January 1921; *Vancouver Sun,* 8 June 1921; *Vancouver World,* 27 April 1921; *Kamloops Telegram,* 16 June 1921; *Times* (London), 24 June 1921; *Victoria Times,* 17 May 1921.

13 Victoria had a small Japanese population and was mainly interested in Chinese immigration. When city council learned that the treaty did not relate to immigration, it did not send a wire to Meighen (*Victoria Times,* 4 July 1921); *Nanaimo Herald,* 17 June 1921; Oliver to Meighen, 13 June 1921, AGR, 1918-17-2060; *Victoria Colonist,* 16 June 1921; Meighen to Oliver, 22 June 1921, POC; Meighen's Private Secretary to City Clerk, Nanaimo, and Others, 4 July 1921, AMP, #17292-303; *Vancouver World,* 19 August 1921; *Vancouver Sun,* 13 August 1921; *Victoria Colonist,* 20 August, 26 October, and 2 November 1921; *Vancouver Province,* 2 November 1921; *Vancouver Sun,* 1 November 1921; Oliver to W.C. Nichol, 10 April 1922, DImm, MfC10652. Through a bureaucratic error, the resolution was not forwarded to the provincial secretary's office for transmission to the lieutenant governor or Ottawa until April 1922 (Oliver to G.S. Hanes, 7 April 1922, POC).

14 The phrase "a white man's country" also appeared in Washington State rhetoric surrounding the campaign there for Japanese exclusion. The *Seattle Star,* for example, ran headlines such as "WILL YOU HELP TO KEEP THIS A WHITE MAN'S COUNTRY?" (Thomas H. Heuterman, *The Burning Horse: Japanese-American Experience in the Yakima Valley, 1920-1942* [Cheney, WA: Eastern Washington University Press, 1995], 19-20).

15 *Prince Rupert Daily News,* 24 September 1921; *Ashcroft Journal,* 30 September 1921; *Penticton Herald,* 1 October 1921; *Cumberland Islander,* 1 October 1921; *Vancouver World,* 9 September 1919; Lukin Johnston, "British Columbia's Oriental Problem," *United Empire* 13 (September 1922): 573; *Ottawa Journal,* 14 January 1920; *Vancouver Province,* 14 January 1920; *Victoria Times,* 26 August 1921; *Winnipeg Free Press,* 26 August 1921.

16 George S. Hougham to Tolmie, 16 March 1921, DImm, Mf10652; *Vancouver World,* 15 April and 27 July 1921; *Victoria Times,* 2 February and 28 July 1921; *Vancouver Province,* 27 July 1921; *British Columbia Retailer* 12 (May 1921): 313, 12 (August 1921): 400-1, 13 (October 1921): 464, and 13 (November 1921): 495; *Victoria Colonist,* 9 December 1921.

17 *Enderby Okanagan Commoner,* 15 September 1921; *Vancouver Province,* 23 May, 22 June, and 27 August 1921; *Winnipeg Free Press,* 29 August 1921; *B.C. Labour News,* 5 August 1921; *Vancouver World,* 29 June and 13 August 1921. The *B.C. Veterans Weekly* conceded that Asians had been of some benefit – for example, in producing cheap foodstuffs – but concluded that their immigration "as at present permitted, is a great evil" (23 June 1921).

18 The federal and provincial governments, for example, spent $148,438.93 on unemployment relief in 1920-21; they spent more than twice that, $348,333.64, in 1921-22. In 1920 the Dominion Bureau of Statistics calculated that the net value of production in the province's primary and secondary industries was $229,138,933; in 1921 it dropped to $198,941,272. It gradually rose until it reached $331,466,014 in 1929 (*British Columbia in the Canadian Confederation: A Submission Presented to The Royal Commission on Dominion-Provincial Relations by the Government of the Province of British Columbia* [Victoria: King's Printer, 1938], 108, 65). Labour Conference, Court House, Vancouver, 10 August 1921, Transcript, in DLab, v. 209; *Vancouver Sun,* 1 November 1921; Verbatim Report of Proceedings of Unemployment Conference Held at Ottawa, 5-7 September 1922, pp. B52 and E10, DLab, v. 113.

19 Vancouver Board of Trade Council, Minutes, 19 May, 20 and 21 July, 11 August, and 29 September 1921; *Vancouver World,* 14 September 1921; *Vancouver Province,* 20 July and 14 September 1921 and 25 August 1926; *Vancouver Sun,* 14 September 1921. The *Vancouver World* cited the resolution to show the value of its campaign for a white British Columbia (17 September 1921).

20 The Imperial Order of the Daughters of the Empire provincial chapter meeting decided that it was "not in a position to definitely voice the opinion of the entire order in British Columbia" (*Victoria Times,* 7 October 1921); *Chilliwack Progress,* 13 October 1921; *Vancouver World,* 17 August 1921; *Vancouver Sun,* 22 November 1921. Mrs. Howard, who, under the penname Hilda Glynn-Ward, had just published *The Writing on the Wall* (Vancouver: Sun Publishing Company, 1921), was a member of the first permanent executive until a reorganization expanded the executive and made it an exclusively male group (*Vancouver World,* 29 October 1921). The executive's president, W.F. Bartlett, was vice president of the Vancouver Trades and Labour Council; the executive's vice president, W.H. Roberts, was a member of the Imperial Veterans' Association (he resigned in late October and was replaced by Col. J. Leckie); the secretary manager was Captain C.F. Macaulay; and the treasurer, Percy Bengough, was secretary of the Trades and Labour Council (*B.C. Federationist,* 16 September 1921).

21 *Vancouver Sun,* 17 August and 12 and 24 September 1921; *Vancouver World,* 17 August and 13 and 24 September 1921. The Japanese Association of Canada, which was dominated by a small group in Vancouver, rejected the request of the Japanese Labour Union for funds to fight exclusion within white unions. That rejection stimulated a reform movement within the Japanese Association (Toshiji Sasaki, "The Japanese Association of Canada: Its Democratic Reform and the Destruction of its Democratic System by Vancouver Consul Kaii," in *The Study of Christianity and Social Problems* 41 [July 1991]: 65); C.F. Macaulay to Secretary of State, 17 November 1921, DImm, Mf10652; Macaulay to Lloyd George, 31 October 1921, DEAR, v. 1285. Downing Street reminded the league that immigration was a Dominion responsibility and sent the correspondence to the Department of External Affairs. It noted widespread Canadian support for "excluding Orientals" but, possibly confusing the league with its predecessor, said that it knew "nothing very good" about Macaulay and his league, whose tactics were "so vicious and extreme that they are more likely to injure their cause than to promote it" (E.M.W. Grigg to Macaulay, 23 November 1921, and Loring Christie to Grigg, 9 December 1921, DEAR, v. 1285); *Vancouver World,* 13 December 1921.

22 With its circulation of approximately 17,669, the *Vancouver World* ranked third among the city's dailies. The *Vancouver Province* had a circulation in 1922 of 59,633, and the *Vancouver Sun* of 21,304 ("Newspapers Published in British Columbia," TDPP). Charles E. Campbell had recently purchased the *Vancouver World* because the *Vancouver Sun* opposed the provincial Liberal government (Campbell to Mackenzie King, 16 May 1921, KP, #50244-5).

23 *Vancouver World,* 27 August 1921 and 9, 24, and 29 September, 21 October, and 15 and 25 November 1921; *Port Alberni News,* 19 October 1921; *Comox Argus,* 27 October 1921; *New Westminster British Columbian,* 13 September and 7 October 1921; *Cowichan Leader,* 6 October 1921; *Prince Rupert Daily News,* 15 December 1921; *B.C. Labour News,* 2 September and 23 December 1921; *Vancouver Sun,* 30 August and 11 November 1921.

24 For a fuller account, see my introduction to the 1974 reprint. Later research revealed that the novel closely follows a serial story published in 1910-11 in *Westward Ho!* (see Patricia E. Roy, *A White Man's Province: British Columbia Politicians and Chinese and Japanese Immigrants, 1858-1914* [Vancouver: UBC Press, 1989], 261); *Vancouver World,* 13 August 1921, reprinted in *Victoria Colonist,* 19 August 1921; *Victoria Colonist,* 24 September 1921; *British Columbia United Farmer,* 15 September 1921, 8; *B.C. Federationist,* 6 January 1922; *Vancouver Sun,* 11 January, 9 July, 12 and 13 August, and 23 October 1921.

25 *Danger: The Anti-Asiatic Weekly,* 20 October 1921, 18-19, and 1 December 1921, 3, 23, 25; *Vancouver Sun,* 29 November 1921. Only two issues of *Danger* appear to have survived. Copies of both are at UBC.

26 Oliver decried Ottawa's failures to accept British Columbia's anti-Asian legislation and suggested that the Bowser government had wanted to use Chinese labour to complete the Pacific Great Eastern Railway. The few Liberals who mentioned Asians noted that for Dominion and imperial reasons, the province could do little about exclusion. William Sloan, the Liberal incumbent in Nanaimo, claimed to be working toward "finally cleaning the Orientals out of the mines"; Conservative leader Bowser retorted that 480 Asians were employed at Cumberland. In Comox, W.W.B. McInnes, who had been active in the Asiatic Exclusion League in 1907, tried to re-enter politics as an Independent. Claiming that the Asiatic question was "more important" than ever, he promised to "work and vote for more drastic laws for their exclusion and curtailment of their employment." None of his rivals disagreed, but most barely mentioned the issue. He came fourth and last. In South Okanagan, J.W. Jones, the successful Conservative, included exclusion, preventing Oriental ownership of land, an educational test for foreign immigrants, and an aggressive immigration policy, especially for Britons, in his campaign planks (*Victoria Colonist,* 12 November 1920; *Vancouver Sun,* 10 November 1920; *Vancouver Province,* 22 November 1920; *Victoria Times,* 17 and 23 November 1920; *Comox Argus,* 11, 18, and 25 November 1920; *Nanaimo Free Press,* 18 November 1920; Roy, *A White Man's Province,* 201; *Cumberland Islander,* 6 November 1920; *Kelowna Courier,* 18 November 1920).

A curious campaign incident was a government-produced film on the oyster industry that showed many Hindus at work. Its final caption identified the opposition leader, William J. Bowser, as the successful owner of oyster beds and noted that the industry gave "many of our Asiatic citizens profitable employment." When Conservatives complained, the film was removed from theatres. In Victoria a Liberal candidate complained that a Conservative, R.H. Pooley, had shown pictures of Chinese labourers working on the construction of the Canadian Northern Railway on Vancouver Island but did not say that they were taken after the railway had passed to the control of the Conservative government (*Vancouver Province,* 26 November 1920; *Victoria Times,* 22 and 24 November 1920).

27 Neither the Meighen nor King papers refer to the "Oriental question" as an election issue. Senator Hewitt Bostock told King that railways, Oriental immigration, and trade were important issues for the new government (Bostock to King, 9 December 1921, KP, #49798-9). John Nelson to the Vancouver Rotary Club, *Vancouver Province,* 15 November 1921;

Vancouver World, 29 November 1921; J.T. Robinson, in the *Kamloops Standard-Sentinel,* 15 November 1921; *Nanaimo Herald,* 18 November 1921.

The Progressives did not run a full slate. For convenience, "Conservative" is used here although Meighen's supporters ran variously as Government, Unionist, or National Liberal Conservatives. The few Socialists were rarely reported in the press. In Vancouver South both Leon Ladner and Victor W. Odlum noted that the Socialist Labour candidate did not oppose Asian immigration. See also: *New Westminster British Columbian,* 11 October 1921; *Penticton Herald,* 16 November 1921; *Prince Rupert Daily News,* 27 October 1921; and *Vancouver Province,* 18 November 1921. During the campaign, the Immigration Department had to deny rumours of the Japanese evading the gentlemen's agreement (H.H. Stevens to J.W. Edwards, 23-24 November 1921, and Blair to Stevens, 28 November 1921, DImm, MfC4751).

28 East Kootenay had 679 Chinese and 107 Japanese residents, and West Kootenay had 679 Chinese and 29 Japanese residents.

29 *Vancouver Sun,* 11 October 1921; *Kamloops Standard-Sentinel,* 18 October and 11 November 1921; *Kamloops Telegram,* 10 November 1921; *Prince George Citizen,* 18 November 1921; *Creston Review,* 2 December 1921; *Trail Daily Times,* 11 November 1921; *Fernie Free Press,* 4 November 1921; *Nelson Daily News,* 3 and 5 November and 1, 2, 3, and 5 December 1921; *Cranbrook Herald,* 3 November 1921 and 1 December 1921; *Trail News,* 2 December 1921.

30 *Prince Rupert Evening Empire,* 10 October 1921; *Prince Rupert Daily News,* 27 October and 20 and 22 November 1921.

31 *Vernon News,* 20 October and 1 December 1921; *Kelowna Courier and Okanagan Orchardist,* 24 November and 8 December 1921; *Okanagan Commoner,* 1 December 1921; *New Westminster British Columbian,* 13 October 1921; *Fraser Valley Record,* 27 October and 3 November 1921; *Chilliwack Progress,* 27 October and 3 November 1921. There is no published record of what Munro said, if anything. Neither weekly newspaper in the riding covered the campaign well and, when they did, displayed their Conservative bias. *B.C. Labour News,* 11 November 1921; *New Westminster British Columbian,* 8, 9, and 16 November 1921; *Vancouver Sun,* 14 November 1921.

32 Burrard had 630 Chinese and 1,527 Japanese residents; Vancouver South had 809 Chinese and 359 Japanese residents. *Vancouver Province,* 15, 18, and 23 November 1921; Campaign Address of Brigadier-General Odlum at Kerrisdale Hall, 17 November 1921, LJLP, v. 13; *Vancouver Sun,* 18 November and 2 and 4 December 1921; *Victoria Colonist,* 2 December 1921; *Vancouver World,* 17 November and 2 December 1921.

33 *Vancouver Province,* 15 and 18 November and 3 December 1921; *Vancouver World,* 2 December 1921. Campaign Address of Brigadier-General Odlum at Kerrisdale Hall, 17 November 1921, LJLP, v. 13; V.W. Odlum to L.J. Ladner, 2 December 1921, LJLP, v. 12; *Comox Argus,* 24 November 1921; *Vancouver Sun,* 1 November and 1, 2, and 4 December 1921; *Victoria Colonist,* 2 December 1921. A Conservative advertisement outlining party policy generally repeated this idea (*Vancouver Province,* 5 December 1921). In Nanaimo, T.B. Booth used an almost identical advertisement (*Nanaimo Free Press,* 5 December 1921). On election eve each Vancouver Liberal candidate had a full-page advertisement in the *Vancouver Sun.* Only Odlum's mentioned immigration policy and only briefly (5 December 1921).

34 The 1911 census recorded 3,458 Chinese residents, and the 1921 census, 3,441. In 1921 there were 225 Japanese residents in the Victoria constituency (David Chuenyan Lai, *Chinatowns: Towns Within Cities in Canada* [Vancouver: UBC Press, 1988], 231). All other census statistics in the following paragraphs are from Canada, *Census,* 1921, v. 1, 380-81. *Victoria Times,* 26 November and 2 and 6 December 1921; *Victoria Colonist,* 26 November 1921. A Conservative advertisement alluded to the admission of Chinese students while Mackenzie King was minister of labour (*Victoria Colonist,* 3 and 4 December 1921).

35 There were 2,064 Chinese and 575 Japanese residents. *Nanaimo Free Press*, 12, 16, 17, 19, 25, and 26 November 1921; *Victoria Colonist*, 16, 18, and 19 November 1921; *Victoria Times*, 15 November 1921; *Cowichan Leader*, 24 November and 1 December 1921. In a purely local issue, Booth tried to embarrass Dickie by referring to his 1902 vote in the legislature against an Asiatic exclusion bill (*Victoria Times*, 21 November 1921; *Nanaimo Herald*, 27 November 1921).

36 *Comox Argus*, 17 and 24 November and 1 December 1921; *Port Alberni News*, 16 and 30 November 1921; *Victoria Times*, 12 November and 2 December 1921. J.E. Armishaw of the Farmer-Labour Party said that he had always stood for a white BC, that he had been secretary of the Asiatic Exclusion League in 1911, and that, if elected, he would continue to fight for a white BC (*B.C. Labour News*, 25 November 1921). Neill won the nomination as an Independent over J.S. Cowper and four others (*Comox Argus*, 3 November 1921). Later in the session, Neill introduced a bill that would have required potential immigrants not of British birth to write from their country of origin requesting permission to enter Canada. This provision, he explained, would allow Canada to reject any immigrants, such as Asians, that it did not want (HCD, 26 May 1922, 2207). The bill did not proceed further.

37 Ladner to Mrs. M. Barber, 17 April 1923, LJLP, v. 7; Leon J. Ladner, Diary, 31 March 1922, LJLP, v. 4; HCD, 8 May 1922, 1509; W.G. McQuarrie to Members of the House of Commons, 4 May 1922, DImm, Mf10652.

38 King, Diary, 5-9 August 1919 and 1 April 1922, KD. King met the Japanese consul on 19 April 1922, but his diary does not record the subject discussed; Percy Reid to W.J. Black, 20 February 1922, A.L. Jolliffe to Scott, 7 February 1922, and Reid to Chilien Tsur, 12 May 1922, DImm, MfC4784; *Victoria Times*, 4 April 1922; *Victoria Colonist*, 13 April 1922; *Vancouver Sun*, 17 April 1922; PC 715, 12 April 1922. The gentlemen's agreement exempted Japanese immigrants from this provision. Because of unemployment, the immigration ban was extended to all immigrants except bona fide farmers or farm labourers, female domestic servants with employment prospects, wives and families of immigrants already in the country, British subjects with "sufficient means of maintenance," Americans whose labour was required, and nationals whose country had special treaty arrangements with Canada (PC 717, 9 May 1922). Jolliffe to Scott, 1 September 1922, DImm, MfC4784. The number of schoolboys seemed likely to increase (Reid to Stewart, 5 January 1923, DImm, Mf10661); HCD, 15 May 1922, 1776.

39 *Vancouver Province*, 6 April, 8 May, and 30 November 1922. Hugh Thornley, later president of the Asiatic Exclusion League, subsequently claimed that the resolution passed because he "flooded the Federal House with the Briefs and other literature" (Thornley to J.W. Jones, 10 January 1924, JWJP). Whether he was working on his own, for the Asiatic Exclusion League, for the Retail Merchants Association, or for some other agency is not clear. G.S. Hougham to King, 28 April 1922, DImm, Mf10652. Many resolutions are in this file. *New Westminster British Columbian*, 26 January and 25 February 1922; L.L. Peltier et al. to King, 28 February 1922, KP, #59049-54; *Victoria Colonist*, 19 January and 30 March 1922; D.H. Elliott to F.A. McGregor, 18 April 1922, DImm, Mf10652; *Victoria Times*, 13 April 1922; *British Columbia United Farmer*, 15 April 1922, 3.

40 HCD, 8 May 1922, 1555.

41 The debate is in HCD, 8 May 1922, 1509-77. According to the *Chilliwack Progress*, Munro absented himself after "the Liberal leadership cracked the whip" (18 May 1922). He was not paired. *Vancouver Province*, 9 May 1922; *Victoria Times*, 17 May 1922; *Nanaimo Herald*, 10 May 1922; *Nanaimo Free Press*, 9 May 1922; *British Columbia Retailer* 13 (May 1922): 703, and 13 (June 1922): 737; *New Westminster British Columbian*, 9 May 1922 (reprinted in the *Chilliwack Progress*, 18 May 1922); *Vancouver World*, 9 May 1922; *British Columbia United Farmer*, 15 May 1922, 6; *Toronto Globe*, 10 May 1922 (reprinted in the *Nanaimo Free Press*, 22 May 1922).

42 *Victoria Times,* 12, 14, and 25 July 1922; J.T. Crowder to Manson, 12 September 1922, Crowder to Manson, 26 May 1922, Manson to Stewart, 18 May 1922, Manson to Crowder, 3 October 1922, and W.F. Ing to Manson, 5 October 1922, AGR, 1918-18-2060; *British Columbia Retailer* 13 (July 1922): 767; *Vancouver Province,* 19 July 1922; *Chilliwack Progress,* 14 December 1922; *Cowichan Leader,* 21 December 1922. Possibly reflecting the waning interest of some Retail Merchants Association members, the resolution carried with an amendment that information be provided to show the question from a retail merchant's point of view (*British Columbia Retailer* 14 [October 1922]: 9); Ing to Stewart, 28 October 1922, DImm, Mf10652; *Vancouver Province,* 14 August 1922; *Vancouver Sun,* 20 July 1922.

43 *Victoria Times,* 23 August and 14 October 1922. M.J. Crehan said practically the same thing at the 1923 convention (*Nanaimo Free Press,* 28 September 1923); *Vancouver World,* 3 June, 23 August, 25 October, and 1 November 1922 and 22 January 1923; *Victoria Colonist,* 1 June 1922; *New Westminster British Columbian,* 31 October 1922; *Nanaimo Free Press,* 3 November 1922; *Kamloops Standard-Sentinel,* 27 October 1922; *Vernon News,* 14 December 1922; J. Castell Hopkins, ed., *The Canadian Annual Review, 1923* (Toronto: Annual Review Publishing, 1924), 494.
    Three years earlier the Victoria Municipal Chapter had called for lifting the head tax for Chinese cooks and domestic servants (*Victoria Times,* 10 October 1919). Trades and Labour Congress of Canada, Memorandum on Legislation, January 1923. When the congress met in Vancouver in 1923, it again called for the total exclusion of Orientals (*B.C. Federationist,* 14 September 1923). At its 1924 interview with the federal Cabinet, the congress took favourable notice of the Chinese Immigration Act (*B.C. Federationist,* 25 January 1924).

44 *British Columbia Retailer* 13 (April 1922): 672, and 15 (June 1923): 7; *Vancouver World,* 1 September 1922; *Vancouver Province,* 2 October 1922; *Nanaimo Herald,* 21 March 1922; *Nanaimo Free Press,* 13 April 1922; *Vancouver Sun,* 14 April 1922. Some groups present, including the city council, separately endorsed Oriental exclusion to support McQuarrie's forthcoming resolution. *Nanaimo Herald,* 19 April 1922; *Victoria Colonist,* 1 March 1922; *Kamloops Standard-Sentinel,* 23 May 1922; *New Westminster British Columbian,* 1 and 9 May 1922; D. Stuart to King, 8 May 1922, DImm, Mf10652.

45 *Victoria Times,* 15 September and 12 October 1922; *Cowichan Leader,* 28 September 1922; *Chilliwack Progress,* 12 October 1922; *Agricultural Journal,* January 1923, 263; C. Sanderson to Stewart, 21 November 1922, DImm, MfC10410. Resolutions from other institutes, including those in Surrey, Duncan, Creston, and Fruitvale, are in this file. *Vancouver Province,* 14 June 1923; *Vernon News,* 18 January 1923; *British Columbia United Farmer,* 1 February 1923. For the relationship between the United Farmers of British Columbia and the Provincial Party, see Ian Parker, "The Provincial Party," *BC Studies,* 8 (Winter 1970-71): 17-21. Not every member of the Provincial Party was happy with the policy. C.H. Tupper suggested that the plank might offend Japan or China since it seemed to give "a preference for the scum of Europe to the Oriental races" (Tupper to A.D. McRae, 25 January 1923, CHTP, b. 26).

46 Kay Anderson, *Vancouver's Chinatown: Racial Discourse in Canada, 1875-1980* (Montreal and Kingston: McGill-Queen's University Press, 1991), 114.

47 *Vancouver Province,* 24 August and 29 September 1922; Oliver to King, 11 October 1922, KP, #67076-7; Oliver to Brenton S. Brown, 11 October 1922, POC; *Vancouver World,* 31 October 1922; BCV&P, 10 November 1922; *Victoria Times,* 29 September and 11 November 1922; *Nanaimo Free Press,* 10 November 1922.

48 *Fraser Valley Record,* 30 November 1922; Oliver to E.A. Riddell, 21 November 1922, and H.P. Thorpe to Oliver, 20 November 1922, POC. The speaker ruled William J. Bowser's amendment out of order. Attorney-General's speech on Oriental Debate, British Columbia Legislature, [15 November 1922] (emphasis in original), Riddell to Oliver, 18 November 1922, and J.M. Paterson to Manson, 4 December 1922, AGR, 2060-17-18; BCV&P, 16 and 20 November

1922; *Victoria Times*, 11, 13, 15, and 16 November 1922; *Victoria Colonist*, 15 and 16 November 1922; *Agricultural Journal*, December 1922, 232; *Vancouver World*, 18 November 1922.

49 King to Oliver, 9 December 1922, KP, #67078-9; Memorandum of Conversation [of W.L.M. King] with Dr. Chilien Tsur, Chinese Consul General, Ottawa, 28 July 1922, KP, #61104-10. The Vancouver Board of Trade investigated industrial scholarships for Chinese students. The Canadian Pacific Railway (CPR), Canadian universities, especially A.W. Currie, a former British Columbian and principal of McGill University, and J.A. Robb, the minister of trade and commerce, liked the idea of students as "active trade missionaries for Canada," but nothing came of the idea. In 1932 Prime Minister R.B. Bennett told Currie that the "drastic" regulations of the Chinese Immigration Act of 1923 were "necessary." Jolliffe to W.D. Scott, 21 March 1922, DImm, MfC10659; R.L. Borden to King, 13 June 1922, KP, #59738; *Victoria Times*, 8 August 1922; *Vancouver Sun*, 27 June 1923. See also *Vancouver Sun* editorials, 16 August and 16 October 1922, 2 February and 15 November 1923, 26 August and 3 December 1924, and 21 February 1925; *Vancouver Province*, 14 February 1923 and 17 September 1931; W. Maugham to Robb, 30 July 1923, KP, #78635; General Passenger Agent to Baird, 21 December 1928, copy in DImm, MfC10661; Currie to King, 8 December 1924, KP, #83913-4; Currie to Bennett, 16 February 1931, RBBP, #231891-2; Robb to King, 2 August 1923, KP, #78634; Bennett to Currie, 6 February 1932, RBBP, #241889-90.

50 Reid to Stewart, 29 August and 7 September 1922 and 22 January 1923, DImm, MfC10661; Loring Christie to King, 3 October 1922, KP, #C61335-9; PC 182, 31 January 1923. The Immigration Department also advised about ways to ensure that those admitted as "merchants" were bona fide merchants (Reid to Stewart, 2 March 1923, DImm, MfC10661); *Vancouver World*, 31 January 1923; *Vancouver Province*, 27 December 1922.

51 HCD, 21 February 1923, 497, 503-9, 513.

52 HCD, 2 March 1923, 768; *Victoria Times*, 1 March 1923; *Vancouver Province*, 17 March and 3 April 1923; *Vancouver World*, 29 March 1923; *British Columbia Retailer* 15 (April 1923): 207, and 15 (June 1923): 9; J.L. Ward, Nanaimo, to Stewart, 24 April 1923, DImm, MfC10661. The New Westminster, Nelson, Kamloops, Victoria, and Vernon branches sent similar resolutions.

53 Ladner to M. Barber, 17 April 1923, LJLP, v. 7; *Vancouver Province*, 3, 24, and 26 April 1923; Percy Reid to J.E. Featherston, 9 April 1923, DImm, MfC10660; *Victoria Times*, 26 April 1923.

54 HCD, 30 April 1923, 2312-13, 2317, 2321-22, 2326; Senate, *Debates*, 26 June 1923, 1123.

55 Rev. W.D. Noyes to Stewart, 7 March 1924; Sixty residents of Ottawa interested in the welfare of the Chinese in Canada to Stewart, 11 April 1923, R.P. Mackay to Charles Stewart, 21 April 1923, S.S. Osterhout, N. Lascelles Ward, and David A. Smith to King, 3 April 1923, and Noyes to Stewart, 7 March 1924, DImm, MfC10661; R.P. Mackay to Smith, 23 May 1923, PCC, BFM, b. 5; *Victoria Times*, 5 April 1923; N.W. Rowell to Borden, 11 May 1923, RLBP, #158166-7. Smith soon criticized Osterhout's views (Smith to Mackay, 22 June 1923, PCC, BFM, b. 5).

56 Their letters and briefs can be found in DImm, MfC10661. Edgar Wickberg, ed., *From China to Canada: A History of the Chinese Communities in Canada* (Toronto: McClelland and Stewart, 1982), 142-45; William Proudfoot, Petition to the Senate of Canada Concerning Chinese Immigration Bill 45 on Behalf of the Chinese Association of Canada, 7 May 1923, DImm, MfC10661; *Vancouver Province*, 11 and 16 May 1923; Edgar Wickberg, "Chinese and Canadian Influences on Chinese Politics in Vancouver, 1900-1947," *BC Studies*, 45 (Spring 1980): 50-51; Paul Yee, *Saltwater City: An Illustrated History of the Chinese in Vancouver* (Vancouver: Douglas and McIntyre, 1988), 54; Lai, *Chinatowns*, 238.

57 Chao-Rsin Chu to Lord Curzon, 3 and 5 May 1923, GGR, G21, no. 332, v. 17b; Sun Yat Sen to Stewart, 17 May 1923, and C.Y. Immanuel Liu to Robb, 17 March 1924, DImm, MfC10661; *Ottawa Journal*, 20 August 1923; *Victoria Times*, 30 August and 6 September 1923; *Vancouver Province*, 5 September 1922; *Vancouver Sun*, 3 and 7 September 1923. The Canadian trade commissioner in Shanghai saw no sign of a boycott but said that "it would not take very

much to arouse some such feeling" (J.W. Ross to Stewart, 6 April 1923, DImm, MfC10661). The *Vancouver World* suggested that Tsur's withdrawal would cause little uneasiness in Canada and not interfere with trade because merchants were exempt (31 August 1923).

58 *Victoria Colonist*, 2 July 1924; *Victoria Times*, 2 July 1924. A similar commemoration was held in Victoria in 1925 (*Victoria Colonist*, 4 July 1925); *Vancouver Star*, 2 July 1924; *Vancouver Chinese Times*, 2 and 4 July 1924 (quoted in Wickberg, *From China to Canada*, 157-58) and 8 July 1924 (quoted in Jiwu Wang, "The Chinese Community's Response to Protestant Missions Prior to the 1940s," *Canadian Ethnic Studies* 33, 2 [2001]: 23); *Vancouver Sun*, 2 July 1924; Lai, *Chinatowns*, 238.

59 H.C. Ellis et al., Eastern Canadian Chinese Mission, to Robert Forke, 25 September 1927, DImm, MfC10661; *Vancouver Star*, 3 July 1924 and 5 May 1927. The Confucian stress on family lineage and the dependence of some Chinese villages on overseas remittances also discouraged female emigration (The Women's Book Committee, Chinese Canadian National Council, *Jin Guo: Voices of Chinese Canadian Women* [Toronto: Women's Press, 1992], 17). Victor W. Odlum owned the *Vancouver Star*, the successor to the *Vancouver World*. Within months an Ottawa report noted that all Chinese residents had registered.

60 *Vancouver World*, 1 June 1923; *Vancouver Province*, 19 May 1923; *New Westminster British Columbian*, 29 August 1923; *Nanaimo Free Press*, 1 September 1923; R.J. Cromie to King, 13 September 1923, KP, #72155; *Vancouver Sun*, 3 September 1923; HCD, 1 April 1925, 1757.

61 Young and Reid, *The Japanese Canadians*, 203; *Victoria Colonist*, 19 May 1921, 13 September 1923, and 21 December 1929; J.K. Adams to Oliver, 9 February 1927, and Oliver to Adams, 10 February 1927, POC. On 19 May 1921 the *Victoria Colonist* suggested a gentlemen's agreement with China.

62 Lai, *Chinatowns*, 62; British Columbia, Legislative Assembly, *Report on Oriental Activities within the Province* (Victoria: King's Printer, 1927), 6, 8.

63 *Port Alberni News*, 9 April 1924; John Nelson, *The Canadian Provinces: Their Problems and Policies* (Toronto: Musson, 1924), 188; HCD, 23 March 1923, 1447-48; *Vancouver World*, 2 March 1922; *Vancouver Sun*, 27 February and 1 March 1923; W.J. Black to Blair, 23 September 1922, DImm, MfC10278; Minister of Foreign Affairs of Japan to Ohta, c. 10 December 1922, Translation, KP, #C61527-31; Interim Translation Left by Ohta, 10 March 1923, DEAR, MfT1751.

64 King to Ohta, 19 March 1923, Ohta to King, 10 April 1923, Ohta to Robb, 12 August 1923, and Joseph Pope to Governor-General's Secretary, 23 July 1923, DEAR, MfT1751; HCD, 23 March 1923, 1447, 30 April 1923, 2328, and 27 June 1923, 4441. Japan could not provide accurate statistics for the summer of 1923 because of confusion and the destruction of records in the earthquake and fires in Tokyo and Yokohama, but the number was well under the limit (N. Matsunaga to King, 1 April 1924, DEAR, MfT1751).

65 HCD, 19 March 1924, 464; 15 April 1924, 1381-86; 11 July 1924, 4348-55; A.W. Neill to J.G. Turgeon, 9 February 1924, KP, #86300-1. T.G. McBride, MP (Progressive, Cariboo) echoed the argument (HCD, 28 April 1924, 1568), and to a lesser extent so did another Progressive, L.W. Humphrey, MP (West Kootenay), who was more concerned about Doukhobors (HCD, 13 May 1924, 2057, and 11 July 1924, 4349-54); *Nanaimo Free Press*, 2 May 1924; *Vancouver World*, 25 March 1921. See Tolmie, quoted in *Nanaimo Free Press*, 2 February 1921; W.D. Gilman, Secretary, Los Angeles County Anti-Asiatic Association, to Ralph G. Ritchie, 2 March 1920, JWJP; V.S. McClatchey to Premier of British Columbia, 25 June 1921, and Secretary to McClatchey, 28 June 1921, POC; McClatchey to Blair, 29 May 1923, DImm, MfC4751.

66 *Vancouver Province*, 14 April 1924; *Vancouver Sun*, 23 April 1924 and 3 April 1925; *Victoria Colonist*, 13 July 1922 and 10 June 1924; *Victoria Times*, 24 April 1924; *Prince Rupert Daily News*, 30 November 1926. Walter N. Sage's paper was published as "Canada on the Pacific, 1866-1925," *Washington Historical Quarterly* 17 (April 1926): 91-104.

67 His Majesty's Ambassador at Tokyo to Foreign Secretary, with J.H. Thomas, to Governor-General, 31 July 1924, DEAR, MfT1750; T. Nagao to King, 2 July 1928, DEAR, MfT1751; *Vancouver Province*, 5 December 1924; Neill to King, 16 December 1924, DEAR, MfT1751.

68 *Victoria Times*, 19 June and 9 and 18 December 1924; *Cumberland Islander*, 31 May 1924; *Vancouver Province*, 10 June and 9 and 18 December 1924; *Nanaimo Free Press*, 11 June 1924; BCLJ, 17 December 1924, 158-59; *Victoria Colonist*, 18 December 1924.

69 F.H. Barber to King, 9 February 1923, and Barber to McQuarrie, 9 February 1923, DImm, MfC10410; Ladner to Mrs. M. Barber, 17 April 1923, LJLP, v. 7; Mrs. Barber to Manson, 21 February 1924, and Thornley to J.W. Jones, 6 April 1925, AGR, 1918-17-2060, and JWJP; Thornley to King, 24 March 1924, DImm, MfC4751; *Farm and Home*, 5 February and 5 March 1925; *Vancouver Star*, 20 and 29 January and 3 February 1925; *Vancouver Province*, 20 January, 3 February, and 1 May 1925; *Vernon News*, 11 February 1925; Thornley to Ladner, 21 May 1925, LJLP.

70 When the Methodist Conference refused to confirm Davies as pastor of Centennial Methodist Church, Victoria, the congregation split, and many joined him in his new church (*Vancouver Province*, 15, 21, and 22 May 1924).

71 *Victoria Times*, 24 March and 28 April 1925; *Victoria Colonist*, 25 and 27 November 1924, 31 March 1925, and 2 March 1926; Clem Davies to Oliver, 25 September 1925, POC; Resolution of 1 March 1926, with Harry Langley, to King, 2 March 1926, DEAR, MfT1751. Reverend Davies argued for the age limitation lest a general refund of the head tax result in the "export of elderly Chinamen, no longer of economic value, to secure for the local merchants repayment of the head tax on such men" (*Victoria Times*, 3 December 1925). Langley to King, 23 March 1925, DEAR, MfT1751. The provincial government forwarded the league's resolution to Ottawa; Immigration Department officials suggested that it was impractical (Acting Deputy Minister to Charles Stewart, 26 January 1926, DImm, MfC4785). Reverend Davies became "imperial lecturer for the Kanadian Knights of the Ku Klux Klan" (*Victoria Colonist*, 19 February 1926).

72 *Vancouver Province*, 22 February 1925; W.J. Egan to King, 20 February 1925, and Memo to King, 20 March 1925, DEAR, MfT1750.

73 *Victoria Colonist*, 27 September 1925; *Vancouver Sun*, 3 April 1925; W.E. Haskins to Editor, *Vancouver Sun*, 7 April 1925.

74 *Vancouver Province*, 30 March 1925; *Victoria Times*, 30 March and 16 and 30 April 1925; Canada was considering applying a policy imposed on European immigrants – that is, not recognizing picture brides. Egan to King, 15 August 1924, DEAR, MfT1750; Interviews, King and Matsunaga, 2 April and 5 and 22 May 1925, Skelton, Memo given to Japanese Consul General, 22 May 1925, Byng to Colonial Secretary, 26 May 1925, and Amery to Byng, 17 June 1925, DEAR, MfT1751.

75 Skelton to Neill, 27 June 1925, DEAR, MfT1750; Byng to Amery, 19 June 1925, Skelton to Matsunaga, 16 July 1925, Skelton, Memo, Interview re Japanese Immigration, 19 August 1925, and Skelton to Matsunaga, 27 August 1925, DEAR, MfT1751.

76 *Vancouver Sun*, 18 and 27 May 1925; *Vancouver Star*, 12 June 1925; *Victoria Colonist*, 26 May 1925; *Vancouver Province*, 5 July and 2 August 1925.

77 Japan wanted a maximum of 300 emigrants per year; Canada wanted a total of 200 with a maximum of 100 women and children and 100 agricultural labourers and domestic servants. Japan would consider a total of 250 with no limit on the proportion of women and children (Skelton, Interview with Japanese Consul-General, 21 September 1925, and L.C. Moyer to King, 2 October 1925, DEAR, MfT1751). *Port Alberni News*, 8 July 1925; *Victoria Times*, 4 December 1924; *Comox Argus*, 24 September 1925; *Victoria Colonist*, 16 October 1925; Neill to Skelton, 29 August 1925, Skelton to Neill, 29 September 1925, Neill to Skelton, 15

October 1925, Neill to Skelton, 30 December 1925, and Neill to Skelton, 3 March 1926, DEAR, MfT1751.

78 J.H. King to Moyer, 19 September 1925, DEAR, MfT1751; *Victoria Colonist,* 9, 13, 20, 23, and 27 October 1925; *Vancouver Province,* 22, 23, and 27 October 1925. The conservative *New Westminster British Columbian* agreed that King's government was pro-Japanese (12 October 1925). *Victoria Times,* 1, 6, 8, and 9 October 1925; *Nanaimo Free Press,* 22 October 1925. Munro explained that he had not expected the vote and had gone home because he was ill.

79 *Vancouver Province,* 23 March 1926; Skelton to King, 23 March 1926, and C. Eliot to Austen Chamberlain, 26 January 1926, DEAR, MfT1751.

80 Skelton to King, 27 April 1926, Chamberlain to Tilley, 30 April 1926, L.S. Amery to Byng, 5 May 1926, Matsunaga to Skelton, 20 May 1926, Memo read by Matsunaga to King, 7 August 1926, Skelton to Matsunaga, 25 May 1926, and Dominions Secretary to Governor-General, 8 September 1926, DEAR, MfT1751. *Vancouver Sun,* 23 and 26 August 1926; *Vancouver Province,* 23 August 1926. King made the governor general's powers an election issue.

81 Oliver to King, 21 January 1927, KP, #124777. Oliver's letter is almost identical to both Manson to Oliver, 10 December 1926, and F.C. Aubrey to Manson, 5 March 1927, AGR, 1918-17-2060; *Victoria Times,* 25 February 1927; *Vancouver Sun,* 25 February 1927; *Vancouver Star,* 25 February 1927; *New Westminster British Columbian,* 15 March 1927 (weekly edition); *Vancouver Star,* 28 June 1927; Speech to Luncheon of Canadian Credit Men's Trust Association, 27 June 1927, HHSPN, v. 3.

In a speech on behalf of the British Israel Association of Greater Vancouver, Professor Edward Odlum, father of Victor W. Odlum, opposed discrimination against the Japanese (E. Odlum, "The Ethnological Relationship of the Ruling Japanese to the Members of the British Columbia Legislature," 23 March 1927, VWOP).

The Ku Klux Klan had recently established a Klan in Vancouver (L. Healy to Members of the House of Commons, 8 February 1927, copy in DImm, MfC10410). Given the Klan's reputation, many recipients of its resolution, such as the Vancouver Trades and Labour Council, the Victoria Chamber of Commerce, and Kamloops City Council, ignored it. Only Nanaimo City Council and the grocers' section of Vancouver's Retail Merchants Association seem to have supported it (*Victoria Colonist,* 17, 19, and 23 February 1927; *Ashcroft Journal,* 12 March 1927; *The Retailer* 19 [April 1927]: 32); *Ottawa Citizen,* 12 October 1927; *Victoria Times,* 13 October 1927; *Vancouver Province,* 18 October 1927.

82 *Ottawa Citizen,* 9 November 1927; J.D. MacLean to King, 12 November 1927, POC; King, Diary, 10 November 1927, KD; *Vancouver Province,* 11 and 12 November 1927; Canada, Dominion-Provincial Conference, 1927, *Précis of Discussion* (Ottawa: King's Printer, 1928), 37; Grant Dexter, *Victoria Times,* 10 December 1927. J.H. King to King, 14 January 1928, KP, #130452.

83 *Victoria Colonist,* 16 December 1927 and 2 and 4 February and 1 March 1928; *Vancouver Province,* 2 and 4 February and 1 March 1928; *Nanaimo Free Press,* 2 February 1928; HCD, 31 January 1928, 61; *Vancouver Sun,* 1 March 1928; *Vancouver Star,* 6 February 1928. Victor W. Odlum, the *Vancouver Star*'s owner, was elected a Liberal MLA for Vancouver in 1924. T. Fukuma to MacLean, 27 January 1928, POC. Negotiations proceeded slowly, partly because a new Japanese government took a new approach ([indecipherable] to Egan, 3 February 1928, DEAR, v. 729).

84 *Vancouver Province,* 12 March 1928; BCV&P, 14 March 1928. Two Labour members said that Labour had been seeking such a measure for forty years (*Vancouver Sun,* 15 March 1928).

85 *Prince Rupert Daily News,* 14 and 16 March 1928; *Vancouver Province,* 15 March 1928; *Victoria Colonist,* 17 February and 17 May 1928; J.E. Armishaw to Premier and Members of the Legislative Assembly, 11 February 1928, AGR, 1918-17-2060. McQuarrie cited the United Farmers of British Columbia resolution in Parliament because it asked all British Columbia members to resign and stand for re-election with exclusion as the issue (HCD, 7 March 1928,

1100); *Cowichan Leader,* 15 March 1928; A. Williamson to MacLean, 17 February 1928, POC; T.R.E. MacInnes to MacLean, 21 April 1928, TDPP, v. 28.

86 HCD, 7 March 1928, 1103, and 8 June 1928, 3980. Skelton to Tomii, 22 May 1928. The correspondence is in DCER, v. 4, 887-89.

87 *Victoria Times,* 13, 15, and 30 June, 18 July, and 28 November 1928; *Nanaimo Free Press,* 14 June 1928; *Maple Ridge & Pitt Meadows Weekly Gazette,* 28 June and 5 July 1928; *Vancouver Star,* 13 July 1928; *Revelstoke Review,* 5 and 18 July 1928; *Vancouver Sun,* 13 and 14 July 1928; *Kelowna Courier,* 12 July 1928; "British Columbia's Next Premier" ([Victoria: Conservative Party], 1928); *Vancouver Province,* 22 June and 10, 11, and 15 July 1928; *Victoria Colonist,* 28 November 1928; T. Nagao to King, 2 July 1928, DEAR, MfT1751.

Chapter 4: "Shoving the Oriental Around"

1 Of Scottish Canadian ancestry, Manson grew up in western Ontario and graduated from Osgoode Hall. He settled in Prince Rupert and in 1916 was elected MLA for the adjacent constituency of Omineca.

2 *Vancouver Province,* 30 April and 1 May 1918; Labour Conference, Court House, Vancouver, 17 August 1921, Transcript of Proceedings, DLab, v. 209; *Victoria Colonist,* 1 January 1921; British Columbia, Department of Labour, *Annual Report,* 1920 (Victoria: King's Printer, 1921), F10; Howard O'Hagan, "Japanese British Columbia," *Montreal Listening Post,* March 1925, 6; *Vancouver Province,* 17 October 1919; R.C.R. Report to D.I. Office, Military District No. 11, 7 August 1919, DNDR, MfC5055; *Vancouver World,* 15 May 1921.

3 Paul Phillips, *No Power Greater* (Vancouver: B.C. Federation of Labour, 1967), 88; *Canadian Congress Journal,* February 1929, quoted in John Manley, "Does the International Labour Movement Need Salvaging? Communism, Labourism, and the Canadian Trade Unions, 1921-1928," *Labour/Le Travail* 41 (Spring 1998): 164; *Victoria Times,* 16 and 28 April 1919; *B.C. Federationist,* 6 April 1923, 2 September 1921, and 20 June and 18 July 1924; George Palmer, "Racial Differences and Labour Disunity," *B.C. Federationist,* 10 September 1920.

4 *Vancouver Province,* 10 February 1919, 5 October 1927, and 22 February 1928; Dorothy Steeves, *The Compassionate Rebel* (Vancouver: Boag Foundation, 1960), 53; *Vancouver Chinese Times,* 10 June 1919; G.O.C. (Victoria) to Adjutant General, 13 June 1919, DNDR, v. 2576; Trades and Labour Congress of Canada, *Report of the Proceedings of the Thirty-Ninth Annual Convention, Hamilton, September 22-27, 1919* (Ottawa: Trades and Labour Congress of Canada, 1919), 124; *Vancouver Sun,* 5 May 1920; Martin Robin, *Radical Politics and Canadian Labour* (Kingston: Industrial Relations Centre, Queen's University, 1968), 266 and ch. 2; *B.C. Federationist,* 16 September 1921 and 20 June 1924. A year later the New Westminster Trades and Labour Council withdrew support from the Canadian Labour Party because the party favoured Asian enfranchisement, an idea that had some support among socialists. See Gillian Creese, "Exclusion or Solidarity? Vancouver Workers Confront the 'Oriental Problem,'" *BC Studies,* 80 (Winter 1988-89): 24-51.

5 *Vancouver Star,* 3 July 1924; *B.C. Federationist,* 21 September 1923; *Victoria Times,* 27 January 1923.

6 For example, Testimony before the Royal Commission on Industrial Relations, quoted in the *Victoria Colonist,* 29 April 1919; *Victoria Times,* 29 April 1919; *New Westminster British Columbian,* 30 April 1919; *Vancouver Province,* 30 April 1919; *British Columbia Financial Times,* 3 September 1921; *B.C. Federationist,* 16 April 1920; British Columbia, Department of Labour, *Annual Report,* 1921 (Victoria: King's Printer, 1922), 48; *Kelowna Courier,* 11 August 1921. One of the main speakers, J.J. Atherton, read a poem about the "downfall under the wiles of a Chinese betrayer of the daughter of an old prospector during his absence in the Yukon." He outlined other popular beliefs about Asians: the danger of assimilation, their unsanitary habits, and their habit of sending money out of the country (*Kelowna Courier,* 30 September 1920).

7 Creese, "Exclusion or Solidarity," 50-51; Gillian Creese, "Organizing Against Racism in the Workplace: Chinese Workers in Vancouver Before the Second World War," *Canadian Ethnic Studies* 19, 3 (1987): 35-46; *Comox Argus,* 18 December 1919; Allen Seager, "Workers, Class and Industrial Conflict in New Westminster, 1900-1930," in *Workers, Capital, and the State in British Columbia,* ed. Rennie Warburton and David Coburn (Vancouver: UBC Press, 1988), 123; Koliang Yih to John Oliver, 9 November 1920, AGR, P180-159; *Penticton Herald,* 10 and 24 March and 1 October 1921. Saanich Municipal Council urged berry growers to hire unemployed white men rather than Chinese labourers, but growers claimed that the necessary bending and "light fingered handling" was an "almost impossible handicap" for most white men (*Victoria Times,* 9 June 1922); *Cowichan Leader,* 17 August 1922.

8 When famine struck northern China in 1920-21, Victoria's Chinese took the lead in raising relief funds. Both Victoria daily newspapers successfully encouraged readers to contribute to relief funds and to attend a benefit performance of *The Merchant of Venice* presented in Chinese at the Chinese theatre, a fundraising bazaar, a concert, and a dance sponsored by the Chinese Benevolent Association. At the time of Japan's earthquake, individuals gave cash through the Red Cross; the federal and provincial governments gave food and lumber respectively, but there were not the same fundraising activities as there had been for China's famine victims. The press complained that the donations were inadequate, for humanitarian reasons and because of Japan's importance as a market for British Columbia products (*Victoria Times,* 5 September 1923; *Victoria Colonist,* 6 September 1923; *Vernon News,* 27 September 1923; *Vancouver Sun,* 20 September 1923; *Vancouver Province,* 5 September 1923).

9 *Victoria Colonist,* 19 January 1922; *Victoria Times,* 28 November 1923. The suggestion of several United Farmers of British Columbia locals that a special tax be imposed on employers of Oriental labour found little support (*Vancouver Province,* 24 January 1922); Ronald A. Shearer, "The Economy of British Columbia," in *Trade Liberalization and a Regional Economy: Studies of the Impact of Free Trade on British Columbia,* ed. R.A. Shearer, J.H. Young, and G.R. Munro (Toronto: University of Toronto Press for the Private Planning Association of Canada, 1971), 17; British Columbia, Department of Labour, *Annual Reports,* 1919-29 (Victoria: King's Printer, 1920-1930). In 1919 it was alleged that about 90 percent of the employees in lumber mills around Vancouver were Oriental, but that was a much exaggerated estimate (*Vancouver Province,* 17 October 1919); *Port Alberni News,* 7 February 1923.

10 *Vancouver Star,* 12 July 1924; *Victoria Colonist,* 16 May 1920; *Prince Rupert Evening Empire,* 30 August and 20 and 22 September 1921; *Prince Rupert Daily News,* 20 September 1921.

11 "History of the Oriental Question," undated memo, and "Herbert," Chief Forester of British Columbia, to Loring Christie, 24 and 30 June 1920, LCP, v. 3.

12 Oliver to S. Ukita, 7 April 1920, Ukita to Cabinet, 28 April 1920, J.W. de B. Farris to Oliver, 3 May 1920, and T.D. Pattullo to Oliver, 1 May 1920, POC; BCV&P, 16 April 1920; Ukita to Oliver, 26 March 1920, Charles Doherty to Oliver, 21 April 1920, and Report of Executive Council, 8 June 1920, AGR, 1918-17-2060; *Vancouver Province,* 19 June 1920; *Victoria Times,* 1 May 1920; *Vancouver World,* 6 May 1920; *Victoria Colonist,* 21 May 1921. The *Vancouver Sun* proposed that it would be better to halt Oriental immigration entirely than to "exercise a harsh discrimination" against people who had been permitted to settle in the province (6 May 1920); Farris to Pattullo, 28 July 1920, AGR, 1918-17-2060; *Kelowna Courier,* 7 October 1920; *Victoria Times,* 23 June 1920 and 2 April 1921; Macdonald, Chief Justice A., Judgement, 16 November 1920, copy in AGR, 1918-17-2060. The text of the decision is in the *Victoria Times,* 19 November 1920.

13 A. Millema, "A Chat with Lumberjacks," *Pacific Coast Lumberman* 5 (August 1921): 36. Some thought that the Japanese were not good loggers because they lacked physical strength (*Pacific Coast Lumberman* 4 [June 1920]: 45); C.H. Tupper to S. Tatesishi, 15 April 1921, S. Shimizu to C.J. Doherty, 4 May 1921, Farris to E.L. Newcombe, 21 May 1921, Newcombe to Farris, 31

May 1921, Farris to Brooks-Bidlake & Whittall, 24 August 1921, M.A. MacDonald to Farris, 21 September 1921, and Farris to MacDonald, 30 September 1921, AGR, 1918-17-2060.

14 *Nelson Daily News,* 5 November 1921; *Vancouver Province,* 23 November 1921; *Victoria Colonist,* 9 September and 2 November 1921; *Vancouver World,* 26 August and 26 October 1921; *Port Alberni News,* 9 November 1921; *Victoria Times,* 2 November 1921.

15 Documentation for Brooks-Bidlake & Whittall vs. Attorney-General for British Columbia and Minister of Lands is in SCC, v. 472, file 4517.

16 David Ricardo Williams, *Duff: A Life in the Law* (Vancouver: UBC Press, 1984), 71.

17 Documentation for this case is in SCC, v. 473, file 4641.

18 James W. St. G. Walker observes that the decision upheld "the right of a province to pass a racially discriminatory act within its legislative fields" (*"Race," Rights and the Law in the Supreme Court of Canada* [Toronto: Osgoode Society/Waterloo: Wilfrid Laurier University Press, 1997], 110).

19 J.A. Ritchie to Attorney-General, [8 April 1922], and Lomer Gouin to Governor-General in Council, 27 March 1922, AGR, 1918-17-2060. Brief summaries of the judgments may be found in *Canada and the Law of Nations,* ed. N.A.M. Mackenzie and L.H. Laing (Toronto: Ryerson, 1938), 265-68, 366-71. *Labour Gazette* (March 1923): 288-90; *Vancouver World,* 9 February 1922; BCV&P, 29 November 1922; *Victoria Colonist,* 22 February and 23 October 1923; *Vancouver World,* 26 February and 13 August 1923; *Victoria Times,* 20 February 1923. A copy of the Privy Council ruling is in SCC, v. 473, file 4641.

20 *Victoria Times,* 2 June, 5 August, and 11 October 1922, 15 August 1923, and 29 November 1924; *Victoria Colonist,* 3 June 1922 and 16 August 1923; Manson to North Pacific Logging Co., 9 June 1922, Manson to D.W. Hampton, 20 October 1922, H.W. Thornton to Manson, 19 November 1922, and F.H. Lamar to Manson, 24 June 1922, AGR, 1918-17-2060; *Nanaimo Free Press,* 25 August 1922; *Vancouver World,* 26 February 1923; *Vancouver Province,* 27 November 1924. The text of the October 1923 decision of the Privy Council, including an outline of the legal aspects of the case, is in Richard A. Olmsted, *Decisions of the Judicial Committee of the Privy Council,* vol. 2 (Ottawa: Queen's Printer, 1954), 384-93; BCV&P, 18 December 1924.

21 There were 1,784 Chinese, 1,147 Japanese, and 565 Hindu labourers in the industry.

22 British Columbia, Department of Labour, *Annual Report,* 1921, 48, 1923, G14, G18, and 1925, G18 (Victoria: King's Printer, 1922, 1924, and 1926); R.H.H. Alexander to Oliver, 13 February 1920, E.W. Hamber to Manson, 3 December 1923, J.G. Robson to Oliver, 29 November 1923, and W. McNeill for Timber Industries Council of British Columbia, Open Letter, 27 November 1923, POC; *Victoria Colonist,* 23 July 1920; *Vancouver World,* 5 March and 17 November 1920 and 29 December 1923; *Victoria Times,* 28 November 1922; *Pacific Coast Lumberman* 5 (December 1921): 21, 34, v. 6 (December 1922): 29, and v. 7 (December 1923): 21; *Victoria Colonist,* 20 December 1923. Professional gardeners who competed with Chinese and Japanese plant jobbers and landscapers asked to have their trade included under the eight-hour law (A.E. Dickson et al. to A.M. Manson, c. 26 October 1927, AGR, 1918-17-2060).

23 *Vancouver World,* 4 and 24 November 1923; British Columbia, Department of Labour, *Annual Report,* 1925 (Victoria: King's Printer, 1926), G10, G17; *Vancouver Province,* 8 March 1925.

24 *New Westminster British Columbian,* 13 March 1919; Canada, National Industrial Conference, Ottawa, September 15-20, 1919, *Official Report of Proceedings and Discussions* (Ottawa: King's Printer, 1919), 108. British Columbia's Female Minimum Wage Act of 1918 was social legislation rather than an anti-Asian measure. *Port Alberni News,* 1 October 1924; *Victoria Times,* 15 November 1924; Labour Conference, Vancouver, 10 August 1921, Transcript of Proceedings, DLab, v. 209; *Vancouver Province,* 9 October 1922. The Saanich Workmen's Association endorsed a minimum wage law as a way of ending Asian competition (*Victoria Times,*

23 June 1922); *Victoria Colonist,* 24 March 1925. A labour representative told the Native Sons of Canada that minimum wage laws were not the answer; capitalists would have the work done in China. For him socialism was the only solution (*B.C. Federationist,* 30 January 1925). Audrey Kobayashi and Peter Jackson, "Japanese Canadians and the Racialization of Labour in the British Columbia Sawmill Industry," *BC Studies,* 103 (Fall 1994): 33-58.

25 *Vancouver Star,* 11 December 1925; BC Loggers' Association to Oliver, 17 December 1925, Robson to Oliver, 14 December 1925, Oliver to J.A. Cochran, 9 February 1925, and Oliver to I.R. Poole, 16 December 1925, POC. See also *British Columbia Lumberman* 10 (January 1926): 22; BCV&P, 19 December 1925, 9; *Vancouver Province,* 20 December 1925. Some Chinese workers feared that equal wages would lead to their dismissal (*Victoria Colonist,* 4 December 1924).

26 *Christian Science Monitor,* quoted in the *Chilliwack Progress,* 18 November 1926; British Columbia, Legislative Assembly, *Report on Oriental Activities within the Province* (Victoria: King's Printer, 1927), 19; British Columbia, Department of Labour, *Annual Report,* 1926 (Victoria: King's Printer, 1927), F42-43; *Vancouver Star,* 19 March 1926; *Canadian Labour Advocate,* 23 April 1926.

27 *British Columbia Lumberman* 10 (November 1926): 20, v. 11 (February 1927): 20, and v. 11 (March 1927): 20; *Victoria Colonist,* 26 September 1926 and 17 February 1927; Alexander, BC Lumber and Shingle Manufacturers' Association, to Oliver, 19 January 1927, printed in *British Columbia Lumberman* 11 (February 1927): 28.

28 *Victoria Times,* 30 October 1926; *Nanaimo Free Press,* 8 December 1926; *Cowichan Leader,* 2 September 1926; *Victoria Colonist,* 27 August 1926; British Columbia, Department of Labour, *Annual Report,* 1926, F43, and 1927, L42 (Victoria: King's Printer, 1927 and 1928); *Prince Rupert Daily News,* 12 July 1928; *Vancouver Sun,* 25 June 1928. A copy of the handbook can be found in TDPP.

29 The case involved two cookhouse workers (who were not Asian). Its early stages are outlined in British Columbia, Department of Labour, *Annual Report,* 1927 (Victoria: King's Printer, 1928), L42ff. A brief summary is in J. Castell Hopkins, ed., *The Canadian Annual Review, 1928-29* (Toronto: Annual Review Publishing, 1929), 522; BC Lumber Manufacturers' Association to S.F. Tolmie, 26 February 1929, POC.

30 BCV&P, 10 November 1922, 3; *Vancouver Province,* 28 February 1919; *Nanaimo Free Press,* 3 March 1919 and 8 May 1920; *Victoria Times,* 28 and 29 April 1919; *Vancouver World,* 13 November 1922; British Columbia, Legislative Assembly, Bill No. 27, 1919; British Columbia, *Statutes,* 1919, ch. 58.

31 Numbers of Asian coal miners (1914-41) are shown in the following table:

Year	Chinese	Japanese	Total Asians	Total employees
1914	702	135	837	6,671
1915[a]	581	124	705	3,242
1916[a]	622	151	773	3,386
1917[a]	638	112	750	3,689
1918[b]	961	99	1,060	4,100
1919[c]	892	82	974	4,391
1920[a]	894	82	976	4,597
1921[c, d]			831	4,640
1922			803	5,150
1923			582	6,149
1924			570	5,418
1925			432	5,443
1926			528	5,322

►

Year	Chinese	Japanese	Total Asians	Total employees
1927			440	5,225
1928			448	5,334
1929			432	5,028
1930			338	4,645
1931			280	4,082
1932			146	3,608
1933			108	3,094
1934			112	2,983
1935			79	2,971
1936			92	2,814
1937			99	3,153
1938			86	2,962
1939			97	2,976
1940			63	2,874
1941			29	2,733

a Coast only.
b Canadian Collieries only.
c Vancouver Island only.
d The *Annual Reports* began grouping Chinese and Japanese that year.
   (Mainland mines rarely employed Asians.)
Source: British Columbia, Department of Mines, *Annual Reports*, 1914-41 (Victoria: King's Printer, various).

32 James Murdock to King, 12 December 1922, and King to H. Thornton, 13 December 1922, KP, #66621-2 and #69549. In 1920 a representative of the Vancouver teamsters complained that the federal government bought coal from dealers who employed Chinese labour (*Vancouver World*, 18 June 1920). In August 1922, when an explosion killed nine miners (four Japanese, two Chinese, and three others), the *Vancouver Sun* reported that "in the work of relief, race prejudice was forgotten. It was a work of mercy and humanity" (31 August 1922). *Cumberland Islander*, 17 and 24 February 1923; *Victoria Times*, 2 May 1923; *Vancouver Sun*, 26 May 1923; *Victoria Colonist*, 2 May 1923; *Nanaimo Free Press*, 11, 12, 18, and 19 June 1924.

33 Phillips Harrison to A.M. Manson, 9 March 1925, and Memo for the Attorney-General, 20 January 1927, AGR, 1918-17-2060; *Victoria Times*, 8 June 1925 and 5 and 25 February 1927; *Victoria Colonist*, 22 October 1925 and 11 February 1927; *Vancouver Province*, 27 October 1925; *Vancouver Star*, 26 November 1926; Chow Kwo-Hsuien to Oliver, 1 March 1927, POC; *Cumberland Islander*, 26 November 1926; British Columbia Legislative Assembly, Bill No. 13, 1926-27; Oliver to Lieutenant-Governor, 27 February 1927, quoted in G.R. Shibley to Deputy Minister of Justice, 29 March 1927, DJust, v. 311, file 457-27.

34 *Vancouver World*, 10 September 1919 and 6 October 1922; *Prince Rupert Evening Empire*, 11 November 1921; *Vancouver Province*, 15 May, 20 and 21 September, and 22 November 1922; *Vernon News*, 14 June 1923; *Victoria Times*, 27 and 28 October 1921 and 17 May 1922; *Nanaimo Free Press*, 15 May 1922; "Some Plain Facts About the Oliver Government," British Columbia Liberal Party, 1924.

35 See Chapter 2.

36 Ontario and Saskatchewan had laws against Chinese businesses employing white women. See Constance Backhouse, *Colour Coded: A Legal History of Racism in Canada, 1900-1950* (Toronto: University of Toronto Press, 1999), ch. 5. In 1919, Manitoba passed a bill designed to put Chinese restaurants out of business in order "to protect hotel men" and to close "all-night resorts, where boys learned evil habits" (*Vancouver Province*, 13 February, 1919);

Vancouver Province, 30 April and 21 December 1919 and 5 August 1921; *Vancouver World,* 4 February and 6 May 1921; *Vancouver Star,* 6 October 1926; *Penticton Herald,* 8 January 1920; *Nanaimo Herald,* 12 and 14 September 1922; *Cowichan Leader,* 26 October 1922; Creese, "Exclusion or Solidarity," 33. The *Vancouver World* suggested that women form an organization to eliminate Chinese domestic servants but found no support (31 July 1923). On Asians limiting opportunities for white female domestic servants, see M.V. Burnham to J. Obed Smith, 6 March 1924, DImm, MfC7368.

37 *Nanaimo Free Press,* 9 December 1927; *Victoria Colonist,* 10 December 1927; British Columbia, Department of Labour, *Annual Report,* 1927 (Victoria: King's Printer, 1928), L39-40; *Vancouver Star,* 24 January 1928; *Victoria Times,* 13 December 1927; *Vancouver Sun,* 14 December 1927; *Vancouver Province,* 16 December 1927.

38 E.S. Johnson to Deputy Attorney-General, 20 November 1922, AGR, 1918-17-2060. In 1939 the Department of National Defence advised officers escorting men to camps to try to avoid patronizing Chinese restaurants (D.M. to A.G., 5 July 1939, DHist, 322.009D361); *Vancouver Sun,* 9 March 1928. Banno's letter set off a debate on the Canadian identity of the Nisei. Many writers agreed with him that they were good Canadians; others, including Hugh Thornley, a well-known anti-Asian agitator, disagreed.

39 Kathryn McPherson, *Bedside Matters: The Transformation of Canadian Nursing, 1900-1990* (Toronto: Oxford University Press, 1996), 298n16; *Vancouver Province,* 29 October 1920; *Vancouver Sun,* 26 November 1920. After a Chinese woman complained, the hospital moved Chinese patients from the basement to the fifth floor, where they could receive equal treatment alongside whites (*Vancouver Chinese Times,* 26 February 1921). Mrs. E.J. Carson in *Western Woman's Weekly* suggested that Orientals should provide "a hospital for their own people ... And with the removal of drug patients to a hospital where they could get all the care they need as well as the insane and inebriates; this would, to some extent at least, relieve the present crowded conditions" (8 January 1921). The provincial normal schools admitted Asians, but school boards did not hire them (see Chapter 2).

40 *Vancouver Chinese Times,* 19 January 1918; *Victoria Times,* 25 June 1921. For details see Joan Brockman, "Exclusionary Tactics: The History of Women and Visible Minorities in the Legal Profession in British Columbia," in *Essays in the History of Canadian Law: British Columbia and the Yukon,* ed. Hamar Foster and John McLaren (Toronto: Osgoode Society, 1995), 519-25. In 1932 it was reported that Inglis Hosang of Lillooet had been admitted as a student at the Inner Temple, London. If he qualified as an English barrister, it was suggested that he could practise in British Columbia (*New Westminster British Columbian,* 23 March 1932).

41 The Chinese traditionally worked on shore in canning and processing plants, and their numbers were declining. To provide more employment for whites, one Vancouver processor hired white girls to replace about fifty Chinese labourers doing such light work as labelling cans (*Prince Rupert Daily News,* 21 January 1925). For details of the "Chinese Contract," which was still in use in the 1950s, see *The Development of the Pacific Salmon-Canning Industry: A Grown Man's Game,* ed. Dianne Newell (Montreal and Kingston: McGill-Queen's University Press, 1989), 16-17, 256; Alicja Muszynski, "Shoreworkers and UFAWU Organization: Struggles between Fishers and Plant Workers within the Union," in *Uncommon Property: The Fishing and Fish-Processing Industries in British Columbia,* ed. Patricia Marchak et al. (Toronto: Methuen, 1987), 272-73.

42 *Vancouver Sun,* 7 February 1919; *Port Alberni News,* 19 February and 5 March 1919; Daphne Marlatt, *Steveston Recollected* (Victoria: Provincial Archives of British Columbia, 1975), 53-54; F.H. Cunningham, Fisheries Inquiry, Proceedings, February 1919, DFish, v. 766, 1176.

43 W.G. McQuarrie, in HCD, 10 April 1922, 855; Canada, Department of Naval Services, Fisheries Branch, *Annual Report,* 1919 (Ottawa: King's Printer, 1920), 50; C.H. Young, and H.R.Y. Reid, *The Japanese Canadians* (Toronto: University of Toronto Press, 1938), 43; *Vancouver*

Province, 3 April 1919; HCD, 13 March 1919, 427; *Nanaimo Free Press,* 25 January 1919; *Port Alberni News,* 9 April 1919. The Fraser River Fishermen's Protective Association shared these views. The situation between white and Japanese fishermen was so strained around Ucluelet in 1921 that most whites "carried guns aboard their boats" (Testimony of John Johnson, Evidence Taken in British Columbia, British Columbia Fisheries Commission, 1922, DFish, v. 1234); *Victoria Times,* 24 March and 21 July 1919; *Nanaimo Free Press,* 8 March 1919; *New Westminster British Columbian,* 1 December 1919; *Port Alberni News,* 15 October 1919; Barclay Sound Fisheries Commission, Hearings at Duncan, October 1919, DFish, v. 767.

44 Department of Marine and Fisheries, Fisheries Branch, *Annual Report,* 1920 (Ottawa: King's Printer, 1921), 9, 47-48. A report that the department would not discriminate between white and Asian British subjects aroused much consternation. The BC Canners Association advised the minister of marine and fisheries that such a policy would mean the slow passing of the whole fishing and canning industry into the hands of the Japanese and the extermination of the salmon in the north, as had happened in the Fraser River (*Victoria Colonist,* 30 November 1919); *Port Alberni News,* 3 December 1919; C.C. Ballantyne to Cabinet, 18 December 1919, DJust, v. 1942, file 1919-3092; *Vancouver Sun,* 2, 11, and 26 January, 16 and 23 February, and 23 August 1920; *Vancouver World,* 19 February 1920.

45 *Vancouver Province,* 14 January, 29 March, and 8 April 1920. The Great War Veterans' Association urged that Japanese licence holders be fingerprinted, presumably to restrict the trade in licences (C.C. Ballantyne to W.G. McQuarrie, 28 May 1920, DFish, v. 756); *New Westminster British Columbian,* 19 January 1921; *Port Alberni News,* 19 and 26 May and 16 June 1920; *Victoria Colonist,* 23 May 1920 and 18 June 1921. McQuarrie noted that the Department of Marine and Fisheries wanted to eliminate Japanese labourers from the fisheries but needed time.

46 *Vancouver World,* 10 October 1921; *Port Alberni News,* 9 November 1921; *Victoria Times,* 1 November 1921; W.A. Found to H.H. Stevens, 15 June 1920, DFish, v. 756. In "The Rising Tide of Asiatics in B.C.," J.S. Cowper claimed that Ottawa's policy of limiting Japanese licences was "locking the stable door" after the horse was out (*Vancouver World,* 20 August 1921); *Comox Argus,* 24 November 1921; *Victoria Colonist,* 29 November 1921.

47 *Port Alberni News,* 9 November 1921 and 26 April 1922; *Comox Argus,* 17 November 1921; *Prince Rupert Daily News,* 25 October 1921; *Prince Rupert Evening Empire,* 14 November 1921; Found to McQuarrie, 29 March 1922, DFish, v. 1813. Geoff Meggs, *Salmon: The Decline of the British Columbia Fishery* (Vancouver: Douglas and McIntyre, 1991), ch. 12, ascribes largely to Found, assistant deputy minister of fisheries in Ottawa, the policy of eliminating the Japanese. Found had no sympathy for the Japanese but was following a policy that appealed to his political masters (Canada, Department of Marine and Fisheries, *Annual Report,* 1922 [Ottawa: King's Printer, 1923], 49). (Japanese fishermen had held about 23 percent of the licences issued.) A.W. Neill to Ernest Lapointe, 8 July 1922, DFish, v. 1233; William Duff to Jacques Bureau, 24 August 1922, DFish, v. 1232; *Port Alberni News,* 14 and 28 June 1922; *Victoria Colonist,* 22 August 1922.

3 HCD, 10 April 1922, 859. The Nova Scotians were the chairman, William Duff, and L.H. Martell. The British Columbia members were C.H. Dickie (Conservative, Nanaimo), McQuarrie (Conservative, New Westminster), Neill (Independent [Liberal], Comox-Alberni), and A.W. Stork (Liberal, Skeena).

● The complaint persisted. In 1929 the Niska Fishermen's Union charged that intensive fishing by the Japanese was depleting the Nass River fish and that canneries gave the Japanese preference on licences, nets, and employment on tender boats over "the natives [who] were here before the Japanese or even the white man" (*Vancouver Sun,* 26 August 1929).

Evidence Taken in British Columbia, British Columbia Fisheries Commission, 1922, DFish, vols. 1233-34.

51 To prevent "wholesale fraud," the commission recommended revising naturalization papers issued to Orientals to include a photograph and fingerprints (Duff et al. to Lapointe, 15 September 1922, DJust, v. 284); W.W.B. MacInnes to King, 11 December 1922. (MacInnes may have been the "éminence grise" of the Asiatic Exclusion League in 1907; see Roy, *A White Man's Province*, 201.) Thos. L. Takahashi to Lapointe, 22 November 1922; No. 2 District Fishermen's Association, Evidence, [c. January 1923]; Robert Laurier to A. Johnston, 5 December 1922; J.J. Cowie to Acting Minister, 28 September 1922; Leon Pettersen to Minister of Marine and Fisheries, 27 November 1922; Neill sought a temporary local relaxation for his constituency (Neill to Motherwell, 13 November 1922; *Port Alberni News*, 17 January 1923); H. Bell-Irving to Lapointe, 27 November 1922, D. McPherson to Lapointe, 30 November 1922, and Gosse-Millerd Ltd. to Alex Johnson, 8 January 1923. All correspondence cited above is in DFish, v. 1233. Wm. A. Found to Acting Minister of Marine and Fisheries, 7 October 1922, DJust, v. 284, file 1924-85.

52 J. Bureau to Neill, 23 December 1922, J.J. Cowie to Acting Minister, 28 September 1922, Found to Acting Minister, 7 October 1922, Memo re British Columbia Commission's Interim Report, 26 February 1923, and Duff to Johnston, 5 March 1923, DFish, v. 1233; L.H. Martell, in HCD, 27 March 1923, 1555; Canada, Royal Commission on British Columbia Fisheries, *Report* (Ottawa: King's Printer, 1923), 11; Fishing License Application, 20 April 1926, DFish, v. 1813; *Victoria Colonist*, 10 March 1923.

53 *Vancouver World*, 4 April and 14 November 1923; *Port Alberni News*, 4 April 1923; *B.C. Federationist*, 6 April 1923; *Vancouver Sun*, 28 March 1923; HCD, 27 March 1923, 1540-58; L.J. Ladner to C.F. Batson, 3 April 1923, and Ladner to Editor, *Vancouver Daily World*, 16 April 1923, LJLP, v. 7; *Vancouver Province*, 14 November 1923; Canada, Department of Marine and Fisheries, *Annual Report of the Fisheries Branch*, 1923-24 (Ottawa: King's Printer, 1925), 57, and 1925-26 (Ottawa: King's Printer, 1926), 53. The numbers varied somewhat according to the branch of the fishery and region. In salmon trolling, the number of Asian licences fell by 25 percent while the number held by whites and by Native Indians rose. A few districts had startling changes. On the east coast of Vancouver Island, the number of salmon trolling licences issued to whites and Native Indians increased by 69.7 percent and 343.4 percent respectively. On the west coast, where conditions were more difficult, the number of all licences declined.

54 When the Japanese Fishermen's Association threatened to strike in northern waters over fish prices, canners threatened to replace them with white men (*Vancouver Star*, 12 June 1924); *Vancouver Star*, 4 March 1925; *Vancouver Sun*, 18 June 1924 and 26 August 1926; *New Westminster British Columbian*, 30 September 1925; *Victoria Times*, 8 November 1923, 30 May 1924, 25 April 1925, and 29 January and 25 May 1926; R. Rowe Holland to Stevens, 2 March 1925, JMRC, v. 27; *Nanaimo Free Press*, 29 April 1926; *Comox Argus*, 24 September 1925; *Port Alberni News*, 25 August 1926; *Vancouver Province*, 25 October 1925 and 31 August 1925. McRae won in 1926. In the 1924 provincial election, Premier Oliver had attacked him for employing large numbers of Asians at his Fraser River and Columbia Valley sawmills.

55 Canada, Department of Marine and Fisheries, *Annual Report of Fisheries Branch*, 1928-29 (Ottawa: King's Printer, 1929), 119; Found, Memorandum, 14 April 1927, W.N. Tilley to Minister of Marine and Fisheries, 16 April 1927, and W.E. Williams to J.A. Motherwell, 3 May 1927, DFish, v. 1045; *Vancouver Province*, 14 July 1927.

56 *Victoria Times*, 14 November 1927; *Nanaimo Free Press*, 14 November and 3 December 1927; *Vancouver Sun*, 28 May 1928; *Vancouver Province*, 13 and 14 November 1927 and 30 May 1928; Neill to King, 28 May 1928, KP, #132459-50; Found to Motherwell, 1 June 1928, Motherwell to Found, 4 June 1929, and J. Chisholm to Deputy Minister of Marine and Fisheries, 3 August 1929, DFish, v. 1045. Documents relating to the Supreme Court case are in SCC, v. 563, file 5424. *Vancouver Sun*, 13 January 1930; Marlatt, *Steveston Recollected*, 54-55.

57 *Victoria Colonist,* 21 August 1928; *Vancouver Sun,* 16 January 1930; R. Rowe Holland to Stevens, 2 March 1925, JMRC, v. 27.

58 See Roy *A White Man's Province,* 248-50; *Penticton Herald,* 18 June 1924; *Vancouver Province,* 28 February 1921, 19 July 1924, and 27 January 1928; Stevens, in HCD, 26 April 1921, 2596; *Cowichan Leader,* 20 January 1921; *Farm and Home,* 15 July 1920. See also *Fraser Valley Record,* 12 August 1920; *Vernon News,* 11 December 1919 and 12 February 1920; F.H. Barber to Jones, 10 November 1922, JWJP.
    On California's campaign, see Roger Daniels, *Asian Americans: Chinese and Japanese in the United States since 1850* (Seattle: University of Washington Press, 1988), 145. Oregon passed a similar law in 1923, but it seems to have gone unnoticed in British Columbia.

59 *Prince Rupert Daily News,* 21 January 1921; *Kamloops Standard-Sentinel,* 4 April 1922; *Vancouver World,* 26 January 1922; *Kamloops Telegram,* 21 July 1921; David Demerrit, "Visions of Agriculture in British Columbia," *BC Studies,* 108 (Winter 1995-96): 29-59; *Comox Argus,* 25 December 1919; *Vancouver Sun,* 21 September 1921.

60 *Okanagan Commoner,* 21 July 1921; *Vancouver Star,* 4 February 1928; *Ashcroft Journal,* 1 November and 13 December 1919, 13 and 20 January, 10 February, and 22 September 1923, and 11 February 1928; *Vancouver Province,* 9 December 1919. The Chinese dominated the tomato growing industry in Ashcroft; in 1926 it was claimed that there were no white growers in the area (*Kelowna Courier,* 4 February 1926). Unfortunately the *Armstrong Advertiser* for this period is missing.

61 *Comox Argus,* 18 and 25 December 1919; *Kelowna Courier,* 20 February 1919; *Penticton Herald,* 30 July 1921; *B.C. United Farmer,* 1 February 1921; *Vancouver Province,* 27 February 1929; *Agricultural Journal,* September 1924, 152; *Victoria Times,* 4 September 1928.

62 *Vancouver Province,* 22 January 1919; *Nanaimo Free Press,* 26 February 1919; G.W. Leckie-Ewing to Oliver, 23 December 1918, and R.C. Wilkinson to Oliver, 4 April 1919, POC; W.A. Robertson to Vancouver City Council, 18 January 1919, VCCCl, v. 75.

63 *Penticton Herald,* 23 December 1919 and 1, 8, 15, and 22 January 1920. In his inaugural address, the victor, J.A. Chambers, proposed to stop Chinese settlement by using health regulations (*Summerland Review,* quoted in *Penticton Herald,* 1 January 1920).

64 The Chinese owned twelve acres and leased another ninety-seven. Statistics prepared by the BC Department of Agriculture, 28 May 1920. British Columbia Fruit Growers' Association, *Annual Report for the Year Ended December 31, 1918,* 12, 20, with D. Warnock to Oliver, 7 June 1921, POC; Margaret A. Ormsby, *Coldstream: Nulli Secundus* (Vernon: Corporation of the District of Coldstream, 1990), 54-55; *Vernon News,* 11 and 18 December 1919 and 15 January 1920; *Kelowna Courier,* 20 March and 24 December 1919; *Vancouver Province,* 5 February 1920; *Vancouver World,* 22 February 1919 and 6 February 1920; Japanese Consulate, Verbal Note, 18 March 1920, POC; Reid to Cory, 10 February 1920, DImm, MfC10652. Before the First World War the Coldstream Ranch employed some Japanese contract labourers. The *Toronto Globe* report is cited in John Oliver to Attorney-General, 13 December 1919, AGP, 1918-17-2060.

65 *Vancouver Province,* 6 February 1920; M. Burrell to George Perley, 12 December 1919, DEAR, v. 305; Oliver to Farris, 13 December 1919, AGR, 1918-17-2060; Wade to Lord Cowdray, 13 January 1920, and W.A. Middleton to Oliver, 24 December 1919, POC; *Vernon News,* 22 January 1920; Copy of Resolution Passed 15 January 1920, JWJP.

66 *Victoria Times,* 24 February 1920; *Vancouver Province,* 5, 6, and 24 February and 20 May 1920; *Victoria Colonist,* 7 February and 28 May 1920; *Vancouver Province,* 20 May 1920; *Vancouver World,* 20 May 1920; *B.C. United Farmer,* 1 June 1920; J.A. MacKelvie to Burrell, 16 February 1920, DJust, v. 1970, file 1115.

67 *Penticton Herald,* 3 June 1920; *Kelowna Courier,* 22 January 1920; C.G.M. McDougald, secretary treasurer, Peachland Great War Veterans' Association, to Jones, 8 January 1920, JWJP.

68 *Victoria Times,* 10 February 1920; *Victoria Colonist,* 10 February 1920; *Vancouver Province,* 10 February and 26 March 1920. A decade later, as a cabinet minister, Jones supported these ideas but claimed that the question was too big to be settled (*Vancouver Province,* 2 November 1929). In the spring of 1919, when Maple Ridge residents complained of Japanese encroachments, Oliver ascertained from Ottawa that land ownership was a provincial responsibility. At the time of the Coldstream Ranch rumour, Oliver had sought an opinion on the effects of any provincial legislation concerning land holding on federal policy and the treaty (Oliver to Burrell, 17 December 1919, POC). Burrell to C.J. Doherty, 25 January 1920, Burrell to N.W. Rowell, 4 March 1920, Burrell to C.G. McDougald, Secretary Treasurer, Peachland Great War Veterans' Association, 27 January 1920, and Burrell to B. Belsen, Secretary Treasurer, Kelowna Great War Veterans' Association, 10 February 1920, DJust, v. 1970, file 1115. The minister of justice did not provide a clear answer since he observed that the Anglo-Japanese Treaty probably protected Japanese nationals, but if the province legislated against a certain race or class, whether they were aliens or British subjects, such a law might be within its competence (C.J. Doherty to Burrell, 12 February 1920, DJust, v. 1970, file 1115).

69 Oliver to W.A. Middleton, 26 December 1919, and D. Warnock to Oliver, 7 June 1921, POC; BCV&P, 31 March 1920 and 1 April 1921; *Victoria Colonist,* 12 February 1921; *New Westminster British Columbian,* 23 February 1921; *Victoria Times,* 28 February and 15 June 1921; *Vancouver Province,* 28 February 1921; *B.C. United Farmer,* 1 March 1921; *Agricultural Journal,* April 1921, 54, and June 1921, 90; British Columbia, *Report on Oriental Activities,* 23.

70 *Victoria Times,* 15 June 1921; *Vancouver Sun,* 3 May 1921; *Vancouver World,* 21 April and 15 June 1921; *B.C. United Farmer,* July 1921; Stevens to Arthur Meighen, 8 August 1921, and Meighen to Stevens, 15 August 1921, AMP, #17313-20; C.H. Armstrong to Meighen, 26 September 1921, AMP, #17977; Attorney-General to C.E. Whitney-Griffiths, 17 January 1921, and Oliver to Meighen, 13 June 1921, AGR, 1918-17-2060; Meighen to Oliver, 22 June 1921, POC; Private Secretary to City Clerk, Nanaimo, and Others, AMP, #17292-303.

71 The Oriental Exclusion Committee of the Retail Merchants Association also urged barring Asians from owning, leasing, or renting property except for residential purposes (Memo, with Stevens, to J. Crowder, 19 September 1922, HHSPV, v. 1). The resolution also reflected uncertainty over timber licences after the disallowance of the Oriental Orders in Council Validity Act (BCV&P, 8 and 16 November 1922); *B.C. Federationist,* 8 December 1922; *Vancouver World,* 29 November and 6 December 1922; *Victoria Times,* 29 September and 22 and 29 November 1922 and 23 November 1923; *Victoria Colonist,* 22 November 1922; *Kelowna Courier,* 25 January 1923; British Columbia Fruit Growers' Association, *Annual Report,* 1923 (Victoria: King's Printer, 1923), 58; E.A. Riddell to A.M. Manson, 18 November 1922, AGR, 1918-17-2060; W.E. Payne to W.L.M. King, 25 January 1923, DImm, MfC10410. The letter's wording closely follows that of a report presented by the Board of Trade Council's Special Oriental Immigration Committee to the board in 1921 (Vancouver Board of Trade Council, Minutes, 11 August 1921, CVA) and of a resolution passed by the Associated Boards of Trade of British Columbia (*Victoria Colonist,* 30 March 1922). The editor of the *Vancouver World* neatly summarized the notion: "The patience, industry and success of the Asiatic farmers on the land is fully conceded ... The difficulty harks back to the unassimilability of the Asiatic as a neighbor and a citizen rather than to his interference as a grower. Social pressure is his strongest force in driving out the white families who pioneered the district he invades. His very industry and success only make his grip of the land more secure" (26 January 1922).

72 Clerk of the Privy Council to the Lieutenant-Governor, 20 January 1923, and Memo from A.M. Manson, 19 October 1922, AGR, 1918-17-2060; Memo by W.D. Carner, 11 July 1923, in "Handbook, 1924," 160, copy in TDPP; BCLJ, 17 December 1924; *Vernon News,* 26 February 1925; *New Westminster British Columbian,* 24 January 1925; *Vancouver Province,* 11 December 1925; BCV&P, 10 December 1925.

73 R.C. Neish to Stevens, 13 February 1926, DJust, v. 1970, file 1115; C.E. Whitney-Griffiths to J.H. King, 15 February 1926, Whitney-Griffiths to O.D. Skelton, 9 April 1926, and Whitney-Griffiths to J.H. King, 15 February 1926, DEAR, MfT1751; *Victoria Times*, 5 March 1926.

74 C.M. Watson and C.C.J. Hart to Stevens, 31 March 1926, KP, #118453ff; Grote Stirling to King, 15 April 1926, KP, #118585-7; King to Stirling, 31 May 1926, KP, #118588-9; King to Watson, 31 May 1926, KP, #118457-8. Japan's Alien Land Law of 1925 took effect 10 November 1926. The law replaced a ban on foreign ownership and permitted aliens or foreign corporations to own land, but it did not guarantee the right to those whose home countries did not allow their Japanese residents to hold land. The Japanese law appears to have been a response to American alien land laws (Skelton to Manson, 17 February 1928, A.V. Pineo, Legislative Counsel, Memo re Bill No. 65, Aliens Amendment, n.d., and Manson to A.F. Barss, 11 May 1927, AGR, 1918-17-2060); *Victoria Colonist*, 16 February 1927; *Vancouver Province*, 4 July 1925 and 25 February and 15 March 1927; Oliver to Lieutenant-Governor Bruce, 28 February 1927, DJust, v. 311, file 457-27; *Nanaimo Free Press*, 20 March 1928.

75 *Victoria Colonist*, 7 February and 11 December 1929; G.F. Young, Secretary, Langley Farmers' Institute, to Tolmie, 3 July 1929, POC; *Vancouver Province*, 6 and 14 November 1929; *Vancouver Star*, 20 February 1930; *Prince Rupert Daily News*, 27 January 1930; R.H. Pooley to C.E. Hope, 16 April 1930, AGR, 1918-17-2060; Neill to Lapointe, 8 April 1930, and Lapointe to Neill, 27 May 1930, DJust, v. 2002, file 1930-834.

76 *Vancouver Sun*, 20 August 1920; *Victoria Colonist*, 24 October 1920; *Agricultural Journal*, February 1921, 356, and July 1921, 114; *Victoria Times*, 17 May 1921; *Comox Argus*, 5 May 1921; Provincial Secretary to Mrs. James Lindey, Secretary, Women's Institute, Rock Creek, 13 April 1922, GR1668, v. 1; *Vancouver World*, 29 March 1923; A.V. Pineo to Manson, 15 March 1927, AGR, 1918-17-2060; Port Alberni would not sell city-owned land to Orientals (*Port Alberni News*, 14 February 1923); South Vancouver also refused to sell a patch of "black muck" unsuitable for residential purposes to Chinese residents who wanted to expand their farm (*Vancouver Province*, 20 June 1924).

77 *Comox Argus*, 28 October 1920; *Vancouver Sun*, 27 July 1921; *Vancouver World*, 27 July 1921; *Vancouver Province*, 1 October and 12 November 1927; *Victoria Colonist*, 20 October 1927; *Nanaimo Free Press*, 15 September 1927; *Victoria Times*, 1 February 1929; *Penticton Herald*, 22 January 1925; British Columbia Fruit Growers' Association, *Annual Report*, 1923, 28, and 1924 (Victoria: King's Printer, 1924), 27; W.G. Donley, "The Oriental Agriculturalist in British Columbia," University of British Columbia, BA essay, 1928, 13.

78 Roy, *A White Man's Province*, 248-50; *Vancouver Sun*, 4 September 1921 and 17 October 1929; *Agricultural Journal*, February 1921, 356, and July 1921, 114; Jas. Greig, Clerk, Municipal Council, Duncan, to Oliver, 20 July 1921, POC; *Prince Rupert Daily News*, 26 July 1921; *Vancouver World*, 28 July 1921; *New Westminster British Columbian*, 1 August 1921; *Cowichan Leader*, 28 July 1921 and 9 February 1922. The BC Press Association unanimously called for the publicizing of all details of land transfers to Asians (*Vernon News*, 31 August 1922).

79 C.E. Whitney-Griffiths to Oliver, 27 June 1921, Oliver to Ministers of Agriculture and Finance, 18 February 1924, John Hart to Oliver, 10 March 1924, A.F. Barss to Oliver, 2 February 1923, and M.C. Ironside to Oliver, 17 July 1927, POC; *Vancouver Province*, 28 April 1926, 7 December 1927, and 12 December 1928; BCV&P, 14 December 1923; British Columbia, *Report on Oriental Activities*, passim; British Columbia Fruit Growers' Association, *Annual Report*, 1923, 69, and 1925 (Victoria: King's Printer, 1925), 11; *Victoria Colonist*, 30 November 1927; BCLJ, 2 February 1928, 20-22, and 11 March 1930, 131; *Vancouver Sun*, 1 February 1929; *Vancouver Star*, 3 February 1928; J.B. Ward to Manson, 11 February 1927, AGR, 1918-17-2060. In 1924, University of Chicago sociologist Robert E. Park made preliminary inquiries in Vancouver for a planned "scientific and comprehensive" study of the Oriental problem on the Pacific Coast. Dr. Theodore Boggs of the University of British Columbia headed the

Survey's regional committee (*Vancouver Province*, 3 March 1924). It did some preliminary work but Japanese exclusionary legislation in the United States made the survey a "dead issue" (Winifred Raushenbush, *Robert E. Park: Biography of a Sociologist* [Durham, NC: Duke University Press, 1979], 116). Lisa Rose Mar kindly gave me a private copy of a paper, "All Politics Is Local: Chinese Canadian Elites and the Construction of Canadian Citizenship," that draws extensively on interviews that Raushenbush conducted with some of the Chinese residents of Vancouver. The paper, presented at the 2003 conference of the Canadian Historical Association, will be part of a major monograph that is now in progress. In 1930 the Standing Committee on Agriculture recommended a survey similar to that of 1925 but nothing came of it (BCV&P, 11 March 1930).

80 *Revelstoke Review*, 2 February 1927; *Vancouver Star*, 4 February 1927; *Farm and Home*, 3 January 1929; *Vancouver Sun*, 29 January 1927; *Vancouver Province*, 15 March 1927.

81 *Vancouver Province*, 20 January 1921, 21 April 1922, 19 July 1924, and 2 March 1925; *Vancouver Star*, 28 September 1926; *B.C. United Farmer*, 15 October 1920, 3, and 1 February 1911, 3; *Prince Rupert News*, 27 October 1925; *Victoria Colonist*, 7 February 1929; British Columbia Fruit Growers' Association, *Annual Report*, 1920 (Victoria: King's Printer, 1921), 19; Robert Wood to Members of the Legislative Assembly, 8 February 1928, AGR, 1918-17-2060. *Vancouver World*, 13 August 1921; *Vernon News*, 18 January 1923; *Revelstoke Review*, 25 February 1925. Eggs imported from China had to be labelled. The Oriental Exclusion Association also endorsed the idea (Resolution of 1 March 1926, DEAR, MfT1751). Tom MacInnes outlined his trade licence plan in *Oriental Occupation of British Columbia* (Vancouver: Sun Publishing, 1927).

82 *Okanagan Commoner*, 22 September 1921; *Farm and Home*, 8 February 1923, 24.

83 *Kelowna Courier*, 3 March 1921, 28 September 1922, and 19 February 1925; *Vernon News*, 26 February 1925; *Farm and Home*, 25 January 1923; Thomas Bulman, in *Proceedings of the Select Special Committee of the House of Commons to Inquire into Agricultural Conditions* (Ottawa: King's Printer, 1924), 59; Canada, House of Commons, *Journals*, 60, Part 1, 1923. A crop share arrangement is described by Victor Cororso in *The Cororso Story* (Okanagan Falls: Rima Books, 1983), 164-66.

84 Japanese Canadian and white rhubarb growers formed a co-operative in 1925 (Anne Doré, "Transnational Communities: Japanese Canadians of the Fraser Valley, 1904-1942," *BC Studies*, 134 [Summer 2002]: 56).

85 T. Fukuma to Tolmie, 25 January 1929, and L.D. Mallory to J. Kumagaya, 22 January 1929, POC; *Vancouver Province*, 24 March and 16 August 1924 and 12 November 1927; R. Rowe Holland to Stevens, 2 March 1925, JMRC, v. 27; British Columbia, *Report on Oriental Activities*, 12; R.G.L. Clarke, Dominion inspector of fruit, reported that the Japanese had increased berry shipments from 1,000 to 9,000 tons in two years (*Victoria Colonist*, 25 January 1930); V. Harbord Harbord, "The Oriental Question in the Fraser Valley," *Vancouver Province*, 2 May 1926; *Farm and Home*, 7 December 1922, 1 March 1923, 26 January 1928, and 16 May 1929; Jean Burton, "Berry Growers Co-operative Union of British Columbia," University of Alberta, MA thesis, 1928, 115; *Fraser Valley Record*, 18 June 1925; British Columbia, Department of Agriculture, *Annual Report*, 1927 (Victoria: King's Printer, 1928), Q43. *Victoria Colonist*, 18 January 1928; *Victoria Times*, 23 March and 15 April 1929.

86 In 1923 white growers controlled 570,930 square feet of greenhouse space; two years later they controlled only 567,357 square feet, while the equivalents for Chinese growers had risen from 382,382 to 654,664. British Columbia, *Report on Oriental Activities*, 22; Timothy Chan, "The Social and Regulatory Relations of Metropolitan Victoria's Commercial Greenhouse Industry: 1900 to 1996," University of Victoria, MA thesis, 1997, 94.

87 *Victoria Times*, 5 and 14 March 1928 and 13 November 1929; *Victoria Colonist*, 31 March 1928; *Vancouver Province*, 3 April 1928.

88 *Victoria Colonist*, 28 May 1921 and 18 March 1923; *Victoria Times*, 15 November 1923 and 4 February 1928; *Vancouver Province*, 3 April 1928.

89 *Vancouver Province,* 20 October and 7 December 1927 and 25 January and 3 and 9 February 1928; *Vancouver Star,* 10 February 1928; *Ashcroft Journal,* 18 February 1928.

90 *Vancouver Sun,* 23 January 1928. The Crown did not proceed with charges for selling below the minimum price. *Victoria Times,* 17 November 1927 and 4 February 1928; *Kamloops Sentinel,* 9 December 1930; *Vancouver Province,* 16 and 17 November 1927 and 16 February 1928. The British Columbia Dry Belt Farmers' Exchange honoured the Marketing Act even though it said that its members opposed the act in principle and even though Chinese growers shipped potatoes to Vancouver and sold them at less than the control price (*Vancouver Province,* 14 February 1928). An example of nonco-operation occurred in Armstrong, where Chinese growers reportedly threatened to let celery rot rather than sell it under a pooling arrangement (*Vernon News,* 31 July 1930).

91 *Vancouver Sun,* 28 June, 5, 16, 18, and 26 July, and 9 August 1928 and 30 October 1929; *Victoria Times,* 15 September 1928; *Vancouver Province,* 22 August 1928 and 8 January 1929; *Victoria Colonist,* 3 August 1928; *Vancouver Star,* 15 January 1929.

92 The BC Certified Seed Potato Growers' Association organized the BC White Potato Growers' Protective Association in the fall of 1928. They complained of Oriental competition and of inaction by the Committee of Direction. *Victoria Times,* 24 August and 30 November 1928; *Vancouver Sun,* 30 November 1928; *Farm and Home,* 22 November 1928, 2; *Vancouver Province,* 22 August 1928; R.A. Coleman to Attorney-General, 11 February 1929, AGR, P302-2-260. One report said that interior fruit growers were helping finance Chinese potato growers in their legal appeal against the act (*Vancouver Province,* 21 February 1929). Some white growers in Ladner wanted a law to prevent Orientals from owning or renting land.

93 W. McLelan to Attorney-General, 11 July 1929, and Attorney-General to McLelan, 10 July 1929, AGR, P302-2-185ff; *Victoria Times,* 1 and 15 February 1929; *Kelowna Courier,* 24 October 1929 and 7 August 1930. In 1928 the legislature amended the act so that Oriental shippers were required to keep legible account books in English, but the quickly drafted legislation was, as Manson later explained, "mainly a declaration of principle" (R.H. Pooley to Judge Ruggles, 25 October 1929, AGR, P302-2-50). The interior committee cancelled the mainland committee's powers, dismissed its chairman, A.W. McLelan, and asked him to turn over its property to them. He complained that the interior committee had left him personally responsible for mainland liabilities (McLelan to William Atkinson, 24 September 1930, AGR, P302-1-127). *Kamloops Sentinel,* 9 December 1930; *Vernon News,* 29 January 1931; *New Westminster British Columbian,* 24 February and 24 April 1930; Pooley to F.M. Black, 2 August 1930, and Pooley to C.F. Fillmore, 2 August 1930, AGR, P302-1-162; *Vancouver Province,* 28 February 1928 and 22 February 1931.

94 E.M. Trowern to R.L. Borden, 3 February 1914, DImm, MfC10410; *Victoria Times,* 1 March 1918, 4 April 1920, 26 June 1923; *Vancouver Sun,* 14 August 1918 and 26 February 1919; *Kamloops Standard-Sentinel,* 31 May 1918; *Victoria Colonist,* 17 April 1919; F. Elworthy to Tolmie, 7 May 1919, SFTP, v. 34; *Vancouver Province,* 14 January and 30 April 1919; *Vancouver Star,* 15 December 1925; British Columbia, *Report on Oriental Activities,* 24.

95 *Vancouver Province,* 8, 24, and 25 February 1919 and 19 April 1923; *Vancouver Sun,* 25 February 1919; Koliang Yih to Vancouver City Council, 28 February 1919, VCCCl; Vancouver City Council, Minutes, 8 March 1919, CVA; Tolmie, in HCD, 22 April 1918, 1002, and 17 June 1919, 3570; *Victoria Colonist,* 20 March 1919. No copies of the *Vancouver Highland Echo* seem to have survived. The reference is from the consul's letter to the mayor on behalf of Chinese merchants who were alarmed by the hostility (Koliang Yih to Mayor R.H. Gale, 23 January 1919, VCCCl, v. 74). An account of the 1919 agitation is in Kay Anderson, *Vancouver's Chinatown: Racial Discourse in Canada, 1875-1980* (Montreal and Kingston: McGill-Queen's University Press, 1991), 119-27.

96 *Victoria Times,* 14 March and 16 May 1919, 23 November 1921, and 4 January 1922; *Victoria Colonist,* 22 March and 3 May 1919.

97 The main correspondence is in AGR, 1918-17-2060; J.B. Williams to William McQueen, 1 May 1923, VCCCl, v. 95.

98 *British Columbia Retailer* 12 (September 1921): 438 and 17 (May 1925): 7; *Vancouver World,* 27 July 1921 and 17 January 1922. James Harkness, chairman of the grocers' section of the Vancouver branch of the Retail Merchants Association, wanted to regulate grocery licences for retired prairie farmers as well as for Orientals ("Licenses: Their Use and Abuse," *British Columbia Retailer* 13 [February 1922]: 592).

99 License Inspector, Victoria, to Attorney-General, 18 March 1925, AGR, 1918-17-2060; Statement re Licenses Issued to Orientals During Years 1920, 1922, 1924, 1926, and 1928, 28 June 1929, VCCCl, v. 139.

100 *Victoria Colonist,* 24 June 1919; *Victoria Times,* 30 March 1920; *British Columbia Retailer* 12 (August 1921): 400-1.

101 *Victoria Colonist,* 17 April and 16 May 1919 and 21 January 1927. A member of the New Westminster Great War Veterans' Association suggested a reverse boycott patronizing only Orientals in order to force merchants to take the "Oriental question" seriously. He found no support (*New Westminster British Columbian,* 3 December 1919); *Victoria Times,* 2 May 1922 and 26 June 1923; *Community Shoppers Guide,* February 1923, copy in DImm, MfC10410; *Vancouver World,* 23 January 1922; *Vancouver Star,* 19 July 1924; *Prince Rupert Daily News,* 26 December 1925; *Victoria Times,* 7 October 1922 and 3 February 1923; *Vancouver Sun,* 8 February 1927.

102 *Vancouver Province,* 12 December 1922, 4 May and 26 November 1926, and 14 October 1928; *B.C. Federationist,* 17 November 1922; *Vancouver Star,* 2 and 4 October 1928; *Victoria Colonist,* 15 August 1922 and 12 October 1928; *Victoria Times,* 29 January 1925; *Vernon News,* 29 April 1923.

103 *Vancouver Province,* 17 January 1919 and 30 October 1924; *Vancouver Chinese Times,* 2 June 1919; *Vancouver Sun,* 22 January 1920 and 20 October 1924; *Vancouver World,* 6 March 1920; *Victoria Colonist,* 24 June 1919, 21 July and 8 October 1925; *Farm and Home,* 15 April 1926; V. Harbord Harbord, "The Oriental Question in the Fraser Valley," *Vancouver Province,* 2 May 1926.

104 The complete draft is an appendix in MacInnes, *Oriental Occupation of British Columbia,* 164-66. Because the Municipal Act did not govern Vancouver, MacInnes drafted a special bill for it. Vancouver businessmen to MacLean, 10 February 1928, AGR, 1918-17-2060; *Vancouver Province,* 14 and 21 February and 11 July 1928; *Victoria Colonist,* 14 and 15 March 1928. Nanaimo City Council asked the province to empower smaller municipalities in order to control licences granted to Orientals (H. Hackwood to J.D. MacLean, 9 March 1928, Mackenzie to MacLean, 23 April 1928); MacInnes to MacLean, 21 April 1928, TDPP, v. 28.

105 Vancouver merchants complained in 1923 that Oriental retailers, by keeping their books in their own language, evaded sales taxes and thus gained a competitive advantage (Vancouver Board of Trade Council, Minutes, 15 July 1923, v. 4, CVA); MacInnes to Tolmie, 4 July 1928, and Memorandum re Delegation from Vancouver Concerning Oriental Question, 10 October 1928, POC; Report of Special Committee, 28 June 1929, and George E. McCrossan to W.H. Malkin, 16 November 1928, VCCCl, v. 139; *Vancouver Province,* 26 March, 27 May, and 13 September 1929; *Vancouver Sun,* 15 October 1929.

106 Manson to E.W. Neel, 24 December 1927, AGR, 1918-17-2060.

Chapter 5: "A Problem of Our Own Peoples"

1 Representatives from the Comox Farmers' Institute, Nanaimo City Council, and the City of Vernon came from outside the lower mainland (Minutes of Meeting Held in the Hotel Vancouver, 27 November 1929, copy in POC); *Victoria Times,* 16 October 1929; Charles E. Hope, "British Columbia's Racial Problem," *Maclean's,* 1 February 1930, 3-4, 62-63; Charles E. Hope and W.K. Earle, "The Oriental Threat," *Maclean's,* 1 May 1933, 12, 54-55.

2 *Vancouver Sun*, 25 and 28 November 1929; Conference, Minutes, 27 November 1929; Hope's executive committee in 1930 included the president of the Property Owners' Association in Vancouver, a member of the Retail Merchants Association, the secretary of the Fishermen's Protective Association, a member of the Farmers' Institute, and the secretary of the School Trustees Association. They appear to have represented themselves rather than their associations.
   S.F. Tolmie to Hope, 4 February 1930, POC; R.H. Pooley to C.E. Hope, 5 April 1930, AGR, 1918-17-206. A founder of the association, J.E. Armishaw of the United Farmers of Canada (B.C. section), asked the United Farmers of Alberta to endorse resolutions for an end to Oriental immigration and the denial of property rights to Asians but received only moral support (*Prince Rupert Daily News*, 24 January 1930).
3 For Hope's publicity work, see Patricia E. Roy, "'Educating the "East"': British Columbia and the Oriental Question in the Interwar Years," *BC Studies*, 18 (Summer 1973): 60-61. Hope's repeated ill-founded reports of illegal immigration alienated Department of Immigration officials (Hope to O.D. Skelton, 22 June 1934, DEAR, MfT1748; Hope to H. Marler, 23 November 1935, DEAR, v. 1756; Hope to T.A. Crerar, 28 February 1936, DImm, MfC10264). "Memorandum on Liberal Action on Federal Labour Matters. Proposed, 1930," KP, #C82763. Neill, who usually supported the Liberals, boasted of having tackled the Asian question, ended Chinese immigration, and restricted Japanese immigration and fishing licences (*Comox Argus*, 17 July 1930; *Port Alberni News*, 17 July 1930); "Liberalism and Labour: Nine Years of Forward Policies," [June 1930], KP, #C81783; King to Neill, 11 February 1930, KP, #152387; Neill to Skelton, 28 October 1936, DEAR, v. 1430; HCD, 11 September 1930, 12, and 19 March 1931, 143; Hope to W.A. Gordon, 3 September 1930, DImm, MfC10264; H. Langley to Hope, 6 January 1931, DImm, MfC10410; *Vancouver Province*, 13 August 1936. The Maple Leaf Association claimed to be Dominion-wide, but there is no evidence that it had many members.
4 *Vancouver Sun*, 17 June 1930; HCD, 26 June 1931, 3120, and 22 April 1932, 2278; *Vancouver Province*, 17 June 1930, 14 April, 7 July, and 25 September 1931, and 31 January 1934.
5 *Vancouver Province*, 24 and 28 November and 13 December 1930, 29 March and 7 June 1931, and 2 March 1932; *Vancouver Sun*, 26 April 1930 and 27 March 1931; *Victoria Times*, 31 March 1931; *Prince Rupert Daily News*, 12 February 1930; J.O. Cameron and N.C. Sawyers, Lumber Committee, Canadian Chamber of Commerce Oriental Tour, 1930 [Report, c. January 1931], and Hope to H.J. Barber, 15 January 1931, POC; Hope to Gordon, 17 December 1930, DImm, MfC10264; James Day and Wm. D. Noyes to King, 28 February 1930; Marler to Secretary of State for External Affairs, 11 October 1930, RBBP, #164215-9; Henry F. Angus, "Kyoto," *Canadian Forum* 10 (March 1930): 197.
6 Stevens to R.B. Bennett, 15 January 1931, RBBP, #241841; Stevens to Gordon, 1 March 1933, RBBP, #142880; Bennett to N.W. Rowell, 4 March 1935, RBBP, #241904; A.L. Jolliffe to Bennett, 29 August 1935, RBBP, #529114-5; Commissioner of Immigration to Gordon, 8 November 1931, DImm, MfC10661; Confidential Memo re Chinese Immigration, July 1931, DEAR, v. 1539; Keenleyside to Skelton, 20 February 1936, DEAR, MfT1728.
7 *New Westminster British Columbian*, 13 August 1930; *Vancouver Province*, 29 April 1930; *Vancouver Star*, 1 April 1930. Among the few complaints was the claim by Vancouver garment manufacturers that those Chinese and Japanese residents who worked at home were not covered by minimum wage laws and were bringing "our white girls a step nearer city relief" (*Vancouver Sun*, 19 May 1933; *New Westminster British Columbian*, 26 July 1934). The Victoria Chamber of Commerce urged citizens to employ white labour whenever possible (George I. Warren, Form Letter, 9 September 1930, copy in AGR 1925-37-L125). In the 1933 provincial election, references to Asian competition were isolated. W.M. Dennies, president of the 5,000-member National Labour Council of Vancouver, who was appointed minister of labour in Premier Tolmie's last-minute attempt to form a Union government, said that preference in employment should be given to whites until no whites were unemployed. He derided the

presence of over 6,000 Asians in provincial industries and another 2,200 in trans-Pacific shipping. Like Tolmie's other supporters, Dennies was defeated (Ian Parker, "Simon Fraser Tolmie: The Last Conservative Premier of British Columbia," *BC Studies*, 11 [Fall 1971]: 34n37); J. Castell Hopkins, ed., *The Canadian Annual Review, 1934* (Toronto: Annual Review Publishing, 1935), 328; *Vancouver Province*, 3 October 1933; A.H. Peterson, Secretary, Duncan Chamber of Commerce, Notes of Meeting, 19 March 1930, and Pooley to Peterson, 28 March 1930, AGR, 1918-17-2060; *Cowichan Leader*, 26 September 1935. In Britain and the United States, "massive new poverty made it painfully real that destitution was not caused by a biological flaw" (Elazar Barkan, *The Retreat of Scientific Racism: Changing Concepts of Race in Britain and the United States between the World Wars* [Cambridge, UK: Cambridge University Press, 1992], 344).

8 *Vancouver Province*, 26 May 1930. Among the members of the council delegation were Percy Bengough, a founder of the Asiatic Exclusion League, and Angus MacInnis, later a champion of the Japanese. Trades and Labour Congress of Canada, *Report of Proceedings* (Ottawa: Trades and Labour Congress, 1931), 153, 157, 180.

9 One case was tragic. In the winter of 1933-34, three Chinese workers employed at a shingle bolt camp near Port Alberni died of beriberi after living for three weeks on boiled rice and clams when a Chinese contractor held up supplies because he could not collect accounts from the camp operator (*Vancouver Province*, 24 January 1934; *Vancouver Sun*, 3 February 1934).

10 In 1931 the Fraser Mills Company denied that it operated on a contract system. In 1934 it began restoring wages but set a minimum scale of thirty-five cents per hour for whites and twenty-five cents for Orientals (*Vancouver Province*, 24 September 1931; *New Westminster British Columbian*, 19, 26, and 31 October 1931 and 30 March 1934; *The Commonwealth*, 20 September 1935; *Vancouver News-Herald*, 15 August 1933; *Port Alberni West Coast Advocate*, 13 May 1937; MacInnis to A.R.M. Lower, 14 September 1938, AMMC, v. 54A). Ernest Bakewell (CCF, Mackenzie) accused large corporations of employing cheap Asian labour (*The Commonwealth*, 15 March 1934), but there is no evidence of this rare complaint being pursued (Gillian Creese, "Organizing Against Racism in the Workplace: Chinese Workers in Vancouver Before the Second World War," *Canadian Ethnic Studies* 19, 3 [1987]: 44).

11 *Comox Argus*, 17 July 1930; *Port Alberni News*, 17 July 1930; HCD, 28 April 1933, 4423; Marler to Secretary of State for External Affairs, 6 June 1933, DEAR, v. 1668.

12 *Prince Rupert Daily News*, 20 January 1930 and 26 November and 5 and 8 December 1931; *Vancouver Province*, 13 January, 14 February, and 29 April 1930, 26 November 1932, and 30 June and 3 July 1934; *The Commonwealth*, 28 December 1934.

13 BCV&P, 9 March 1931; E.C. Carson, Secretary, Select Standing Committee on Agriculture, to Tolmie, 24 March 1932, and Tolmie to Carson, 22 April 1932, POC. The matter was outside the scope of the conference, and there are no further references. *Vancouver Province*, 20 November 1930 and 16 December 1937; *Cowichan Leader*, 9 September and 23 December 1937; *Prince Rupert Daily News*, 24 January 1930; Vancouver Island Farmers' Institutes to Pattullo, 27 November 1937, and J.S. Taylor to Crerar, 28 March 1938, DImm, MfC4752; *Nanaimo Free Press*, 1 February 1938.

14 R.R. Robinson to Stevens, 30 April 1936, and Stevens to Robinson, 30 April 1936, HHSPN, v. 59; *Country Life in B.C.* 20 (July 1936): 6; *Victoria Colonist*, 19 October 1937; *New Westminster British Columbian*, 22 January 1938; *Victoria Times*, 27 January 1938; *Prince Rupert Evening Empire*, 3 February 1938; *Vancouver Sun*, 29 October 1938; BCV&P, 11 March 1930 and 9 March 1931; E.C. Carson, Secretary, Select Standing Committee on Agriculture, to Tolmie, 24 March 1932, POC. Tolmie referred the matter to Stevens, but there is no record of a follow-up. In a few instances, farmers raised the Asian question when they feared the sale of land in their areas to Asians (M.D. Wilson to Tolmie, 15 March 1930, POC).

15 *Vancouver Sun,* 1 March 1935; Report of A.E. Richards, 1935, quoted in Ian MacPherson, "Creating Stability amid Degrees of Marginality: Divisions in the Struggle for Orderly Marketing in British Columbia, 1900-1940," *Canadian Papers in Rural History 7* (1990): 328-29; *Vernon News,* 21 June and 12 July 1934. The tomato and cucumber marketing board collapsed in 1938 (Timothy Chan, "The Social and Regulatory Relations of Metropolitan Victoria's Commercial Greenhouse Industry: 1900 to 1996," University of Victoria, MA thesis, 1996, 100).

16 *Vernon News,* 10 January, 11 and 18 April, and 29 August 1935; *Kamloops Sentinel,* 6 September and 10 October 1935; *Victoria Times,* 12 September 1940. The tomato industry declined after the Second World War; the Ashcroft cannery closed in 1959. See John Stewart, "The Kamloops Canneries: The Rise and Fall of a Local Industry, 1913-1990," *BC Studies,* 93 (Spring 1992): 30-47.

17 C.H. Young and H.R.Y. Reid, *The Japanese Canadians* (Toronto: University of Toronto Press, 1938), 56; J.B. Shimek to Bennett, 18 December 1933, RBBP, #471448-9; *New Westminster British Columbian,* 5 February and 29 December 1932, 11 April 1933, 15 January and 27 September 1934, 8, 9, and 21 February 1935, 16 March 1937, and 8 January 1940; *Vancouver Sun,* 22 July 1933 and 8 January 1937; A.A. Milledge, Solicitor, BC Producers' Co-Operative Exchange, to Gordon Wismer, 26 July 1937, AGR, P302; *Vancouver Province,* 19 August 1935; *Country Life in B.C.* 19 (September 1935): 11-13; Board of Review, Special Japanese Investigator, Report, 31 July 1938, DEAR, v. 1867. Yamaga was re-elected in 1934. See also Anne Doré, "Transnational Communities: Japanese Canadians of the Fraser Valley, 1904-1942," *BC Studies,* 134 (Summer 2002), 56-58.

18 *New Westminster British Columbian,* 7 September 1935; L. Hagen to Select Standing Committee on Agriculture of the British Columbia Legislature to Investigate the BC Coast Vegetable Marketing Board and Its Agencies, 16-20 November 1936, 140, 205; W. Hutcherson, *Landing at Ladner* (New York: Carlton Press, 1982), 117.

19 *Ladner Weekly Optimist,* 14 June and 29 November 1934 and 19 September 1935; *Vancouver Sun,* 22 and 23 July and 13 August 1935; BC Coast Vegetable Marketing Board to K.C. Macdonald, 12 August 1935, and Les Gilmore to Gordon Sloan, 30 September 1935, AGR, P302; *Cowichan Leader,* 25 July and 29 August 1935. One board member, A.H. Peterson of Duncan, argued that "if we permit the Orientals to win this time, then God help the white man" (*Cowichan Leader,* 29 August 1935). *New Westminster British Columbian,* 27 September 1934 and 20 and 27 September and 5 October 1935; *Vancouver Sun,* 6 and 13 September 1935. The board claimed that Chinese wholesalers illegally dumped Ashcroft potatoes in Vancouver. A Japanese grower, convicted of selling potatoes without inspection tags, received a suspended sentence. The board said that only 24 of 468 Chinese growers owned their land but that 209 of 273 Japanese growers were owners, with the Japanese producing an average of 7.75 tons to the acre. The board admitted that, contrary to the assumption that Asians grew 80 percent of the potatoes and vegetables, they produced less than 20 percent of the potatoes (*Vancouver Province,* 17 August and 7 December 1935; *Vancouver Sun,* 28 December 1935).

 0 BC Coast Vegetable Marketing Board to K.C. Macdonald, 12 August 1935, and Officer in Charge, E Division, BC Police, to Commissioner, 17 September 1935, AGR, P302. Other correspondence on the police inspection of Chinese potato shipments is in this file. *Vancouver Sun,* 13 August and 22 October 1935; *Langley Advance,* 5 December 1935; *Kamloops Sentinel,* 12 November 1935; *Victoria Times,* 11 October 1935; *Vancouver Province,* 7 December 1935.

 1 MacPherson, "Creating Stability amid Degrees of Marginality," 326-27; *Vancouver Province,* 7 January 1937; *Victoria Colonist,* 3 February 1937. In another case, the court ruled that the British Columbia Coast Vegetable Marketing Board had illegally collected fees from a Chinese grower after the Dominion legislation had been declared *ultra vires.* The previous summer the Low Chong Company had been the centre of a conflict between the Vegetable Board

and Chung Chuck when the board's special constables attempted to load four tons of onions onto a government truck as Chung and his helpers tried to move the onions into a warehouse. The constables soon gave up because onions had fallen from their sacks and been squashed underfoot, making it difficult to see. Adding insult to the constables' injury, they had acted under misapprehension; an injunction prevented the seizure of vegetables destined for the Low Chong Company (*Victoria Colonist,* 29 August 1936).

22 *Vancouver Province,* 24 October and 3, 4, 13, and 14 November 1936; *Vancouver News-Herald,* 3 November 1936; *New Westminster British Columbian,* 5 March 1935. The speaker ruled that the motion was not urgent and that only the government could introduce motions calling for the spending of public money (BCLJ, 3 November 1936, 10); Select Standing Committee on Agriculture of the British Columbia Legislature to Investigate the BC Coast Vegetable Marketing Board and Its Agencies, 172, 229 (copy in Victoria, Legislative Library of British Columbia).

23 *Victoria Colonist,* 12 January 1937; *Vancouver Province,* 12 and 23 February and 2 March 1937; *Ladner Weekly Optimist,* 11 March 1937.

24 *Vancouver Sun,* 1 and 2 March 1937; *Vancouver Province,* 1 March and 27 April 1937; Officer Commanding, E Division, to Commissioner, C.I.B., 2 March 1937, AGR, P302; China's consul general wrote to Attorney General Gordon Sloan about the "alleged fracas," expressing his hope that "Chinese interests are impartially treated with due regard in the sense of justice" (C.H. Bao to Sloan, 5 March 1937, AGR, P302).

25 A.W. Greenwood, Chairman, Grocers' Section, Retail Merchants Association, to Editor, *Vancouver Province,* 5 March 1937; Chunhow H. Pao to Gordon Sloan, 5 March 1937, AGR, P302; *Vancouver Province,* 2 and 6 March 1937; *Vancouver Sun,* 3 March 1937. The Congress of Canadian Organizations praised Attorney General Sloan for enforcing the Marketing Act "irrespective of whether the offender be white or Oriental" (H.G. Mackenrot to Sloan, 11 March 1937, AGR, P302); G. Stewart, Secretary, Maple Leaf Assembly, Native Sons of Canada, to Sloan, 8 March 1937, AGR, P302.

26 *Nanaimo Free Press,* 31 March 1937; *Vancouver Sun,* 3 March 1937; *Vancouver Province,* 14 and 15 May 1937; J.H. Johnson to Officer Commanding, E Division, BC Police, 7 May 1937, and A.H. Peterson to T.D. Pattullo, 18 May 1937, AGR, P302.

27 A.H. Peterson to Gordon Wismer, 16 August 1937, AGR, P302; British Columbia, Department of Agriculture, *Annual Report,* 1937 (Victoria: King's Printer, 1938), K23; *Vancouver Sun,* 11 June and 3 and 9 September 1937; *Vancouver Province,* 4 June, 29 July, 11 August, 3, 17, and 18 September, 2 and 25 October, and 20 November 1937; *New Westminster British Columbian,* 5 June, 28 August, 18 September, and 23 October 1937; *Nanaimo Free Press,* 5 November 1937.

28 *Vancouver Sun,* 3 September 1937; *Nanaimo Free Press,* 19 October 1937; *Vancouver News-Herald,* 9 December 1937; *Vancouver Province,* 16 December 1937 and 27 July 1938; Convention of Vancouver Island Farmers' Institutes to Pattullo, 27 November 1937, and Pattullo to Vancouver Island Farmers' Institutes, 2 December 1937, DImm, MfC4752; *Prince Rupert Daily News,* 13 December 1937; *Cowichan Leader,* 9 September 1937.

29 A.P. Slade, Memorandum, with F.W. Taylor, to Keenleyside, 10 June 1938, DEAR, v. 1867; *Vancouver Sun,* 22 October and 16 November 1938 and 14 July 1941; *Victoria Times,* 25 October 1941; *Vancouver Province,* 14 July 1941. A magazine published by Canadian Industries Limited, a major producer of agricultural chemicals, suggested that Oriental market gardeners in the Fraser Valley took scientific care of the soil (quoted in the *Kamloops Sentinel,* 2 September 1938); Don Mason and J.G. Scully, "John Chinaman, Gardener," *Country Life in B.C.* 23 (February 1939).

30 *New Westminster British Columbian,* 21 November 1938; *Vancouver Sun,* 31 July, 31 October, and 24 and 25 November 1941; A.M. Harper, "Report of Inquiry into the Natural Products Marketing Act [British Columbia]" (Victoria: King's Printer, 1942), 27-28.

31 *Vancouver Province,* 21 March, 11 April, 1 June, and 8 July 1933; W.J. McGuigan to Committee on Market, Exhibition and Industries, 29 April 1933, 19 February and 10 September 1934, and 20 June 1938, VCCCl, vols. 173, 183, 222.

32 *The Retailer* 26 (January 1934): 14, and 26 (September 1934): 8; *Vancouver Province,* 15 March and 15 May 1934; *Vancouver Sun,* 31 May 1934; *Vancouver News-Herald,* 15 May 1934; W.J. McGuigan to Committee, 21 May 1934 and 20 June 1938, VCCCl, vols. 183, 222; *Prince Rupert Daily News,* 12 April 1932; *Victoria Colonist,* 19 April 1932; *New Westminster British Columbian,* 25 May 1932, 31 July 1934, and 26 March 1935; *Kamloops Sentinel,* 17 February 1939; *Kaslo Kootenaian,* 27 April 1939. Burnaby Municipal Council tabled a request from a Chinese produce firm that it be given some relief business.

33 In 1932 the Canadian Association of Seamen began a campaign to reduce the number of Asians on Canadian ocean and coastal vessels. It claimed that over 2,500 Asians worked out of Vancouver while many white seamen were unemployed. The Victoria and Vancouver city councils endorsed the idea, and Thomas Reid, with the support of Angus MacInnis, took it up in Parliament (HCD, 28 April 1933, 4407-12, 2 March 1934, 1140, and 28 January 1935, 230). Trans-Pacific shipping companies replied that hiring whites would be more costly, require better crew accommodation, and displease passengers, most of whom were Asian (*Vancouver Sun,* 9 April 1935). A parliamentary committee agreed but urged the companies to employ as many white Canadians as possible (HCD, 13 June 1935, 3595). It was a minor issue in the 1935 federal election. The new Liberal government accepted the advice of the Canadian Pacific Railway (CPR), which had a mail subsidy for the ships, that change was impractical. China suggested that any change might impair trade. Only in February 1941 when some Chinese seamen refused to enter the Pacific war zone did the CPR begin replacing them with white seamen (*Vancouver News-Herald,* 14 February 1941).

34 The surviving issue is dated 11 March 1935.

35 *Victoria Times,* 17 June 1931 and 20 July 1932 (by H.B.W., a pseudonym of Bruce Hutchison. Peter Stursberg, *Those Were the Days: Victoria in the 1930s* [Victoria: Horsdahl and Schubert, 1993], 78). See also Bruce Hutchison, *Victoria Times,* 24 January 1938. *The Spokesman,* 1 March 1930; *Victoria Colonist,* 22 December 1931; *Vancouver Sun,* 23 December 1931 and 22 January 1932; *Victoria Times,* 17 June 1931; *Vancouver Province,* 22 January 1932. Lee shot himself following the murder, so there was no trial.

36 *Vancouver Province,* 6 September 1933. On the Japanese birth rate, see Young and Reid, *The Japanese Canadians,* 25-33.

37 Young and Reid, *The Japanese Canadians,* 213; *New Westminster British Columbian,* 3 August 1933; *Vancouver Province,* 12 January, 9 February, and 19 March 1930; *Cowichan Leader,* 27 March 1930. On two occasions Arthur Laing, a Richmond school trustee, asked the provincial government for "special grants to school districts charged with educating large numbers of children whose parents or guardians are practically non-taxable" (*Vancouver Province,* 24 September 1931; *Vancouver News-Herald,* 22 September 1939). The province was anxious that Asians not escape taxes. Minister of Finance J.W. Jones boasted that his 1 percent super tax on incomes over a certain minimum would affect casual Asian labourers who previously had contributed almost nothing to the provincial treasury. Minister of Education Joshua Hinchliffe said that every cent paid by Asians and transients would help reduce the burden on others. Despite the province's serious financial problems, the *Vancouver Star* chastised Hinchliffe for using racial prejudice to defend a tax and noted that Asians not affected by income tax paid the poll tax (*Vancouver Star,* 10 and 11 March 1931; *Vancouver Province,* 4 May 1931); *Vancouver Province,* 11 May 1934; *New Westminster British Columbian,* 15 May 1934.

38 *Vancouver Star,* 15 April 1930; *Vancouver Sun,* 11 May 1934 and 27 February 1936; *Vancouver Province,* 11 May 1934; *Cowichan Leader,* 12 September 1935; *Victoria Times,* 27 August 1937. J. Sutherland Brown to Secretary, Department of National Defence, 11 March 1930, DNDR, D1,

v. 15. The Japanese community gave Brown a six-week tour of Japan in the summer of 1930 (*Vancouver Star,* 15 April 1930).

39 HCD, 26 June 1931, 3122; *Vancouver Province,* 14 March and 17 June 1930; *Cowichan Leader,* 6 March 1930; *Vancouver Star,* 20 February and 19 March 1930; W.J. Bonavia, Superintendent of Farmers' Institutes, to Tolmie, 15 January 1930, POC; *Prince Rupert Daily News,* 27 January 1930. One member of the advisory board, J.Y. Copeman of Cowichan, compared the position of Asians in British Columbia to that of Jews in medieval England. He said that Jews were now accepted members of society in England and warned that a similarly "repellent" situation might occur in British Columbia (*Vancouver Star,* 20 February 1930).

40 *Prince Rupert Weekly Empire,* 25 January 1930; H. Glynn-Ward to Editor, *Vancouver Star,* 14 May 1930; *The Spokesman,* 4 January 1930; *Kamloops Sentinel,* 19 January 1930; *Vancouver Province,* 7 March 1930.

41 *Vancouver Star,* 17 April 1930; *Vancouver Province,* 14 March 1930; *Kamloops Sentinel,* 8 April 1930.

42 *Victoria Times,* 28 December 1929; *Prince Rupert Daily News,* 15 and 20 November 1939.

43 *New Westminster British Columbian,* 1 December 1932; *Victoria Colonist,* 29 February 1936; *Fraser Valley Record,* 15 April 1937; *Prince Rupert Daily News,* 16 November 1934 and 30 April 1937; *Victoria Times,* 25 February 1938; *Vancouver News-Herald,* 25 February 1938; *Vancouver Province,* 19 June 1931.

44 *Vancouver Province,* 22 May and 19 June 1931 and 4 January 1939; *Vancouver Sun,* 3 April 1928; *Vancouver Star,* 14 April and 6 July 1931; *Victoria Colonist,* 18 September 1940.

45 *Cowichan Leader,* 8 August 1940; Union of British Columbia Municipalities, Resolutions, 17-18 September 1940, to Premier and Cabinet, GR1222, v. 156. *New Westminster British Columbian,* 25 January 1940; *Port Alberni West Coast Advocate* quoted in *Victoria Times,* 2 October 1940; *Vancouver Sun,* 4, 5 and 10 February 1941; *Vancouver Province,* 4 and 11 February 1941; *News-Herald,* 4 February 1941; Florence Allen to Mayor and Council, 19 February 1941, CVA, RG2A1, v. 248; Laura E. Jamieson to Vancouver City Council, 21 February 1941, VCCCl, v. 248; *The Federationist,* 6 February 1941. E.G. Perrault, *Tong: The Story of Tong Louie, Vancouver's Quiet Titan* (Madeira Park, BC: Harbour Publishing, 2002), 9, 92-96.

46 E.g., *Victoria Colonist,* 1 July 1932; *Vernon News,* 28 July 1932; *Vancouver Province,* 5 May 1937. See also the *Vancouver News-Herald,* 27 March 1937. Suichi Kusaka, who graduated in honours mathematics and physics, came to Canada as a child and was educated in Vancouver schools. His parents returned to Japan, leaving him with his brother-in-law. The federal Department of Mines and Resources denied any discrimination; 4,500 students had applied for 950 positions (Daniel L. Lee to R.K. Finlayson, 8 January 1938, and Finlayson to Lee, 4 February 1938, RBBP, #330765-6).

47 See also Nora Kelly, *Quest for a Profession: The History of the Vancouver General Hospital School of Nursing* (Vancouver: Evergreen Press, 1973), 83-86. The first Asian nurses graduated from Vancouver General Hospital in 1936. Five years later a Chinese Canadian graduate ranked first in the provincial registered nurses examinations; a Nisei came third (*Vancouver Province,* 30 January 1932; *Vancouver Sun,* 15 May 1936 and 7 May 1941; *Prince Rupert Daily News,* 11 August 1934).

48 HCD, 27 May 1931, 2023, 2026; "Figures Showing Number of Orientals in B.C. and Work They are Engaged In," 23 March 1931, SFTP, b. 26; C.E. Hope to Bennett, 30 March 1931, DImm, MfC10264; Skelton to Tokugawa, 3 May 1934, RBBP, #294087-9. In 1935, in reporting the application for naturalization of the chef at Government House, Cheong Chung, the *Victoria Times* noted that "no Oriental of the yellow races has been naturalized here for years" but thought that an exception might be made for Cheong (19 September 1935). Hope to Tolmie, 17 March 1931, POC; Trades and Labour Congress of Canada, *Proceedings,* 1931 (Ottawa: Trades and Labour Congress of Canada, 1931), 190-91. In 1931 Professor Henry F.

Angus said that few, if any, certificates of naturalization had been granted to Orientals since 1923 ("The Legal Status in British Columbia of Residents of Oriental Race and Their Descendants," *The Canadian Bar Review* 9 [January 1931]: 10).

49 *Vancouver Sun*, 21 January 1928 and 19 October 1926.

50 *Vancouver Province*, 8 and 13 July and 28 August 1931; *Vancouver Star*, 18 and 29 August 1931; Circular, "To All Registrars from Committee of the Executive Council on Unemployment Relief," 10 August 1931, Chairman of the Committee of the Executive Council on Unemployment Relief to Hoiki Chow, Chinese Consul, Vancouver, 22 August 1931, and Masanori Yamada to Tolmie, 8 September 1931, POC; Chinese Benevolent Association to Mayor and Council, 30 November 1931, VCCCl, v. 154; *Victoria Times*, 26 October 1932.

51 W.R. Bone to L.D. Taylor, 4 May 1932, VCCCl, v. 171. The city relief office gave the Anglican Mission nine dollars per month for the care of a Chinese resident who had had his leg amputated. The arrangement was made through the mission so that the recipient had "no knowledge that the city is assuming the cost of his care" (*Vancouver Sun*, 23 January 1934). In 1934 Chinese citizens collected $1,281 for the fund and said that they were "privileged" to participate "because they were always anxious to accept their community responsibilities along with other citizens" (*Vancouver Province*, 28 November 1934).

52 *Vancouver Sun*, 26 April 1934 and 6 March 1935; Hilda Hellaby, Report on Chinese Relief under Anglican Board of Oriental Missions, and J.W. McIntosh to Mayor and Council, 23 February 1935, VCCCl, v. 193; Provincial Workers Council to Pattullo, 19 February 1935, RBBP, #492749. The Benevolent Association denied any involvement in a parade of Chinese "reliefers" at the provincial relief office.

53 *Vancouver Province*, 9 January 1935; *The Commonwealth*, 5 April and 21 June 1935; J.H. McVety, General Superintendent, Employment Service of Canada, to Gordon Sloan, 15 April 1935, IAMP, v. 19; *Port Alberni West Coast Advocate*, 13 May 1937. Until 1936 Vancouver did not list relief recipients by racial origin (W.R. Bone to H.J. DeGraves, 25 March 1938, HDWP); *Vancouver Sun*, 4 July 1935; Gordon to Tolmie, 12 December 1931, RBBP, #49201; *Victoria Colonist*, 13 January, 20 May, and 25 December 1932; *Victoria Times*, 16 January and 24 December 1932; *New Westminster British Columbian*, 1 March 1934; Philip C.P. Low, *Memories of Cumberland Chinatown* (Vancouver: P.C.P. Low, 1993), 81; *Comox District Free Press*, 21 November 1940; Bone to W.W. Smith, 29 June 1936, VCCCl, v. 207; Chief Controller of Chinese Immigration to Magladery, 31 January 1936, DImm, MfC10661.

In the case of a disaster, such as the destruction by fire of Chilliwack's small Chinatown for the second time in two years, civic authorities and charitable organizations arranged temporary assistance for the homeless, but most assistance came from Chinese residents elsewhere in the province (*Vancouver Sun*, 27 August 1934; *Chilliwack Progress*, 6 and 20 September 1934).

54 *Prince Rupert Daily News*, 25 February and 2 March 1937; J.H. McVety to F.W. Taylor, 16 January 1935, DImm, MfC4751; Bone to DeGraves, 25 March 1938, HDWP; Young and Reid, *The Japanese Canadians*, 29, 245; G.S. Pearson to Gordon Sloan, 20 January 1936, IAMP, v. 19; Memo for Skelton, 19 March 1936, DEAR, v. 1430; Keenleyside to Skelton, 30 March 1938, and Skelton to Keenleyside, 5 April 1938, DEAR, v. 1867. The provincial Unemployment Relief Branch did not segregate the Japanese on relief lists but estimated that in the winter of 1937-38 fewer than 500 received assistance (E.W. Griffith to Premier's Secretary, 31 March 1938, TDPP, v. 73). In 1939 Thomas Reid said that few Japanese residents had applied for relief because, fearing deportation, they had gone undercover, denied destitution, or depended on friends (HCD, 14 March 1939, 1884).

55 *New Westminster British Columbian*, 12 September 1935; W.W. Foster to G.G. McGeer, 15 December 1937, GGMcGPA, v. 1; *Victoria Times*, 5 February 1938; Helen Gregory MacGill, "The Oriental Delinquent in the Vancouver Juvenile Court," *Sociology and Social Research* 22 (May-June 1938): 430, 434-35.

56 S.I. Hayakawa, "The Japanese-Canadian: An Experiment in Citizenship," *Dalhousie Review* 16 (April 1936): 17. In a special UBC issue of the *Vancouver Sun*, Shinobu Higashi made a similar comment (4 February 1936); *Vancouver Province*, 2 April 1931. David Lim Yuen, the son of a clergyman, spoke to the Rotary Club later that year on the Manchurian Crisis. In 1932 he secured the highest marks in the district and the fourth highest in the province in the junior matriculation exams (*Vernon News*, 30 April and 31 December 1931 and 28 July 1932).

57 *Vancouver Province*, 2 November 1935; BCV&P, 31 March 1931; *Victoria Colonist*, 31 March 1931; *Victoria Times*, 1 April 1931; Vancouver's Japanese residents marked the victory with a pilgrimage to the Japanese war memorial in Stanley Park (*Vancouver Province*, 12 April 1931).

58 S.S. Osterhout, of the United Church, had urged "less invidious discrimination in the franchise" (*Orientals in Canada* [Toronto: United Church of Canada, 1929], 208).

59 *Vancouver Sun*, 13 May 1936; *Western Recorder*, August 1936; *Vancouver Province*, 3 October 1936, 3 September 1937, and 25 May 1938; *Victoria Times*, 22 May 1937; United Church, Committee on Christianity and Racial Relations, BC Conference, Report, May 1935, copy in HDP; *Victoria Colonist*, 21 December 1937 and 6 January and 15 May 1938; *Nanaimo Free Press*, 12 June 1937 and 26 February 1941; *New Westminster British Columbian*, 2 September 1937; *Vernon News*, 13 June 1935. Despite the presence of some Japanese delegates, the First Annual Greater Vancouver and New Westminster Youth Congress replaced a resolution favouring the enfranchisement of all Canadian-born citizens with one calling for an inquiry into the matter. The Youth Congress claimed to represent forty-eight organizations, including Japanese and Caucasian young people's church groups, Young Liberals, Young Communists, and the Vancouver Trades and Labour Council (Resolutions of the First Annual Greater Vancouver and New Westminster Youth Congress, 27-29 March 1937, copy in HDWPV, 551-A-5). Minutes of British Columbia Conference of United Church, May 1933, HDP; *Vancouver Province*, 13 May 1936 and 25 September 1931; Trades and Labour Congress of Canada, *Proceedings*, 1931 (Ottawa: Trades and Labour Congress of Canada, 1931), 141-42. The *New Westminster British Columbian*, 20 December 1933, printed the *Ubyssey* editorial without comment; Shinobu Higashi, Notes Taken on an Address by Sherwood Lett, 27 November 1934, MMP; Skelton to Stevens, 11 August 1933, DEAR, v. 3193.

60 C.F. Davie demanded that the university ask for Angus's resignation or at least censure him and, in future, require the Department of Education to censor in advance any speech by a university professor (*The Spokesman*, 7 June 1930). Davie's views were extreme, but the normally tolerant editor of the *Vancouver Star*, who thought Canadian-born Asians should have citizenship rights, wondered why in immigration matters British Columbia "should be offered up on the altar of Pacific Ocean peace" (17 February, 19 April, and 22 and 28 May 1930); *Vancouver Province*, 26 May 1930; Henry F. Angus, Inventory of Papers, HFAP, v. 36. In his unpublished memoirs, Angus said that he thought the *Queen's Quarterly* article was his first publication on the subject, but it was not. He had made similar arguments in "Kyoto," *Canadian Forum* 10 (March 1930): 196-97; Henry F. Angus, "Underprivileged Canadians," *Queen's Quarterly* 38 (Summer 1931): 460. Angus's article in the magazine section of the *Vancouver Province*, "More than a Tenth of B.C. Is Asiatic and There's the Problem" (1 September 1934), set off such a flurry that the editor cut off debate after a month. *Vancouver Province*, 27 March, 23 June, 6 October, and 19 November 1934; *Vancouver News-Herald*, 27 March and 19 June 1934; F.C. Aubrey, Recording Secretary, Native Sons of British Columbia, Post No. 3, to Editor, *Vancouver Province*, 23 June 1934; *New Westminster British Columbian*, 25 April and 22 May 1934.

61 *Victoria Times*, 31 March 1936 and 5 May 1938; *Nanaimo Free Press*, 23 January 1937; *Vancouver Province*, 10 February and 8 September 1937; *Victoria Colonist*, 13 March 1937; HCD, 12 May 1938, 2789-90. Prime Minister King communicated with Chief Commissioner N.W. Rowell, but Angus had spoken as an individual on a matter outside the commission's

jurisdiction. The Victoria Assembly of the Native Sons of Canada also complained *(Victoria Colonist,* 15 May 1938).

62 A 1935 survey of second generation Japanese residents revealed that more than 1,205 Japanese Canadians had reached the age of 21 *(Vancouver Sun,* 4 February 1936). The Dominion Franchise Act disqualified anyone, except veterans of the Canadian forces, who was disqualified by race from voting in the elections of the province in which he or she resided (Canada, *Statutes,* 24-5 Geo 5, ch. 51, sec 4 [xi]).

63 HCD, 22 June 1934, 4206. Woodsworth was misinformed; Saskatchewan disfranchised Chinese residents from 1908 to 1944. *Vancouver Sun,* 7 November 1934. In 1923 he had said that "to a very large extent the people of British Columbia ought to decide who are the right and proper persons to be taken into their citizenship" (HCD, 3 May 1923, 2456); *The Commonwealth,* 16 August and 15 and 22 November 1934. The small "People's Party," headed by J.E. Armishaw, withdrew support from the CCF because it could not endorse its "pro-Oriental policy" and the determination of its leaders to create "a complete socialist state" (The People's Party of British Columbia, "Challenge to the C.C.F. and the Liberal Party of British Columbia to Take Action to Bring to an Immediate End the Unnecessary Poverty in British Columbia" (copy in RBBP, #529146-7). Armishaw wrote to the *Vancouver Province,* attacking CCF policy on the franchise (14, 15, and 17 November 1934). Woodsworth's announcement inspired H.T. Gaetz and Peter Simonds of Vancouver to form the Anti-Japanese Expansion Society. Although they gave a radio talk, spoke to the New Westminster Kiwanis Club and a Vancouver post of the Native Sons of British Columbia, and occasioned a few press reports, their movement disappeared within a month *(New Westminster British Columbian,* 16 and 18 July 1934; *Vancouver Province,* 18 July, 10 August, and 26 October 1934; *Vancouver Sun,* 11 August 1934).

64 BCLJ, 23 March 1935; *Vancouver Province,* 14 July and 19 October 1934.

65 *Victoria Times,* 4 and 12 October 1935; *Victoria Colonist,* 12 October 1935; *The Commonwealth,* 27 December 1935; Typescript of a Radio Address by Angus MacInnis, 20 August 1935, AMMC, b. 17; *Vancouver Sun,* 8 and 12 October 1935; *Comox District Free Press,* 5 September 1935; *Cowichan Leader,* 22 August 1935; *Maple Ridge-Pitt Meadows Weekly Gazette,* 10 October 1935.

66 *Vancouver Province,* 7 and 8 October 1935; *Vancouver News-Herald,* 8 and 9 October 1935; *Vancouver Sun,* 7 and 8 October 1935; *Victoria Times,* 2, 5, and 11 October 1935; J. Edward Sears, *Orientals and the C.C.F.* (Vancouver: n.p., 1935); *Kelowna Courier,* 26 September 1935; *Prince Rupert Daily News,* 3 and 5 October 1935; *The Commonwealth,* 10 October 1935. In reporting Mackenzie's meeting, the *Vancouver Sun* did not mention Mrs. McClung's statement. The *Vancouver Province* reported that it had "aroused a storm of abuse" (9 October 1935). See Henry F. Angus, "Liberalism Stoops to Conquer," *Canadian Forum* 15 (December 1935): 389-90.

67 Howard C. Green to W.A. Gordon, 22 April 1935, DImm, MfC4751. Grote Stirling endorsed the resolution, but the minister of immigration, while sympathetic to "protecting our own people," believed that immigration laws were being "strictly observed" (Stirling to Gordon, 29 April 1935, and Gordon to Green, 4 May 1937, DImm, MfC4751); *Prince Rupert Evening Empire,* 19 September 1935; *Vancouver Sun,* 12 October 1935; *Vancouver News-Herald,* 10 and 12 October 1935; *Nanaimo Free Press,* 7 and 11 October 1935; *New Westminster British Columbian,* 7 and 10 October 1935; *Victoria Times,* 26 September and 5 and 11 October 1935. In the Fraser Valley, H.J. Barber had his own variation on the advertisement *(Fraser Valley Record,* 3 October 1935; *Maple Ridge-Pitt Meadows Weekly Gazette,* 3 October 1935). In Nanaimo and Vancouver East, CCF candidates won. In Victoria the CCF candidate was a close second to the Conservative incumbent, D.B. Plunkett. Mackenzie, the incumbent in Vancouver Centre, was the only Liberal to win and by only 136 votes over the CCF candidate; HCD, 20 February 1936, 373.

68 HCD, 27 February 1936, 573, 576; E.A. P[ickering], Notes on Proposed Resolution of Mr.
    MacInnis, 19 February 1936, KP, #C122720ff.
69 *Prince Rupert Daily News,* 10 March 1936; *Vancouver Province,* 10 February 1936; *Ladner Weekly
    Optimist,* 5 March 1936; Bruce Hutchison, *Victoria Times,* 1 April 1936; *Vancouver News-
    Herald,* 1 April 1936; BCV&P, 5 March 1936, 5, and 31 March 1936, 8. The Japanese consul
    complained about the resolution to Pattullo, who tried to persuade Pooley to withdraw the
    motion (Ko Ishii to Pattullo, 1 April 1936, and Pattullo to Ishii, 4 April 1936, GR1222, b.
    124); MacInnis to T. Umezuki, 17 February 1936, AMMC, b. 54A; Japanese Canadian Citizens League,
    Vancouver Chapter, Minutes of the Executive Meeting, 4 March 1936, JCCL, v. 7. For details see
    Ken Adachi, *The Enemy That Never Was* (Toronto: McClelland and Stewart, 1976), 160-65.
70 The Japanese Canadian Citizens League incorporated an older group, the Japanese Cana-
    dian Citizens Association (Adachi, *The Enemy That Never Was,* 160).
71 Muriel Kitagawa, "Material for 'Crucible': Autobiographical Pieces," n.d., NWFP, file 2; Adachi,
    The Enemy That Never Was, 160-64; Muriel Kitagawa, *This Is My Own: Letters to Wes & Other
    Writings on Japanese Canadians, 1941-1948,* ed. by Roy Miki (Vancouver: Talonbooks, 1985),
    29; "In the Matter of the Dominion Franchise Act 1934 and the Dominion Election Act 1934
    and in the Matter of the Disqualification of Certain Persons in the Province of British Co-
    lumbia from Being Registered and Voting Under the Said Acts," 12 May 1936, T.G. Norris
    Papers, UBC; Canada, House of Commons, Special Committee on Elections and Franchise
    Acts, *Minutes of Proceedings and Evidence* (Ottawa: King's Printer, 1936), passim.
72 Adachi, *The Enemy That Never Was,* 160-64; *Vancouver Sun,* 22 May 1936; *New Westminster
    British Columbian,* 2 September 1937; Canada, House of Commons, Special Committee on
    Elections and Franchise Acts, *Minutes of Proceedings and Evidence,* 254; *Vancouver News-
    Herald,* 15 June 1936; *Victoria Colonist,* 15 August 1936 and 31 March 1937; *Vancouver Province,*
    11 and 16 March 1937. The Native Sons of British Columbia sought information from the
    Sons of the Golden West, a similar organization in California. In Victoria representatives of
    the Native Sons and Daughters, the Naval Veterans' Branch, the Canadian Legion, the De-
    fence of Canada League, and the Conservative and Liberal associations met to organize op-
    position (*Vancouver Province,* 19 December 1936). Native Sons of British Columbia, *Argument
    Advanced by Native Sons of British Columbia in Opposition to Granting of Oriental Franchise*
    (New Westminster: Native Sons of British Columbia, [1937]). "Brief Opposing Oriental Fran-
    chise in the Province of British Columbia Submitted by Tom Reid, MP," 14 March 1935, copy
    in HDWP; Kitagawa, "Material for 'Crucible,'" NWFP, file 2.
73 *Vancouver Sun,* 15 and 21 May 1937; *Vancouver Province,* 14 and 15 May 1937; *Kamloops Senti-
    nel,* 28 May 1937; *Comox District Free Press,* 3 June 1937; *Langley Advance,* 27 May 1937; *Victo-
    ria Colonist,* 8 and 29 May 1937; *Prince Rupert Daily News,* 17 and 21 May and 1 June 1937. At a
    Vancouver rally, Grey Turgeon, MP (Liberal, Cariboo), attacked a *Vancouver Province* edito-
    rial by suggesting that if the CCF's franchise plank was not an issue, then no CCF assertion
    was an issue.
74 Conservative Convention, Vancouver, 29 and 30 June 1936; *Victoria Colonist,* 27 April 1937;
    Vancouver Province, 19 and 27 August 1936. Patterson came third, behind the successful Lib-
    eral and a CCF candidate.
75 *Comox District Free Press,* 13 and 20 May 1937; *Cowichan Leader,* 20 May 1937; *Victoria Colo-
    nist,* 27 and 30 May 1937; *Victoria Times,* 31 May 1937; *Vancouver News-Herald,* 1 June 1937;
    Vancouver Sun, 18 May 1937; *Vancouver Province,* 19 and 29 May 1937; *Penticton Herald,* 22
    May 1937. The provincial government estimated that there were 25,886 Japanese and 21,740
    Chinese residents in the province in 1936 and that the total Asian population had been de-
    clining in recent years at the rate of about 1,000 per year (*British Columbia in the Canadian
    Confederation* [Victoria: King's Printer, 1938], 62); Herbert Anscomb, Radio Speech, Trail,
    BC, 30 April 1937, LJLP, v. 21.

76 *Vancouver Province,* 18 May 1937; *Kamloops Sentinel,* 18 May 1937; *Powell River News,* 27 May 1937; *Vancouver Sun,* 7 June 1937; *Prince Rupert Daily News,* 20 and 31 May 1937; *Prince Rupert Evening Empire,* 20 May 1937; *Comox District Free Press,* 27 May 1937; *Port Alberni West Coast Advocate,* 20 May 1937; *Victoria Colonist,* 29 May and 1 June 1937; *Victoria Times,* 29 May 1937; *B.C. Federationist,* 3 March 1938. The CCF vote decreased from 32 percent in 1933 to 29 percent, and the Liberal vote from 42 percent to 37 percent (Elections British Columbia, *Electoral History of British Columbia, 1871-1986* [Victoria: Queen's Printer, 1988], 173, 183).

77 The royal couple had expected to return to Japan via the United States but changed their plans for fear of demonstrations there. Their return trip was surrounded by "war-time secrecy," and the Vancouver police asked the press not to refer to the visit until it was over. The royal party went directly from the train to their ship (Frank E. Dorchester to R.B. Bennett, 7 April 1937, RBBP, #524317; *Vancouver Sun,* 29, 30, and 31 March and 6 April 1937; *Vancouver Province,* 29, 30, and 31 March 1937; H.L. Keenleyside, *Memoirs: Hammer the Golden Day* [Toronto: McClelland and Stewart, 1981], 478; Vancouver Police Chief Foster to Editors of the Sun, Province, and News-Herald, 27 September 1937, VMC, v. 24; *Vancouver Province,* 1 October 1937; *New Westminster British Columbian,* 31 March and 1 October 1937). The visit to Victoria was also low-key, but 200 people, including many Japanese residents, waited to see them at the dock. The lack of official ceremony was "at the request of the Japanese government" (*Victoria Colonist,* 2 October 1937).

78 E. Banno et al. to Editor, *Vancouver Sun,* 10 April 1937; Memo to T.G. Norris, TGNP, v. 31; Lt. Commr F.R.W.R. Gow to DeGraves, 9 April 1937, DNDR, v. 11917. The Nisei, who suspected that Planta had written the letter, secured a photostat of the original and asked Norris, their lawyer, to have the typing and signature compared with some of Planta's letters. There is no record of any results of this investigation. Bruce A. McKelvie, grand factor of the Native Sons of British Columbia, protested criticism of the cartoon, but his letter was not published. He claimed that the Japanese consul had given the *Vancouver Sun* two pages of advertising in return for not publishing any more critical letters (McKelvie to Bennett, 5 October 1937, RBBP, #522398-401); *New Westminster British Columbian,* 18 January 1946.

79 *Victoria Colonist,* 17 July 1931; *Kelowna Courier,* 4 March 1937; *Victoria Times,* 5 and 11 August 1937 and 13 November 1940; *Vancouver Province,* 7 August 1937; *Vancouver Sun,* 7 August and 20 December 1937 and 12 October 1941; *New Westminster British Columbian,* 1 June 1939.

80 Walter N. Sage, "Vancouver: The Rise of a City," *Dalhousie Review* 17 (April 1937): 54; *Vancouver Sun,* 13, 17, and 18 July 1936. Kay Anderson suggests that the Chinese village was a precursor to the emergence of Chinatown as a tourist attraction (*Vancouver's Chinatown: Racial Discourse in Canada, 1875-1980* [Montreal and Kingston: McGill-Queen's University Press, 1991], 155-58), but Vancouver residents had long shown Chinatown to prominent tourists seeking exotic sights (Patricia E. Roy, *A White Man's Province: British Columbia Politicians and Chinese and Japanese Immigrants, 1858-1914* [Vancouver: UBC Press, 1989], 15).

81 Hope to Marler, 23 November 1935, DEAR, v. 1756; *Vancouver Province,* 7 April 1937.

Chapter 6: Inflaming the Coast

1 *Vancouver Province,* 25 August 1937; *Toronto Globe and Mail,* 11 November 1937; *Toronto Star,* 17 November 1937. Memo to Mackenzie, 5 February 1938, IAMP, v. 34; C.E. Hope to Herbert Marler, 23 November 1935, DEAR, v. 1756. The *Halifax Herald,* 18 November 1937, gave the story some attention, but its headline ("Mystery Ships Ply Waters Off Pacific Coast?") ended with a question mark. The *Montreal Star,* the *Winnipeg Free Press,* and the *Calgary Herald* had only short versions of the Canadian Press story; the *Toronto Globe and Mail* did not mention it.

2 Former prime minister Bennett had recently observed that British Columbians were "not making any real complaint" about the vulnerability of their coast to sabotage from Japanese

residents (R.B. Bennett to R.S. Hanna, 15 November 1937, RBBP, #524343); *Vancouver Province,* 18 November 1937; *Prince Rupert Daily News,* 23 November 1937; *Cowichan Leader,* 25 November 1937; *Nanaimo Free Press,* 18 November 1937. The Japanese naval attaché in Ottawa dismissed Scott's "propaganda" as "utterly ridiculous and dangerous" (*Toronto Star,* 19 November 1937; *Vancouver Sun,* 19 November 1937); W.W. Foster to Mayor G.C. Miller, 17 November 1937, CVA, RG3, v. 24.

3 See Patricia E. Roy, *A White Man's Province: British Columbia Politicians and Chinese and Japanese Immigrants, 1858-1914* (Vancouver: UBC Press, 1989), 259-63; *Vancouver Province,* 24 November 1919 and 6 February 1925; *Victoria Colonist,* 2 November 1920, 20 August 1921, and 30 August 1929; C.H. Dickie, HCD, 8 May 1922, 1524; *Victoria Times,* 2 November 1920 and 2 February 1925; *Vancouver Sun,* 6 February 1925 and 6 April 1933; *Prince Rupert Evening Empire,* 27 September 1935; Constable Kennedy to Robert Mudy, D/S/Sgt, 25 October 1920, and A.E. Jukes to F.E. Davis, 19 August 1919, DNDR, MfC5055; Commissioner, RCMP, to Defence Committee, 24 March 1921, and Willougby Gwatkin to J.H. MacBrien, 24 October 1921, DHist, S-1009, v. 3; *Fraser Valley Record,* 12 August 1920; *Penticton Herald,* 12 October 1921; *Cumberland Islander,* 5 November 1921; *Nanaimo Free Press,* 8 November 1921.

4 C.H. Stuart Wade's "The Pacific War of 1910," *Westward Ho!* June 1910, was the first instalment of a story published over the next year; H. Glynn-Ward, *The Writing on the Wall* (Vancouver: Sun Publishing Company, 1921, reprinted 1974 by University of Toronto Press). This issue of *Danger: The Anti-Asiatic Weekly* has not survived. *Vancouver World,* 10 October and 3 and 13 November 1921; *Vancouver Sun,* 7 August 1921 and 17 March 1922; *Victoria Colonist,* 2 November 1921; *Cowichan Leader,* 16 November 1922. James W. Davidson, a fellow of the Royal Geographic Society, author of several books on the Orient, and former US consul at Shanghai, warned that Stevens's "most regrettable" statement would make diplomatic relations with Japan more difficult. In any case, Davidson observed, the Japanese had no reason to chart the coast since they could buy detailed charts from the Canadian and American governments (*Vancouver Province,* 20 March 1922).

5 Professor Edward Odlum, a Vancouver newspaper publisher and financier, wrote from Yokohama that Japan was "as reliable, as honorable and dependable" as any nation (*Vancouver Sun,* 10 May 1922); *Vancouver Sun,* 15 August 1922; *Victoria Colonist,* 27 November 1924; *Comox Argus,* 17 October 1929; *Victoria Times,* 19 October 1929. When a few alarmists worried about China's military awakening, the *Vancouver Sun* cautioned that "the Oriental menace, if there be one, is not an Oriental armed, but an Oriental suspicious, unacquainted and isolated from Western civilization, by international prejudice and superstitious ill will" (9 May 1922). The newspaper was not consistent; three years later it argued that "if this continent ever becomes Asiatic, it will not be by immigration, but by the sword" (27 May 1925).

6 H.H. Matthews to Major M.A. Pope, 15 June 1926, DNDR, v. 2670; G.A. Youle to Commander in Charge, Esquimalt, 25 October 1932, DNDR, MfC5853; C.E. Hope and W.K. Earle, "The Oriental Threat," *Maclean's,* 1 May 1933, 12, 54-55; "Annual Report on Japanese in British Columbia," October 1933, and F.R.W.R. Gow, Naval Staff Officer, Esquimalt, to Director of Naval Intelligence and Plans, Department of National Defence, Ottawa, 10 March 1937, DNDR, v. 11917; Constable Tweedhope to Parsons, 8 December 1934, DNDR, MfC5853. Another claim of Japanese fishermen boasting of being former Japanese naval officers drew no public response (*Vancouver Province,* 3 July 1934); HCD, 29 May 1936, 3249.

7 *Vancouver Province,* 3 February 1925.

8 *Vancouver Sun,* 10 May and 6 October 1932. F. Leighton Thomas, author of *Japan: The Octopus of the East* (Vancouver: F.L. Thomas, 1932) and a Vancouver resident, was a self-described "Veteran of the Imperial British Army." The keen anti-Asian, C.E. Hope, came across the pamphlet only by chance (Hope to Tolmie, 27 April 1932, POC). When Japan intimated unhappiness with Reid's allegations, the Department of External Affairs told the Canadian

legation in Tokyo to inform Japanese officials that there was no basis for Reid's claim, "that much latitude exists in debate" (Skelton to Marler, 12 July 1933, v. 1666. See also *Comox Argus*, 17 October 1929; *Vancouver Province*, 29 April 1933). Around 1932 an unnamed magazine returned an article by the British Columbia writer Francis Dickie that pointed "out the criminal defencelessness of this coast, the danger from Japan, etc." with the comment that "it was too fantastically out of the question" (Dickie to H.N. Moore, 28 June 1939, FDP, v. 2). B.K. Sandwell of *Saturday Night* returned one of Dickie's articles on the "Japanese menace" with the comment that it would do good only "to some out-of-office politician" (Sandwell to Dickie, 4 August 1938, FDP, v. 2). HCD, 28 April 1933, 4423, and 29 May 1936, 3249; *Vancouver Sun*, 27 May 1933, magazine, and 26 and 27 February and 5 March 1936.

9 *Vancouver Province*, 5 April 1933; *Vancouver Sun*, 5 April 1933. The Canadian Japanese Association contributed $500 to help entertain the crew (Annual Report on Japanese in British Columbia, October 1933, DNDR, MfC5853). A number of Communist groups, mainly in Ontario, protested the visit. Their letters are in RBBP, MfM890. After paying its bills, the Canadian Japanese Association asked the mayor to find it "some useful and worthy purpose for its surplus." Mayor Taylor recommended using the funds to prevent tuberculosis (L.D. Taylor to Vancouver City Council, 5 May 1933, VCCCo, v. 174); *Vancouver Sun*, 11 and 14 June 1935. When the *Kaiwo Maru* visited Prince Rupert in 1937, Japanese residents provided most of the hospitality, but, possibly because of the novelty of the visit, service clubs entertained the officers and crew. On Armistice Day, 1937, the Canadian Japanese Association arranged an observance on board a Japanese liner visiting Vancouver and invited both Canadian and Japanese members of the Canadian Legion. Several politicians, including Mayor G.C. Miller of Vancouver, participated (*Vancouver Sun*, 13 November 1937); Acting Secretary of State of External Affairs to Chargé, Tokyo, 31 October 1936, and *Visit to Canada of Their Imperial Highnesses the Prince and the Princess Chichibu of Japan 1937* (Ottawa, 1937), GGR, MfT2530; H.L. Keenleyside, *Memoirs: Hammer the Golden Day* (Toronto: McClelland and Stewart, 1981), 476. Keenleyside, who had recently returned from the Tokyo legation, acted for the federal government; honorary aides-de-camp represented the governor general and lieutenant governor (*Vancouver Sun*, 29 March and 6, 8, and 9 April 1937).

10 *Vancouver Sun*, 10 April and 28 September 1940; P.W. Luce, *Saturday Night*, 3 June 1939; *Victoria Colonist*, 24 September 1939. Further details may be found in DEAR, v. 2809. The winners, A.D.M. Doyle of the University of British Columbia and Morris Shumiatcher of the University of Alberta, reported receiving considerable publicity in Japan (*Vancouver Province*, 25 September 1940). As a lawyer, Shumiatcher later acted for the Government of Saskatchewan in appealing the Orders in Council directed at the Japanese in Canada.

11 For example, *Prince Rupert Evening Empire*, 22 October 1931; *Victoria Times*, 23 and 28 January 1932; *Vancouver Province*, 28 January and 1 February 1932; *Vernon News*, 4 and 11 February 1932; *Vancouver Sun*, 17 September 1932; *Prince Rupert Daily News*, 24 January 1933; *Victoria Colonist*, 7 February and 4 November 1932; Weekly Intelligence Reports, MD No. 11, 17 November and 9 January 1932, DNDR, v. 2576.

12 *Victoria Colonist*, 22 February 1933; *Victoria Times*, 14 November 1936; *Prince Rupert Evening Empire*, 10 April 1935 and 16 March and 14 August 1936; *New Westminster British Columbian*, 29 April 1935; *Vancouver Sun*, 23 July, 30 September, 10 October, and 27 December 1935; Mackenzie, Radio Speech, Hastings Park, 31 July 1935, IAMP, v. 4; C.J. Woodsworth, *Canada and the Orient* (Toronto: Macmillan, 1941). The *Japan Advertiser* on 19 November quoted *Nichi Nichi*, a major Japanese newspaper, as saying that it was pleased that Mackenzie King intended to cultivate "wholesome trade relations." However, it reminded Canada that "its attitude towards Japanese residents ... has stood in the way of friendship," that they were losing rights to fish, and that Japanese born in Canada were "so discriminated against that they are virtually without Canadian citizenship" (Enclosure, with Marler, to King, 21 November 1935, KP, #179659).

13 *Prince Rupert Evening Empire,* 23 May 1936; *Vancouver Province,* 8 February 1936; Memo for Dr. Skelton, 16 July 1937, DEAR, v. 1839; Gow to Director Naval Intelligence, 10 March 1937, G.C. Jones, Commander, i/c Esquimalt, to Director, Naval Intelligence, Department of National Defence, 7 January 1936, J.M. McClinton, NCO, i/c Prince Rupert, to OC, D Division, BC Provincial Police, 9 September 1936, T.W.S. Parsons to NIO/RCN/Esquimalt, 10 December 1936, D.W. Taylor, Constable, BC Provincial Police, Prince Rupert, Report, 5 December 1936, M.R. Dafoe, BC Provincial Police, to NCO, i/c Prince Rupert, 22 March 1937, and McClinton to Parsons, 24 March 1937, DNDR, v. 11917.

14 *Prince Rupert Daily News,* 1 May and 16 December 1936; Keenleyside to Beaudry, 28 October 1936, Prince Rupert Chamber of Commerce to King, 9 November 1936, and Note re Pattullo's Proposal for a U.S.-Canada Fishery Treaty, 10 January 1939, DEAR, v. 1799; *Vancouver Province,* 18 May 1937; *Nanaimo Free Press,* 5 December 1937; *Victoria Colonist,* 27 April 1938; HCD, 30 June 1938, 4483; *New Westminster British Columbian,* 4 January 1939; King to Pattullo, 14 January 1939, KP, #233279; J.C.E. Bayer to King, 8 December 1939, KP, #223729; *Prince Rupert Evening Empire,* 17 January 1940; *Vancouver Sun,* 3 June 1941; *B.C. Federationist,* 5 June 1941.

15 *Vancouver Province,* 2 November 1938 and 30 March 1941; *Prince Rupert Evening Empire,* 30 May 1941; *Vancouver Sun,* 20 December 1937; *Cowichan Leader,* 26 January 1939; *Vernon News,* 6 July 1939.

16 *Vancouver Sun,* 7 April 1937. The contract was renewed in March 1940 (*Victoria Times,* 27 March 1940); *Vancouver Province,* 2 April and 5 July 1937; *Victoria Times,* 8 February 1938; Maj.-Gen. C.F. Constantine, Memo, 16 July 1937, DEAR, v. 1803; C.N. Senior to A.W. Gray, 5 August 1937, IAMP, v. 29; Chief of the General Staff to Mackenzie, 13 November 1937, IAMP, v. 30. The Department of External Affairs recommended expanding intelligence services (L.C. C[hristie], Memorandum, 25 August 1937, DEAR, v. 1839).

17 *Victoria Times,* 14 November 1936, 13 and 28 September and 2 and 16 November 1937, and 20 and 25 January and 5 and 19 February 1938; *Toronto Star,* 24 November 1937. E.E. Winch, a CCF MLA, asked the minister of lands about any tariff preference that lumber and minerals from these properties might receive in Japan (BCV&P, 3 November 1937); *New Westminster British Columbian,* 15 July, 2 September, 23 and 26 October, and 6 and 10 November 1937; *Langley Advance,* 1 July 1937; *Vancouver Province,* 22 March and 23 October 1937 and 18 February 1938; *Victoria Colonist,* 10 and 27 November 1937; *Vancouver Sun,* 25 March 1938.

18 Pattullo to King, 26 January 1938, and King to Pattullo, 5 February 1938, TDPP, v. 75; Pattullo to King, 9 March 1939, KP, #233287-8; Keenleyside to Skelton, 16 March 1939, DEAR, MfT1750; King to Pattullo, 25 April 1939, TDPP, v. 73; *Vancouver Province,* 18 February 1938.

19 Memo to Mackenzie, 5 February 1938, IAMP, v. 34; Grant MacNeil to King, 27 February 1939, KP, #231059-60; HCD, 13 May 1939, 4035. Copies of these resolutions against nationals of aggressor nations investing in companies dealing with the export of raw materials, dated July and August 1939, are in GR1222, v. 156.

20 For details of the national campaign and an overall view of Canada's relations with Japan, see John D. Meehan, "Steering Clear of Great Britain: Canada's Debate over Collective Security in the Far Eastern Crisis of 1937," *International History Review* 25 (June 2003), 253-81.

   Vancouver Sun, 2 March 1939; *Vancouver Province,* 2 March 1939; *Vancouver News-Herald,* 5 August 1939. In July 1940 M.J. Coldwell, MP (CCF, Rosetown-Biggar), criticized the government for letting Japanese interests obtain valuable ore and timber limits near defence preparations (HCD, 31 July 1940, 2193). Coldwell repeated this in a radio broadcast during the October 1941 provincial election. In the same campaign, the Liberal attorney general claimed that G.H. Andrews, a Vancouver lumberman, a friend of the Japanese, and a Conservative, was exporting raw materials to Japan (*Vancouver Province,* 18 October 1941). In December 1938 opponents of Colonel Nelson Spencer, who was running for mayor in Vancouver, cited the need for "self-preservation," alleging that there was Japanese money or control in his lumbering business. Spencer vigorously denied the accusation but ran third with fewer than half the votes of Lyle Telford, the winner (*Vancouver Sun*, 5 and 12 December 1938; *Vancouver Province*, 29 November and 2, 13, and 15 December 1938). H.R. MacMillan to Clarence R. Fraser, 23 August 1938, HRMP, v. 6. MacMillan and other Canadian exporters lost their remaining business late in 1938 when Japan announced that it would purchase all forest products from the Pacific Northwest through a new Japanese firm, the American Importers' Association, whose staff was entirely Japanese and which bought all services, even printing, from Japan (MacMillan to W.D. Euler, 4 January 1939, HRMP, v. 92). As put by C.L. Shaw, a *Vancouver Province* reporter, "the Japanese intend to corral the business from sawmill or logging camp to the ultimate consumer in Japan or China" (22 December 1938). Canada could do nothing (Euler to MacMillan, 12 January 1939, HRMP, v. 92). Some Japanese-run logging operations continued. In September 1940 the Deep Bay Logging Company was fined $375 for failing to keep records of hours worked in English and to observe laws relating to hours of work, minimum wages, and the payment of monthly wages (*Victoria Times*, 7 September 1940).

21 *Vancouver Province*, 6 October 1937; *Vancouver Sun*, 23 November 1937; *Victoria Times*, 7, 15, and 23 December 1937; *Vancouver News-Herald*, 5 and 7 January 1938; *Victoria Colonist*, 17 February 1938. At the League of Nations, China's delegate complained that Canada sold raw materials to Japan (*Vancouver Sun*, 16 November 1937). In a private communication, R.B. Bennett suggested that King believed it was "more important for Canada to gather in a few dollars from the sale of products to Japan than to take the position which honour dictates we should take with respect to the conduct of Japan" (Bennett to Norman F. Priestley, 28 December 1937, RBBP, #524344).

An attempt to bomb a Japanese ship in Seattle caused little excitement. In January 1938 R.E. Forsyth, an unemployed chick-sexer with a master's degree in agriculture from the University of British Columbia, drowned while attempting to put a time bomb under a dock near where the *Hiya Maru* was anchored. One story suggested that Chinese interests based in San Francisco had hired him and an accomplice, also a Vancouver resident; another suggested that Japanese interests had hired him to create an incident (*Vancouver Sun*, 21 and 24 January 1938; *Victoria Times*, 25 January 1938).

22 Freda Utley, *Japan's Feet of Clay* (New York: W.W. Norton, 1937), 14. *Victoria Times*, 28 October 1938. The book had considerable circulation. H.R. MacMillan loaned his copy to the editor of the *Penticton Herald* (R.J. McDougall to MacMillan, 24 October 1938, HRMP, v. 6). A surviving date due sheet, at least the second, on a Victoria Public Library copy shows that it circulated twenty-six times between September 1939 and April 1947. Utley, who was born and educated in Britain, joined the Communist Party, married a Russian, and moved to Russia. At the time of her tour, she was living in the United States, where she remained for the rest of her life. While in British Columbia, she spoke at the university and at a meeting sponsored by the Medical Aid for China Committee, which unanimously supported an embargo (*Vancouver Province*, 4 November 1938).

3 *Victoria Times*, 10 December 1937, 2, 3, and 30 November 1938, and 27 February 1939; Macdonald, "The Question of an Embargo on the Sale of Canadian Raw Materials to Japan," 16 February 1938, DEAR, MfT1748; *Nanaimo Free Press*, 21 December 1938; *New Westminster British Columbian*, 23 January 1939; *Nelson Daily News*, 12 March 1939; *Prince Rupert Daily News*, 6 July 1939; New Westminster Board of Trade, Executive Meeting, 2 February 1939 (Mf in New Westminster Public Library); *Vancouver Sun*, 2 December 1938 and 24 January 1939; Mayhew to King, 15 February 1939, KP, #232622; HCD, 12 May 1939, 3997, and 13 May 1939, 4035. The embargo movement was not confined to British Columbia; delegates from Washington State attended the Pacific Northwest Embargo Conference in Vancouver in April 1939 (Pacific Northwest Embargo Conference, Report, Vancouver, April 22 and 23, 1939, copy in HDP).

24 King, Diary, 8 March and 1 August 1939, KD. One exception was Dr. V.J. Sipprell, who thought that such sanctions "would just stir things up" (*Victoria Times*, 8 December 1938). A.D.P. Heeney to A. Beauchene, 17 May 1939, KP, #223613; H.T. Allen to King, 17 April 1939, KP, #223339; G.H. Dunn, Kelowna, to King, 20 July 1939, KP, #226437; *Victoria Colonist*, 12 and 15 August 1939. King recognized a political problem and sought advice from the Department of External Affairs on how to comment. Skelton's observation that Australia and New Zealand had insisted on similar shipments being loaded, albeit "a good many months ago," was not very useful (Mackenzie to Skelton, 21 August 1939, and Skelton to King, 22 August 1939, DEAR, MfT1750; Skelton, Memo, 8 June 1939, DEAR, MfT1792).

25 King, Diary, 11 March 1940, KD; Henry F. Angus, *Canada and the Far East, 1940-1953* (Toronto: University of Toronto Press, 1953), 12; *Vancouver Province*, 20 and 28 June 1940. The matter of copper exports even arose in the British House of Commons (*Vancouver Province*, 19 September 1940). In the case of lead, the Department of External Affairs reported plentiful stocks, for which Japan was the only available export market. If Canada had stopped shipping lead, Japan would have obtained it from Mexico (N.A. Robertson to Skelton, 2 August 1940, DEAR, MfT1792; CWC, 13 August 1940); *Vancouver Sun*, 5 and 24 August and 7 October 1940; *Victoria Times*, 17 June and 1 August 1940; *Vancouver News-Herald*, reprinted in *Victoria Times*, 22 July 1940. In the spring of 1940, a small, unofficial Canadian trade commission that included Mayne D. Hamilton, superintendent of the Pacific Coast branches of the Canadian Bank of Commerce, accepted an invitation from the Japanese Foreign Trade Association to visit Japan. On his return Hamilton said that Japan was keen to have Canadian raw materials in order "to keep her manufacturing industries busy" (*Victoria Times*, 3 May and 20 June 1940). When some of his comments were misunderstood, Hamilton publicly criticized the militarists who controlled Japan's government (*Vancouver Province*, 19 July 1940).

26 W.E. Payne, Vancouver Board of Trade, to Mackenzie, 4 October 1940, and Reid to Mackenzie, 7 October 1940, IAMP, v. 24; H.R.L. Henry to J.L. Telford, 26 October 1940, VMC, 1940; *Victoria Colonist*, 2 October 1940; *Victoria Times*, 28 September and 7 October 1940; *Vancouver Sun*, 27 September and 9 October 1940; *New Westminster British Columbian*, 17 October and 2 November 1940; *Vancouver Province*, 7, 8, and 10 October 1940; *Prince Rupert Daily News*, 30 September 1940; *Kelowna Courier*, 10 October 1940. The *Victoria Colonist* called the copper embargo "logical" (10 October 1940). The *Prince Rupert Daily News* had earlier suggested that it might be better to have the revenue since Japan would buy copper elsewhere (1 May 1940); CWC, Minutes, 8 October 1940. Japan protested the discrimination since it was Canada's only major customer for copper outside the United States and the British Empire (Japanese Legation to External Affairs, 22 October 1940, DEAR, MfT1792).

27 G.E. Wellburn, Duncan Chamber of Commerce, to King, 15 February 1941, KP, #271283. The Canadian Chamber of Commerce endorsed the resolution (R.J. Magor to King, 1 March 1941, KP, #262618). The Duncan Chamber of Commerce had Captain J.D. Groves investigate when longshoremen loading logs onto Japanese ships at Ladysmith "found the cargoes below the decks of every one were largely made up of copper in various forms, huge steel ingots and brass scrap" (*Victoria Times*, 8 July 1940 and 13 February 1941; *Cowichan Leader*, 13 February and 13 March 1941; *Prince Rupert Evening Empire*, 21 April 1941; *Vancouver Province*, 18 December 1940; *Victoria Colonist*, 21 June 1940).

28 *Cowichan Leader*, 10 April 1941; Memo for Mackenzie King, 19 April 1941, DEAR, MfT1793; Memo "Re Canadian-Japanese Trade, Wheat and Wood," in King, Diary, 28 April 1941, KD. Concern about arousing "antagonistic feelings" and "risking the possibility of riots" led King to dither for over six weeks before letting the British divert to Vancouver for examination and possible seizure of cargo any Japanese merchant vessels suspected of carrying contraband for shipment to Germany. Before the examination facilities were set up, the Pacific war

began (King, Diary, 28 January 1941, KD; King to Chargé d'Affaires, Washington, 28 January 1941, DEAR, MfT1792; King to Secretary of State for Dominion Affairs, London, 11 February 1941, KP, #266664). The press reported that Britain and the United States were discussing putting an inspection post on the west coast of Vancouver Island, but Ottawa denied knowing anything about it (*Victoria Times*, 29 February 1940; Memo for King, 19 April 1941, DEAR, MfT1793; CWC, Minutes, 23 April and 1 May 1941). See HCD, 10 June 1941, 3782-85, for King's statement on trade with Japan.

29 *Vancouver Sun*, 7 June and 26 July 1941; Robertson to King, 10 May 1941, DEAR, MfT1809; Robertson to King, 10 June 1941, DEAR, MfT1793. Robertson admitted that the policy was determined "primarily by domestic political considerations" and by the fear that demonstrations against exports "could easily exacerbate the strong anti-Japanese sentiments in British Columbia" (Robertson to King, 23 April 1941, CWC). He noted that wheat exports might be possible through Prince Rupert, where there was less of a chance of longshoring problems or demonstrations. The *Victoria Times* twice broke the censor's ban. In June, in calling for an end to exports to Japan, it declared, "we know ... the government of this province and the government at Ottawa know, that ships are being loaded in our ports ... with goods for Japan that conceivably may be either converted to war materials for use against China," shipped through Russia to Germany, or eventually used against Canada and its allies (*Victoria Times*, 16 June and 28 July 1941); *Prince Rupert Daily News*, 13 June 1941; *Prince Rupert Evening Empire*, 11 June 1941; King to Canadian Minister at Washington, 26 July 1941, KP, #260574; King to Chargé d'Affaires, Tokyo, 26 July 1941, KP, #261462. *Victoria Times*, 28 July 1941; Henry F. Angus to F.J. Hume, 25 July 1941, DEAR, v. 2007; Report of Special Committee on Measures to Be Taken in the Event of War with Japan, 24 July 1941, DEAR, MfT1809.

30 *Nanaimo Free Press*, 6 December 1937; *Victoria Colonist*, 8 October 1937; *Vancouver Sun*, 30 October 1937; *Prince Rupert Daily News*, 18 December 1937.

31 *Vancouver Province*, 1 and 8 October 1937; *Victoria Times*, 24 September, 8 October, and 17 and 21 December 1937. *Victoria Colonist*, 7 December 1937. The pamphlet, *Sino-Japanese Conflict Elucidated*, and a printed circular of 23 October 1937 are in RBBP, #524328; Angus MacInnis to Canadian Japanese Association, 11 December 1937, AMacIP, v. 54A.

32 A.M. Stephen, a poet and president of the League Against War and Fascism, wrote a pamphlet, *War in China ... What It Means to Canada* (Vancouver: China Aid Council and the National Salvation League, [c. 1938]). Stephen, an old-time Socialist, was expelled from the CCF in 1937 for associating with the league (Dorothy Steeves, *The Compassionate Rebel* [Vancouver: Boag Foundation, 1960], 114-15; *New Westminster British Columbian*, 18 November 1937; Pacific Northwest Embargo Conference Report, Vancouver, 22 and 23 April 1939, HDP). The League for Peace and Democracy repeated its demonstration against the import of Japanese oranges in 1938 (*Vancouver Province*, 23 November 1938). British Columbia apple growers, who had a vested interest in cutting orange sales, endorsed the orange boycott but denied any motives other than patriotism. They claimed that 425,000 boxes of Japanese oranges had been imported in 1938 and 750,000 in 1939. They sought a tariff on Japanese oranges. South Vancouver Island Women's Institutes and the Provincial Council of Women revived the campaign against imported oranges in 1940. By the fall of 1941 foreign exchange restrictions had ended their import. Several branches of the British Columbia Fruit Growers' Association called for a boycott of all Japanese goods (*Vancouver Province*, 15 January 1941; *The Retailer* 34 [January 1941]: 9; *Vancouver Sun*, 14 January and 16 November 1940; *Kelowna Courier*, 14 and 21 November 1940; *Prince Rupert Daily News*, 26 November 1940; *Victoria Colonist*, 20 November 1940; *Kaslo Kootenaian*, 31 October 1940; *Victoria Times*, 18 and 21 November and 3 December 1940 and 14 January and 15 November 1941). Japan's chargé d'affaires in Ottawa complained that Toronto department stores Eaton's and Simpson's were not buying Japanese goods (L. Beaudry to Skelton, 20 September 1940, DEAR, v. 2007).

Wholesalers offered California oranges but imported Japanese oranges. Japanese growers would have suffered any loss since oranges were sold on consignment (*Cowichan Leader,* 1 November 1940; *Vancouver Sun,* 16 November 1940).

33 T.M., "The Japanese Boycott," *B.C. Lumber Worker,* 26 January 1938; *Vancouver Sun,* 16 March, 27 April, and 2 December 1938 and 29 September 1941; *Vancouver Province,* 19 January 1938 and 4 January and 6 February 1939.

34 *Victoria Colonist,* 3 September and 23 October 1937, 27 April 1938, and 18 March, 25 September, and 3 October 1940; *Vancouver Province,* 17 June 1938; *Cowichan Leader,* 5 January 1939; *Cranbrook Courier,* 26 January 1939; *Nanaimo Free Press,* 17 December 1937 and 24 January and 13 and 21 February 1939; *Kamloops Sentinel,* 18 April 1939; *Victoria Times,* 21 August and 5 October 1937, 22 October 1940, and 8 February, 16 May, 25 July, and 24 September 1941; *New Westminster British Columbian,* 1 June 1938; *Prince Rupert Daily News,* 19 April 1940; *Vancouver Sun,* 8 February and 21 June 1941; Wilson to Foon Sien, 17 March 1938, HDWPV, 551-D-2. Chinese communities throughout Canada and in Newfoundland raised funds to aid China. After the outbreak of the European war, their applications for permission to send funds to China may be found in NAC, Chinese Consulate (Canada) Fonds, v. 3.

Most of the controversy concerned the film *China Strikes Back,* which the League for Peace and Democracy proposed to show in order to raise money for medical aid for the Chinese army (*Vancouver Sun,* 14 February 1938). Military and police officials feared disturbances between Chinese and Japanese residents in British Columbia (Chief of the General Staff to Ashton, 21 August 1937, DNDR, v. 2671). Police in Vancouver, where clashes were most likely because of the size of the Chinese and Japanese populations and the proximity of Chinatown to "Little Tokyo," persuaded Chinese and Japanese organizations to agree not to refer to the Sino-Japanese war at public meetings. Individual Chinese residents refused to patronize Japanese businesses, and some Japanese leaders advised their countrymen not to patronize Chinese cafés in order to prevent trouble (W.W. Foster to Brig. D.J. MacDonald, Commanding, MD No. 11, 31 August 1937, VMC, v. 24). Teachers reported no problems in Vancouver schools. At the university, Chinese and Japanese students maintained friendships. As a Japanese student put it, "we are British subjects first, and Orientals afterwards" (*Vancouver Sun,* 20 December 1937). A report of a Japanese potato digger assaulting a Chinese man working in the same field at Cloverdale was newsworthy only because such incidents were rare (*New Westminster British Columbian,* 7 November 1940). Victoria's Chinese residents organized their own Air Raid Protection branch with instructions in both English and Chinese (*Victoria Colonist,* 16 January 1941); W.S. Chow to Minister of Finance, 6 December 1940, DImm, MfC10661. The only concession the Canadian government made to Chinese immigration was an extension – from one year to two years beyond the termination of the war – of the period during which landed immigrants might remain out of Canada (PC 10160, 31 December 1941).

35 MacMillan to Arthur Meighen, 21 April 1936, HRMP, v. 4. Ishimaru argued that England must abandon tariff and immigration discrimination (Tota Ishimaru, *Japan Must Fight Britain* [London: Hurst and Blackett, 1936], 155, 271, 280). According to a memorandum prepared for Minister of National Defence Mackenzie, Canada's chief military problem in the Pacific was "the risk of involvement in a war which might occur between the United States and some other Pacific power" (Memorandum for Mackenzie, 26 May 1937, KP, #203758); *Vancouver Sun,* 4 April 1936; Inglis Hosang, *Vancouver Province,* 11 April 1936.

36 *Vancouver News-Herald,* 9 April and 16 September 1936; *Vancouver Province,* 9 April 1936; *Victoria Colonist,* 15 September 1936; *Vancouver Sun,* 9 January 1937; *Port Alberni West Coast Advocate,* 21 January 1937; *Prince Rupert Evening Empire,* 2 January 1936; *Prince Rupert Daily News,* 4 March and 3 and 9 October 1936 and 22 February 1937.

37 The by-election followed the death of Simon Fraser Tolmie. W.N. Saunders to Mackenzie, 8 July 1937, Despard Twigg to Mackenzie, 13 July 1937, and L.R. LaFleche to Mackenzie, 28 July 1937, IAMP, v. 29; F.A. Willis to Mackenzie, 8 October 1937, IAMP, v. 27; *Nanaimo Free Press*, 18 August 1937; *Victoria Colonist*, 10 November 1937; *Victoria Times*, 25 November 1937; McKelvie to Bennett, 5 October 1937, RBBP, #522898-401; *Cowichan Leader*, 14 October 1937; *Victoria Colonist*, 9 October 1937. The *Prince Rupert Daily News* used McKelvie's arguments to justify constructing a highway to Alaska (30 October 1937); Barber to Bennett, 1 December 1937, RBBP, #522412-3. McKelvie did not cite Asian issues in explaining his defeat (McKelvie to Bennett, 4 December 1937, RBBP, #522416-8), a fact that Bennett had already observed (*Vancouver Province*, 30 November 1937). The CCF candidate, J. King Gordon, found it paradoxical that Canada was increasing its defences while exporting raw materials to Japan (*Victoria Colonist*, 18 November 1937); "Victoria By-Election," Speech Notes, IAMP, v. 38.

38 King, Diary, 30 September and 3 November 1936 and 7 and 11 January 1938, KD; *Prince Rupert Daily News*, 22 February 1937; *Nanaimo Free Press*, 6 August 1937 and 4 February 1938; *Victoria Times*, 18 November 1937; *Vancouver Province*, 14 December 1937 and 4 January 1938. The *Vancouver Sun* complained that the plans were "a good beginning" but inadequate (18 January 1938). The arrival of these destroyers in November 1938 doubled the destroyer fleet in Esquimalt and marked the first time that four destroyers had been moored there at one time (*Vancouver Province*, 7 November 1938).

39 *Vancouver Province*, 14 December 1937. The *Prince Rupert Daily News* also noted the need "to defend our shores" (8 January 1938); the *Prince Rupert Evening Empire* suggested that the government would not make such expenditures unless there was sound reason to do so (7 January 1938); *Victoria Times*, 7, 8, 25, and 27 January and 25 April 1938.

40 *Victoria Times*, 7 and 10 January and 6 April 1938; *New Westminster British Columbian*, 29 June 1938; New Westminster Board of Trade, General Meeting, 28 June 1938; Maj. J.G. Rycroft to DMAI, National Defence Headquarters, 22 January 1938, DNDR, v. 2671; *Penticton Herald*, 10 March 1938. This was a good example of the British Columbia complaint that "the East" did not understand their "Oriental problems." See Patricia E. Roy, "'Educating the "East"': British Columbia and the Oriental Question in the Interwar Years," *BC Studies*, 18 (Summer 1973): 50-69.

41 *Vancouver Sun*, 4 April 1938; HCD, 1 April 1938, 1966-68; *Vancouver Province*, 20 April 1938.

42 *Victoria Colonist*, 9 February 1938; *Victoria Times*, 2 March 1938; *Vancouver Province*, 1 March and 4 May 1938 and 30 September 1939; *Nelson Daily News*, 3 March 1938. The *Trail Daily Times* rarely commented on Asian matters, but an editorial on Japanese immigration mentioned the need to strengthen Canada's defences. After spy stories faded, it commented that "one of the things the Japanese did whole-heartedly absorb from the Occident was its espionage legend of actual fact and fiction" (3 March and 1 June 1938); *Vancouver Sun*, 1 March and 27 May 1938; Privy Council Office, Memorandum of Defence Council and Emergency Council 1938-39, and Memo of Chiefs of Staff Discussed at Meeting of Defence Committee of the Cabinet, 5 September 1939, PCOR, 7C, v. 1.

43 J.A. Clark, speech in Vancouver, 8 March 1940, JACP, v. 12; *Victoria Times*, 14 March 1940; *Prince Rupert Evening Empire*, 23 March 1940; *Vancouver Sun*, 6 March 1940. All Liberal incumbents were returned.

44 *Victoria Times*, 26 April, 11 June, and 25 September 1940; *Vancouver Sun*, 7 October 1940; *Vancouver News-Herald*, reprinted in *Victoria Times*, 27 June 1940; HCD, 28 June 1940, 1229.

45 *Nanaimo Free Press*, 18 September 1940; *Prince Rupert Daily News*, 14 February and 29 April 1941. Professor Henry F. Angus also admitted that war with Japan was likely (*Vancouver Province*, 21 October 1940); CWC, 8 October 1940; T.W.S. Parsons, "Position of the Japanese in British Columbia," 24 September 1940, Escott Reid to Skelton, 14 October 1940, and R.R.

Tait to Keenleyside, 28 October 1940, DEAR, v. 1867; Stockwell to Department of National Defence, 10 October 1940, DHist, 169.012 (D2). The Department of External Affairs determined that the United States Navy Department had similar concerns about Japanese residents in the United States although the State Department was less concerned (Tait to the Commissioner, 28 October 1940, RCMPR, v. 3564).

46 *Vancouver Province,* 27 September and 4 November 1940; Telford to Ralston, 27 September 1940, VMC, v. 41; Fire Chief to Fire and Light Committee, 29 October 1940, HDWP; Muriel Kitagawa, "Material for 'Crucible': Autobiographical Pieces," n.d., NWFP, file 2.

47 *Nanaimo Free Press,* 27 September 1940. As the situation deteriorated, the *Free Press* repeated such warnings (e.g., 18 and 21 February 1941); *B.C. Financial News,* quoted in *Victoria Times,* 7 October 1940; *Victoria Colonist,* 9, 10, and 11 October 1940.

48 King, Diary, 6 September 1939, 27 September 1940, and 17 November 1941, KD; "Notes on Far Eastern Situation," [c. 17 July 1940], DNDR, D1, v. 776; Memo re Meeting of Cabinet War Committee, 20 June 1940, High Commissioner in Great Britain to King, 18 July 1940, and H.G.D. Crerar to Cabinet War Committee, 26 July 1940, PCOR, 7C, v. 1; Pattullo to King, 8 August 1940, TDPP, v. 73; King to Pattullo, 21 August 1940, TDPP, v. 75. The outgoing letter is in KP, #248359. A few weeks later, King said that he expected Japan to "strike against British power" (King, Diary, 15 September 1940, KD). The Cabinet War Committee discounted an alarming cable from Vincent Massey, the high commissioner in the United Kingdom, which suggested that Japan might be planning an attack on the coast and that Japanese settlers in British Columbia had "their duties" (Vincent Massey to King, 28 February 1941, KP, #262971ff). See Patricia E. Roy, J.L. Granatstein, Masako Iino, and Hiroko Takamura, *Mutual Hostages: Canadians and Japanese during the Second World War* (Toronto: University of Toronto Press, 1990), 54; King to Massey, 14 June 1941, KP, #254012.

49 "Appreciation Defence of Pacific Coast of Canada," 18 November 1941, DNDR, MfC8366; Charles M. Cree, Staff Officer, to the C.O., Pacific Coast, re Conference with Col. Mulally, 6 August 1941, DNDR, v. 11764; King to Churchill, 2 March 1941, KP, #266870-3. Related correspondence and cabinet deliberations are in CWC, 5 March 1941; *Kamloops Sentinel,* 26 June 1941. The minister of national defence invited journalists to spend a few days with the Pacific fleet in Esquimalt in the fall of 1939 (*Vancouver Province,* 18 November 1939); Maj. H.C. Bray to Secretary, Department of National Defence, 29 April 1941, DNDR, v. 2671; *Nanaimo Free Press,* 11 July 1940 and 21 August 1941; *Kelowna Courier,* 6 March 1941; *Victoria Times,* 23 April 1941; *Vancouver Sun,* 15 August 1941. A Duncan newspaper encouraged readers to buy war savings bonds by citing Alexander's warning that "developments in the international situation bring the potential and possible dangers of actual conflict nearer to us" (*Cowichan Leader,* 6 November 1941).

50 *Prince Rupert Daily News,* 28 July 1941; *Cowichan Leader,* 21 August 1941; *Kamloops Sentinel,* 4 September 1941; *Nanaimo Free Press,* 5 and 17 September 1941; *Victoria Times,* 4 June, 5 September, and 1, 8, 15, and 18 October 1941; *Vancouver Sun,* 1, 13, and 22 August, 5 September, and 18 October 1941. Captain MacGregor Macintosh, MLA, called Wismer's tour "on alleged" Air Raid Protection (ARP) work "into places where there was not the slightest fear of a raid" an "example of Liberal organization and Liberal propaganda" (*Nanaimo Free Press,* 17 September 1941).

51 *Prince Rupert Daily News,* 14 July and 2 December 1941. See also *Prince Rupert Evening Empire,* 26 July 1941; *Cowichan Leader,* 4 September 1941; J.W. Cornett to King, 31 October 1941, KP, #256177; A. McGavin to R.W. Mayhew, 5 December 1941, IAMP, v. 26; *Vancouver Sun,* 15 September 1941.

52 Col. B.R. Mulally, "Comments on Developments in the Far East," 28 November 1941, DNDR, v. 11764; *Victoria Times,* 3 November 1941; *Vancouver Sun,* 26 November and 2 December 1941.

Chapter 7: "Poisoned by Politics"

1 Born in Glasgow, Scotland, Macintosh emigrated to Canada as a boy. He went overseas with a university group in the First World War, losing an arm, but made the army a career. In 1926 he married a daughter of Richard Mcbride.

2 *Victoria Colonist*, 19 January 1938; *Vancouver Province*, 19 January 1938. Thomas Reid, MP, endorsed Macintosh's charges but sought credit for having raised them some years earlier, after which, he claimed, 400 Japanese residents had been deported and 700 had disappeared (*Victoria Times*, 20 January 1938); Victor Okano, President, Japanese Young People's Association, to Editor, *Vancouver Province*, 16 January 1938; Herbert [indecipherable] to Halford Wilson, 17 December 1937, HDWPV, 551-A-6; Marie Elliott, *Mayne Island and the Outer Gulf Islands: A History* (Mayne Island: Gulf Islands Press, 1984), 57, 65-68.

3 *Victoria Times*, 9 February and 4 March 1938; *Victoria Colonist*, 1 February 1938; *Vancouver Province*, 9 February and 1, 16, and 23 March and 8 April 1938; *Vancouver Sun*, 9 and 26 February and 23 March 1938; *New Westminster British Columbian*, 22 March 1938.

4 *New Westminster British Columbian*, 28 January 1941; *Vancouver Sun*, 8 February 1940 and 16 February 1941; *Victoria Times*, 27 January 1941.

5 See Patricia E. Roy, "'Educating the "East"': British Columbia and the Oriental Question in the Interwar Years," *BC Studies*, 18 (Summer 1973): 50-69. In October 1941, in a report to the United Church, Rev. C.E. Silcox, director of the Canadian Council of Christians and Jews, suggested that a low Japanese standard of living would threaten that of other Canadians (Carmela Patrias and Ruth A. Frager, "'This Is Our Country, These Are Our Rights': Minorities and the Origins of Ontario's Human Rights Campaigns," *Canadian Historical Review* 82 [March 2001]: 5-6).

6 *Victoria Times*, 11 October 1935 and 24 January 1938; *New Westminster British Columbian*, 8 March 1938; *Vancouver Sun*, 23 February 1938 and 26 August 1940; *Kamloops Sentinel*, 12 November 1935; *Langley Advance*, 31 March 1938; *Nanaimo Free Press*, 26 April 1938.

When McGill University added to its staff Dr. Forrest E. La Violette, an expert on Japanese settlement on the Pacific Coast, the *Vancouver Sun* remarked that "the announcement says he has spent several summer holidays in Vancouver studying the situation in British Columbia. We hope so, because the people of Eastern Canada require much education on this Dominion's Oriental problem" (30 September 1940).

7 *Vancouver Province*, 22 February 1938; *Victoria Times*, 31 January 1938. See John Nelson, "Will Canada be Yellow?" *Maclean's*, 1 November 1921, 11-12, 45-47; Lukin Johnston, "The Case of the Oriental in B.C.," *Canadian Magazine*, August 1921, 315-18; C.L. Shaw, "The Rising Sun's Dark Shadow over Canada," *Liberty*, 11 November 1939, 14-17; Jim Marshall, "The Japanese Invasion," *Colliers*, 14 October 1939. P.W. Luce's regular "British Columbia Letter" in *Saturday Night* often reported on the situation and had such special articles as "Problem of the Native-born Japanese in B.C.," 31 December 1938, and "Vancouver Chinese Assimilate," 9 September 1939. One of B.K. Sandwell's essays appeared in *Saturday Night* on 4 February 1939; C.H. Young and H.R.Y. Reid, *The Japanese Canadians* (Toronto: University of Toronto Press, 1938); C.J. Woodsworth, *Canada and the Orient* (Toronto: Macmillan, 1941); *La Presse* (Montreal), 18 February and 16 April 1938, clipping in DImm, MfC4752; *Toronto Star*, 14, 16, 17, and 23 August 1938; Harold Dingman, in the *Toronto Globe and Mail*, 6 August 1938. The *Toronto Star* repeated a milder form of the allegations but carried a retraction two days later (6 and 8 August 1938). A.I. Jolliffe to file, 9 August 1938, DImm, MfC4752. In British Columbia only the *Nanaimo Free Press* seems to have picked up the story of the fleeing Japanese, which it hoped would remove the prime minister's "qualms" about abrogating the gentlemen's agreement (9 August 1938). Morton L. Bennett, "Rising Sun Sinks in West," *Winnipeg Free Press*, 9 November 1940, reprinted in *Victoria Times*, 7 December 1940; *Toronto Telegram*, quoted in *Vancouver Sun*, 26 August 1941.

8   *Vancouver News-Herald,* 16 April 1938; HCD, 24 May 1938, 3199; Marjory L. Gilbard to King, 4 June 1938, DEAR, v. 1430; copy of Canadian Daughters' League resolution, in KP, #C129390; *Victoria Times,* 5 October 1938; Vancouver Junior Board of Trade, "Fifteen Reasons Why the 'Gentlemen's Agreement' with Japan Should be Cancelled," with E.T. Orr, to Ernest Lapointe, 24 July 1939, and Orr to Lapointe, 29 March 1938 and 24 July 1939, ELP, v. 25; Orr to King, 29 March 1938, KP, #218291; *Prince Rupert Daily News,* 13 April 1938; *Trail Daily Times,* 28 May 1938; *Vancouver Province,* 28 October 1938.

9   Resolutions Passed at the National Conservative Convention, Ottawa, July 5, 6, and 7, 1938, RBHP, v. 48; Ian Mackenzie used the resolution to urge the prime minister to take more action (Mackenzie to King, 18 July 1938, DEAR, MfT1751). *Vancouver Sun,* 6 and 7 July and 22 October 1938; *Vancouver Province,* 22 October 1938 and 20 and 28 July 1939; *Vancouver News-Herald,* 8 August 1939.

10   The professor was K.W. Taylor of McMaster University. *Burnaby Broadcast,* quoted in *Langley Advance,* 2 September 1937; *Vancouver Sun,* 20 August, 9 September, and 11 December 1937; *Victoria Times,* 18 August 1937; *New Westminster British Columbian,* 23 October 1937 and 13 December 1937; Minutes of BC Conservative Association, Executive Meeting, 15 January 1938, WACBP, v. 6; *Vancouver Province,* 8 and 14 December 1937; *Fraser Valley Record,* 6 January 1938. The Canadian Legion's national convention referred the resolution to its incoming executive (*Vancouver News-Herald,* 4 February 1938).

11   Bruce Hutchison, in the *Vancouver Province,* 29 January 1938. Hutchison wrote a series of articles based on Carrothers's findings over the next two months. In Vancouver the number of Japanese births declined from nearly 1,600 in 1930 to fewer than 600 in 1938 (*Vancouver Province,* 20 May 1939). In October 1941 the city's medical health officer reported that the Japanese had a birth rate of 20.45 per thousand and a death rate of 7.92. The averages for all other non-Asian races combined were 17.73 and 11.58 respectively. With a birth rate of 8.86 and a death rate of 15.53, the Chinese, he said, faced extinction (*Vancouver Province,* 15 October 1941); *Victoria Times,* 22 January 1938; *Vancouver Province,* 3 January and 21 February 1938; *Vancouver Sun,* 1 March 1938; *Victoria Colonist,* 23 January 1938; *New Westminster British Columbian,* 22 and 24 January 1938.

12   *Vancouver Sun,* 10 and 12 February 1938; *Vancouver Province,* 11 February and 13 April 1938; *Nanaimo Free Press,* 19 February 1938; *B.C. Federationist,* 17 February 1938; *Vancouver News-Herald,* 11 February 1938. The *Nanaimo Free Press* supported Macintosh's call to investigate the "Oriental problem" (10 February 1938). *Victoria Times,* 24 January 1938; *Vancouver Sun,* 20 January 1938; *Prince Rupert Evening Empire,* 20 January 1938. Hutchison argued that "the only way" to stop the Japanese "from flooding this province" was to encourage them to raise their living standards by having smaller families (*Victoria Times,* 25 February 1938). Hutchison also wrote for the *Vancouver Sun* and the *Vancouver Province.* See also the *New Westminster British Columbian,* 9 December 1937.

13   *Vancouver Province,* 26 January 1938; *Victoria Colonist,* 27 January 1938; Pattullo to King, 26 January 1938, DEAR, MfT1751; *New Westminster British Columbian,* 16 February 1938; *Victoria Times,* 15 February 1938.

14   *Vancouver Sun,* 12, 14, 19, and 26 February 1938; *Nanaimo Free Press,* 3 February 1938; Mrs. R. Bancroft, East Burnaby-Edmonds Liberal Association, to King, 9 March 1938, KP, #210132. Resolutions from Vancouver Point Grey, Vancouver East, and Alice Arm, TDPP, v. 62; *Country Life in B.C.* 22 (March 1938): 18; C.E. Hope to King, 24 February 1938, RBBP, #529354-6; *Maple Ridge-Pitt Meadows Gazette,* 28 January 1938; *Vancouver News-Herald,* 8 March 1938; *Kamloops Sentinel,* 1 March 1938. The congress may have been an umbrella for several anti-Asian groups.

15   HCD, 9 March 1938, 1161-62. O.D. Skelton noted that because it would probably bar Hebrew speakers, though that was not its intention, the bill might find support in "unexpected quarters" (Skelton to King, 24 March 1938, KP, #C122852-8). Neill claimed that the language

bill overcame a principal objection to his other bill since it mentioned neither Japan nor exclusion (HCD, 10 May 1938, 2737). Though later regretting his decision, because the bill would have been "easy to debate and defeat," the prime minister had the bill ruled out of order on a technicality (King, Diary, 10 May 1938, KD; HCD, 10 May 1938, 2735-43, 24 May 1938, 3202, and 31 May 1938, 3410). Thomas Reid, Grant MacNeil, H.J. Barber, T.J. O'Neill, Grote Stirling, Angus MacInnis, and J.S. Taylor spoke. British Columbia had sixteen members.

16 *Port Alberni West Coast Advocate*, 3 March 1938; *Vancouver News-Herald*, 29 January 1938; *Trail Daily Times*, 3 March 1938; *Vancouver Province*, 19 and 24 February and 12 August 1938; *Vancouver Sun*, 14, 15, 19, and 28 February 1938; *New Westminster British Columbian*, 22 March 1938.

17 *Vancouver Province*, 10 February 1937. In 1942 the provincial secretary reported that in 1941 there had been eight mixed marriages in which one party was Oriental. Six Chinese grooms had white brides; two Japanese brides had white grooms. There were forty all-Chinese marriages and 174 that were all-Japanese (BCV&P, 21 January 1942).

18 R.T. Elson, in the *Vancouver Province*, 12 April 1938; *Vancouver Sun*, 26 April 1938; B.H. Warden, Acting City Clerk, to King, 26 April 1938, KP, #222651. Eight British Columbia members promised unconditional support. Mackenzie said that he would consider it; G.G. McGeer (Liberal, Vancouver-Burrard) referred it to the Department of Immigration, and a Conservative, Grote Stirling, noted that it had already been referred to a committee. Only Angus MacInnis questioned it, as he chastised Liberals and Conservatives for not supporting his 1936 resolution linking immigration and the franchise and warned that "trouble will be built up" if discrimination "towards Orientals in B.C." continued (*Vancouver Province*, 17 May 1938).

19 HCD, 17 February 1938, 550-57, 22 March 1938, 1589-92, and 24 May 1938, 3199. Keenleyside, who drafted much of King's speech, favoured appointing a Royal Commission to halt debate, provide authentic information for policy making, and satisfy British Columbia agitators (Keenleyside to Skelton, 3 February 1938, DEAR, MfT1751). Before the debate, King showed a secret British dispatch to Neill and to R.B. Bennett, leader of the opposition, but could not turn them against the bill (King, Diary, 16 and 17 February 1938, KD). Bennett, who believed that the sooner the gentlemen's agreement was "terminated the better it will be for this country," would only accept a delay in implementation to allow time for diplomatic negotiations (HCD, 31 January, 38 and 17 February 1938, 566); *Vancouver Sun*, 18 February and 12 May 1938; *Vancouver Province*, 18 February 1938; *Victoria Colonist*, 18 February 1938. Mackenzie absented himself from a debate (King, Diary, 22 March 1938, KD) rather than vote against the government and went through considerable intellectual contortions before voting against the bill (HCD, 24 May 1938, 3202).

20 *Victoria Times*, 18 February 1938; *Vancouver News-Herald*, 19 February 1938; *Vancouver Province*, 24 March 1938; see also the *New Westminster British Columbian*, 8 March 1938. A Swedish language newspaper, the *Vancouver Posten*, complained that thousands of Scandinavians were suffering from Japanese competition and criticized Parliament for killing Neill's exclusion bill (*Vancouver Province*, 19 February and 1 April 1938). *Vancouver Sun*, 18 February, 2 March, and 2 June 1938; *Nanaimo Free Press*, 19 February and 10 March 1938; *New Westminster British Columbian*, 8 March 1938; *Prince Rupert Evening Empire*, 19 February 1938; *Port Alberni West Coast Advocate*, 16 June 1938. On another occasion, The *B.C. Federationist* argued that Asian immigration continued only because the federal Liberal government wanted it (2 September 1938).

21 HCD, 17 February 1938, 575; *Victoria Times*, 18 February 1938. King promised Pattullo that he would consider checking for illegal immigrants. Skelton believed that the "fundamental cause" of anti-Oriental feeling was economic rather than racial, but reasons for objections varied among individuals (King to Pattullo, 10 February 1938, TDPP, v. 73; Skelton to Mrs. W.A. Hambly, 16 February 1938, DEAR, v. 1430; Skelton, "The Oriental Problem in

British Columbia," 28 February 1938, KP, #C122760-2; Skelton, Memo, 16 February 1938, DEAR, MfT1751; F.C. Blair to T.A. Crerar, 17 February 1938, and Blair, Memorandum, 28 February 1938, DImm, MfC4752). After the Yoshi scandal of 1931, a number of illegal immigrants, mainly deserting seamen or individuals using fraudulent birth or naturalization certificates, were found. The RCMP investigated illegal entries until 1936, when the Immigration Department refused to pay the cost (Memo for Skelton, 3 March 1938, DEAR, MfT1751). Early in 1938 the press reported the deportation of two Japanese residents who had entered in 1920 and 1921 respectively with false passports (*Vancouver Province,* 14 February 1938). Keenleyside, "Japanese in Canada," c. 15 March 1938, KP, #129335.

22 Mackenzie to King, 26 February 1938, KP, #216060; *Vancouver Sun,* 3 and 4 March 1938. See King's statement in HCD, 4 March 1938, 1035; The *Prince Rupert Evening Empire* expressed similar sentiments (15 March 1938).

23 King, Diary, 9 March 1938, KD; Skelton to King, 4 March 1938, DEAR, MfT1751. According to Keenleyside, the RCMP, with "more enthusiasm than judgment," planned "to spend thousands of dollars in pursuing illegal entrants all over the Province by car, boat and plane – to establish in short a 'reign of terror' among the Japanese residents of British Columbia." He warned that such a campaign would do little or no good, cause "unpleasant incidents," and encourage illegal entrants to escape to cities where they could hide. Moreover, the RCMP's only interpreter was working for him (Keenleyside to Blair, 2 May 1938, DImm, MfC4751). *Vancouver Province,* 21 March 1938; Board of Review, *Report* (Ottawa: King's Printer, 1939); *Nanaimo Free Press,* 25 March 1938; *Vancouver Sun,* 24 March 1938; *Victoria Times,* 26 March 1938.

24 Keenleyside to Blair, 29 and 31 March 1938, DImm, MfC4751; Minutes of Interdepartmental Committee, 7 March 1938, DEAR, MfT1751; *Vancouver Province,* 16 March 1938; *Vancouver Sun,* 16 March 1938; *British Columbia in the Canadian Confederation: A Submission Presented to the Royal Commission on Dominion-Provincial Relations by the Government of the Province of British Columbia* (Victoria: King's Printer, 1938), 59-64, 353; Royal Commission on Dominion-Provincial Relations, Report of Proceedings, 16 March 1938, 4858, British Columbia Legislative Library; D.A. McGregor, *Vancouver Province,* 17 March 1938. Because the subject needed to be handled "with care," the president of the provincial Conservative Association suggested that it might "better be left alone" (J.H. Morgan to B.A. McKelvie, 23 April 1938, BAMP, v. 4); *Vancouver Sun,* 30 March 1938; *Vancouver News-Herald,* 29 March and 5 April 1938; *Vancouver Province,* 29 March 1938; Pattullo to King, 20 October 1939, TDPP, v. 69; Skelton to King, 5 April 1938, KP, #C114416; BCLJ, 9 December 1938.

25 *Vancouver Province,* 10 August 1939; *Vancouver Sun,* 14 February 1940. An *Ottawa Citizen* reporter, noting Britain's plans to remove Japanese residents from England, suggested that a similar policy would enable Canada to settle districts vacated by Japanese residents with refugees from Britain or other friendly countries (Eric C. Jamieson, reprinted in *Victoria Times,* 20 November 1940). The *Vancouver Sun* favoured repatriation (21 July and 31 October 1939). Carrothers's paper on Oriental standards of living was published as an appendix to Young and Reid, *The Japanese Canadians,* without his knowledge (*Victoria Times,* 13 October 1938).

26 Keenleyside to Blair, 29 and 31 March and 5 April 1938, DImm, MfC4752; Keenleyside to Neill, 13 March 1941, and Hope to Keenleyside, 24 October 1938, DEAR, v. 1867; *Kamloops Sentinel,* 22 April 1938; *Kelowna Courier,* 5 May 1938; *Vancouver Province,* 13 May 1938; *The Retailer* 31 (May 1938): 6. Noting that it had "virtually no Oriental problem," Penticton did not make an official submission (*Penticton Herald,* 21 April 1938).

27 Ronald Morris Wynd, born in Japan to missionary parents, came to Canada via Edinburgh University and the Royal Air Force in 1924. He had served in the Royal Canadian Air Force but was at the time in question a commercial flier based in Toronto (Blair, Memorandum, 21 March 1938, DImm, MfC4752).

28 *Vancouver Province,* 10 May 1938; *Vancouver Sun,* 10 May 1938; *Victoria Times,* 10 May 1938; H.L. Keenleyside, *Memoirs: Hammer the Golden Day* (Toronto: McClelland and Stewart, 1981), 480-81; Keenleyside to Blair, 5 April and 2 May 1938; Board of Review (Immigration), Interim Report and Supplement, 14 May 1938, DImm, MfC4752; Keenleyside to Blair, 14 April 1938, DEAR, v. 1867; Keenleyside to Blair, 20 September 1938, DEAR, MfT1751. A "sit-down strike" of unemployed workers in Vancouver took police away from the immigration investigation. The government probably did not plan to publish the report but did so to halt further stories of illegal immigrants (F.W. Taylor to Blair, 30 May 1938, DImm, MfC4752); Blair to Charles Camsell, 18 June 1938, DCIR, v. 119; Neill to Skelton, 19 November 1938; Keenleyside to Skelton, 7 January 1939, Keenleyside to G.W. Fish and F.W. Taylor, 12 January 1939, and Skelton to Blair, 14 October 1940, DEAR, v. 1867; Keenleyside to Skelton, 9 October 1940, DEAR, v. 2007.

29 Neill to Skelton, 30 January 1938, DEAR, v. 1867; J.A. Young, Detective, British Columbia Police, to Lt. A.T. Morrell, H.M.C.S. Nootka, 15 December 1939, DNDR, v. 11913; *Vancouver Province,* 17 and 18 January 1939; *Vancouver Sun,* 17 January 1939.

30 *Vancouver Province,* 23 and 25 January 1939; Crerar to J.S. Taylor, 5 April 1938, DImm, MfC4752; Blair to file, 8 June and 21 July 1938, and "Orientals in British Columbia: Economic Competition with White Residents," c. 7 June 1938, DImm, MfC4752; Hugh Thornley to King, 24 March 1924, DImm, MfC4751; Thornley to J.W. Jones, 6 April 1925, JWJP. Even among those involved, there was confusion as to the precise relationship between the Board of Review and the interdepartmental committee (J.W. Pickersgill to King, 31 January 1939, KP, #C122618). The White Canada Research Committee report was prepared as a submission to the Royal Commission on Dominion-Provincial Relations, but the commission refused to receive the report because the subject was outside its jurisdiction (Confidential Report to Council on the Oriental Problem in Canada, with F.C. Blair, to King, 30 August 1938, KP, #210488-99 [italics in original]); HCD, 30 January 1939, 430, and 30 May 1939, 4731; Interdepartmental Committee on Orientals in Canada, 20 July 1938, DEAR, v. 1867. In providing background for King's speeches on the exclusion bill, Keenleyside revived the idea of reciprocal agreements (Keenleyside, Memorandum, 4 February 1938, KP, #C122589). Officials continued to consider ways of halting Asian immigration ("Japanese Immigration into Canada: Alternative Solutions," DEAR, v. 1867). King's advisors reported that China's government had not protested but that commercial and nationalistic organizations had expressed opposition, as had similar bodies in Japan; they noted, however, that serious protests had been few in recent years ("Notes for Sessional Folder on Japanese Immigration," c. fall 1938, KP, #C122693ff). Keenleyside proposed trying to negotiate an agreement whereby British Columbia would end political and legal discrimination against Orientals in return for an end to immigration, the deportation of illegal immigrants, and the issuing of identification cards to all Japanese residents (Keenleyside to Skelton, 28 October and 10 December 1938, DEAR, v. 1867).

31 Keenleyside, *Hammer the Golden Day,* 432. The Tokyo legation also dealt with China. Keenleyside to Skelton, 24 September 1935, and Hope to King, 24 September 1937, DEAR, v. 3193; Keenleyside to Skelton, 20 February 1936, DEAR, MfT1748; "Canada and China: A Summary," 31 March 1936, KP, #C111316-351; Hope to King, 23 November 1934, DEAR, v. 1756; Skelton to King, 4 February 1938, DEAR, MFT1751; HCD, 17 February 1938, 570; King, Diary, 23 March 1938, KD; interview with Keenleyside, 11 December 1980, in F.J. McEvoy, "A Symbol of Racial Discrimination: The Chinese Immigration Act and Canada's Relations with China, 1942-1947," *Canadian Ethnic Studies* 14, 3 (1982): 25-26.

2   Confidential Report to Council, 30 August 1938, KP, #210488-99; King, Diary, 23 and 24 May 1938, KD. That summer, King told Tomii, in the presence of Matsunaga, the former consul general, that he needed their help in stopping migration to avoid an exclusion law (King, Diary, 26 August 1938, KD). Mackenzie and Turgeon voted with the government; two Liberals, G.G. McGeer (Vancouver-Burrard) and R.W. Mayhew (Victoria), were absent (HCD, 24

May 1938, 3201); King to Malcolm MacDonald, 10 January 1939, DEAR, v. 1430; R.R. Bruce to King, 16 December 1938, KP, #C122614ff; Keenleyside to Skelton, 13 December 1938, KP, #C112612; MacDonald to King, 25 January 1939, KP, #234879-80; E.D. McGreer to King, 30 January 1939, KP, #229736-7. With King's permission McGreer consulted the American ambassador in Tokyo, who concurred (McGreer to King, 3 February 1939, KP, #229739). There was little follow-up, but the Department of External Affairs remained sensitive to Japan's feelings. In August 1940 the chargé in Tokyo, with the agreement of the British ambassador, suggested that if any Canadians were apprehended during Japan's anti-British campaign, he should be empowered to notify the Foreign Office of the cancellation of the gentlemen's agreement. Keenleyside warned that this would cause bitterness and that Japan might retaliate by expelling Canadians (Keenleyside to Skelton, 7 August 1940, DEAR, v. 1430; King, Diary, 30 and 31 January 1939, KD; HCD, 23 February 1939, 1346, 14 March 1939, 1884, and 3 April 1939, 2556).

33 Anticipated questions on immigration did not arise (Skelton to Blair, 9 April 1940, and M.C. Ironside to Department of Mines and Resources, 21 July 1938, DImm, MfC4752). *Port Alberni West Coast Advocate*, 23 June 1938; *Vancouver Province*, 5 and 26 August 1938; Resolutions for British Columbia Liberal Convention, 8 August 1938, TDPP, v. 61; *Vancouver Sun*, 26 August and 4 November 1938; Memo of Discussion with Pattullo and His Colleagues, 26 September 1938, KP, #C114445; *Kamloops Sentinel*, 27 September 1938; Resolutions Passed at the British Columbia Conservative Party Convention, Kamloops, 23 and 24 September 1938, WACBP, MG 1/1, b. 6; Torchy Anderson, *Vancouver Province*, 17 November 1938; Bruce Hutchison, *Vancouver Sun*, 17 November 1938; BCV&P, 23 November and 9 December 1938; *Victoria Times*, 4 November 1938.

34 *Vancouver Sun*, 10 December 1938; *Victoria Times*, 9 December 1938; Pattullo to King, 6 January 1939, TDPP, v. 70. On financial matters, Pattullo still had an amiable relationship with King (Robin Fisher, *Duff Pattullo of British Columbia* [Toronto: University of Toronto Press, 1991], 316-17); Memo of Conference with Mr. Pattullo, 10 January 1939, KP, #C114460; King, Diary, 10 January 1939, KD; Mackenzie to King, 19 December 1938, KP, #216254; *Vancouver Province*, 27 June and 25 July 1939; *B.C. Federationist*, 10 August 1939.

35 *Vancouver Province*, 21 February and 23 and 25 March 1940; *Comox District Free Press*, 7, 14, and 21 March 1940; *Vancouver Sun*, 23 March 1940; *Vancouver News-Herald*, 1 March 1940; *New Westminster British Columbian*, 7, 8, 9, 14, and 21 March 1940.

36 *Prince Rupert Daily News*, 7 and 8 March 1937, 1 and 21 February 1938, and 11 March 1940. The chamber complained that half of the gas boat licences had been issued to Japanese residents (*Prince Rupert Daily News*, 5 March 1938).

37 J.F. Booth to J.G. Gardiner, 9 April 1936, and Hugh Dalton, BC Salt Fish Board, to W.C. Hopper, 26 March 1936, DAgri, v. 3354; J.M. Buchanan to G.S. Pearson, 12 July 1938, HDWP; *Port Alberni West Coast Advocate*, 20 May 1937; *Vancouver Province*, 13 January 1938; *Victoria Colonist*, 20 September 1938; Pattullo to Kenji Nakauchi, 4 September 1939, GR1222, v. 96. Explaining that he had no direct interest in Japanese canners who were "not citizens of my country," the Japanese consul asked the premier to reconsider a decision affecting international trade (Nakauchi to Pattullo, 28 September 1939, GR1222, v. 96). The chargé in Ottawa also emphasized trade (G. Omori to King, 2 October 1939, KP, #227227).

38 HCD, 23 February 1938, 733-37; Canada, Department of Fisheries, *Annual Report*, 1937-38 (Ottawa: King's Printer, 1938), 23; *Vancouver Province*, 2 October 1940. When Koichi Imai was charged with failing to produce a gill-net licence, rumours of a "big fund" for his defence suggested that this was a test case. Although his lawyer intimated that Imai would appeal his fine of twenty-five dollars and costs, no appeal appears to have followed (*Vancouver Sun*, 24 February 1938; *Nanaimo Free Press*, 24, 25, and 26 February 1938; *New Westminster British Columbian*, 5 March, 5 April, and 9 September 1938). H.R. MacMillan agreed that

they lived "for almost nothing" and sent most of their earnings to Japan (MacMillan to W. A. Carrothers, 18 March 1938, HRMP, b. 6). According to Geoff Meggs, who provides no documentation, the abolition of boat pullers' licences followed prolonged efforts by two fisheries officials, J.A. Motherwell and W.A. Found, to reduce the number of Japanese fishermen (*Salmon: The Decline of the British Columbia Fishery* [Vancouver: Douglas and McIntyre, 1991], 131). Keenleyside said that the matter had not been handled well, had not been widely demanded, was opposed even by Neill, and faced a possible court challenge (Keenleyside to Skelton, 30 June 1938, DEAR, v. 1874). The interdepartmental committee recommended spreading the reduction over four years (Minutes, 20 June 1938, DEAR, v. 1874; Chairman of Committee to King, 21 June 1938, DImm, MfC4752; J.E. Michaud to Mackenzie, 17 January 1940, IAMP, v. 19; *Vancouver Province,* 14 and 28 March 1939).

39 BCLJ, 8 December 1938; *Vancouver Province,* 24 February and 19 November 1938 and 17 January, 13 March, and 7 December 1939; MacMillan to Sandwell, 7 August 1938, HRMP, v. 24; *Vancouver Sun,* 13 March 1939; *Nanaimo Free Press,* 5 June 1940. After some debate, Bruhn withdrew his motion.

40 Wilson to A.V. Hill, 20 April 1940, and Blair to Michaud, 29 May 1940, HDWP; MacMillan to Sandwell, 23 August 1938, HRMP, v. 24; A.L. Jolliffe to Skelton, 29 May 1940, DImm, MfC4752; *Vancouver Sun,* 26 July 1941; Commanding Officer, Pacific Coast, Memo, 2 May 1941, DNDR, v. 11867.

41 Young and Reid, *The Japanese Canadians,* 55-56, 270; *Vancouver Sun,* 5 October 1938; *Vancouver Province,* 12 December 1938.

42 HCD, 23 February 1938, 735; *B.C. Federationist,* 10 and 17 March 1938; *Vancouver Sun,* 16 February 1938; *Vancouver Province,* 16 March 1938; *New Westminster British Columbian,* 12 and 17 March 1938.

43 *Vancouver Province,* 30 November 1939; P.W. Luce, "Vancouver Chinese Assimilate," *Saturday Night,* 9 September 1939.

44 *Vancouver Sun,* 15 August, 13 October, and 12 December 1933, 6 September 1935, and 25, 26, and 28 March 1938; *Vancouver Province,* 20 March and 13 December 1934; Patricia E. Roy, *Vancouver: An Illustrated History* (Toronto: James Lorimer, 1980), 123; "Mayor McGeer's Fight against Crime in Vancouver, Radio Speech, CKWX, 15 September 1935," GGMcGPA, v. 7; A. Grundy to G. Miller, 10 May 1937, VMC, v. 24; *New Westminster British Columbian,* 25 March 1938. For an overview of the police response to Chinese gambling, see Greg Marquis, "Vancouver Vice: The Police and the Negotiation of Morality," in *Essays in the History of Canadian Law: British Columbia and the Yukon,* ed. Hamar Foster and John McLaren (Toronto: Osgoode Society, 1995), 246-52; Report on Clubs, Gambling and Lottery Conditions in the City of Vancouver, 12 January 1939, VMC, v. 33; Donald McKay to L.J. Telford, 4 November 1938, VMC, v. 32.

45 *Vancouver News-Herald,* 10 October 1935; *Vancouver Province,* 14 October 1936 and 1 February 1937. Wilson complained about the consumption of liquor in enclosed booths and boxes in restaurants. The police said that such immorality was "practically non-existent" and that Asians operated fewer than half of the 138 restaurants with such facilities (W. Grinsdall to C.E. Tisdall, 11 April 1935, and Urquhart to Tisdall, 13 April 1935, VCCCl, v. 182; Urquhart to Finance Committee, 22 January 1936, VCCCl, v. 203); *Victoria Times,* 30 November 1936; *Vancouver Sun,* 10 October 1935; Foster to Miller, 5 and 27 February and 6 March 1937, and Dennis Murphy to Miller, 6 May 1937, VMC, v. 26. For a fuller account, see Kay Anderson, *Vancouver's Chinatown: Racial Discourse in Canada, 1875-1980* (Montreal and Kingston: McGill-Queen's University Press, 1991), 158-65.

.6 See Roy, *Vancouver,* 123; Foster to Miller, 3 September 1937, VMC, v. 26; Foster to Fred Howlett, November 1937, VCCCo, v. 213; *New Westminster British Columbian,* 23 June 1937; *Vancouver Province,* 23 and 30 June 1937.

47 *Vancouver Sun,* 16 and 18 September, 12 October, and 19 November 1937 and 15 August 1938; Denis Murphy to Oscar Orr, 29 September 1937, VMC, v. 26; *Vancouver Province,* 21 March 1939. Note, 26 September 1938, on H.A. Urquhart, to City Council, 9 September 1938, VCCCl, v. 222. To reinforce his arguments, Foster later sent Mayor Telford a statement from a woman, recently arrested for prostitution, who said that "the finest thing that has ever been done for the moral welfare of white girls [is] to ban them out of Chinatown cafés and they should always be kept out" (Foster to Telford, 28 April 1939, VMC, v. 32). The city police were trying to suppress prostitution as part of a provincial venereal disease control campaign. Police found young girls who prostituted themselves in Chinese residences and then tipped off their pimps or friends, who robbed Chinese clients carrying large sums of money. Files on the campaign contain relatively little relating to Chinese residents (A.S. Rae to W.W. Foster, 9 May 1939, VMC, v. 32). Other Canadians also wanted to limit the employment of white women by Orientals. At a convention in Montreal in December 1938, the Canadian Federation of Labour approved a resolution from Calgary asking for laws to make it illegal for white girls under the age of twenty-one to work in Oriental establishments and for all white girls to work in them after 10 p.m. (*Vancouver Sun,* 8 December 1938).
48 In what may have caused an interesting family debate, in 1941 Wilson's mother chose Kimi Miramatsu to give the welcoming address to the diocesan meeting of the Church of England Girls Auxiliary (*Vancouver News-Herald,* 11 March 1941).
49 A.W. Greenwood, in *The Retailer* 29 (November 1936): 1; *Vancouver Province,* 5 March and 6 July 1937.
50 Wilson to R.B. Bennett, 28 January 1938, RBBP, #529349; Wilson to "Attorney-General, Parliament Buildings, Washington, D.C.," 3 February 1938, HDWP; (*Vancouver Sun,* 21 February and 1 March 1938); *B.C. Federationist,* 17 March 1938. Wilson briefly revived the idea in the summer of 1939 by suggesting restricting Orientals to their own districts "unless we can get rid of them entirely." He proposed that the city register a covenant on its property "forbidding it ever to be sold or rented to or occupied by Orientals" (*Vancouver Province,* 8 August 1939; *Vancouver News-Herald,* 8 August 1939). The city owned extensive undeveloped land within its boundaries, a fact that would have denied Asians access to new subdivisions.
51 *Vancouver Province,* 8, 24, and 29 March and 15 May 1938; *Vancouver Sun,* 23 March 1938. In presenting his weekly list of applications for new licences or transfers, the licence inspector did not mention race or nationality, but when new applicants had Chinese or Japanese names, he referred to the health bylaw. From time to time, he recommended cancelling licences of Chinese and Japanese stores that violated closing hour bylaws (see VCCCl, v. 222). Among the few to endorse Wilson's campaign were the Native Daughters of British Columbia (*Vancouver News-Herald,* 11 May 1938). Wilson to A.H. McRobbie, 13 December 1938, HDWPV, 551-A-6. DeGraves headed a civic inquiry into alleged price fixing by the Japanese-dominated Consolidated Cod Fishermen's Association. The inquiry found no price fixing but recommended a quota on cod fishing licences issued to Asians, which Federal Fisheries Inspector J.A. Motherwell pointed out was already in effect (*Vancouver Sun,* 11 and 14 October 1938). The association's lawyer, T.G. Norris, rightly accused DeGraves of attempting to use racial prejudice for publicity (*Vancouver Province,* 5 May 1938); *Vancouver News-Herald,* 12 July 1938; *Vancouver Sun,* 12 July 1938; D.E. McTaggart to Fred Howlett, City Clerk, 26 February 1938, VCCCl, v. 226. The *Vancouver Sun* thought that if the city could deny licences to businesses "inimical to the welfare of the city" or exclude industries from certain areas, it could say that "a Japanese store in a white district is contrary to public welfare and should not be permitted to continue" (*Vancouver Sun,* 23 February 1938); *Vancouver Sun,* 28 February 1938, 15 November 1939, and 26 April 1940; *Vancouver Province,* 15 October 1938.
52 See Patricia E. Roy, "Protecting Their Pocketbooks and Preserving Their Race: White Merchants and Oriental Competition," in *Cities in the West,* ed. A.R. McCormack and Ian

MacPherson (Ottawa: National Museum of Man, 1975), 116-38; Wilson and DeGraves, "Brief on the Oriental Situation in British Columbia in the Year 1938," Submitted to Keenleyside, Board of Review, 6 May 1938, HDWPV.

53 W. Peter Ward, "The Oriental Immigrant and Canada's Protestant Clergy, 1858-1925," *BC Studies*, 22 (Summer 1974): 40-55; *Victoria Times*, 25 February 1938; *Vancouver News-Herald*, 9 March 1938 and 9 July 1939; *Vancouver Province*, 15 November 1938.
   At a meeting sponsored by the Vancouver League of Nations Society and the General Ministerial Association, 2,500 people condemned Germany's treatment of its Jewish minority and urged the Canadian government to open Canada's doors "to an appreciable number of Jewish refugees" (*Vancouver Sun*, 21 November 1938). Victor W. Odlum chaired the meeting. Among the speakers were W.M. Duke, Roman Catholic archbishop of Vancouver; Rev. Geo. Biddle; Rev. G. Harrison Villett; Bertram Lewis; Canon W. Cooper; Mrs. F. Rolston, head of the Provincial Council of Women; A.E. Jamieson of the Trades and Labour Council; and Dr. W.G. Black of the University of British Columbia. Both major Vancouver newspapers saw the presence of Asians as a problem but recognized their need to make a living (*Vancouver Sun*, 16 and 23 November and 18 October 1938). The *Vancouver Province* hoped that the issue might bring an "apathetic" Parliament's attention to "the urgency and seriousness of the Oriental menace to British Columbia." At a Conservative Club meeting, Howard C. Green praised Wilson's efforts and advised his audience that "if we don't take a stand on it, the rest of Canada won't" (*Vancouver Province*, 16, 19, and 23 November 1938).

54 *Vancouver Province*, 13 and 27 September 1938 and 12, 20, 22, 27, and 29 April 1939; *Vancouver Sun*, 25 October and 16 November 1938 and 12 and 25 April 1939; *The Retailer* 31 (December 1938). On the election, see also Wilson's advertisement in *Labour Statesman*, May 1939, a publication of the Trades and Labour Council; *Vancouver News-Herald*, 25 April 1939. Jamieson received 3,730 votes, Corey, 3,587, and Wilson, 3,572 (Elections British Columbia, *Electoral History of British Columbia, 1871-1986* [Victoria: Elections British Columbia, 1988], 190).

55 In fact, the rate of natural increase among Japanese residents in British Columbia – that is, the excess of births over deaths – had been steadily declining from a peak of 598 in 1934 to 362 in 1939 ("Vital Statistics of Japanese in British Columbia Compiled from the Bulletin of the B.C. Board of Health by Dr. M. Miyazaki," Canadian Japanese Association, MMP). Preliminary reports from the Department of Vital Statistics indicated that the trend was continuing; in 1940 there were only 263 more Japanese births than deaths (*Victoria Times*, 5 April 1941).

56 DeGraves retired. Jones, a former city clerk and a licence inspector, promised to check penetration of Orientals in the retail trade (*Vancouver News-Herald*, 26 September and 9 December 1939; *Vancouver Province*, 19 and 20 July, 15 August, 20 September, 25 October, and 9 and 12 December 1939 and 10 and 16 January 1940; *Vancouver Sun*, 15 November 1939 and 10 January 1940; Wilson to Mayor and Council, 22 May 1940, HDWP). The Municipal Act did not affect Vancouver, which had its own charter, but the attorney general's office said that such a measure would be *ultra vires* the 1911 treaty. In 1938, New Westminster refused to issue licences to Orientals but reached a compromise before the courts ruled (*Vancouver Province*, 18 October 1938).

57 *Nanaimo Free Press*, 20 August and 4 September 1940; *Victoria Times*, 29 May 1940; *Victoria Colonist*, 27 September 1940.

58 *Vancouver Sun*, 22 November 1940; *Vancouver Province*, 4 and 30 October and 13 November 1940. Mayor Telford said that the amendment was unnecessary. Attorney General Wismer was sympathetic but privately explained that the legislature had no power to legislate for a "particular race" and thought it unwise to regiment an entire community to deal with "a very few people" (Wismer to Wilson, 28 December 1940, HDWP; *Victoria Colonist*, 14 November 1940; *Vancouver News-Herald*, 29 October 1940).

59 *Mount Pleasant Review,* 16 October 1940, and *Vancouver Parashooter,* n.d.; *Vancouver Province,* 10 and 12 December 1940 and 18 March and 13 August 1941; *Vancouver Sun,* 4, 10, and 12 December 1940 and 18 March 1941; Keenleyside to Skelton, 11 June 1940, DEAR, v. 2007; Keenleyside to T.C. Davis, 7 February 1941, DEAR, v. 1867.

60 *Victoria Times,* 10 and 25 January 1938; R.L. Cadiz, A/Commr, E Division, RCMP, Report, 19 November 1937, and D.C. Tweedhope to OC, A Division, Victoria, 10 January 1938, DNDR, v. 11917. The provincial police in Chemainus investigated a report of illegal immigrants replacing ex-servicemen returning to Japan but found no evidence of this claim or of Japanese drilling (S. Service, Cpl. 126, Chemainus Detachment, to N.C.o. District, Duncan, 4 February 1938, DImm, MfC4752). *Cowichan Leader,* 20 January 1938; *Maple Ridge Leader,* 3 February and 14 April 1938; *Vancouver Province,* 2 March 1938; Percy Rosomon to Mackenzie, 23 December 1937, IAMP, v. 34; Gordon Sloan to Mackenzie, 18 January 1938, and S.T. Wood to Lt.-Col. H.D.G. Crerar, 24 February 1938, IAMP, v. 30; *Vancouver Sun,* 22 December 1937.

61 C.H. Hill, Superintendent, E Division, to Commissioner, 25 August 1938, DImm, MfC4752; F.R.W.R. Gow, Naval Staff Officer, Esquimalt, to Admiral Nugent (ret), 5 December 1937, and Gow to Director of Naval Intelligence and Plans, 9 February 1938, DNDR, v. 11917; LaFleche to F.C. Blair, 1 and 15 June 1938, DHist 322.009 (D538).

62 MacMillan to Sandwell, 7 August 1939, HRMP, v. 24; MacMillan to Davis, 25 April 1941, Hope to Keenleyside, 12 May 1941, and Keenleyside to Hope, 19 May 1941, DEAR, v. 2007; *Nanaimo Free Press,* 8 March 1938; *Vancouver Sun,* 8 March 1938; *Kamloops Sentinel,* 1 March 1938; *Prince Rupert Daily News,* 28 July 1941.

63 On 7 September 1939 the *Kelowna Courier* said that Japanese residents were suspected of having good knowledge of every vulnerable point in British Columbia but that war with Japan was not immediately expected. It called for protecting bridges, power plants, and other utilities against German saboteurs. H. Napier Moore, Editor, Maclean's, to Francis Dickie, 13 July 1939, FDP, v. 2; J.K. Barnes, Reports, 28 August and 16 December 1939, DEAR, v. 1867.

64 *Vancouver Sun,* 24 August 1939, 3 and 6 February 1940, and 10 June 1941; *Nanaimo Free Press,* 15 March 1940 and 28 and 29 July 1941; *Prince Rupert Daily News,* 5 August 1940, 17 March, and 17 April 1941; *Victoria Times,* 7 December 1939; *New Westminster British Columbian,* 19 and 24 January and 28 November 1940; *Cowichan Leader,* 22 February 1940; *Prince Rupert Evening Empire,* 29 January 1940 and 17 March 1941; *Comox District Free Press,* 15 February 1940. There is an extensive file on contributions in VMC, v. 41; *Vancouver News-Herald,* 9 August 1940; Young and Reid, *The Japanese Canadians,* 111; Ken Adachi, *The Enemy That Never Was* (Toronto: McClelland and Stewart, 1976), 123; *Vancouver Province,* 10 August 1940.

65 Tsutae Sato to J.W. Cornett, 11 January 1941, HDWP; Gar Macpherson, *Vancouver Sun,* 15 January 1941; Wilson and DeGraves, "Brief on the Oriental Situation in British Columbia in the Year 1938," Submitted to Keenleyside, Board of Review, 6 May 1938, 13, HDWPV; *Vancouver Sun,* 14 January and 26 July 1941; *Vancouver Province,* 14 January 1941; Arthur Laing to G.M. Weir, 20 August 1940, GR1222, v. 27; P.W. Luce, "British Columbia Letter," *Saturday Night,* 26 April 1941; *New Westminster British Columbian,* 14 March 1941; *Cowichan Leader,* 20 February 1941; *Victoria Times,* 4 March 1941. Wilson quoted the director of public school medical services as saying that extended schooling hours harmed the health of students (*Vancouver Sun,* 15 January 1941).

66 *Vancouver Sun,* 11 November 1940. The League did not speak for all Japanese Canadians. Its Vancouver chapter enrolled only 200 of nearly 1,000 eligible members (Minutes of Vancouver Chapter, 5 May 1941, JCCL). In 1939, in accepting the League's gift of a silver cup as a prize for presentation at an annual oratorical competition at Victoria High School, a trustee commented that young Japanese residents in Victoria accepted the ideals of Canada and the British Empire (*Victoria Colonist,* 30 September 1939). Despite the school board's refusal to allow them to use facilities at Victoria College "in view of the international situation," the

League met in Victoria in 1941. Mayor Andrew McGavin welcomed them as people who "were as loyal to their country as any other group of settlers in Canada" (*Victoria Times*, 11 June and 10 October 1941).

67 *New Canadian*, 15 September 1940; R. Ovens to Commissioner, BC Provincial Police, 24 September 1940, TDPP, v. 73; *Victoria Times*, 25 September and 17 October 1940; *Vancouver Sun*, 24 September and 5 October 1940; *Prince Rupert Daily News*, 7 October 1940; *Vancouver News-Herald*, 2 October 1940; *Vancouver Province*, 25 September 1940. In September 1940 the *Empress of Asia* suffered slight damage when Japanese fliers "accidentally" bombed it. The Japanese consul said that Nisei should enjoy full privileges of Canadian citizenship but cautioned them against using military service to bargain for political rights (*Nanaimo Free Press*, 30 September 1940). For details see Patricia E. Roy, "The Soldiers Canada Didn't Want: Her Chinese and Japanese Citizens," *Canadian Historical Review* 59 (September 1978): 341-58.

68 In a by-election in Dewdney in 1938, Liberals and Conservatives used the issue to embarrass CCF candidate Mildred Osterhout (*Vancouver Province*, 19 May and 4 July 1938; *Vancouver Sun*, 19 May and 4 July 1938; *Maple Ridge-Pitt Meadows Gazette*, 6 May 1938). The CCF's National Council believed that a plebiscite was contrary to its principles of equality of status and asked the British Columbia branch of the party to reconsider (MacInnis to A.R.M. Lower, 14 September 1938, AMMC, v. 54A); *Langley Advance*, 1 July 1937; *Port Alberni West Coast Advocate*, 7 July 1938; *Victoria Times*, 7 December 1939; *Victoria Colonist*, 17 November 1937; *Vancouver Province*, 23 March and 8 April 1938; *Vancouver News-Herald*, 27 July 1939.

69 Pattullo to King, 23 September 1940, CWC, v. 2; Wismer to J.L. Ralston, 23 September 1940, DEAR, v. 1867; Pattullo to King, 23 September 1940, TDPP, v. 70. Wismer claimed that call-ups would interfere with plans to disarm Chinese and Japanese residents, whose loyalty they doubted. In November 1941 Pattullo agreed not to oppose Japanese enlistments if enlistees knew that they would "not now" have the right to vote and were sent out of the province as soon as possible (Pattullo to R.O. Alexander, 22 November 1941, GR1222, v. 99). By then Pattullo was a political lame duck; King's staff drafted a reply, but it was not sent (J.A. Gibson to N.A. Robertson, 5 December 1941, DEAR, MfT1809).

Vancouver Province, 26 November and 3 December 1940 and 3 and 10 October 1941; *New Canadian*, 6 December 1940; *Vancouver News-Herald*, 2 October 1941; *Vancouver Sun*, 7 October 1941. Vancouver East was a two-member constituency; the CCF won both seats, with the Liberals coming third and fourth (Elections British Columbia, *Electoral History*, 198). Henry F. Angus, "The Effect of the War on Oriental Minorities in Canada," *Canadian Journal of Economics and Political Science* 7 (November 1941): 515-16; *Victoria Times*, 26 May 1941; Neill to Keenleyside, 2 June 1941, DEAR, v. 337.

70 Cabinet War Committee, 26 September and 1 and 3 October 1940; King to Pattullo, 25 October 1940, TDPP, v. 70. The committee hoped to employ the special knowledge of Sir George Sansom, former commercial counsellor at the British Embassy in Tokyo, who Keenleyside said knew "more about Japanese history and civilization than any other foreigner" and whose presence would strengthen any recommendations the committee might make (Keenleyside to Skelton, 23 October 1940, KP, #C249316-8). Sansom acted only as an advisor.

71 Keenleyside to Skelton, 5 November 1940, DEAR, MfT1809; T.W.S. Parsons, Diary, 8 November 1940, TWSPP, v. 1. Parsons's cryptic comment does not indicate whether British Columbia desired this immediately or only in the case of war. The committee suggested that university authorities could decide on Japanese participation in the Canadian Officers Training Corps (Special Committee on Orientals, *Report* [Ottawa: King's Printer, 1941]).

72 Keenleyside to Sparling, Mead, and Sansom, 2 January 1941, DEAR, v. 1867; CWC, 2 January 1941. On 7 August 1941 the Cabinet War Committee noted that the government did not plan any wholesale internment of Japanese residents but in October agreed, after some discussion, that in the case of a war between the United Kingdom and Japan, the RCMP "should

proceed with the internment of such Japanese as they thought should be interned for cause" (CWC, 7 August and 22 October 1941; Keenleyside to King, 2 December 1940, KP, #244808-10; A.D.P. Heeney to Mackenzie, 6 January 1941, IAMP, v. 24; *Vancouver Sun,* 16 June 1937; *Vancouver News-Herald,* 16 June 1937).

73 King, Diary, 8 January 1941, KD; *Victoria Times,* 9 January 1941; *Vancouver Province,* 9 January 1941; Keenleyside to Robertson, 23 February 1941, DEAR, MfT1808; Bruce Hutchison, *Vancouver Sun,* 18 February 1941.

74 The National Resources Mobilization Act compelled all Canadians over the age of sixteen to register for possible war service. Where numbers warranted, Chinese and Japanese residents volunteered as interpreters at special offices. The Vancouver press reported that the Chinese used these offices but that few Japanese registrants needed special assistance and thus registered at regular offices. Wilson complained that many Japanese registration officers were illegal immigrants. There was some confusion at Steveston, where a Japanese national registered forty individuals (*Vancouver Sun,* 15, 20, and 21 August 1940; *Vancouver Province,* 15 August 1940 and 9 and 10 January and 21 March 1941; R.D. MacLachlan to King, 12 March 1941, KP, #262127; *Prince Rupert Daily News,* 10 January 1941; Harry Naganobu to King, 9 January 1941, DEAR, v. 1867; *New Canadian,* 10 January 1941; G.A. Ishiwara, Japanese Canadian Citizens League, to King, 15 January 1941, DEAR, v. 2007; Luce, "British Columbia Letter," *Saturday Night,* 15 February 1941; Reid to Mackenzie, 14 January 1941, IAMP, v. 24).

75 HCD, 25 February 1941, 1018-21; *Vancouver Sun,* 10 and 14 January 1941; *Vancouver Province,* 9, 10, and 14 January 1941; *Vancouver News-Herald,* 9 and 14 January 1941.

76 *Victoria Times,* 26 February 1941; *Vancouver News-Herald,* 19 and 27 February 1941; Neill to Keenleyside, 13 March 1941, DEAR, v. 1867; *Vancouver Province,* 30 July 1941, reprinted in *Victoria Times,* 9 August 1941; *Vancouver Highland Echo,* 20 February 1941. The Department of External Affairs drafted a letter notifying Japan of Canada's intention to terminate the agreement (King to Japanese Minister to Canada, 28 July 1941, DEAR, v. 1430; a note on the document reads: "Hold. No decision yet taken re termination of Immigration Agreement 9.8.41").

77 The provincial Bureau of Vital Statistics provided lists of name changes, delayed birth registrations, and current birth and death registrations (J. Marshall to G.F. Amyot, 10 March 1941, GR1222, v. 155; F.J. Hume to King, 26 February 1941, DEAR, MfT1809; Hume to King, 15 August 1941, KP, #259042ff; *Victoria Times,* 16 April 1941; Keenleyside to Hume, 1 March 1941, DEAR, v. 337 quoted King's statement to Parliament, HCD, 25 February 1941, 1047; Insp. D.L. McGibbon to F.J. Mead, 1 April 1941, DEAR, v. 337; *Vancouver Province,* 15 August 1941); Henry F. Angus, Report of Special Committee, Measures to Be Taken in the Event of War with Japan, 24 July 1941, and Meeting, 25 and 30 July 1941, CWC. For some who thought they had been naturalized through their fathers, registration was a shock. Because the RCMP kept their documents, they had "no proof of their status here." They were issued cards indicating that they were Japanese Nationals, which, among other things, made them ineligible for fishing licences. The loss of their documents made some Japanese suspicious of Etsuji Morii, their liaison with the RCMP (Barnes to Mead, 3 December 1941, DEAR, v. 2638).

78 Cabinet War Committee, 15 July 1941, CWC; Special Committee, Measures to Be Taken in the Event of War with Japan, 24 July 1941, and Meeting, 25 and 30 July 1941, CWC; Angus to Hume, 25 July 1941, DEAR, v. 2007; Hume to King, 15 August 1941, KP, #259042ff; G.O.C. Pacific Command to National Defence Headquarters, 15 February 1941, and "Appreciation Defence of Pacific Coast of Canada," 18 November 1941, DNDR, MfC8366.

79 *Vancouver News-Herald,* 4 December 1941.

80 Spy stories continued to intrigue the *Toronto Star.* Also, on 1 October 1938, the *Star Weekly,* a popular national magazine, ran a story, "Rising Sun over B.C.," whose author, James Culver, related spy stories he had heard. *Kelowna Courier,* 6 June 1940; *New Westminster British*

Columbian, 6 June 1940; *Victoria Colonist,* 28 May 1940; *Vancouver Sun,* 14 May 1940; Telford to Board of Police Commissioners, 17 May 1940, VMC, 1940; *Victoria Times,* 25 June 1940; MacMillan to Sandwell, 23 August 1939, and MacMillan to Sherwood Lett, 31 August 1939, HRMP, v. 24; MacMillan to M.E. Nicholls, 2 July 1940, HRMP, b. 7. Lett, a prominent lawyer, endorsed the idea of dismissing Japanese servants from the Vancouver Club (Lett to MacMillan, 5 September 1939, HRMP, v. 27); J.A. Clark to Ralston, 24 July 1940, JACP, b. 12.

81 Maude M. Studholme, "New and Old in Vancouver," *Vancouver Province,* 17 February 1940, magazine; *Vancouver Sun,* 8 May 1940. The chief press censor in Vancouver understood that the agitation resulted from "the activities of a number of aliens and British-born people who have communistic leanings" (Lew Gordon to C.J. Hanratty and F. Charpentier, 7 May 1940, PCOR, v. 5979; Wilson, Speech to British Canadian Allies Club, 16 May 1940, VMC, v. 41. *Vancouver Province,* 30 May 1940; Telford to McGeer, McInnis, and Green, 17 May 1940, and Kenji Nakauchi to Mayor, 13 June 1940, VMC). Nakauchi sent a copy of his letter to Premier Pattullo, who replied that he deprecated "insulting remarks towards groups of individuals within our Province" but had not heard of the likelihood of "any attempt against Japanese nationals in Vancouver" (Pattullo to Nakauchi, 19 June 1940, GR1222, v. 153; Tomii to Skelton, 10 June 1940, DEAR, MfT1792; Keenleyside to Angus, 28 June 1940, DEAR, v. 1867; Telford to Nakauchi, 8 July 1940, VMC, 1940). It is not known if this potentially interesting lunch took place (Keenleyside to Skelton, 11 June 1940, DEAR, v. 2007). Telford drafted a speech in which he said that "recent attacks upon the Japanese are unwarranted and unjust" and recalled the assistance of Japanese nationals during the First World War, but there is no evidence that he gave the speech (Draft Speech, 17 June 1940, VMC, 1940). There is no record of a reply from the Department of External Affairs despite Consul Tomii's request for one (Tomii to Skelton, 26 June 1940, DEAR, v. 2007).

82 *Vancouver Sun,* 5 and 10 August 1940, 31 July and 11 August 1941; *Vancouver Province,* 7 and 13 August 1940; *Vancouver News-Herald,* 7 and 13 August 1940; Howlett to Telford, 8 August 1940, VMC. Wilson told J.G. Gardiner, the minister of war services, that "numerous citizens of Vancouver" were anxious about "the status of many thousands of Japanese in our city and along the coast of British Columbia" (Wilson to Gardiner, 15 August 1940, HDWP; *Vancouver Sun,* 15 August 1940). The Japanese government quietly showed its displeasure over Wilson's repeated outbursts by cancelling a newspaper interview with a cabinet minister who was passing through Vancouver because he had "a cough in the early stage" (W.W. Murray, Chief Telegraph Censor, to T.A. Stone, 7 October 1940, DEAR, MfT1792); Muriel Kitagawa to Wes Fujiwara, 15 August 1940, NWFP.

83 *New Canadian,* 7 August 1940; Kunio Shimizu to L.J. Telford, 7 August 1940, VMC, 1940; *Vancouver Sun,* 13 August 1940; *B.C. Federationist,* 10 October 1940; *Vancouver Province,* 15 and 24 October 1940. To prevent Hallowe'en violence, Telford hired 150 special constables, who dispersed gangs of "near-adult hoodlums" marching toward Powell Street (*Vancouver Province,* 1 November 1940; *Vancouver Sun,* 1 November 1940; *Vancouver News-Herald,* 19 October 1940). There were precedents for Hallowe'en incidents. In 1936 seven Asian shopkeepers (whether they were Chinese or Japanese was not stated) reported the theft of merchandise and, in some cases, personal assaults (*Vancouver News-Herald,* 2 November 1936). The *Prince Rupert Evening Empire* claimed that in Vancouver over a thousand special police had been sworn in (23 October 1940); the *Nanaimo Free Press* suggested that hundreds of police patrolled "special areas of the city" (1 November 1940).

84 According to Skelton, Wilson's claims about dual nationality were not "thoroughly correct." In 1934 a Canadian Order in Council declared that the secretary of state would issue naturalization papers only to Japanese residents who had certificates saying that they had complied with the Japanese law allowing abandonment of that nationality. Thus no one could simultaneously be a naturalized Canadian and a Japanese national. Skelton understood that

the Japanese no longer registered their children with the local consulate in order to retain Japanese nationality (Skelton to Davis, 12 September 1940, DEAR, v. 2638). In 1924, Japan changed its law of nationality so that children born abroad to Japanese citizens did not become citizens of Japan unless they specifically applied for Japanese nationality (King to John Oliver, 6 December 1924, KP, #90190-1). *Vancouver Province,* 16 and 27 August 1940; Wilson to Capt. J. Bowen Colthurst, 8 January 1940, and Wilson to Civic Finance Committee, 24 September 1940, HDWP; *Vancouver News-Herald,* 17 August 1940; BC Provincial Police, Report on Inaugural Meeting, BC Special Committee, 1 October 1940, DHist, 332.009 (D358).

85 *Victoria Times,* 23 January 1940; *Prince Rupert Daily News,* 7 June 1940. In March 1938 a member of the Japanese Diet spoke to the Japanese Canadian Citizens Association to clear up misunderstandings caused by the Sino-Japanese conflict and "gave good encouraging words to the Second Generation people" (Minute Book, JCCA, v. 1). Mr. Kawaski, who succeeded Nakauchi as consul in Vancouver, told Colonel B.R. Mullaly that because of "underlying racial animosity" in British Columbia, he "insisted upon strict discipline in the community in order to avoid any pretext for agitation by the hostile elements." Because they did not want to endanger their positions and livelihoods, he said that there was no danger of their participating in activities that might do so. As for the Canadian-born, he said, they were "first and foremost Canadians and had little in common with native-born Japanese" (Memo of Interview between Col. B.R. Mullaly and Japanese Consul, Vancouver, 1 October 1941, DNDR, MfC5853). Kawaski described Wilson as a "Japanese baiter" (*Vancouver Sun,* 31 July 1941).

86 Tomii to Skelton, 10 June 1940, DEAR, MfT1792. In a census of all Japanese on the American continent, Japan did not include the Canadian-born (*Vancouver Sun,* 23 October 1940). In May 1941 Nisei applauded when the consul said that "unlike the situation in the Orient the Japanese in Canada are placed in a humiliating position due to racial prejudice of the white Canadians." Stressing that they might obtain full citizenship rights, but that "de facto" discrimination resulting from their "Oriental physiognomy" would never disappear, he urged Nisei to be "more ambitious, more united, and to be more on alert in discovering possible avenues to better living." He suggested copying "the methods of the Jews in attaining financial independence and greater powers" (Minute Book, Vancouver, JCCA, v. 1).

87 CWC, Minutes, 5 September 1940; Skelton, Memorandum, 28 August 1940, DEAR, MfT1792; *Vancouver Sun,* 4 October 1940; *New Westminster British Columbian,* 4 October 1940.

88 *Vancouver Sun,* 5 February 1940 and 10 February, 10 April, 14 October, and 18 November 1941; *Vancouver Province,* 25 September 1940; *Victoria Times,* 13 November 1940.

89 "The Japanese Hazard in BC," *Financial Times,* 11 October 1940; Telford to Ralston, 27 September 1940, and Mayor to Press, 4 October 1940, VMC, v. 41; *Victoria Times,* 1 October 1940; Mead to Commissioner, RCMP, 5 October 1940, DNDR, MfC5055; *Vancouver Sun,* 30 September and 1 October 1940; *Vancouver Province,* 27 September and 1 October 1940. Mead thought that Wilson was getting "ammunition" from the Communist Party, and Lieutenant General H.G.D. Crerar, chief of the General Staff, agreed that Communist agitation could lead to trouble with the Japanese (Mead to Commissioner, RCMP, 21 August 1940, and Crerar to Wood, 2 September 1940, DNDR, v. 2730); Mead to Commissioner, RCMP, 5 October 1940, DNDR, MfC5055; Wilson to Mead, 9 October 1940, and Mead to Wilson, 17 October 1940, HDWP; H. Naganobu and K.T. Shoyama, Japanese Canadian Citizens League, to Lapointe, 9 October 1940, IAMP, v. 24; *Vancouver Province,* 15 October 1940. Premier Pattullo told the Japanese Canadian Citizens League that he would speak to Wilson, but his secretary later explained that although Wilson had not come to Victoria as expected, the premier was interested in learning of the minister of justice's reply to their letter (Pattullo to Shoyama, 17 October 1940, and Secretary to Shoyama, 24 October, 1940, GR1222, v. 155).

90 Minutes of Meeting, 1 October 1940, at Invitation of the Attorney-General of British Columbia, copy in VMC, 1940; Mead to Commissioner, RCMP, 5 October 1940, DNDR,
MfC5055; Keenleyside to Davis, 7 February 1941, and Angus to Keenleyside, 25 January
1941, DEAR, v. 1867; Keenleyside to Angus, 22 January 1941, DEAR, v. 2007. Skelton decided
to allow the debate to proceed about an hour before his sudden death (Keenleyside to
Angus, 29 January 1941, DEAR, v. 1867); Keenleyside to Skelton, 18 September 1940, DEAR,
MfT1809; (A.D.P. Heeney to King, 24 December 1940, KP, #C249353). The publication of a
tabloid, the *Vancouver Parashooter,* suggested that Wilson was back in business. Advertisers were mainly cleaners and dyers. The first issue had patriotic articles but nothing specifically anti-Asian.

91 King, Diary, 19 June and 26 July 1940, KD; CWC, 9 July 1940; "An Appreciation of the Situation in B.C. in the Event of War with Japan," 24 June 1940, DNDR, v. 8366; A.E. Godfrey, C.V.
Stockwell, and V.G. Brodeur, "Memorandum of the Joint Service Committee, Pacific Coast,
on the Matter of the Defences of the Pacific Coast of Canada," 12 July 1940, DNDR, v. 2730;
R.M. Wynd to Senior Air Staff Officer, 24 June 1940, DImm, MfC4752.

92 Wismer to Lapointe and C.G. Power, 28 June 1940, TDPP, v. 73; G.G. McGeer to Lapointe, 2
July 1940, and McGeer to P.J. Cardin, 13 July 1940, copies in JWdeBFP, v. 6.

93 *Vancouver Sun,* 25 July and 7 October 1940; *New Westminster British Columbian,* 25 July 1940;
Vancouver Province, 29 August 1940; *Victoria Colonist,* 20 June and 1 August 1940; *Victoria
Times,* 24 July, 8 August, 3 and 14 September, and 29 November 1940; *Kelowna Courier,* 1
August 1940; *Nanaimo Free Press,* 5 and 28 August 1940. Without giving much detail, Wismer
sought more money for policing, saying that secret police reports revealed "an alarming
situation" (*Victoria Times,* 29 November 1940; Wismer to Pattullo, 2 August 1940, TDPP, v.
73; Wismer to Pattullo, 3 August 1940, TDPP, v. 66). According to Arthur G. Slaght, an Ontario Liberal MP, Wismer's July visit to Ottawa "in connection with a 'very important problem' was of great value" to British Columbia and the Dominion as a whole (*Victoria Colonist,*
31 December 1941; CWC, 17 July and 8 October 1940; Wismer to Lapointe and Power, 28 June
1940, TDPP, v. 73). Some young Japanese Canadians proposed using bows and arrows for
hunting (*Vancouver Province,* 26 January 1941). When the ban on explosives caused problems for farmers, the Maple Ridge Municipal Council accepted their suggestion that if a
British neighbour sponsored and supervised them, they might secure police and council
approval to obtain stumping powder for land clearing (*New Westminster British Columbian,*
5 and 27 November 1940). On 20 September 1940 the *Vancouver Sun* reported that Asians in
Vancouver, mainly the Japanese, were tardy in surrendering firearms and that about two
thousand Japanese residents had hunting licences. In announcing a special canvass to find
unregistered guns, Wismer denied that the search was directed at the Japanese (*Vancouver
Province,* 5 October 1940). The *Kelowna Courier* argued that a planned house-to-house "canvass" challenged the "freedom and manner of living" for which the war was being fought (10
October 1940). The New Westminster Air Raid Protection (ARP) organization complained
that it had no time for a canvass that was not ARP work (*New Westminster British Columbian,*
9 October 1940).

94 In the summer of 1941, an air force intelligence officer neither found nor expected to find
evidence of subversion among "the Japanese population as a whole" because "such doings
are kept secret." Nevertheless, he thought that "widespread disaffection and disorder" were
possible if "irresponsibly organized disorder and official restrictive measures to combat this"
forced them "into a desperate situation." He recommended supervision and the internment
of suspicious Japanese residents but thought that large-scale evacuation or internment would
probably cause more trouble and expense than it would save (W.A. Nield to D.I.A. Wing
Commander R.A. Logan, 27 July 1941, DHist, 181.009 [D5546]); Meeting of Interdepartmental Committee on Aliens and Alien Property, 31 May 1939, and J.E. Read to L.R. LaFleche, 9

June 1939, DEAR, v. 1805; "Plan for the Defence of Pacific Coast of Canada Based on Forces and Equipment Available, 10 July 1940," DHist, 169.012 (D12); Godfrey, Stockwell, and Brodeur, "Memorandum of the Joint Service Committee, Pacific Coast, on the Matter of the Defences of the Pacific Coast of Canada," 12 July 1940, C.V. Stockwell to Secretary, DNDR, 4 September 1940, and R.O. Alexander, Godfrey, and W.J.R. Beech, "Memorandum of the Joint Service Committee, Pacific Coast, on the Subject of Dealing with Persons of Japanese Origin in the Event of an Emergency," 20 September 1941, DNDR, v. 2730; Wismer to Lapointe, 2 July 1940, and Wismer to Power, 3 July 1940, TDPP, v. 73; H. Stethem to Adjutant-General, 25 July 1941, DNDR, MfC5394; "Appreciation Defence of Pacific Coast of Canada," 18 November 1941, DNDR, MfC8366.

95 The Permanent Joint Board on Defence (PJBD) agreed that the two governments should consult to bring about "policies of a similar character" (PJBD, Journal of Discussion and Decisions, 10-11 November 1941, KP, #220838); Alexander, Godfrey, and Beech, "Memorandum," 20 September 1941, DNDR, v. 2730; "Memorandum of an Interview between Colonel B.R. Mullaly, Attached, Pacific Command, and Representatives of the Japanese Community in British Columbia," 4 October 1941, KP, #C249374ff; C.E. Hill to Commissioner, RCMP, 3 December 1941, DEAR, v. 2007. One American study of the situation on the west coast also determined "that the Japanese are in more danger from the whites than the other way around" (John Franklin Carter to F.D. Roosevelt, 22 October 1941, quoted in Greg Robinson, *By Order of the President: FDR and the Internment of Japanese Americans* [Cambridge, MA: Harvard University Press, 2001], 66).

96 [R.B.C.] Mundy to Commander Hart, 8 August 1940, and "Vancouver" to Officer Commanding, RCMP, Vancouver, 13 and 19 July 1940, DNDR, v. 11913. Early in 1941 Vancouver newspapers reported that city police had apprehended a new member of the consulate staff and his movie camera because he was taking pictures of the Jericho air station. The local RCMP commander recommended prosecution to "allay anti-Oriental feeling" and to demonstrate that regulations against taking photographs in restricted areas would be enforced. His commander in Ottawa and Norman A. Robertson of the Department of External Affairs, however, said that prosecution would likely have the opposite effect (the correspondence is in DEAR, v. 2855). A few weeks later, Vancouver city police seized film from two Japanese residents photographing a baby near the Canadian National Railway (CNR) dock. They said that they did not know that Defence of Canada regulations forbade taking photographs in the harbour area. The police did not lay charges (*Victoria Times*, 8 February 1941). The RCMP had a list of Japanese residents who might be considered for internment in the case of war with Japan (Wood to Crerar, 8 August 1940, DNDR, v. 2730).

97 *Vancouver Province*, 3 August 1940; *Vancouver News-Herald*, 5 August 1940. In an editorial on Britain and the Tokyo-Berlin link, the *Victoria Colonist* suggested that Japanese residents were spying on Canada's Pacific Coast (4 August 1940). Pattullo to King, 8 August 1940, KP, #248358; *Vancouver Sun*, 3 August 1940; R.R. Tait to OC, E Division, 25 April 1941, and Hill to Commissioner, 8 May 1941, RCMP, v. 3564; Thomas Barker to Pattullo, 12 May 1941, TDPP, v. 73; Norman A. Robertson advised Pattullo that the Department of National Defence, the RCMP, and the provincial police had the situation "well in hand" (Robertson to Pattullo, 24 May 1941, TDPP, v. 73); Hope to Keenleyside, 12 May 1941, and Neill to Robertson, 17 March 1941, DEAR, v. 2007; Neill to Intelligence Section, RCMP, 30 April 1941, RCMP, v. 3564. What especially upset Neill was his belief that most fishermen came from Brechin, near Nanaimo, where "Koyani, the Jap who runs the store, where most of them hang out, is reported to be an officer in the Japanese navy." The RCMP found no one named Koyani or any evidence of a Japanese storekeeper in the small community having ever served in the Japanese army or navy (Hill to Commissioner, 6 June 1941, RCMP, v. 3464; Keenleyside to Neill, 13 June 1941, DEAR, v. 337).

98 *Vancouver Sun,* 10 October 1941; Kitagawa to Fujiwara, 14 October 1941, NWFP; Keenleyside to V.C. Best, 14 October 1941, and G. Upton, s/constable, RCMP, Report, 27 October 1941, DEAR, v. 2007; *Victoria Times,* 15 October 1941; Leaflet for Dr. A.F. Barton, Liberal Candidate, Salmon Arm, TDPP, v. 62; *Vancouver News-Herald,* 15 October 1941; Kunio Shimizu to King, 10 October 1941, KP, #270152-3.
99 Fisher, *Duff Pattullo,* 342-44.

Conclusion

1 David Theo Goldberg, *Racist Culture: Philosophy and the Politics of Meaning* (Oxford: Blackwell, 1993), 59.
2 "Memorandum of an Interview between Colonel B.R. Mullaly, Attached, Pacific Command, and Representatives of the Japanese Community in British Columbia," 4 October 1941, KP, #C249374-7.
3 Alicja Muszynski, *Cheap Wage Labour: Race and Gender in the Fisheries of British Columbia* (Montreal and Kingston: McGill-Queen's University Press, 1996), 243.
4 W.E. Payne to W.L.M. King, 25 January 1923, DImm, MfC10410.
5 C.M. Watson and C.C.J. Hart to Stevens, 31 March 1926, KP, #118453ff.
6 Edward Said, *Orientalism* (New York: Vintage, 1979), 3.
7 Henry Yu, *Thinking Orientals: Migration, Contact and Exoticism in Modern America* (New York: Oxford University Press, 2001), 190.
8 Patricia E. Roy, *A White Man's Province: British Columbia Politicians and Chinese and Japanese Immigrants, 1858-1914* (Vancouver: UBC Press, 1989), 268.
9 *Kamloops Standard-Sentinel,* 4 April 1922.
10 Wing Chung Ng, *The Chinese in Vancouver, 1945-80* (Vancouver: UBC Press, 1999), 6.
11 *The Japanese Contribution to Canada* (Vancouver: Canadian Japanese Association, 1940), 44.
12 Manson to Neel, 24 December 1927, AGR, 1918-17-2060.
13 *B.C. Federationist,* 10 October 1940; *Vancouver Sun,* 3 April 1925 and 27 August 1940.
14 Some of this has been discussed in Patricia E. Roy, J.L. Granatstein, Masako Iino, and Hiroko Takamura, *Mutual Hostages: Canadians and Japanese during the Second World War* (Toronto: University of Toronto Press, 1990).
15 For examples see Patricia E. Roy, "A Tale of Two Cities: The Reception of Japanese Evacuees in Kelowna and Kaslo, B.C.," *BC Studies,* 87 (Autumn 1990): 23-47, and "If the Cedars Could Speak: Japanese and Caucasians Meet at New Denver," *BC Studies,* 131 (Autumn 2001): 81-92.
16 Patricia E. Roy, "Lessons in Citizenship, 1945-1949: The Delayed Return of the Japanese to Canada's Pacific Coast," *Pacific Northwest Historical Quarterly* 93 (Spring 2002): 69-80.

Index

Hanson, Olof, 202
Hanson, R.B., 223
Harkness, Rev. Nelson A., 52, 209
Harper, Andrew M., 143-44
Harris, Cole, 12
Harrison, Paul Phillips, 100
Hawthornthwaite, J.H., 20
Hayakawa, S.I., 153, 160
Hepburn, Mitchell, 192
Hill-Tout, Charles, 148
Hinchliffe, Joshua, 289n37
Hirota, Koki, 213
Hodges, Nancy, 175
Hope, C.E., 34, 65, 118, 131-33, 136, 150, 154, 165, 193, 198, 200, 213, 229, 285n2, n3
Hope, Joseph, 75, 180
Hoskins, Joseph, 125
hospitals, 102-3, 149, 151, 276n39
hotel workers, 17, 18, 101, 246n12, n13
Hougham, George S., 60
Hughes, William, 59
Hume, F.J., 132, 178, 217, 220, 221
Humphrey, L.W., 64
Hutchison, Bruce, 4-5, 137, 145, 147, 173, 175, 182, 190, 193, 289n35, 306n11, n12
Hyakutake, Vice Admiral, 170
Hyodo, Hideko, 39, 160

Immigration restrictions, 265n38; proposed in the B.C. Legislature, 71-72, 80, 85, 87; proposed in Ottawa, 158, 200-1. *See also* Chinese Immigration Act (1923); gentlemen's agreement *under* Japan
inassimilability, 9, 26-54, 72, 85-86, 131, 150, 154, 193, 195, 201, 225, 231, 243n26, 250n19, 280n71. *See also* assimilation; miscegenation
India, immigrants from, 14, 244n54, 262n9; *Komagata Maru*, 14
Institute of Pacific Relations, 154
Ishimaru, Tota, 181, 302n35
Italians, 220, 222
Ito, Minoru, 148
Iwashita, K., (of Camp and Mill Workers), 179
Iwashita, K., (of Kelowna) 27, 114, 121

Jackson, Peter, 9

Jamieson, Laura, 209
Japan: as an ally, 14-15, 167, 170, 297n9; boycott of imports, 178-80, 301n32; embargo on war materials, 175-78, 299n23, n26, 300n24, n25, n28, 301n29; gentlemen's agreement, 58, 68, 69, 82-85, 88, 133, 152, 191, 192, 194, 201, 217, 218-19, 223, 261n9, 265n38, 268n64, 269n77, 270n83, 307n19, 316n76; immigration, illegal, 133, 189, 192-94, 197-99, 235, 305n7, 308n21, 309n28; immigration restrictions, proposed, 78-79, 189, 194-96, 265n36, 307n18, 309n30, n32; investment in British Columbia, 171, 172-75, 181, 298n17, n20; military ambitions, 105, 168-70, 181, 208, 215, 220-21, 238-39 (*see also* defence); "spies" and "fifth columnists," alleged, 15, 105-6, 135, 166-69, 190, 197, 204, 210, 212-13, 221-23, 227-29, 238, 245n5, 296n2, n4, n8, 303n42, 314n63, 316n80, 320n96, n97; trade, 15, 28, 82, 87, 133, 171, 175, 177-78, 202, 220, 237, 248n5, 251n20, 272n8, 297n12, 298n17, n20, 299n21, 300n27, n28, 310n37
Japanese Canadians: birth rate, 56, 146, 193, 210, 259n3, 289n37, 306n11; conflict within the community, 11, 159, 223, 245n9, 262n21; distinguished from Japan, 172, 179-80, 190, 193, 210, 219, 223, 225, 236; dual nationality, 213, 224, 251n20, 317n84; employment on crown lands and public works, 15, 20, 115 (*see also* Brooks-Bidlake & Whittall *under* lumber industry; employment *under* lumber industry); immigration numbers, 25, 57, 58-59, 78, 146, 192; loyalty to Canada demonstrated, 15-16, 163-64, 213-15, 220, 223; loyalty to Canada doubted, 213-14, 226, 276n38; "picture brides," 88, 269n74; population statistics, 6, 55-56, 146, 192-93, 294n75, 313n55; registration, 217-20, 221, 316n74, n77; relief, 291n54; service in the Canadian armed forces, 16, 21, 41, 153, 215, 223, 228, 245n9, 255n48, 315n67, n69, n71; sojourning, 31; wartime treatment, proposals, 204, 216-17, 220, 227-28, 315n72, 319n94. *See also* Chinese and Japanese compared; Nisei

Japanese diplomats: employment restrictions, 20, 93, 95, 101; franchise, 41; immigration, 78, 79, 82-83, 87, 200, 217, 294n69, 309n32; investment capital, 112; Japanese in Canada, 39, 113, 115, 315n67, 317n81, n82, 318n85, n86; promoting goodwill, 15, 36, 224; response to agitation and rumours, 190, 222; trade, 87, 133

Japanese labour organizations: Amalgamated Association of Japanese Fishermen, 108; Japanese Fishermen's Association, 278n54; Japanese Labour Union, 11, 262n21; Japanese Workers' Union, 62; Mill and Camp Workers Union, 91, 134, 135, 179; Northern British Columbia Resident Fishermen's Association, 202; Steveston Fishermen's Benevolent Association, 8

Japanese organizations: Japanese Association of Canada, 262n21; Japanese Canadian Citizens League (JCCL), 159-60, 214-15, 218, 223, 229, 294n70, 314n66; Japanese Students' Club, 153

Jay, George, 39

Jewish refugees, 313n53

Johns, Albion, 126

Johnston, V.H., 62

Jolliffe, A.L., 68

Jones, Charles, 210, 224, 313n56

Jones, J.W., 92, 114, 268n68, 289n37

Judicial Committee of the Privy Council, 95-96, 109, 143

Kabayama, Commander, 14

Kamloops, 70, 123, 137, 180, 198, 238

Keenleyside, H.L., 7, 133, 173, 196, 197-99, 200, 213, 217, 222, 229, 297n9, 307n19

Kelowna, 27, 92, 111, 112, 114, 117, 121, 164, 221, 224, 271n6

Kemp, Mrs., 23

Kenney, E.T., 215

Keremeos, 92

Ketchen, H.D.B., 182

King, J.H., 69, 84, 86, 88, 117

King, William Lyon Mackenzie: Anglo-Japanese treaties, 173; anti-Japanese agitation, 220, 226; Asian immigration, 66, 69, 72, 86; assimilation, 26; Chinese immigration, 58, 68, 72, 74; defence, 181-84, 185-86, 226; election (1935), 171; embargoes, 176-78; employment restrictions, 100; franchise, 42, 159; Japanese immigration, 78, 81-83, 88, 196, 200-1, 217, 218; military service for Asians, 216; race, 231; riots feared, 178, 188, 238; trade, 171

Kitagawa, Muriel (née Fujiwara), 27, 160

Kobayashi, Audrey, 9

Kobayashi, Minoru, 160

Kootenays, 5, 52, 64, 184, 238, 264n28

Koyama, Frank, 214

Ku Klux Klan, 80, 86, 269n71, 270n81

Kusaka, Suichi, 290n46

Kuwahara, Setsuo, 148

Kwong, Charlie, 137

Labour unions: British Columbia Federation of Labour, 15, 19, 25, 43, 232; Brotherhood of Locomotive Engineers, 120; Canadian Lumber Workers' Association, 98; Cooks and Waiters Union, 101; One Big Union, 91, 92; Relief Project Workers' Union, 180; Retail Clerks Union, 209; Shingle Weavers' Union, 135; United Mine Workers of America, 19, 100; Vancouver Waiters and Caterers Union, 102; Workers' Unity League, 135. *See also* fishermen's organizations; Japanese labour organizations; Trades and Labour Congress of Canada; Trades and Labour Councils

Ladner, 138-39

Ladner, Leon J., 51, 52, 53, 65-66, 67, 73, 80, 84, 107-8, 158

Laing, Arthur, 214, 218, 289n37

land acquisition. *See* alien land laws

Langley, Harry, 34

language, 248n5

Lapointe, Ernest, 107-8

laundries and dry cleaners, 17, 18, 60, 101, 127, 208-9, 246n12

Laurier, Wilfrid, 64, 245n4

La Violette, Forrest E., 305n6

League against War and Fascism, 179

League of Nations, 59, 181, 261n11

League of Nations Society, 180
Leary, Sid, 127
Leckie, J., 262n20
Lee, Alfred Quan, 27
Lee, Dick, 145, 289n35
Lee, W., 207
Lefaux, Wallis, 156
Legal Professions Act, 103
Lemieux, Rodolphe, 40, 254n46
Letson, H.F., 182
Lew, David C., 48
liquor, 17, 258n72, 311n45
"Little Tokyo," 17
Lloyd George, David, 62
Loh Tsei, 180
Lougheed, N.S., 88, 133, 150
Louie, Tong, 149
Low Chong Company, 139, 142
Lucas, W.T., 69
Lum Fun Ting, 207
lumber industry: Brooks-Bidlake &
  Whittall (legal case), 93-96, 109; employ-
  ment, logging, 20, 93-96, 232, 286n9;
  employment, mills, 18-19, 47, 92-99, 135,
  246n15, 272n9, 273n21, 286n10; exports,
  177, 298-99n20; mills, Canadian Western
  Lumber Company, 62 (*see also* Fraser
  Mills); mills, Rat Portage Mill, 97
lumber industry, trade organizations:
  British Columbia Loggers' Association,
  96; British Columbia Lumber Manufacturers' Association, 99; British Columbia
  Shingle Manufacturers' Association, 95,
  96; Shingle Agency of B.C., 93; Timber
  Industries Council, 97. *See also* minimum wage
Lytton, 44

Macaulay, C.F., 34, 52, 53, 62, 63, 70, 262n20
McBride, Richard, 5, 14, 15, 17, 19, 93, 231,
  254n45
McBride, T.G., 55, 64, 74
McClatchey, V.S., 79
McClung, Nellie, 12, 157, 293n66
Macdonald, K.C., 114, 139, 142, 143, 161
MacDonald, M.A.: Asian immigration,
  64-66; Chinese immigration, 77;
  employment of Asians, 94, 246n17;

franchise, 42; Japanese immigration, 59;
  land holding, 118
McDonald, Robert A.J., 10
McGavin, Andrew, 50
McGeer, G.G. (Gerry), 108, 181, 202, 206, 227
MacGill, Helen Gregory, 153
MacGill, J.H., 28
McGuigan, W.J., 144
MacInnes, T.R.E. (Tom), 87, 129, 278n51,
  282n81
MacInnis, Angus, 62, 135, 156, 158, 159, 161,
  218, 223, 237, 286n8
McIntosh, J.C., 22
Macintosh, MacGregor, 4, 189-90, 192-93,
  195, 197, 201, 204, 217, 229, 232, 235,
  304n50, 305n1, n2
McKay, E.A., 141
Mackay, Rev. John, 29
McKelvie, Bruce A., 181
MacKelvie, J.A., 65, 71, 73, 114
Mackenzie, D.D., 70, 73
Mackenzie, Ian: federal election (1935), 157;
  franchise, 156; franchise for veterans, 41,
  237; immigration of Chinese merchants,
  133; Japanese immigration, 194, 196, 202,
  306n9; land ownership, 116; minimum
  wage law, 98-99; national defence, 166,
  173, 181-83, 184; relief, 129; trade with
  Japan, 171
McLachlan, Mrs., 71
MacLean, J.D., 86, 88, 129
MacMillan, H.R., 3, 204, 213, 221, 232,
  310n38
McMullin, J.H., 198
MacNeil, Grant, 174, 176
McNiven, J.D., 98, 102
McPherson, Dougal, 87
McQuarrie, W.G., 43, 65, 67-68, 70, 73, 78,
  80, 85, 87, 104, 118, 126, 270n85, 277n45
McRae, A.D., 3, 62, 108, 232, 278n54
McRae, W., 47, 50
McVety, J.H., 21
Mah Bing Mo, 143
Mah Chong, 125
Maitland, R.L., 177, 191, 193, 215-16, 225
Malkin, W.H., 48, 128
Manion, R.J., 201, 202
Manitoba, 43, 256n57, 275n36

Manson, A.M., 271n11; agricultural marketing, 142; Asian immigration, 69, 72; birth
rate, 55; drugs, illegal, 53; economic
competition, 90, 92, 95-96, 99, 123, 126,
129, 231; land holding, 116-17; miscegena-
tion, 4, 32-33, 72, 85-87, 231; naturalization, 251n20; public opinion, 130
Maple Ridge, 112, 121, 205, 280n68
Marler, Herbert, 170, 200
Massey, Vincent, 304n48
Matsunaga, Rev. Fumio, 16
Mayhew, R.W., 176, 181, 184
Mayne Island, 189
Mead, F.J., 216, 217, 223, 225
Meighen, Arthur, 42, 58, 59-60, 64, 66, 78,
85, 94, 115
merchant seamen, 289n33
Miles, Robert, 7-8
Miller, G.C. (mayor of Vancouver), 166,
206, 208
Miller, George, 204
Milne, G.L., 82
minimum wage, 9, 19-20, 97-99, 102, 135,
158, 232, 235, 247n17, n18, 257n58, 273n24,
274n25, n29, 285n7
miscegenation, 32-34, 86, 148, 195, 250n18,
251n22, 307n17. *See also* inassimilability
"Miss Astrid," 207
Mission, 23, 35, 151-52
Miyata, Lieutenant, 14
Morii, Etsuji, 223, 228
Morley, H.B., 114
Motherwell, W.R., 70, 107-8
Mullaly, B.R., 228
Munro, E.A., 65, 84, 265n41, 270n78
Murdock, James, 70
Murphy, Emily ("Janey Canuck"), 50
Murray, G.M., 136
Muszynski, Alicja, 3, 4, 8, 232

Nakashima, T., 138
Nakauchi, Kenji, 224
Nanaimo, 52, 70, 71, 84, 100, 119, 134, 175, 210
National Conference of University
Students, 154
National Resources Mobilization Act, 215,
218, 316n74
Native Indians. *See* Aboriginal peoples

Native Sons (and Daughters) of British
Columbia, 9, 34, 41, 59, 86, 118, 132, 154,
160, 181, 193, 251n20, 294n72
Native Sons of Canada, 80, 160, 176, 177,
217-18
Natural Products Marketing Act, 122-23,
137-44 *(passim)*
naturalization, 33, 93, 95, 116, 149-50, 250n20,
254n45, 278n51, 290n48, 316n77, 317n84
Neelands, R.H., 116
Neill, A.W.: Asian immigration, 73, 132,
265n36; Chinese immigration, 77; federal
elections (1921), 67, 265n36; (1930),
285n3; (1940), 202; fisheries, 105, 108-10,
135, 136, 172; franchise, 42, 155, 156, 158,
160, 216; Japanese immigration, 73, 78-
79, 83-85, 191, 194-96; racism, 218; "spies,"
alleged, 169-70, 229; toleration, 147
Neish, R.C., 117, 120
Nelson, 175
Nelson, John, 6, 59, 78
Nelson, Orlando H., 21
New Brunswick, 60
New Westminster, 27, 57, 65, 70, 84, 128, 129,
163-64, 221, 284n101, 313n56
New Zealand, 73
newspapers, 12-13, 244n57, 263n22, 268n59
Nisei, 6, 9, 148, 153, 159-60, 162-64, 276n38;
sympathy for, 147-48, 193, 219, 225, 236,
243n39, 315n66. *See also* Japanese
Canadian Citizens League *under*
Japanese organizations
Norris, T.G., 159, 161
North, Joseph, 49
Nova Scotia, 60
nursing, 102-3, 149, 290n47

Oak Bay, 66, 125
O'Brien, Mrs. James, 51, 53, 70
Ocean Falls, 20, 96, 172
Oda, Yoshio, 106
Odlum, Edward, 270n81
Odlum, Victor W., 64, 65-66, 129, 184,
268n59, 270n83
Ogasawara, S.G., 137
Okanagan Valley, 22, 23, 61, 65, 112-15, 120,
201, 221, 235, 238
Old Age Pension, 150

retail and wholesale trade, 60, 125-30, 140,
144, 208-11, 235, 312n51
Revelstoke, 119
Richmond, 119; Richmond School Board, 39
riots, apprehended, 42, 48, 73, 104, 178, 185,
188, 190, 193, 196, 212, 216-17, 220, 221,
222, 225, 227, 235, 238, 300n28, 317n83
Roberts, W.H., 262n20
Robertson, Norman A., 178
Robson, J.G., 97, 98
Roediger, David, 10
Rogers, Norman, 152, 214
Rome-Berlin-Tokyo Axis, 177, 185, 213
Roosevelt, F.D., 182
Rotary Club, 51, 61, 62
Royal Canadian Mounted Police (RCMP):
and illegal drugs, 53; investigations of
Japanese Canadians, 168, 185, 196, 197,
198-99, 212, 213, 216, 220, 228, 229, 308n23
Royal Commission on the British Colum-
bia Fisheries, 106-7
Royal Commission on Dominion-
Provincial Relations (Rowell-Sirois), 154,
197, 215, 230, 292n61, 309n30

Saanich, 66, 72, 119, 272n7
Sage, Walter N., 79, 164-65, 187
Said, Edward, 233
Saita, Aiko, 163
Sandiford, Peter, 35, 252n30
Sandwell, B.K., 191, 297n8
Sansom, George, 315n70
Sapiro, Aaron, 120
Saskatchewan, 40, 43, 130, 275n36, 293n63
Sato, Tsutae, 214
Sato, Y., 39
Scandinavians, 307n20
schools and schooling. *See* education
Scott, Archdeacon F.G., 166, 181, 184, 191, 212
Scott, H.G., 181
Sears, J. Edward, 157
Seattle, bombing of Japanese ship, 299n21
segregation, social, 27, 35
Selkirk, T.R., 202
Seymour Narrows, 229
Shaw, Mrs. E.B., 42
Shaw, Mary, 145
Shearer, Sam, 179-80

Shimizu, Rev. K., 148
Shoyama, Thomas, 153, 223
Shue Moy, 48
Shumiatcher, Morris, 297n10
Simonds, Peter, 293n63
Sino-Japanese War, 166, 169-72, 179, 180,
181, 190, 203, 302n34
Sivertz, Christian, 253n35
Skeena, 64-65
Skelton, O.D., 83, 84, 85, 88, 117, 154, 196,
200, 224, 306n15, 307n21
Skillings, Waldo, 229
Sloan, Gordon, 212
Sloan, William, 19, 20, 71, 79-80, 99, 100,
108, 109, 117
Small Storekeepers Association, 126
Smith, David A., 75
Smith, Janet K., 44, 256n57
Smith, Mary Ellen, 43, 51, 127
Smithers, 144
Sommerville Canneries Case, 109
South Vancouver, 281n76
Spallumcheen, 119
Sparling, A.W., 216, 217, 220, 227
Special Committee on the Chinese and
Japanese in British Columbia, 216-17, 220
Special Committee on Measures to Be
Taken in the Event of War with Japan,
178
Spencer, Chris, 51
Spofford, Mrs. Cecelia, 37
sports and recreation, 27, 224. *See also*
celebrations and entertainments
Stacey, F.B., 64, 65
Standing Committee on Orientals, 178, 217,
220
Stanley, Timothy J., 11, 37
Steeves, Dorothy, 175, 209
Stephen, A.M., 301n32
Stevens, H.H.: Asian immigration, 69, 73,
86; Chinese immigration, 58, 74, 133;
defence, 168-69; drugs, illegal, 52;
franchise, 154, 239, 255n51; Japanese
immigration, 64, 66; labour, 22-23; land
holding, 115, 118, 136-37; miscegenation,
32, 250n19
Stevenson, L.F., 187
Stewart, Charles, 67, 69-70, 73

Praise for *A White Man's Province: British Columbia Politicians and Chinese and Japanese Immigrants, 1858-1914*

"A fascinating and readable account of the early history of anti-Orientalism in Canada ... a fair and lucid account of the roots of legalized racism in British Columbia ... Roy's clear and dispassionate eye makes this book a particularly useful addition to other recent histories of the Chinese in Canada."
– Margaret Cannon, *Globe and Mail*

"An important contribution to knowledge [which] should be read by anyone with an interest in the issues of racism, immigration policy, British Columbia history, and minority groups in Canada."
– Victor Satzewich, *Canadian Historical Review*

"I particularly like [Roy's] conclusion that 'white man's province' is not an expression of simple racism. It seems to me that she has gone part of the way towards shifting the focus of explanation from where it has been to where it could more fruitfully lie."
– Edgar Wickberg, *BC Studies*

"Roy's solid, well-researched book helps us understand the response of British Columbia politicians to Chinese and Japanese immigration."
– Gunther Barth, *Pacific Northwest Quarterly*

"*A White Man's Province* should become required reading for all those interested in BC history."
– George Brandak, *Canadian Book Review Annual*